Frommer's®

P9-BZD-281

New York City with Kids

10th Edition

by Holly Hughes

Here's what the critics say about Frommer's:

"Amazingly easy to use. Very portable, very complete."

—*Booklist*

"Detailed, accurate, and easy-to-read information for all price ranges."
—*Glamour Magazine*

"Invaluable in planning your family's pit stops."

—*San Diego Family*

"Frommer's Guides have a way of giving you a real feel for a place."
—*Knight Ridder Newspapers*

BICENTENNIAL
1807
WILEY
2007
BICENTENNIAL

Wiley Publishing, Inc.

About the Author

Holly Hughes is a freelance writer and editor who lives on the Upper West Side of Manhattan with her husband and three children. She is the author of *Frommer's 500 Places To Take Your Kids Before They Grow Up*, has been series editor for *Frommer's Irreverent Guides*, and has been an executive editor of *Fodor's Travel Guides*. She is also the editor of the annual *Best Food Writing* anthology (Avalon Publishing).

Published by:

Wiley Publishing, Inc.

111 River St.
Hoboken, NJ 07030-5774

ISBN: 978-0-470-04210-6

Editor: Alexia Meyers Travaglini
Production Editor: Eric T. Schroeder
Cartographer: Guy Ruggiero
Photo Editor: Richard Fox
Production by Wiley Indianapolis Composition Services

Front cover photo: New York City skyline, young girl pointing at skyscraper

For information on our other products and services or to obtain technical support, please contact our Customer Care Department within the U.S. at 800/762-2974, outside the U.S. at 317/572-3993 or fax 317/572-4002.

Wiley also publishes its books in a variety of electronic formats. Some content that appears in print may not be available in electronic formats.

Manufactured in the United States of America

5 4 3 2

Contents

List of Maps

An Invitation to the Reader

In researching this book, we discovered many wonderful places—hotels, restaurants, shops, and more. We're sure you'll find others. Please tell us about them, so we can share the information with your fellow travelers in upcoming editions. If you were disappointed with a recommendation, we'd love to know that, too. Please write to:

Frommer's New York City with Kids, 10th Edition
Wiley Publishing, Inc. • 111 River St. • Hoboken, NJ 07030-5774

An Additional Note

Please be advised that travel information is subject to change at any time—and this is especially true of prices. We therefore suggest that you write or call ahead for confirmation when making your travel plans. The authors, editors, and publisher cannot be held responsible for the experiences of readers while traveling. Your safety is important to us, however, so we encourage you to stay alert and be aware of your surroundings. Keep a close eye on cameras, purses, and wallets, all favorite targets of thieves and pickpockets.

Other Great Guides for Your Trip:

Frommer's Irreverent Guide to Manhattan
Frommer's Memorable Walks in New York
Frommer's Portable New York City
Frommer's New York City from $90 a Day
Frommer's Wonderful Weekends from New York City

Frommer's Star Ratings, Icons & Abbreviations

Every hotel, restaurant, and attraction listing in this guide has been ranked for quality, value, service, amenities, and special features using a **star-rating system.** In country, state, and regional guides, we also rate towns and regions to help you narrow down your choices and budget your time accordingly. Hotels and restaurants are rated on a scale of zero (recommended) to three stars (exceptional). Attractions, shopping, nightlife, towns, and regions are rated according to the following scale: zero stars (recommended), one star (highly recommended), two stars (very highly recommended), and three stars (must-see).

In addition to the star-rating system, we also use **six feature icons** that point you to the great deals, in-the-know advice, and unique experiences that separate travelers from tourists. Throughout the book, look for:

Finds	Special finds—those places only insiders know about
Fun Fact	Fun facts—details that make travelers more informed and their trips more fun
Moments	Special moments—those experiences that memories are made of
Overrated	Places or experiences not worth your time or money
Tips	Insider tips—great ways to save time and money
Value	Great values—where to get the best deals

The following **abbreviations** are used for credit cards:

AE	American Express	DISC	Discover	V	Visa
DC	Diners Club	MC	MasterCard		

Frommers.com

Now that you have the guidebook to a great trip, visit our website at **www.frommers.com** for additional travel information on more than 3,500 destinations. We update features regularly to give you instant access to the most current trip-planning information available. At Frommers.com, you'll find scoops on the best airfares, lodging rates, and car rental bargains. You can even book your travel online through our travel booking partners. Other popular features include:

- Online updates to our most popular guidebooks
- Vacation sweepstakes and contest giveaways
- Newsletter highlighting the hottest travel trends
- Online travel message boards with featured travel discussions

What's New in New York City

With tourism levels remaining strong, the cost of visiting New York City is still high and lines at the most popular attractions can be long at peak times; plan your trip well ahead and make reservations for hotels and restaurants as early as possible, especially for moderate- and low-priced accommodations, which tend to book up quickly. The good news in New York City is that falling crime rates and a brisk pace of real-estate development have resulted in the city looks cleaner and feeling safer than ever.

WHAT TO SEE & DO Two major tourist attractions have been temporarily closed for major renovation—the **Liberty Science Center** (✆ 201/200-1000; www.lsc.org) right across the river in Jersey City, New Jersey, and the **Intrepid Sea-Air-Space Museum** (✆ 212/245-0072; www.intrepidmuseum.org) on the Hudson River in west Midtown. Both may re-open as early as summer 2007; call or log onto their websites for updated information. Two other attractions, however, have re-opened after extensive makeovers: the stately **Morgan Library,** 225 Madison Avenue at East 36th Street (✆ 212/685-0008) and the snazzy **Top of the Rock** observation deck at 30 Rockefeller Center (the entrance is on West 50th Street between Fifth and Sixth avenues; ✆ 212/698-2000), which is atop the GE Building, also the headquarters of the NBC television network.

Out in Brooklyn, the new **Jewish Children's Museum** opened in Crown Heights at 792 Eastern Parkway and Kingston Avenue, (✆ 718/467-0600), with a host of interactive exhibits dedicated to explaining Judaism to children of all faiths.

Farther in the future, visitors to New York City can look forward to the new state-of-the-art **water park** (New York City's first) on Randall's Island in the East River, projected to open in the summer of 2008; and the construction of new-and-improved baseball stadiums, adjacent to their current ballparks, for both the **New York Mets** (scheduled to open for the 2009 season) and the **New York Yankees** (scheduled to open in 2010). The proposed development of an in-town stadium for the **New York Jets,** however, is still mired in political wrangling.

To learn all about New York City's best sightseeing attractions for families, see chapter 6.

DINING The Manhattan outpost of the **Hard Rock Café** has moved from its former 57th Street location down to Times Square and now serves up excellent burgers and rock-'n'-roll memorabilia at 1501 Broadway between West 43rd and 44th streets (✆ 212/343-3355). An East Side branch has opened for the charmingly eccentric **Alice's Tea Cup** at 156 East 64th Street and Lexington Avenue (✆ 212/486-9200). A sister restaurant to the roadhouse-style Duke's barbecue restaurant near Gramercy Park has now opened in East Midtown: **Earl's,** 560 Third Avenue at East 37th Street (✆ 212/949-5400).

Two new fast-food chains have significantly raised the bar for take-out hamburgers, with organic ingredients and health-conscious cooking techniques: **New York Burger Co.** at 303 Park Avenue South between East 23rd and 24th streets (© 212/254-2727), and 678 Sixth Avenue between West 21st and 22nd streets (© 212/229-1404); and **Better Burger,** which has four branches, at 1614 Second Avenue and East 84th Street (© 212/734-6644), 587 Ninth Avenue at West 42nd Street (© 212/629-6622), 561 Third Avenue at East 37th Street (© 212/949-7528), and 178 Eighth Avenue at West 19th Street (© 212/989-6688). See chapter 5 for full reviews of these and other kid-friendly New York restaurants.

IN THE PARKS   Development on the Hudson riverfront continues apace, with the west side bike path completed and many new facilities being opened in **Hudson River Park.** Check out more recreational options in chapter 8.

SHOPPING   Not long after the successful opening of American Girl Place at Fifth Avenue and 49th Street, **Build-A-Bear Workshop** opened a similar destination store three blocks away at 565 Fifth Avenue, at East 46th Street (© 212/871-7080). A considerably larger version of the Build-A-Bear outlets as seen in shopping malls around the country, the bright and busy Manhattan flagship is designed for children to customize their own stuffed animals (as well as soft cloth dolls in the attached Friends2BMade shop), buy several only-in-New-York items, enjoy various activities, and eat in a nifty kid-friendly cafe (a good thing to know about if you're hungry in Midtown). Continuing this trend, the famous toy store

FAO Schwarz at 767 Fifth Avenue at East 58th Street, (© 212/644-9400) has opened an appealing soda shoppe on its ground floor, with its own handy entrance at the corner of Madison Avenue and East 58th Street.

For more information on these and other stores, see chapter 9.

ACCOMMODATIONS   The famous wedding-cake **Plaza Hotel** at 57th Street and Fifth Avenue has been closed and converted to condominium apartments, although once renovation is complete (by the fall of 2007), a small section of the building will be re-opened as a boutique hotel within the apartment building.

Hotel room rates have definitely been on the rise in Manhattan, though seasonal swings and package deals reveal deep discounts to offset the high rack rates. Several new hotels have been built in the current real-estate boom but, unfortunately, most of them cater to the high-end business traveler. See chapter 4 for complete details on a wide range of family-friendly lodgings.

ENTERTAINMENT   With the continued development of sports and entertainment facilities on Randall's Island in the East River, the touring company of **Cirque du Soleil** (© 800/678-5440 or 514/790-1245, www.cirquedusoleil.com) now sets up its delightfully gaudy blue-and-yellow tents every April through July, becoming a regular fixture on New York City's entertainment calendar. The Disney organization has expanded its family-oriented theatrical offerings, with four shows currently running at various Broadway theaters: *Aida, Beauty and the Beast, The Lion King,* and *Tarzan.* See chapter 10 for other entertainment options that appeal to families.

How to Feel Like a New York City Family

In those first few grim weeks after the September 11, 2001, attack on the World Trade Center, just about every family we knew asked themselves The Big Question: Does it still make sense to live in New York City? Not that we hadn't asked ourselves before—that always goes with the territory. New York, and especially Manhattan, is expensive, crowded, and hard to navigate even if you know all the secrets. In those haunted months of late 2001, it was awfully hard to remember why we had always answered The Big Question with a resounding "Yes."

And yet no one I knew moved out. If anything, New Yorkers' collective outpouring of kindness, generosity, and community spirit in the tragedy's aftermath made us feel more rooted than ever. (That image of NYC as a cold, heartless urban jungle? Blown forever.) The T-shirt motto that started appearing everywhere says all you need to know: I STILL ♥ NY. More than that: We still think it's the greatest place on earth to raise children.

It goes without saying that this is a city of unparalleled cultural richness, but what isn't so widely known is how much of it is accessible to families. In my New York years BC—Before Children—I did all the things folks think Manhattanites do: I went downtown to CBGBs to hear head-banging new bands; I did the standing-room thing at the Met and Carnegie Hall; I saw experimental theater pieces in dingy alternative spaces way downtown; I stood in line all day to get free tickets to Shakespeare in the Park. After my husband and I had our first baby, I thought my life as a Manhattanite was over. If we wanted to stay out late, we had to pay a fortune to a babysitter, and if we ordered tickets to anything in advance, we'd end up giving away our seats when the baby came down with an ear infection. We went out to eat as a family, but only at pizza, Chinese, and burger joints, where baby wails and spilled Cheerios would be tolerated.

Well, we've got three kids now, and I've come full circle. I feel as though I never really got to know Manhattan until I began exploring it with children. We actually talk to passersby now—there's no better way to strike up conversations with New Yorkers than by the simple virtue of having a baby strapped to your chest in a Snugli. (Alec Baldwin actually stopped *me* to have a chat when he spotted my week-old daughter, Grace.) Taxi drivers, most of them immigrants from far-flung lands, teach our kids about their native countries and coach them to speak words in their own languages. Deli clerks slip them tidbits; greengrocers pop extra strawberries into our pint cartons. When we pass fire stations, they're allowed to go inside and climb onto the hook-and-ladder truck, not to mention pat the firehouse dog.

I used to rush around the city underground, crammed into subway cars at rush hour; now we take buses at off-peak hours, peering out the windows as the city rolls past, or we stroll across Central Park, stopping frequently to feed ducks or watch horses on the bridle trail. We still go to museums, but we go to the same ones over and over; I've been to the American Museum of Natural History at least 100 times, and I'm ready to go again today if the kids so choose. After much trial and error, we know which restaurants are kid-friendly and still manage to have palatable food for adults. (Along the way, I've learned to accept that a toddler will be just fine if he or she eats only bread or french fries for one night.) We started our kids early with children's theater and puppet shows and dance concerts; and now they're happy to go with us to Broadway musicals, Philharmonic concerts in the park, and even the Metropolitan Opera. They're just about ready to see the head-banging bands at whatever grungy downtown clubs have replaced CBGBs—but I'm afraid they'll have to do that on their own.

Many families we know ditch the city every weekend to flee to a country house in the Hamptons or Connecticut, but we're rarely free to visit them. If we haven't got a soccer or baseball game in Central Park (or Riverside Park or out on Ward's Island), we have tickets to a show or concert or ballgame. En route, we may wander through a street fair, join a nature walk in Central Park, ride along the Hudson River bike path, or thread our way through the glitz and glitter of Times Square. On weekends we take the kids on subways, which they happen to love—what's not to love about whooshing through a dark underground tunnel in an air-conditioned stainless-steel bullet?—because that's the best way to get out to the Bronx Zoo, the Brooklyn Botanic Garden, or Shea Stadium.

The pulse and tempo of New York City can be dizzying at first if you're not used to it—I'll grant you that—but once you attune yourself, you'll find it tremendously exciting, even for youngsters. When my kids return to the city after an idyllic 2 weeks at the beach, they stride down the sidewalks and look around eagerly, glad to be back in a place where there's something happening every few yards. They love the fact that when they go to a playground, there's always someone else to play with. World-class museums are their after-school classrooms, where they encounter more art, science, and history than I'd been exposed to by the time I graduated from college. Central Park is their backyard, all 840 acres of it, and it provides them with nature ponds, tennis courts, horseback riding, ice-skating, and on and on and on.

Serendipity is the name of the game in New York City, all the more so if you've got kids. So many things come at you all the time, you can't help but stumble upon something interesting. Let me tell you about one Sunday we spent. Right after breakfast, from our own apartment windows, we heard via loudspeakers the pope—*the pope!*—saying mass in Central Park. Walking outside afterward, we saw legions of the faithful trooping home, festooned with pope pennants and memorabilia. As we rode the subway downtown, we were explaining who the pope is and why so many people wanted to see him—that is, until we changed trains and got distracted by the guy who plays electric harmonica on the N, R platform in Times Square. We went on to a SoHo furniture store where we saw performance artist Eric Bogosian trying out the rocking chairs (my kids weren't impressed, but my 5-year-old admitted that Bogosian's young son's leather jacket was pretty cool). When we ran into Bogosian and Bogosian, Jr., minutes later down the street at the Fire Museum, we all smiled at one another with recognition. ("Your kids bugging you to buy souvenir fire engines, too?" Bogosian's weary chuckle seemed to say to us.) Then, on the subway ride home, we sat next to Sarah Jessica Parker, who kept sneaking eye contact with our baby. By the time we got home, it was too late to cook, so we ordered in Chinese food; my older son, aka the Bok Choy Boy, snarfed down Buddhist Delight with his chopsticks like an old pro, while our toddler delicately dismantled an egg roll on her plate and smeared her face with cold sesame noodles. A whole family of satisfied customers.

We've come to realize that Manhattan isn't one monolithic city but a palimpsest of different cities sharing the same space. Just as the Alternative Art New York is worlds apart from the Wall Street New York, so is New York with Kids a quite different place from Singles New York—a sort of parallel universe, like in *A Wrinkle in Time* or *The Chronicles of Narnia*. It just takes time to scout out the turf. I've been scouting it for nearly 18 years now, and yet there's always something new for me to discover—some fresh reason to proclaim I STILL ♥ NY.

1 Frommer's Favorite New York City Family Experiences

- **Watching One of the Parades of All Nations:** Every one of the many nationalities that share New York City gets its own day in the sun— generally a national holiday celebrated with a parade down Fifth Avenue. St. Patrick's Day is the biggie—it's celebrated more festively here than it is even in Ireland—but there are scores of others, from the German Steuben Day Parade in September to the Puerto Rican Day Parade in June, complete with floats, marching bands, and loads of costumes from the old country. Scout out the uptown parts of the parade route (some parades get rowdy once they near Midtown). If crosstown traffic seems tied up on a fair-weather Saturday, hurry on over to Fifth— chances are there's a parade in progress. See "Kids' Favorite New York City Events," in chapter 2.

- **Taking the Ferry Ride to the Statue of Liberty and Ellis Island:** In many ways, the boat ride over is the best thing about this de rigueur sightseeing excursion—out on the sparkling waters of New York Harbor, with the wind in your hair and the seagulls shrieking overhead, you'll see the Manhattan skyline in all its glory. Even if there's a bit of a wait for the ferry at Battery Park, there are usually street musicians on hand to entertain you. Ride on the upper deck if you really want a dose of salt air and sun. See "Getting Around," in chapter 3.

- **Eating a Piece of New York Pizza:** Thin-crust pizza may have been invented in Naples, but New Yorkers know it was brought to perfection right here: oversize triangles with flat, crisp crusts, dripping with tangy tomato sauce and sloppy melted mozzarella. Even the most basic corner pizza stands usually have a couple of tables where you can sit and often feature open glass counters where kids can watch the pizza being made— toss the dough, smear the sauce, scatter on some cheese, fling on a few rounds of pepperoni, and presto! For some suggestions, see chapter 5.

- **Spending a Sunday Afternoon at the American Museum of Natural History:** Weekends are definitely family time at this magnificent big museum on the Upper West Side, but the more, the merrier—these dim, cool, high-ceilinged halls never seem too crowded. We never even bother with extra-charge activities like the planetarium show or the IMAX film; we head for back corners where there are old-fashioned dioramas we know

New York City Dateline

1524   Sailing under the French flag, Italian Giovanni da Verrazano is the first European to enter what's now New York Harbor.

1609   Henry Hudson sails up the Hudson River, exploring for the Dutch East India Company.

1626   The Dutch settle in Nieuw Amsterdam and make it a fur-trading post; Peter Minuit, governor of Nieuw Amsterdam, buys Manhattan Island from the Algonquin Indians for trinkets worth 60 florins (about $24).

1664   English invaders take Nieuw Amsterdam from the Dutch (wooden-legged Peter Stuyvesant is the Dutch governor).

1673   The Dutch take back Manhattan.

1674   Under the Treaty of Westminster, the Dutch finally give Nieuw Amsterdam to the English, who rename it New York after James, duke of York.

1776   American colonists topple the statue of King George on Bowling Green on July 9, but by year's end New York becomes a British stronghold for the rest of the American Revolution.

1783   Victorious Gen. George Washington bids farewell to his troops at Fraunces Tavern in Lower Manhattan.

1789   Washington is inaugurated as the first president at Federal Hall in New York City, the first capital of the new United States.

1790   Philadelphia deposes New York City as the nation's capital.

1792   The first U.S. stock exchange is founded in New York City, making it the country's financial capital.

1811   The city north of 14th Street is laid out, using an orderly grid system.

1853   The World's Fair is held in New York's Bryant Park.

1858–73   Central Park is laid out by Frederick Law Olmsted and Calvert Vaux.

and love (Asian Peoples and North American Woodlands are two faves) or stop by the Natural Science Center in the early afternoons for hands-on puttering with plants and live animals (for ages 4 and older). See p. 143.

- **Watching Sea-Lion Feeding Time at the Central Park Wildlife Center:** Check out the feeding schedule as you walk in the front entrance— the Sea Lion Pool is the centerpiece of this tidily landscaped little gem of a zoo, and an audience starts to gather well in advance. Claim a spot on the top steps where short people can most easily view the frisky sea lions. Don't expect fancy tricks, but there'll be enough barking and diving and splashing to satisfy everybody. See p. 153.

- **Hanging Out at Rockefeller Plaza:** The sunken plaza beneath the golden Prometheus statue truly is a locale for all seasons: In winter it's a tiny ice rink lively with the clash of blades and the tinny blare of piped-in music; in summer it's an open-air cafe with big umbrellas. In December it's an especially thrilling holiday sight, with the city's biggest Christmas tree (a real doozy) twinkling with lights. A railing surrounds the plaza at street level, where onlookers hang over and take in the scene; overhead, colorful flags

1883   The Brooklyn Bridge is completed, linking Manhattan and Brooklyn.

1885–86   The Statue of Liberty is erected in New York Harbor.

1892   Ellis Island opens as an immigration station.

1898   The newly consolidated New York City incorporates all five boroughs.

1904   Construction begins on the New York City subway system.

1929   The stock market crashes on October 29, sending not only Wall Street but also the entire nation into an economic tailspin that results in the Great Depression.

1939   New York's second World's Fair is held in Flushing Meadows, Queens.

1964–65   New York's third World's Fair is held in Flushing Meadows, Queens.

1970s   New York nearly declares bankruptcy.

1973   The World Trade Center opens.

1983   South Street Seaport's restoration begins.

1986   The Statue of Liberty's centennial is celebrated in gala style.

1990   Ellis Island reopens as a museum after a spectacular 6-year renovation.

1997   The restored New Amsterdam Theater launches the rehabilitation of West 42nd Street.

2001   Terrorists fly two 747s into the World Trade Center, laying waste to the site and killing thousands. Rescue and recovery efforts continue for months, with people from all across America rallying to New York City's support.

2004   On July 4, the cornerstone is laid for the new Freedom Tower, on the site of the former World Trade Center.

2005   Throughout February, tourists from around the world stroll through Christo & Jeanne Claude's *The Gates*, an immense celebratory artwork that fills Central Park with orange draperies fluttering from temporary arches.

flap from a rank of tall flagpoles. You really feel at the heart of the Big City. See "Midtown" in chapter 7.

- **Doing the Times Square Hustle:** With kids? Yes, indeed, because the panhandlers and hookers have been displaced by theme stores and restaurants, and the neon is more brilliant than ever. The Toys "R" Us store, the Hard Rock Cafe, Madame Tussaud's New York, the ESPN Zone, a picture window into the MTV studios, or David Letterman's antics up the street—it has an only-in-New-York energy and excitement you won't get anywhere else. See "Midtown," in chapter 7.

- **Heading to a Playground on a Weekday Afternoon:** Choose a neighborhood playground, pack a picnic lunch, and head for the sandpits, swings, and slides where New York kids hang out. Mornings are when parents with infants and toddlers congregate; preschoolers arrive after lunch; and the bigger kids hit the ground at 3 or 4pm, when schools let out. In summer many playgrounds have sprinklers that help youngsters cool off without getting all wet. See "The Playground Lowdown," in chapter 8.

- **Enjoying a Sunny Afternoon at a World-Famous Ballpark:** You've got two choices in New York: Yankee Stadium in the Bronx, where the Bronx Bombers play; and Shea Stadium in Flushing, Queens, where the Mets play. Both are handy to the subway, and unless there's a full-blown pennant race in swing, you can usually buy tickets that day, at least in the upper-level "nosebleed" sections (bring your mitt in hopes of high foul balls). Nobody minds if your kids make noise, you can leave early if they get tired, and there's plenty of food available—especially the overpriced hot dogs that are so much a part of the experience. See "Spectator Sports" in chapter 10.

2 The Best Hotel Bets

• **Most Family-Friendly:** The **Doubletree Guest Suites,** 1568 Broadway (© **800/222-8733** or 212/719-1600; p. 72), not only provides standard two-room accommodations sleeping four or six, but also kitchenettes, baby equipment, childproof rooms, and a super toddler playroom. The Upper East Side's **The Mark,** 25 E. 77th St. (© **800/843-6275** or 212/744-4300; p. 70), offers kids all sorts of amenities with its weekend packages, and **Le Parker Meridien,** 118 W. 57th St. (© **800/543-4300** or 212/245-5000; p. 73) has special welcoming packets for young guests; concierges at both of these hotels are full of great tips for kids visiting NYC.

• **Best Suite Deals:** The **Doubletree Guest Suites,** 1568 Broadway (© **800/222-8733** or 212/719-1600; p. 72), is a sensible family option, sleeping the whole crew in one unit for a relatively easy price. The **Embassy Suites Hotel,** 102 North End Ave. (© **800/EMBASSY** or 212/945-0100; p. 83), offers some very favorable rates on weekends for its roomy, sleek suites.

• **Most Peace & Quiet:** It's all relative in New York, of course, but the **Excelsior,** 45 W. 81st St. (© **800/368-4575** or 212/362-9200; p. 64) is buffered by Central Park and the park surrounding the Natural History, and the **Gracie Inn,** 502 E. 81st St. (© **212/628-1700;** p. 72), is tucked away on an Upper East Side street near the East River. Even in Midtown you can find residential quiet at the **Millennium U.N. Plaza,** 1 United Nations Plaza (© **800/222-8888** or 212/758-1234; p. 80), and the **Holiday Inn Midtown 57th Street,** 440 W. 57th St. (© **800/HOLIDAY** or 212/581-8100; p. 75).

• **Best Views:** Two downtown hotels feature dynamite New York Harbor views starring Lady Liberty and Ellis Island: The **Ritz-Carlton New York,** 2 West St. (© **800/241-3333** or 212/344-0800; p. 83), wins hands-down for its glorious open westward views from a majority of guest rooms, but there are several rooms with great harbor views also at the **Marriott New York Financial Center,** 80 West St. (© **800/228-9290** or 212/385-4900; p. 85). Central Park panoramas are worth requesting at **The Mark,** 25 E. 77th St. (© **800/843-6275** or 212/744-4300; p. 70).

• **When Price Is No Object:** My vote goes to **The Carlyle,** 35 E. 76th St. (© **800/227-5737** or 212/744-1600; p. 69), for its dignified East Side calm; its well-nigh-perfect service; and the spaciousness of its designer-decorated rooms, which really deserve to be called apartments. Spring for a suite with a Central Park view and a grand piano. The **Four Seasons,** 57 E. 57th St. (© **800/332-3442** or 212/ 758-5700; p. 77), has a stylish Midtown address, sleek if somewhat small rooms (but then, you can afford a suite, right?), fabulous service, and a surprisingly kid-friendly gourmet restaurant.

- **When Price Is Your Main Object:** You can't go wrong with the **Travel Inn,** 515 W. 42nd St. (© **800/869-4630** or 212/695-7171; p. 76), which delivers roomy, clean, fairly quiet motel rooms, plus a huge pool and free parking, for around $150 to $200 a night. Families willing to sleep in bunk beds and forgo en suite bathrooms should pounce on the very clean and safe, if somewhat spare, **Vanderbilt YMCA,** 224 E. 47th St. (© **212/756-9600;** p. 81) and **West Side YMCA,** 5 W. 63rd St. (© **212/ 875-4100;** p. 68).

- **Best Lobby:** You've gotta love the classic Art Deco lobby of the **Waldorf= Astoria,** 301 Park Ave. (© **800/ WALDORF,** 800/HILTONS, or 212/ 355-3000; p. 78), with its marble-faced pillars, deep carpeting, ornamental plasterwork, the magnificent Park Avenue entry chandelier, and that amazing clock near the front desk.

- **Best Pool:** The pool at the **Millennium U.N. Plaza Hotel,** 44th Street and First Avenue (© **800/222-8888** or 212/758-1234; p. 80), has it all: views, cleanliness, handsome tilework, and not much of a crowd.

- **Tops for Toddlers:** When all is said and done, the **Hotel Wales,** 1295 Madison Ave. (© **212/876-6000;** p. 71), wins for its Carnegie Hill location, friendly staff, breakfast buffet, residential calm, and Puss-in-Boots theme. The **Doubletree Guest Suites,** 1568 Broadway (© **800/222-8733** or 212/719-1600; p. 72), scores big here, too, for its suite convenience and toddler playroom.

- **Tops for Teens:** Budding bohemians may want to be in Greenwich Village at the **Washington Square Hotel,** 103 Waverly Place (© **800/222-0418** or 212/777-9515; p. 82), while trendsetters will gravitate to the way-cool decor and hipster cachet of **The Paramount,** 235 W. 46th St. (© **800/ 225-7474** or 212/764-5500; p. 75), or the art-jazzed vibe of the **Gershwin Hotel,** 7 E. 27th St. (© **212/545-8000;** p. 82).

3 The Best Dining Bets

- **Most Kid-Friendly Service:** Kudos to these family favorites, where every waiter and waitress I've ever encountered is friendly, uncloying, and unflappable: **American Girl Café,** 609 Fifth Ave. (© **877/247-5223;** p. 112); **Two Boots,** in the East Village at 37 Ave. A (© **212/505-2276;** p. 132); and **Ellen's Stardust Diner,** just north of Times Square at 1650 Broadway (© **212/956-5151;** p. 137).

- **Best Kids' Menu:** To most Manhattan restaurants, a kids' menu means burgers, chicken fingers, and spaghetti and meatballs, with maybe a hot dog or a grilled cheese sandwich thrown in. But **Gabriela's,** 688 Columbus Ave. (© **212/961-9600;** p. 101) makes kids' tacos and roast chicken that are wonderfully savory and free of spicy sauces. **Friend of a Farmer,** near Gramercy Park at 77 Irving Place (© **212/477-2188;** p. 122), adds some comfort foods like macaroni and cheese and chicken with pasta; and the publike **Telephone Bar & Grill,** at 149 Second Ave. (© **212/529-5000;** p. 129), includes such English-nanny favorites as shepherd's pie.

- **Best Views:** The **Rock Center Café,** 20 W. 50th St. (© **212/332-7620;** p. 115), features a movie-perfect view of Rockefeller Plaza's lower plaza—in winter you can watch ice-skaters through the windows, and in summer you can dine at tables set out on the plaza. Uptown, the **Boat Basin Café,** West 79th Street at the Hudson River in Riverside Park (© **212/496-5542;** p. 104), gives you a glorious river horizon, along with houseboats bobbing charmingly in the foreground.

- **Most Fun Decor:** The East Village's funky **Two Boots,** 37 Ave. A (© **212/ 505-2276;** p. 132), litters the dining room with a goofy collection of cowboy boots in every shape, color, and size; the Western motif at **Cowgirl Hall of Fame,** 519 Hudson St. (© **212/633-1133;** p. 126), is lively too, though a little more packaged. While there are plenty of retro diners in town, Midtown's **Prime Burger,** 5 E. 51st (© **212/759-4729;** p. 121), is the real thing: a 1950s coffee shop that time has passed by. Kids love the seats with the lift-up wooden trays.

- **Best Burgers:** My favorite just might be the perfectly grilled burgers at the Upper East Side's **Luke's Bar & Grill,** 1394 Third Ave. (© **212/249-7070;** p. 109), though a close runner-up would be the succulent O'Neal burger served not only at **O'Neal's,** 49 W. 64th St. (© **212/787-4663;** p. 101), but also at its fair-weather park satellites, including **Boat Basin Café,** West 79th Street at the Hudson River (© **212/496-5542;** p. 104). Village burger lovers have enshrined the **Corner Bistro,** 311 W. 4th St. (© **212/242-9502;** p. 126), for its big and meaty hamburgers. If you're partial to "sliders," those moist miniburgers steamed with onions, know that **Sassy's Sliders,** 1530 Third Ave. (© **212/828-6900;** p. 112),

puts the White Castle version to shame.

- **Best Breakfast:** TriBeCa's **Bubby's,** 120 Hudson St. (© **212/219-0666;** p. 137), welcomes kids for breakfast until 4pm daily; the weekend brunches are especially popular. At **NoHo Star,** 330 Lafayette St. (© **212/925-0070;** p. 126), breakfasts are blissfully relaxed and uncrowded. If it's lox and bagels you're after, the place to go is the famous **Barney Greengrass,** 541 Amsterdam Ave. (© **212/724-4707;** p. 103).

- **Best Brunch: Elephant and Castle,** 68 Greenwich Ave. (© **212/243-1400;** p. 126), is a longtime Village favorite for leisurely weekend brunches that won't break the bank.

- **Best Milkshakes:** In Midtown, head for **Route 66,** 858 Ninth Ave., (© **212/977-7600;** p. 121), which has a great variety of shakes and smoothies. The **Lexington Candy Shop,** 1226 Lexington Ave. (© **212/ 288-0057;** p. 111), has perfect classic milkshakes and malts in an authentic vintage coffee-shop setting. On the Upper West Side, my older son is partial to the shakes at **Homer's,** 487 Amsterdam Ave. (© **212/496-0777;** p. 105), though his brother is addicted, and I mean *addicted,* to their blue raspberry slushies.

- **Best Chinese:** While many Chinatowners roll out the dim sum carts only on Sunday, **Jing Fong,** at 18 Elizabeth St. (© **212/964-5256;** p. 135), makes every day a dim sum day, offering small servings of dumplings, skewers, rolls, and other delectables right at your table. Outside of Chinatown, **Ollie's Noodle Shops,** at 2315 Broadway (© **212/ 362-3111;** p. 106), 1991 Broadway (© **212/595-8181;** p. 106), and 200 W. 44th St. (© **212/921-5988;** p. 120), are can't-miss choices for not-too-exotic but still delicious Chinese fare.

• **Best Pizzas:** I'm treading on controversial ground here, in this pizza-loving city, but I'll have to give the nod to **John's Pizza;** the original Greenwich Village location, at 278 Bleecker St. (© 212/243-1680; p. 127), is still the best, but the branches at 408 E. 64th St. (© 212/935-2895; p. 111) and 260 W. 44th St. (© 212/391-7560; p. 120) serve up thin-crust brick-oven pies that are pretty darn close to perfection. I'm also partial to Midtown's **Angelo's Coal Oven Pizza,** 117 W. 57th St. (© 212/333-4333; p. 119) and 1043 Second Ave. (© 212/521-3600. Our neighborhood favorite is another thin-crust pie, on the Upper West Side at **Pizzabolla,** 654 Amsterdam Ave. (© 212/579-4500; p. 106).

• **Best Pastas:** Forget Little Italy: The best Italian pastas I've found, outside of a couple of expensive places I could never take kids, are at **Mangia e Bevi,** 800 Ninth Ave. (© 212/956-3976; p. 117), and sleek but casual **Bella Luna,** 584 Columbus Ave. (© 212/877-2267; p. 99).

• **Best Chicken Fingers:** Here's the lowdown from my son Tom, who's been seriously researching chicken fingers around the world for the past several years: the hands-down best in Manhattan are at **Artie's Delicatessen,** 2290 Broadway (© 212/579-5959; p. 103).

• **Grandma's Favorites:** For every dressed-up special meal, linen and china and all, I'd pick **Petaluma,** 1356 First Ave. (© 212/772-8800; p. 107). Afternoon tea couldn't be cozier than at the whimsical **Alice's Tea Cup,** at 102 W. 73rd St. (© 212/799-3006) or 156 E. 64th St. (© 212/486-9200).

• **Grandpa's Favorites:** At 42 Central Park S., **Mickey Mantle's** (© 212/688-7777; p. 114) celebrates the sports stars Granddad has actually heard of—plus it's handsome, the food's pretty darn good, and there are lots of big TVs so you won't miss the big game. Granddads also get a kick out of burgers and pig-out ice-cream sundaes at fun and friendly **Serendipity 3,** 225 E. 60th St. (© 212/838-3531; p. 109).

• **Most Fun Menu:** I love the wacky names of various dishes at **Chat 'n' Chew,** 10 E. 16th St. (© 212/243-1616; p. 123).

• **Best Floor Show:** Most waiters in Manhattan are really actors waiting for their break; the guys and gals at **Ellen's Stardust Diner,** 1650 Broadway (© 212/956-5151; p. 137), get to belt out their favorites to a karaoke machine in this Times Square cafe's weekend dinner shows. But for my sons, the flying knives of the teppanyaki chefs at **Benihana,** 47 W. 56th St. (© 212/581-0930; p. 113), are pretty hard to beat.

2

Planning a Family Trip to New York City

New York City is much more kid-friendly than most visitors anticipate—the trick lies in planning your trip to take advantage of it. Timing is everything, as is fortifying yourself with all the printed information you can snare.

1 Visitor Information

Once you decide to visit Manhattan, contact the **New York Convention & Visitors Bureau's Information Center,** 810 Seventh Ave., 3rd Floor, New York, NY 10019 (© **800/NYC-VISIT** or 212/397-8222; www.nycvisit.com), to ask for an Official NYC Visitor Kit, which includes a map, hotel lists, brochures, and sightseeing suggestions. The kit costs $5.95 for domestic orders and $9.95 for rush delivery and international orders. You can also order the *Official NYC Guide,* which is the heart of the kit, for free. If you have specific questions to ask, call visitor-center counselors at © **212/484-1222.** Other useful websites to consult are www.times squarenyc.org, www.gocitykids.com, and www.nycgovparks.org. The local parents' monthly **Big Apple Parent** (9 E. 38th St., 4th Floor, New York, NY 10016 (© **212/ 889-6400**) has a very useful site at www. parentsknow.com. Parents of infants may want to go online to check out **Urban Baby.com** (http://newyork.urbanbaby. com), which zeros in on topics such as maternity clothing stores, nursery furnishings, havens for nursing mothers, and baby-friendly playgrounds.

2 Entry Requirements & Customs

ENTRY REQUIREMENTS
PASSPORTS

For information on how to get a passport, go to **"Passports"** in the **"Fast Facts"** section of chapter 3—the websites listed provide downloadable passport applications as well as the current fees for processing passport applications. For an up-to-date, country-by-country listing of passport requirements around the world, go to the "Foreign Entry Requirement" Web page of the U.S. State Department at **http://travel.state.gov**. International visitors can obtain a visa application at the same website.

VISAS

For information on how to get a Visa, go to **"Visas"** in the **"Fast Facts"** section of chapter 3.

The U.S. State Department has a **Visa Waiver Program** allowing citizens of the following countries (at press time) to enter the United States without a visa for stays of up to 90 days: Andorra, Australia, Austria, Belgium, Brunei, Denmark, Finland, France, Germany, Iceland, Ireland, Italy, Japan, Liechtenstein, Luxembourg, Monaco, the Netherlands, New Zealand, Norway, Portugal, San Marino, Singapore,

Slovenia, Spain, Sweden, Switzerland, and the United Kingdom. Citizens of these nations need only a valid passport and a round-trip air or cruise ticket upon arrival. If they first enter the United States, they may also visit Mexico, Canada, Bermuda, and/or the Caribbean islands and return to the United States without a visa. Further information is available from any U.S. embassy or consulate. Canadian citizens may enter the United States without visas; they need only proof of residence.

Citizens of all other countries must have (1) a valid passport that expires at least 6 months later than the scheduled end of their visit to the United States, and (2) a tourist visa, which may be obtained without charge from any U.S. consulate.

MEDICAL REQUIREMENTS

Unless you're arriving from an area known to be suffering from an epidemic (particularly cholera or yellow fever), inoculations or vaccinations are not required for entry into the United States. If you have a medical condition that requires **syringe-administered medications,** carry a valid signed prescription from your physician—the Federal Aviation Administration (FAA) no longer allows airline passengers to pack syringes in their carry-on baggage without documented proof of medical need. If you have a disease that requires treatment with **narcotics,** you should also carry docu-mented proof with you—smuggling narcotics aboard a plane is a serious offense that carries severe penalties in the U.S.

For **HIV-positive visitors,** requirements for entering the United States are somewhat vague and change frequently. For up-to-the-minute information, contact **AIDSinfo** (© **800/448-0440,** or 301/519-6616 outside the U.S.; www.aidsinfo. nih.gov) or the **Gay Men's Health Crisis** (© **212/367-1000;** www.gmhc.org).

CUSTOMS
WHAT YOU CAN BRING INTO NEW YORK

Every visitor more than 21 years of age may bring in, free of duty, the following: (1) 1 liter of wine or hard liquor; (2) 200 cigarettes, 100 cigars (but not from Cuba), or 3 pounds of smoking tobacco; and (3) $100 worth of gifts. These exemptions are offered to travelers who spend at least 72 hours in the United States and who have not claimed them within the preceding 6 months. It is altogether forbidden to bring into the country foodstuffs (particularly fruit, cooked meats, and canned goods) and plants (vegetables, seeds, tropical plants, and the like). Foreign tourists may carry in or out up to $10,000 in U.S. or foreign currency with no formalities; larger sums must be declared to U.S. Customs on entering or leaving, which includes filing form CM 4790. For details regarding U.S. Customs and Border Protection, consult your nearest U.S. embassy or consulate, or **U.S. Customs and Border Protection** (© **202/927-1770;** www. customs.ustreas.gov).

WHAT YOU CAN TAKE HOME FROM NEW YORK
Canadian Citizens

For a clear summary of Canadian rules, write for the booklet *I Declare,* issued by the **Canada Border Services Agency** (© **800/461-9999** in Canada, or 204/983-3500; **www.cbsa-asfc.gc.ca**).

U.K. Citizens

For information, contact **HM Customs & Excise** at © **0845/010-9000** (from outside the U.K., 020/8929-0152), or consult their website at **www.hmce.gov.uk**.

Australian Citizens

A helpful brochure available from Australian consulates or Customs offices is *Know Before You Go.* For more information, call the **Australian Customs Service** at © **1300/363-263,** or log on to **www. customs.gov.au**.

New Zealand Citizens

Most questions are answered in a free pamphlet available at New Zealand consulates and Customs offices: *New Zealand Customs Guide for Travellers, Notice no. 4.*

For more information, contact New Zealand Customs, The Customhouse, 17–21 Whitmore St., Box 2218, Wellington (© 04/473-6099 or 0800/428-786; www.customs.govt.nz).

3 Money

KEEPING COSTS LOW

New York is a notoriously expensive destination to visit, but there are definitely ways to keep expenses under control. The first is to aggressively look for **hotel discounts,** through a travel agent or on the Internet (see "The 21st-Century Traveler," below). Many Midtown hotels offer excellent weekend or summer packages. Once you arrive, use **public transportation** instead of taxis as often as possible; subways are wonderfully fast and safe, and buses, though prone to traffic slowdowns, are a great way to see the city. Use the **TKTS booth** or other theater discount schemes to get half-price tickets to Broadway shows; even though the season's hottest seats may be excluded, you're bound to get into something memorable. And make **smart restaurant choices;** theme restaurants may be exciting for kids, but you'll pay double the price for a mediocre hamburger there. Sample New York's coffee shops and ethnic storefront restaurants instead, and if there's no children's menu per se, don't be shy about asking to have your children share one adult-size entree—that is, if you can get two siblings to agree on an entree!

ATMs

Nationwide, the easiest and best way to get cash away from home is from an ATM (automated teller machine), sometimes referred to as a "cash machine," or "cashpoint." Walk-up ATMs can be found every few blocks in New York City, at various bank branches, hotels, grocery stores, and delis. Look at the back of your bank card to see which network you're on—**Cirrus** (© **800/424-7787;** www.mastercard.com) or **PLUS** (© **800/843-7587;** www.visa. com)—then call or check online for ATM locations at your destination. Be sure you know your personal identification number (PIN) and daily withdrawal limit before you depart. *Note:* Remember that many banks impose a fee every time you use a card at another bank's ATM, and that fee can be higher for international transactions (up to $5 or more) than for domestic ones (where they're rarely more than $2). In addition, the bank from which you withdraw cash may charge its own fee. To compare banks' ATM fees within the U.S., use **www. bankrate.com**. For international withdrawal fees, ask your bank.

Tips Easy Money

You'll avoid lines at airport ATMs by exchanging at least some money—just enough to cover airport incidentals and transportation to your hotel—before you leave home.

When you change money, ask for some small bills or loose change. Petty cash will come in handy for tipping and public transportation. Consider keeping the change separate from your larger bills, so that it's readily accessible and you'll be less of a target for theft.

Tips **Small Change**

Try to keep on hand small bills or loose change, which will come in handy for tipping, bus fares, and taxi fares (New York cabbies quickly run out of singles and fives when one passenger after another pays with a crisp $20 bill fresh from a cash machine).

CREDIT CARDS & DEBIT CARDS

Credit cards are the most widely used form of payment in the United States: **Visa** (Barclaycard in Britain), **MasterCard** (EuroCard in Europe, Access in Britain, Chargex in Canada), **American Express, Diners Club,** and **Discover.** They also provide a convenient record of all your expenses, and they generally offer relatively good exchange rates. You can withdraw cash advances from your credit cards at banks or ATMs, provided you know your PIN.

Visitors from outside the U.S. should inquire whether their bank assesses a 1% to 3% fee on charges incurred abroad.

In New York City, most hotels and restaurants accept all major credit cards, except for some storefront restaurants; those that do not are noted in this book's listings.

It's highly recommended that you travel with at least one major credit card. You must have one to rent a car, and hotels and airlines usually require a credit card imprint as a deposit against expenses.

ATM cards with major credit card backing, known as **"debit cards,"** are now a commonly acceptable form of payment in most stores and restaurants. Debit cards draw money directly from your checking account. Some stores enable you to receive "cash back" on your debit-card purchases as well. The same is true at most U.S. post offices

TRAVELER'S CHECKS

Traveler's checks are widely accepted in the U.S., but foreign visitors should make sure that they're denominated in U.S. dollars; foreign-currency checks are often difficult to exchange.

You can buy traveler's checks at most banks. Most are offered in denominations of $20, $50, $100, $500, and sometimes $1000. Generally, you'll pay a service charge ranging from 1% to 4%.

The most popular traveler's checks are offered by **American Express** (© 800/807-6233; © 800/221-7282 for card holders—this number accepts collect calls, offers service in several foreign languages, and exempts Amex gold and platinum cardholders from the 1% fee.); **Visa** (© 800/732-1322)—AAA members can obtain Visa checks for a $9.95 fee (for checks up to $1,500) at most AAA offices or by calling © 866/339-3378; and **MasterCard** (© 800/223-9920).

If you do choose to carry traveler's checks, keep a record of their serial numbers separate from your checks in the event that they are stolen or lost. You'll get a refund faster if you know the numbers.

4 When to Go

New York buzzes every day, with pretty much everything open year-round. All school vacation seasons—late December, spring vacation, and summer—tend to be busy times; lots of museums schedule special programs then, because New York schoolchildren are looking for something to do, too. December is particularly jam-packed, with lots of annual holiday entertainment (the *Nutcracker,* the Big Apple Circus, the Radio City Christmas Spectacular). Fall is traditionally the prime

What Things Cost in New York City	U.S.$
Hot dog at corner umbrella cart	1.25–1.50
Hot pretzel at corner umbrella cart	1.25–1.50
12-oz. soft drink in a deli	1.00
16-oz. apple juice in a deli	1.25
Takeout bagel with cream cheese	1.00–1.50
Slice of plain pizza	1.50–2.50
McDonald's McNuggets Happy Meal	3.55–3.99
Local telephone call	0.50
Movie ticket	10.00–11.00 adult, 7.50–8.00 child
Taxi ride from the American Museum of Natural History to American Girl Place	10.00 (plus $2.00 tip)
Taxi ride from South Street Seaport to Rockefeller Center, depending on traffic	17.00 (plus $3.50 tip)
Package of Pampers/Huggies	11.00
32-oz. can prepared Similac formula	6.00

season for culture, with new plays opening on Broadway and classical-music venues booked solid, but even in summer, music series at Lincoln Center and star-studded limited-run plays fill the boards. Spring and summer weekends really bustle, with street fairs all over town and what seems like an endless succession of parades, one for every ethnic group in the city, filing down Fifth Avenue.

There's no "high" or "low" season as far as hotel rates go, though it may be particularly tough to get a reservation around Christmas or during the fall and spring fashion shows. Hotels are slightly less crowded on weekends, when business travelers clear out of town; many even offer weekend package rates.

In terms of weather, winter tends to be cold but not intolerably so, whereas July and August can be sweltering and muggy—but that never stops hordes of visitors from descending on the city every summer. For up-to-date forecasts, visit **www.intellicast.com** or **www.weather.com**.

New York's Average Temperature & Rainfall

	Jan	Feb	Mar	Apr	May	June	July	Aug	Sept	Oct	Nov	Dec
Daily Temp. (°F)	38	40	48	61	71	80	85	84	77	67	54	42
Daily Temp. (°C)	3	4	9	16	22	27	29	29	25	19	12	6
Days of Precipitation	11	10	11	11	11	10	11	10	8	8	9	10

KIDS' FAVORITE NEW YORK CITY EVENTS

The following information is always subject to change. Always confirm information before you make plans around a specific event. Call the venue or the NYCVB at ✆ 212/484-1222, go to **www.nycvisit.com**, or pick up a copy of **Time Out New York** once you arrive in the city for the latest details.

January

New York National Boat Show. Slip on your Top-Siders and head to the Jacob K. Javits Convention Center, which promises a leviathan fleet of boats and marine products from the world's leading manufacturers. Call ℂ 212/984-7000, or point your Web browser to www.newyorkboatshow.com or www.javitscenter.com. First or second week in January.

February

Black History Month is observed with some very good programs for kids at museums around town. Throughout February.

Chinese New Year rattles the streets of lower Manhattan with parades, dragon and lion dancers, firecrackers, and fun. Call the NYCVB (ℂ 212/484-1222) or visit www.nycvisit.com for details on this year's celebration.

The **Westminster Kennel Club Dog Show** at Madison Square Garden (ℂ 212/465-MSG1; www.thegarden.com or www.westminsterkennelclub.org) brings champion pooches of every breed to the city. Besides watching the judging, it's fun just to walk around outside the ring, where the dogs and handlers hang out. Mid-February.

March

The **St. Patrick's Day parade** rolls down Fifth Avenue with over 150,000 marchers—it's the world's largest civilian parade. The parade usually starts at 11am, but go extra early if you want a good spot. Call ℂ 212/484-1222 for more information. March 17.

The **Ringling Bros. Barnum & Bailey Circus** begins its annual month-long run at Madison Square Garden. For dates and ticket information, check out the website at www.ringling.com or contact Madison Square Garden (ℂ 212/465-MSG1, www.thegarden.com). Late March to mid-April.

April

The annual **Central Park Easter egg hunt** is held on Easter weekend near the Bandshell, with activities, giveaways, and visiting celebrities.

The **Easter Parade** is a stroll down Fifth Avenue that anyone can join—the bigger the bonnet, the better. The parade generally runs from about 10am to 3 or 4pm. Call ℂ 212/484-1222. Easter Sunday.

May

Bike New York: The Great Five Boro Bike Tour. The largest mass-participation cycling event in the United States attracts about 30,000 cyclists from all over the world. After a 42-mile (68km) ride through the five boroughs, finalists are greeted with a traditional New York–style celebration of food and music. Call ℂ 212/932-BIKE (2453) or visit www.bikenewyork.org. First or second Sunday in May.

The Brooklyn Botanic Garden's annual **Cherry Blossom Festival** takes a cue from Japanese tradition in celebrating the flowering pink trees around its pond. Call ℂ 718/623-7200 or visit www.bbg.org. Early May.

Fleet Week welcomes a host of U.S. and foreign naval ships to the Hudson River piers around Memorial Day weekend, highlighted by a parade of ships. Call ℂ 212/484-1222. Late May.

June

Museum Mile Festival. Fifth Avenue from 82nd to 106th streets is closed to cars from 6 to 9pm as 20,000-plus strollers enjoy live music from Broadway tunes to string quartets, street entertainers from juggling to giant puppets, and free admission to nine Museum Mile institutions, including the Metropolitan Museum of Art and the Guggenheim. Call ℂ 212/606-2296 or check www.museummilefestival.org

or any of the participating institutions for details. Usually the second Tuesday in June.

SummerStage. A summer-long festival of outdoor performances in Central Park, featuring world music, pop, folk, and jazz artists ranging from Fiona Apple to the New York Grand Opera (always performing Verdi) to the Chinese Golden Dragon Acrobats. Performances are often free, but certain events require purchased tickets (usually around $35). Call © 212/360-2756 or visit www.summerstage.org. June through August.

July

Macy's July 4 Fireworks Spectacular explodes in the skies over the East River. The best vantage point is from the FDR Drive, which closes to traffic several hours before sunset. Call Macy's Visitor Center at © 212/494-4495. July 4th.

August

The **Lincoln Center Out-of-Doors Festival** turns the plaza around the arts complex into one big street fair, with crafts and food stalls and loads of free performances. Call © 212/546-2656 or visit www.lincolncenter.org for this year's schedule. Throughout August.

The **U.S. Open Tennis Championships** are played in Flushing Meadows, Queens, for 2 weeks starting just before Labor Day. Tickets go on sale in May or early June and often sell out immediately; call © 866/OPEN-TIX or 718/760-6200 well in advance; visit www.usopen.org for additional information. Late August to early September.

September

The **Feast of San Gennaro** fills the streets of Little Italy with carnival booths and Italian food stands for a week around the saint's day, September 19. Call © 212/768-9320 or visit www.sangennaro.org for more information.

October

The **Feast of St. Francis** turns the Cathedral of St. John the Divine into a menagerie of animals for its Blessing of the Animals on the first Sunday of the month. Call © 212/316-7490 or visit www.stjohndivine.org.

The **Big Apple Circus** settles in for its annual 3-month run at Lincoln Center's Damrosch Park. Call © 212/307-4100 or check out www.bigapple circus.org.

The **Greenwich Village Halloween Parade** marches up lower Sixth Avenue. Call the Village Voice Parade hot line at © 212/475-3333, ext. 14044, or visit www.halloween-nyc.com. October 31.

November

The **Radio City Christmas Spectacular** at Radio City Music Hall ushers in the holiday season early, beginning a 2-month run. Call © 212/247-4777 or visit www.radiocity.com for exact dates; buy tickets at the box office or via Ticketmaster's Radio City Hot line at © 212/307-1000 or www.ticketmaster. com.

The **Macy's Thanksgiving Day Parade** runs from 77th Street and Central Park West down to Broadway and 34th Street; sidewalk viewing along the route is first-come, first-served. The evening before, the parade's mighty balloons are blown up on 77th and 81st streets, around the Museum of Natural History; go early, as it gets to be a mob scene by 8pm. Call Macy's Visitor Center at © 212/494-4495.

December

The **Christmas Tree Lighting** at Rockefeller Center is accompanied by an ice-skating show and a huge crowd. The tree stays lit around the clock until after the new year. Contact © 212/332-6868 or www.rockefellercenter. com for this year's date.

The *Nutcracker* ballet, performed by the New York City Ballet every year at Lincoln Center, is a perpetual delight. Call © **212/870-5570** or visit www. nycballet.com.

The Lighting of the Giant Hanukkah Menorah at Grand Army Plaza (Fifth Ave. and 59th St.) is performed on the world's largest menorah (32 ft. high) each evening during Hanukkah.

New Year's Eve is celebrated famously in Times Square; although this is hardly an event for kids (or for parents who aren't crazy about lunatic crowds), several other events around town capitalize on the holiday. Contact www. timessquarenyc.org for helpful information. December 31 to January 1.

5 What to Pack

If you plan to go out to a fancy dinner or the theater, you'll want at least one **dressy outfit,** which means a jacket and tie for men (boys may be able to get by without the tie). Most restaurants have no dress code, though.

It's important to remember that this is preeminently a walking city. There's almost always a bit of a walk from the subway to wherever you're going, and even if you intend to cab it everywhere, you'll have to sprint for a taxi or two or trudge a few blocks when no cabs are in sight—which will happen. So bring **sturdy low-heeled shoes,** and don't skip **socks** unless you're wearing well-broken-in sneakers. Sandals aren't a good option, because the streets can be dirty, and your bare toes are vulnerable to being run over by a kamikaze bicycle messenger, a rolling dress rack or hot dog cart, or any of a dozen other urban vehicles.

Walking a lot also makes **strollers** a must for any young children who can't hike at least a mile without complaining. Strollers can be a hassle, though, when getting in and out of cabs or up and down subway stairs; make sure you've got one that folds easily. If you have an infant, a **soft carrier** is a better idea.

July and August can be miserably hot and sticky, conditions worsened by the fact that subway platforms are like saunas, thanks to the heat thrown off by the subway trains' air-conditioning (subway cars are glacially cool, by the way).

Short-sleeved T-shirts and **shorts** are best—the roomier, the better. **Sun hats** are helpful, and a **folding hand fan** is a great idea—if nothing else, it could distract the kids from how hot it is. If you don't own such a thing, buy one in Chinatown while you're here.

January and February may be cold, but all the buildings around you in Manhattan retain heat, so it's never as cold here as it is outside the city. Still, this is the Northeast, so **gloves, hats,** and **scarves** are advisable if you arrive from November to March. If it does snow, the streets are plowed swiftly, and sidewalks get shoveled fast: It takes a really big blizzard to stop Manhattan in its tracks. But plowed banks of snow can stand for weeks, getting filthier and filthier. **Boots** are a good idea in winter, just in case, because sewers quickly back up, and lake-size puddles form at curbs—too big for kids to jump over.

If you're bringing an infant, call ahead to your hotel to check what baby equipment it can provide—besides a crib, it may help to have a bathing ring and a high chair in your room. You may want to pack a few **outlet covers** so you can childproof your room when you arrive. Of course, you can buy diapers, wipes, formula, and no-tears shampoo here, but it might be handier to bring your own **bottles, spout cups, feeding dish,** and **infant spoon,** which you can bring to restaurants.

Accidents do happen, so bring **extra changes of clothes** for your children; for infants and for toddlers who haven't mastered the fine art of using the potty, make that two or three changes of clothes for each day. You'll also want a **tote bag** full of toys, preferably toys without lots of separate pieces (imagine trying to pick up dozens of spilled Lego bricks off the floor of an airplane!). Older kids may want to carry their own **backpacks** with books, colored markers and pads, a deck of cards, handheld electronic games, a personal CD player, or whatever keeps them happy.

6 Travel Insurance

The cost of travel insurance varies widely, depending on the cost and length of your trip, your age and health, and the type of trip you're taking, but expect to pay between 5% and 8% of the vacation itself. You can get estimates from various providers through **InsureMyTrip.com**. Enter your trip cost and dates, your age, and other information, for prices from more than a dozen companies.

TRIP-CANCELLATION INSURANCE

Trip-cancellation insurance will help retrieve your money if you have to back out of a trip or depart early, or if your travel supplier goes bankrupt. Permissible reasons for trip cancellation can range from sickness to natural disasters to the State Department declaring a destination unsafe for travel.

For more information, contact one of the following recommended insurers: Access America (© 866/807-3982; www.accessamerica.com); Travel Guard International (© 800/826-4919; www.travelguard.com); Travel Insured International (© 800/243-3174; www.travel insured.com); and Travelex Insurance Services (© 888/457-4602; www.travelex-insurance.com).

MEDICAL INSURANCE

Although it's not required of travelers, health insurance is highly recommended. Most health insurance policies cover you if you get sick away from home—but verify that you're covered before you depart, particularly if you're insured by an HMO.

International visitors should note that unlike many European countries, the United States does not usually offer free or low-cost medical care to its citizens or visitors. Doctors and hospitals are expensive, and in most cases will require advance payment or proof of coverage before they render their services. Good policies will cover the costs of an accident, repatriation, or death. Packages such as **Europ Assistance's "Worldwide Healthcare Plan"** are sold by European automobile clubs and travel agencies at

---

Travel in the Age of Bankruptcy

Airlines go bankrupt, so protect yourself by **buying your tickets with a credit card.** The Fair Credit Billing Act guarantees that you can get your money back from the credit card company if a travel supplier goes under (and if you request the refund within 60 days of the bankruptcy). **Travel insurance** can also help, but make sure it covers against "carrier default" for your specific travel provider. And be aware that if a U.S. airline goes bust mid-trip, a 2001 federal law requires other carriers to take you to your destination (albeit on a space-available basis) for a fee of no more than $25, provided you rebook within 60 days of the cancellation.

attractive rates. **Worldwide Assistance Services, Inc.** (© 800/777-8710; www. worldwideassistance.com) is the agent for Europ Assistance in the United States.

Though lack of health insurance may prevent you from being admitted to a hospital in nonemergencies, don't worry about being left on a street corner to die: The American way is to fix you now and bill the living daylights out of you later.

INSURANCE FOR BRITISH TRAV-ELERS Most big travel agents offer their own insurance and will probably try to sell you their package when you book a holiday. Think before you sign. **Britain's Consumers' Association** recommends that you insist on seeing the policy and reading the fine print before buying travel insurance. **The Association of British Insurers** (© 020/7600-3333; www.abi. org.uk) gives advice by phone and publishes *Holiday Insurance,* a free guide to policy provisions and prices. You might also shop around for better deals: Try **Columbus Direct** (© 0870/033- 9988; www.columbusdirect.net).

INSURANCE FOR CANADIAN TRAV-ELERS Canadians should check with their provincial health plan offices or call **Health Canada** (© 866/225-0709; www. hc-sc.gc.ca) to find out the extent of their coverage and what documentation and receipts they must take home in case they are treated in the United States.

LOST-LUGGAGE INSURANCE
On flights within the U.S., checked baggage is covered up to $2,500 per ticketed passenger. On flights outside the U.S. (and on U.S. portions of international trips), baggage coverage is limited to approximately $9.07 per pound, up to approximately $635 per checked bag. If you plan to check items more valuable than what's covered by the standard liability, see if your homeowner's policy covers your valuables, get baggage insurance as part of your comprehensive travel-insurance package, or buy Travel Guard's "BagTrak" product.

If your luggage is lost, immediately file a lost-luggage claim at the airport, detailing the luggage contents. Most airlines require that you report delayed, damaged, or lost baggage within 4 hours of arrival. The airlines are required to deliver luggage, once found, directly to your house or destination free of charge.

---

7 Health & Safety

STAYING HEALTHY
New York City has no less healthy an environment than that of any other large city: The climate is temperate, public hygiene is relatively good, and the water supply is highly drinkable (in fact, in blind taste tests, New York tap water often scores higher than bottled waters). Although most visitors don't think of New York as an outdoor destination, if you plan to be in the parks a good deal during warm weather, insect repellent is advised, as mosquito- and tick-borne illnesses like the West Nile virus and Lyme disease can be contracted here as readily as anywhere in the Northeast.

If you or your child suffers from conditions like epilepsy, diabetes, or heart problems, wear a **MedicAlert identification tag** (© 888/633-4298; www.medic alert.org), which will immediately alert doctors to your condition and give them access to your records through MedicAlert's 24-hour hot line.

WHAT TO DO IF YOU GET SICK AWAY FROM HOME
There is one great advantage to getting sick in the city that never sleeps: Drugstores and hospital emergency rooms are open 24 hours a day, should you need them, and the quality of medical care is very high. (See "Fast Facts," in chapter 3,

Healthy Travels to You

The following government websites offer up-to-date health-related travel advice.
- **Australia:** www.dfat.gov.au/travel/
- **Canada:** www.hc-sc.gc.ca/index_e.html
- **U.K.:** www.dh.gov.uk/PolicyAndGuidance/HealthAdviceForTravellers/fs/en
- **U.S.:** www.cdc.gov/travel/

for the one nearest you, as well as contacts for local doctors, dentists, and poison control.) To streamline matters, however, bring an extra supply of any **prescription medications** you or your child may be taking, and carry them in their original containers, with pharmacy labels—otherwise, they won't make it through airport security. Divide them between carry-on and checked luggage so that if you lose a bag, you won't be left in the lurch. It's also a good idea to contact your pediatrician before you leave to get a written prescription for any medicines you might lose or run out of and to obtain a reference for a New York City pediatrician in case of a sudden illness. Failing that, your hotel's front desk should be able to put you in touch with a local doctor if illness flares up during your New York City stay. To be on the safe side, bring a supply of any over-the-counter medication your child often needs—why waste vacation time looking for the one brand of diaper ointment that works on your baby's bottom or searching for the only flavor of Tylenol your child is willing to take?

8 Words of Wisdom & Helpful Resources

I can understand how intimidating it must be to families who come here as tourists, not knowing a single local soul, trying to navigate and negotiate around the sights. In New York's heavily touristy areas, the prices are high, the traffic is dense, and the crowds are pushy and rude. Outside those areas, certain pockets of town may be dingy and even downright scary. And when you're traveling with kids, one bad experience can send you home shaking your head and wondering why anybody would live in a place like New York City.

So let's deal with some of the negatives head-on. First of all: **Yes, there's crime in New York,** but it's by no means America's crime capital (perhaps the biggest coup of Rudolph Giuliani's mayorship was the city's plummeting crime rate in all categories). Stay alert, and follow the tips in "Health & Safety" above.

Second: **Yes, it's deliriously easy to spend money here.** Right off the bat, a lot of it gets eaten up by transportation, which surprises folks who are used to driving everywhere they go. Even if you take public transportation, you'll be spending $8 every time your family of four jumps on a bus (whereas a short trip by taxi might cost only $6). So be strategic in your sightseeing: Visit several sites in one neighborhood at a time, and walk between neighborhoods if you've got the stamina and time (in Manhattan, there's always enough to gaze at en route that you won't be bored). Buy MetroCard passes if you plan to crisscross the city. On the other hand, sometimes an extra block's walk may save you money on a restaurant or store; don't fall for tourist traps. And at the beginning of your visit, set a firm limit on souvenir buying, because your kids will be enticed at every turn.

Three Invaluable Tips

- **Eat outdoors whenever you can.** If a restaurant has tables in a courtyard or on the sidewalk, grab them (your fellow diners won't hear your kids' racket, and the passing show will distract your restless offspring). If the weather's decent, pick up food from a deli or hot dog stand, and eat in a park—you'll save money and have fun.
- **Never be shy about asking directions.** New Yorkers may look like they're in a rush, but most are such incurable know-it-alls, they're always happy to tell you where to go. Even lifelong Manhattanites can get disoriented when emerging from a subway station, so verifying that you're headed the right way doesn't brand you as a tourist. Don't wear your kids out with needless walking—ask.
- **Don't spend all your time in Midtown.** Granted, most visitors' hotels are in Midtown, and there are some boffo attractions for kids here—the Empire State Building, the Sony Wonder Technology Lab, Toys "R" Us, American Girl Place, the New Victory Theater—but you can't really understand New York City unless you get out to the neighborhoods. They're quieter, safer, cheaper, and more kid-friendly. The Upper West Side, the Upper East Side, Greenwich Village, Chelsea, and Brooklyn Heights—this is where New Yorkers with children live. Go thou and do likewise.

Yet another reality of life in New York is the **street people.** The number of beggars and homeless people has fallen drastically since the late 1980s; panhandlers aren't allowed to hassle people on the subways anymore (though a few still do). Nevertheless, you and your kids may spot a diehard vagrant or two sleeping in doorways or pawing through corner trash bins. Act like it's no big deal, and your kids will take their cue from you.

The reason folks are more likely to run into desperate characters like this in New York is really not because New York has such a high percentage of weirdos, wackos, and wastrels. It's simply because you're always out walking on the streets here, not whizzing around in the isolation of your car. With so many millions of human beings coexisting in a relatively small area, you'll come into contact with lots of people in the course of a day, and by the law of averages, some of those people will have

more of an edge to them than you'd like. But to my mind that's just the flip side of one of this city's great pluses: Everybody, from the Wall Street banker to the greengrocer to the starving actor waiting tables, shares the streets. The rich can't ignore the poor, the young can't ignore the old, the Republicans can't ignore the Democrats, and vice versa. My kids are aware of how tough it is for people in wheelchairs to get around because they often have to wait on a city bus while such folks haul themselves aboard. They know that not everyone in the world speaks English because there's a constant counterpoint of French, Greek, Urdu, or Japanese swirling around them. A million different agendas clash every day in the Manhattan melee, and it keeps us all in touch with reality. Kids who grow up in New York City tend to have street smarts—not a bad thing to have, in my opinion.

FAMILY TRAVEL RESOURCES

Recommended family travel websites include **Family Travel Forum** (www.familytravelforum.com), a comprehensive site that offers customized trip planning; **Family Travel Network** (www.familytravelnetwork.com), an award-winning site that offers travel features, deals, and tips; **Traveling Internationally with Your Kids** (www.travelwithyourkids.com), a comprehensive site offering sound advice for long-distance and international travel with children; and **Family Travel Files** (www.thefamilytravelfiles.com), which has many vacation ideas for families traveling with children.

FOR SINGLE PARENTS

Online, the **Single Parent Travel Network** (www.singleparenttravel.net) offers excellent advice, travel specials, a bulletin board, and a free electronic newsletter. The **Family Travel Forum** (www.familytravelforum.com) also hosts a single-parent travel bulletin board for tips from fellow travelers.

FOR GRANDPARENTS

Mention the fact that you're a senior citizen when you make your travel reservations. Check with your airline (especially America West, Continental, and American) to see if they offer senior discounts; many hotels also offer discounts for seniors. In most cities, people over the age of 60 qualify for reduced admission to theaters, museums, and other attractions, as well as discounted fares on public transportation.

One reliable agency that targets traveling grandparents is **Elderhostel** (© 877/426-8056; www.elderhostel.org), which arranges study programs for those aged 55 and over in the U.S. Most courses last 5 to 7 days in the U.S. and many include airfare, accommodations in university dormitories or modest inns, meals, and tuition.

Members of **AARP** (© 888/687-2277; www.aarp.org) get discounts on hotels, airfares, and car rentals. AARP offers members a wide range of benefits, including *AARP: The Magazine* and a monthly newsletter. Anyone over 50 can join.

FOR FAMILIES WITH SPECIAL NEEDS

Many travel agencies offer customized tours and itineraries for travelers with disabilities. Among them are **Flying Wheels Travel** (© 507/451-5005; www.flyingwheelstravel.com); **Access-Able Travel Source** (© 303/232-2979; www.access-able.com); and **Accessible Journeys** (© 800/846-4537 or 610/521-0339; www.disabilitytravel.com). **Avis Rent a Car** has an "Avis Access" program that offers such services as a dedicated 24-hour toll-free number (© 888/879-4273) for customers with special travel needs; special car features such as swivel seats, spinner knobs, and hand controls; and accessible bus service.

Organizations that offer assistance to disabled travelers include **MossRehab** (www.mossresourcenet.org); the **American Foundation for the Blind** (AFB; © 800/232-5463; www.afb.org); and **SATH (Society for Accessible Travel & Hospitality;** © 212/447-7284; www.sath.org). **AirAmbulanceCard.com** is now partnered with SATH and allows you to preselect top-notch hospitals in case of an emergency.

GAY & LESBIAN PARENTS

New York City is renowned for its large, active gay community and a very gay-friendly general population. **The International Gay and Lesbian Travel Association (IGLTA;** © 800/448-8550 or 954/776-2626; www.iglta.org) is the trade association for the gay and lesbian travel industry, and offers an online directory of gay- and lesbian-friendly travel businesses; go to their website and click on "Members." **Gay.com Travel** (© 800/ 929-2268 or 415/644-8044; www.gay. com/travel or www.outandabout.com), an excellent online successor to the popular *Out & About* print magazine, provides regularly updated information about gay-owned, gay-oriented, and gay-friendly lodging, dining, sightseeing, nightlife, and shopping establishments worldwide. The following travel guides are available at many bookstores, or you can order them on line: *Spartacus International Gay Guide* (Bruno Gmünder Verlag; www.spartacusworld.com/gayguide/) and *Odysseus: The International Gay Travel Planner* (Odysseus Enterprises Ltd.); and the *Damron* guides (www.damron. com), with separate, annual books for gay men and lesbians.

FOR AFRICAN-AMERICAN FAMILIES

Black Travel Online (www.blacktravel online.com) posts news on upcoming events and includes links to articles and travel-booking sites. **Soul of America** (www.soulofamerica.com) is a comprehensive website, with travel tips, event and family-reunion postings. Agencies and organizations that provide resources for black travelers include: **Rodgers Travel** (© 800/825-1775; www.rodgers travel.com); the **African American Association of Innkeepers International** (© 877/422-5777; www.africanamerican inns.com); and **Henderson Travel & Tours** (© 800/327-2309 or 301/650-5700; www.hendersontravel.com), which has specialized in trips to Africa since 1957. For more information, check out the following collections and guides: *Go Girl: The Black Woman's Guide to Travel & Adventure* (Eighth Mountain Press), a compilation of travel essays by writers including Jill Nelson and Audre Lorde; *The African American Travel Guide* by Wayne Robinson (Hunter Publishing; www.hunterpublishing.com); *Steppin' Out* by Carla Labat (Avalon); *Travel and Enjoy Magazine* (© 866/ 266-6211; www.travelandenjoy.com); and *Pathfinders Magazine* (© 877/ 977-PATH; www.pathfinderstravel.com), which includes articles on everything from Rio de Janeiro to Ghana as well as information on upcoming ski, diving, golf, and tennis trips.

9 Planning Your Trip Online

SURFING FOR AIRFARE

The most popular online travel agencies are **Travelocity** (**www.travelocity.com**, or www.travelocity.co.uk); **Expedia** (**www. expedia.com,** www.expedia.co.uk, or www. expedia.ca); and **Orbitz** (**www.orbitz. com).**

In addition, most airlines now offer online-only fares that even their phone agents know nothing about. For the websites of airlines that fly to and from your destination, go to "Getting There," p. 28.

Other helpful websites for booking airline tickets online include:

- www.biddingfortravel.com
- www.cheapflights.com

- www.hotwire.com
- www.kayak.com
- www.lastminutetravel.com
- www.opodo.co.uk
- www.priceline.com
- www.sidestep.com
- www.site59.com
- www.smartertravel.com

SURFING FOR HOTELS

In addition to **Travelocity, Expedia, Orbitz, Priceline,** and **Hotwire** (see above), the following websites will help you with booking hotel rooms online:

- www.hotels.com
- www.quickbook.com;
- www.travelaxe.net

Frommers.com: The Complete Travel Resource

For an excellent travel-planning resource, we highly recommend **Frommers. com** (www.frommers.com), voted Best Travel Site by *PC Magazine*. We're a little biased, of course, but we guarantee that you'll find the travel tips, reviews, monthly vacation giveaways, bookstore, and online-booking capabilities thoroughly indispensable. Among the special features are our popular **Destinations** section, where you'll get expert travel tips, hotel and dining recommendations, and advice on the sights to see for more than 3,500 destinations around the globe; the **Frommers.com Newsletter,** with the latest deals, travel trends, and money-saving secrets; and our **Travel Talk** area featuring **Message Boards,** where Frommer's readers post queries and share advice, and where our authors sometimes show up to answer questions. Once you finish your research, the **Book a Trip** area can lead you to Frommer's preferred online partners' websites, where you can book your vacation at affordable prices.

- www.travelweb.com
- www.tripadvisor.com

It's a good idea to **get a confirmation number** and **make a printout** of any online booking transaction.

SURFING FOR RENTAL CARS

For booking rental cars online, the best deals are usually found at rental-car company websites, although all the major online travel agencies also offer rental-car reservations services. Priceline and Hotwire work well for rental cars, too; the only "mystery" is which major rental company you get, and for most travelers the difference between Hertz, Avis, and Budget is negligible.

10 The 21st-Century Traveler

INTERNET ACCESS AWAY FROM HOME
WITHOUT YOUR OWN COMPUTER

Aside from formal cybercafes (see "Internet Access" under "Fact Facts" in Chapter 3), most **youth hostels** and **public libraries** offer Internet access. Avoid **hotel business centers** unless you're willing to pay exorbitant rates.

Most major airports now have **Internet kiosks** scattered throughout their gates. These give you basic Web access for a per-minute fee that's usually higher than cybercafe prices.

WITH YOUR OWN COMPUTER

More and more hotels, cafes, and retailers are signing on as Wi-Fi (wireless fidelity) "hotspots." Mac owners have their own networking technology, Apple AirPort. **T-Mobile Hotspot** (www.t-mobile.com/ hotspot) serves up wireless connections at more than 1,000 Starbucks coffee shops nationwide. **Boingo** (www.boingo.com) and **Wayport** (www.wayport.com) have set up networks in airports and high-class hotel lobbies. IPass providers (see below) also give you access to a few hundred wireless hotel lobby setups. To locate other hotspots that provide **free wireless networks** in cities around the world, go

Online Traveler's Toolbox

Veteran travelers usually carry some essential items to make their trips easier. Following is a selection of handy online tools to bookmark and use.

- **Airplane Food** (www.airlinemeals.net)
- **Airplane Seating** (www.airlinequality.com)
- **Foreign Languages for Travelers** (www.travlang.com)
- **Maps** (www.mapquest.com)
- **Subway Navigator** (www.subwaynavigator.com)
- **Time and Date** (www.timeanddate.com)
- **Travel Warnings** (http://travel.state.gov, www.fco.gov.uk/travel, www.voyage.gc.ca, www.dfat.gov.au/consular/advice)
- **Universal Currency Converter** (www.xe.com/ucc)
- **Visa ATM Locator** (www.visa.com), **MasterCard ATM Locator** (www.mastercard.com)
- **Weather** (www.intellicast.com; and www.weather.com)

to **www.personaltelco.net/index.cgi/ WirelessCommunities**.

For dial-up access, most business-class hotels in New York offer dataports for laptop modems, and several now offer free high-speed Internet access. In addition, major Internet Service Providers (ISPs) have **local access numbers** around the world, allowing you to go online by placing a local call. The **iPass** network also has dial-up numbers around the world. You'll have to sign up with an iPass provider, who will then tell you how to set up your computer for your destination(s). For a list of iPass providers, go to www.ipass.com and click on "Individuals Buy Now." One solid provider is **i2roam** (www.i2roam.com; © **866/811-6209** or 920/235-0475).

Wherever you go, bring a **connection kit** of the right power and phone adapters, a spare phone cord, and a spare Ethernet network cable—or find out whether your hotel supplies them to guests.

For information on electrical currency conversions, see "Electricity," in the "Fast Facts" section in Chapter 3.

CELLPHONE USE IN THE U.S.

Just because your cellphone works at home doesn't mean it'll work everywhere in the U.S. (thanks to our nation's fragmented cellphone system). If you need to stay in touch at a destination where you know your phone won't work, **rent** a phone that does from **InTouch USA** (© **800/872-7626**; www.intouchglobal.com) or a rental car location, but beware that you'll pay $1 a minute or more for airtime.

Visitors from overseas may be appalled at the poor reach of our **GSM (Global System for Mobiles) wireless network,** which is used by much of the rest of the world. To see where GSM phones work in the U.S., check out www.t-mobile.com/coverage/.

It's a good bet that your phone will work in New York City, but inside large buildings or on occasional blocks that fall into a quirky "dead zone," your coverage may fail; walk a short distance outside and coverage should pick up.

11 Getting There

BY PLANE

Almost every major domestic carrier serves the New York area. Here's a handy list of toll-free numbers and websites: **American** (© 800/433-7300; www.aa. com), **Continental** (© 800/525-0280; www.continental.com), **Delta** (© 800/ 221-1212; www.delta.com), **Northwest** (© 800/225-2525; www.nwa.com), **United** (© 800/241-6522; www.united. com): and **U.S. Airways** (© 800/235-9292; www.usair.com).

In recent years, there has been rapid growth in the number of start-up, no-frills airlines serving New York. You might check out Atlanta-based **AirTran** (© 800/ AIRTRAN; www.airtran.com), Chicago-based **ATA** (© 800/225-2995; www.ata. com), Denver-based **Frontier** (© 800/432-1359; www.flyfrontier.com), Milwaukee-and Omaha-based **Midwest Airlines** (©800/452-2022; www.midwestairlines. com), or Detroit-based **Spirit Airlines** (© 800/772-7117; www.spiritair.com). The JFK-based cheap-chic airline **jetBlue** (© 800/JETBLUE; www.jetblue.com) offers low fares and classy service to cities throughout the nation. The nation's leading discount airline, **Southwest** (© 800/ 435-9792; www.iflyswa.com), flies into MacArthur (Islip) Airport on Long Island, 50 miles (80km) east of Manhattan.

Most of the major international carriers also fly into New York—see appendix A for details.

NEW YORK AREA AIRPORTS

New York City has three major airports. **John F. Kennedy (JFK) International** (© 718/244-4444; www.kennedy airport.com), in southeastern Queens 15 miles (about an hour's drive) from Manhattan, is largely served by international flights, though some domestic flights are routed through. **LaGuardia** (© 718/533-3400; www.laguardiaairport.com), chiefly for domestic flights, is also in Queens, though only 8 miles from Manhattan — a shorter ride (30–45 min.) into Midtown. In nearby New Jersey, **Newark Liberty International** (© 888/EWR-INFO; www.newarkairport.com) serves both domestic and international flights; it's 16 miles form Manhattan, about 45 to 60 minutes by car. If you need to make connections at another airport, you can contact **New York Airport Service** (© 718/ 875-8200; www.nyairportservice.com), which shuttles travelers between LaGuardia and JFK for $13 one-way.

IMMIGRATION & CUSTOMS CLEARANCE Foreign visitors arriving by air, no matter what the port of entry, should cultivate patience and resignation before setting foot on U.S. soil. Clearing

Tips Prepare to Be Fingerprinted

As of January 2004, many international visitors traveling on visas to the United States will be photographed and fingerprinted at Customs in a new program created by the Department of Homeland Security called **US-VISIT**. Non-U.S. citizens arriving at airports and on cruise ships must undergo an instant background check as part of the government's efforts to deter terrorism by verifying the identity of incoming and outgoing visitors. Exempt from the extra scrutiny are visitors entering by land or those (mostly in Europe; see p. 12) that don't require a visa for short-term visits. For more information, go to the Homeland Security website at **www.dhs.gov/dhspublic**.

New York Metropolitan Area

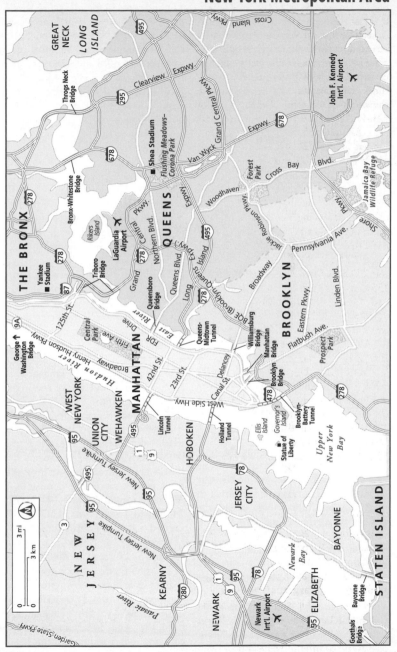

immigration control can take as long as 2 hours. This is especially true in the aftermath of the September 11, 2001, terrorist attacks, when U.S. airports considerably beefed up security clearances. People traveling by air from Canada, Bermuda, and certain Caribbean countries can sometimes clear Customs and Immigration at the point of departure, which is much faster.

GETTING INTO TOWN FROM THE AIRPORT

With young kids in tow, it's best to take a **cab** from the airport into the city. All three airports have orderly taxi stands where you line up until it's your turn for the uniformed dispatcher to help you into a licensed cab (only yellow cabs are licensed to pick up passengers from JFK and LaGuardia; New Jersey cab companies work from Newark). Cab fares from JFK into Manhattan are set at $45, which comes to around $60 once you've added bridge and tunnel tolls and a 15% to 20% tip; the total from Newark, including tolls and tip, is also about $60, and from LaGuardia it's more like $35-$40. There's no charge for extra people or for luggage, though yellow cabs add a 50¢ surcharge on weekends and from 8pm to 6am, and a $1 surcharge weekdays from 4 to 8pm. New Jersey cabs are allowed to tack on a $10 fee for crossing the state line (stay alert, for New Jersey cab drivers have been known to get lost on the way to Midtown). Passengers are expected to pay bridge and tunnel tolls, though the driver may pay the toll and then add it to your fare.

If your kids are older, and you don't have loads of luggage, you can save money by taking a **New York Airport Service** bus (© **718/875-8200,** www.ny airportservice.com) running from either JFK or LaGuardia to Manhattan. Buses leave clearly marked stops at the terminals every 20 minutes. The trip in **from JFK** costs $15 and takes about an hour;

from LaGuardia to Midtown it costs $12 and takes 45 minutes. New York Airport Service buses stop at Grand Central Terminal (Park Ave. and 42nd St.) and the Port Authority Bus Terminal (Eighth Ave. between 40th and 42nd sts.). If you hail a cab from Grand Central, Port Authority, or Penn Station, the fare should be $7 to $9 to most Midtown hotels, though catching a cab at these busy terminals can be stressful. All three have taxi stands.

From Newark Airport, **Coach USA** (© **212/964-6233;** www.coachusa.com) operates a 30-minute bus ride to Port Authority Bus Terminal and Grand Central Terminal; the ride costs $14 one-way ($23 round-trip) and buses leave every 20 to 30 minutes. **SuperShuttle** (© **212/ 315-3006;** www.supershuttle.com) operates a minibus service between all three airports and a number of Manhattan hotels for $9-$35; reserve 24 hours in advance. **AirTrain Newark** connects passengers to Newark International Airport Station, where you can transfer to a NJ Transit train with stops in Manhattan. The trip into Manhattan can take as little as 20 minutes, and the one-way fare is $11 (children under 5 ride free) (© **800/ 297-7433;** www.airtrainnewark.com).

To have a limousine (actually, a luxury sedan—don't promise the kids a stretch limo) pick you up, call before you fly (at least a day in advance) to arrange pickup from private car-service companies like **All State Car and Limo** (© **212/741-7440**) and **Tristate** (© **212/777-7171**); the cost is about $44 from LaGuardia and $58 from JFK or Newark, not counting tolls and tips. **Carmel** (© **800/9CARMEL** or 212/666-6666; www.carmellimo.com) charges even lower rates, provided that you book an ordinary car rather than a luxury sedan—$37 from LaGuardia, $46 from JFK, and $45 from Newark, not counting tolls, parking, and tips.

There are public transportation options that are cheaper, though they take longer.

Getting Through the Airport

- Arrive at the airport 1 hour before a domestic flight and 2 hours before an international flight; if you show up late, tell an airline employee and he or she will probably whisk you to the front of the line.
- Beat the ticket-counter lines by using airport electronic kiosks or even online check-in from your home computers, from where you can print out boarding passes in advance.
- Bring a current, government-issued photo ID such as a driver's license or passport. Children under 18 do not need government-issued photo IDs for flights within the U.S., but they do for international flights to most countries.
- Speed up security by removing your jacket and shoes before you're screened. In addition, remove metal objects such as big belt buckles. If you've got metallic body parts, a note from your doctor can prevent a long chat with the security screeners.
- Use a TSA-approved lock for your checked luggage. Look for Travel Sentry certified locks at luggage or travel shops and Brookstone stores (or online at www.brookstone.com).

For only $5, the monorail **AirTrain JFK** (© 877/JFK-Airtrain) takes passengers from Kennedy airport to either Howard Beach or Jamaica stations in Queens, where you can pick up a Long Island Rail Road train to Penn Station ($6.75) or A, E, J, or Z subway service ($2 subway fare). From LaGuardia, you can take a local **Q33 bus** (fare $2) to the subway's Roosevelt Avenue station, where you can transfer to the no. 7 train to Midtown; or the local **Q48 bus** (fare $2) to the 111th Street station, also on the no. 7 line to Manhattan. The **M60 bus** (fare $2) goes directly from LaGuardia to Manhattan, where it makes stops along 125th Street and then down Broadway, terminating at 106th Street; you can transfer to the no. 1 or 9 train at 116th or 110th Street and head down the Upper West Side from there. Any of these trips can take well over an hour. *Note:* If you don't have a MetroCard (sold at subway station fare booths), you can pay the $2 bus fare in change (no pennies); as soon as you pay your fare, ask the bus driver for a transfer

card so you can enter the subway system for the next leg of your trip.

FLYING FOR LESS: TIPS FOR GETTING THE BEST AIRFARE

- Passengers who can book their ticket either **long in advance or at the last minute,** or who **fly midweek** or **at less-trafficked hours** may pay a fraction of the full fare. If your schedule is flexible, say so, and ask if you can secure a cheaper fare by changing your flight plans.
- Search **the Internet** for cheap fares (see "Planning Your Trip Online").
- Keep an eye on local newspapers for **promotional specials** or **fare wars,** when airlines lower prices on their most popular routes. You rarely see fare wars offered for peak travel times, but if you can travel in the off-months, you may snag a bargain.
- Try to book a ticket **in its country of origin.** If you're planning a one-way flight from Johannesburg to New York, a South Africa–based travel agent will

probably have the lowest fares. For foreign travelers on multi-leg trips, book in the country of the first leg; for example, book New York–Chicago–Montréal–New York in the U.S.

• **Consolidators,** also known as bucket shops, are great sources for international tickets, although they usually can't beat Internet fares within North America. Start by looking in Sunday newspaper travel sections; U.S. travelers should focus on the *New York Times, Los Angeles Times,* and *Miami Herald.* U.K. travelers should search in the *Independent, The Guardian,* or *The Observer. Beware:* Bucket shop tickets are usually nonrefundable or rigged with stiff cancellation penalties, often as high as 50% to 75% of the ticket price, and some put you on charter airlines, which may leave at inconvenient times and experience delays. Several reliable consolidators are worldwide and available online. **STA Travel** has been the world's lead consolidator for students since purchasing Council Travel, but their fares are competitive for travelers of all ages. **Flights.com** (© 800/TRAV-800; www.flights.com) has excellent fares worldwide, particularly to Europe. They also have "local" web-sites in 12 countries. **FlyCheap** (© 800/FLY-CHEAP; www.flycheap.com) has especially good fares to sunny destinations. **Air Tickets Direct** (© 800/778-3447; www.airtickets direct.com) is based in Montreal and leverages the currently weak Canadian dollar for low fares; they also

book trips to places that U.S. travel agents won't touch, such as Cuba.

• Join **frequent-flier clubs.** Frequent-flier membership doesn't cost a cent, but it does entitle you to better seats, faster response to phone inquiries, and prompter service if your luggage is stolen or your flight is canceled or delayed, or if you want to change your seat. And you don't have to fly to earn points; **frequent-flier credit cards** can earn you thousands of miles for doing your everyday shopping. With more than 70 mileage awards programs are on the market, consumers have never had more options. Investigate the program details of your favorite airlines before you sink points into any one. Consider which airlines have hubs in the airport nearest you, and, of those carriers, which have the most advantageous alliances, given your most common routes. To play the frequent-flier game to your best advantage, consult Randy Petersen's **Inside Flier** (www.insideflyer.com). Petersen and friends review all the programs in detail and post regular updates on changes in policies and trends.

FLYING WITH KIDS

If you plan carefully, you can make it fun to fly with your kids:

• **Reserve a seat in the bulkhead row** if you have babies or toddlers. You'll have more legroom, your children will be able to play on the floor underfoot, and the airline might provide bassinets (ask in advance).

Tips **Don't Stow It—Ship It**

Though pricey, it's sometimes worthwhile to travel luggage-free. Specialists in door-to-door luggage delivery include **Virtual Bellhop** (www.virtualbellhop.com), **SkyCap International** (wwww.skycapinternational.com), **Luggage Express** (www.usxpluggageexpress.com), and **Sports Express** (www.sportsexpress.com).

⌒ Tips Coping with Jet Lag

Jetlag is a pitfall of traveling across time zones. If you're flying north–south and you feel sluggish when you touch down, your symptoms will be the result of dehydration and the general stress of air travel. When you travel east–west or vice-versa, however, your body becomes thoroughly confused about what time it is, and everything from your digestive system to your brain is knocked for a loop. Traveling east, say from San Francisco to Boston, is more difficult on your internal clock than traveling west, say from Atlanta to Hawaii, because most peoples' bodies are more inclined to stay up late than fall asleep early.

Here are some tips for combating jet lag:

- **Reset your watch** to your destination time before you board the plane.
- **Drink lots of water** before, during, and after your flight. Avoid alcohol.
- **Exercise and sleep well** for a few days before your trip.
- If you have trouble sleeping on planes, **fly eastward on morning flights.**
- **Daylight** is the key to resetting your body clock. At the website for **Outside In** (www.bodyclock.com), you can get a customized plan of when to seek and avoid light.

- **Pack items for your kids in your carry-on luggage,** such as books, snacks, and toys. Be sure to bring self-contained compact toys with few pieces, like magnetic checker sets. Be aware that electronic games can interfere with the aircraft navigational system, and their noisiness may annoy your adult neighbors. Small coloring books and crayons work well, as do card games like Go Fish.

- **Have a long talk with your children** before you depart for your trip, explaining to them what to expect at takeoff, landing, and during the flight. Explain to your kids the importance of good behavior in the air—how their own safety can depend upon their being quiet and staying in their seats during the trip.

- **Pay extra attention to the safety instructions** before takeoff. Consult the safety chart behind the seat in front of you, and show it to your children. Be sure you know how to operate the oxygen masks, as you'll be expected to secure yours first and then help your children with theirs.

Locate the emergency exits before takeoff, and plot out an evacuation strategy for you and your children, just in case.

- **Be sure your child's seatbelt remains fastened properly,** and try to reserve the seat closest to the aisle for yourself. This will make it harder for your children to wander off—in case, for instance, you're taking the red-eye or a long flight, and you happen to nod off. You will also protect your child from jostling passersby and falling objects. It's impossible for a parent to hold onto a child in the event of a crash, and children often die of impact injuries. Sudden turbulence is also a danger to a child who is not buckled into his or her own seat restraint.

- **Try to sit near the lavatory,** though not so close that your children are jostled by the crowds that tend to gather there. Make as few trips there as possible, and anticipate times—for instance, during meal service—when carts may block the aisles. (On crowded flights, the flight crew may

need as much as an hour to serve dinner; suggest a restroom visit *before* the attendants begin to serve.) **Always accompany children to the lavatory.**
• Some airlines **serve children's meals first.** When you board, ask a flight attendant if this is possible, especially if your children are very young or seated toward the back of the plane. After all, if your kids have a happy flight experience, everyone else in the cabin is more likely to as well.

BY CAR

Having a car in Manhattan isn't an asset. Drive here only if you must. If you do, my best advice is to get to your destination, put your car in a garage, and keep it there. Yes, hotel and independent garages charge exorbitant rates, but street parking can be a nightmare, and you don't want to deal with having your car broken into while you're on vacation.

North–south **I-95** runs up through New Jersey, jogs across the northern tip of Manhattan and the Bronx, and heads up to New England. From the south, you can exit I-95 (the New Jersey Tpk.) at I-78 in Jersey City, which takes you to the **Holland Tunnel** ($6 toll) into downtown; at I-495 in Union City, which takes you to Midtown's **Lincoln Tunnel** ($6 toll); or after crossing the **George Washington Bridge** ($6 toll), where NY 9A (the **Henry Hudson Parkway**) goes down the west side of Manhattan. I-278 branches off I-95 south of Elizabeth, New Jersey, crossing east to Staten Island, then into Brooklyn across the **Verrazano Narrows Bridge** ($9 toll westbound into Staten Island; no toll eastbound into Brooklyn).

From the north, I-95 connects with the **Bruckner Expressway** (I-278), which swings down to the **Triborough Bridge** ($4.50 toll), leading you into Manhattan on the East Side's **FDR Drive.** If you're going to the west side of Manhattan, stay on I-95 as it becomes the **Cross Bronx Expressway,** and take the last exit in

Manhattan to the **Henry Hudson Parkway** (NY 9A). Other useful routes from the north include the **Merritt Parkway/ Hutchinson Parkway/Cross County Expressway** from New England and the **Taconic Parkway** from upstate New York. Both feed into the **Saw Mill Parkway,** which crosses into Manhattan at the **Henry Hudson Bridge** ($2.25 toll) and becomes the Henry Hudson Parkway (NY 9A).

I-87 leads down from upstate New York; either exit south onto the **Palisades Parkway** into New Jersey and take that down to the George Washington Bridge ($6 toll), or stay on I-87/287 as it turns east and crosses the Hudson at Tarrytown, New York, then exit onto the **Saw Mill Parkway** and continue south across the Henry Hudson Bridge ($2.25 toll) into Manhattan.

From the west, **I-80** feeds into the George Washington Bridge ($6 toll). **I-280** branches off I-80 out near Morris Plains, New Jersey, heading southeast to join **I-95;** from there, you can pick up **I-78** to the Holland Tunnel ($6 toll) or **I-495** to the Lincoln Tunnel ($6 toll). **I-78** is another Interstate highway coming into New York from the west; it leads into the Holland Tunnel downtown.

BY TRAIN

The major long-distance rail terminal in Manhattan is **Pennsylvania Station,** known to all as Penn Station, between Seventh and Eighth avenues and 31st to 33rd streets. **Amtrak** trains (© **800/USA-RAIL;** www.amtrak.com) come through Penn Station from all across the country. Two commuter train lines, **New Jersey Transit** (© **800/626-RIDE;** www.nj transit.com) and the **Long Island Rail Road** (© **718/217-5477;** www.mta.nyc. ny.us), also come into Penn Station, so it can be a madhouse at rush hour, especially on the lower-level LIRR platforms. Plans are in the works to convert the neoclassical main post office on Eighth Avenue between 31st and 33rd streets (across from the current Penn Station) into a new Penn Station—stay tuned. **Grand Central Terminal,** at 42nd Street and Park Avenue, is the city's other train station, used today only by **Metro North** commuter trains (© **212/532-4900;** www.mta.nyc.ny.us), serving Connecticut and New York State. **PATH** commuter trains (© **800/234-PATH;** www.panynj.gov/path) from New Jersey have their own underground stations in Manhattan: Christopher Street, West 9th Street, West 14th Street, West 23rd Street, and 33rd Street and Sixth Avenue; the fare is $1.50.

There are **taxi stands** at both Penn Station and Grand Central. Penn Station has subway stations on the A, C, E, 1, 2, 3, and 9 lines. Grand Central subway station serves the 4, 5, 6, and 7 lines and the S shuttle to Times Square.

Tip: Even if you don't catch a train from Grand Central, take your kids to see the gloriously restored main hall, a grand marble cavern with a star-spangled ceiling.

BY BUS

The **Port Authority Bus Terminal,** at Eighth Avenue between 40th and 42nd streets (© **212/564-8484;** www.panynj.gov), still has its grubby corners, despite the remarkable transformation of the nearby Times Square area. On the whole, however, this cheerless big station is well lit and well patrolled, with lots of discount shops and fast-food restaurants lining the main hall. Greyhound, Trailways, Bonanza, Peter Pan, and other long-distance bus lines stop here, along with various commuter bus lines, including NJ Transit.

Upon arrival, head straight for the taxi stand on Eighth Avenue, where a dispatcher can get you a cab. The fare won't be more than $6 or $7 to most Midtown hotels, barring traffic jams. The A, C, and E subways also stop at Port Authority, and a long underground tunnel leads you to Times Square and the 1, 2, 3, 7, 9, N, Q, R, S, and W trains.

12 Show & Tell: Getting the Kids Interested in New York City

Several corny old songs come in handy as memory guides for New York City geography: Start with "I'll take Manhattan / The Bronx and Staten Island too" to teach your kids about the city's five boroughs, the other two being Brooklyn and Queens. Then there's "New York, New York, a wonderful town / The Bronx is up and the Battery's down / The people ride in a hole in the ground." Discuss the subway lines—rendered in different colors on the map—and talk about the neighborhoods and sights they pass through. New York's subways have been cleaned up incredibly since the early 1980s, and it's perfectly safe to take your kids for rides on these underground trains.

Current TV shows tend to present New York either as a hangout for self-involved singles or as a gritty battlefield for cops and killers. For a more fun image of Manhattan, try two of my kids' favorite New York movies, *Ghostbusters* and *Splash. Crocodile Dundee* is a light-hearted look at how an outsider might view New York. *The Muppets Take Manhattan* captures the city in its own wacky, cartoony spirit. *Stuart Little* and *Home Alone II* show kids adventuring in NYC; the Olsen twins' *New York Minute* is a 'tweens' fantasy of NYC escapades. For a kids'-eye view of grownup New York, try the Tom Hanks classic *Big* or its more recent girl equivalent, *13 Going on 30.* Older kids interested in downtown lifestyle might like *Desperately Seeking Susan* or Adam Sandler's *Big Daddy.* Digging deep into the classics vaults, you could get *Miracle on 34th Street,* the musical *On the Town,* or the priceless *Breakfast At Tiffany's.* For particular neighborhoods, *You've Got Mail* is a love letter to the Upper West

Top Kids' Books Set in New York City

Picture Books

- *The Adventures of Taxi Dog* by Debra and Sal Barracca (Dial; ages 2–6). This, or any of the Barraccas' books about Maxi the Taxi dog, is a lovable look at the city from the seat of a yellow cab.
- *Tar Beach* by Faith Ringgold (Crown; ages 2–5). This charming book recounts evocative memories of a Harlem childhood and hot summer nights up on the roof.
- *The Escape of Marvin the Ape* by Caralyn and Mark Buehner (Dial; ages 3–6) portrays a fugitive gorilla happily losing himself in New York City's parks, museums, stores, and ballparks.
- *The Little Red Lighthouse and the Great Gray Bridge* by Hildegarde H. Swift and Lynd Ward (Harcourt Brace; ages 4–7). A Hudson River lighthouse feels superceded by the new George Washington Bridge, until one dark and stormy night. . . . Kids can still see both landmarks today.
- *Eloise* by Kay Thompson (Simon & Schuster; ages 4–8). This irrepressible 6-year-old growing up in the Plaza Hotel definitely has an exotic view of life. Perfect for the precocious.

Chapter Books

- *The Cricket in Times Square* by George Selden (Farrar, Straus and Giroux or Yearling paperback; ages 6–10). A Connecticut cricket winds up in the Times Square subway station and becomes the toast of Manhattan.
- *Stuart Little* by E. B. White (Harper & Row; ages 7–10). The Little family's mouse-size young son has adventures in and around Central Park.
- *All of a Kind Family* by Sydney Taylor (Dell Yearling; ages 7–10). This portrait of a Jewish family living on the Lower East Side is a window into turn-of-the-20th-century New York.
- *The Saturdays* by Elizabeth Enright (Puffin Books; ages 7–10). Four siblings pool their resources to explore New York City on weekends; it's set in the 1940s but is not as dated as it may seem.
- *Harriet the Spy* by Louise Fitzhugh (HarperTrophy; ages 8–11). Spunky sixth-grader Harriet M. Welch keeps tabs on her East Side friends and neighbors.
- *From the Mixed-Up Files of Mrs. Basil E. Frankenweiler* by E. L. Konigsburg (Simon & Schuster or Aladdin paperback; ages 8–12). A 12-year-old Connecticut girl and her younger brother hole up in the Metropolitan Museum and become involved in an art mystery.
- *Gossip Girls* by Cecily von Ziegesar (Little Brown; ages 13 and up) is a paperback series depicting the lives and loves of Upper East Side private-school brats; trashy and a little risqué, it's like *Sex and the City* for teens

Side; *Crossing Delancey* captures the Lower East Side; and *Everybody Says I Love You* (along with most other Woody Allen films) serenades the Upper East Side. For outer-borough views, consult *Moonstruck* or *Saturday Night Fever* (Brooklyn) or *Raising Helen* (Queens).

New York City's skyline is a famous sight—prime your youngsters for that first glimpse of it. Buildings to identify include the Empire State Building, with its tall antenna tower up which the original King Kong climbed; the Chrysler Building's chrome-tipped Art Deco spire, looking for all the world like a hood ornament; the riverside United Nations, a vertical plane of sheer glass anchored by the dome of the General Assembly; the slant-roofed white Citibank Building; and the Chippendale-style crest on the Sony Building. The Statue of Liberty is another indelible New York landmark to show your kids pictures of ahead of time. Yet another is Rockefeller Plaza, where a giant gilded statue overlooks an ice-skating rink in winter and an outdoor cafe in summer—and where the even-more-giant Rockefeller Center Christmas tree sparkles during the holiday season.

Older kids may have strong associations with New York's battery of sports teams—depending on the season, watch some innings of Yankees or Mets baseball; a Jets or Giants football game; a Rangers, Devils, or Islanders hockey match; or a Knicks or Nets basketball game.

3

Getting to Know New York City

At first glance, New York can be a very intimidating town, especially when you have a flock of youngsters under your wing. Take time from the outset to get a grasp of the city's layout and the best navigating methods.

1 Orientation

VISITOR INFORMATION

New York City visitor centers are scattered around Manhattan; the most comprehensive one is at **810 Seventh Ave.** between 52nd and 53rd streets ((*C*) **212/484-1222**), which is open Monday to Friday 8:30am to 6pm and Saturday and Sunday 9am to 5pm. There are also kiosks in **City Hall Park** (Broadway and Park Row, downtown) and **Chinatown** (at the triangle where Canal, Walker, and Baxter streets meet). Stop by to pick up maps, brochures, and sightseeing suggestions, along with "twofers" for savings on Broadway and off-Broadway plays. You can call the **New York Convention & Visitors Bureau's** 24-hour information hot line at (*C*) **800/NYC-VISIT** or visit its website, **www.nycvisit.com.** Helpful staff members at (*C*) **212/484-1222** will answer questions during daily office hours.

The **Times Square Alliance** (www.timessquarenyc.org) is a good source for information about Broadway theater, Midtown hotels and restaurants, and special events; it operates the **Times Square Information Center** (Seventh Ave. between 46th and 47th sts.). For recorded listings of **Lincoln Center** events, call (*C*) **212/546-2656** or visit its website at www.lincolncenter.org. For upcoming **events in city parks,** call (*C*) **888/NY-PARKS** or visit www.nycgovparks.org; for **Central Park events,** go to www.centralpark.org.

CITY LAYOUT

MAJOR ARTERIES IN MANHATTAN The limited-access **FDR Drive** runs along Manhattan's East River shore, from the Brooklyn Battery Tunnel (which links to Brooklyn) north to the Triborough Bridge (which links to Queens and to I-95). The **West Side Highway** goes from Battery Park up along the Hudson, eventually becoming the limited-access **Henry Hudson Parkway** running all the way to Manhattan's northern tip and on through the Bronx (Riverdale), where it becomes the **Saw Mill Parkway.**

Broadway is Manhattan's spine, beginning at Battery Park and angling north all the way through Washington Heights (from there on, as U.S. 9, it continues all the way to Albany). Since Manhattan's axis is skewed to the northeast, Broadway—which runs due north—seems to run at an angle, and every time it crosses a major avenue in the Manhattan grid, there's a significant traffic junction: **Union Square** at 14th Street, **Madison Square** at 23rd Street, **Herald Square** at 34th Street, **Times Square** at 42nd

Manhattan Neighborhoods

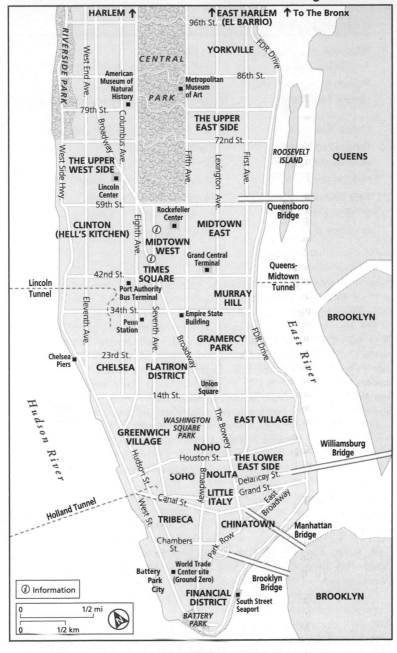

A Street by Any Other Name

When the street sign says . . .	It's the same as . . .
Amsterdam Avenue	Tenth Avenue (above 59th St.)
Avenue of the Americas	Sixth Avenue
Central Park North	West 110th Street (between Fifth Ave. and Central Park W.)
Central Park South	59th Street (between Fifth and Eighth aves.)
Central Park West	Eighth Avenue (from 59th to 110th sts.)
Columbus Avenue	Ninth Avenue (above 59th St.)
Fashion Avenue	Seventh Avenue (from 34th to 42nd sts.)
Park Avenue	Fourth Avenue (above 14th St.)
St. Mark's Place	8th Street (from Third Ave. to Ave. A)
West End Avenue	Eleventh Avenue (from 59th to 107th sts.)

Street, **Columbus Circle** at 59th Street, **Lincoln Square** at 66th Street, **Verdi Square** at 72nd Street, and **Straus Park** at 106th Street. Above 59th Street, where Central Park divides Manhattan, Broadway is the West Side's main drag.

The other big avenues in the grid are one-way, with the exception of the Upper West Side's **Central Park West** and the East Side's **Park Avenue.** The avenues that run uptown (north) are **First Avenue, Third Avenue, Madison Avenue, Sixth Avenue** (also called **Ave. of the Americas**), **Eighth Avenue,** and **Tenth Avenue** (called **Amsterdam Ave.** above 59th St.). To go downtown (south), take **Second Avenue, Lexington Avenue, Fifth Avenue, Seventh Avenue, Ninth Avenue** (called **Columbus Ave.** above 59th St.), or **Eleventh Avenue** (called **West End Ave.** from 59th to 107th sts.).

In the older areas of town, below 8th Street, the grid doesn't apply, and you'll need a map to navigate. **Hudson Street** is a major northbound thoroughfare on the West Side; on the East Side it's **Fourth Avenue** (the southern section of Park Ave.), which is created when the **Bowery** splits into Third and Fourth avenues.

Most cross streets in the grid are one-way; generally, in Manhattan even-numbered streets are eastbound and odd-numbered streets are westbound. The following major cross streets, however, are two-way: **Canal Street,** which cuts across the island from the Manhattan Bridge to the Holland Tunnel; **Houston Street,** which funnels traffic from the Williamsburg Bridge to the Holland Tunnel; and **14th Street, 23rd Street, 34th Street, 42nd Street, 57th Street, 59th Street** (aka Central Park S.), **72nd Street, 79th Street, 86th Street, 96th Street,** and **110th Street** (aka Central Park N.). Above the park, **125th Street** is Harlem's major two-way commercial street.

Central Park bisects Manhattan between 59th Street and 110th Street, dividing the Upper East Side from the Upper West Side. To cross Central Park **from the Upper East Side,** your choices are 66th Street, 72nd Street (open weekday rush hours only), 79th Street, 85th Street, and 97th Street. If you're going east **from the Upper West Side,** your options are 65th Street, 81st Street, 86th Street, and 96th Street. All other car entrances to the park feed into the circular drive, open only during weekday rush hours.

Tips **Getting Oriented**

Cross streets are listed for every destination in this book, but be sure to ask for the cross street (or avenue) if you're ever calling for an address.

When you give a taxi driver an address, always specify the cross streets. New Yorkers, even most cab drivers, probably wouldn't know where to find 994 Second Ave., but they do know where to find 51st and Second. If you're heading to the restaurant La Bonne Soup, for example, tell them that it's on 55th Street between Fifth and Sixth avenues. The exact number (in this case, no. 48) is given only as a further precision.

MAJOR ARTERIES IN THE OUTER BOROUGHS   The **Grand Central Parkway** leads from the Triborough Bridge to LaGuardia Airport, in northern Queens, and on to Long Island. The **Long Island Expressway (I-495)** goes from the Queens Midtown Tunnel across Queens, through Forest Hills and Flushing, and out to Long Island. **Northern Boulevard** is one of Queens's major commercial thoroughfares.

The **Brooklyn-Queens Expressway**—known as the BQE—runs north–south, linking Brooklyn and Queens; you can get on it from the Grand Central Parkway, from the 59th Street Bridge (also called the Queensboro Bridge), from the Queens-Midtown Tunnel, and from the three Brooklyn-Manhattan bridges: the Williamsburg, the Manhattan, and the Brooklyn. At the southern end of Brooklyn, the BQE links with the **Verrazano Bridge** (toll $9 westbound only) from Staten Island, then (as the **Belt Parkway**) swings around the coast past Coney Island and the Rockaways, feeding into **Southern Parkway,** which heads out to Long Island. Radiating out from Brooklyn Heights, **Atlantic Avenue, Flatbush Avenue,** and (starting near Prospect Park) **Ocean Parkway** fan out across Brooklyn.

The **Cross-Bronx Expressway (I-95)** is the major highway cutting across the Bronx; the **Bronx River Parkway** runs up through Bronx Park, where you'll find the Bronx Zoo and the Botanical Garden.

MANHATTAN NEIGHBORHOODS IN BRIEF

Manhattan was settled from its southern tip northward, so the oldest area is **Lower Manhattan,** roughly everything south of Canal Street. Within this, the **Financial District,** concentrated around Wall Street and lower Broadway, has pretty much obscured traces of the early colonial settlement with its battery of skyscrapers, but you'll still find a few venerable churches tucked away, and some of the skyscrapers themselves are early-20th-century landmarks. The only really historic quarter left is on the East River waterfront at **South Street Seaport.**

Southwest of the Seaport, you'll find City Hall, other municipal buildings, and an imposing set of courthouses clustered around Foley Square. Over on the Hudson side of the narrow island, you'll get some open green space at Battery Park and the planned community of **Battery Park City,** which has a great riverside promenade. Ground Zero, the site of the World Trade Center tragedy, lies just inland from Battery Park City. The nickname **TriBeCa** derives from the *Tri*angle *Be*low *Ca*nal Street, but the label is used for only the northwestern chunk

---

Value **Free New York City Tours**

If you'd like to tour a specific neighborhood with an expert guide, call **Big Apple Greeter** (© **212/669-2364**; www.bigapplegreeter.org) at least 1 week ahead of your arrival. This nonprofit organization has specially trained volunteers who take visitors around town for a free 2- to 4-hour tour of a particular neighborhood. And they say New York isn't friendly!

---

of that triangle, a hypercool neighborhood of converted industrial lofts dotted with trendy restaurants and a few galleries.

Above South Street Seaport and the courts, **Chinatown** occupies the East River side of the below-Canal area, but it burst its boundaries long ago to spill north of Canal Street, engulfing the old tenements of **Little Italy,** which still clings to Mulberry Street as its main drag. East of Little Italy lies the **Lower East Side,** for years the Jewish immigrant district, more recently a hot spot for young urban bohemians. To the west of Little Italy, a derelict 19th-century industrial zone was converted in the 1970s to the lofts and boutiques of artsy **SoHo** (*So*uth of *Ho*uston St.— pronounced, by the way, "*How*-stun," never "*Hew*-stun").

Above Houston Street you enter the Villages—**Greenwich Village,** from Broadway west to the Hudson River; and the **East Village,** from Broadway on east across Avenues A, B, C, and D. Greenwich Village still has a certain bohemian cachet, and its quiet side streets, with their redbrick town houses, make a good place to ramble. The East Village is funkier and grittier, just the place to bring teenagers who think their parents are so uncool they don't want to be seen with them. (Just walk five paces behind them, okay?) Teens may also want to hang out in the New York University area, which sprawls around the Village's focal

point, Washington Square Park, or in the now chic northwest corner of the West Village, still called the Meatpacking District for its (ever-dwindling) butchers' trade.

Above 14th Street the Manhattan grid falls into place, and the city starts to get more buttoned-down. Between 14th and 30th streets, **Chelsea** occupies the area from Sixth Avenue west. This is now a very hot area for art galleries, fashion industry types, and gays; at its far west end, the Chelsea Piers sports complex on the river is a major draw for families. East of Sixth Avenue is what's called the **Flatiron District** (named after the famous Flatiron Building at 23rd St. and Broadway), a trendy area for restaurants and nightlife, and the quiet older neighborhoods around **Gramercy Park,** the city's only private park. North of Gramercy lies **Murray Hill,** a largely residential neighborhood.

Midtown is the major business district, sprawling across the island from about 34th Street to 59th Street. Big department stores and elegant shops march up Fifth Avenue, with a handful of museums set on side streets; the **Theater District** clusters around Times Square (42nd St. and Broadway). By far the greatest number of Manhattan hotels are in Midtown, and many restaurants as well. But with its crowded sidewalks and restaurants packed with impatient workaday New Yorkers, it's not necessarily where families want to

Tips Manhattan's Bridges & Tunnels

Manhattan's an island—to get on or off it, you have to go over or under the water. Going clockwise around the island, starting from the northern tip, you can take the **Henry Hudson Bridge** (on the Henry Hudson Pkwy.; $2.25 toll), the **Triborough Bridge** ($4.50 toll), the **59th Street/Queensboro Bridge** (no toll), or the **Queens-Midtown Tunnel** (part of I-495; $4.50 toll). A trio of toll-free bridges into Brooklyn—the **Williamsburg,** the **Manhattan,** and the **Brooklyn**—all connect handily with the Brooklyn-Queens Expressway, as does the **Brooklyn Battery Tunnel** ($4.50 toll) at the island's southern tip. Two big tunnels cross the Hudson on Manhattan's west side—the **Holland Tunnel** ($6 toll only into Manhattan), which funnels into Canal or Houston Street; and the **Lincoln Tunnel** ($6 toll only into Manhattan), which funnels into 40th Street—and the **George Washington Bridge** (part of I-95; $6 toll only into Manhattan) crosses above the water up at 175th Street.

Drivers can zip through bridge and tunnel toll booths much faster if they have **E-ZPass,** a small device that drivers can post on their windshields to have tolls electronically deducted from a credit card account. Certain lanes at toll stations are designated for E-ZPass users only, so stay alert (there are no toll attendants at those booths). To set up an account, call ℂ **800/333-TOLL** or go online at **www.e-zpassny.com**. Note that E-ZPass devices are also compatible with the New Jersey, Pennsylvania, and Massachusetts turnpikes; the New York State Thruway; Delaware River bridges; and the Atlantic City Expressway.

concentrate their time. Come here to shop and to gawk at the tall buildings, but venture away from Midtown, and you'll get a better idea of how New York families experience the city.

The **Upper West Side** occupies the part of Manhattan directly west of Central Park—here you'll find great museums for kids, lots of kid-friendly restaurants, toy stores, and playgrounds in both Central and Riverside parks. The **Upper East Side,** everything east of Central Park, is also very child-oriented but less casual; you'll see packs of uniformed kids from tony private schools gathering in pizza parlors and Gaps. The East Side is rich in museums, especially along the park on Fifth Avenue.

Above Central Park to the west is **Morningside Heights,** dominated by Columbia University and two magnificent churches—Riverside Church and the Cathedral of St. John the Divine. East of Morningside Park, **Harlem** takes over the island north of Central Park. Many tourists visit Harlem as part of a guided tour, though you can certainly check it out on your own. However, your kids' interest in the social-history aspects of a Harlem guided tour may lag if they're under 10. Unless you're visiting The Cloisters (the Metropolitan Museum's medieval-art branch in Fort Tryon Park), there's not much reason for you to tour **Washington Heights,** which lies above Harlem.

Fun Fact **Fun Fact**

Population-wise, even if they were counted as separate cities, New York City's five boroughs would still rank high in the list of U.S. cities. Brooklyn on its own would be the nation's third-largest city, right after Los Angeles and Chicago; Queens would be fourth-largest, and Manhattan sixth (just after Houston), with the Bronx ranking ninth right after Phoenix. Even relatively less populous Staten Island would come in 40th, after Albuquerque, New Mexico, and before Kansas City, Missouri.

THE OUTER BOROUGHS IN BRIEF

New York City's other four boroughs surround the island of Manhattan. To the north and east lies the **Bronx,** which only partly deserves its bad rap as a crime-infested slum. Parts of the Bronx are rotten indeed, but the Bronx also includes suburban Riverdale, along the Hudson, and the middle-class Fordham area, anchored by Fordham University and Bronx Park (where the zoo and the botanical garden are). The New York Yankees are called the Bronx Bombers because Yankee Stadium is at 161st Street in the Bronx; crowds of baseball fans make it safe around game time, and the subway takes you directly to the stadium.

The landmass directly east of Manhattan (the western end of Long Island) contains the two most populous boroughs: Brooklyn and Queens. Immortalized (rightly or wrongly) as Archie Bunker territory, **Queens** is the city's great middle-class borough, where hardworking immigrant groups have colonized various neighborhoods from Astoria to Flushing. Directly across the river from Manhattan, Long Island City and Williamsburg are havens for young artists, and Forest Hills in the middle of Queens is a manicured residential area. Further-out areas of Queens, like St. Albans, Little Neck, and Douglaston, are basically suburban neighborhoods.

Brooklyn on the whole is more urban and edgy, though it has some of the city's loveliest residential areas, notably brownstone-lined Brooklyn Heights, right across the Brooklyn Bridge from Manhattan, and nearby gentrified row-house neighborhoods such as Cobble Hill, Carroll Gardens, Fort Greene, and Park Slope (the last has the advantage of bordering Prospect Park, Central Park's Brooklyn cousin). Facing Staten Island across the Narrows, Bay Ridge is a vast middle-class enclave; Brighton Beach, on Brooklyn's southern shore, is a former Jewish area now heavily colonized by immigrant Russians. But other Brooklyn neighborhoods, like Bedford-Stuyvesant, Brownsville, and East New York, aren't for the uninitiated. If you visit Brooklyn, know where you're going.

That leaves **Staten Island,** the most suburban of the boroughs, the one that's always threatening to secede from the city—which actually makes sense, because Staten Island is geographically part of New Jersey. Staten Island's attractions for visitors—the restored historic village at Richmond Town, a zoo, a children's museum, a couple of historic houses—don't lure many New Yorkers across the water, which suits most Staten Islanders just fine. Still, the Staten Island Ferry ride is one of those classic New York things to do, a pleasant way to spend an hour or so crossing the harbor—and it's free.

2 Getting Around
BY SUBWAY

Not only are subway stations brighter and better lit than they used to be, but the trains themselves are also now clean, graffiti-free, and blessedly air-conditioned in summer. Rush-hour crowds can still be pushy, and derelicts, panhandlers, and thugs still disturb riders' peace from time to time. Trains don't run as often as they should, either. But the subway is truly a viable alternative, especially for long daytime rides, when you'll save time as well as money by gliding under the streets instead of getting mired in city traffic.

The **Metropolitan Transit Authority** (© **718/330-1234;** www.mta.nyc.ny.us) operates the city's buses and subways, which run 24 hours. Even mildly adventurous visitors should feel comfortable underground from 7am to 8pm—however, the morning and evening rush hours (generally 8–9:30am and 5–6:30pm weekdays) make the trains so crowded you'd be better off not traveling then, especially with a family to squeeze in. Currently the **fare** is $2, and for your two bucks you can ride as long and far as you like, changing lines at any of more than 50 transfer points. Children under 44 inches tall ride free; in practice, kids under 6 can just duck under the turnstile bar, and no one challenges them. (In some neighborhoods, even 12 year olds can duck under the turnstile and no one will blink.)

New Yorkers use multiride **MetroCards,** with magnetic strips that automatically deduct one fare every time you slip them through a groove in a turnstile; each time you run your card through a turnstile, your remaining balance is displayed. MetroCards can be bought in various denominations from $3 to $80 and can be refilled at fare booths or at vending machines in many stations. Up to four passengers traveling together can use the same MetroCard—just slide it through the turnstile once for each rider.

Bonuses of 20% are offered for buying MetroCards of $10 or more; unlimited-ride passes are also available, costing $76 for 30 days, $24 for 7 days, and $7 for 1 day (expires at 3am). All of these except the 1-day pass (the Fun Pass) are available at fare booths and vending machines; the Fun Pass can be bought only in the vending machines or at newsstands and shops around town (look for blue-and-yellow METRO-CARDS SOLD HERE signs). *Only one catch:* Unlimited-ride passes cannot be used by more than one passenger, so to take advantage of the discounts, you'll have to buy each member of your family a separate card.

MetroCards allow riders **free transfers** to and from city buses. If you're coming from a city bus, just slide your card through the subway turnstile's groove, and the machine should indicate that this is a transfer. Note that transfers do expire after a certain amount of time; sometimes you'll be pleasantly surprised when you reenter the system half an hour after one ride to find that your second ride registers as a transfer, but don't count on it.

Maps are posted inside stations (usually out by the token booths, so you can make sure where you're going before you enter) and in most cars. Near the token booths, many stations now also feature detailed street maps of the immediate area, so you can get oriented before you hit the street.

BY BUS

There are two ways to pay your $2 bus fare: with a **MetroCard** (the same one you use for the subway) or $2 in exact change (no pennies). You can't buy MetroCards onboard, however; you have to get them at a subway station. Children under 44 inches tall ride free (there's a line near the driver's seat against which to measure your child), but in practice kids under 6 are usually allowed to ride free, regardless of height.

Art Down Under

Many Manhattan subway stations were renovated in the 1990s, and more will be in the new century. The tile walls along waiting platforms often feature work by local artists or symbols appropriate for that particular neighborhood. Some of our favorites: the fossils and critters crawling over the walls of the **West 81st Street** stop on the B, C lines (beneath the American Museum of Natural History); the artwork by local schoolchildren at the **West 86th Street** stop on the 1, 9 line and at the **Columbus Circle** station (A, B, C, D, 1, 9 trains); the scenes from famous operas and ballets at **West 66th Street/Lincoln Center** station on the 1, 9 line; the fanciful cartoon characters peeking out from the floors and ceilings of the **14th Street** stop on the A, C, E lines; the sea creatures slithering over the **Houston Street** station (1, 9 line), and the scurrying beavers at the **Astor Place** stop on the 6 line (obscure reference: Astor Place is named after 19th-c. tycoon John Jacob Astor, whose fortune originally came from beaver furs).

To transfer for free to a second bus, dip your MetroCard into the fare box slot; if you've just come from the subway or another bus, the machine will register this as a transfer (reading "Xfer OK" or "2 Xfers OK" if two passengers are using the same card). Transfers expire after a certain amount of time, but you probably can slip into a shop between buses and still have your second ride count as a transfer. *Note:* If more than one passenger is using the same MetroCard, when you are transferring to a second bus or train, *dip only once for the transfer.* (Dip a second time, and an additional fare will be deducted.)

If you're using coins, request a transfer card from the driver of the first bus *when you pay your fare.*

Each bus's destination is displayed above its front windshield; routes are posted at most bus stops. Look for blue-and-red bus stop signs along sidewalks; at transfer points, a glassed-in shelter often accompanies them. Within Manhattan, bus stops are stationed every 2 or 3 blocks along avenues or major crosstown streets. Once you're riding a bus, if you wish to get off at the next stop, press any one of several electronic strips posted around the bus. A sign at the front of the bus should light up, reading STOP REQUESTED, and the driver will then pull over at the next stop.

If you're trying to get around the downtown area, you should also know about the free **Downtown Connection** bus service organized by the Downtown Alliance (© 212/566-6700; www.downtownny.com). Running about every 10 to 15 minutes between 10am and 7:30pm, these buses travel from the northern end of Battery Park City around Manhattan's southern tip to South Street Seaport, making 16 stops en route.

BY TAXI

The only taxis authorized to pick up passengers hailing them on the street are **yellow cabs,** which have an official Taxi and Limousine Commission medallion screwed onto the hood. So-called gypsy cabs, working for car services, sometimes stop illegally for passengers on the street, but because they have no meter, you'll have to negotiate your own fare with the driver, and you'll have no legal recourse if there's a problem (besides, some gypsy cabs are filthy rattletraps). To know whether a yellow taxi is available, look for the lit-up center sign on the roof of the cab; off-duty cabs (side sections of the roof sign lit) may pick up passengers at their own discretion.

Taxi meters calculate the fare: $2.50 when you get in, plus 40¢ for each one-fifth of a mile or 120 seconds of waiting time in traffic. The meter should "click" every 4 blocks in normal traffic or once every crosstown block. There's an extra 50¢ charge from 8pm to 6am, a $1 surcharge for peak weekday service (Mon–Fri 4–8pm), and passengers pay any bridge or tunnel tolls. A 15% to 20% tip is expected, unless the service is bad. For complaints or inquiries about lost property, dial © **311** or go online at **www.nyc.gov/taxi**.

Technically, a taxi doesn't have to take more than four passengers (with adults, this is possible only if one sits in the front seat next to the driver). But if your kids are small, most cabbies will let you all squeeze in, which is good news for families of five. All New York yellow cabs are supposed to have working seat belts. If your kids are car-seat-size, technically you could haul around a car seat and strap it in every time you get in a cab, but the only person I've ever known to do this did it only once, when cabbing her newborn home from the hospital. Most cabbies are cool about letting kids sit on laps or even kneel on the seat to look out the cab window. Occasionally you'll get one who'll hassle you about your 2-year-old getting his sneakers on the backseat upholstery. I never fight the cabbies on this one—hey, it's their cab.

BY FERRY

The free **Staten Island Ferry** (© **718/727-2508**) at Battery Park remains the best way to enjoy views of the Manhattan skyline, New York Harbor, and the Statue of Liberty. To reach the South Ferry terminal take the R, W train to Whitehall Street or the 1, 9 to South Ferry. If you don't have any business on Staten Island, simply disembark from the ferry, go through the turnstiles, and turn around for the return trip.

The **New York Waterway Ferry System** (© **800/53-FERRY;** www.nywaterway. com) runs a number of commuter ferries. Most cost $3 to $5 one-way; they link New Jersey (from Jersey City, Weehawken, Hoboken, or Liberty Harbor) to Midtown (W. 39th St.) and Downtown (the World Financial Center in Battery Park City, Pier A in Battery Park, or Pier 11 at Wall St.) **Liberty Landing Marina** (© **201/985-8000;** www.libertylandingmarina.com) runs service every 20-30 minutes from 6am to 9pm, from Liberty Landing State Park in New Jersey to the World Financial Center. Fares are $5 for adults, $3 for children under 12.

BY CAR

Cars are the least efficient way to get around town, but if you must drive, keep in mind that car-rental rates at the airports are often lower than those in Midtown. All the big national chains operate several locations, including at all three major airports: **Avis** (© 800/331-1212; www.avis.com), **Budget** (© 800/527-0700; www.budget. com), **Dollar** (© 800/800-3665; www.dollar.com), **Enterprise** (© 800/261-7331; www. enterprise.com), **Hertz** (© 800/654-3131; www.hertz.com), and **National** (© 800/ 227-7368; www.nationalcar.com).

If you're visiting from abroad and plan to rent a car in the United States, you probably won't need the services of an additional automobile organization. If you're planning to buy or borrow a car, automobile-association membership is recommended. **AAA, the American Automobile Association** (© **800/222-4357; http://travel.aaa.com**), is the country's largest auto club and supplies its members with maps, insurance, and, most important, emergency road service. *Note:* Foreign driver's licenses are usually recognized in the U.S., but you should get an international one if your home license is not in English.

PARKING   On the streets, look for parking signs stating what days or hours you can park curbside. In Midtown and other spots where police feel it's vital to keep traffic flowing, your illegally parked car will be towed in minutes, so don't even think of violating parking laws. In residential neighborhoods, "alternate side of the street parking" means that everybody's expected to shift their cars to the opposite curb once a day. Officers are required to complete any parking ticket they start to fill out, so pleading will do no good. If your car does get towed, call the **Borough Tow Pound** at ✆ 212/971-0770 to find out where it is; you'll have to pay $185 in cash to retrieve it.

Space is so tight in New York that some residents are willing to pay over $400 a month for parking-garage spaces. Public garages dot Manhattan streets every 2 blocks or so, with rates averaging about $12 to $15 for less than 2 hours, $20 to $30 for half a day, and $40 overnight. Better-known commercial parking-garage operators include **Rapid Park, Manhattan Parking,** and **GMC.** Prices are sometimes lower at night or on weekends in business districts and during the day in residential areas; outdoor lots are less expensive, when you can find them. Few hotels offer parking. Some Midtown hotels provide valet parking at about $35 per night, often with the requirement that guests not take their cars from the garage between arrival and final departure. The city government's website at **www.nyc.gov** provides maps of licensed parking facilities, as well as information about how to obtain the **NYC Parking Card** (✆ 718/786-7042), which gives you access to certain municipal metered parking. Otherwise, street metered parking costs 25¢ for 10 minutes—if you can find a free space, which isn't easy.

DRIVING RULES   Every passenger is supposed to wear a seat belt, and all kids 5 and under should be in car seats of some kind. Except for major crosstown streets and a few north–south avenues (Broadway, Park Ave.), most of Manhattan's streets are one-way, so sometimes you'll have to circle around a couple of blocks to get to a specific address. Right turns on red are not legal, and left turns are prohibited in some major intersections (watch for signs). Several major avenues have designated bus lanes (marked on the pavement), which are off-limits to cars during rush hours.

Midtown Manhattan streets are prone to the phenomenon known as *gridlock.* Beware of edging into an intersection in slow-moving traffic—if you don't manage to get through the intersection before the light changes, you can get stranded in the path of oncoming cross-traffic. If a police officer's watching, you may be ticketed for "blocking the box."

3 Planning Your Outings

Everything is relatively close together in Manhattan, but if you're traveling by cab, traffic jams can make even a few blocks' travel take half an hour; waiting for frequent changes of buses or subways can add up to lots of wasted time; and plodding long distances on foot could tire out the kids (or yourself) before you get to the sights you want to see. Instead, plan carefully and you may be able to spend the entire day within a few blocks' radius, wasting little time on street travel. If you do have to hop from one part of town to another, don't underestimate travel time—snarled traffic or sluggish subways or buses can make a 40-block journey seem to take forever.

A Museum Note

One thing to take into account is museum closing days—many are closed on Monday. For a list of those that will be open, see "Rainy Days & Mondays," in chapter 6.

Prime areas for families are the **Upper West Side,** with the American Museum of Natural History and the Children's Museum of Manhattan; **SoHo,** with the Children's Museum of the Arts and the Fire Museum; **Midtown,** where you'll find the Sony Wonder Technology Lab, Rockefeller Center, the Empire State Building, and the Museum of Modern Art; **Lower Manhattan,** with South Street Seaport; and the Upper East Side stretch of Fifth Avenue known as **Museum Mile.** If you're going to **Brooklyn** to see the Botanic Garden or Prospect Park Zoo, take in the Transit Museum and Brooklyn Heights on the same day. The same ferry goes to both the **Statue of Liberty** and **Ellis Island,** so it's a natural to do both the same day—but after waiting in all those lines, you probably won't have time to do much else that day. The **Bronx Zoo** and the **New York Botanical Garden** are right next to each other, but it'd be pretty exhausting to do both sprawling venues in a day.

FINDING A RESTROOM

If you've got a recently toilet-trained toddler in tow, better think ahead, because in Manhattan it's not easy to find a bathroom at sudden notice. The **Times Square subway station** does have four clean attended bathrooms, for which there's often a line; **Grand Central Terminal** has a few, but they're not what you'd call clean. Restrooms can be found in **Central Park** and **Riverside Park** (see chapter 8 for locations), as well as in **Bryant Park,** which is at 42nd Street and Sixth Avenue behind the **New York Public Library;** the library itself has nice large bathrooms. Another option may be to use the bathrooms at various skyscrapers' shopping atriums, notably those at the **Sony Building** (56th St. and Madison Ave.), **Trump Tower** (56th St. and Fifth Ave.), the **Citicorp Building** (between Lexington and Third aves. and 53rd and 54th sts.), and the **Time-Warner Center** at Columbus Circle (59th St. and Columbus Ave.). **Barnes & Noble** bookstores, which are all around the city (see chapter 9), usually have decent bathrooms available. And here's one good thing about the number of **Starbucks** coffee shops dotting Manhattan: Nobody seems to mind if you stroll in just to use the bathroom. Major hotel lobbies are other good bets, although some of them require guest-room card keys for entry. In a pinch, if your child looks very distressed, you may be able to talk sympathetic waiters or store owners into letting you use their facilities. (I even once got the manager of a D'Agostino's grocery store to let me take my 2-year-old down to the employees' john in the basement—a real adventure.)

Best advice: Always use the potty at your hotel before you leave, and stop in the restroom before you leave any museum or restaurant.

FAST FACTS: New York City

Area Codes The area codes for New York City are 212, 646, 917, and 347. Make sure to dial the area code before your call, even if you are in the same area.

ATM Networks See "Money," p. 14.

Babysitting Many New York hotels provide babysitting services or keep a list of reliable sitters. If your hotel doesn't, call the **Baby Sitters Guild** (© 212/682-0227) or the **Frances Stewart Agency** (© 212/439-9222). Both services provide in-room child care, as well as on-request trips to the playground, the Central Park Zoo, and so on, for children of all ages, with licensed, bonded, insured sitters (baby nurses are trained in CPR) who speak a range of languages.

Business Hours The city that never sleeps truly doesn't. Although Midtown and Downtown **stores** tend to close at 6pm, shops in residential areas often stay open to 7pm or so, with drugstores and groceries usually going strong until 9pm or later, and delis and corner produce markets lasting on into the wee hours. Most stores (except for Midtown and Upper East Side boutiques) are open on Sunday, though they may not open until noon. **Restaurants** stay open late, usually at least until 11pm, and most are open 7 days a week. Many **museums** are closed on Monday, but several have late hours—until 9 or 10pm—on Thursday, Friday, or Saturday. **Banks** tend to keep more standard hours—Monday to Friday 9am to 3pm.

Car Rentals See "Getting Around," p. 44.

Cashpoints See "Money," p. 14.

Currency The most common bills are the $1 (a "buck"), $5, $10, and $20 denominations. There are also $2 bills (seldom encountered), $50 bills, and $100 bills (the last two are usually not welcome as payment for small purchases).

Coins come in seven denominations: 1¢ (1 cent, or a penny); 5¢ (5 cents, or a nickel); 10¢ (10 cents, or a dime); 25¢ (25 cents, or a quarter); 50¢ (50 cents, or a half dollar); the gold-colored Sacagawea coin, worth $1; and the rare silver dollar.

For additional information see "Money," p. 14.

Disability Services **Majestic Transportation** (© 212/410-2227) provides ambulette service for those with disabilities for around $130 round-trip within Manhattan. Note that the subway system remains largely inaccessible to travelers with disabilities, but 95% of the city's buses are equipped to carry wheelchairs.

Doctors **Dial-A-Doctor** (© 516/521-7040) sends physicians on house calls 24 hours a day throughout the five boroughs. **TravelMD.com** offers 24-hour urgent care and full-service travel medicine (© 212/737-1212, www.travelmd.com).

Drinking Laws The legal age in New York for purchase and consumption of alcoholic beverages is 21; proof of age is required and often requested at bars, nightclubs, and restaurants, so it's always a good idea to bring ID when you go out. You can also be fined for drinking publicly from an open container—which means if you do want to enjoy a bottle of beer or wine during a picnic in Central Park, be certain it's covered in a brown paper bag.

Driving Rules See "Getting Around," p. 44.

Drugstores Several **Duane Reade** stores are open 24 hours a day; **www.duane reade.com** lists them all. Some centrally located ones are at Broadway and 57th Street (© 212/541-9708), Broadway and 94th Street (© 212/663-1580), Third Avenue and 74th Street (© 212/744-2668), Columbus Circle at 58th Street (© 212/265-2302, pharmacy closes 9pm weekdays, 7pm weekends), Lexington and 47th Street (© 212/682-5338; pharmacy closes 8:30pm weekdays, 5pm weekends), and Third Avenue at 14th Street (© 212/529-7140; pharmacy closes 9pm). For **Rite-Aid** 24-hour locations, consult **www.riteaid.com**; these include the Lower East Side location at Grand and Clinton streets (© 212/529-7115) and Second Avenue between 30th and 31st streets (© 212/213-9887).

Electricity Like Canada, the United States uses 110 to 120 volts AC (60 cycles), compared to 220 to 240 volts AC (50 cycles) in most of Europe, Australia, and

New Zealand. Downward converters that change 220–240 volts to 110–120 volts are difficult to find in the United States, so bring one with you.

Embassies & Consulates All embassies are located in the nation's capital, Washington, D.C. Some consulates are located in major U.S. cities, and most nations have a mission to the United Nations in New York City. If your country isn't listed below, call for directory information in Washington, D.C. (© **202/555-1212**) or log on to **www.embassy.org/embassies**.

The embassy of **Australia** is at 1601 Massachusetts Ave. NW, Washington, DC 20036 (© **202/797-3000**; www.austemb.org). There are consulates in New York, Honolulu, Houston, Los Angeles, and San Francisco.

The embassy of **Canada** is at 501 Pennsylvania Ave. NW, Washington, DC 20001 (© **202/682-1740**; www.canadianembassy.org). Other Canadian consulates are in Buffalo (New York), Detroit, Los Angeles, New York, and Seattle.

The embassy of **Ireland** is at 2234 Massachusetts Ave. NW, Washington, DC 20008 (© **202/462-3939**; www.irelandemb.org). Irish consulates are in Boston, Chicago, New York, San Francisco, and other cities. See website for complete listing.

The embassy of **New Zealand** is at 37 Observatory Circle NW, Washington, DC 20008 (© **202/328-4800**; www.nzemb.org). New Zealand consulates are in Los Angeles, Salt Lake City, San Francisco, and Seattle.

The embassy of the **United Kingdom** is at 3100 Massachusetts Ave. NW, Washington, DC 20008 (© **202/588-7800**; www.britainusa.com). Other British consulates are in Atlanta, Boston, Chicago, Cleveland, Houston, Los Angeles, New York, San Francisco, and Seattle.

Emergencies Call © **911** for police, fire, and ambulance service. Fires can also be reported in Manhattan by dialing © **212/628-2900** or 212/999-2222. Other emergency numbers include the **Crime Victims Hotline** (© **212/577-7777**), **Animal Bites** (© **212/676-2483**), **Poison Control** (© **212/340-4494**), **gas leaks or electric emergency** (© **212/683-8830**, and the Salvation Army's **Homeward Bound** visitor assistance program (© **718/935-0439**).

Gasoline (Petrol) At press time, in the U.S., the cost of gasoline (also known as gas, but never petrol), is abnormally high, usually topping $3 per gallon. Taxes are already included in the printed price. One U.S. gallon equals 3.8 liters or .85 imperial gallons. Fill-up locations are known as gas or service stations.

Holidays Banks, government offices, post offices, and many stores, restaurants, and museums are closed on the following legal national holidays: January 1 (New Year's Day), the third Monday in January (Martin Luther King, Jr., Day), the third Monday in February (Presidents' Day), the last Monday in May (Memorial Day), July 4 (Independence Day), the first Monday in September (Labor Day), the second Monday in October (Columbus Day), November 11 (Veterans' Day/Armistice Day), the fourth Thursday in November (Thanksgiving Day), and December 25 (Christmas). The Tuesday after the first Monday in November is Election Day, a federal government holiday in presidential-election years (held every 4 years, and next in 2008).

For more information on holidays see "Calendar of Events," earlier in this chapter.

Hospitals The following hospitals have full-service emergency rooms: **New York University Medical Center,** 550 First Ave., at 33rd Street (© 212/263-7300); **New York Presbyterian Hospital,** 510 E. 70th St. (© 212/746-5454); **St. Vincent's Hospital,** 12th Street and Seventh Avenue (© 212/604-7000); and **St. Luke's-Roosevelt Hospital,** 59th Street and Tenth Avenue (© 212/523-6800).

Hot Lines For information on theater, music, and dance performances, check out **NYC On Stage** on line at www.tdf.org/search. Review current offerings at **Lincoln Center** (© 212/LINCOLN, www.lincolncenter.org). The **City Parks Special Events Hot line** (© 888/NY-PARKS, www.nycgovparks.org) gives details on outdoor concerts and performances and New York Roadrunner Club events. Listings of commercial films are available through **Moviefone** (© 212/777-FILM) or **Fandango** (© 800/326-3264), which also allow you to prepurchase movie tickets via credit card. **Sports Scores** (© 212/976-1717) gives updates on the most recent pro sports events.

Internet Access **Cybercafe** (© 212/333-4109) offers Internet access with coffee and noshing in the Times Square area at 250 W. 49th St. (between Broadway and Eighth Ave.).

Legal Aid If you are "pulled over" for a minor infraction (such as speeding), never attempt to pay the fine directly to a police officer; this could be construed as attempted bribery, a much more serious crime. Pay fines by mail, or directly into the hands of the clerk of the court. If accused of a more serious offense, say and do nothing before consulting a lawyer. In the U.S. the burden is on the state to prove a person's guilt beyond a reasonable doubt, and everyone has the right to remain silent, whether he or she is suspected of a crime or actually arrested. Once arrested, a person can make one telephone call to a party of his or her choice. International visitors should call your embassy or consulate.

Lost & Found Be sure to tell all of your credit card companies the minute you discover your wallet has been lost or stolen and file a report at the nearest police precinct. Your credit card company or insurer may require a police report number or record of the loss. Most credit card companies have an emergency toll-free number to call if your card is lost or stolen; they may be able to wire you a cash advance immediately or deliver an emergency credit card in a day or two. Visa's U.S. emergency number is © 800/847-2911 or 410/581-9994. American Express cardholders and traveler's check holders should call © 800/221-7282. MasterCard holders should call © 800/307-7309 or 636/722-7111. For other credit cards, call the toll-free number directory at © 800/555-1212.

If you need emergency cash over the weekend when all banks and American Express offices are closed, you can have money wired to you via **Western Union** (© 800/325-6000; www.westernunion.com).

Mail At press time, domestic postage rates were 24¢ for a postcard and 39¢ for a letter. For international mail, a first-class letter of up to 1 ounce costs 84¢ (63¢ to Canada and Mexico); a first-class postcard costs 75¢ (55¢ to Canada and Mexico); and a preprinted postal aerogramme costs 75¢. For more information go to **www.usps.com** and click on "Calculate Postage."

If you aren't sure what your address will be in the United States, mail can be sent to you, in your name, c/o General Delivery at the main post office of the city or region where you expect to be. (Call © **800/275-8777** for information on the nearest post office.) The addressee must pick up mail in person and must produce proof of identity (driver's license, passport, etc.). Most post offices will hold your mail for up to 1 month, and are open Monday to Friday from 8am to 6pm, and Saturday from 9am to 3pm.

Always include zip codes when mailing items in the U.S. If you don't know your zip code, visit www.usps.com/zip4

Libraries At any branch of the **New York Public Library,** you can pick up a monthly brochure listing all the kids' activities planned—films, story hours, puppet plays, and the like—at the system's many branches. These are usually wonderful programs, and they're absolutely free. The **Donnell Library,** 20 W. 53rd St. (© **212/621-0636**), has the main children's room for the entire system, with lots of scheduled readings and events. Branches with good children's rooms include **Jefferson Market,** 425 Sixth Ave., at West 10th Street (© **212/243-4334**); **Yorkville,** 222 E. 79th St. (© **212/744-5824**); **Epiphany,** 228 E. 23rd St. (© **212/679-2645**); and **St. Agnes,** 444 Amsterdam Ave., at 82nd Street (© **212/877-4380**).

The **Early Childhood Resources & Information Center** at 66 Leroy St. (© **212/929-0815**) has lots of parenting books, as well as a big indoor play space for kids 6 and under. The **central research library** on Fifth Avenue at 41st Street is worth a stop to see its magnificent main reading room; there are frequent free guided tours and fascinating exhibits, but these are usually more interesting for parents than for kids.

Newspapers & Magazines New York City has three vigorous newspapers: the well-known *New York Times,* the somewhat racier morning tabloid the *Daily News,* and the afternoon tabloid the *New York Post.* The *Wall Street Journal* is also published here, though its scope is national rather than local. Weekly newspapers include the downtown-oriented *Village Voice* and the uptown-oriented *New York Observer,* printed on distinctive peach-colored paper. Weekly magazines with comprehensive cultural listings include *New York Magazine, Time Out,* and the *New Yorker.*

Passports **For Residents of Australia:** You can pick up an application from your local post office or any branch of Passports Australia, but you must schedule an interview at the passport office to present your application materials. Call the **Australian Passport Information Service** at © **131-232,** or visit the government website at www.passports.gov.au.

For Residents of Canada: Passport applications are available at travel agencies throughout Canada or from the central **Passport Office,** Department of Foreign Affairs and International Trade, Ottawa, ON K1A 0G3 (© **800/567-6868;** www.ppt.gc.ca). *Note:* Canadian children who travel must have their own passport. However, if you hold a valid Canadian passport issued before December 11, 2001, that bears the name of your child, the passport remains valid for you and your child until it expires.

For Residents of Ireland: You can apply for a 10-year passport at the **Passport Office,** Setanta Centre, Molesworth Street, Dublin 2 (© **01/671-1633;** www.irl gov.ie/iveagh). Those under age 18 and over 65 must apply for a 3-year passport.

You can also apply at 1A South Mall, Cork (℃ **021/272-525**) or at most main post offices.

For Residents of New Zealand: You can pick up a passport application at any New Zealand Passports Office or download it from their website. Contact the **Passports Office** at ℃ **0800/225-050** in New Zealand or 04/474-8100, or log on to www.passports.govt.nz.

For Residents of the United Kingdom: To pick up an application for a standard 10-year passport (5-year passport for children under 16), visit your nearest passport office, major post office, or travel agency or contact the **United Kingdom Passport Service** at ℃ **0870/521-0410** or search its website at www.ukpa.gov.uk.

Police Dial **911.**

Post Offices The **main post office** at Eighth Avenue between 31st and 33rd streets (℃ **212/330-3668**) is open daily 24 hours. There are many other branches around town. Call the **Postal Answer Line** at ℃ **800/ASK-USPS** (275-8777) for information.

Radio On the AM dial, **WINS** (1010 AM) and **WCBS-AM** (880 AM) are all news; **WFAN** (660 AM) and **WEPN** (1050 AM) are all sports; and **Radio Disney** (1560 AM) broadcasts programs for children. On the FM dial, **WFUV** (90.7 FM) is an excellent National Public Radio affiliate out of Fordham University, and **WKCR** (89.9 FM) plays an eclectic mix out of Columbia University; **WQXR** (96.3 FM) is devoted to classical music; **Jazz 88** (88.3 FM) specializes in jazz; **WLTW** (106.7 FM) is the Lite FM station; **Q 104** (104.3 FM) plays classic rock; **WCBS** (101.1 FM) features the so-called "Jack format"; and **Z-100** (100.3 FM), **WPLJ** (95.5 FM), and **WQHT** (97.1 FM) are rock stations that are popular with teens and 'tweens.

Restrooms See "Finding a Restroom," above.

Safety Areas to avoid after dark if you're not a local: the deserted after-hours Wall Street area, the Lower East Side, the East Village east of First Avenue, Midtown west of Ninth Avenue, and Uptown north of 96th Street (except for the corridor along Broadway up to 120th St.).

Smoking New York's laws against smoking in public places are among the country's strictest. There is no smoking allowed inside theaters, museums, stores, buses, or subways; on trains, you must find a designated smoking car; and in restaurants or bars, unless they are large enough to include a designated smoking area, smoking is off limits. When you book a hotel room, specifically request a smoking room or you may be placed on a no-smoking floor.

Taxes The United States has no value-added tax (VAT) or other indirect tax at the national level. New York City's **sales tax** is 8.25%; this tax will not appear on price tags. It is not charged on groceries, takeout food, or any clothing and shoe purchases under $110. **Hotels** add a 13.25% hotel tax to room rates.

Telephones For directory assistance, dial ℃ **411** or [area code] + **555-1212.** There are public phones on every other street corner in Manhattan, though not all are in what you'd call working order; large hotels generally have a bank of public phones off the lobby, too. A local call costs 50¢. Pay phones do not accept pennies, and few will take anything larger than a quarter.

Generally, hotel surcharges on long-distance and local calls are astronomical, so you're better off using your **cellphone** or a **public pay telephone**. Many convenience groceries and packaging services sell **prepaid calling cards** in denominations up to $50; for international visitors these can be the least expensive way to call home. Many public phones at airports now accept American Express, MasterCard, and Visa credit cards.

Most long-distance and international calls can be dialed directly from any phone. **For calls within the United States and to Canada,** dial 1 followed by the area code and the seven-digit number. **For other international calls,** dial 011 followed by the country code, city code, and the number you are calling.

Calls to area codes **800, 888, 877,** and **866** are toll-free. However, calls to area codes **700** and **900** (chat lines, bulletin boards, "dating" services, and so on) can be very expensive—usually a charge of 95¢ to $3 or more per minute, and they sometimes have minimum charges that can run as high as $15 or more.

For **reversed-charge or collect calls,** and for person-to-person calls, dial the number 0 then the area code and number; an operator will come on the line, and you should specify whether you are calling collect, person-to-person, or both. If your operator-assisted call is international, ask for the overseas operator.

Telegraph and telex services are provided primarily by Western Union. You can telegraph money, or have it telegraphed to you, very quickly over the Western Union system, but this service can cost as much as 15 to 20 percent of the amount sent.

Most hotels have **fax machines** available for guest use (be sure to ask about the charge to use it). Many hotel rooms are even wired for guests' fax machines. A less expensive way to send and receive faxes may be at stores such as **The UPS Store** (formerly Mail Boxes Etc.),

Time New York City is in the **Eastern Time Zone**. (The continental United States has four time zones, each one hour apart: Eastern, Central, Mountain, and Pacific, with Alaska and Hawaii having their own zones.) From November through early March, it is on Eastern Standard Time (**EST**), which is 5 hours behind Greenwich Mean Time; **daylight saving time (EDT)** takes effect at 2am the second Sunday in March and holds sway until the 2am the first Sunday in November, moving the clock 1 hour ahead of standard time.

Tipping Tips are a very important part of certain workers' income, and gratuities are the standard way of compensating them for services provided. In hotels, tip **bellhops** at least $1 per bag ($2–$3 if you have a lot of luggage) and tip the **chamber staff** $1 to $2 per day (more if you've left a disaster area for him or her to clean up). Tip the **doorman** or **concierge** only if he or she has provided you with some specific service (for example, calling a cab for you or obtaining difficult-to-get theater tickets). Tip the **valet-parking attendant** $1 every time you get your car.

In restaurants, bars, and nightclubs, tip **service staff** 15% to 20% of the check (25% in cheaper restaurants, especially if your waiter has provided extra attention to keep your children happy). Tip **checkroom attendants** $1 per garment, package, or stroller.

Tip **cab drivers** 10%-20% of the fare; tip **skycaps** at airports at least $1 per bag ($2–$3 if you have a lot of luggage); and tip **hairdressers** and **barbers** 15% to 20%.

Toilets See "Find a Restroom," above.

Useful Phone Numbers U.S. Dept. of State Travel Advisory © 202/647-5225 (manned 24 hrs.)

U.S. Passport Agency © 202/647-0518

U.S. Centers for Disease Control International Traveler's Hotline: © 404/332-4559

For local **time** and **weather,** call © **212/976-2828** or **212/976-4111** (you'll also get current winning lottery numbers).

Visas For information about U.S. Visas go to **http://travel.state.gov** and click on "Visas." Or go to one of the following websites:

Australian citizens can obtain up-to-date visa information from the **U.S. Embassy Canberra,** Moonah Place, Yarralumla, ACT 2600 (© **02/6214-5600**) or by checking the U.S. Diplomatic Mission's website at **http://usembassy-australia. state.gov/consular.**

British subjects can obtain up-to-date visa information by calling the **U.S. Embassy Visa Information Line** (© **0891/200-290**) or by visiting the "Visas to the U.S." section of the American Embassy London's website at **www.usembassy. org.uk.**

Irish citizens can obtain up-to-date visa information through the **Embassy of the USA Dublin,** 42 Elgin Rd., Dublin 4, Ireland (© **353/1-668-8777;** or by checking the "Consular Services" section of the website at **http://dublin.usembassy.gov.**

Citizens of **New Zealand** can obtain up-to-date visa information by contacting the **U.S. Embassy New Zealand,** 29 Fitzherbert Terrace, Thorndon, Wellington (© **644/472-2068**), or get the information directly from the "For New Zealanders" section of the website at **http://usembassy.org.nz.**

4

Family-Friendly Accommodations

One big problem families have with New York hotels is that the overwhelming majority are in Midtown, between 30th and 59th streets—just about the least desirable part of town for parents to stay in with their children. There's traffic, there's noise, there's hardly any greenery, and there's no resident population to fill the sidewalks at night. Besides, Midtown's tourist attractions—the Theater District, Fifth Avenue and Madison Avenue shopping, gourmet restaurants—don't matter so much when you've got kids in tow. Of course, Midtown does have some superb hotels whose facilities and service level more than compensate for the location; there are also decent moderately priced hotels that cater well to families. But the list of hotels I recommend is deliberately skewed to include more choices in other neighborhoods. If you can, why not stay near Central Park or the American Museum of Natural History or the Metropolitan Museum of Art? Lower-Manhattan hotels are close to South Street Seaport, the Statue of Liberty/Ellis Island ferry, and Hudson River Park, and they often have incredible weekend discount packages.

Which brings us to the other big problem: cost. Manhattan hotels sit on some very expensive real estate, pay staff wages in a top urban job market, and, since they're often the flagships of various lodging chains, definitely tilt toward the high end of the luxury spectrum. New York City has one of the highest average room rates in the country, and hotels here don't have to discount to fill their beds—citywide occupancy rates regularly hover in the 90% range and up. Many hotels are designed to target business travelers and conventioneers, whose expense accounts presumably cover those hotel bills—so why court cost-conscious families? (Never mind that more and more business travelers and conventioneers are trying to bring their families with them, turning a business trip into a family vacation as well.)

If a swimming pool is important to you and your kids, I warn you now: Few Manhattan hotels have them, and some that do have pools sell memberships to adult New Yorkers, who may resent having a bunch of kids doing cannonballs in the deep end when they're trying to get some laps in on their lunch hour. I've listed nearly every hotel that does have a pool but tried to give you an idea of how welcoming those pools really are for families.

One thing my family always makes use of when traveling is a kitchenette—if you can throw together breakfasts and lunches in your room, you can easily save $100 a day, not to mention keep your children happy by not requiring them to use their restaurant manners three times a day. Suite hotels in general get my vote whenever they include some kind of kitchen facilities; they're also great with younger kids because you can put toddlers to bed at 8pm and retreat to the other room for

Uptown Accommodations

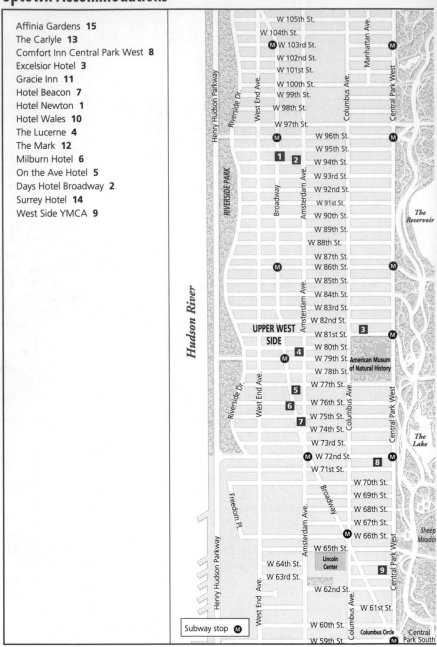

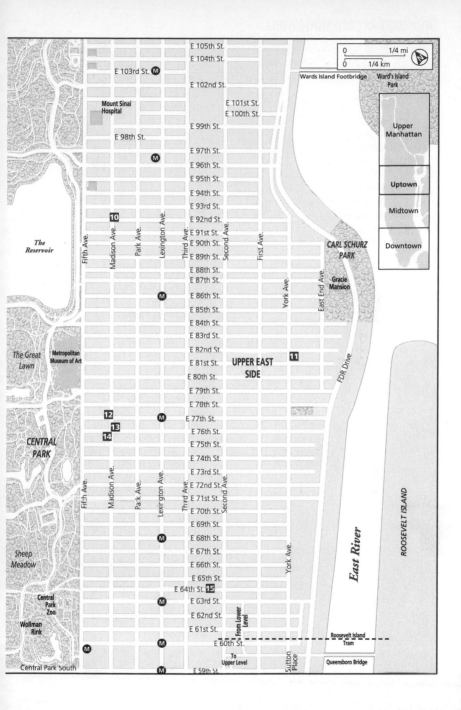

E 105th St.
E 104th St.
E 103rd St. Ⓜ
E 102nd St.
E 101st St.
E 100th St.
Mount Sinai
Hospital
E 99th St.
E 98th St.
E 97th St.
Ⓜ
E 96th St.
E 95th St.
E 94th St.
E 93rd St.
E 92nd St.
10
E 91st St.
E 90th St.
E 89th St.
E 88th St.
E 87th St.
Ⓜ
E 86th St.
E 85th St.
E 84th St.
E 83rd St.
E 82nd St.
E 81st St.   **11**
E 80th St.
E 79th St.
E 78th St.
Ⓜ   E 77th St.
12
13   E 76th St.
14   E 75th St.
E 74th St.
E 73rd St.
Ⓜ   E 72nd St.
E 71st St.
E 70th St.
E 69th St.
Ⓜ   E 68th St.
E 67th St.
E 66th St.
E 65th St.
E 64th St. **15**
Ⓜ   E 63rd St.
E 62nd St.
E 61st St.
Ⓜ   E 60th St.
Ⓜ   E 59th St.

Fifth Ave.
Madison Ave.
Park Ave.
Lexington Ave.
Third Ave.
Second Ave.
First Ave.
York Ave.
East End Ave.

The
Reservoir

The Great
Lawn

Metropolitan
Museum of Art

CENTRAL
PARK

Sheep
Meadow

Central
Park
Zoo

Wollman
Rink

Central Park South

From Lower Level
To Upper Level

Sutton
Place

0   1/4 mi
0   1/4 km

Wards Island Footbridge   Ward's Island
Park

Upper
Manhattan

Uptown

Midtown

Downtown

CARL SCHURZ
PARK

Gracie
Mansion

FDR Drive

UPPER EAST
SIDE

East River

ROOSEVELT ISLAND

Roosevelt Island
Tram

Queensboro Bridge

Midtown Accommodations

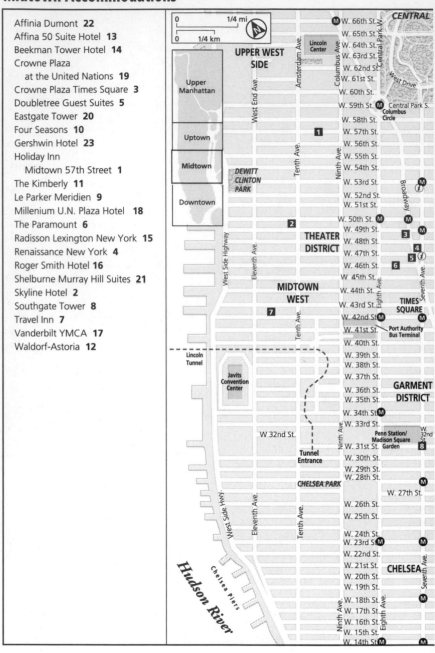

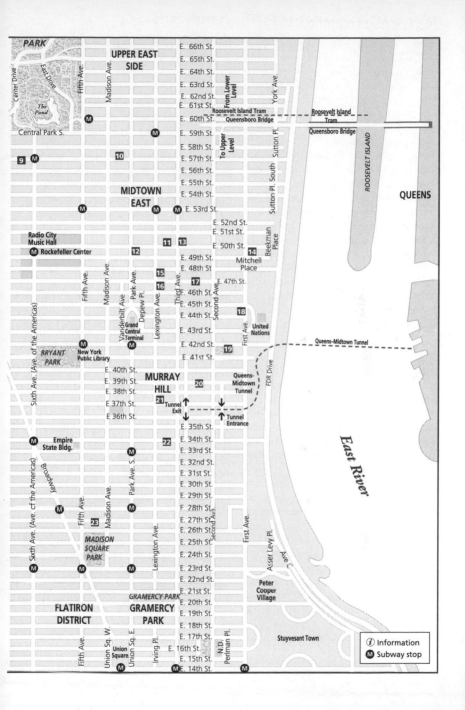

a room-service dinner, a movie on cable TV, whatever. Seems a shame to spend your evening this way when you're in Manhattan, but for 1 or 2 evenings of a 1-week stay, it can be restful.

On this built-up island, there just isn't the range of properties you'd find even in other expensive markets like London and Paris. You've got fleabags, you've got palaces—and not a whole lot in between. But face it: In between is where most families need to be. I've concentrated on ferreting out midrange hotels that are at least decent, if not always charming and atmospheric. When I do include some of the high-priced four-stars, it's because they offer something families especially value—not necessarily stunning decor, hushed privacy, and meticulous valet service (three things that don't mix well with small children anyway), but a pool, a kids' program, or a family-friendly location.

WHEN IS HIGH SEASON? Some hotels report that their slow time is January to early March; others say that July and August are their slow times. Just about all hotels, however, are booked way in advance from Thanksgiving to mid-December. When a big convention hits town, it can be impossible to find a room for love or money. Moral of the story: Call for reservations as soon as you know you're coming to New York to make sure you won't get shut out. But the other side of the coin is also true—call at the last minute, and you may get lucky even at one of the most popular properties.

Because New York attracts lots of business visitors as well as tourists, some hotels, especially those in Midtown or downtown, are more likely to have rooms free on weekends. Always ask about weekend packages if that's when you plan to check in.

RESERVATION SERVICES Quikbook (© 800/789-9887; www.quikbook. com) will book you into any of more than 80 hotels, including all the Affinia Group suite hotels, the Doubletree Guest Suites, the Crowne Plazas, and Le Parker Meridien; there's no charge, and they can often get you discounts of 25% to 40%. The nationwide **Central Reservation Service** (© 800/873-4683; www.reservation-services.com) also offers a discount, quoted as 10% to 40%, when they help you book rooms in New York. **Hotels.com** (© 800/246-8357; www. hotels.com) offers discount hotel booking in several large cities across the country, including New York.

A NOTE ABOUT HOTEL SERVICES Certain services are so standard in Manhattan hotels I haven't noted them in individual reviews. Because tall buildings here interfere badly with TV reception, every hotel that offers in-room TVs—and that's virtually all of them—offers **cable TV,** which means you'll have a range of channels to surf. Most hotels also have Spectravision or pay-per-view or some other **in-room movie service** feeding into the TVs. In the past couple of years, **high-speed Internet service** has become standard in all of the more expensive hotels; accommodations in lower price ranges may charge extra or offer it on a terminal in the lobby, but it's always available somewhere on-site. In the more expensive hotels, **dry cleaning** and **laundry services** are usual. Nearly all hotels

---

Best Hotel Bets

See chapter 1 for a list of my hotel favorites—the most family-friendly, the best views, and more.

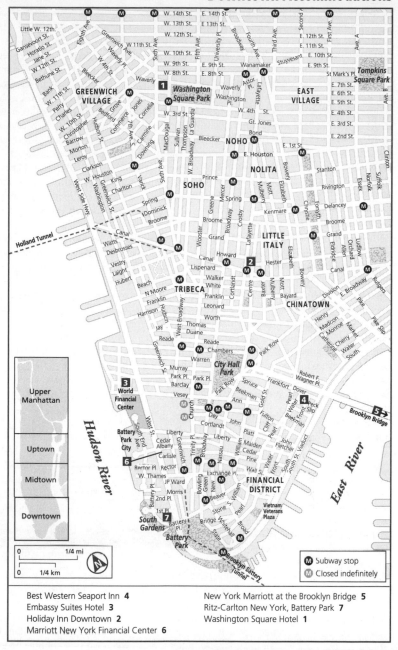

Downtown Accommodations

Best Western Seaport Inn **4**
Embassy Suites Hotel **3**
Holiday Inn Downtown **2**
Marriott New York Financial Center **6**
New York Marriott at the Brooklyn Bridge **5**
Ritz-Carlton New York, Battery Park **7**
Washington Square Hotel **1**

M Subway stop
Ⓜ Closed indefinitely

have some rudimentary **secretarial services;** if these are important to you, verify before booking that a hotel has the business capabilities you need. **Hair dryers** and **irons** can generally be obtained from the front desk if they aren't provided in the guest rooms.

Just about every concierge or front desk has a list of **babysitters** they've used, usually provided by one of the city's many bonded child-care agencies. Rates can be steep—around $20 per hour, with additional fees for more children, plus cab fare to get home afterward ($15–$20). What you'll get will be professional babysitters, many of them from Europe, Asia, or South America as well as North America. They'll come to your hotel room and take care of your children there.

Parking at just about all these Manhattan hotels, whether the hotel has its own garage or merely gives you a discount at nearby garages (the latter being more usual), is based on a per-night rate that assumes you won't be taking your car in or out during the day. Once you start moving the car, you'll have to pay more. Just another reason for not using your car while you're visiting.

A NOTE ABOUT PRICES I've categorized hotels according to a fairly basic rate for a family of four. In some hotels, that'll be the price for a double room with two double beds. In others, it may require a connecting pair of double rooms (though hardly any hotels will guarantee you'll get two rooms that connect—they're covering themselves in case the folks next door don't check out as expected—but in general, if you request connectors, you'll get them). In some hotels I've had to base things on the assumption that a small suite will be the best family deal. At any rate, I call a hotel **inexpensive** if that fictional family of four can stay for less than $225 a night; **moderate** if their bill will run $225 to $300; **expensive,** $300 to $400; and **very expensive,** over $400. (Those terms are, of course, relative to the Manhattan lodging price structure in general—and remember, that's for four people.) Quoted rates don't include the 13.375% New York City hotel tax or the occupancy tax, which is $3.50 per room per night.

These are based on "rack rates," the hotel's standard rates for peak times: Corporate discounts and package deals can bring them in at as much as $100 lower a night, so I've also noted which hotels regu offer good discounts. Some hotels regularly offer summer packages, while others are likely to activate package deals at the last minute, when occupancy rates appear to be falling short of projected levels. (Yield management is the name of the game.) Even if you've already secured a room at rack rates at a lower-priced hotel, just before you arrive, you might call a couple of pricier places to see if any special deals have kicked in. You could get a premium room for less, if you're lucky.

1 The Upper West Side
VERY EXPENSIVE

Excelsior Hotel 👶👶 This longtime neighborhood bargain hotel—perfectly situated right across the street from the city's top family attraction, the American Museum of Natural History—has been transformed into a smart upscale hotel, with a French provincial motif in soothing greens and soft rosy browns. The bathroom fixtures are up-to-date, with nice country-French tile accents. The rooms are good-size—a family of four could fit into one of the double-doubles (double room with two double beds), though a one-bedroom suite, with its pullout couch in the smallish sitting room, would give even more privacy (some one-bedroom suites have two doubles in the bedroom, so request this if your family needs to sleep more than four). The small but handsome wood-paneled lobby has an ornate plasterwork ceiling, much like many of the grand old apartment houses around the corner up Central Park West. Unfortunately, there's no room service, but complimentary continental breakfast is available on-premises in a breakfast room.

You can't deny that the location is superb—facing the wooded side yard of the American Museum of Natural History, on a clean and relatively quiet West Side block of luxury apartment buildings. You're half a block from Central Park, and there are loads of good restaurants and stores nearby on Columbus Avenue. The Excelsior is popular, particularly on weekends—reserve a couple of months ahead, if you can.

45 W. 81st St. (btwn Central Park W. and Columbus Ave.), New York, NY 10024. © 800/368-4575 or 212/362-9200. Fax 212/721-2994. www.excelsiorhotelny.com. 198 units. $369–$379 double; $549–$579 suite. Children under 14 stay free in parent's room. Rollaway $20; crib free. AE, DC, DISC, MC, V. Parking garages nearby. Subway: B, C to 81st St./Museum of Natural History. **Amenities:** Breakfast; fitness center; concierge; conference room; library. *In room:* A/C, TV, safe.

On the Ave Hotel   Definitely the hip choice on the Upper West Side. The trendy lobby looks very minimalist, with pale stone walls, a slick dark-wood floor, and a few scattered pieces of black leather furniture. It's been smartly renovated upstairs as well, with a Japanese-like simplicity—neutral carpet, gauze curtains, stainless-steel sinks, a sleek panel of varnished wood morphing from headboard into canopy over the bed. Rooms are smallish and contain only a king or queen bed, which means that a family will need to snag connecting rooms (of which there are about 30 in the hotel) or go for the penthouse suites, which have sitting areas and, often, balconies. This stylish hotel is very popular, especially with hip younger travelers; the location is convenient, with the American Museum of Natural History only 2 blocks away and Lincoln Center a 10-block stroll down Broadway. There's also a marvelous cityscape view accessible to all guests from a common-area balcony. There's no restaurant, but there is 24-hour room service.

2178 Broadway (entrance on 77th St.), New York, NY 10023. © 800/509-7598 or 212/362-1100. Fax 212/787-9521. www.ontheave.com. 253 units. $350–$425 double; $495–$650 suite; $695–$895 penthouse suite. Rollaway $20. AE, DC, MC, V. Parking $37 in nearby garage. Subway: 1 to 79th St. **Amenities:** Concierge; 24-hr. business center; 24-hr. room service; laundry service; dry cleaning. *In room:* A/C, TV, dataport, coffeemaker, fridge (on request).

EXPENSIVE

The Lucerne ⌅   Just a block from the American Museum of Natural History, in an area rich with restaurants and shopping, The Lucerne has all the earmarks of a chic boutique hotel, but it still works well for families. It's set in a gorgeous 1904 landmark building of plum-colored brownstone with baroque ornamentation running riot around its columned entrance; the small lobby gleams like a jewel, with marble floors, big potted plants, and deep settees. Glossy, traditional room decor features striped and floral fabrics, thick carpeting, and framed prints. The good-size, tidy bathrooms gleam with ivory-hued tilework, brown polished granite, and top-of-the-line fixtures. For dramatic views, be sure to ask for a room that looks out onto the Hudson River.

Fire laws prohibit rollaways in the double rooms, so unless you've only got one infant, you'll need a suite, but there are several of these, with either two queen-size beds or a king-size bed plus a foldout couch, and all the suites have kitchenette areas. You'll be happy (or not) to know that the in-room TV options include Nintendo games. The service level of this hotel lifts it above other neighborhood options, with a concierge in the lobby, business services, and a pocket-size fitness center. Hotel guests get a 20% discount at the downstairs Nice Matin restaurant, which is very popular in the neighborhood.

201 W. 79th St. (at Amsterdam Ave.), New York, NY 10024. ℭ 800/492-8122 or 212/875-1000. Fax 212/721-1179. www.thelucernehotel.com. 185 units. $310 double; $430 suite. Crib free. AE, DC, DISC, MC, V. Parking $29 (valet parking $42). Subway: 1 to 79th St. **Amenities:** Restaurant; fitness center; concierge; 24-hr. room service; dry cleaning. *In room:* A/C, TV w/Nintendo, microwave, fridge, coffeemaker in suites.

MODERATE

Comfort Inn on Central Park West   Despite the tony-sounding name, this budget-priced chain hotel isn't on classy Central Park West, but on a side street just off the park, in a narrow converted apartment building clad in a dour gray stone. But it *is* near the park, and near the American Natural History Museum, and within walking distance of Lincoln Center—a handy location that, given the price, is hard to beat. The small modern lobby hasn't got much charm, nor do the rooms—floral bedspreads, bland traditional furniture with a shiny cherrywood finish, new but small standard bathrooms—and the doubles are too tight to accommodate more than three guests, once you've wedged in a crib. Still, at the right season these rooms are cheap enough that you can book two for your family and still be in the moderate range, and the free continental breakfast (limited as it is) is an nice bonus. It's a decent choice for a short stay if you plan to be out on the town most of the time anyway.

31 W. 71st St. (btwn Central Park West and Columbus Ave.) ℭ 877/424-6423 or 212/721-4770. Fax 212/579-8544. www.comfortinn.com. 100 units. $199–$309 double. AE, DC, DISC, MC, V. Parking $30–$40 nearby. Subway: 1, 2, 3 to 72nd St. **Amenities:** Fitness center; concierge; free breakfast. *In room:* Hair dryer, iron.

Hotel Beacon 𝕲𝕲   Converted from an apartment building in the early 1990s, the Beacon offers just what we need more of in this city: clean, respectably furnished rooms with all the important amenities and none of the glitzy frills, in a neighborhood great for kids. Riverside Park is 2 blocks west and Central Park is 3 blocks east; the American Museum of Natural History and the Children's Museum of Manhattan are just a few blocks up the street, and Lincoln Center isn't far down Broadway. You'll find a quiet marble-clad lobby; wide, well-lit corridors; and good-size rooms freshly done up in a traditional decor (glossy dark Queen Anne–style furniture, muted rose and tan color schemes, and framed botanical prints on the walls). There's a full kitchenette with a microwave in every room; the baths aren't large but look sparkling clean and have proper drinking glasses and tidy little amenities baskets.

Even the doubles are big enough for a family, because they have two double beds and enough space for a crib or rollaway. Suites add on a sitting room with a foldout couch; if you've got more than four people staying in a suite, there's a $15 charge per extra adult. There's no room service, but a coffee shop is right on the corner. Though this is a busy stretch of Broadway, the windows are pretty well soundproofed (internal walls could use a little more soundproofing, unfortunately); since the 25-story hotel is one of the tallest buildings in the neighborhood, the upper-floor rooms facing west have nice views over Riverside Park and the Hudson. The Beacon gets a steady stream of business, so reserve as far in advance as possible, especially in June and October; weekdays tend to be less busy than weekends, so plan accordingly.

2130 Broadway (at 75th St.), New York, NY 10023. ℭ 800/572-4969 or 212/787-1100. Fax 212/724-0839. www.beaconhotel.com. 237 units. $235–$265 double; $280–$550 suite. Children 12 and under stay free in parent's room. Rollaway $15; crib free. AE, DC, DISC, MC, V. Parking $31. Subway: 1, 2, 3 to 72nd St. **Amenities:** 24-hr. restaurant; business center; laundry room. *In room:* A/C, TV, wireless internet, kitchenette, fridge, coffeemaker, hair dryer, iron, safe.

Cool Pools

You'll get fabulous views year-round at the snazzy, glass-enclosed atrium pool at **Le Parker Meridien** (p. 73), which is 42 stories up, with panoramas of Central Park and the Midtown skyline. The enclosed pool at the **Millennium U.N. Plaza Hotel** (p. 80) may be only 27 stories up, but it's right on the East River, which means not only river views but also unobstructed skyline views south. What's more, the Millennium U.N. Plaza's pool features gorgeous tilework and a canopy overhead. Also in Midtown, the **Crowne Plaza Times Square** (p. 74) has a gleaming 50-foot indoor lap pool with a nice view, if that matters to you.

Farther west, the **Skyline Hotel** (p. 76) has a smallish enclosed rooftop pool of an earlier vintage, squirreled away in a hard-to-find upstairs nook; the plus here is big windows grabbing a bit of a Hudson River view. Hours are limited, however. The largest hotel pool in town is the blue Olympic-size one at **Travel Inn** (p. 76), which is outdoors (hence open seasonally only), surrounded by wings of the hotel; a very pleasant patio area provides space for lounging poolside. The **Holiday Inn Midtown 57th Street** (p. 75) has a small outdoor rooftop pool, open Memorial Day through Labor Day.

Downtown, the 50-foot indoor pool at **Marriott New York Financial Center** (p. 85) has no views but is sparkling clean and quiet. Across the East River in Brooklyn, the **New York Marriott at the Brooklyn Bridge** (p. 86) has a 75-foot-long lap pool where kids can cavort after a day of sightseeing.

INEXPENSIVE

Days Hotel Broadway   Don't let the unglamorous upper Broadway environs put you off: You're half a block from an express subway stop, where trains can whisk you to the Theater District in minutes, and with several good casual restaurants nearby (not to mention top playgrounds and sports facilities in both Riverside and Central parks), this neighborhood works very well for families. Friends of ours lived here for several weeks after the World Trade Center attack drove them from their Battery Park City home, and given the horrific circumstances, they felt the Days Hotel did them quite well.

The hotel itself is unexceptional, with tight corridors, a ho-hum traditional decor (subtly patterned wallpaper, mauve carpeting, rose-hued bedspreads, cherry-veneered reproduction furniture), and window air conditioners (not that there's any view to block). Bathrooms, though neatly modernized, are on the small side. Still, a double room with two double beds puts you in the inexpensive rate category, and the suites aren't that much more (a junior suite, with a queen bed and a foldout couch, is a good option for families). Lots of tour operators know about this place, so book well ahead. Weeknights are considerably cheaper than weekends, and summer means lower rates, though even then rooms book up fast. There's no room service, but there are plenty of nearby coffee shops. It's a sensible, no-fuss option for families who plan to be out and about most of the time anyway.

215 W. 94th St. (btwn Broadway and Amsterdam Ave.). (℃ **800/228-5151**, 800/834-2972, or 212/866-6400. Fax 212/866-1357. www.daysinn.com. 350 units. $120–$600 double; $200–$600 junior suite. Rollaway $20; crib free. AE, DC,

MC, V. Parking $30–$40 in nearby garages. Subway: 1, 2, 3 to 96th St. *In room:* A/C, TV, fridge ($15 extra), coffeemaker.

Hotel Newton   With a cheerful, eager-to-please staff and clean, simple rooms, the Newton offers guests a way to see New York on a budget and still have a good time. The lobby is bright and has a comfy seating area, while restful guest rooms are neatly done up in beiges and browns with soft carpeting and functional wooden furniture. A deluxe room with two double beds would accommodate a family, but for a little more you could upgrade to the junior suite, which also has a sitting area and kitchenette. Bathrooms are small, with only adequate fixtures and bland tan tilework, but house-keeping keeps them sparkling. So what if the only views are of other buildings, the elevator is tiny, and the hallways narrow; there's an express subway stop right outside the hotel door, the neighborhood is friendly and safe, and you weren't planning to spend all your time in your hotel room anyway, were you? The Key West Diner downstairs is a shiny, up-to-date coffee shop with a huge menu, serving three meals a day, and the nearby area has loads of other family-friendly dining options.

2528 Broadway (btwn 94th and 95th sts.), New York, NY 10025. ℂ 800/643-5553 or 212/678-6500. Fax 212/678-6758. www.thehotelnewton.com. 100 units. $150-275 double; $195-300 suite. Rollaway $25; crib free. AE, DC, MC, V. Parking $22–$27. Subway: 1, 2, 3 to 96th St. **Amenities:** Restaurant; room service (6am–11pm). *In room:* A/C, TV; kitchenettes in suites.

Milburn Hotel 🧒   As a happy mother checking out reported to me the day I visited, "What's not to like? It's clean, cheap, and friendly to kids." The Milburn Hotel has a lot to offer at a great price. The hallways are narrow, but the rooms are decent-size (a few even have small outdoor terraces), with simple, traditional furnishings crisply maintained. Adding a crib or rollaway would make one of the doubles seriously snug; a family should probably go for a suite, which adds a sitting room with foldout couch. Kitchenettes have been smartly tucked into all rooms, with a microwave, minifridge, and tiny sink. Keeping kids happy in the room becomes easier with the in-room VCRs (with a free video library downstairs) and PlayStations available from the front desk.

The Milburn's entrance is just around the corner from Broadway, making it convenient for shopping and restaurants; though the Milburn has no restaurant, it offers a dining plan with discounts at good local restaurants. Considering you'll have a kitchenette, it's good to know that food shopping is especially great in this neighborhood, with the Fairway market and Citarella's fish store a couple blocks south, and H&H Bagels and Zabar's gourmet emporium a few blocks north. Riverside Park is only 2 blocks away, too. All told, an excellent deal.

242 W. 76th St. (btwn Broadway and West End Ave.), New York, NY 10023. ℂ 800/833-9622 or 212/362-1006. Fax 212/721-5476. www.milburnhotel.com. 122 units. $139–$249 double; $159–$269 suite. Rollaway $15; crib free. AE, DC, MC, V. Parking $25. Subway: 1 to 79th St.; 1, 2, 3 to 72nd St. **Amenities:** Pool privileges nearby; fitness room; 24-hr. room service. *In room:* A/C, TV/VCR, kitchenette, fridge, coffeemaker, safe.

West Side YMCA (Value)   One of the best lodging bargains in New York—if you're lucky enough to snag a room; it's the sort of place where Manhattan newcomers live for weeks, waiting to get situated, and someone else moves in as they finally check out. The Y has both single and double rooms, and they are small and no-frills but quite neat, many with snug little modern bathrooms. The building, however, is a knockout, a landmark Romanesque beauty with arches and medieval encrustations all over the brick-and-limestone exterior, and an expansive low-ceilinged lobby richly tiled in warm shades of brown; you almost feel as it you are stepping into a European monastery, except for the continual buzz of young people coming in and out. The athletic facilities of the Y are excellent, and room guests get to use them—pools, gyms, handball and squash courts, dance studios, the works. The location is brilliant, too, five minutes' walk from Lincoln Center and only steps from Central Park. If you're trying to see New York on a budget, make this your first call.

5 W. 63rd St. (btwn Central Park West and Broadway) ℭ 212/875-4273. Fax 212/875-4291. www.ymcanyc.org. 480 units. $105–$140 double; $72–$89 with shared bathroom. AE, MC, V. Parking $30–$40 nearby. Subway: A, B, C, D, 1 to Columbus Circle/59th St. **Amenities:** Cafe; 2 indoor pools; aerobics studios; fitness classes; basketball, racquetball, and squash courts; sauna; concierge; tour desk; coin-op laundry. In room: A/C, TV.

2 The Upper East Side
VERY EXPENSIVE
The Carlyle ℭℭℭ   In my opinion, this is the best hotel in Manhattan—and lots of people seem to agree with me. The roster of celebrity guests includes everyone from Jack Nicholson to JFK, from Brooke Astor to David Bowie, from Jessica Lange and Sam Shepard to Goldie Hawn and Kurt Russell. Many of the staff, from the bellmen to the concierges, make working at The Carlyle a lifetime career, delivering white-glove service that's rare indeed. Surprisingly enough, all this makes The Carlyle is a great family hotel, if the prices aren't beyond your budget. The neighborhood is wonderfully quiet and well behaved, and the rooms are huge—even a double is big enough for a smaller family, with a crib or rollaway brought in.

All the rooms are done up in beautiful traditional style, with gorgeous chintzes and drapes and thick carpets; from its first decorator in the 1930s, Dorothy Draper, to more recent refurbishments by Mark Hampton, The Carlyle has been furnished by Manhattan society's top residential designers. "Residential" is the key word—if a room has shelves, they'll be stocked with books; vases and china dishes and ormolu clocks are set out on the occasional tables; every sitting room and bedroom has its own entertainment center with a VCR and CD player. More than a dozen rooms have grand pianos, some of them Steinways, others Baldwins. The suites have sleek modern kitchens, while even the double rooms at least have an alcove with a sink and well-stocked minibar. The baths are big and gleaming, with Givenchy toiletries, thick towels and terry-cloth robes, and makeup mirrors; most tubs have whirlpools in them.

The Carlyle's dining choices have always attracted locals, from the plush and intimate Carlyle Restaurant decorated in the style of an English manor (breakfast, lunch, and dinner, with a lavish Sun brunch) and Café Carlyle, a renowned cabaret venue with regular performers like Bobby Short, to the Gallery, a Turkish-style red-velvet lobby area with a few small tables which is the place for breakfast coffee and afternoon tea, as well as post-theater snacks. But best of all for kids is the atmospheric Bemelmans Bar, with its fanciful murals painted by Austrian artist Ludwig Bemelmans, creator of the *Madeline* books ("In an old house in Paris, covered in vines, lived twelve little girls in two straight lines. . . .") where a special Madeline tea is held on weekends (see p. 112).

The hotel is 35 stories tall, so if you're lucky enough to snag a room overlooking Central Park, you'll have a view you could gaze at for hours, day or night. Carlyle guests are near enough to the park to scamper right over and play, as well as being close to the Fifth Avenue museums and to the glorious children's shops of upper Madison Avenue.

35 E. 76th St. (at Madison Ave.), New York, NY 10021. ℭ 800/227-5737 or 212/744-1600. Fax 212/717-4682. www.thecarlyle.com. 179 units. $500–$825 double; $900–$3,200 suite. AE, DC, MC, V. Parking $50. Subway: 6 to 77th St. **Amenities:** Restaurant; lounge; cafe/cabaret; bar; small fitness center with sauna and steam room; concierge;

secretarial services; 24-hr. room service. *In room:* A/C, TV/DVD, dataport, kitchen in suites, minibar, hair dryer, CD player, safe.

The Mark 😺😺   Compared to its near neighbor The Carlyle (see above), The Mark looks hipper and more corporate, though it's still one of the city's finest hotels. Many of its guests are visiting New York on business, and 40% of the clientele is European. But families still fit into the mix pretty well, especially because summers and weekends—prime times for family travel—are less busy here. Families are, in fact, actively courted with kid-savvy concierges and special offers such as the Little Fans package, which includes stuffed animals and backpacks and complimentary tickets to nearby attractions children like.

The Mark offers one thing that few other uptown hotels do: connecting doubles that can be closed off with their own private doorway and vestibule. Double rooms have either twin beds or a king-size bed, and rooms are plenty large enough for a crib to be brought in. The so-called executive suite is a good option for families, with a queen-size bed in one room and a foldout couch in the other. The plush decor feels residential, with warm browns or greens, well-stuffed chairs, and eye-catching draperies. The bathrooms are bigger than average, with stunning black-and-white tiles and fixtures, including deep tubs, separate shower stalls, and heated towel bars (my kids always find these a kick for some reason—well, it is pretty nice to swathe yourself in a warm towel when you step out of a bath). The neighborhood is restful, with a sort of moneyed calm; Central Park is only a block away. At 16 stories, The Mark offers views over many neighboring rooftops, and large windows fill the rooms with light.

The well-regarded on-site restaurant, Mark's, serves all meals as well as Sunday brunch and afternoon tea; it's a handsome clublike dining room with velvet banquettes, brass railings, mahogany armchairs, and tables spaced well apart.

25 E. 77th St. (at Madison Ave.), New York NY 10021. ℂ **800/843-6275,** 800/526-6566, or 212/744-4300. Fax 212/744-2749. www.themarkhotel.com. 180 units. $720–$750 double; $880–$1,900 suite. Children under 17 stay free in parent's room. Rollaway $30; crib free. Corporate, weekend, and summer packages available. AE, DC, DISC, MC, V. Parking $45. Subway: 6 to 77th St. **Amenities:** Restaurant; bar; small fitness center with sauna and steam room; concierge; twice-daily shuttle to Wall St.; weekend shuttle to the Theater District; business services; 24-hr. room service. *In room:* A/C, TV/VCR, kitchenette in many units, minibar, safe.

Surrey Hotel 😺   If you haven't got the dough to stay nearby at The Carlyle or The Mark (see above), you can still enjoy this ace East Side neighborhood with a somewhat more affordable suite at the Surrey. Its clean, well-maintained rooms are positively huge—you could easily fit a crib or rollaway into the so-called studio suites. The one-bedroom suites could sleep six, with two double beds in the bedroom and a foldout sofa in the sitting room. The decor is tasteful, if not fussy, with Chippendale-ish reproductions. The bathrooms are sparkling clean, though the fixtures aren't necessarily luxurious. Every unit has a kitchen or kitchenette with cutlery and plates, and guests here really do seem to use their kitchens—the staff will even do your food shopping for only $5 (plus the cost of the groceries, of course). If cooking is not your idea of a vacation, there are scads of restaurants within a short walk, and room service is provided by the kitchen of one of Manhattan's most stellar chefs, Daniel Boulud, whose Café Boulud is downstairs.

The ample reception area, with marble columns, a chandelier, and a genteelly faded Oriental rug, resembles many Upper East Side apartment building lobbies—indeed, staying here is one way to discover what it's like to live in New York as a family, as you troll the Madison Avenue children's shops and hang out at the East 76th Street Playground in

Central Park. The Surrey's residential air is enhanced by the fact that many guests are on long stays—corporate relocations, local families holing up during apartment renovations. Nevertheless, the Surrey welcomes short-stay guests, especially on weekdays and in the July/August slow period, so don't hesitate to check if there's a room, even on short notice.

20 E. 76th St. (at Madison Ave.), New York, NY 10021. © 866/AFFINIA or 212/288-3700. www.affinia.com. Fax 212/628-1549. 131 units. $369–619 studio suite/1-bedroom suite; $990-2060 2-bedroom suite. Rollaway $30; crib free. Weekly and monthly discount rates available. AE, DC, DISC, MC, V. Valet parking $47. Subway: 6 to 77th St. **Amenities:** Fitness center; room service (7:30am–10pm); concierge; secretarial service; coin-op laundry; nonsmoking floors; grocery shopping service. In room: A/C, TV/VCR, kitchen or kitchenette, fridge.

EXPENSIVE

Affinia Gardens   Manhattan East Suites hotels offer great deals for extended-stay visitors or families: roomy suites with fully equipped kitchens, along with essential hotel services. (There's no restaurant, but several nearby restaurants will deliver, and there are loads of family-friendly restaurants near by.) The Affinia Gardens attracts a lot of business from the cluster of hospitals around 68th Street and York Avenue, but this relatively residential neighborhood also makes sense for families on a short stay. From the stylish small lobby, with its tranquil waterfall wall, the decor is spare, Zen-like, and contemporary—serene surroundings to crash in after a long day. Request a junior suite with a pullout couch as well as a king or two double beds, or go for the one- or two-bedroom suites, which have separate bedrooms and sitting rooms, with sleeper sofas. In general, the staff seems helpful and friendly, accommodating whatever requests guests have.

215 E. 64th St. (btwn Second and Third aves.), New York, NY 10021. © 866/AFFINIA or 212/355-1230. Fax 212/758-7858. www.affinia.com. 130 units. $379–$679 suite. Children under 11 stay free in parent's room. Rollaway $20; crib free. AE, DC, DISC, MC, V. Valet parking $38. Subway: 4, 5, 6 to 59th St.; 6 to 68th St.; N, R, W to Lexington Ave./59th St. **Amenities:** Fitness center; concierge. In room: A/C, TV, kitchenette.

Hotel Wales ⚜   There's more than a touch of Edwardian Kensington to this charming century-old hotel in Carnegie Hill, a historic Upper East Side neighborhood full of top-notch private schools and well-off families. Only a block from Central Park and Museum Mile, the hotel is smack in the middle of upper Madison's strip of upscale children's shops. The lobby looks like the entry hall in a private mansion, with its marble staircase, carved wood banisters, dark wainscoting, and striped wallpaper, and the room decor is tastefully traditional—beautiful restored woodwork, original cabinets, and cedar-lined closets. The Pied Piper Room, where guests can help themselves to a granola-and-muffins breakfast, is a big comfy space with potted palms and Victorian settees where chamber music is played at teatime and on Sunday evening.

Absolutely the only drawback to staying in this hotel is that the rooms are so small you can barely fit in a crib—better to go for a suite, which consists of a fair-size bedroom and an adjoining sitting area with a pullout sofa. (There are no connecting doubles.) The bathrooms are tiny yet outfitted with top-quality fixtures. Kids get a kick out of the hotel's Puss-in-Boots theme, discreetly carried out with framed prints on the walls and designs on the bath toiletries. Every room has a VCR, and you can tell how popular the Wales is with families when you see how many kids' movies there are in its video library. Separately owned Sarabeth's Restaurant, popular with East Side families for brunch, is right downstairs.

1295 Madison Ave. (at 92nd St.), New York, NY 10128. © 212/876-6000. Fax 212/876-7139. www.waleshotel.com. 87 units. $270–$399 double; $370–$699 suite. Rates include continental breakfast. Extra person $20. Rollaway $20;

crib free. AE, DC, DISC, MC, V. Valet parking $40–$42. Subway: 6 to 96th St. **Amenities:** Breakfast room; fitness room; concierge; room service. *In room:* A/C, TV/VCR, fridge on request, CD player.

INEXPENSIVE

Gracie Inn *(Finds* If only New York had more places like the Gracie Inn! First off, there's the neighborhood: the Upper East Side, on a side street near the East River, not far from Carl Schurz Park—the part of the East Side where middle-class families live and shop and go to school. Then there are the thoughtful service and quiet un-hotel-like atmosphere, which make this a welcome retreat from Manhattan bustle—the sort of bed-and-breakfast boutique hotel you can find all over Europe but rarely in the States.

Once you get past the unprepossessing exterior and minuscule lobby, the five-story townhouse (with elevator) has individually decorated suites. Antiques, stenciled wallpapers, rag rugs, hardwood floors, and lace curtains go for a country-inn look that's never too frilly or precious; fresh flowers are set out in the rooms, and plump snowy duvets are on the beds. Every suite has a tidy little kitchen with all utensils, and a continental breakfast is brought to your room each morning. Cribs or rollaways could fit handily even in the studios, though a one- or two-bedroom suite would be better for a family, especially the penthouse duplex (kids will have a blast running up and down the snug wooden staircase). With skylights, a greenhouse wall, and weathered wood terraces, the penthouse suites get loads of sun, but even rooms on the lower floors are fairly light. Don't expect to walk to the subway—York Avenue is a long way east from the subway line—but buses and taxis are easy to find, and the neighborhood has plenty of good, reasonably priced restaurants.

502 E. 81st St. (btwn York and East End aves.), New York, NY 10028. © **212/628-1700.** Fax 212/628-6420. www. gracieinn.com. 12 units. $179–$189 studio suite; $199–$215 1-bedroom suite; $279–$350 penthouse. Rates include continental breakfast. Discounts offered for weekly and monthly stays. Rollaway free; crib free. AE, DC, DISC, MC, V. Parking garages nearby. Subway: 6 to 77th St. **Amenities:** *In room:* A/C, TV, dataport, kitchen.

3 Midtown West

EXPENSIVE

Doubletree Guest Suites *GG* Quite possibly the most family-oriented hotel in Manhattan, the Doubletree more than makes up for what might be an off-putting location, smack dab on Times Square. There are two entire floors fitted out for families with younger children—plastic drinking cups, childproofed power outlets, padded bump guards on furniture edges, spout covers in the tubs. The suite concept is a natural for families anyway, because you automatically get sleeping space for four or six, depending on whether you request a king-size bed or two doubles in the bedroom (there's a foldout sofa in the sitting room). All suites have kitchenettes with a microwave, a stocked minibar, and TVs in both rooms. The low-key contemporary decor features calm grays and subdued geometric designs that don't show spills.

Now let's get to the really unusual ways the Doubletree provides for families: There's no charge for cribs, playpens, and strollers, and you can request that the cable movie service be shut off if you're worried your kids will go wild with the remote. Next to the restaurant and health club is a delightful large playroom with a stunning Statue of Liberty design on the carpet; it's equipped with well-chosen picture books, big stuffed animals, colorful large foam blocks, and a clever wall-mounted city maze around which kids can steer small taxis. Security is good, though not forbidding: There's a ground-floor foyer with monitored elevators leading up to the guest lobby, and a separate bank of elevators goes up to guest-room floors. After 11pm guests have to show their key card to be admitted into the guest-room elevators. At 43 stories, the Doubletree does have some high-floor rooms with Midtown views, but what's more important about the height is that it means there are lots of rooms, so more families can take advantage of this great deal.

The Center Stage Café has whimsical wall murals carrying out its Broadway theater theme—face one way, and you'll feel like an audience watching the stage; face the other, and you'll feel like performers looking up at the audience in the painted balcony. The restaurant serves a breakfast buffet, lunch, and dinner and has a kids' menu, naturally.

1568 Broadway (at 47th St. and Seventh Ave.), New York, NY 10036. ⓒ 800/222-8733 or 212/719-1600. Fax 212/921-5212. www.doubletree.com. 460 units. $315–$640 suite. Children 17 and under stay free in parent's room. Crib free. AE, DC, DISC, MC, V. Valet parking $35–$40. Subway: 1 to 50th St.; N, R, W to 49th St.; B, D, F, V to 47th–50th sts./Rockefeller Center. **Amenities:** Restaurant; fitness room; children's playroom; concierge; room service (5:30am–11:30pm). *In room:* A/C, TV, VCR by request, kitchenette, minibar, fridge, coffeemaker, safe.

Le Parker Meridien ⭐⭐⭐   The property looks chic enough, with a marble-columned lobby and a sleek, Zen-like guest-room decor—but Le Parker Meridien does a good job of making families feel welcome. On arrival, kids are given the hotel's own hand-drawn coloring book; the elevators play continual cartoons and classic silent slapstick comedies; and kids can borrow a Razor scooter from the front desk to whiz around the neighborhood. Not only does the concierge know what's on for kids, but guests can also consult an online concierge even before arrival to scope out kid-friendly activities. Naturally, items like highchairs, nightlights, bottle warmers, and safety plugs are available on request.

With its splendid glass-enclosed atrium pool, sun deck, ⅛-mile rooftop jogging track, and top-notch health club, this family-owned hotel is a super choice for any athletic family. The 57th Street location is close to Midtown attractions, yet only 2 blocks from Central Park; several rooms on the 42-story hotel's upper floors—say, from 20 on up—offer green park views. The artfully uncluttered guest rooms are of a good size by Manhattan standards—a double with two double beds could accommodate a family for a short stay—though the Tower Suites aren't a bad deal, with a king-size bed in one room, a pullout couch in the other, a bathroom, a kitchenette, and an awesome skyline view on upper floors. The suites have full kitchenettes with pots, plates, and condiments available upon request. But best of all, at least from my son's point of view, is the rotating blond-wood entertainment console—which, naturally, has video games on tap as well as movies.

Norma's serves gargantuan gourmet breakfasts, all the way through lunchtime, and Seppi's is an atmospheric wine-bar/bistro. But face it, the restaurant kids will dig the most here is the no-name burger den hidden off the lobby, which serves nothing but dang good burgers, cheeseburgers, and fries. Look for a neon burger hung discreetly near the concierge desk, and follow.

118 W. 57th St. (btwn Sixth and Seventh aves.), New York, NY 10019. ⓒ 800/543-4300 or 212/245-5000. Fax 212/307-1776. www.parkermeridien.com. 700 units. $295–$580 double; $675 and up suites. Rollaway or crib $30. Weekend packages available. AE, DC, DISC, MC, V. Valet parking $45. Subway: N, Q, R, W to 57th St./Seventh Ave. **Amenities:** 2 restaurants; bar; indoor pool; fitness center with squash and racquetball courts; spa; sauna; jogging track; concierge; courtesy car to Wall St.; business center; 24-hr. room service. *In room:* A/C, TV/DVD, kitchenette in suites, minibar, CD player.

Renaissance New York   Sleek and corporate-looking as it is, the Renaissance isn't the kind of hotel families automatically gravitate to, but those who do wind up here

might be very pleasantly surprised. First, you're right in the thick of the exciting Times Square action, but in a good way—the famous Coca-Cola sign hangs on the hotel's south wall; the TKTS discount ticket booth is a few steps away, many rooms look out onto one or another of the fabled supersigns; and Foley's, a wedge-shaped restaurant off the lobby with dark glass windows on three sides, offers the best panoramic view of the Times Square intersection. (You couldn't ask for a better ringside seat on New Year's Eve.) Yet the riffraff gets screened out by the ground-floor security lobby (the guest lobby is up on the third floor), and double-paned windows do an amazing job of keeping out traffic noise.

Inside, everything is mahogany and brass and marble and truly handsome. Families can fit nicely into the doubles, which are roomier than most Midtown doubles—go with a king-size-bedded room with a rollaway or a room that has two double beds. Suites consist of a king-size-bedded sleeping room and a sitting room with a pullout couch. Minibars are set under a marble countertop which makes a handy place for fixing snacks or lunches. The hotel isn't too buttoned-down to have a sense of fun: Instead of pillow mints, you get apples at turndown (because you're in the Big Apple, get it?), and there are board games at the front desk to while away the time.

714 Seventh Ave. (btwn 47th and 48th sts.), New York, NY 10036. © 800/468-3571, 800/228-9290, or 212/765-7676. Fax 212/765-1962. www.nycrenaissance.com. 305 units. $350–$549 double; $375–$850 suite. Children 15 and under stay free in parent's room. Rollaway or crib free. AE, DC, DISC, MC, V. Valet parking $44. Subway: N, R, W to 49th St.; B, D, F, V to 47th–50th sts./Rockefeller Center; 1 to 50th St. **Amenities:** Restaurant; breakfast room; lounge; small fitness center; concierge; 24-hr. room service. *In room:* A/C, TV/VCR, minibar, coffeemaker.

MODERATE

Crowne Plaza Times Square ⚐   In the new, spiffed-up Times Square, the Crowne Plaza is nicely positioned to be a major player. With a reception area one floor up from Broadway (security is thorough but not oppressive) and tight soundproofing, you can feel removed from the tumult but not bunkered in—many windows overlook the razzmatazz, including some around the pool and at the end of every corridor. The guest floors begin on the 16th story (several floors of offices are in between the lobby and the guest rooms), giving many rooms great skyline or river views. Yet this contemporary 46-story building sticks firmly to the middle of the road, in style as well as rates. Its lobby has some marble and brass and plush touches, but it's not overbearing; the room decor is traditional and corporate, with greens and browns and lots of table lamps; the restaurants are generally casual, with a breakfast buffet (or if you really want to get going fast in the morning, pick up coffee, juice, and muffins to go from the lobby bar).

Families have several layout options: a double room with two double beds; connecting doubles; a smallish sitting room with your choice of one or two bedrooms connecting; or a large sitting room (complete with a minibar/serving area and dining table) with your choice of one or two bedrooms connecting. Along with pullout sofas, the Crowne Plaza has some pull-down Murphy beds, which kids might enjoy. Some extra amenities (terry bathrobes, a jar of hard candies) are offered on Crowne Plaza Club floors, but it might be worth it if only because you can get continental breakfast free in the lounge, a huge windowed parlor with dynamite views; once the corporate travelers have cleared out at 9am or so, the room is virtually empty. The health club is an obvious attraction for families, though there are some caveats: The fitness center is run by the New York Sports Club, whose members get priority over hotel guests weekdays at lunchtime and after work. The 50-foot lap pool, however, is open to guests at all times; if you want to make sure there's room, call ahead to reserve a lane.

1605 Broadway (btwn 48th and 49th sts.), New York, NY 10019. © **800/2-CROWNE**, (800/980-6429), or 212/977-4000. Fax 212/333-7393. www.crowneplaza.com. 770 units. $239–$479 double; $599–$1,200 suite. Children 18 and under stay free in parent's room. Rollaway $30; crib free. AE, DC, DISC, MC, V. Valet parking $39–$44. Subway: 1 to 50th St.; N, R, W to 49fth St. **Amenities:** 3 restaurants; bar; indoor pool; fitness center with classes; sauna; concierge; theater and tour desk; business center; shopping arcade; room service (6am–2pm and 5–10pm); massage; concierge-level rooms. *In room:* A/C, TV, minibar, coffeemaker.

The Paramount   Not many families stay here, maybe because the parents feel intimidated by the aggressively hip Philippe Starck decor: Stepping into the minimal-ist gray lobby with its asymmetrical rug, cartoonishly shaped armchairs, and freestand-ing stairway of brushed stainless steel can be unnerving. Young singles who look like *Sex and the City* extras stare meaningfully at each other over tiny tables at the Brasserie; the Dean & Deluca espresso bar is way cooler than a Starbucks, and the Whiskey Bar has a definite happy-hour vibe. Heading upstairs, you may be disoriented by the deeply colored lighting inside the elevators. The rooms have severe-looking white linen bedcovers, black-and-white checkerboard carpets, and oversize gilt frames for headboards; the bathrooms have an inverted cone of brushed steel for a sink.

Truth to tell, though, it's stunning, and kids might really get into its futuristic weirdness. And who would have expected it'd have a children's playroom, with an almost psychedelic Looney Tunes decor? If the guest-room decor's not a problem, the size may be—some double rooms do have two double beds, but that doesn't leave a whole lot of space. The west-of-Times-Square location is close to Broadway theaters and Eighth Avenue's mixed bag of restaurants. All in all, I think this is a super place for a few nights' stay, provided your kids are sophisticated enough to appreciate the hypercoolness.

235 W. 46th St. (btwn Broadway and Eighth Ave.), New York, NY 10036. © **800/436-3542** or 212/764-5500. Fax 212/354-5237. www.nycparamount.com. 608 units. $259–$400 double. Rollaway $25; crib free. AE, DC, DISC, MC, V. Parking $45. Subway: A, C, E to 42nd St./Port Authority; C, E to 50th St.; N, Q, R, S, W, 1, 2, 3, 7 to 42nd St./Times Sq. **Amenities:** 3 restaurants; coffee bar; bar; fitness room; children's playroom; concierge; business center; 24-hr. room service. *In room:* A/C, TV/VCR, minibar, iron, hair dryer.

INEXPENSIVE

Holiday Inn Midtown 57th Street   This reassuring motor inn in a residential area of Midtown's far west fringe is a very workable option for families. If you're driving into Manhattan, the low parking rate from the attached garage may appeal to you, especially because this property is close to the West Side Highway. And if your kids can't survive a vacation without a pool handy, the outdoor rooftop pool (open in sum-mer only) may be a draw. Yes, it's a long walk from here to Midtown attractions, but the relative quiet and calm may make all the difference, and the immediate neighbor-hood has lots of casual, locals-only restaurants that'll welcome you and your kids.

The paneled front-desk area is low-key and pleasant, with a lobby bar (the restau-rant and breakfast room are down a hallway). Although the guest room layouts are chain-motel-predictable, with large windows looking out at nothing particularly sce-nic, the double rooms are of decent size by Manhattan standards—they do hold two double beds comfortably, which means a whole family may be able to fit in. There are a number of connecting doubles, if your family wants more space to spread out. Rooms have neutral-toned contemporary-style furnishings; those who are interested in swimming might try to snag one in the south tower, where the pool is.

440 W. 57th St. (btwn Ninth and Tenth aves.), New York, NY 10019. ℭ **800/315-2621** or 212/581-8100. Fax 212/581-7739. www.sixcontinentshotels.com/holiday-inn. 599 units. $209–$367 double; $350–$700 suite. Rollaway $15; crib free. AE, DC, DISC, MC, V. Valet Parking $23; regular parking free. Subway: A, B, C, D, 1 to 59th St./Columbus Circle. **Amenities:** Restaurant; cafe; bar; fitness center; outdoor pool; room service (6:30am–11pm). *In room:* A/C, TV, coffeemaker.

Skyline Hotel *Value*   With the transformation of the gritty Hell's Kitchen neighborhood into respectable Clinton, the Tenth Avenue location of the Skyline is no longer a drawback. Guest rooms are tastefully decorated—green carpets, mottled rosy walls, flowered bedspreads—with up-to-date bathrooms (though small, most have bathtubs); so-called deluxe floors have a newer, more contemporary decor and added amenities, including a minifridge. Most rooms are large enough to hold two double beds, which means that families may be able to get by with one room; junior and one-bedroom suites comfortably sleep six. We're talking bargain here, and many European travelers have already found it, so book well ahead. The small rooftop indoor pool is freshly tiled with lots of surrounding windows, but there's a catch: It's open weeknights and weekends only. For these prices, people are happy to work around such minor inconveniences.

Off the lobby, Restaurant 1050 is a casual spot serving American bistro-style food, three meals a day, and it will deliver to your room (though you can't charge it to your room bill). There's a wealth of fun restaurants just a block away on Ninth Avenue, too. Yes, it's a trek from here to most sights, but it's generally easy to hail a cab outside the hotel door. Now that it's no longer scary to walk this far west on 49th or 50th streets, the Skyline makes a lot of sense if you're trying to save a buck or two.

725 Tenth Ave. (btwn 49th and 50th sts.), New York, NY, 10019. ℭ **800/433-1982** or 212/586-3400. Fax 212/582-4604. www.skylinehotelny.com. 230 units. $159–$250 double; $175–$340 suite. Rollaway $20; crib free. AE, DC, DISC, MC, V. Parking $8 (no in/out during stay). Subway: A, C, E to 50th St. **Amenities:** Restaurant; indoor pool; concierge. *In room:* A/C, TV, Nintendo, wireless internet.

Travel Inn *Kids Value*   One of New York's very best deals is this bright, clean, sprucely decorated motor inn way at the end of 42nd Street—beyond Theater Row, in an area of warehouses and parking lots and not much else. One reason to stay here is you get free parking; of course, what you save in parking you could easily spend in taxi fare, because the only attractions close at hand are the Circle Line boat tours. Still, the Travel Inn remains very busy—there are many times when it's sold out months and months in advance—partly because it's handy for the nearby Javits Convention Center; partly because it has a pool; and, well, did we mention the parking is *free?*

If you don't mind the concrete surroundings (the hotel certainly seems secure enough), you could save a whole lot by staying here: A family could fit comfortably in these rooms, which have two double beds, a desk, a dresser, and upholstered chairs. The decor is standard hotel-room traditional but very nicely kept; the bathrooms are spotless. And as befits a true motor inn, there's a big lap pool (open May–Oct), set in a spacious tiled area with lots of lounge chairs and room to stroll around. A number of rooms overlook the pool area from balconied walkways—request one of these, as opposed to the ones overlooking the street. The fitness room with weights and exercise machines is small but serviceable. The attached Broadway Bagel deli will deliver up to your room 6am to 8pm, and a host of other area delis are happy to deliver as well.

515 W. 42nd St. (btwn Tenth and Eleventh aves.), New York, NY 10036. ℭ **800/869-4630** or 212/695-7171. Fax 212/967-5025. www.thetravelinnhotel.com. 160 units. $140–$250 double. Rollaway $15; crib free. AE, DC, DISC, MC, V. Free parking. Subway: A, C, E to 42nd St./Port Authority. Bus: M42. **Amenities:** Outdoor pool; fitness room; tour desk. *In room:* A/C, TV, dataport.

4 Midtown East

VERY EXPENSIVE

Four Seasons   Now owned by Ty Warner of Beanie Baby fame, this stunning 57th Street hotel designed by I. M. Pei sets high standards for service, upscale chic, and high prices. The tortoiseshell onyx skylight and soaring octagonal limestone columns in the cathedral-like foyer instill a sense of awe, and everything from there on is hushed and knowingly subtle. Smartly dressed guests wander through the lobby toting the right designer shopping bags; the attentiveness of the staff is wonderful, without a trace of fawning or condescension. This hotel manages to be decorous without being uptight (and kid radar can register uptightness a mile away). The guest rooms are outfitted with understated but sleek modern furnishings, beautifully streamlined stuff Frank Lloyd Wright would approve of. The marble baths are huge and superbly appointed, with roomy adjacent dressing areas.

The room layouts aren't particularly handy for families: A maximum of one extra bed is allowed per room (crib or rollaway), and there are only a few adjoining doubles that could be set off by shutting a common door to the corridor. Larger families will have to go for a suite, which knocks you up into the $1,000-plus range. Some of the suites are on the higher floors, 31 and above (the hotel is 52 stories tall), which gives many of them stunning Central Park views. But the Four Seasons chain is known for valuing its young guests; special amenities for kids include a well-focused kids menu and a collection of toys, videos, and DVDs to borrow.

57 E. 57th St. (btwn Madison and Park aves.), New York, NY 10022. (© **800/487-3769** or 212/758-5700. Fax 212/758-5711. www.fourseasons.com. 368 units. $595–$625 double; $775–$2,550 suite. Extra person $50. Rollaway or crib free for 18 and under. AE, DC, DISC, MC, V. Parking $42. Subway: 4, 5, 6 to 59th St. **Amenities:** Restaurant; lounge with light food; fitness center; spa services; Jacuzzi; sauna; business center; concierge; 24-hr. room service. *In room:* A/C, TV, VCR upon request, minibar, fridge, CD player.

EXPENSIVE

Beekman Tower Hotel 𝒢   In many respects, the Beekman Tower offers the best of all worlds. You're convenient to Midtown but in the posh residential East 50s, where peace and safety reign. You have all the roominess of a small apartment but with lots of hotel services. You get some super views but don't have to pay through the nose for them.

This orange-brick Deco tower rising on a slope just north of the United Nations is known to New Yorkers for the Top of the Tower, a pleasant and unpretentious restaurant and lounge with a wonderful view of the skyline and East River. What New Yorkers don't seem to know is what a great deal this all-suite hotel is. Its smallest suite, the studio, will work only for a small family—it has a queen- or full-size bed and a small sofa (not all of them foldout), but there's plenty of room for a crib or rollaway, and it has a kitchenette. The one-bedroom suites are perfectly fine, with a foldout couch in the spacious living room and a separate bedroom with a king- or queen-size bed. And they have full kitchens—a four-burner stove; a full refrigerator; a big sink; a microwave; pots and pans; and, incredibly enough, a dishwasher. With clean, up-to-date appliances and a grocery-shopping service, these are kitchens people really can use. Ask for a "C-line suite" and you'll also get a dynamite East River view. The traditional room decor is easy to live with; deluxe suites also have VCRs, in-room fax machines, and, on top floors, balconies. July and August are particularly good times to snag a room, and significant discounts may be offered all times of year, so inquire when you book.

Tips A Family of Hotels

The Beekman Tower is part of **Affinia** hotels, as are the Surrey Hotel (p. 70) and Affinia Gardens (p. 71). Affinia is a very good company to know about because their suite layouts are so convenient for families. Other Affinia hotels in Midtown are the **Affinia Dumont**, 150 E. 34th St., between Third and Lexington avenues (© **212/481-7600**); **Eastgate Tower**, 222 E. 39th St., between Second and Third avenues (© **212/687-8000**); the **Affinia 50 Suite Hotel**, 155 E. 50th St., at Third Avenue (© **212/751-5710**); the **Shelburne Murray Hill Suites**, 303 Lexington Ave., at 37th Street (© **212/689-5200**); and the **Southgate Tower**, 371 Seventh Ave., at 31st Street (© **212/563-1800**). All are in roughly the same price category, and reservations at any of them can be made by calling © **866/ AFFINIA.**

---

3 Mitchell Place (First Ave. at 49th St.), New York, NY 10017. © **866/AFFINIA** or 212/355-7300. Fax 212/753-9366. www.affinia.com. 174 units. $219 studio suite; $379–$439 1-bedroom suite; $619 2-bedroom suite. Rollaway $20; crib free. AE, DISC, MC, V. Valet parking $37. Subway: E, V to Lexington Ave./53rd St.; 6 to 51st St. **Amenities:** Restaurant; cafe; fitness center; concierge; room service till 6:30pm. *In room:* A/C, TV, kitchenette, coffeemaker.

The Kimberly *Finds* More people ought to know about this plush smaller hotel on a spruce Midtown East block heading toward the townhouses of Turtle Bay. The small lobby, full of pale shiny marble and gilt rococo furnishings, has pizzazz but not a high snobbery quotient, thanks to a friendly, unpretentious veteran staff. Because the 30-story building was designed in the mid-1980s as an apartment building (though it was turned into a hotel immediately), the rooms are all big—even the standard doubles don't feel crowded when they have two double beds in them (a great setup for families on a short visit). The closets are sizable, as are the nicely appointed baths. Most units in the hotel are suites; the one-bedroom suites could sleep six, with two double beds in the bedroom and a pullout couch in the sitting room. The decor is traditional, with quality furniture in dark woods; vases and framed prints and other accents give each room a residential flair. All suites have galley kitchens with cooking burners, pots and pans, and full-size refrigerators. Almost every room has a balcony where you can sit and have breakfast or cocktails while watching the Manhattan ad execs, lawyers, and publishing types scurry to or from their offices far below. Though there's no pool on-site, guests get free use of the New York Health & Racquet Club's pool, where there's a Saturday-morning swim session just for families.

145 E. 50th St. (btwn Lexington and Third aves.), New York, NY 10022. © **800/683-0400** or 212/755-0400. Fax 212/ 486-6915. www.kimberlyhotel.com. 186 units. $289–$629 1-bedroom suite; $529–$885 2-bedroom suite. Children under 18 stay free in parent's room. Rollaway or crib free. Weekend rates and summer packages available. AE, DC, DISC, MC, V. Valet parking $30. Subway: 6 to 51st St.; E, V to Lexington Ave./53rd St.; 6 to 51st St. **Amenities:** 2 restaurants; 2 bars; fitness room; complimentary access to New York Health & Racquet Club; concierge; business center; room service (6am–11pm). *In room:* A/C, TV, dataport, kitchenette in suites, fridge.

Waldorf=Astoria *★★* This is my sentimental favorite among Manhattan's grand hotels because I stayed here at age 13 when my dad came to New York for a convention. That was long before the Waldorf became a Hilton, but the chain regularly renovates this flagship property beautifully, devoting a lot of taste and money to maintaining its character. The wide stately corridors, the vintage Deco door fixtures, the white-gloved bellmen, the luxe shopping arcade, and that knockout lobby all trumpet Grand Hotel, and there's a certain electric thrill about being here. Enter from the Park Avenue side and you'll cross a stunning round mosaic under an immense crystal chandelier; in the main lobby, the four-sided freestanding Waldorf clock, covered with bronze relief figures, should fascinate your children as much as it did me all those years ago.

Upstairs, the wide plush-carpeted corridors seem to run on forever. The room decor is pleasant, if unremarkable—a sort of traditional English country-house look. The standard double rooms are plenty spacious; request a room with two double beds if you've got more than one kid. A mini suite, combining one king-size-bedded room with a sitting room, might work better, though not all have foldout couches; some suites have kitchenettes, so ask for one if that's important. There's also a number of connecting doubles you can request. The staff seems unfailingly gracious, though in such a large hotel you won't get the personal service you might at a smaller place. Do inquire about special discounts, because they pop up all year round. There are 244 rooms in the Waldorf Towers, with a separate entrance; the duke and duchess of Windsor and John F. Kennedy are among the guests who've resided here. Staying in the pricier Towers, which have more distinctive antique-laden decor, snags you some extra amenities, like complimentary continental breakfast and hors d'oeuvres in a lounge on the 26th floor.

The Waldorf's restaurants really are major players in the New York restaurant universe: Oscar's, the ornate Peacock Alley, the Japanese Inagiku, and the clubby steak-and-seafood Bull and Bear. Sir Harry's Bar, fitted out like an African safari, serves drinks.

301 Park Ave. (btwn 49th and 50th sts.), New York, NY 10022. © 800/WALDORF, 800/HILTONS, or 212/355-3000. Fax 212/872-7272. www.waldorf.com. 1,245 units. $299–$700 double; $449–$950 suite. Children under 18 stay free in parent's room. Rollaway $25–$50 per stay; crib free. DC, DISC, MC, V. Parking $45. Subway: 6 to 51st St. **Amenities:** 4 restaurants; bar; fitness center with steam rooms (day-use fee $14); concierge; business center; shopping arcade; 24-hr. room service. *In room:* A/C, TV, minibar.

MODERATE

Crowne Plaza at the United Nations
Down at the quiet end of 42nd Street lies this European-like boutique hotel, known for years as the Hotel Tudor (look high on the west-facing facade for the neon HOTEL TUDOR sign, protected as a city landmark). Now run by the Crowne Plaza folks, it's often booked solid September through December, when diplomats flock into town for General Assembly sessions at the nearby United Nations. It's a great bet for families, though, convenient to Midtown sights yet in a peaceful area on the fringe of residential Tudor City. Weekend and summer rates are in the moderate range, although September-to-May weekday rates would bump you up into the expensive price category.

Hallways are narrow but bright, and the rooms are comfortably sized, with a traditional decor in a restrained rose-and-green color scheme. The up-to-date bathrooms have red marble vanities. I like the hushed lobby, narrow but very deep (linking the hotel's two towers) with old-fashioned touches like red plush armchairs, marble floors, columns, drapes, and potted palms. The staff, many of whom have worked here for years, are very friendly and accommodating. Go for superior rooms with two double beds, or even better, take the upgrade to executive rooms, which also have a sitting area and access to a lounge serving complimentary continental breakfast.

304 E. 42nd St. (btwn First and Second aves.). © 212/986-8800. Fax 212/986-1758. www.sixcontinentshotels.com/crowneplaza. 300 units. $230–$330 double; $335–$570 executive unit; $569–$689 suite. Crib free. AE, DC, DISC, MC, V. Parking $40. Subway: S, 4, 5, 6, 7 to 42nd St./Grand Central. **Amenities:** Restaurant; fitness room; spa; sauna; concierge; business center; room service (6:30am–10:30pm); concierge-level rooms. *In room:* A/C, TV, dataport, minibar, coffeemaker.

Millennium U.N. Plaza Hotel The Millennium U.N. Plaza's neighborhood hardly qualifies as Midtown—across from the United Nations, it's deliciously quiet, safe, and residential. When you combine that with the peerless views (all rooms are on the 28th floor or above, overlooking the East River or the skyline, uptown or downtown), the premium prices start to make sense. The clientele is heavily international, with foreign businesspeople as well as some United Nations visitors. Although it's a sleek corporate-style hotel, families may well be attracted not only by the neighborhood but also by the fact that it has a great pool—what may well be the prettiest pool in town, with a harem-like canopy hanging overhead and those dynamite views from windows on two sides.

There are two towers to choose between, connected by a disconcertingly slick lobby: the original East Tower, built in 1976, and the newer West Tower, built in 1980. While the East Tower is on the same elevator bank as the pool and has a more contemporary decor (think blond wood, opaque glass, and neutral fabrics), the West Tower makes up for it with floor-to-ceiling windows and warm-toned furnishings that feel homelike (homelike, that is, if you're a wealthy international diplomat). The east wing's sleek minimalist design carries into the bathrooms, which feel a bit bigger than those in the west wing. The wall hangings are framed museum-quality international textile pieces. Double rooms have only a king-size bed or two twins (two kids could fit in one of these European-size twins), and fire laws permit only one rollaway. Most families go for a junior suite or duplex one-bedroom suite, or spring for a spacious two-bedroom suite.

1 United Nations Plaza (44th St. and First Ave.), New York, NY 10017. ✆ 800/972-3160 or 212/758-1234. Fax 212/702-5051. www.millenniumhotels.com. 427 units. $219–$309 double; $350–$800 and up suite. Rollaway $35; crib free. Weekend packages available. AE, DC, DISC, MC, V. Valet parking $35–$40. Subway: S, 4, 5, 6, 7 to 42nd St./Grand Central. **Amenities:** Restaurant; indoor pool; indoor tennis court; fitness center with sauna; concierge; business center; 24-hr. room service. *In room:* A/C, TV, minibar, coffeemaker.

Roger Smith Hotel _{Value} The Roger Smith is decidedly quirky, which may be why so many musicians and artists and Europeans choose to stay here. The small oval lobby is a mini gallery in itself, with paintings, sculptures, and polished wainscoting (there's more art next door in an actual art gallery run by Roger Smith). Upstairs, however, the look is more like a country inn, with individually decorated rooms featuring such items as canopy beds, stocked bookshelves, and chintz upholstery and bedspreads. Lots of hotels boast of a homey feeling, but the rooms here really do qualify. There are a variety of room layouts, including some connecting rooms and a junior suite that has a double bed and a foldout couch in the same room. Bathrooms are somehow homelike as well, not lavish but trim and up-to-date. For the price of a double at the Waldorf or The Plaza, here you can get a suite that includes not only a pullout couch in the sitting room and a double bed in the bedroom, but also a second cozy bedroom with a twin bed.

Though none of the rooms has a full kitchen, all suites have pantries with a refrigerator and coffeemaker. And as if that weren't enough, continental breakfast is included (rare enough in New York hotels), served every morning in Lily's, a spunky little bistro with gaudy murals; Lily's also serves an interesting Continental menu for lunch and dinner (closed weekends). This lively, fun hotel does a pretty brisk business, but its slowest months are July and August—peak family travel time—so cross your fingers and call ahead if you're visiting New York in the summer.

501 Lexington Ave. (at 47th St.), New York, NY 10017. ✆ 800/445-0277 or 212/755-1400. Fax 212/758-4061. www.roger smithhotel.com. 133 units. $259–$350 double; $400–$600 suite. Rates include continental breakfast. Extra person

$20. Rollaway or crib free. AE, DC, DISC, MC, V. Valet parking $35. Subway: S, 4, 5, 6, 7 to 42nd St./Grand Central. **Amenities:** Restaurant; health club access ($25/day); concierge; 24-hr. room service; email center. *In room:* A/C, TV, fridge, coffeemaker, hair dryer, iron, library.

Radisson Lexington New York ⚲   This handsome 1920s vintage property along Lexington's Midtown hotel strip looks like an upscale boutique hotel, but at 27 stories and 700-plus rooms, it's much larger than it feels. Look and listen, and you'll notice it has a sophisticated international clientele (not surprising in the U.N. vicinity). The architecture is a heady blend of Art Deco and Gothic elements: Kids will enjoy spotting the terra-cotta figures on the facade, the griffins and dragons prancing over the vaulted ceiling of the Lexington Avenue entryway, and the birds and lizards etched onto the elevator's brass doors. But from the spiffy porte-cochere above the 48th Street entrance to the two-story mahogany-paneled lobby with textured fabrics and brushed-nickel fixtures, the Radisson East Side has been smartly renovated for a contemporary look without sacrificing the property's charm.

The guest-room decor shows quiet verve, with a palette of muted earth tones, nubbly carpeting, pleated gauze shades that let in loads of light, and framed black-and-white art photographs on the walls. Bathrooms have been tidily modernized, with gray marble floors and modern white fixtures. Amenities like full-length mirrors, large desks, and dataports with high-speed Internet access bespeak the Radisson's attention to traveling executives. What families may appreciate more, though, is room size: The one-bedroom suites are positively rambling, with a huge bedroom and sitting room (some even have little terraces where you can step outside and study the skyscrapers all around). Business-class rooms are large doubles with either two double beds or a king bed and foldout couches; the great thing about these is that they have two bathrooms. Deluxe rooms have either a king, queen, or two single beds, but there's plenty of room for a rollaway. The whole place seems well run, with thoughtful, friendly service; it's dignified enough to be restful, but not at all stuffy.

Breakfast, lunch, and dinner are served in Raffles, a cheery diner-like corner coffee shop; the hotel's upscale restaurant is J. Sung Dynasty, a lovely gourmet Chinese restaurant that does a brisk lunch and dinner business with nonguests as well as guests.

511 Lexington Ave. (at 48th St.), New York, NY 10017. ⓒ 800/448-4471 or 212/755-4400. Fax 212/308-0194. www. lexingtonhotelnyc.com. 701 units. $179–$599 double; $239–$799 suite. Rollaway $25; crib free. AE, DC, DISC, MC, V. Parking nearby $40 for 24 hr. Subway: 6 to 51st St.; S, 4, 5, 6, 7 to 42nd St./Grand Central. **Amenities:** 3 restaurants; coffee shop; bar; fitness center; concierge; business center; room service (7am–10pm). *In room:* A/C, TV, dataport, minibar upon request, coffeemaker, safe.

INEXPENSIVE

Vanderbilt YMCA *(Value)*   This clean, big, friendly Midtown East Y is a great money-saving option. A quad room (two sets of bunk beds) would work for a family, or if your kids are old enough, book separate doubles. The rooms are pleasant if dorm-like, but they do have curtains and mirrors and a TV on a stand in the corner, and the down-the-hall bathrooms are quite clean; many rooms have washbasins, which means you don't have to trot down the hall every time you want to wash your face or brush your teeth. En-suite rooms have an adjoining bathroom (shower only) and private phones. And the location can't be beat, on a clean, safe block not far from the United Nations. The on-site International Café serves decent, cheap deli fare, but there are so many good restaurants nearby, you probably won't use it much. Best of all, the Y has truly impressive sports facilities, including an indoor jogging track, loads of classes for kids, and two sparkling indoor pools, which guests can use for free during their stay.

224 E. 47th St. (btwn Second and Third aves.), New York, NY 10017. © **212/756-9600.** Fax 212/752-0210. www. ymcanyc.org. 370 units, 1 per floor with private bathroom. $105–$140 double; $72–$89 with shared bathroom. AE, MC, V. Parking $20–$30 nearby. Subway: E, V to Lexington Ave./53rd St.; 6 to 51st St.; S, 4, 5, 6, 7 to 42nd St./Grand Central. **Amenities:** Cafe; 2 indoor pools; 2 aerobics studios; fitness classes; basketball, racquetball, and squash courts; sauna; concierge; tour desk; coin-op laundry. *In room:* A/C, TV.

5 The Flatiron District & Greenwich Village

MODERATE

Gershwin Hotel This creative-minded, Warholesque hotel caters to up-and-coming artistic types—and well-established names with an eye for good value—with its bold modern art collection and wild style. Standard rooms are clean and bright, with Picasso-style wall murals and Philippe Starck-ish takes on motel furnishings. Superior rooms are newly renovated and well worth the extra money; all have either a queen bed, two twins, or two doubles, plus a newish private bathroom with cute, colorful tilework. The hotel is more service-oriented than you usually see at this price level, and the staff is very professional. Two-room suites are the best option for families, and the bohemian ambience works better for teens than tots.

7 E. 27th St. (btwn Fifth and Madison aves.), New York, NY 10016. © **212/545-8000.** Fax 212/684-5546. www. gershwinhotel.com. 150 units. $109–$199 double; $249-329 family room. Check website for discounts, 3rd-night-free specials, or other value-added packages. AF, MC, V. Parking $25 3 blocks away. Subway: N, R, W to 28th St. **Amenities:** Bar; tour desk; babysitting; dry cleaning; laundry service; Internet-access PC. *In room:* A/C, TV, dataport, hair dryer, iron.

Washington Square Hotel ⭐ ⓥalue With its fantastic location at the corner of Washington Square Park, the focal point of Greenwich Village—Bob Dylan and Joan Baez lived here when it was the Hotel Earle in the folkie 1960s—the Washington Square Hotel would probably do well even if it weren't so nice. The good news is that this small hotel is a winner on its own account: clean, cheery, tastefully furnished—and very reasonably priced. Book a room here as soon as you know you're coming to New York, because lots of people have found out about this gem and it's nearly always full, especially on weekends

The rooms are just big enough to accommodate a crib or rollaway, but a family might as well spring for a quad room, which has two double beds; request no. 902, the largest, which is in front with a super view of leafy Washington Square Park. (Any front room on the fifth through ninth floors has good park views.) If you need connecting doubles, request rooms 219 and 220, which share a bathroom. All other rooms have their own small but spruce white-tiled baths; the bedrooms sport a snazzy Art Deco look, with rose-colored walls, frosted glass light fixtures, mahogany and pink granite accents, black leather headboards, and crisp white duvets. There are plenty of generous-size mirrors and reading lamps, operating on the novel assumption that guests might actually like to read in bed.

At the back of the Parisian-looking little lobby, with its wrought-iron gate and marble staircase, there's an atmospheric tea lounge and bar; the attached C III restaurant draws locals on its own merits. There's no room service, but this part of the Village is crawling with restaurants in all price ranges that stay open all hours, and walking around here is a pleasure at night. True, street musicians may be performing into the wee hours in the park across the street, but compared to the bustle of Midtown, that's a minor annoyance.

103 Waverly Place (btwn Sixth Ave. and MacDougal St.), New York, NY 10011. ℂ **800/222-0418** or 212/777-9515. Fax 212/979-8373. www.washingtonsquarehotel.com. 160 units. $230–$250 double. Rates include continental breakfast. Crib free. AE, MC, V. Parking $38. Subway: A, B, C, D, E, F, V to W. 4th St. **Amenities:** Restaurant; cafe; small fitness room. *In room:* A/C, TV, dataport, hair dryer, iron, safe.

6 Lower Manhattan
VERY EXPENSIVE
Ritz-Carlton New York, Battery Park 🦋   Facing out onto New York Harbor, this luxury high-rise has without a doubt the best views of any Manhattan hotel. It finally opened in January 2002 (its original opening date of Oct 2001 was derailed by the World Trade Center attacks), a much-heralded emblem of downtown's triumphant rebound. A majority of rooms face the harbor, and every room with harbor views has its own telescope so you can zoom in on each spike in Lady Liberty's crown. The signature decor details are lots of warm wood paneling; a discreet Art Deco–inspired lobby; heartwarming tones of gold, ochre, and green; and artworks specially commissioned from living New York artists—that and big windows everywhere, to drink in those wide-open harbor views.

Even the standard double rooms are large enough for a family; request one with two double beds, or take advantage of a pullout sofa or rollaway bed. Suites don't necessarily add bed space so much as they add entertaining space (and a super home-theater system, which would indeed be great for parents relaxing in the room after the kids have gone to sleep). And while weeknights are busy here, weekend visitors may be able to net some serious rate discounts. Anchoring the lower end of Battery Park City (like a bookend to balance the Embassy Suites a few blocks north), the Ritz-Carlton is marvelously convenient to downtown attractions such as the Ellis Island/Statue of Liberty ferry, the Museum of Jewish Heritage (right behind the hotel), the Skyscraper Museum, and the National Museum of the American Indian. The beautifully landscaped South Cove portion of Battery Park City is the hotel's backyard.

Lest you think the Ritz-Carlton is too upscale to welcome children, know that every youngster who visits finds his or her own (to keep!) Ritz-Carlton teddy bear waiting on the pillow; the entertainment armoire has Nintendo; you can just phone downstairs to get board games and kid movies; and you can call for the hotel's bath butler to draw a perfectly calibrated bubble bath. On-site restaurants and room service include a well-tailored kids' menu; all meals, including afternoon tea, are served downstairs in either the 2 West restaurant or the Art Deco Lobby Lounge. My 12-year-old son, however, was more intrigued by the prospect of eating in the Rise bar on the 14th floor, with its grassy outdoor terrace and wraparound views; its casual light menu includes dim sum, tapas-like snacks, and (oh, yes) extravagant desserts.

2 West St. (at Battery Place), New York, NY 10004. ℂ **800/241-3333** or 212/344-0800. Fax 212/344-3804. www.ritz carlton.com. 298 units. $450–$800 double; $850–$4,500 and up for suites. Children 12 and under stay free in parent's room. Weekend packages available. AE, DC, DISC, MC, V. Parking $60. Subway: 4, 5 to Bowling Green. **Amenities:** Restaurant; lounge; bar; fitness center and spa; concierge; complimentary shuttle around downtown; business center; 24-hr. room service. *In room:* A/C, TV with Nintendo, dataport, minibar, safe.

EXPENSIVE
Embassy Suites Hotel 🦋   This classy property in Battery Park City, with views of the harbor on one side and of the downtown skyline on the other, can be a great deal for families on weekends, when the rates fall well down into the moderate category. (On weekdays, you may slide up into very expensive.) Every unit is totally suitable for

a family, with a king-bedded bedroom and a separate living room with foldout couch (larger families may gravitate toward one of the rooms with two double beds in the bedroom). Bathrooms are roomy, with tubs, and there's always a table big enough for paperwork or art projects, not to mention room-service meals. The place has a with-it sort of buzz, from the curvy bright yellow wall behind the reception desk, to the soaring atrium dominated by an 11-story purple-and-blue Sol LeWitt abstract painting, to the sleek room decor, all neutral tones and textured fabrics and striking art prints commissioned expressly for the hotel. A complimentary breakfast buffet is served each morning, which I know for my crew is always a huge plus. And my son wants me to make sure to tell you that there are Sony PlayStations provided in every suite.

The Embassy Suites building also contains several other restaurants (Lili's Noodle Shop and Grill; PacRim Sushi; and the somewhat more plebian Appleby's, Chevy's, and Pick-a-Bagel), as well as an 11-screen movie theater. The well-outfitted New York Sports Club is a handy on-site add-on for hotel guests. The excellent playgrounds of Hudson River Park are only steps from the hotel, as is the gorgeous riverside promenade of Battery Park City. Right outside the hotel's door is one of the coolest memorials ever: the Irish Hunger Memorial, a tilting acre of Irish sod complete with a ruined crofter's cottage. You're within decent walking distance of the Museum of Jewish Heritage, the National Museum of the American Indian, the ferry to Ellis Island and the Statue of Liberty, and across West Street from the former World Trade Center site. No rooms have direct views of World Trade Center construction, as the hotel is slightly north of the site.

102 North End Ave. (btwn Murray and Vesey sts.), New York, NY, 10282. © 800/EMBASSY or 212/945-0100. Fax 212/945-3012. www.embassynewyork.com. 463 units. $299–$430 double. Rate includes full breakfast and cocktail reception. Crib free. Children under 18 stay free in parent's room, restrictions on rollaways in some rooms. AE, DC, DISC, MC, V. Valet parking $55. Subway: A, C, 1, 2, 3 to Chambers St. **Amenities:** 5 restaurants; 2 bars; fitness center; concierge; tour desk; business center; 24-hr. room service. In room: A/C, TV/VCR, dataport, minibar, kitchenette, coffeemaker, CD player.

MODERATE

Best Western Seaport Inn   This spunky little hotel in a converted 19th-century redbrick building has an offbeat location—on a cobbled street just north of the Fulton Fish Market, a couple of blocks up from South Street Seaport, in the lee of the Brooklyn Bridge's Manhattan entrance ramps (a delightful *trompe l'oeil* mural on a brick building just east of the hotel shows you what the view through the bridge's arches would look like if the building weren't in the way). Walk through the front door to find a spruce country-style decor and a cheerful staff. Upstairs are quiet, bright corridors and quite decent guest rooms; some have two double beds, while others have a queen-size bed plus a foldout couch. The baths are up-to-date and dazzlingly clean—so what if they have wrapped plastic drinking tumblers? (This *is* a Best Western.) While you don't get kitchenettes, there's an unstocked minifridge in every room, as well as a VCR (pick up a tape in the lobby). Some upper-floor rooms have Astroturf terraces with lawn furniture and partial views of the East River and Seaport; some have whirlpools. The complimentary continental breakfast is a nice plus, as are the fresh-baked cookies offered daily and the board games on hand at the front desk for kids to borrow.

The immediate area has been transformed lately by a spate of residential co-op buildings, bringing in its wake more foot traffic and street-level businesses. Pace University is a block away, and there's no trouble getting cabs at night if you walk the block to Pearl Street. Though the inn has no restaurant and no room service, local restaurants will deliver, and Chinatown is just as close as the Seaport for nighttime forays. For what you save on frills, you can easily afford to spend a little money on cabs by staying here.

33 Peck Slip (btwn Front and Water sts.), New York, NY 10038. ℂ **800/HOTEL-NY** or 212/766-6600. Fax 212/766-6615. www.bestwestern.com. 72 units. $240-300 double. Rates include continental breakfast. Children 17 and under stay free in parent's room. Rollaway $25; crib free. AE, DC, DISC, MC, V. Parking $20 nearby. Subway: 4, 5, 6 to City Hall; J, M, Z to Chambers St. **Amenities:** Fitness room; concierge; tour desk. *In room:* A/C, TV/VCR, dataport, fridge, coffeemaker.

Holiday Inn Downtown

At the nexus of Chinatown, Little Italy, and SoHo, this modern midrange hotel occupies a converted factory/warehouse a block north of Canal Street. Take your basic contemporary Holiday Inn decor and add Asian accents—a stylized floral still life here, a subtle woven wallpaper there—and you've got an idea of what this place looks like: sparkling clean and only a bit impersonal-looking (the staff, many of whom are Asian, are very helpful).

The lobby is one floor up from the busy, grubby commercial street; there are 12 stories of rooms above that. The rooms haven't been well soundproofed, and the windows are a bit high, which makes things feel institutional. The rooms aren't large (high ceilings make them look smaller), so only a limited number of doubles contain two double beds; larger families may want to get connecting doubles, which might have a king-size or a queen-size bed or two twin beds. The Pacifica restaurant serves all meals, including a big breakfast buffet, with a menu that straddles Western and Chinese cuisine. About 40% of the clientele is foreign, which may simply mean that travel agents in other countries can spot a good deal when they see one.

138 Lafayette St. (btwn Canal and Howard sts.), New York, NY 10013. ℂ **800/HOLIDAY** or 212/966-8898. Fax 212/966-3933. www.holiday-inn.com. 227 units. $189–$330 double; $350– $700 suite. Rollaway $15; crib free. AE, DC, DISC, MC, V. Valet parking $34. Subway: N, Q, R, W, 6 to Canal St. **Amenities:** Restaurant; concierge; tour desk; room service (7am–11pm); laundry service; dry cleaning. *In room:* A/C, TV, dataport, coffeemaker.

Marriott New York Financial Center

A good downtown choice for families, the Marriott Financial Center has wonderful skyline and harbor views and its own 50-foot pool. So what if the pool has no views? When they're splashing in the water, kids don't care if there are glorious vistas at hand.

The small lobby's traditional marble-and-mahogany look is pleasantly unintimidating, almost cozy. Though guest rooms here don't give you the same kind of space to stretch out in as the Embassy Suites, the double rooms with two double beds are roomy enough to take a crib or rollaway, and there are plenty of connecting doubles. The executive suite is a decent option for families. Bathrooms are a good size. Rooms are decorated in glossy reproduction furniture, deep-piled patterned carpeting, and dark print fabrics, and have large windows to drink in those views. The main restaurant, Roy's New York, serves a standout Hawaiian fusion cuisine (never fear, the buffet breakfasts are American-style). The other on-site restaurant, 85 West, serves light grill food. If you're going to be in Manhattan for the weekend, ask if weekend packages are in effect—they could save you nearly $100 a night over the weekday rates, plus throw in a complimentary breakfast. Summer packages plunge even lower. You'll be right across from Battery Park City, within walking distance of the Statue of Liberty/Ellis Island ferry, and not far from South Street Seaport and have a very comfy hotel room to boot.

85 West St. (at Albany St.), New York, NY 10006. ℂ **800/228-9290** or 212/385-4900. Fax 212/227-8136. www.marriott.com. 504 units. $230–$579 double; $549–$2,000 suite. Rollaway or crib free. Weekend and summer

packages available. AE, DC, DISC, MC, V. Valet parking $40. Subway: E to World Trade Center; R, W to Rector St. **Amenities:** Indoor pool; fitness room; concierge; business center; room service (6am–midnight); concierge-level rooms. *In room:* A/C, TV, minibar.

7 Brooklyn

MODERATE

New York Marriott at the Brooklyn Bridge   Brooklyn Heights is said to be America's first suburb, and many Manhattanites still have the notion that Brooklyn is not quite "New York." But anyone who's spent time there knows better. In addition to having its own attractions (including a top-notch children's museum), Brooklyn is very much part of New York City, not to mention wonderfully convenient to downtown Manhattan—the Wall Street area, Battery Park, and the Statue of Liberty ferry are only one subway stop away. Located in downtown Brooklyn, near picturesque Brooklyn Heights, the Marriott is also a mere 7-minute subway ride from trendy SoHo and, of particular interest to families, only a few blocks away from the famous Brooklyn Bridge, with its pedestrian walkway where energetic kids can run off steam while their parents enjoy breathtaking views. Don't be put off by the location on Adams Street, a busy, nondescript thoroughfare feeding the Brooklyn Bridge; the hotel itself is spacious, comfortable, attractive, and well organized without being the least bit uptight or intimidating.

Kids will love the domed ceiling that soars above the entryway and mezzanine lobby, a stunning mural of the sky behind a white trellised gazebo. As you sweep up to the lobby on the escalator between huge potted plants, for a split second you feel as if you're flying. Otherwise, there's a businessy feel to the place, with its network of conference rooms off the main lobby. Guest rooms (and their views) are unremarkable, with standard hotel antique reproduction furniture, but high ceilings make rooms feel spacious. There are some connecting rooms, and the doubles themselves have two double beds and just enough extra space to fit a crib or cot. Room decor is reasonably cheery, with red, gold, and green patterned bedspreads and soft green carpeting.

The Archives restaurant off the lobby lounge takes its name from the Brooklyn memorabilia it proudly exhibits (on loan from the Brooklyn Historical Society); it serves breakfast, lunch, and dinner. Kids will also enjoy some of the reasonably priced family restaurants on nearby Montague Street in Brooklyn Heights, a 5-minute walk from the hotel. Another plus for families is the 75-foot lap pool; several kids were swimming happily the day we visited.

333 Adams St., Brooklyn, NY 11201. ⓒ **888/436-3759** or 718/246-7000. Fax 718/246-0563. www.marriott.com. 376 units. $199–$400 double; $425–$800 suite. Rollaway free; crib free. AE, DC, DISC, MC, V. Parking $13–$18. Subway: A, C, F to Jay St./Borough Hall; 2, 3, 4, 5 to Borough Hall; M, R to Court St. **Amenities:** Restaurant; indoor pool; fitness center; car-rental desk; concierge; business center; salon; room service (6am–1am); concierge-level rooms. *In room:* A/C, TV, minibar.

5

Family-Friendly Dining

In the gastronomic universe, New York has a fair number of star-quality restaurants, but are they worth it if you're eating out with your kids? Fuhgeddaboudit. Le Bernardin and Nobu be damned—what I look for these days is a restaurant that's noisy and casual, where the service is relatively speedy, and the menu includes at least one or two items from my kids' major food groups: chicken fingers, burgers, pasta, pancakes, and pizza, any or all of which could come with a side of fries. You can find plenty of such restaurants in New York, and they won't cost you an arm and a leg.

DINING OUT WITH YOUR KIDS

You know a restaurant welcomes kids when they've printed up a place mat for young customers to color and when you get to keep the crayons you're given to color it with. If they've gone to the trouble of developing a specific children's menu, that's even better. A number of tourist-dependent restaurants around Times Square go this route, and we're grateful for them in a pinch. For us adults, however, the food is generally mediocre, and the only thing that's relaxing about the ambience is that we don't have to do the dishes afterward.

So we try to venture beyond Pizzeria Uno and T.G.I. Friday's. **Ethnic restaurants** are one good option—our kids will always eat pasta and rice—and New York, this great immigrant city, is rich in these. **Coffee shops** are another choice, and I don't mean just the corner Greek joints with the revolving showcase of whipped cream–topped desserts. A number of trendy retro coffee shops have opened in recent years, adding upscale parent-pleasing food to the traditional menu of burgers, omelets, and grilled cheese sandwiches.

As soon as the weather warms up, many families opt for restaurants with **sidewalk seating.** The open-air arrangement minimizes the impact of noisy children on other diners, provides endless distraction, and makes messes less important (there's always a pigeon or two around to peck up dropped french fries after you've cleared off).

Knowing that many Manhattan restaurants don't work for smaller children, for the most part I've tried to steer you towards those that do, although I also suggest some that appeal best to older kids. If your youngsters are well-behaved, adventurous eaters, your choice of eating places is obviously much broader.

As far as **hours** go, most Manhattan restaurants serve continuously—you can generally order dinner as early as 5pm if that's what you're used to, though most New Yorkers eat around 7 or 8pm. If you're dining anywhere in the Theater District (the W. 40s) or near Lincoln Center (the W. 60s), you'll be competing with lots of other people trying to finish dinner before an 8pm curtain time; unless you're trying to make that curtain, too, delay your arrival until 7:30pm or so, when most of these restaurants are ready to draw a sigh of relief and relax. Similarly, Midtown and Lower Manhattan restaurants can be very busy from 11:30am to 2:30pm.

I've noted in this chapter if a given restaurant doesn't take **reservations** or if reservations are generally necessary to ensure a table. If there's no notation about reservations, you have a fair chance of being seated even if you haven't called ahead, but making a reservation is always smart. Although a few posh Manhattan restaurants still cling to formal dress codes, requiring men to wear a jacket and tie, none of the restaurants I list here do.

Because we do eat out regularly, we long ago stopped bringing toys to keep the kids occupied at the table (especially when the restaurant has a jukebox or a big picture window to view the passing street show). Our 16-year-old is finally willing to try stuff like fondue and crab cakes and mesclun salad. Even my picky-eater middle son has graduated from hamburgers to tempura shrimp and grilled chicken. With all the wonderful restaurants in New York City, the world is their oyster (just so long as we don't expect them to *eat* oysters—at least not yet . . .).

A NOTE ABOUT PRICES   The following reviews include a range of specific menu prices as often as possible; I've also categorized the restaurants as expensive, moderate, or inexpensive, based on rough estimates of what it would cost to feed a family of four—two parents and two children, assuming that one of the kids is young enough to be satisfied with either a kids' meal or a half portion or just an appetizer. If this mythical family would have to spend $80 or more for dinner (excluding any bar tab), I've classed that restaurant as **expensive;** between $60 and $80, **moderate;** under $60, **inexpensive.**

THE CHAIN GANG   Besides the restaurants covered in detail below, there are a number of kid-friendly chains— some local, some national—with several properties in New York City that can be handy if you're in the neighborhood. I don't indicate a specific price category for them, but their prices are uniformly low.

Among the local burger restaurant chains, **Jackson Hole** offers burgers so thick and juicy they'll make your buns soggy (whatever that means), as well as grilled chicken sandwiches, some salads, and less successful Mexican dishes. If you want your fast food organic, check out the various branches of **Better Burger,** which also adds a number of salads, pastas, meatloafs, and veggie burgers to its burgers-fries-and-dogs menu; the kids' meal there is a healthy $5.95. A local ethnic chain worth seeking out is **Lemongrass Grill,** for Thai food. **Blockhead's Burritos** is a fun addition to the city's dining scene, with a menu of tortilla-wrapped meals that go well beyond the Mexican standards (like the West Indian vegetable casserole tortilla or the Bar-B-Cuban Chicken); teenagers in particular like its hipster decor and healthy emphasis on fresh vegetables, lean meats, and lard-free cooking. Bargain-hunters like the casual **Dallas BBQ** restaurants, where you can get big portions for under $10. The menu holds no surprises: barbecued chicken, barbecued baby back ribs, barbecued sliced beef, half-pound burgers (turkey or beef). Just beware if you see a tour bus parked out front.

Pizzeria Uno is a known commodity: swift, cheery service; child-friendly amenities (kids' menu, crayons, flimsy activity booklet, drinks served in lidded plastic cups); and a saloonish decor with wooden booths, black-and-white tiled floors, and exposed-brick walls. Both the deep-dish and the thin-crust pizzas are decent; it's when they go beyond pizzas that you can't always be sure of what you'll get.

A NOTE ABOUT FAST FOOD   The reality of eating out with small children is that fast-food joints are sometimes a blessing. Most of those in high-traffic areas of Manhattan are spanking clean and recently renovated; somehow, there's always a McDonald's or a Burger King or a Sbarro's just where you need one.

There's also a McDonald's delivery service operating in Manhattan (how New Yorkers do love to phone out for their food): Call ☏ **212/337-3278** to get your Happy Meals and Big Macs brought to your door.

1 Restaurants by Cuisine

AMERICAN

American Girl Café ✮✮✮ (Midtown, $$$ p. 112)

Barking Dog Luncheonette ✮ (Upper East Side, $$, p. 108)

Big City Bar and Grill (Upper East Side, $$, p. 108)

Boat Basin Café ✮✮ (Upper West Side, $, p. 104)

Bubby's Pie Company ✮✮ (TriBeCa, $, p. 137)

Chat 'n' Chew ✮ (Flatiron District, $, p. 123)

Edward's (TriBeCa, $$, p. 137)

Elephant and Castle (Greenwich Village, $, p. 126)

ESPN Zone (Midtown, $$, p. 116)

Fanelli's (SoHo, $, p. 133)

Fetch ✮ (Upper East Side, $$, p. 108)

Flight 151 (Chelsea, $, p. 124)

Friend of a Farmer (Gramercy Park, $$, p. 122)

Good Enough to Eat ✮ (Upper West Side, $$, p. 101)

Hard Rock Cafe (Midtown, $$, p. 117)

Homer's ✮✮ (Upper West Side, $, p. 105)

Jekyll & Hyde Club (Midtown, $$$, p. 114)

Jekyll & Hyde Pub (Greenwich Village, $$$, p. 125)

Kitchenette ✮ (TriBeCa, $, p. 138)

Luke's Bar & Grill ✮✮ (Upper East Side, $$, p. 109)

Mickey Mantle's (Midtown, $$$, p. 114)

NoHo Star ✮ (Greenwich Village, $$, p. 126)

Odeon ✮ (TriBeCa, $$$, p. 136)

O'Neal's ✮ (Upper West Side, $$, p. 101)

Peanut Butter & Co. (Greenwich Village, $, p. 128)

Planet Hollywood (Midtown, $$, p. 118)

Popover Café (Upper West Side, $$, p. 102

Prime Burger ✮ (Midtown, $, p. 121)

Route 66 ✮ (Midtown, $, p. 121)

Tavern on the Green (Upper West Side, $$$, p. 99)

Telephone Bar & Grill ✮ (East Village, $$, p. 129)

Vesuvio Bakery Café (SoHo $$, p. 134)

Virgil's Real Barbecue ✮ (Midtown, $$, p. 118)

BAGELS

H&H Bagels (Upper West Side, $, p. 100)

H&H Bagels East (Upper East Side, $, p. 100)

Ess-a-Bagel (Murray Hill and Midtown East, $, p. 100)

Kossar's Bialys (Lower East Side, $, p. 100)

BARBECUE

Brother Jimmy's Bait Shack (Upper East Side, $, p. 110)

Brother Jimmy's BBQ (Upper East Side, $, p. 110)

Brother Jimmy's BBQ & Booze (Upper West Side, $, p. 104)

Duke's (Flatiron District, $, p. 123)

Earl's (Midtown, $, p. 120)

Rodeo Grill (Flatiron District, $, p. 124)

Virgil's Real Barbecue ✮ (Midtown, $$, p. 118)

Key to Abbreviations: $$$$ = Very Expensive $$$ = Expensive $$ = Moderate $ = Inexpensive

Uptown Dining

Alice's Tea Cup **29, 64**
Artie's Delicatessen **17**
Barking Dog Luncheonette **38, 59**
Barney Greengrass **11**
Barron's Pizza **39**
Bella Luna **9**
Better Burger **50**
Big City Bar & Grill **43**
Big Nick's Burger & Pizza Joint **24, 32**
Blockhead's Burritos **52**
Boat Basin Café **21**
Brother Jimmy's **20, 41, 58**
California Pizza Kitchen **70**
The Carlyle **55**
Carmine's **7**
Crumbs **26, 56**
Dallas BBQ **33, 61**
Dougie's BBQ and Grill **30**
EJ's Luncheonette **19, 60**
Fetch **40**
Gabriela's **4,**
Good Enough to Eat **15**
Googie's Luncheonette **57**
Gray's Papaya **31**
H&H Bagels **22**
H&H Bagels East **53**
Hampton Chietney Co. **16**
Harry's Burritos **32**
Homer's **12**
Hunan Balcony **2**
Jackson Hole **13, 42, 49, 65**
John's Pizza **66**
La Caridad Luncheonette **24**
Lemongrass Grill **3**
Lexington Candy Shop **51**
Lili's Noodle Shop and Grill **48**
Luke's Bar & Grill **54**
Mary Ann's **6**
O'Neal's **37**
Ollie's Noodle Shop **14, 35**
Papaya King **45**
Patsy's Pizzeria **28, 63, 67**
Petaluma **62**
Pizzabola **5**
Pizzeria Uno **21, 46**
Popover Café **10**
Rain **18**
Ruby Foo's **25**
Saigon Grill **8**
Sassy's Sliders **44**
Serendipity 3 **68**
T & R Pizzeria **23**
Tavern on the Green **36**
Tony Di Napoli **50**
Trattoria Sambucca **34**
Two Little Red Hens **47**
V & T Pizzeria-Restaurant **1**
Vinnie's Pizzeria **27**

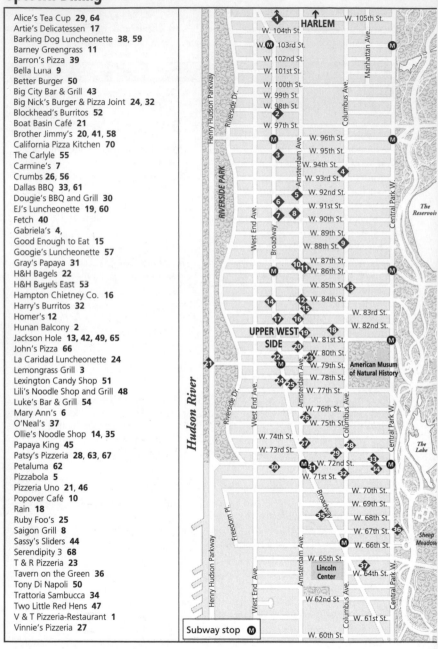

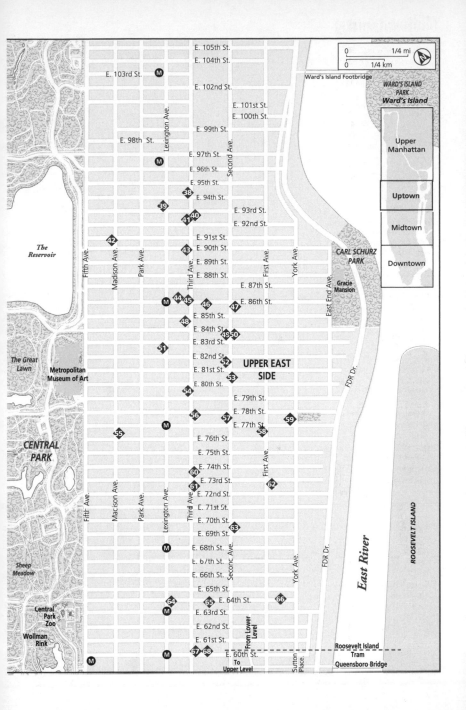

Midtown Dining

American Girl Café **36**
Angelo's Coal Oven Pizza **25, 29**
Benihana **28**
Better Burger **14, 21, 42**
Blockhead's Burritos **7, 34, 47**
Buttercup Bake Shop **33**
Café SFA **35**
Carmine's **12**
Carnegie Deli **3**
Chat 'n' Chew **58**
Chelsea Market food court **23**
Comfort Diner **37, 51**
Cupcake Café **17**
Dallas BBQ **18**
Duke's **56**
Earl's **41**
Ellen's Stardust Diner **6**
Empire Diner **20**
ESPN Zone **16**
Ess-a-Bagel **32, 54**
Flight 151 **22**
Friend of a Farmer **57**
Grand Central Dining Concourse **40**
Great American Health Bar **27**
H&H Bagels **9**
Hard Rock Cafe **1**
Jackson Hole **44**
Jekyll & Hyde Club **26**
John's Pizza **11**
Kelly and Ping **50**
Kosher Delight **43**
La Bonne Soupe **30**
Lemongras's Grill **45**
Mangia e Bevi **5**
Mickey Mantle's **24**
New York Burger Co. **52, 53**
Ollie's Noodle Shop **13**
Patsy's Pizzeria **19, 46**
Planet Hollywood **10**
Prime Burger **31**
Rock Center Café **41**
Rodeo Grill **49**
Route 66 **2**
Ruby Foo's **8**
Stage Deli **4**
T Salon **27**
Tony's de Napoli **38**
Virgil's Real Barbecue **39**
Won Jo **48**

Downtown Dining

Angelo's of Mulberry Street **50**
Arturo's Restaurant-Pizzeria **16**
Benny's Burritos **3, 39**
Bubby's **18**
Caffé Napoli **52**
Caffé Roma **47**
Chevy's **22**
Cloister Café **33**
Corner Bistro **2**
Cowgirl Hall of Fame **9**
Crif's Dogs **36**
Dallas BBQ **32, 35**
Dawgs on Park **37**
De Robertis Pasticceria **30**
Edward's **19**
Elephant and Castle **4**
Ellen's Café & Bake Shop **59**
Emack & Bolio's Ice Cream **1**
Famous Ray's Pizza
    of Greenwich Village **5**
Fanelli's **45**
Ferrara **48**
Great New York Noodletown **57**
Grimaldi's **63**
Harry's Burritos **12**
Il Fornaio **53**
Jekyll & Hyde Pub **10**
Jing Fong **54**
John's of Bleeker Street **11**
Johnny Rockets **35**
Kelley & Ping **40, 44**
Kitchenette **21**
Kossar's Bialys **49**
Lemongrass Grill **25, 60**
Lin's Dumpling House **58**
Lombardi's Pizza **46**
Magnolia Bakery **5**
Mitali East **38**
Nha Hang **56**
NoHo Star **43**
Odeon **20**
Old Devil Moon **26**
Pasticceria Bruno **15**
Patsy's Pizzeria **27**
Peanut Butter & Co. **13**
Pier 17 food court **62**
Pizza Box **14**
Pizzeria Uno **7, 28, 61**
Pommes Frites **34**
Rocco's **15**
Sal Anthony's SPQR **51**
Tai Hong Lau **55**
Telephone Bar & Grill **31**
Two Boots **4, 41, 42**
Veniero's **29**
Vesuvio Bakery Café **17**
World Financial Center food court **23**

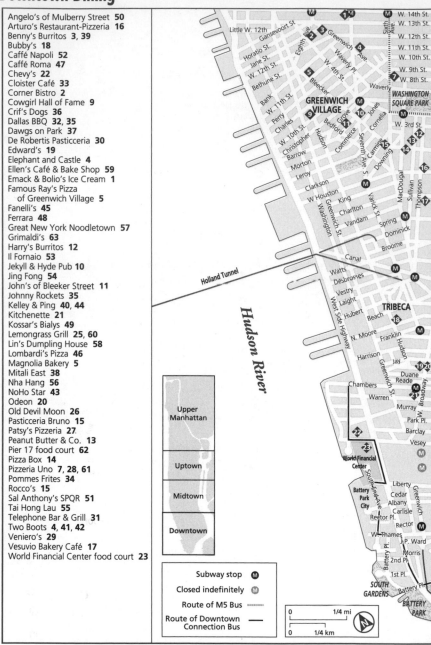

Subway stop Ⓜ
Closed indefinitely Ⓜ
Route of M5 Bus ·······
Route of Downtown
    Connection Bus ———

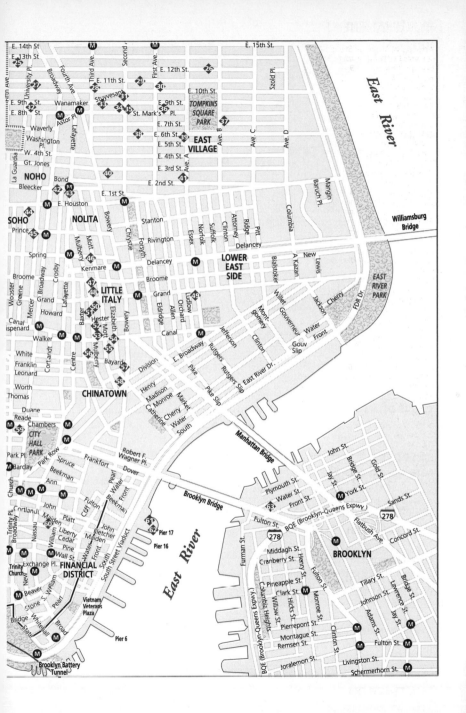

BRITISH

Alice's Tea Cup ✦✦ (Upper West Side and Upper East Side, $, p. 102 and 110)

Telephone Bar & Grill ✦ (East Village, $$, p. 129)

BURGERS

Better Burger (Upper East Side, Midtown, and Chelsea, $, p. 112, 122, and 125)

Big Nick's Burger & Pizza Joint (Upper West Side, $, p. 103)

Corner Bistro (Greenwich Village, $, p. 126)

Hard Rock Cafe (Midtown, $$, p. 117)

Homer's ✦✦ (Upper West Side, $, p, 105)

Johnny Rockets (Greenwich Village, $, p. 127)

Luke's Bar & Grill ✦✦ (Upper East Side, $$, p. 109)

Prime Burger ✦ (Midtown, $, p. 121)

Sassy's Sliders (Upper East Side, $, p. 112)

CALIFORNIAN

California Pizza Kitchen (Upper East Side, $, p. 110)

CHINESE

Hunan Balcony (Upper West Side, $, p. 105)

Jing Fong (Chinatown, $, p. 135)

Lili's Noodle Shop and Grill (Upper East Side, $, p. 111)

Lin's Dumpling House ✦ (Chinatown, $, p. 136)

Great NY Noodletown (Chinatown, $, p. 135)

NoHo Star ✦ (Greenwich Village, $$, p. 126)

Ollie's Noodle Shop (Upper West Side and Midtown, $, p. 106 and 120)

Tai Hong Lau (Chinatown, $$, p. 135)

CONTINENTAL

Carlyle Hotel (Upper East Side, $$, p. 112)

Cloister Café (East Village, $$, p. 129)

Tavern on the Green (Upper West Side, $$$, p. 99)

CUBAN-CHINESE

La Caridad Luncheonette (Upper West Side, $, p. 105)

DELI

Artie's Delicatessen ✦✦ (Upper West Side, $, p. 103)

Barney Greengrass (Upper West Side, $, p. 103)

Carnegie Deli (Midtown, $$, p. 116)

Stage Deli (Midtown, $, p. 121)

DESSERTS

Alice's Tea Cup ✦✦ (Upper West Side and Upper East Side, $, p. 102 and 110)

Buttercup Bake Shop (Midtown, $, p. 113)

Caffé Roma (Little Italy, $, p. 134)

Crumbs (Upper West Side and Upper East Side, $, p. 113)

Cupcake Cafe (Midtown, $, p. 113)

Ferrara (Little Italy, $, p. 135)

Magnolia Bakery (Greenwich Village, $, p. 113)

Two Little Red Hens (Upper East Side, $, p. 113)

Serendipity 3 (Upper East Side, $$, p. 109)

DINER

Comfort Diner ✦ (Midtown and Chelsea, $, p. 120 and 123)

EJ's Luncheonette (Upper West Side and Upper East Side, $$, p. 100 and 108)

Ellen's Stardust Diner ✦✦ (Midtown and Lower Manhattan, $$, p. 116 and 137)

Empire Diner (Chelsea, $$, p. 122)

Googie's Luncheonette (Upper East Side, $$, p. 109)

Lexington Candy Shop ✦✦✦ (Upper East Side, $, p. 111)

Prime Burger ☆ (Midtown, $, p. 121)

Serendipity 3 (Upper East Side, $$, p. 109)

ECLECTIC

Alice's Tea Cup ☆☆ (Upper West Side and Upper East Side, $, p. 102 and 110)

Big City Bar and Grill (Upper East Side, $$, p. 108)

Café SFA ☆ (Midtown, $$, p. 115)

Chat 'n' Chew ☆ (Union Square, $, p. 123)

Ellen's Stardust Diner ☆☆ (Midtown, $$, p. 116)

Fetch ☆ (Upper East Side, $$, p. 108)

Hampton Chutney Co. (Upper West Side, $, p. 104)

Old Devil Moon (East Village, $$, p. 129)

Tavern on the Green (Upper West Side, $$$, p. 99)

T Salon (Chelsea, $$, p. 124)

FRENCH

La Bonne Soupe ☆☆☆ (Midtown, $$, p. 117)

Pommes Frites (East Village, $, p. 131)

HOT DOGS

Crif Dogs (East Village, $, p. 130)

Dawgs on Park (East Village, $, p. 130)

F&B (Chelsea, $, p. 130)

Gray's Papaya (Upper West Side, $, p. 130)

Papaya King (Upper East Side, $, p. 130)

INDIAN

Mitali East (East Village, $, p. 130)

Hampton Chutney Co. (Upper West Side, $, p. 104)

ITALIAN

Angelo's Coal Oven Pizza ☆☆ (Midtown, $, p. 119)

Angelo's of Mulberry Street (Little Italy, $$, p. 133)

Arturo's Restaurant-Pizzeria (Greenwich Village, $$, p. 125)

Bella Luna ☆☆☆ (Upper West Side, $$, p. 99)

Caffè Napoli (Little Italy, $$, p. 133)

Carmine's (Upper West Side and Midtown, $$, p. 99 and 115)

Mangia e Bevi (Midtown, $$, p. 117)

Patsy's Pizzeria (Midtown, Chelsea, Greenwich Village, Upper West Side, Upper East Side, $, p. 121, 124, 127, 106, and 111)

Petaluma ☆ (Upper East Side, $$$, p. 107)

Pizzabolla ☆☆ (Upper West Side, $, p. 106)

Rock Center Café ☆ (Midtown, $$$, p. 115)

Sal Anthony's SPQR (Little Italy, $$$, p. 132)

Tony's di Napoli (Upper East Side and Midtown, $$, p. 109 and 118)

Trattoria Sambucca ☆ (Upper West Side, $$, p. 102)

Two Boots ☆☆ (East Village, $, p. 132)

V & T Pizzeria-Restaurant (Upper West Side, $, p. 107)

Vinnie's Pizzeria (Upper West Side, $, p. 107)

JAPANESE

Benihana ☆☆ (Midtown, $$$, p. 113)

KOREAN

Won Jo (Midtown, $$, p. 119)

KOSHER

Great American Health Bar (Midtown, $, p. 131)

Kosher Delight (Midtown, $, p. 131)

Dougie's BBQ and Grill (Upper West Side, $$, p. 131)

MEXICAN

Benny's Burritos (East Village, $, p. 129)

Chevy's (Lower Manhattan, $, p. 137)

Gabriela's ✿✿✿ (Upper West Side, $$, p. 101)

Harry's Burritos (Upper West Side and Greenwich Village, $, p. 105 and p. 127)

Mary Ann's (Upper West Side, $, p. 106)

PAN-ASIAN

Kelley & Ping ✿ (Gramercy Park, East Village, and SoHo, $$, p. 124, 130, and 134)

Rain (Upper West Side, $$, p. 102)

Ruby Foo's (Upper West Side and Midtown, $$$, p. 99 and 115)

PIZZA

Angelo's Coal Oven Pizza ✿✿ (Midtown, $, p. 119)

Arturo's Restaurant-Pizzeria (Greenwich Village, $$, p. 125)

Barron's Pizza (Upper East Side, $, p. 110)

Big Nick's Burger & Pizza Joint (Upper West Side, $, p. 103)

California Pizza Kitchen (Upper East Side, $, p. 110)

Famous Ray's Pizza of Greenwich Village (Greenwich Village, $, p. 126)

Grimaldi's (Brooklyn, $, p. 138)

Il Fornaio (Little Italy, $, p. 133)

John's of Bleecker Street (Greenwich Villlage, $, p. 127)

John's Pizza ✿✿ (Upper East Side and Midtown, $, p. 111 and 120)

Lombardi's Pizza (Little Italy, $, p. 134)

Patsy's Pizzeria (Midtown, Chelsea, Greenwich Village, Upper East Side, and Upper West Side, $, p. 121, 124, 127, 111, and 106)

Pizzabolla ✿✿ (Upper West Side, $, p. 106)

Pizza Box (Greenwich Village, $, p. 128)

T & R Pizzeria (Upper West Side, $, p. 107)

Two Boots ✿✿ (East Village $, p. 132)

V & T Pizzeria-Restaurant (Upper West Side, $, p. 107)

Vinnie's Pizzeria (Upper West Side, $, p. 107)

SOUTHERN

Brother Jimmy's Bait Shack (Upper East Side, $, p. 110)

Brother Jimmy's BBQ (Upper East Side, $, p. 110)

Brother Jimmy's BBQ & Booze (Upper West Side, $, p. 104)

Duke's (Flatiron District, $, p. 123)

Earl's (Midtown, $, p. 120)

Old Devil Moon (East Village, $$, p. 129)

TEX-MEX

Cowgirl Hall of Fame ✿ (Greenwich Village, $$, p. 126)

Rodeo Grill (Flatiron District, $, p. 124)

THAI

Lemongrass Grill (Upper West Side, $$, p. 101)

Rain (Upper West Side, $$, p. 102)

VIETNAMESE

Saigon Grill (Upper West Side, $, p. 107)

Nha Hang (Chinatown, $, p. 136)

2 The Upper West Side

EXPENSIVE

Ruby Foo's PAN-ASIAN The Suzy Wong–style decor of this bi-level rice palace is eye-popping, and the menu hits all the high notes of Asian cuisine, from dim sum to sushi to maki rolls to Thai curries. Compared to more authentic Chinese, Japanese, or Thai restaurants, the food is only competent, but the stunning setting makes up for it—you'll feel like you're inside a jewel-toned lacquered box, with Chinese lanterns glowing overhead, your linen napkin crisply folded into a fan, chopsticks set before you in a gleaming metal stand. Don't expect to get in without a reservation, and don't expect the service to be speedy. The restaurant does, however, offer a coloring sheet and crayons to keep the kids busy. They will even make a good ol' PB&J or grilled cheese sandwich for those kids who will not try the Asian cuisine.

2182 Broadway (at 77th St.). ℂ 212/724-6700. www.brguestrestaurants.com. Kids' menu, high chairs, boosters. Reservations recommended. Lunch $15–$25; dinner $27–$40; kids' menu $9–$15 (average per person, including drinks). AE, DISC, MC, V. Sun 11:30am–midnight; Mon–Thurs 11:30am–12:30am; Fri–Sat 11:30am–1am. Subway: 1 to 79th St.

Tavern on the Green AMERICAN/CONTINENTAL/ECLECTIC   Local wisdom has it that only tourists go to Tavern on the Green, drawn by scores of movies featuring this huge Central Park site with its Tiffany glass lamps, crystal chandeliers, surrounding gardens, and twinkling outdoor lights. To celebrate a special event, however, even New Yorkers find themselves considering this undeniably enchanting place. The menu changes seasonally, but expect such American dishes as grilled salmon, roasted rack of lamb, and prime rib, along with a handful of Italian dishes and fancy salads. The children's menu is surprisingly ordinary—rigatoni, chicken fingers, hot dogs—but it does indicate a commitment to family business. I'd save this place for a special celebration, and only with kids old enough to appreciate the glitz and glamour, because the service can be deadly slow and careless—and you know how fatal that is when you've got restless children.

In Central Park at W. 67th St. ℂ 212/873-3200. www.tavernonthegreen.com. Kids' menu, sassy seats. Reservations recommended. Lunch $20–$34; dinner $24–$50; kids' menu $17–$19. AE, DC, DISC, MC, V. Mon–Thurs 11:30am–10pm; Fri 11:30am–11:30pm; Sat 10am–11:30pm; Sun 10am–10pm. Subway: 1 to 66th St.; B, C to 72nd St.

MODERATE

Bella Luna ✶✶✶ ITALIAN   This cool and sophisticated restaurant with art-hung white walls and dreamy lights rimming the plate-glass windows looks like it'd be strictly for grown-ups, but from day 1 the place has been extremely easygoing about young diners, always happy to bring them a small portion of plain pasta. The Tuscan-style pasta dishes are truly superior, as are the veal and fish dishes, the bruschetta, and the glorious mixed antipasto starter (practically a meal in itself); my kids often fill up on the crusty, dense bread. We eat here just as often without the kids as we do with them, even bringing clients—the food's that good.

584 Columbus Ave. (btwn 88th and 89th sts.). ℂ 212/877-2267. www.bellalunanyc.com. High chairs, boosters. Reservations recommended. Main courses $9–$19. AE, MC, V. Daily noon–11pm. Subway: B, C, 1 to 86th St.

Carmine's ITALIAN   The original location of this popular northern Italianer (see also p. 115) still is tough to get into, so be sure to make a reservation. That said, this lively, hearty restaurant is fun, with a décor that's a 1960s throwback (dark wood trim, chrome bar stools) and the aroma of garlic hanging in the air. The menu features superbly executed standards like shrimp scampi, rigatoni with sausage, chicken Marsala, veal scaloppine, and big thick steaks. The dining room can be noisy, but it's a cheerful rumble, so conversation isn't impossible. Portions are served family-style and are legendarily huge, so order accordingly—insist on your children splitting a dish with you, even if they're big eaters. We always over-order, though; the menu's so tempting, we just can't help it.

The Best of the Bagels

Why is it that bagels in other cities just don't taste as good as New York bagels? There can't be such a mystery, after all, to baking what's essentially a chewy bread doughnut. Yet we know many transplanted New Yorkers who beg us to bring real bagels with us when we come to visit. (Even New Jersey suburbanites make special treks into the city to get their bagels.) And bagels are such a great kid-pleasing food—New Yorkers even use them to pacify teething infants—that we'd hardly know what to do without them.

In my opinion, the premier outlet is **H&H Bagels,** 2239 Broadway, at 80th Street (*©* **212/595-8000**), and 639 W. 46th St., between Eleventh Avenue and the West Side Highway (*©* **212/765-7200;** call *©* **800/NY-BAGEL** for shipping anywhere). Besides selling bagels hot out of the oven to the public, H&H supplies bagels to delis and grocery stores all around the city, so look for signs boasting WE HAVE H&H BAGELS. The problem with H&H is that it has no seating and doesn't serve bagels with any spread (in local parlance, a "schmear"), though you can buy separate little tubs of cream cheese, chopped liver, egg salad, herring in cream sauce, whatever. At least the store has finally installed a coffee machine so you can get a cup of coffee to go. **H&H Bagels East,** 1551 Second Ave., near 80th Street (*©* **212/734-7441**), is a former branch that had to litigate for the right to keep using the name; it too has wonderfully chewy bagels, with the added convenience of a deli counter where countermen can cut and dress your bagels. I know many people who'd award the crown to **Ess-a-Bagel,** 359 First Ave., at 21st Street (*©* **212/260-2252**), and 831 Third Ave., at 51st Street (*©* **212/980-1010**), which is a full-service bagel deli where you can sit down and eat. But if you really want to get authentic, you might journey down to the Lower East Side to try **Kossar's Bialys,** 367 Grand St., between Essex and Norfolk streets (*©* **212/473-4810**).

2450 Broadway (btwn 90th and 91st sts.). *©* **212/362-2200.** High chairs, boosters. Reservations recommended. Family-style main courses (serve 2–4 people) $20–$28 (more for porterhouse steaks and lobsters). AE, DC, MC, V. Sun–Thurs 11:30am–11pm; Fri-Sat 11:30am–midnight. Subway: 1 to 86th St.

EJ's Luncheonette DINER   With its blue leatherette banquettes, pressed-tin ceiling, and chrome-trimmed Formica-topped tables, this is a museum-perfect replica of a classic American diner, and the menu strives to match—burgers, omelets, salads, sandwiches—though it gives away its upscale 21st-century character with a number of vegetarian specials. Sandwiches on the kids' menu may be served with whole-grain bread, so ask specifically to avoid violating your children's eating codes (better yet, opt for a fluffy stack of flapjacks). A feel-good sorta place, it couldn't be nicer to kids, at least at lunchtime. Halfway between the Children's Museum of Manhattan and the American Museum of Natural History, it's a natural for the family trade.

447 Amsterdam Ave. (btwn 81st and 82nd sts.). *©* **212/873-3444.** Kids' menu, high chairs, boosters. Reservations not accepted. Breakfast $6.20–$11; lunch and dinner $6.50–$11. No credit cards. Daily 8am–11pm. Subway: 1 to 79th St.

Gabriela's 🐸🐸🐸 MEXICAN   Gabriela's serves up astonishingly good regional dishes that go well beyond rote Mexican combo platters. The roast chicken is a marvel, succulent and delicately spiced; quesadillas are light, crisp, and flavorful; and you can't go wrong with any of the marvelous spicy casseroles and soups. As for kids, there are simple tacos (served without hot red sauce—hooray!), accompanied by rice and beans, as well as a number of fruit drinks, fruit shakes, and exotic Mexican soft drinks. The staff is cordial and accommodating; the softly lit stucco walls have a golden glow that's very relaxing, even when the restaurant is packed to the gills, as it usually is.

688 Columbus Ave. (btwn 93rd & 94th sts.). ℭ 212/961-9600. www.gabrielas.com. Subway: B, C, 1, 2, 3 to 96th St. Kids' menu, high chairs, boosters. Reservations recommended. Main courses $14–$22; kids' menu $7.95. AE, MC, V, DISC. Mon–Thurs 11:30am–11pm; Fri–Sat 11:30am–midnight; Sun 11:30am–10pm.

Good Enough to Eat 🐸 AMERICAN   This charming little restaurant grew out of a bakery, so you can bet the pies and cakes are excellent. Tables are small, with weathered wood pickets around to strike a rustic note; cut flowers add another farmhouse touch. Though the menu focuses on old-fashioned American dishes like mac 'n' cheese, meatloaf, and a classic turkey dinner, chef/owner Carrie Levin trained at the Russian Tea Room and the Four Seasons, and is perfectly capable of turning out stunning daily fish specials, lemon Parmesan chicken breast, and a vegetable napoleon that's memorable indeed. Pasta and chicken fingers are still available on the kids' menu, never fear, so you can keep finicky eaters happy while indulging grown-up palates as well.

483 Amsterdam Ave. (btwn 83rd and 84th sts.). ℭ 212/496-0163. Kids' menu. Reservations not accepted. Main courses $9–$23, kids' menu $4.75-$6.75. AE, MC, V. Mon–Thurs 8am–10:30pm, Fri 8:30am-11pm, Sat 9am-11pm, Sun 9am-10:30pm. Subway: 1 to 86th St.

Lemongrass Grill THAI   Succulent spring rolls and grilled skewers of chicken start you off right at this dependable Thai restaurant with its restful tropical-colonial decor (ceiling fans, bamboo, wooden rafters). Our youngsters feast on those appetizers and plain white rice, while we indulge in basil beef and green-chili chicken and spicy pork chops. The tables are set close together, and things can get pretty busy, but the upside is that no one minds kids' messes and noise—the staff actually seems to like children, and the service is attentive, if not chatty.

2534 Broadway (at 95th St.). ℭ 212/666-0888. High chairs. Reservations recommended for groups of 5 or more. Main courses $7–$15. AE, DC, MC, V. Mon–Thurs noon–10:30pm; Fri–Sat noon–11:30pm; Sun 1–11:30pm. Subway: 1, 2, 3 to 96th St.

O'Neal's 🐸 AMERICAN   Opened in 1964 as The Ginger Man, this perennial Lincoln Center-area favorite is a great place, so long as you can steer around the pre-performance rush. The staff is adept at getting diners out in time for the 8pm curtain, but if you want a relaxed meal, come for dinner after 8pm, or do weekday lunch or an early weekend brunch. The rambling dining rooms have the authentic look of a turn-of-the-20th-century saloon—brass fittings, wood trim, tile floors—and the unpretentious menu runs the gamut from burgers to seafood with more than a bit of panache. The chicken paillard and broiled shrimp curry are two unfailing winners, but the daily specials are always worth considering. The burgers are some of the best in town.

49 W. 64th St. (btwn Broadway and Central Park W.). ℭ 212/787-4663. Kids' menu, high chairs, boosters. Reservations recommended, especially for dinner or brunch. Main courses $9.50–$34. AE, DC, DISC, MC, V. Mon–Fri 11:30am–midnight; Sat 11am–midnight; Sun 10am–10:30pm. Subway: 1 to 66th St.

Popover Café AMERICAN   This pleasantly upscale cafe's signature teddy bears lined up in the front windows have always deluded folks into thinking it's a restaurant for kids—but it's not particularly so, and the staff has been burned enough by unsupervised brats that they've added a note on children's manners to their menu. With an unpretentiously handsome decor (red plaid banquettes, cadet-blue walls, granite-speckled Formica tabletops), it serves the West Side equivalent of the East Side ladies-who-lunch crowd, wholesome chic types who appreciate sprout-bedecked salads and soul-warming soups accompanied by a light-as-air baked popover. The owner seems somewhat to have accepted the family fate, serving milk in a lidded paper cup and adding a kids' menu of sorts—yet a grilled cheese cooked on hearty home-baked peasant bread isn't necessarily as good as one made with Wonder Bread if you're 4 years old. Avoid weekend brunch, when the lines can be ridiculous.

551 Amsterdam Ave. (at 87th St.). © 212/595-8555. Kids' menu, high chairs, boosters. Reservations not accepted. Lunch $8.95–$16; dinner $12–$22; kids' menu $3.95–$6.95. AE, MC, V. Mon–Fri 8am–10pm; Sat–Sun 9am–10pm. Subway: B, C, 1 to 86th St.

Rain PAN-ASIAN/THAI   The dreamy Maughamesque decor of this upscale West Sider perfectly matches its exotic cuisine, principally Thai but borrowing accents from Malaysia and Vietnam—peanut sauces; coconut-milk soups; grilled meats; stir-fries; and lemongrass, chile, and lime flavorings. Though there's no kids' menu, many young diners are happy with the chicken skewers, noodle dishes, and rice. The place certainly is family-friendly, especially at lunch, despite the romantic calm of its softly lit dining room, with lots of drapes and rattan chairs and potted plants and fringed lampshades. *An added plus:* It's very handy to the Natural History Museum—repair here after a morning in the Asian-animals gallery, and you'll feel you've really been to the Far East.

100 W. 82nd St. (at Columbus Ave.). © 212/501-0776. High chairs. Reservations recommended. Lunch $6.50–$15; dinner $15–$24. AE, DC, DISC, MC, V. Mon-Thurs noon–11pm; Fri noon–midnight; Sat noon–midnight; Sun noon–10pm. Subway: 1 to 79th St.; B, C to 81st St./Museum of Natural History.

Trattoria Sambucca ⚘ ITALIAN   We like to come here for family birthday celebrations; the waiters are very friendly, you can color on the paper tablecloths, and the food is straightforward Italian classics, served in robust portions. (We have to remind our kids not to fill up on the delicious bread beforehand.) Dishes are served family-style, so don't over-order—our family of five chose two entrees and left a lot of food on the platters. The chicken piccata was a real winner, as was the penne with eggplant and mozzarella. The dining room is pleasantly soft-hued and contemporary, with sponged orange walls, iron sconces, and Tuscan painted pottery on wall brackets. Very casual, but you still get that special dining-out feeling.

20 W. 72nd St. (btwn Columbus Ave. and Central Park W.). © 212/787-5656. Kids' menu, high chairs, boosters. Reservations recommended. Main courses $25-30 (family-size portions); kids' menu $11. AE, DC, DISC, MC, V. Mon–Thurs 5–10pm; Fri–Sat 5–11pm; Sun 3–10pm. Subway: B, C, 1, 2, 3 to 72nd St.

INEXPENSIVE

Alice's Tea Cup ⚘⚘ *Finds* BRITISH/ECLECTIC/DESSERTS   My daughter and her friends adore this unique little spot snuggled into a West Side brownstone, with its shabby-chic jumble of secondhand furniture and mismatched china. Lewis Carroll quotes are stenciled onto the walls, and the gift shop in front is full of treasures. While it's perfect for tea parties—the menu of teas is encyclopedic, brownies and cookies arrive freshly baked and buttery, and crumbly scones are served with clotted cream and preserves—Alice's is brilliant for lunch or dinner, too, serving around-the-world favorites like cucumber sandwiches, curried chicken salad, and croque-monsieurs. Eating here is a special treat indeed.

102 W. 73rd St. (btwn Columbus and Amsterdam aves.). (C) 212/799-3006. www.alicesteacup.com. Kids' menu, high chairs. AE, DISC, MC, V. Salads and sandwiches $8–$14, kids' menu $6–$14; $22–$35 high tea. Mon–Thurs 8am–8pm; Fri 8am–10pm; Sat 10am–10pm; Sun 10am–8pm. Subway: B, C, 1, 2, 3 to 72nd St.

Artie's Delicatessen DELI   My son, whom I suspect is secretly working on his own guidebook called *Best Chicken Fingers in the Northeast,* insists that the ones at this retro deli/coffee shop are his New York City favorites. Pastrami is a cornerstone of the huge menu, though I was disappointed by it. Now that I've discovered the scrumptious meatloaf, I'll never order anything else. I also love the pickles that come standard with table service and the crisp, tangy coleslaw. My teenager is a fan of the hot chicken wings; he insisted we order a bucket for our annual Super Bowl party, and they were gone in 3 minutes. Hot dogs, potato pancakes, and grilled cheese sandwiches are other kid-friendly choices. Service is quick and friendly, and the white-tiled setting is always noisy enough that no one minds if kids add to the din. Okay, so it's only a decade old, as opposed to burnished veterans like the Carnegie Deli or Barney Greengrass; Artie's still has good classic deli food, at least a couple of old-timer waiters, and a sort of go-figure nonchalance that's very kid-friendly and very New York.

2290 Broadway (at 83rd St.). (C) 212/579-5959. www.arties.com. Kids' menu, high chairs, boosters. Reservations not accepted. Sandwiches $6–$13; main courses $11–$16; kids' menu $6–$7.75. AE, DISC, MC, V. Daily 9am–11pm. Subway: 1 to 86th or 79th St.

Barney Greengrass (Finds) DELI   As authentic as Artie's (see above) is contrived, Barney Greengrass has been a West Side institution since 1908, and it looks like it hasn't been redecorated in half a century—the chipped Formica tabletops, beige linoleum floor, stained brownish wallpaper, and fluorescent lighting are an aggressive statement of the fact that the food's so good, you come here anyway. I'm not a smoked-salmon expert, but the fish here is so silky, so meltingly tender, it converted me for life (problem is, nobody else's lox is ever gonna live up to this standard). The service is famously laconic, even gruff, but food arrives quickly. Sodas come in cans; the plates are plain white institutional china—who cares? Your kids may not get the time-warp charm of this place, but if they're at all inclined to try classic deli food—lox, chopped liver, cold borscht, chopped herring, whitefish salad, with omelets and bagels as safe alternatives—they'll love it. Especially good for breakfast.

541 Amsterdam Ave. (at 86th St.). (C) 212/724-4707. www.barneygreengrass.com. Reservations not accepted. Egg dishes $4.50–$15; sandwiches $6.25–$11; smoked fish platters $20–$75. No credit cards. Tues–Fri 8am–4pm; Sat–Sun 8am–5pm. Closed 1st 2 weeks in Aug. Subway: 1, 9 to 86th St.

Big Nick's Burger & Pizza Joint BURGERS/PIZZA   Cacophonous, crowded, and utterly unpretentious, this burger joint is great for kids. You squeeze in past a long counter with chrome stools, hoping one of the cramped leatherette booths in the back is free. Head shots of customers, famous or not, fill the brick-faced walls alongside hand-scrawled signs advertising dozens of specials (all this on top of a menu that's almost bewilderingly extensive). Even the regular burgers are obscenely huge—my carnivore son, Tom, could barely get his hands around one—and the pizzas are gooey with crisp crusts (whole pies only, no slices). There are also steaks; pot pies; sandwiches; and lots of Greek dishes such as souvlakia, spanakopita, and gyros, all in huge

portions. But keep one thing in mind: Big Nick's sees greasy food as a good thing. If you agree, you will be tremendously happy here.

(1) 70 W. 71st St. (at Columbus Ave.). © **212/799-4444**. Subway: B, C, 1, 2, 3 to 72nd St. (2) 2175 Broadway at 77th St. © **212/799-4450**. Subway: 1 to 79th St. Main courses $8–$15; weekday lunch specials $4.95. AE, DC, DISC, MC, V. Daily 10am–5am.

Boat Basin Café 🐸🐸 AMERICAN   A stroke of genius, to put a restaurant here overlooking the houseboat marina in lower Riverside Park. Not only are there great views west over the Hudson (time it right, and you'll get a sunset show to die for), but the arched stone vaults of this open-air structure also have a kind of Venetian charm all their own. And the food is head-and-shoulders above what you'd expect at an outdoor cafe: superb burgers, zestfully seasoned salads and sandwiches, and excellent grilled seafood. The trappings are supercasual: checked vinyl tablecloths, sturdy plastic chairs, folding tables, and fries heaped in a plastic basket on wax paper. The service can dawdle, but our kids didn't seem to mind, they were so busy counting boats on the river. They're smart enough to serve the kids'-menu sandwiches on white bread and not to blacken the hot dogs on the grill; the lemonade was too sour for our kids, but once they realized they could pour packets of sugar into their glasses, they were delighted. This cafe is run by the management of the excellent **O'Neal's** restaurant (see above), which also operates a similar seasonal restaurant, the **Hudson Beach Café** in Riverside Park at about 105th Street.

W. 79th St. at the Hudson River, in Riverside Park. © **212/496-5542**. www.boatbasincafe.com. Kids' menu. Reservations not accepted. Main courses $13–$25; kids' menu $2.50–$3.50. AE, DC, MC, V. Early May to late Sept (weather permitting) Mon–Fri noon–11:30pm; Sat–Sun 11–11:30. Subway: 1 to 79th St.

Brother Jimmy's BBQ & Booze BARBECUE/SOUTHERN   As the evening wears on, this low-lit, cluttered joint becomes a noisy, beery, Southern frat party, especially on nights when UNC and Duke square off in basketball. But the three Brother Jimmy's restaurants definitely like kids and prove it by letting the under-12 set eat free (two free kids' meals per each paid adult entree). And the barbecue is some of the city's best, with meaty, spicy ribs, pulled pork, and chicken cooked slowly over hickory wood and slathered with a tangy sauce. Add a little cornbread, candied yams, corn on the cob, and black-eyed peas, and it's a welcome break from pizza and burgers.

428 Amsterdam Ave. (btwn 80th and 81st sts.). © **212/501-7515**. www.brotherjimmys.com. Kids' menu, high chairs, boosters. Reservations accepted for groups of 8 or more only. Main courses $7.75–$22; salads and sandwiches $4.75–$9.25; kids' menu $4.50. AE, DC, DISC, MC, V. Mon–Thurs 5pm–midnight; Fri 5pm–1am; Sat noon–1am; Sun noon–11pm; Wed–Sun noon–midnight during summer months. Subway: B, C, 1, 9 to 79th St.

Hampton Chutney Co. INDIAN/ECLECTIC   This bright, casual sandwich shop serves up sandwiches with an interesting twist—they're not served on bread at all but folded up in dosas (light, crispy rice-lentil crepes) or served open-face on uttapams (fluffy rice-lentil pancakes). Okay, there are regular bread sandwiches too, but the Indian breads are the most fun. You can order them topped with curried chicken or masala (a spicy Indian potato filling) or with boring stuff like grilled chicken or smoked turkey. The kids menu is very down-to-earth with simple versions like cheese or scrambled eggs on a dosa. It's right around the corner from the Children's Museum of Manhattan, so there always seems to be a healthy number of pre-schoolers around; there are even board books and toys kept in the roomy front window seat to buy parents a few extra minutes for a cup of chai tea.

464 Amsterdam Ave. (btwn 82nd and 83rd sts.) ℂ 362-5050. www.hamptonchutney.com. Kids' menu, high chairs. Reservations not accepted. AE, DC, MC, V. Sandwiches $6.95–$12, kids menu $4.95–$7.95. Daily 10am–10pm. Subway: 1 to 86th St.

Harry's Burritos MEXICAN If your children can even get their hands around the overstuffed burritos here, more power to them. The menu also features standards like tacos, fajitas, and quesadillas, as well as some salads and fish; fresh ingredients and a consistent hand with the spices makes this outpost of the Village burrito haunt (see p. 127) a reliable bet. The kids menu has gringo options like chicken fingers, fish sticks, and cheeseburgers alongside the taco and burritos. The look is casual, simple, and blessedly free of kitschy South-of-the-Border decoration.

241 Columbus Ave (at 71st St.). ℂ 212/580-9494. www.harrysburritos.com. Kids' menu, high chairs. Main courses $4.25–$20; kids' menu $4.95. AE, MC, V. Sun–Thurs 11am–midnight, Fri-Sat 11am–1am. Subway: B, C, 1, 2, 3 to 72nd St.

Homer's ⭐⭐ *(Finds)* AMERICAN/BURGERS My kids clamor to go here on a regular basis—regular meaning every weekend night. What's the draw? Well, the burgers are just right, and the french fries (Homerfries) are some of the city's best; the chicken tenders are indeed tender, the chili hot and gutsy, shakes and malteds creamy and thick. Hot dogs come in several variations, and the slushies are . . . well, they're slushies, which you can't get in most restaurants. There is no kids menu, precisely because the entire menu consists of food with time-tested kid appeal; check the blackboards for daily specials which may include offbeat stuff like deep-fried Snickers. Don't worry, grownups, there are tasty soups and salads, too. The name refers to home runs (the owner used to play baseball), not to Homer Simpson, although Homer Simpson would be happy here, especially with the freshly made doughnuts. You'd expect a place with this sort of throwback menu to be loaded with kitsch, but the decor is streamlined and bright—the better to focus on the big-screen TVs, invariably tuned to either cartoons or sports.

487 Amsterdam Ave. (btwn 83rd and 84th sts.). ℂ 212/496-0777. www.homersworldfamous.com. High chairs, boosters. Reservations accepted. Main courses $2.75–$7.75. AE, DC, DISC, MC, V. Mon–Thurs 8am–11pm; Fri–Sun 8am–1am. Subway: 1 to 86th St.

Hunan Balcony CHINESE The Upper West Side has long been well served by Chinese restaurants, and Hunan Balcony is the granddaddy of them all. It's a big operation, smartly run, with a menu that tries hard to meet everybody's tastes—noodles, seafood, steamed items, spicy Hunan dishes, even sushi, plus the classic chow meins and egg rolls that characterized another American generation's idea of Chinese food. Purists will realize that the cooking isn't as authentic as you'll find in Chinatown, but it's usually delicious (I've eaten here so often over the past 20 years that I've occasionally hit an off night, but that's rare). Dishes are served family-style; children can drop all the rice they want and no one seems to mind.

2596 Broadway (at 98th St.). ℂ 212/865-0400. High chairs, boosters. Reservations recommended. Main courses $6–$15. AE, DC, MC, V. Daily 11:30am–1am. Subway: 1, 2, 3 to 96th St.

La Caridad Luncheonette *(Value)* CUBAN-CHINESE There's often a line at this cheap, authentic corner storefront spot, but customers move in and out fast—a hearty meal materializes on your Formica-topped table minutes after you order. The clientele seems split pretty evenly between those ordering white-rice dishes (savory Chinese stir-fries, chop sueys, and soups) and those going for the yellow-rice side of the menu (pork chops, fried chicken cracklings, and a divine Cuban pot roast my daughter attacked with gusto). This isn't a place for picky eaters—the mere sight of yucca and fried plantain side dishes send my boys into total appetite arrest—but anyone who's willing to try the food comes away happy. Though the place is cramped, crowded, and crazily busy, the taciturn Asian waiters never blink at a stroller blocking the aisle or a bread crust flung on the floor. What you see is what you get, and what you get is delicious.

2199 Broadway (at 78th St.). (℘ 212/874-2780. Reservations not accepted. Main courses $7–$16. No credit cards. Mon–Sat 11:30am–midnight; Sun 11:30am–10:30pm. Subway: 1 to 79th St.

Mary Ann's MEXICAN   The West Side branch of this Mexican chain is its most kid-friendly, with a junior menu that includes quesadillas, tacos, chicken fajitas, and a red-cheese enchilada. The earth-toned decor is movie-set Mexican, with tile-topped tables and a sombrero or two on the walls; the food is fairly standard, not too fiery, with tomatillo salsa and handmade tortillas. A decent choice for families.

2452 Broadway (at 91st St.). (℘ 212/877-0132. Kids' menu, high chairs, boosters. Reservations accepted for groups of 8 or more only. Main courses $8–$17; kids' menu $3.95–$4.25. MC, V. Sun-Tues noon-10pm, Weds-Sat noon–11pm. Subway: 1 to 86th St.; 1, 2, 3 to 96th St.

Ollie's Noodle Shop CHINESE   The roast poultry hanging in the front window is a promising sign, and the cheery bustle inside carries out the promise of simple, filling Chinese food—nothing too exotic to challenge the taste buds. Besides the usual spring rolls, dumplings, and steamed buns for appetizers, the menu features lots of fish, grilled or steamed or braised or sautéed, and a fairly classic range of Chinese dishes (lemon chicken, double-sautéed pork, eggplant sautéed in garlic sauce). Be careful about dishes marked with little jalapeño peppers on the menu—those are way too hot for most kids. My kids usually opt for lo mein noodles or the broader chow fun noodles, topped with chunks of chicken and a few shredded vegetables. The service is brisk and tolerant; it can get pretty crowded on a weekend night, but tables empty quickly.

(1) 2315 Broadway (at 84th St.). (℘ 212/362-3111. Subway: 1 to 86th St. (2) 1991 Broadway (near 68th St.). (℘ 212/595-8181. Subway: 1 to 66th St. (3) 2957 Broadway (at 116th St.) (℘ 212/932-3300. Subway: 1 to 116th St. Reservations not accepted on weekends. Main courses $7–$21; lunch specials $6.45. AE, MC, V. Sun–Thurs 11:30am–midnight; Fri–Sat 11:30am–1am.

Patsy's Pizzeria PIZZA/ITALIAN   Expanding beyond its original East Harlem location, the chain branches of Patsy's have discarded the married-to-the-mob ambience in favor of wood paneling and potted plants and marble-topped tables, perfect for serving up savory pizza pies, crisp salads, and satisfying pastas. The Upper West Side branch is only a few blocks from the American Museum of Natural History, another plus.

64 W. 74th St. (at Columbus Ave.). (℘ 212/579-3000. www.patsyspizzeriany.com. High chairs, boosters. Reservations not accepted. Pizzas $14–$21; pasta $10–$16. No credit cards. Sun–Thurs noon–11pm; Fri–Sat noon–midnight. Subway: B, C, 1, 2, 3 to 72nd St.

Pizzabolla ✺✺ (Finds) PIZZA/ITALIAN   This casual corner spot, with an upscale trattoria decor of brick facing and mustard-colored walls, never fails us. The menu isn't huge, but we still have a hard time choosing—the tangy thin-crust pizza? A meatball hero? The superb chicken tenders? A satisfying Caesar salad? The staff is friendly and responsive; it's just the right place to plunk yourself down and relax after a dizzying day, and so unpretentious you may be surprised to realize how good the food is.

654 Amsterdam Ave. (at 92nd St.). (℘ 221/579-4500. Kids' menu, high chairs, boosters. Main courses $8–$18, kids' menu $5–$6. AE, DISC, MC, V. Sun–Wed 11:30am–10pm; Thurs–Sat 11:30am–11pm. Subway: 1, 2, 3 to 96th St.

Saigon Grill VIETNAMESE   Ever since my daughter discovered sticky rice (white rice soaked in sweet coconut milk), she badgers us to come here whenever we eat out. While it lacks the romantic ambience of Rain or Monsoon (see above), this big, clean, busy restaurant often has a line out the door, but it usually doesn't take long to be seated or to be served once you're at the table. Appetizer skewers of beef or chicken sate make a fine meal for a picky eater; otherwise main course dishes like curry chicken, basil prawns, and ginger-honey pork stir fry are big enough to share, family-style. And don't forget that sweet sticky rice!

620 Amsterdam Ave. (at 90th St.). ✆ 212/875-9072. High chairs. Lunch $4.50–$7.95; dinner $6.50–$14. AE, DC, MC, V. Daily 11am–midnight. Subway: 1 to 86th St.

T & R Pizzeria PIZZA   Need a pizza near the Natural History Museum? Here's the place for a quick slice or a pie to go—a very dependable neighborhood storefront pizzeria. No fancy airs or graces, just good pizza.

411 Amsterdam Avenue (at 79th St.). ✆ 212/787-4093. Reservations not accepted. Pizzas $12–$16. No credit cards. Mon–Tues 10am–midnight; Wed 10am–1am; Thurs–Sat 11am–3am; Sun 10am–11pm. Subway: 1, 9 to 79th St.

V & T Pizzeria-Restaurant PIZZA/ITALIAN   With its brick walls, painted murals, low lighting, and red-checkered tablecloths, V & T looks just like the campus pizza joint it is, the campuses in question being nearby Columbia and Barnard. The pizzas are fabulous, with thin crusts, runny cheese, and robust tomato sauce; other southern Italian dishes, like lasagna and baked ziti, are heartwarmingly good, too. Not much on ambience, but then, you don't get a lot of attitude, either.

1024 Amsterdam Ave. (btwn 110th and 111th sts.). ✆ 212/663-1708. High chairs. Main courses $6–$17. AE, DC, DISC, MC, V. Daily 11:30am–midnight. Subway: 1 to 110th St.

Vinnie's Pizzeria PIZZA/ITALIAN   One of the best by-the-slice walk-in pizzerias in the city, Vinnie's also provides table service if you want to go beyond the wonderful pies and order pasta, antipasti, or salads. At $2 for a plain cheese slice, the pizza is a good deal, flavorful and nicely goopy. The location is handy too.

285 Amsterdam Ave. (btwn 73rd and 74th sts.). ✆ 212/874-4382. Reservations accepted. Pizza $2–$3 slice, $10–$17 pie; pasta $7–$12. No credit cards. Daily 11am–11:30pm. Subway: 1, 2, 3 to 72nd St.

THE CHAIN GANG

Handy to the American Museum of Natural History is the **Pizzeria Uno Chicago Bar and Grill,** 432 Columbus Ave., at 81st Street (✆ 212/595-4700). There's a **Dallas BBQ** at 27 W. 72nd St., between Central Park West and Columbus Avenue (✆ 212/873-2004). The **Jackson Hole** at 517 Columbus Ave., at 85th Street (✆ 212/362-5177), has sidewalk seating and lots of parked strollers on weekends.

3 The Upper East Side

EXPENSIVE

Petaluma ✦ ITALIAN   A good place to take a well-behaved child for a special meal out, the atmosphere is indeed friendly to kids, and the thin-crust pizzas from the brick oven go down well with youngsters. With such upscale food—risotto with porcini mushrooms, spinach gnocchi, swordfish with tomatoes, capers, and olives—it'd be nice to have a child appreciate it. The dining room is mellow and contemporary, with saffron-colored walls and plenty of room between tables; service is attentive but low-key.

1356 First Ave. (at 73rd St.). ✆ 212/772-8800. High chairs, boosters. Main courses $15–$31. AE, DC, DISC, MC, V. Mon–Thurs 11:30am–11pm, Fri 11:30am–11:30pm, Sat noon–11:30pm, Sun noon–11pm. Subway: 6 to 68th St.

MODERATE

Barking Dog Luncheonette ⓖ AMERICAN   The Barking Dog isn't automatically a family restaurant, but that's what I like about it. Convenient to the 92nd Street Y and Carl Schurz Park, this sleek retro diner is suffused with a mellow glow from golden walls, wood-trimmed booths, and parchment-shaded lamps at every table. The dog motif amuses my daughter: Posters, cookie jars, and even bulldog hood ornaments from Mack trucks put dogs all around the room, and there's a dog bar outside, a blue-tiled corner trough with a polished spigot. But what really makes this place work for families is that it serves breakfast until 4pm—kids can feast on waffles or blueberry pancakes while parents get a chance to eat something suitably grown-up, like a salad of field greens with goat-cheese croutons or a grilled fillet of salmon sandwich. For dinner, there's a good fried chicken with real mashed potatoes, baked ham, pot roast, and a homey meatloaf, as well as more sophisticated stuff like the pan-roasted breast of chicken with piquant Mediterranean-flavored ragout. Bribe your children with old-fashioned ice cream sodas and sundaes served from a vintage soda fountain.

(1) 1678 Third Ave. (at 94th St.). ℂ 212/831-1800. Subway: 6 to 96th St. (2) 1453 York Ave. (at 77th St.). ℂ 212/861-3600. Subway: 6 to 77th St. Boosters, sassy seats. Reservations not accepted. Main courses $13–$22; sandwiches and salads $6–$13. No credit cards. Daily 7:30am–11pm.

Big City Bar and Grill AMERICAN/ECLECTIC   Though it looks like so many other noisy dinner saloons along the Third Avenue dining strip—dark wood furnishings, plate-glass windows, and a large central bar area—Big City actually has a good-size children's menu, simply offering smaller versions of popular items from the adult menu. The kitchen's repertoire ranges beyond the expected burgers, steaks, and Caesar salads to include items like jalapeño poppers, Santa Fe salad, an herb-garlic wrap with Thai chicken, and seared-ginger tuna steak. The staff is friendly and the bar scene not too overpowering.

1600 Third Ave. (at 90thSt.). ℂ 212/369-0808. Kids' menu, high chairs, boosters. AE, DC, DISC, MC, V. Dinner $7.95–$16; kids' menu $4.95. Mon–Fr noon–midnight, Sat–Sun 11am–4am. Subway: 4, 5, 6 to 86th St

EJ's Luncheonette DINER   Breakfast is an especially good time to check out this old-style lunch-counter diner, which like its West Side sibling (p. 100) has a big choice of pancakes, waffles, and French toast for breakfast. The classic repertoire of burgers, salads, and sandwiches—plus daily specials like skinless fried chicken and turkey meatloaf—makes it a good bet for lunch or dinner, too, so long as you can get in. The tile floor and high ceiling usually ring with noise.

1271 Third Ave. (at 73rd St.). ℂ 212/472-0600. Kids' menu, high chairs, boosters. Reservations not accepted. Breakfast $6.20–$12; lunch and dinner main courses $6.50–$11. No credit cards. Daily 8am–11pm. Subway: 6 to 77th St.

Fetch ⓖ AMERICAN/ECLECTIC   A welcoming environment and friendly staff go a long way to make this neighborhood favorite work for kids; what really seals the deal is the dog theme, with snapshots of beloved family pups covering every inch of the warm yellow walls (hence the restaurant's name). The ever-popular burgers and fries, plus delicious salads, omelets, soups, and pastas give you a decent range of options, with grilled fish and roast chicken added at dinner; it's hard to resist the Philly cheese steak. Truly a place to yap about.

1649 Third Ave. (btwn 92nd and 93rd sts.). ℂ 212/289-2700. www.fetchny.com. Kids' menu, high chairs, boosters. Reservations recommended. Main courses $8–$19, kids' menu $6–$7. AE, DC, DISC, MC, V. Mon–Fri 11am–3pm and 5–11pm; Sat–Sun 10am–3pm and 5–midnight. Subway: 4, 5, 6 to 96th St.

Googie's Luncheonette DINER   This upscale coffee shop's bright, clean, pastel-toned decor lacks the sassy retro atmosphere of EJ's or the Barking Dog (see above), but the food is perfectly fine, especially if your kids, like mine, are pasta omnivores. It's usually bustling, and though the service can be slipshod, no one will hurry you out the door. The menu features a fair number of Italian dishes along with typical diner fare—burgers, club sandwiches, omelets, or even a fairly decent sirloin steak, to be accompanied if at all possible with the excellent shoestring fries. The pasta sauces are a little less spicy than I like, but my kids seem to prefer 'em that way. Googie's is a useful option for a late breakfast, with Italian frittatas in addition to standard waffles, pancakes, and French toast.

1491 Second Ave. (at 78th St.). ✆ 212/717-1122. High chairs, boosters. Sandwiches $6.75–$9.50; main courses $8–$17. AE, MC, V. Sun–Wed 9am–midnight; Thurs 9am–1am; Fri 9am–1:30am; Sat 9am–2am. Subway: 6 to 77th St.

Luke's Bar & Grill 🐸🐸 AMERICAN/BURGERS   It's hard for me to analyze why I like Luke's—it just seems to me like a very civilized place where children are included as a matter of course. Lots of brick and wood give it a warm, clubby look that's also somehow young and casual; there's definitely an active bar scene here, but it never overwhelms the pleasant, relaxing restaurant. Luke's burgers are really wonderful, firm and yet juicy, with an ever-so-slightly charred outside, and the salads are big, fresh, and well conceived. My younger ones go for the grilled cheese sandwich, roast chicken, or one of the pasta dishes. There's no attitude on the part of the waiters: They seem genuinely happy to serve youngsters, even babies. If only more restaurants were like this.

1394 Third Ave. (btwn 79th and 80th sts.). ✆ 212/249-7070. Boosters, sassy seats. Reservations accepted. Main courses $7–$23. No credit cards. Daily 11:30am–1am. Subway: 6 to 77th St.

Serendipity 3 DINER/DESSERTS   This cheery, bright restaurant with its snugly deep booths and Tiffany-style lamps has a classic coffee-shop menu, with especially good burgers. But it's best known in the under-12 population as a source for huge, wickedly rich desserts; fountain sodas; and ice cream sundaes. The Outrageous Banana Split is priced at $19 and worth every penny. Because space is tight, strollers and carriages cannot be accommodated within the restaurant.

225 E. 60th St. (btwn Second and Third aves.). ✆ 212/838-3531. www.serendipity3.com. Boosters. Reservations accepted for full meals only. Main courses $7.50–$20. AE, DC, DISC, MC, V. Sun–Thurs 11:30am–midnight; Fri 11:30am–1am; Sat 11;30am–2am. Subway: 4, 5, 6 to 59th St.

Tony's di Napoli ITALIAN   Hearty southern Italian food is served family-style at this genial Upper East Side neighborhood spot, which opens a big sidewalk cafe in fair weather. Polaroids of satisfied customers in the front window and black-and-white head shots of race-car drivers on the yellowed plaster walls give it the look of a vintage family-owned red-sauce joint, though in fact it's part of the Dallas BBQ restaurant empire. Sunday lunch is the most popular time for families (Tony's doesn't serve lunch on weekdays), but you'll find kids sprinkled around the boisterous dining room on weeknights, too. The family-style menu is strong on pasta dishes, with several chicken and veal offerings as well, plus a two-person steak for dedicated carnivores. If your family can't agree on dishes, half portions can be ordered for individuals, as well as kid-size portions of pasta (there's no separate kids' menu). Though I prefer the similar food at Carmine's (p. 99 and 115), the scene here is less trendy, and the prices are certainly reasonable, considering that you can get away at $20 a head, including wine for adults. Note that there isn't room to park strollers beside tables.

1606 Second Ave. (btwn 83rd and 84th sts.). © **212/861-8686**. High chairs, boosters. Reservations recommended. Main courses (serve 2–4 people) $16–$45. AE, DC, DISC, MC, V. Mon–Fri 5pm–midnight; Sat–Sun 2pm–midnight. Subway: 4, 5, 6 to 86th St.

INEXPENSIVE

Alice's Tea Cup 🎯🎯 BRITISH/DESSERTS/ECLECTIC   Chapter Two of the popular West Side tearoom has the same boho-grunge assortment of castoff furniture and china, and the same delightful menu of sandwiches, omelets, salads, and pastries, with fuller selections available for dinner. The after-school snack menu attracts lots of private-school girls and their nannies.

156 E. 64th St. (at Lexington Ave.). © **212/486-9200**. www.alicesteacup.com. Kids' menu, high chairs. AE, DISC, MC, V. Salads and sandwiches $8–$14, kids' menu $6–$14; $22–$35 high tea. Mon–Thurs 8am–8pm; Fri 8am–10pm; Sat 10am–10pm; Sun 10am–8pm. Subway: 6 to 68th St.

Barron's Pizza *(Finds* PIZZA   We stumbled into this pizzeria one Sunday noontime and had some of the best pie of our lives—tangy sauce, fresh mozzarella, crisp chewy crust—along with friendly counter service. The decor is a little different from your standard storefront pizza shop, with mosaic tile designs and wrought-iron cafe chairs. This is the sort of place you might not seek out without a recommendation, so take it from me: It's well above average. We go back whenever we're in the neighborhood.

1426 Lexington Ave. (at 93rd St.). © **212/410-6600**. Slice $2.25; plain pie $14–$16. No credit cards. Daily 7am–11pm. Subway: 6 to 96th St.

Brother Jimmy's Bait Shack BARBECUE/SOUTHERN   The rowdy roadhouse charm of Brother Jimmy's always appeals to kids—blackened catfish and peel-and-eat shrimp are featured on a menu otherwise heavy on barbecued chicken, ribs, and pork. The kitchen doesn't stint on the spices, and beer flows plentifully. But kids are welcomed warmly, with a kids-eat-free policy that can't be beat anywhere else in town (two under-12s per parent, so long as the adult buys an entrée rather than a sandwich). A variety of nightly "events" like All-U-Can-Eat Sundays and White Trash Wednesdays make every evening a party here.

1644 Third Ave. (at 92nd St.). © **212/426-2020**. www.brotherjimmys.com. Kids' menu, high chairs, boosters. Reservations accepted for groups of 8 or more only. Main courses $7.75–$22; salads and sandwiches $4.75–$9.25; kids' menu $4.50. AE, DC, DISC, MC, V. Mon–Fri 5pm–midnight; Sat noon–1am; Sun noon–11pm. Subway: 6 to 96th St.

Brother Jimmy's BBQ BARBECUE/SOUTHERN   With a jumble of frat-party paraphernalia littering the walls, low-lit Brother Jimmy's brings hickory-smoked Carolina barbecue—both Northern and Southern versions—to New York City. Thick 'n' meaty ribs, brisket, and chicken are served up in hefty dinners that also include cornbread and a choice of country sides; if your kids aren't into collard greens (yeah, right), you can satisfy them with creamed corn, french fries, or macaroni and cheese. As with the Upper West Side location (p. 104), it may be best to get here early, before the frat party swings into high gear.

1485 Second Ave. (btwn 77th and 78th sts.). © **212/288-0999**. www.brotherjimmys.com. Kids' menu, high chairs, boosters. Reservations accepted for groups of 8 or more only. Main courses $7.75–$22; salads and sandwiches $4.75–$9.25; kids' menu $4.50. AE, DC, DISC, MC, V. Mon 5pm–midnight, Tues-Thurs noon-midnight, Fri-Sat noon-1am, Sun noon-11pm. Subway: 6 to 77th St.

California Pizza Kitchen PIZZA/CALIFORNIAN   Frankly, I think the idea of a pizza topped with barbecued chicken or shrimp is an abomination, but this cheery chain restaurant surmounts that objection for me because it's so darned kid-friendly.

The menu does include other items, like salads and soups and pasta dishes, and you can order more traditional pizzas, which come out of a brick oven on the ground floor. My younger son pronounced the pepperoni pizza the best he'd ever had (but remember, he was under the influence of being given crayons, an activity sheet, and a take-home plastic cup); his older brother and dad are partial to the barbecued chicken pizza, which is surprisingly good. Service is decently prompt, and the kids' menu is smartly focused on pizza and pasta, including perfectly plain (no sauce) spaghetti and penne. The black-and-yellow decor is clean and modern, neither beachy nor barlike, and the noise level is just right—we could hear one another talk but didn't feel self-conscious when the kids became exuberant. It's a middle-of-the-road option that comes in real handy.

201 E. 60th St. (at Third Ave.). © 212/755-7773. Kids' menu, high chairs, boosters. Reservations accepted for parties of 8 or more only. Main courses $10–$16; kids' menu $5. AE, DC, MC, V. Sun–Thurs 11:30am–10pm; Fri–Sat 11:30am–11pm. Subway: 4, 5, 6 to 59th St.; E, N, R, V, W Lexington Ave.

John's Pizza ☆☆ PIZZA   The great Village pizzeria chain (see p. 120 and 127 later on in this chapter) has opened this East Side branch for thin-crust, brick-oven pies, substantial green salads, and a few well-executed pasta dishes. The menu's limited, but every dish on it is delectable.

408 E. 64th St. (btwn First and York aves.). © 212/935-2895. Reservations accepted for groups of 5 or more only. Pizzas $11–$14, toppings $2–$3; pastas $8.75–$12. AE, MC, V, DISC. Daily 11:30am–11:30pm. Subway: 4, 5, 6 to 59th St.

Lexington Candy Shop ☆☆☆ *Finds* DINER   Walking through the door of the Lexington Candy Shop is like passing through a time warp: Inside is a perfectly preserved old luncheonette that makes EJ's Luncheonette (above) look like Planet Hollywood. It's been around since 1925 and looks it. There's a counter with chrome-rimmed stools, along with a handful of wooden booths, where you can down creamy milkshakes and malteds, fresh lemonade, buttery grilled cheese sandwiches, super BLTs, outstanding cheeseburgers, and crinkle fries. And best of all, the staff seems to positively perk up when they see kids coming. The candy-shop component doesn't consist of much more than a rack of Milky Ways and Hershey Bars just inside the door; the front window is also crammed full of stuffed animals for sale, which guarantees that my children never pass by without stopping. And I don't mind because it's the sort of place that warms the cockles of my heart.

1226 Lexington Ave. (at 83rd St.). © 212/288-0057. Boosters, sassy seats. Main courses $5.75–$12. AE, DC, DISC, MC, V. Mon–Sat 7am–7pm; Sun 9am–6pm. Subway: 4, 5, 6 to 86th St.

Lili's Noodle Shop and Grill CHINESE   My kids are big fans of this kind of noodle-shop/rotisserie food, and Lili's is their favorite place for it. The food is delicately spiced and not too greasy, which is a feat considering how barbecue-roasted pork and chicken can be. We also like the noodle dishes, even plain lo mein; the soups come in enormous bowls and can be a challenge to finish, but the broth is light and flavorful, filled with fresh noodles and vegetables. Light varnished woods and streamlined shapes give the decor a smart, modern feel, and the service is efficient, casual, and friendly.

1500 Third Ave. (btwn 84th and 85th sts.). © 212/639-1313. High chairs, boosters. Main courses $12–$37. AE, DC, DISC, MC, V. Sun–Thurs 11am–11pm; Fri–Sat 11am–midnight. Subway: 4, 5, 6 to 86th St.

Patsy's Pizzeria PIZZA/ITALIAN   Superb thin-crust pizza and wonderful filling pastas make these casual pizzerias a worthwhile destination for families. Though there no kids' menu per se, smaller-sized pizzas and small portions of pasta make good child options, so everybody can be satisfied with different choices from the menu.

1312 Second Ave. (at 69th St.). (C) 212/639-1000. Subway: 6 to 68th St. (2) 200 E. 60th St. (at Third Ave.) (C) 212/688-9707. Subway: 4, 5, 6 to 59th St. High chairs, boosters. Reservations not accepted. Pizzas $14–$21; pasta $10–$16. No credit cards. Sun–Thurs noon–11pm; Fri–Sat noon–midnight.

Sassy's Sliders *Value* BURGERS   The decor is very 1950s—wall tiles, Formica tables, and linoleum, all in Fiestaware colors—and so is the fast-food concept: 2-inch hamburgers steamed with onions, so small and moist they slide whole down your throat, hence the name "sliders." I've been addicted to them ever since I was a kid going to White Castle, and I've turned my older son into a fan as well. But Sassy's Sliders are much better than White Castle's, and with other choices like grilled chicken, ground turkey, and veggie burgers, this nifty little spot should satisfy everyone in the family. The slider is a perfect-size burger for a kid anyway, and at these incredibly low prices, you may be able to feed the whole gang for less than $20. Most of its business is takeout and delivery, but there are a few tables inside.

1530 Third Ave. (at 86th St.). (C) 212/828-6900. www.sassyssliders.com. Reservations not accepted. Burgers $1.18–$1.31. AE. Mon–Thurs 11:30am–11pm; Fri–Sat 11am–midnight, Sun 11:30am–10pm. Subway: 4, 5, 6 to 86th St.

AFTERNOON TEA

Carlyle Hotel CONTINENTAL   Beneath the charming Ludwig Bemelman murals in the luxe surroundings of Bemelman's Bar, this tony East Side hotel (see p. 69) offers a storybook Madeline's Tea every Friday through Sunday from noon to 4pm. Finger sandwiches and delicate little pastries accompany finely-brewed tea and other beverages, served on bone china, of course. French convent-school uniforms optional.

In the Carlyle Hotel, 35 E. 76th St. (at Madison Ave.). (C) 212/570-7192. www.thecarlyle.com. AE, DC, DISC, MC, V. Full tea $31 adults, $24 kids. Fri–Sat noon–4pm (except Aug). Subway: 6 to 77th St.

THE CHAIN GANG

The Carnegie Hill branch of **Jackson Hole,** 1270 Madison Ave., at 91st Street ((C) 212/427-2820), is perpetually mobbed after 3pm with kids from the clutch of private schools nearby; the main thing here is the burgers, which are fat and juicy (prepare to wipe your child's chin). There are two other East Side Jackson Holes, at 232 E. 64th St., between Second and Third avenues ((C) 212/371-7187), and 1611 Second Ave., between 83rd and 84th streets ((C) 212/737-8788). A somewhat healthier and still tasty alternative is the organic burgers at **Better Burger,** 1614 Second Ave., at 84th St. ((C) 212/734-6644). A good-size **Pizzeria Uno** at 220 E. 86th St., between Second and Third avenues ((C) 212/472-5656), a **Dallas BBQ** at 1265 Third Ave., between 72nd and 73rd streets ((C) 212/772-9393), and a **Blockhead's Burritos** at 1563 Second Ave., at 81st St. ((C) 212/879-1999) round out the neighborhood.

4 Midtown

EXPENSIVE

American Girl Café ★★★ AMERICAN   Girls would have begged to come to American Girl Place's house restaurant anyway, but parents will be gratified to discover that the food is actually good. Advance reservations are essential, up to 6 months ahead at busy seasons, but it never hurts to stop by the front desk as you enter the store just to see if there are any free slots. Prix-fixe pricing simplifies everything, as does the small, well-chosen menu. As soon as you sit down, you're offered warm,

The Cupcake Craze

Whether it's the crowns of butter cream frosting, the portable charm of a cake that fits in your palm, or an automatic response to fond childhood memories, Manhattanites old and young alike crave cupcakes. And cupcakes abound. Scattered throughout the city, bakeries that feature shiny glass cases full of these beloved treats have multiplied, with some small shops drawing not only neighborhood crowds but also citywide fame.

Among the most popular are **Magnolia Bakery,** located at 401 Bleecker St. (at W. 11th St.; ✆ **212/462-2572**), and the **Cupcake Cafe,** on the outskirts of midtown (522 Ninth Ave., at 40th St.; ✆ **212/465-1530**), probably the two joint progenitors of the cupcake frenzy. (Frequent mentions on *Sex and the City* didn't hurt Magnolia's fame any.) For these bakeries, the story is in the frosting; Whether piled on in flowerets or cloudlike curls, there's always enough to trump the cake. Both shops produce and sell thousands of the miniature cakes daily and have loyal customer followings. Farther north, **Two Little Red Hens** on the Upper East Side (1652 Second Ave., at 85th St.; ✆ **212/452-0476**) and the two locations of **Crumbs** (321½ Amsterdam Ave., at 75th St., ✆ **212/712-9800,** and 1371 Third Ave., at 78th St., ✆ **212/794-9800**) feature decadent goods—we're talking frosting you can really sink your teeth into. And in the middle of it all, the **Buttercup Bake Shop,** a descendent of Magnolia located at 973 Second Ave. (at 51st St.; ✆ **212/350-4144**), offers a challenge to even the most determined sweet tooth. Both cake and frosting are overwhelmingly sweet—combined, they could send you into sugar shock. For the faint of heart or appetite, it might be best to split.

—Connor Puleo

gooey cinnamon buns (don't bypass these). At lunch and dinner there's one choice of appetizer (an arrangement of crudités, dips, cheeses, and breads that's already on the table when you arrive), and everybody gets the same dessert, a yummy little pudding in a chocolate cup. Special touches make all the difference, as with the kids' pizza, decorated with veggies to look like tic-tac-toe, or the baby-size hamburgers with curly fries. Best of all, there are special doll seats where girls can prop their American Girl dolls while they eat (the dolls get their own tea sets, and you wouldn't believe how many girls carefully feed their dolls). If you haven't brought a doll, they'll even lend you one for the meal. The waitstaff is unfailingly patient and kind, and the decor is sophisticated yet girly. The experience will make your daughter's day, and—surprise, surprise—yours too.

609 Fifth Ave. (at 49th St.). ✆ **877/AG-PLACE.** www.americangirl.com. High chairs, boosters. Reservations required. Brunch $18; lunch $22; tea $19; dinner $24. AE, DISC, MC, V. Subway: E, V to Fifth Ave./53rd St.

Benihana ✮✮ JAPANESE   Watching the Benihana chefs at work with their flying knives, slicing and dicing the meat, seafood, and vegetables they'll grill on the teppanyaki right at your table, is endlessly fascinating to my kids and their friends. (Best trick: the onion transformed into a smoking volcano or the shrimp tail flipped into the top of the chef's hat.) As far as Japanese food goes, this doesn't require as adventurous a palate as, say, sushi does, so it's a good choice for kids—these kitchen samurai even managed to get my son to try shrimp for the first time (he promptly fell in love with it). For adults, the grilled food is a decent nongreasy option; small portions on the grill turn out to be a very hearty meal when they're all added up. What with the teahouse decor and the low tables, kids may feel they're getting an exotic Eastern experience, though this operation is clearly tourist-oriented, and truth be told, some of the chefs look bored with their work. But even if you don't get one of the show-off types, you'll find you can't take your eyes off the cook at work, and folks sharing the communal tables are oddly drawn together by the experience.

47 W. 56th St. (btwn Fifth and Sixth aves.). ☎ 212/581-0930. Boosters. Reservations recommended. Lunch $7.25–$15; dinner $15–$42. AE, DC, DISC, MC, V. Mon–Thurs 11:30am–11pm, Fri 11:30am–11pm, Sat noon–11pm, Sun noon–10pm (closed weekdays 2:30–5pm). Subway: E, V to Fifth Ave./53rd St.; F to 57th St.; N, Q, R, W to 57th St./Seventh Ave.

Jekyll & Hyde Club AMERICAN   When they were younger, my kids were terrified of this place—I could barely get them to walk past the entrance where ghoulish skull heads dangle and there are always throngs of older kids lined up, dying to get in. Other theme restaurants have staid display cases full of memorabilia; Jekyll & Hyde delivers a thrill-ride experience, from the crashing ceiling in the vestibule to the creepy artwork that stares back at you from the walls. The waiters all look decked out for Halloween, and there's a continual floor show of ghastly figures telling even ghastlier jokes—expect an extra $2.50 per person slapped onto your bill to cover the entertainment. As with the Village location (p. 125), the food is somewhat beside the point, but for the record, I'll tell you that they serve burgers, popcorn shrimp, pizzas, pastas, baby back ribs, and more. The kitchen's general strategy seems to be to smother things with cheese if at all possible and to grill anything that's grillable.

1409 Sixth Ave. (btwn 57th and 58th sts.). ☎ 212/541-9505. www.jekyllandhydeclub.com. Kids' menu. Reservations accepted for groups of 15 or more only. Main courses $14–$32; kids' menu $13. AE, DC, DISC, MC, V. Mon–Thurs 11:30am–11pm; Fri 11:30am–1am; Sat 11am–1am; Sun 11:30am–11pm. Subway: F, N, Q, R, W to 57th St./Seventh Ave.

Mickey Mantle's AMERICAN   Young fanatics hungering for a brush with athletic celebrity may not get the point of this sleek blond-wood sports shrine owned by the late, great baseball star Mickey Mantle: The autographed jerseys hung on the walls belonged to Ted Williams, Hank Aaron, Stan Musial, Yogi Berra, and Joe DiMaggio, names from long-ago baseball cards, back in the days when they gave you bubble gum with your cards. Oh, yeah, there's a Shaquille O'Neal autographed basketball, but who's this Johnny Unitas whose name is scrawled on the football next to it? What the place lacks in ESPN glitz, however, it gains in food and a smart, friendly, casual atmosphere. A couple of upscale dishes like grilled yellowfin tuna, herb-roasted chicken, and lobster ravioli with grilled shrimp grace the menu, but most of it is studiedly downhome. Mick's own picks include chicken-fried steak, Texas barbecued ribs, and grilled sirloin chili with blue-corn tortillas. The Little League menu has the usual range of chicken fingers, grilled cheese, spaghetti, and burgers. TV monitors everywhere are usually tuned to some sports event, and oil paintings of baseball players festoon the walls of the quieter, carpeted back room.

42 Central Park S. (btwn Fifth and Sixth aves.). ☎ 212/688-7777. www.mickeymantles.com. Kids' menu, high chairs, boosters. Reservations recommended. Main courses $14–$30; kids' menu $9.95. AE, DC, DISC, MC, V. Sun–Thurs 11am–10:30pm; Fri-Sat 11am–11pm. Subway: N, R, W to Fifth Ave./59th St.

Rock Center Café ⭐ ITALIAN   If it weren't in the very heart of Midtown, this restaurant might have cause to be snooty about children, with its sleek mahogany-trimmed contemporary decor and upscale Italian food (stylish pastas, roasted chicken, fish, and steak). But as they say in the real estate biz, location is everything, and this location couldn't be more of a tourist magnet: set right on the lower plaza of Rocke-feller Plaza, where you can watch the ice skaters in winter and sit out under Prometheus in summer. (And if that isn't enough of a thrill, you can ride a tiny glass-enclosed ele-vator down from sidewalk level to the restaurant.) Where tourists flock, there are bound to be children, and the Rock Center Café has shrewdly decided to make the most of them with a decent children's menu—chicken tenders, handmade penne pasta, and a grilled cheese sandwich made with fontina cheese on Italian bread. Every-thing about this place spells Special Event.

20 W. 50th St. (at Rockefeller Center). 🕐 212/332-7620. Kids' menu, high chairs. Reservations recommended, espe-cially for lunch. Lunch $16–$35; dinner $18–$35; kids' menu $14. AE, DC, MC, V. Mon–Thurs 7:30am–10pm, Fri 7:30am–11pm, Sat 11am–11pm, Sun 11am–10pm. Subway: B, D, F, V to 47th–50th sts./Rockefeller Center.

Ruby Foo's PAN-ASIAN   This Theater District location of the Asian-themed chain (p. 99) is good for special events—the decor is as stunning as a movie set, the food precisely presented, the whole atmosphere trendily abuzz. The menu ranges all over Asia, with dim sum, sushi, hand rolls, and Thai curries. Best for older kids who can appreciate the setting and are willing to sample exotic dishes.

1626 Broadway (at 49th St.). 🕐 212/489-5600. High chairs, boosters. Reservations recommended. Lunch $15–$25; dinner $27–$40. AE, DISC, MC, V. Sun–Thurs 11:30am–midnight; Fri–Sat 11:30am–1am. Subway: 1 to 50th St.

MODERATE

Café SFA ⭐ ECLECTIC   Many things recommend this department store cafe for lunch or afternoon tea: its high-floor views over Rockefeller Center and St. Patrick's (insist on a window table), elegant weekday tea service from 3 to 5pm, and the smart kids' menu—soup and sandwich, miniburgers, a hot dog, or a PB&J sandwich, with a choice of drinks that includes chocolate milk. Grown-ups will feel very ladies-who-lunch-ish with selections like grilled salmon, turkey club, Cobb salad, a portobello focaccia sandwich, and an asparagus-and-mushroom risotto. The decor is thick-car-peted and pleasant, with golden hues and mahogany-stained wood trim. A great, relaxing place to go to get out of the Midtown crush.

In Saks Fifth Avenue, 611 Fifth Ave. (btwn 49th and 50th sts.), 8th floor. 🕐 212/940-4080. Kids' menu, high chairs. Reservations accepted. Main courses $16–$35; afternoon tea $22; kids' menu $6.25–$8. AE, DC, DISC, MC, V. Tues–Sat 11am–5pm (Thurs until 7pm); Sun noon–5pm. Subway: E, V to Fifth Ave./53rd St.; B, D, F, V to 47th–50th sts./Rockefeller Center.

Carmine's ITALIAN   Northern Italian, and lots of it. Family-style dinners make this a natural if you're eating out with kids, especially if yours are the kind to suck up spaghetti with gusto. The noisy, casual atmosphere absorbs a lot of tantrums, and once you've got a table, service is prompt (if you can't move customers in and out quickly in the Theater District, you're done for). The original branch is on the Upper West Side (p. 99).

200 W. 44th St. (btwn Broadway and Eighth aves.). 🕐 212/221-3800. High chairs, boosters. Reservations after 6pm accepted for groups of 6 or more only. Family style main courses (serve 2–4 people) $20–$28 (porterhouse steaks and lobsters more). AE, DISC, DC, MC, V. Sun 11am–11pm, Mon 11:30pm–11pm, Tues 11:30am–midnight, Wed 11am–midnight, Thurs-Fri 11:30am–midnight, Sat 11am–midnight. Subway: N, Q, R, S, W, 1, 2, 3, 7 to 42nd St./Times Sq.

Carnegie Deli DELI   A classic delicatessen restaurant, straight out of Woody Allen's *Broadway Danny Rose,* the Carnegie Deli may borrow its name from nearby Carnegie Hall, but the atmosphere is anything but refined and stuffy. Every table has a little bowl of crisp dill pickles on it, and the sandwiches are piled so high you can hardly get your mouth around them—corned beef, pastrami, brisket, chopped liver, the works, with Russian dressing the condiment of choice. You can also get kosher dairy dishes like blintzes, pirogue, and matzo brei, or eastern European home-cooking like chicken paprikash, Hungarian goulash, and stuffed cabbage. The menu is as huge as the servings. Ya wanna know what New York was like in the 1940s and '50s? Come here; order an egg cream, borscht, or gefilte fish; and schmooze away.

854 Seventh Ave. (btwn 54th and 55th sts.). (C) 212/757-2245. www.carnegiedeli.com. High chairs, boosters. Reservations not accepted. Breakfast $8–$13; sandwiches and main courses $13–$23. No credit cards. Daily 6:30am–4am. Subway: B, D, E to Seventh Ave.

Ellen's Stardust Diner DINER/ECLECTIC   This *Happy Days*–style diner is a block from my husband's office, and it's our kids' favorite place to eat when we visit Dad at work. Enter through what looks like a vintage red subway car, and you're in a nostalgic time warp—streamlined chrome trim, turquoise vinyl and Formica, vintage movie posters and ads, and a wall full of subway posters introducing a bevy of Miss Subways (owner Ellen Hart was herself voted Miss Subways in 1959). But what my kids like best are the model train zipping around on an elevated track above our heads and the TV monitors showing old black-and-white TV shows. The food—your basic grab bag of burgers and fries, salads, omelets, tacos, and club sandwiches—tastes decent and comes in good-size portions; Nick at Niters may get a kick out of the cutesy names for menu items, like Fred Mertz-arella Sticks or the Cesar Romero Salad. The waitstaff is supercongenial, and Wednesday through Saturday nights they even sing, as part of a slightly goofy dinner-hour floor show. They totally embarrassed my 9-year-old by making him stand in the spotlight while the whole place sang "Happy Birthday" to him—his older brother couldn't get enough of it.

1650 Broadway (at 51st St.). (C) 212/956-5151. www.ellensstardustdiner.com. Kids' menu, high chairs, boosters. Reservations accepted only for groups of 10 or more. Breakfast $3–$10; lunch and dinner entrees $7–$24; kids' menu $8. AE, DISC, MC, V. Mon–Thurs 7am–midnight, Fri-Sat 7am–1am, Sun 7am–11pm. Subway: 1 to 50th St.

ESPN Zone AMERICAN   It's definitely a theme-restaurant scene, with a line out front, a gift shop, multiple floors, an arcade upstairs, and big-screen TVs putting sports in your face everywhere you turn. But the streamlined blond-wood decor is not too cluttered; the noise level is tolerable; and the menu offers a decent range of standard dishes, with salads and pizzas and lighter food amid all the fried stuff that kids and jock types are expected to love. Meat is, however, a linchpin of the menu: steaks, ribs, cheese steak, burgers, and barbecued pork, along with tailgate-party-worthy appetizers like chicken wings, queso chips, and cheese fries. Though the kids' menu is pretty standard, there are two unusual items—sliders (mini-hamburgers) and a chicken breast with broccoli—and maybe the best thing about the place is the upstairs game room, which is the city's best arcade—clean, well-lit, and spacious, with tons of great sports-themed games to play. That alone made it worth the visit for my kids.

1472 Broadway (at 42nd St.). (C) 212/921-3776. www.espnzone.com/newyork. Kids' menu, high chairs, boosters. Sandwiches $11–$13; main courses $12–$26; kids' menu $5.99. AE, DC, DISC, MC, V. Mon–Thurs 11:30am–12:30pm; Fri-Sat 11am–1am; Sun 11am–midnight. Subway: N, Q, R, S, W, 1, 2, 3, 7 to 42nd St./Times Sq.

Hard Rock Cafe AMERICAN/BURGERS   Right in the pulsing heart of Times Square, under a big revolving neon guitar, this brassy burger joint promotes its rock-and-roll theme with such memorabilia as a pair of John Lennon's wire-rims with a cracked lens, a red feather boa of Janis Joplin's, Jimi Hendrix's purple velvet suit, and a complete set of collarless suits worn by the Beatles on the *Ed Sullivan Show*. Various trippy 1960s slogans pepper the place, scripted in neon or proclaimed on posters, but the target audience isn't baby boomers nostalgic for Woodstock: It's teenagers, who regard the place as a museum of their parents' goofy past. Despite its lowbrow Disney-land-ish cachet, the Hard Rock is really not so bad; the burgers and milkshakes are perfectly fine, the prices aren't out of sight, and there's something infectious about the blaring rock soundtrack. And if you've got teenagers in tow, the fact that the place is packed with callow teenagers might even be a plus. (Unless, of course, your teenager is too sophisticated for the place already.)

1501 Broadway (btwn 43rd and 44th sts.). (© 212/343-3355. www.hardrock.com. Reservations accepted for groups of 15 or more only. Main courses $7.95–$14. AE, DC, DISC, MC, V. Sun–Thurs 11am–12:30am, Fri–Sat 11am–1:30am. Subway: N, Q, R, S, W, 1, 2, 3, 7 to 42nd St./Times Sq.

La Bonne Soupe ✦✦✦ (Finds FRENCH   One rainy Sunday, we left the Museum of Modern Art, all five of us starving, not knowing where to go for lunch. (Yes, it happens to us, too.) We wandered into La Bonne Soupe simply because there wasn't much else open nearby on a Sunday, and it was one of the most pleasant discoveries we ever made. This is a cozy, charming bistro, French but not snooty, which truly welcomes *les enfants*. The quiches are splendid, as is the onion soup gratiné, and there are a few fine fondue dishes (talk about throwbacks). Omelets, salads, and filet mignon fill out the menu. My kids ordered from the kids' menu *steak haché*—aka chopped steak, aka hamburger—and were astonished when it arrived with no bun and no ketchup. But the accommodating waitress quickly sliced up French bread and discovered some ketchup in the kitchen, and *voilà!*—we were all set. There are two floors, the lower one softly lit and paneled, the cheery upper floor more like an Alpine chalet, checkered tablecloths and all. Service isn't speedy, but it's pleasant. A delightful change of pace.

48 W. 55th St. (btwn Fifth and Sixth aves.). (© 212/586-7650. Kids' menu. Reservations recommended. Main courses $11–$25; kids' menu $11. AE, MC, V. Mon–Sat 11:30am–11pm; Sun 11:30am–10pm. Subway: F, N, Q, R, W to 57th St./Seventh Ave.

Mangia e Bevi ITALIAN   Graffiti-ish murals outside do their best to stop traffic on Ninth Avenue, drawing customers to this hearty Italian restaurant on the western edge of Midtown. *Boisterous* is the word to describe what goes on inside, with the small tables crammed together and speakers pouring out standard Italian music (we actually heard *O Sole Mio*). The decor is pointedly rustic, with rough white plaster, wood trim, and red-checkered tablecloths, though no true Adriatic taverna would cover the tablecloth with paper and give diners Crayolas. But the southern Italian food is up to Manhattan standards—savory gourmet pastas, grilled seafood, and some of the best bruschetta I've ever tasted. Many pasta dishes are available in half orders to suit small appetites, but my three kids shared a pizza with a divinely thin, crispy crust and big splatters of fresh mozzarella, plenty big enough for three. Our waiter was a tad sullen but totally efficient, and everybody in the restaurant seemed delighted to have the kids there, even our 20- and 30-something fellow diners.

800 Ninth Ave. (at 53rd St.). (© 212/956-3976. High chairs, boosters. www.mangiaebevirestaurant.com. Reservations recommended. Main courses $13–$21. AE, DC, DISC, MC, V. Mon–Fri 11:30am–midnight, Sat 11am–midnight, Sun 11pm–midnight. Subway: C, E to 50th St.

Pizza Etiquette

Sometimes it seems there's a narrow little neighborhood pizzeria on every corner in New York City (though, of course, when you really need one you may not find one for blocks). Most kids, even picky eaters, like pizza, and between the tomato sauce and the cheese, it actually makes a fairly well balanced meal. In most neighborhood pizzerias, a single slice of plain cheese pizza will cost between $2 and $3, with higher prices for additional toppings. But the New York preference for huge triangles of thin-crust pizza with satiny thin sauce can make it hard to eat without utensils. The local solution: Fold the triangular slice in half lengthwise, hold it by the thick end, and eat it like a sandwich from the narrow end up. Younger kids may need to have their pizza cut up, which is tricky when you're sawing away on a thin paper plate with a plastic knife. Try slicing it into long triangular strips.

Planet Hollywood *(Overrated* AMERICAN The Times Square location makes this movie-themed restaurant more convenient for tourists than when it was on 57th Street, but it has lost much of its pizzazz. Large display cases in the high-ceilinged rooms feature a thinned-out collection of film memorabilia (with the nationwide proliferation of Planet Hollywoods, there must not have been enough to go around); what's left is mostly costumes and weapons from movies you never heard of. Forget the classics: We're talking action movies and music videos (no surprise, considering that the founders were Bruce Willis, Sylvester Stallone, and Arnold Schwarzenegger). Service is lackluster, and the menu is squarely middle-of-the-road, with hamburgers, steaks, and grilled fish. But on the plus side, the restaurant is big enough that you may not have to wait in line to get in, especially if you go before 8pm, and there's a kids' menu of standards like spaghetti and meatballs, chicken tenders, and pizza. The dramatic central room still has a bit of buzz, though the upstairs bar seems to be where it's happening. No matter where you're seated, tour the room to see all the displays; eventually you'll find something cool.

1540 Broadway (at 45th St.). (*C* 212/333-7827. www.planethollywood.com. Kids' menu, high chairs, boosters. Reservations not accepted. Main courses $13–$26; kids' menu $8. AE, DC, DISC, MC, V. Sun–Thurs 11am–midnight; Fri–Sat 11am–1am. Subway: Subway: N, Q, R, S, W, 1, 2, 3, 7 to 42nd St./Times Sq.

Tony's DiNapoli ITALIAN Heaping platters of satisfying Italian food are served up at this boisterous, good-natured Theater District branch of the Upper East Side favorite (p. 109). The menu offers lots of pasta choices, but also veal, chicken, fish, and Tuscan-style steaks; the waiters really bustle to get folks out in time for their theater curtain.

147 W. 43rd St. (btwn Sixth and Seventh aves.). (*C* 212/221-0100. High chairs, boosters. Reservations recommended. Main courses (serve 2–4 people) $17–$45. AE, DC, DISC, MC, V. Mon–Fri 5pm–midnight; Sat–Sun 2pm–midnight. Subway: B, D, F, V to 42nd St., N, Q, R, S, W, 1, 2, 3, 7 to 42nd St./Times Sq.

Virgil's Real Barbecue *ᴋ* AMERICAN/BARBECUE Your cutlery is wrapped in a maroon hand towel atop the plastic tablecloth, which tells you all you need to know about Virgil's—this is barbecue, and you're expected to get messy eating it. Along with the wood-smoked barbecued specialties, you get sides of down-home stuff like turnip greens, a slaw made with mustard greens, and buttery cornbread, as well as more mainstream choices like french fries and coleslaw for folks whose home isn't below the Mason-Dixon line. Kids who can't handle ribs are offered some safer choices, like grilled cheese and hot dogs. The decor is roadhouse chic, with polished wood paneling, ceiling fans, and a clutter of vintage livestock photos. Casual and friendly as it is, Virgil's has a postmodern self-consciousness—come on, that woodpile inside the front door is not there just to stoke the barbecue. But you might as well play along with the game when the food is this good, this hearty, and this authentic.

152 W. 44th St. (btwn Broadway and Sixth Ave.). © 212/921-9494. www.virgilsbbq.com. Kids' menu, high chairs, boosters. Reservations recommended. Main courses $13–$25; kids' menu $5.95. AE, DC, MC, V. Sun–Mon 11:30am–11pm; Tues–Sat 11:30am–midnight. Subway: N, Q, R, S, W, 1, 2, 3, 7 to 42nd St./Times Sq.

Won Jo KOREAN   Skip the Japanese sushi bar downstairs, and head straight upstairs for do-it-yourself barbecue, Korean-style. Each of the wooden tables has a small built-in grill, and you choose what you want to grill on it—beef, pork, chicken, or mushrooms. The result is food that can be as simple as you want it and an experience that's fun for kids (the same kids who'd be bored to death watching you cook at home). Just make sure they're old enough to refrain from burning themselves on the grill. Other Korean specialties are kimchi (pickled vegetables), a variety of buckwheat noodle dishes, and broiled fish. There are a lot of authentic Korean restaurants in the immediate vicinity, but this one's a standout.

23 W. 32nd St. (btwn Broadway and Fifth Ave.). © 212/695-5815. High chairs. Reservations recommended. Main courses $13–$25. AE, MC, V. Daily 24 hr. Subway: B, D, F, N, Q, R, V, W to 34th St./Herald Sq.

INEXPENSIVE

Angelo's Coal Oven Pizza ✹✹ PIZZA/ITALIAN   Yet another claimant to the title of New York's most authentic pizza. With ties to the Patsy's dynasty, Angelo's (which is actually run by Angelo's nephew, John) is an upscale two-level pizzeria dishing up crisp thin-crust pies as well as calzones, salads, and pastas. The glossy decor features wood trim, green marble-topped tables, and parchment yellow walls; you can't get a single slice of pizza here, but you can get a superb cannoli. I dragged my famished older son here during a shopping trip, and it completely won him over (it helped

---

⌐ *Fun Fact* **Who's Ray & Why Does He Own So Many Pizza Joints?**

The overwhelming majority of pizza places in New York have the name *Ray* somewhere in the title: Famous Ray's, World Famous Ray's, Famous Original Ray's, Original Ray's, Ray's Famous, Ray's House of Pizza, Ray's Real Pizza. Most of these are trying to cash in on the enormous success of **Famous Ray's Pizza of Greenwich Village** (p. 126), where you'll often have to stand in line just to buy a slice to go. (Considering the equal popularity of the Village's **John's of Bleecker Street**, it could just as easily have been that every pizzeria in town was named John's.) Litigation has been useless in trying to convince these lesser Rays to change their names. Just for fun, ask your kids to keep a running log of Ray sightings as they ramble around the city—you may be surprised by how many they'll turn up.

that the service was quick). I still wouldn't rate it as high as John's (see below), but it's an excellent choice for a Midtown meal.

(1) 117 W. 57th St. (btwn Sixth and Seventh aves.). © **212/333-4333**. Subway: F, N, Q, R, W to 57th St./Seventh Ave.; B, D, E to Seventh Ave. (2) 1045 Second Ave. (at 55th St.). © **212/521-3600**. Subway: E, V to Lexington Ave./53rd St. Pizzas $14–$16; pasta courses $7.50–$16. AE, MC, V. Daily 11:30am–11pm.

Comfort Diner ⚘ DINER   This chain diner (p. 123) is a great place to know about if you're visiting the U.N. or staying in one of the Midtown East hotels. The Comfort Diner certainly lives up to its name, with generous portions of satisfying diner classics—mac 'n' cheese, open-faced hot turkey sandwiches, chili, tuna melts, BLTs, and burgers, as well as a substantial breakfast menu served all day. The clean, cheery look is classic, too, with booths and banquettes and a long chrome-trimmed counter with stools; you almost expect the waitress to call you "honey." Service is quick, and kids are welcomed with a joke-laden menu they can color. The kids' menu is wonderfully sensible, with PB&J sandwiches, pancakes, and buttered noodles ("with no green stuff") along with the usual burger/grilled cheese/macaroni and cheese stuff. Somebody running this place must have young children.

214 E. 45th St. (btwn Second and Third aves.). © **212/867-4555**. www.comfortdiner.com. Kids' menu, high chairs, boosters. Reservations not accepted. Main courses $6–$20; kids' menu $5.75–$6.50. AE, DC, DISC, MC, V. Mon–Thurs 7:30am–10pm, Fri 7:30am–11pm, Sat 9am–11pm, Sun 9am–10pm. Subway: S, 4, 5, 6, 7 to 42nd St./Grand Central.

Earl's BARBECUE/SOUTHERN   Handy to both the Empire State Building and the Morgan Library, this roadhouse-style hangout—a sibling of Duke's (p. 123)—is a good stop for barbecue, burgers, fried chicken, and salads, with an easygoing atmosphere that puts young'uns right at home. If you get a hankering for a catfish po' boy or a mess of collard greens, they've got those, too.

560 Third Ave. (at 37th St.) © **212/949-5400**. www.earlsnyc.com. Kids' menu, high chairs, boosters. Reservations required for groups of 6 or more. Main courses $8–$22; kids menu $6.95. AE, MC, V. Sun–Wed noon–11pm; Thurs noon–midnight; Fri–Sat noon–1am. Subway: 6 to 33rd St.

John's Pizza ⚘⚘ PIZZA   As good as all the John's branches are (p. 111 and 127), this one deserves special mention because it fills such a need in the Theater District for a quick, unpretentious, fabulous meal. The simple white-walled space is stunning, too, a two-story dining room converted from a church, with a stained-glass dome in its upper reaches. Pizzas slide out of the brick ovens with incredibly thin, crisp crusts; the satisfying green salads are huge enough for two; and the stuffed homemade rolls are a special treat. They don't take reservations, so expect up to an hour's waiting time in the height of the pre-theater crush, but the food's worth it, and service is prompt enough to get you out before your curtain.

260 W. 44th St. (btwn Broadway and Eighth Ave.). © **212/391-7560**. High chairs, boosters. Reservations not accepted. Pizzas $11–$14, toppings $2–$3; pastas $8.75–$12. AE, DISC, MC, V. Daily 11:30am–11:30pm. Subway: N, Q, R, S, W, 1, 2, 3, 7 to 42nd St./Times Sq.; A, C, E to 42nd St./Port Authority.

Ollie's Noodle Shop CHINESE   The Midtown branch of this popular Upper West Side noodle shop (p. 106) does a brisk business in the Chinese standards Americans are most comfortable with—egg rolls, barbecued spare ribs, wonton soup, sweet-and-sour pork—with a nod to newer favorites like Mandarin noodle soups, a sizzling tofu platter, and a grilled tuna kabob with teriyaki sauce. At these prices, who could complain? Fast, noisy, casual, and dependable, it may work better for families if you can avoid the pre-theater madhouse.

200 W. 44th St. (btwn Broadway and Eighth aves.). ℭ **212/921-5988.** High chairs. Reservations accepted for groups of 6 or more only. Main courses $7–$21. AE, MC, V. Mon–Thurs 11:30am–midnight; Fri–Sat 11:30am–1am; Sun 11:30am–11:30pm. Subway: N, Q, R, S, W, 1, 2, 3, 7 to 42nd St./Times Sq.; A, C, E to 42nd St./Port Authority.

Patsy's Pizzeria PIZZA/ITALIAN   Not far from the Empire State Building, this branch of the great pizzeria chain makes a good lunchtime choice for families, especially in this less-touristy section of Murray Hill. The kids can feast on a small pizza while parents go for satisfying, if not fancy, pastas and salads.

(509 Third Ave. (btwn 34th and 35th sts.). ℭ **212/689-7500.** High chairs, boosters. Reservations not accepted. Pizzas $14–$21; pasta $10–$16. No credit cards. Sun–Thurs noon–11pm; Fri–Sat noon–midnight. Subway: 6 to 33rd St.

Prime Burger 𝒦 *Finds* AMERICAN/BURGERS/DINER   Behind an unprepossessing Midtown coffee shop facade is this amazing slice of the 1950s (Truman Capote mentions it in *Breakfast at Tiffany's* under its former name, Hamburg Heaven). The decor is all chrome and Formica and fake wood paneling, with a long counter and spinning stools. Food is served on melamine plates; drinks, in plastic tumblers; and your order gets to your table unbelievably fast, all of which makes this great for young ones. But what my kids remember best are the seats at the front, which have wooden trays you swing in front of you in lieu of a table; they insist on waiting for these, even if there's room at the counter. The hand-formed hamburgers are small—maybe 5 inches in diameter—which I find a welcome relief from most diners' too-big-to-finish wads of ground beef. French fries are crisp, tasty, and perfectly salted. The menu has many other offerings—chicken in a basket, BLTs, club sandwiches, grilled cheese, omelets, even retro choices like canned peaches with cottage cheese—but burgers— and the seats with the trays—are the main event.

5 E. 51st St. (btwn Madison and Fifth). ℭ **212/759-4729.** Kids' menu, high chairs, boosters. No credit cards. Mon–Sat 7am–7pm; closed Sun. Main courses $4–$8.50; kids menu $5. Subway: 6 to 51st St.

Route 66 𝒦 AMERICAN   The open-road murals and the clutter of artifacts decorating this place give it a nice, breezy, Southwestern feel; the food is contemporary casual stuff, some of it with a Southwestern accent (a little jalapeño thrown in here and there), but nothing too contrived or exotic. Grilled portabello mushroom salad and lobster ravioli all sound good, but somehow we always end up with fat juicy burgers and the Popeye salad (spinach, naturally), or one of the many fluffy omelets. Shakes and smoothies of all flavors are another option we find hard to resist. We like it for Sunday brunch, after soccer games, or before plays at Theatreworks USA. Tables are set close together, and the noise level is . . . well, lively, but everybody seems happy and relaxed.

858 Ninth Ave. (btwn 55th and 56th sts.). ℭ **212/977-7600.** High chairs, boosters. Reservations accepted except for weekend brunch. Breakfast dishes $5–$12; sandwiches, salads, and burgers $5–$13; main courses $12–$25. AE, DC, DISC, MC, V. Daily 7:30am–midnight. Subway: 1, A, B, C, D to 59th St./Columbus Circle.

Stage Deli DELI   Doggedly trying to compete with the Carnegie Deli up the street (p. 116), the Stage Deli promotes more of a theatrical connection; besides the requisite black-and-white glossies of stars plastered all over the place, near the door there's a large display case of Polaroids taken of more recent stars (I use the term loosely for folks like Pauly Shore and David Faustino, along with reliables like Dom DeLuise— who, judging from the numbers of pictures posted in restaurants around town, must've eaten everywhere). On many factors—the overstuffed sandwiches, dill pickles on every table—the Stage Deli competes head-to-head with its rival, and there are some who even claim its corned beef is better; the cheesecake here is smooth as satin and of heroic proportions. The menu is more limited than Carnegie's, sticking mostly to sandwiches. On the whole, the Stage Deli is less atmospheric than the Carnegie, if ambience is what you're after. Lunch and pre-theater hours are crazed, which may mean impatient service, something you don't need when you're with kids.

834 Seventh Ave. (btwn 53rd and 54th sts.). © 212/245-7850. Kids' menu, high chairs. Reservations accepted only for parties of 8 or more. Sandwiches $10–$17; main courses $14–22; kids' menu $6–$11. AE, DISC, MC, V. Daily 6am–2am. Subway: B, D, E to Seventh Ave.

THE CHAIN GANG

Better Burger has two useful Midtown locations for families looking to refuel fast and still eat healthy: 587 Ninth Ave. at 42nd St. (© **212/629-6622**) and 561 Third Ave. at 37th St. (© **212/949-7528**). There's a **Jackson Hole** fairly near the Empire State Building at 521 Third Ave., at 35th Street (© **212/679-3264**); **Lemongrass Grill** also is near the Empire State, at 138 E. 34th Street, between Park Avenue South and Lexington Ave. (© **212/213-3317**). **Dallas BBQ** has a Theater District outpost at 241 W. 42nd St., between Seventh and Eighth aves. (© **212/221-9000**). **Blockhead's Burritos** has three Midtown locations: 499 Third Ave., between 33rd and 34th streets (© **212/213-3332**); 954 Second Ave., between 50th and 51st streets (© **212/750-2020**); and 322 W. 50th St., in the plaza between Eighth and Ninth avenues (© **212/307-7070**).

FOOD COURT

The **Grand Central Dining Concourse** is definitely a smart option, even if you're not taking a train into or out of the city. There's loads of seating under the cool marble arches, and a few of the participating restaurants, like **Two Boots** (pizza and Cajun food), **Zocalo** (trendy Mexican), and **Junior's** (classic deli), have sit-down table-service areas as well as carry-out. The globe-spanning assortment of vendors aren't the usual tired food-court chains but respected New York restaurants coaxed into this high-profile location, so expect to eat well.

5 Chelsea, the Flatiron District & Gramercy Park

MODERATE

Empire Diner DINER   The enduring popularity of this Deco-ish chrome diner, stretching like a waiting limo along Chelsea's far west Tenth Avenue, is no doubt because it stays open until all hours of the morning—the club-happy crew that tramps through here at 5am is a sight to behold. There's only one booster seat in the whole joint, which tells you how little they value family business. But if your kids are older and have developed some restaurant smarts, this is a dependable choice, especially for breakfast. The whimsically footnoted menu is big on omelets, burgers, meatloaf, and the like, which won't threaten a youngster's palate, but you can still find chic dishes like grilled portobello and goat-cheese salad or linguine with smoked salmon. One thing you can be sure of—you'll feel like you're in Manhattan.

210 Tenth Ave. (at 22nd St.). © 212/243-2736. Boosters. Reservations not accepted. Main courses $11–$14; salads and sandwiches $4.75–$14. DISC, MC, V. Daily 24 hr. (except closed Tues 4am–8am). Subway: C, E to 23rd St.

Friend of a Farmer *Finds* AMERICAN   Like a little piece of upstate New York plunked down just south of Gramercy Park, rustic low-ceilinged Friend of a Farmer does the country cafe thing right—fresh-baked breads and muffins, hearty soups, filling casseroles, and potpies on a menu that also offers steaks, roast chicken, pastas, and salads. It's an excellent choice for lunch (dinner gets a little more formal), when young farmhands can choose from macaroni and cheese, chicken fingers, grilled cheese, or scrambled eggs with cheese. Casual and low-key it may be, but the wooden tables are small and set close, service can dawdle a bit, and the lunching neighborhood folks may look askance if rowdy juveniles shatter the usual calm. All the same, I keep coming here to get the kind of home cooking I never have time to do at home.

77 Irving Place (btwn 18th and 19th sts.). © **212/477-2188.** www.friendofafarmer.com. Kids' menu, high chairs, boosters. Reservations not accepted. Lunch $8.75–$13; dinner $10–$20; kids' menu $6.95. AE, DC, DISC, MC, V. Mon–Fri 8am–10pm; Sat–Sun 10am–11pm. Subway: N, Q, R, W, 4, 5, 6 to 14th St.; L to Union Sq.

INEXPENSIVE

Chat 'n' Chew ✦ *Finds* AMERICAN   Are they serious about that name? Of course not, and neither should you be. Something about this cozy place just makes me smile as soon as I walk in the door. Maybe it's the (nudge, nudge) "down-home" decor— red-painted floors, dark-stained wood, farm implements and road signs on the walls— or maybe it's the casual, friendly way they treat you. The menu's fun to read, with names like the Cesar Romero Salad, Uncle Red's Addiction (honey-dipped fried chicken), 110% Veggie Chili, and the Holy Cow (a 9-oz. hamburger); the fried catfish po' boy is especially moist and delicious, and the meatloaf comes with "skin-on" smashed potatoes. Kids get offered a fairly standard menu of favorites, but the names will intrigue them: Flying Saucer Pancakes, for example, or Tarzan Sticks (chicken fingers). Tongue-in-cheek it may be, but it's not too hip to welcome families.

10 E. 16th St. (btwn Fifth Ave. and Union Sq. W.). © **212/243-1616.** www.chatnchew.citysearch.com. Kids' menu, high chairs, boosters. Reservations not accepted. Main courses $8.25–$14; salads and sandwiches $7–$11; kids' menu $3.95 at brunch, $4.95 at lunch and dinner. AE, MC, V. Mon–Fri 11am–midnight; Sat 10am–midnight; Sun 10am–11pm. Subway: N, Q, R, W, 4, 5, 6 to 14th St.; L to Union Sq.

Comfort Diner ✦ DINER   Right next to Madison Square, this satellite of Midtown's Comfort Diner (p. 120) brings diner classics to the Flatiron District. Besides a range of burgers, sandwiches, and salads, there's an all-day breakfast menu and some more creative lunch choices like pecan-crusted catfish or a spicy jerk-chicken wrap. The retro diner look is cheery and sassy, and kids feel at home here.

25 W. 23rd St. (btwn Fifth and Sixth aves.). © **212/741-1010.** www.comfortdiner.com. Kids' menu, high chairs, boosters. Reservations not accepted. Main courses $6–$20; kids' menu $5.75–$6.50. AE, DC, DISC, MC, V. Mon 7:30am–10pm, Tues–Fri 7:30am–11pm; Sat 9am–11pm, Sun 9am–10pm. Subway: 6 to 23rd St.

Duke's BARBECUE/SOUTHERN   Yet another haven for transplanted Southerners, this roadhouse-style hangout believes in huge portions, a steady noise level, and friendliness to kids. Expect a rock-and-roll soundtrack, vintage clutter on the weathered-looking walls, and Tennessee-style barbecue (ribs, chicken, fish), along with down-home favorites like meatloaf, blackened catfish, and fried chicken with cream gravy. The kids' menu consists of your usual burgers, chicken fingers, mac 'n' cheese, and the like, but meals include a drink and a hot fudge sundae, which makes it a decent deal. It doesn't have quite the kitschy sense of fun as Chat 'n' Chew (above), but we thought the food was a half notch above Rodeo Grill (see below), with a similar down-home atmosphere.

99 E. 19th St. (btwn Park Ave. S. and Irving Place). © **212/260-2922.** www.dukesnyc.com. Kids' menu, high chairs, boosters. Reservations required for groups of 6 or more. Main courses $8–$22. kids menu $6.95. AE, MC, V. Sun–Wed noon–11pm; Thurs noon–midnight; Fri–Sat noon–1am. Subway: N, Q, R, W, 4, 5, 6 to 14th St.; L to Union Sq.

Flight 151 AMERICAN   This relaxed neighborhood hangout is a welcome spot for families at lunch and early dinner, before the drinking crowd settles in for the night. Vintage plane memorabilia decorates the space, an added plus for aircraft-loving kids. The food is middle-of-the-road standards—burgers, pastas, crab cake sandwich, steak, chicken Marsala—with chicken fingers, hot dogs, and grilled cheese on the kids' bill of fare. Service is friendly and blessedly tolerant.

151 Eighth Ave. (btwn 17th and 18th sts.). ℂ 212/229-1868. Kids' menu, boosters. Main courses $6–$15; kids' menu $4.95. AE, MC, V. Sun–Thurs 11am–1am; Fri-Sat 11am–2am. Subway: A, C, E, to 14th St.; L to Eighth Ave.

Kelley & Ping PAN-ASIAN   Over in the Gramercy Park area, this low-key noodle shop offers a change of pace for families who've had too many burgers and chicken fingers; like its urban-chic SoHo parent (p. 134), it's sophisticated, but not too snobbish to welcome kids who don't mind a few spices.

340 Third Ave. (at 25th St.). ℂ 212/871-7000. Kids' menu (dinner only), high chairs, boosters. Reservations accepted for parties of 6 or more. Lunch $4–$13; dinner $6.50–$22; kids' menu $7. AE, MC, V. Daily 11:30am–11pm. Subway: 6 to 33rd St.

Patsy's Pizzeria PIZZA/ITALIAN   A few blocks east of Chelsea Piers, this branch of the stalwart pizzeria chain makes a dependable place to refuel, especially for kids who won't go much beyond pizza and plain pasta. A casual meal that won't take too long.

318 W. 23rd St. (btwn Seventh and Eighth aves.). ℂ 646/486-7400. High chairs, boosters. Reservations not accepted. Pizzas $14–$21; pasta $10–$16. No credit cards. Sun–Thurs noon–11pm; Fri–Sat noon–midnight. Subway: C, E, 1 to 23rd St.

Rodeo Grill BARBECUE/TEX-MEX   Someone had a lot of fun decorating this bi-level space, with the feed-grain silo on the upper landing and the huge stuffed bison on a ledge above the bar. The weathered-wood walls are hung with old highway signs and lots of animal horns; Western music twangs, and a basket of taco chips arrives on your table in a flash. Children are a welcome part of the mix—on Monday night they even eat free. The menu is heavy on burgers, steaks, barbecue, fajitas, and burritos, but there are a fair number of vegetarian items and a short list of salads as well. French fries come piled high, which made my kids very happy. I found the salsa and hot sauce pretty acrid, but our family enjoyed our meal nevertheless, which just goes to prove that dining out with kids isn't about eating good food.

375 Third Ave. (at 27th St.). ℂ 212/683-6500. Kids menu, high chairs, boosters. Reservations accepted. Main courses $9–$24; kids menu $3.50. AE, DC, DISC, MC, V. Daily 11:30am–2am. Subway: 6 to 28th St.

AFTERNOON TEA

T Salon ECLECTIC   This cozy bohemian-chic spot is full of artistic types brooding over cups of fragrant brew (herbal as well as caff and no-caff) chosen from a list as long as the wine list at most restaurants. And who knew that tea could come in so many delicious forms? Macrobiotic foods, organic ice creams, shakes, smoothies, all of them tea-based, and all of them quite tasty indeed. It's got the sort of trendy vibe that teenagers eat up.

In the Chelsea Market, 75 Ninth Ave. (btwn 15th and 16th sts.) ℂ 212/358-0506. www.tsalon.com. Boosters. Set-course afternoon tea $18–$50. AE, DC, DISC, MC, V. Daily 7am–1am. Subway: A, C, E to 14th St.

FOOD COURT

Definitely the coolest place to eat in Chelsea is at the **Chelsea Market,** 75 Ninth Ave., between 15th and 16th streets (entrance also on Tenth Ave.), a rambling series of food shops set in a rehabbed Nabisco factory. Older kids with a sense of style will appreciate the industrial chic look, with scrubbed brick walls, exposed pipes, and utilitarian light fixtures; the focal point is a ripped-open water main gushing into a crumbling brick cavity in the floor. Among fish stores and produce stalls, you'll find hip little takeout eateries like Amy's Bread, Sarabeth's Bakery, Fat Witch Bakery, Eleni's Cookies, and Hale and Hearty Soups, all with tiny cafe tables nearby where you can enjoy the food.

THE CHAIN GANG

There's a branch of **Better Burger** handy at 178 Eighth Ave., at 19th St. (℃ **212/989-6688**) ; a similar healthy fast-burger chain, **New York Burger Co.,** has two Chelsea locations, at 303 Park Ave. South, between 23rd and 24th sts. (℃ **212/254-2727**), and 678 Sixth Ave., between 21st and 22nd sts. (℃ **212/229-1404**). The **Dallas BBQ** at Eighth Avenue and 23rd Street (261 Eighth Ave.; ℃ **212/462-0001**) is good to know about in a pinch.

6 Greenwich Village

EXPENSIVE

Jekyll & Hyde Pub AMERICAN   The original outpost of this horror-themed restaurant, the Village's Jekyll & Hyde is slightly more casual than the Midtown spot (p. 114), in a dining room that opens right onto Seventh Avenue South, and waiting in line is less of a factor here. The menu is slightly different but still features a fairly standard range of burgers, salads, pizza, pasta, fish, and steaks, gussied up with hokey names. And it has its own repertoire of spooky special effects, with an ongoing floor show that definitely goes for corny punch lines; on weekends an extra $1.50 per person is tacked on as an entertainment fee. Boasting an extensive range of international beers, plus exotic drinking vessels to quaff your brew from, Jekyll & Hyde shoots for an adult crowd, which is all the more reason why adolescents think it's cool.

91 Seventh Ave. S. (btwn Barrow and W. 4th sts.). ℃ **212/989-7701.** www.jekyllandhydeclub.com. Kids' menu, boosters. Reservations accepted. Sandwiches $13–$17; main courses $15–$19; kids' menu $11. AE, DC, DISC, V. Sun–Thurs noon–2am; Fri–Sat noon–4am. Subway: 1, 9 to Christopher St./Sheridan Sq.

MODERATE

Arturo's Restaurant-Pizzeria ITALIAN/PIZZA   Crowded, dimly lit, and busy, this vintage hangout right on the border between the Village and SoHo—near the Italian part of the West Village, around Father Demo Square—serves some very good thin-crust pizzas; they're slung on your table fresh from a coal-fired oven, so hot the mozzarella could burn the roof of your mouth. You can get various pasta dishes, too (go for the baked stuff like ziti and lasagna), or even surf and turf, though that seems a bit beside the point here: Pizzas are the thing to order. Several notches above storefront by-the-slice pizzerias, it's still a casual sort of place where drinks come in plastic tumblers and side salads come in plastic fake-wood bowls, which bodes well if you've got kids in tow. You may have to wait in line, though, and at particularly frantic mealtimes, it can be hard to get your waiter's attention. There's live jazz every night, which may make waiting easier. Arturo's is certainly as authentic as any place officially in Little Italy—and a good deal less touristy.

106 W. Houston St. (at Thompson St.). ℃ **212/677-3820.** High chairs, boosters. Reservations not accepted on weekends. Pizzas $14 and up; main courses $16–$24. AE, DC, MC, V. Mon–Thurs 4pm–1am; Fri–Sat 4pm–2am; Sun 3pm–midnight. Subway: 1 to Houston St.

Cowgirl Hall of Fame ☞ TEX-MEX   Think the Old West motif of this West Village theme spot is corny? You're darn tootin' it's corny, and that's why kids get into it. Cowboy hats, boots, and lassos adorn the walls; steer horns poke from the mirrors and antlers from the chandeliers; younger customers are handed crayons to color a paper Indian headdress. Passable barbecue, hearty chili, and a mess of fried catfish are included in the menu round-up; kids' options feature some offbeat items such as corn dogs and Frito pie along with the obligatory chicken fingers.

519 Hudson St. (at 10th St.). ☎ 212/633-1133. Kids' menu, high chairs, boosters. Reservations recommended. Lunch entrees $7.95–$12; dinner entrees $11–$18; kids' menu $4.50–$6.25. MC, V. Mon–Fri 11am–midnight, Sat 10am–midnight, Sun 11am–11pm. Subway: 1 to Christopher St./Sheridan Sq.

NoHo Star ☞ AMERICAN/CHINESE   Just a block above Houston Street, this airy loftlike space has a very SoHo-ish feel, with brightly painted columns and an arty tile mural of a newspaper (the fictional NoHo Star). Burgers, pastas, and very good omelets are winners for lunch and brunch; the dinner menu goes upscale with items like seared sea scallops, shrimp with string beans, a top-drawer Caesar salad, and a range of superb, zestfully spiced Chinese dishes. The best time to come, though, is at breakfast, when it's quiet and never crowded—kids can dive into a stack of pancakes while parents nurse a cup of good coffee. The atmosphere is always relaxed and relaxing, and the waiters are totally friendly to kids.

330 Lafayette St. (at Bleecker St.). ☎ 212/925-0070. Boosters. Reservations not accepted. Breakfast $6–$12; lunch and dinner $16–$24. AE, DC, DISC, MC, V. Mon–Fri 8am–midnight; Sat–Sun 10:30am–midnight. Subway: 6 to Bleecker St.

INEXPENSIVE

Corner Bistro *Finds* BURGERS   Here are your choices: hamburger, cheeseburger, bacon cheeseburger, or chicken sandwich; only recently have they expanded the menu to include grilled cheese, chili, and BLT. No doubt about it, this place is a bar, and a dark and smoky one at that, the kind where people huddle in wooden booths and initials have been carved into the tabletops. Which is precisely why some kids will think it's totally cool to come here; others will simply dig into the thick, juicy burgers and piles of fine fries. And if that's not enough, there's a pretty darn good jukebox. Though the Corner Bistro can get full of drinkers later in the night, at midday or in the early evening, it's wonderfully mellow, and kids aren't out of place.

331 W. 4th St. (btwn Jane St. and Eighth Ave.). ☎ 212/242-9502. Reservations not accepted. Main courses $2.75–$5.75. No credit cards. Daily 11:30am–4am. Subway: A, C, E, 1, 2, 3, 9 to 14th St.; L to Eighth Ave.

Elephant and Castle AMERICAN   Like a holdover from the 1970s, this mellow-eats parlor continues to churn out good burgers and crepes, fluffy omelets, and other grub kids will generally accept, while parents can get a little more gourmet with stuff like smoked chicken salad or a roasted portobello-mushroom sandwich. A cheery, well-lit space, it's best for leisurely brunches; bring a few toys for your offspring and a copy of the Sunday *Times* for you to browse through. Though it isn't inherently child-oriented, E&C is informal and friendly enough that families blend right in.

68 Greenwich Ave. (at 11th St.). ☎ 212/243-1400. Boosters. Reservations not accepted. Main courses $6.75–$16. AE, DC, DISC, MC, V. Mon–Fri 8:30am–midnight; Sat–Sun 10am–midnight. Subway: 1, 2, 3 to 14th St.; L to Sixth Ave.

Famous Ray's Pizza of Greenwich Village PIZZA   Definitely the most renowned corner pizzeria in town is Famous Ray's—the Ray's that all those other ersatz Ray's Pizzas around town are hoping you'll confuse them with. Set right in the midst of the Village's prettiest townhouse streets, Ray's is easy to spot by the lines snaking out onto the sidewalk, with all sorts of people hungry for a slice to go. Many pizza lovers rave about the extra-cheese pizza here; I find it a bit excessive, but I do like the plain pizza's chewy crust and tangy sauce. All sorts of designer toppings are also available—pesto, eggplant, lettuce, even pineapple and ham (say it ain't so, Ray!)—but why mess around with a classic?

465 Sixth Ave. (at 11th St.). ℂ 212/243-2253. Reservations not accepted. Pizza $2.25 (slice), $15 (pie). AE, DC, DISC, MC, V. Sun–Thurs 11am–2am; Fri–Sat 11am–3am. Subway: F, V to 14th St.; L to Sixth Ave.; A, B, C, D, E, F, V to W. 4th St.

Harry's Burritos *Value* MEXICAN   Casual, cheap, and often crowded, Harry's is the kind of homey little Village student joint everyone drifts into sooner or later. The burritos can be truly gargantuan; the menu also offers salads and fish as well as the more traditional quesadillas, tacos, and sizzling fajitas. Try the chicken tortilla pie, a layered casserole that's sort of a Mexican lasagna—mouth-watering. Bring a hearty appetite.

76 W. 3rd St. (at Thompson St.). ℂ 212/260-5588. Kids' menu, high chairs. Main courses $4.25–$12; kids' menu $4.95. AE, MC, V. Mon–Sat 11am–midnight; Sun 1–8:30pm. Subway: 1, 2, 3 to 14th St.; L to Sixth Ave.

Johnny Rockets BURGERS   As chains go, this is one that doesn't feel plastic: The 1950s soda shoppe look is executed smartly, with lots of gleaming white tile and chrome, and the menu really works for kids. You get perfectly fine burgers, creamy milkshakes, good fries that aren't too greasy—and get this, a jukebox at every table (though our waiter confessed to me that they don't always work, and it's a pain to find mechanics who can fix them). With $4–$5.25 kids' meals and menus to color, this is a good bet to please most kids. The staff seems cheerful enough, at least at lunchtime, and the NYU crowd hasn't taken over (not grungy enough for students, I suppose, and the music on the jukes is too old-fashioned).

42 E. 8th St. (at Greene St.). ℂ 212/253-8175. Kids' menu, high chairs, boosters. Burgers $5.50–$7.50. AE, DC, DISC, MC, V. Daily 10:30am–midnight. Subway: N, R, W to 8th St./NYU; 6 to Astor Place.

John's of Bleecker Street *Finds* PIZZA   This is the kind of place that's often described as having no ambience, when in fact it has plenty—classic no-frills pizzeria ambience, with harsh lighting, worn linoleum, cheap paneling, bare wooden booths, and an open view of the brick ovens where the pizzas are baked. Folks in the Village always lament that John's doesn't sell pizza by the slice, but families should have no problem polishing off a whole pie. The crust is crunchy thin, with savory tomato sauce, bubbly melted mozzarella, and a host of fresh toppings to pick among (nothing too trendy, though). After eating at John's, you can say you've truly sampled New York pizza at its best.

278 Bleecker St. (btwn Seventh Ave. and Morton St.). ℂ 212/243-1680. Reservations not accepted. Pizzas $12–$23; pasta $5.50–$8. No credit cards. Mon–Sat 11:30am–midnight; Sun noon–midnight. Subway: 1, 9 to Christopher St./Sheridan Sq.

Patsy's Pizzeria PIZZA/ITALIAN   On this restaurant strip just north of the New York University campus, this branch of the Patsy's chain finally gives Village pizza lovers a good alternative if their legs are too tired to walk west to the original John's Pizza on Bleecker Street (see above). Boasts a classic pizzeria look and an informal atmosphere that works great with kids.

67 University Place (btwn 10th and 11th sts.). ℂ 212/533-3500. High chairs, boosters. Pizzas $14–$21; pasta $10–$16. No credit cards. Sun–Thurs 11:30am–11pm; Fri–Sat 11:30am–midnight. Subway: N, R to 8th St./NYU; N, Q, R, W, 4, 5, 6 to 14th St.; L to Union Sq.

Peanut Butter & Co. *Finds* AMERICAN Born of owner Lee Zalben's obsession, this is a quirky little store/restaurant that serves mostly, you guessed it, peanut butter. Peanut butter memorabilia decorates the golden-hued little cafe, and jars of the house brand are for sale, along with jam and marshmallow Fluff and other suitable accompaniments. The menu's a hoot, with items like Ants on a Log (a celery stalk coated with peanut butter and raisins), your traditional Fluffernutters, and the Elvis (grilled peanut butter sandwich with bananas and honey). If you really must, you can also get a grilled cheese, a tuna-fish sandwich, or a baloney sandwich, you spoilsport you. But the peanut butter is superb, freshly ground from high-quality peanuts with only enough oil to make it spreadable, just like Mom used to make (honest, my mom used to make it just like this, in her Waring blender). Every sandwich is served with potato chips and carrot sticks, and they'll even cut off the crusts for you. You should be drinking milk with your PB&J, but Welch's grape juice is also available, as are fountain treats such as egg creams and milkshakes. And for dessert, what else but peanut butter cookies or chocolate peanut butter pie?

240 Sullivan St. (btwn Bleecker and W. 3rd sts.). ℂ 212/677-3995. www.peanutbutterco.com. Kids' menu, high chairs, boosters. Sandwiches $5–$9. AE, DC, DISC, MC, V. Sun–Thurs 11am–9pm; Fri–Sat 11am–10pm. Subway: A, B, C, D, E, F, V to W. 4th St.

Pizza Box *Value* PIZZA The hippielike scruffiness of this stretch of Bleecker Street reminds you that you're close to a major university campus (NYU), but among the cheap ethnic hole-in-the-walls lies this pleasant and unpretentious pizza spot, worth noting for its restful back garden, open in fair weather. The pizza is perfectly fine, though connoisseurs may want to head west to John's (see above). At least it does have waiter service at tables, unlike Famous Ray's (see above). If you've OD'd on pizza, but your child is clamoring for it, you can indulge him or her here while you have pasta or a hero and enjoy the garden.

176 Bleecker St. (btwn MacDougal and Sullivan sts.). ℂ 212/979-0823. Reservations not accepted. Pizza $2.50 (slice), $15 (pie). No credit cards. Daily 11am–midnight. Subway: A, B, C, D, E, F, V to W. 4th St.

ICE CREAM & SWEETS

The West Village has a branch of New England's top ice cream vendor, **Emack & Bolio's,** 56 Seventh Ave., at 14th Street (ℂ 212/727-1198), starring flavors like grasshopper pie, cosmic crunch, and vanilla bean speck. Pastry hounds should find happiness on the traditional Italian strip of Bleecker Street between Sixth and Seventh avenues, where next-door neighbors **Rocco's** (243 Bleecker St.; ℂ 212/242-6031) and **Pasticceria Bruno** (245 Bleecker St.; ℂ 212/242-4959) prove that competition can be very healthy. Decide the local debate over which is better: Get a cannoli from one and a napoleon from the other, and compare for yourself.

THE CHAIN GANG

The first **Pizzeria Uno** branch in the city was the bustling one at 391 Sixth Ave., at 8th Street (ℂ 212/242-5230). There are two **Lemongrass Grills** in the Village, one at 9 E. 13th St. between 5th Ave. and University Pl., in the Japanese Restaurant Uzu (ℂ 646/486-7313), and another at 37 Barrow Street, between Bleecker and Bedford streets (ℂ 212/242-0606).

7 The East Village

MODERATE

Cloister Café CONTINENTAL   The main reason to come here is for the court-yard garden, with umbrella-shaded tables set out on crooked paving stones and a tiny fountain trying its best to gurgle. The menu's rather predictable fare runs a tired range from salads (the avocado salad isn't bad) to pastas (cheese ravioli, linguine with clam sauce) to veal, chicken, and seafood dishes (grilled red snapper, shrimp scampi). The lemonade is refreshingly sour; kids may want to add their own sugar. Service can be slapdash at times, but the garden is a treat, day or night, and things are plenty casual enough to come here with kids.

238 E. 9th St. (btwn Second and Third aves.). ℭ 212/777-9128. Reservations accepted. Main courses $6–$28. MC, V. Daily 11am–midnight. Subway: 6 to Astor Place.

Old Devil Moon ECLECTIC/SOUTHERN   The junk-shop decor of this urban Love Shack is a little out of hand, though it's often too dark inside to see all the stuff on the walls. Younger kids may be overwhelmed, but for preteen would-be hipsters and for anyone who appreciates Southern home cooking, it's a worthy stop. Not that this is necessarily traditional Southern cooking—not with items like chicken fried tofu on the menu. But hey, you're in the East Village, so get over it. The catfish, jerk chicken, and po' boy sandwiches are plenty satisfying, and the jambalaya and greens 'n' beans taste like they've been simmering on the stove for hours, swapping their juices deliciously around. Best of all are the pies for dessert (the pecan pie will require several days of penance afterward). Come here on weekends, too, for breakfasts of country ham, grits, and fresh-baked biscuits. Whoo-*eee!*

511 E. 12th St. (btwn Ave. A and Ave. B). ℭ 212/475-4357. Boosters. Reservations recommended. Main courses $9–$20. AE, MC, V. Mon–Thurs 5–11pm, Fri 5pm–midnight; Sat 10am–midnight; Sun 10am–11pm. Subway: L to First Ave.

Telephone Bar & Grill ℱ AMERICAN/BRITISH   Instead of East Village grunge, what you get here is an ersatz British pub, as signaled by the red phone box out front. This place has been around for years, serving Stuyvesant Square squares more than Tompkins Square hipsters; its very middle-of-the-roadness is the key to its survival. There are several sidewalk tables, or you can go inside for brick-walled coziness. The shepherd's pie and the fish and chips are quite decent, and you'll get them on the kids' menu as well, along with hamburgers and grilled cheese sandwiches. The rest of the adult menu covers all the American bases, from salads to burgers to steaks and seafood. Weekend brunch is popular here; the restaurant also serves a proper Irish breakfast every morning, with oatmeal and Irish bacon.

149 Second Ave. (btwn 9th and 10th sts.). ℭ 212/529-5000. www.telebar.com. Kids' menu, high chairs. Lunch $5–$20; dinner $11–$20. AE, DC, MC, V. Mon–Thurs 11:30am–midnight; Fri–Sat 11:30am–1:30am; Sun 10:30–midnight. Subway: 6 to Astor Place; N, Q, R, W, 4, 5, 6 to 14th St.; L to Union Sq.

INEXPENSIVE

Benny's Burritos ℱalue MEXICAN   Monster-size burritos and other hearty, healthy Mexican fare are dished up at this East Village branch of the Greenwich Village Harry's (p. 105).

93 Ave. A (at E. 6th St.). ℭ 212/254-2054. Boosters. Reservations not accepted. Main courses $4.25–$20; kids' menu $4.95. AE, MC, DISC, V. Daily 11am–midnight. Subway: 6 to Astor Place.

Hot Dog!

The ubiquity of the New York hot dog may be due to the century-old Coney Island frankfurter shrine of **Nathan's Famous,** 1310 Surf Ave., Brooklyn (✆ **718/946-2202**), site of the annual world hot-dog-eating contest. But a recent crop of East Village hot-dog emporiums have been standing Nathan's franks on their ends. **Dawgs on Park,** 178 E. 7th St., near Avenue B (✆ **212/598-0667**), has a dog-centric theme, posting photos of customers' dogs; its signature offering is the deep-fried chili dog (beef, turkey, or tofu franks). Its rival is **Crif Dogs,** 113 St. Mark's Place, between First Avenue and Avenue A (✆ **212/614-2728**), which has wacky slogans scrawled on the walls and offers over-the-top treats like a deep-fried bacon-wrapped hot dog topped with avocado and jalapeños. The frankfurters dished out at Chelsea's **F&B,** 269 W. 23rd St., between Seventh and Eight avenues (✆ **646/486-4441**), put a European spin on the standard hot dog; a few dollars will buy you beignets and pommes frites along with specialties like the Great Dane (a hot dog with remoulade, roasted onions, and cucumber slices).

Uptown, your hot doggery choices are more limited and less retro-chic. **Gray's Papaya,** 2090 Broadway, at 72nd Street (✆ **212/799-0243**), may not tempt youngsters with its milky, sweet, refreshing papaya juice (there's also fruit punch and soda), but you can't complain about the plump, succulent hot dogs, which still cost about a buck—an absurdly quick and cheap meal, which you can eat stand-up at the counter or on the go as you walk on down the street. Gray's Papaya's Upper East Side counterpart is **Papaya King,** at the northwest corner of 86th Street and Third Avenue (✆ **212/369-0648**).

Kelley & Ping PAN-ASIAN   This cafeteria-style noodle shop, a branch of the original SoHo Kelley & Ping's, is a smart lunchtime option in the East Village—casual and hip, with noodles as spicy (or not) as you want them.

325 Bowery (at 2nd St.) ✆ 212/475-8600. Kids' menu (dinner only), high chairs, boosters. Reservations accepted for parties of 6 or more. Lunch $4–$13; dinner $6.50–$22; kids' menu $7. AE, MC, V. Daily 11:30am–11pm. Subway: 6 to Bleecker St.

Mitali East INDIAN   Though there are good Indian restaurants all around Manhattan, my kids get a special kick out of visiting the "Little India" on East Sixth Street, where several mostly Bengali restaurants compete side by side for diners' attention. On a summer night, when waiters stand outside the lit-up entrances beckoning customers inside, there's a definite bazaarlike flavor to the street. One of the most dependable choices is Mitali East, a cozy downstairs spot where Indian fabrics drape the walls, a water fountain splashes at the back of the dining room, and recorded sitar and raga music weaves through the air. Reliable choices includes the spicy curries, *murgha tikka* (boneless chicken pieces cooked in a tandoori oven), *biryanis* (meats and vegetables mixed with rice), and masalas. The *papadoms* (thin, crisp lentil wafers) are downright addictive. Because this is Bengali cooking, the menu includes beef, but no pork, with plenty of seafood and vegetarian alternatives. Service is leisurely, the atmosphere low-lit and hushed, yet somehow it's kid-friendly, too, and a pleasant place to chill.

Kosher Restaurants

Even if you don't maintain a kosher diet, New York offers the best kosher family dining outside of Israel. The important thing to remember is that a kosher restaurant will be meat, dairy, or pareve (*pareve* means the food doesn't contain either meat or dairy products)—you won't find a cheese-burger or chicken parmigiana on any menu unless either the meat or the cheese is really an imitated product. This may sound restricting, but restaurants have learned to make do and become extremely creative in the process.

In Midtown, **Kosher Delight,** 1365 Broadway, at 36th Street (*©* **212/563-3366; meat**), is the kosher answer to McDonald's and Burger King. Grilled burgers and chicken sandwiches are standard, but you can also choose from a small Chinese menu and Middle Eastern specialties like falafel. Kosher Delight also has free delivery to any location in Manhattan (although it's not guaranteed your food will arrive hot or within a reasonable amount of time). The **Great American Health Bar,** 35 W. 57th St., between Fifth and Sixth avenues (*©* **212/355-5177; dairy**), proves that healthy food doesn't have to be boring and flavorless, offering a varied menu from salads to veg-etarian chili to pastas. There are wonderful fresh-fruit health shakes blended with milk and yogurt, and kids may get a kick out of the pita pizza—tomato sauce, melted cheese, and vegetables baked on top of pita bread. Unlike most of these restaurants, the Health Bar also serves breakfast, opening at 8am; it's also the only one of these restaurants that doesn't close Friday night and Saturday for the Sabbath.

The West Side's popular **Dougie's BBQ and Grill,** 222 W. 72nd St., between Broadway and West End Avenue (*©* **212/724-2222; meat**), offers crayons on all tables to keep kids occupied while they're waiting for their food. The service is fast-paced and friendly. Burgers and hot dogs are popular items, but the ribs and pasta dishes shouldn't be passed up.

Note: Because of the Sabbath, most kosher restaurants vary their hours on Friday and Saturday, depending on when sundown is on Friday night and when the Sabbath ends on Saturday night. (Some simply close all day Fri.) Call ahead to be sure when they'll be open if you plan to dine on Fri-day or Saturday.

334 E. 6th St. (btwn First and Second aves.). *©* 212/533-2508. Main courses $7.75–$20. AE, DC, MC, V. Reserva-tions accepted. Daily noon–midnight. Subway: 6 to Astor Place; F, V to Lower East Side/Second Ave.

Pommes Frites FRENCH   Not really a restaurant but a narrow storefront takeout joint with a bill of fare that's pretty straightforward: nothing but thin, crispy, Belgian-style french fries with all manner of sauces to dip them into. Considering that my chil-dren often eat nothing but fries anyway at sit-down restaurants, this isn't such a bad option for a lunchtime pit stop.

123 Second Ave. (at 9th St.). *©* 212/674-1234. French fries $4–$7.50. No credit cards. Sun–Thurs 11am–1am; Fri–Sat 11am–3:30am. Subway: 6 to Astor Place.

Two Boots ⚘ PIZZA/CAJUN/ITALIAN This dandy East Village restaurant couldn't be better for kids. To start, you've got witty junk-shop decor (strings of Christmas lights shaped like red chiles, old movie posters, and a pair of cowboy boots hanging on a pink wall); then when you're seated, the kids are handed coloring books. You know these people are used to dealing with kids when you see that the milk is served in plastic cups; grown-ups get their drinks in glass mugs shaped like boots, which our boys find hilarious. The service can be pretty casual, but the waitresses relate to kids instantly, which always seems to make my children behave better. For kids, probably the most popular choice is the Pizza Face, an individual-sized pizza with vegetables arranged to form eyes, nose, and grin. Bigger pizzas are served on cake stands, which is also a kick. I opt for a spicy Cajun sandwich on good chewy bread, a po' boy—the kind of food I can't normally get in the kinds of restaurants my kids like. We all walk out with smiles on our faces.

(1) 37 Ave. A (at 2nd St.). ℂ **212/254-1919.** High chairs, boosters. Reservations accepted for groups of 6 or more only. Main courses $9–$13; pizzas $6–$22. AE, DISC, MC, V. Daily 11:30am–12:30am. Subway: F, V to Lower East Side/Second Ave. (2) 74 Bleecker St. (btwn Broadway and Crosby St.). ℂ **212/777-1033.** Subway: B, D, F, V to Broadway/Lafayette St. (3) 200 W. 11th St. (at Seventh Ave.) ℂ **212/633-9096.** Subway: 1 to Christopher St./Sheridan Sq.

ICE CREAM & SWEETS

Two family-owned Italian pastry shops have held on in the East Village for a century, vestiges of an earlier immigrant community—and there's a reason they've survived. The better-known one is **Veniero's,** 342 E. 11th St., between First and Second avenues (ℂ **212/674-7070;** www.venierospastry.com), a spiffed-up dessert cafe that's open until midnight to accommodate crowds of people craving after-dinner delights from cakes to cookies to cannoli, plus cappuccino and espresso that put Starbucks to shame. With kids, come in the afternoon, when you'll have no trouble getting a table. A more relaxed local crowd skips the lines at Veniero's and drifts over to **DeRobertis Pasticceria,** 176 First Ave., between 10th and 11th streets (ℂ **212/674-7137**), which gives its around-the-corner neighbor a run for its money, serving creamy cannoli and cheesecake along with anise cookies and fruit tarts. The back room, with its pressed-tin ceiling and small marble tables, feels as authentic as any place in Little Italy. It shuts down completely for 2 weeks in July—hey, a family's got to take a vacation.

THE CHAIN GANG

Beatniks must be turning in their graves to see St. Mark's Place, that bastion of bohemian hipness, invaded by **Dallas BBQ** at 132 Second Ave. (ℂ **212/777-5574**). Next thing you know, **Pizzeria Uno** will be moving in around the corner . . . oops, it already has, at 55 Third Ave., between 10th and 11th streets (ℂ **212/995-9668**).

8 SoHo and Little Italy

EXPENSIVE

Sal Anthony's SPQR ITALIAN Lots of bustle and brightness define this big, high-ceilinged dining hall, where people on all sides are happily digging into Italian food: High-gloss as it is, you can tuck your napkin into your collar here with no fear. Despite the brick walls and potted plants, the look is modern, not vintage trattoria. But what it lacks in coziness and atmosphere, it more than makes up in efficiency, big portions, and party spirits; it seems there are always a few large tables occupied by extended families, bonding over fusilli and linguine. Pastas are consistently good, as are the hearty meat dishes, especially the macho veal chop. A first-rate place to celebrate a special family event.

133 Mulberry St. (btwn Grand and Hester sts.). ℂ 212/925-3120. www.salanthonys.com. High chairs, boosters. Reservations recommended. 2-course fixed-price lunch $15–$17; fixed-price dinner $30 or $44; dinner entrees $12–$35. AE, MC, V. Sun–Thurs noon–11pm; Fri–Sat noon–midnight. Subway: N, Q, R, W, 6 to Canal St.

MODERATE

Angelo's of Mulberry Street ITALIAN   This crowded, crowd-pleasing Little Italy favorite, which has been around since 1902, turns out an incredibly long list of southern Italian pasta dishes with zestful flavor, most around $13. Make a reservation so you won't get stuck in the line of tourists waiting to get in, but don't be dissuaded by the place's low-brow popularity—this is Little Italy, after all, where tourists flock to eat, and no restaurant here that's any good would be without a line. Order anything with garlic, or anything with tomato sauce. If your kids like their pasta plain, as mine do, even they'll benefit from the fresh homemade quality of the food.

146 Mulberry St. (btwn Grand and Hester sts.). ℂ 212/966-1277. Sassy seats. Reservations recommended. Main courses $12–$17. AE, DC, MC, V. Tues–Thurs and Sun noon–11:30pm; Fri noon–12:30am; Sat noon–1am; closed Mon. Subway: N, Q, R, W, 6 to Canal St.

Caffé Napoli ITALIAN   Though there's a string of more renowned "fine-dining" restaurants to the north on Mulberry Street, for a leisurely dinner out with family I'd rather go to a place like Caffé Napoli and its annex, **Trattoria Canta Napoli** (ℂ 212/226-8705). The food is upscale enough to feel like a treat, with seafood alongside the pasta dishes (Naples is a seaport, remember); specialties include the stuffed veal chop and the pasta malefemmina. The softly lit dining room has been tastefully decorated—Neapolitan pictures and artifacts are strewn about, but there's no attempt to make it look like "the Old Country." Diners are encouraged to linger over their meals; waiters are attentive but not intrusive. And families are definitely welcome—they'll cheerfully do half portions of pasta for kids.

191 Hester St. (at Mulberry St.). ℂ 212/226-8705. High chairs. Reservations not accepted. Lunch prix fixe $7.50 or $13; dinner entrees $9–$33. AE, DC, DISC, MC, V. Daily 11am–2am. Subway: N, Q, R, W, 6 to Canal St.

INEXPENSIVE

Fanelli's Finds AMERICAN   This 19th-century saloon claims to be the second-oldest drinking spot in the city, being descended from a grocery store that opened on this site in 1847 and soon had a good side business as a "porter shop" (saloon); it became a speakeasy after Michael Fanelli bought it in 1922. Atmospheric Fanelli's still has the requisite carved mahogany bar, pressed-tin ceilings, beery smell, and filtered light, but the fare is refreshingly simple pub grub—burgers, omelets, quiches, pastas, fried chicken, shepherd's pie. Families gravitate to the back room, which is a little sunnier and quieter, for casual lunches and early dinner; later on, it might be hard to compete with the drinking scene. The service is friendly and laissez-faire.

94 Prince St. (at Mercer St.). ℂ 212/226-9412. Reservations not accepted. Main courses $8–$15. AE, MC, V. Sun–Thurs 10am–12:30am; Fri–Sat 10am–2am. Subway: N, R, W to Prince St.

Il Fornaio Value PIZZA   The sign outside is explicit: KIDS WELCOME. And it goes without saying, no one will get too upset about spills or crying or food left on the plate in this unpretentious cafe. It's small enough that you can't miss the shouted exchanges between waiters and cooks, but the pizza here has a longstanding reputation for excellence, so don't be surprised if you have to wait a few minutes for a table on a weekend.

(And once you get in, don't be startled if you're hustled back out again fairly soon—not a bad thing if you're with kids.) Pizza, pasta, calzones, and muffalettas—the menu has many kid-friendly choices, so who needs a chicken-fingers-and-burgers kids' menu?

132A Mulberry St. (btwn Canal and Hester sts.). ℂ 212/226-8306. Reservations recommended. Main courses $7–$21. AE, DC, DISC, MC, V. Daily 11:30am–10:30pm. Subway: N, Q, R, W, 6 to Canal St.

Kelley & Ping ℛ PAN-ASIAN   With its pressed-tin ceiling and wooden factory floor, Kelley & Ping looks very SoHo, but its friendliness to kids is unusual in this hyper-urban-chic neighborhood. It started out as an Asian grocery store but soon added an open kitchen in the center of the room; there are still stocks of bottled sauces and woks for sale along the walls. The noodles, stir-fries, and grilled meats (Vietnamese crispy duck, Thai grilled shrimp) go down well with children, though some dishes can be superspicy—ask for your waiter's guidance. There are also branches in the East Village (p. 130) and Gramercy Park (p. 124).

127 Greene St. (btwn Houston and Prince sts.). ℂ 212/228-1212. Kids' menu (dinner only), high chairs, boosters. Reservations accepted for parties of 6 or more. Lunch $4–$13; dinner $6.50–$22; kids' menu $7. AE, MC, V. Daily 11:30am–11pm Subway: N, R, W to Prince St.; B, D, F, V to Broadway/Lafayette St.

Lombardi's Pizza PIZZA   Claiming to be a resurrection of New York's first pizza restaurant, which opened at 53 Spring St. in 1905—and where all the other pizza maestros learned their trade—the new Lombardi's is owned by a grandson of the original Gennaro Lombardi, and it does have an authentic coal oven, taken over from an old bakery. It's a bit far north from the main Little Italy strip along Mulberry Street, but the look is nice and atmospheric, with the obligatory red-checkered tablecloths, brick walls, and white tiled floor. Its wonderful pizzas more than hold their own among the top contenders (John's, Patsy's, Angelo's), with lightly charred thin crusts and totally fresh ingredients. The clam pie is so good that it actually justifies the weird idea of putting seafood on a pizza. Don't expect to just pick up a slice: Sit your family down in a booth, and apply yourselves to consuming a whole pie.

32 Spring St. (btwn Mott and Mulberry sts.). ℂ 212/941-7994. Boosters. Reservations accepted for parties of 6 or more. Pizzas $13–$16. No credit cards. Mon–Thurs 11:30am–11pm; Fri–Sat 11:30am–midnight; Sun 11:30am–10pm. Subway: 6 to Spring St.

Vesuvio Bakery Café *Finds* AMERICAN   When SoHo starts feeling too trendy for words, here's a refuge: a tiny brick-walled cafe at the western edge of the artsy district where you can rest your feet briefly at one of the few tiny tables while fortifying yourself with a salad, wrap, panini, muffin, or omelet. You'll be in and out fast, with a minimum of fuss. The bakery part has been here since the 1920s, and it's still owned by the same family.

160 Prince St. (btwn W. Broadway and Thompson St.). ℂ 212/925-8248. Reservations not accepted. Sandwiches: $7–$8.50. No credit cards. Sun–Thurs 8am–7pm; Fri–Sat 8am–11PM. Subway: N, R, W to Prince St.

ICE CREAM & SWEETS

In the heart of shrinking Little Italy, a pair of venerable pastry shops still convey the flavor of the old neighborhood. With its hexagonal-tile floors and tiny wrought-iron cafe tables, **Caffè Roma,** 385 Broome St., at the corner of Mulberry Street (ℂ 212/226-8413), is a great place to duck into for cannoli, those ricotta-filled roll-ups of sweet crisp pastry. Kids can drink frothy hot chocolate or chilled lemonade while parents indulge in cappuccino or espresso, made the classic way (no half-caffè mocha double latte here). Follow Mulberry down to Grand Street, and you'll find the somewhat larger and brighter (and more crowded) **Ferrara,** 195 Grand St., between Mulberry and Mott streets (© **212/226-6150**), its refrigerated display cases crowded with mouthwatering pastries to go or to stay. If your kids want to sample Italian gelato (ice cream), this is a good place for that, too.

9 Chinatown

Finding a place to eat in Chinatown isn't difficult—just stroll along Mott or Mulberry streets south of Canal Street, or along Bayard Street between Mott Street and the Bowery, and you'll pass dozens of decent restaurants with menus posted outside so you can check out what's on offer. They may not accept credit cards, and communicating with your waiter may require lots of menu-pointing and sign language, but so long as you order prudently, the food should be good. These restaurants depend on the tourist trade and have every incentive to please you. The following are some tried-and-true options.

MODERATE

Tai Hong Lau CHINESE   With its chandeliers, carpeting, and white tablecloths, Tai Hong Lau is much more dignified than the other places listed here and therefore should be saved for special occasions with older children. If you don't want to splurge on the Peking duck, you can still dine well on a number of Cantonese specialties such as boneless chicken with lemon sauce; the menu is strong on seafood and bean-curd dishes, so vegetarian teenagers may be pleased. The restaurant is open for dim sum until late afternoon, but be prepared: It's very hard to keep track of how many of those tempting-looking delicacies you've chosen from the little carts being wheeled about, and the price can mount up fast.

70 Mott St. (btwn Bayard and Canal sts.). © 212/219-1431. Reservations recommended. Main courses $8.95–$19, except for Peking duck ($38, but only $18 on Mon). AE. Mon–Fri 10am–11:30pm; Sat–Sun 9am–11:30pm; dim sum daily 10am–3:30pm. Subway: N, Q, R, W, 6 to Canal St.

INEXPENSIVE

Great NY Noodletown ⟨*Value*⟩ CHINESE   Noodles are one Asian food that even picky-eater kids can often be persuaded to try, and the noodles in this bustling Chinatown spot are delectable, simmered in broth or coated with various savory sauces; a wide range of menu choices mix 'n' match the noodles with grilled or roasted meats and stir-fried veggies. Be prepared to elbow your way in and endure hurried service; smaller kids may have to sit in your lap, as there are no boosters or high chairs.

28½ Bowery (at Bayard St.). © 212/349-0923. Reservations recommended. Main courses $4–$19. No credit cards. Daily 9am–4am. Subway: N, Q, R, W, 6 to Canal St.

Jing Fong CHINESE   If you're looking to give the kids a memorable Chinatown experience, try this vast, chandeliered Hong-Kong-style dim sum parlor. The place can easily become a madhouse, as soon as the ladies start wheeling out the carts; tiny dishes with all kinds of delectable dumplings and skewers and rolls are laid out on the carts, and diners choose whatever looks good to them. At the end of the meal, they count up your dishes and tell you how much you owe. You don't have to read a menu or communicate with the cart ladies—just point to choose yourself a meal full of wonderful surprises (you may never learn the name of certain mouthwatering dishes). Eating dim sum is a novel experience that can be loads of fun for older kids who are willing to blindly sample new foods, though no item is really that far from standard

Chinese dishes. The only problem may be discovering how high a bill you've run up, taste-testing all those tempting morsels.

18 Elizabeth St. (near Canal St.). ℭ 212/964-5256. Boosters. Reservations accepted for dinner only. Main courses $9–$24. AE, MC, V. Daily 10am–10pm; dim sum daily 10am–3:30pm. Subway: J, M, Z, 6 to Canal St.

Lin's Dumpling House ℱ CHINESE Though my kids aren't dumpling fans (foods aren't supposed to touch each other, you see), a lot of kids do like them, and this is the place to come for very succulent dumplings. The pork-with-leek dumpling is especially delicious. Other recommended dishes are the sesame shrimp; the romantically named Romeo and Juliet (prawns and flank steak with peppers and water chestnuts); and the Chicken Delight, which is chunks of chicken fried with vegetables. But face it, you won't get kids to try the pig's intestine with sour cabbage. This place is a good choice for families who are put off by the hole-in-the-wall look of most of the other restaurants in this price category: It's a soothing, respectable setting, with lots of dark wood, etched glass panels, and green tablecloths.

25 Pell St. (btwn Bowery and Mott sts.). ℭ **212/577-2777**. Main courses $4.25–$15; dumplings $4.75–$6.25; lunch special $5.25. AE, MC, V. Daily 11am–11pm. Subway: N, Q, R, W, 6 to Canal St.

Nha Hang VIETNAMESE The first Vietnamese restaurant interloper in Chinatown, Nha Hang made it easier for the others to follow because its popularity spread the word. The space is bright, modern, and simply decorated, with lightly varnished wood furnishings—nothing too exotic, until you taste the food. Less sauce-driven than Chinese food, Vietnamese cooking is big on spices and grilling, so watch out for those red stars on the menu if you don't like hot foods (there are plenty of soothing noodle soups for those who prefer to play it safe, as well as more subtly spiced dishes). My kids like both spring rolls and barbecued beef, so the dish that combines the two of those on vermicelli noodles was a hit; there are also a fine green papaya salad with beef and a curry shrimp with string beans and coconut milk over rice that'll really clear your sinuses.

73 Mulberry St. (btwn Bayard and Canal sts.). ℭ 212/233-8988. Boosters. Reservations recommended. Main courses $4–$15. AE, MC, V. Daily 10:30am–10pm. Subway: N, Q, R, W, 6 to Canal St.

10 TriBeCa, Lower Manhattan & Brooklyn
EXPENSIVE

Odeon ℱ AMERICAN The mellow Art Deco look of Odeon, with its wooden blinds and comfy banquettes, helped make it one of TriBeCa's first hot spots way back in the early 1980s. Standards have been kept up surprisingly well into the 21st century, and now it's not too hip to welcome families. The brasserie menu is inventive and constantly changing, but there's always simple classic food like burgers, roast chicken, steak frites, and pastas. On past visits, I've enjoyed a seared tuna sandwich with arugula and wasabi mayonnaise, as well as a grilled stuffed chicken breast with melted Gruyère cheese. This is also a good place to make a meal of two appetizers, with some excellent salads and a fine country pâté available. While there's no kids' menu, kids' options are available upon request. There's very little attitude and a lot of smart cooking going on here—no wonder Odeon has survived.

145 W. Broadway (at Thomas St.). ℭ 212/233-0507. www.theodeonrestaurant.com. High chairs. Reservations recommended. Brunch $10–$19; lunch $10–$20; dinner $11–$24. AE, DC, DISC, MC, V. Mon–Fri 11:45am–2am; Sat–Sun 10am–2am. Subway: A, C, 1, 2, 3, 9 to Chambers St.

MODERATE

Edward's AMERICAN   The brasserie menu at this retro diner is reminiscent of that at its more famous neighbor, Odeon (see above): burgers, omelets, roast chicken, grilled tuna, steak frites. The kids' menu isn't much more adventurous, but it does throw in scrambled eggs and pancakes alongside the fish sticks, chicken nuggets, and hot dogs, and there is a pizza offering. Brunch is served Saturday and Sunday from 10am to 5pm. Informal and totally kid-friendly, Edward's allows parents to feel like hip extras from *Sex and the City* while their children loll happily on the Naugahyde banquettes.

136 W. Broadway (btwn Thomas and Duane sts.). © 212/233-6436. Kids' menu, high chairs, boosters. Lunch $8–$15; dinner $8.50–$22; kids' menu $6.50. AE, DC, DISC, MC, V. Daily 9am–midnight. Subway: 1 to Franklin St.; A, C, 1, 2, 3 to Chambers St.

Ellen's Stardust Café DINER   Though it caters largely to the Wall Street lunch crowd, this downtown branch of Ellen Hart's diner empire is now open evenings as well, which is very handy for the greater numbers of people who have come to live downtown. The look is more saloonish than Ellen's Stardust Diner in Midtown (p. 116), but the atmosphere is 100% kid-friendly. The wide-ranging menu includes omelets, salads, burgers, and sandwiches, not to mention a brimming display case of yummy baked goods by the front door.

270 Broadway (at Chambers St.). © 212/962-1257. Boosters, sassy seats. Reservations recommended. Main courses $15–$20. AE, DC, DISC, MC, V. Mon-Sat 7:30am–midnight; Sun 7:30am–11pm. Subway: R, W, 4, 5, 6 to City Hall; 2, 3 to Park Place; A, C to Chambers St.

INEXPENSIVE

Bubby's Pie Company 🐾🐾 AMERICAN   "Homey" is the word for this comforting TriBeCa restaurant, with its wooden chairs, soft recorded jazz, and kitschy clutter. The food is comforting as well, with sandwiches, burgers, pastas, and a great selection of pies—not to mention breakfast food served until 4pm, good to know if you've got kids who like scrambled eggs and French toast for lunch. There are also more upscale salads and chicken and fish dishes to please adults. It's the sort of place that understands that kids may like their spaghetti with butter and Parmesan instead of tomato sauce and that cooked carrots go down better if you drizzle maple syrup on top. Service may dawdle a bit, but the laid-back ambience somehow makes children willing to linger. The Saturday and Sunday brunch tends to be very popular. On Sundays, kids under 8 eat free at dinner.

120 Hudson St. (at N. Moore St.). © 212/219-0666. www.bubbys.com. Kids' menu, high chairs, boosters. Reservations recommended; no reservations accepted for weekend brunch. Lunch $8–$15; dinner $10–$15; kids' menu $2–$6. DC, MC, V. Mon–Thurs 8am–11pm; Fri 8am–midnight; Sat 9am–midnight; Sun 9am–10pm; closed 4-6pm Sat and Sun. Subway: 1 to Franklin St.; A, C, E to Canal St.

Chevy's MEXICAN   This Mexican chain restaurant, located in the base of the Embassy Suites hotel (right around the corner from the new Regal Cineplex) offers families a decent option in a neighborhood where restaurants are all too often geared to Wall Streeters. The menu is fairly standard: burritos, quesadillas, fajitas, chimichangas, occasionally with a little Texas-style barbecued chicken thrown in. Some safer alternatives show up on the kids' menu, to take care of little gringos who don't do spicy food—stuff like burgers and chicken fingers. Expect a rock soundtrack, roadhouse decor, and some rowdy spirits, especially at happy hour.

102 North End Ave. (entrance on Vesey St. between West St. and North End Ave.), in Battery Park City. (C) **212/786-1111**. Kids' menu, high chairs, boosters. Main courses $9–$20; kids' menu $7. AE, DC, DISC, MC, V. Mon–Sat 11am–midnight, Sun 11am–10pm. Subway: E to World Trade Center.

Grimaldi's PIZZA   Yet another contender for the title of Best Pizza in New York, Grimaldi's lays legitimate claim to honors in the coal-oven category, with gooey home-made mozzarella and chunky tomato sauce topping a wonderfully thin but not tough crust. Like its rivals Anthony's and Lombardi's, it doesn't serve slices, and there are often lines out the door on summer evenings waiting for a table. Persevere: The line moves quickly enough, and you'll have views of the Manhattan skyline to entertain yourselves while you wait. (Better yet, come in the late afternoon, when there's no crush.) Inside, just as you'd expect, the tables are covered in red-checkered cloths, and Sinatra and Pavarotti dominate the jukebox as well as the photos on the walls. If your kids are into pepperoni, be sure to order some on your pizza—Grimaldi's uses the best in town. Make a Grimaldi's pizza your kids' reward for walking over the Brooklyn Bridge (it sits right underneath the bridge, by the old Fulton ferry landing), and top it off with a post-pizza ice cream cone down by the river at the Brooklyn Ice Cream Works.

19 Old Fulton St. (btwn Front and Water sts.), Brooklyn. (C) **718/858-4300**. Boosters. Reservations not accepted. Pizzas $14 and up. No credit cards. Sun–Thurs 11:30am–10:45pm; Fri 11:30am–11:45pm; Sat noon–11:45pm. Subway: A, C to High St.

Kitchenette ⋆ AMERICAN   This artfully weathered little cafe looks like it belongs on Cape Cod or in upstate New York, not in the shadow of downtown skyscrapers. Farmhouse-style breakfasts, featuring things like blueberry pancakes and buttermilk biscuits, start out weekdays; the lunch menu starts to drift toward hipness with choices like goat-cheese sandwich, or Tuscan tuna salad alongside your standard grilled cheese, B.L.T., and tuna melt. The house-special turkey meatloaf with mashed potatoes is really, really good. It's the best of both worlds: The kids eat happy, you can eat upscale, and everything's copacetic.

156 Chambers St. (btwn Greenwich St. and W Broadway) (C) **212/267-6740**. High chair. Breakfast $6–$9.50; main dishes $12–$18. AE, MC, V. Mon–Fri 7:30am–10pm; Sat–Sun 9am–10pm. Subway: A, C, 1, 2, 3 to Chambers St.

THE CHAIN GANG

If you're at South Street Seaport, and your kids hate fish, head for that old standby **Pizzeria Uno,** 89 South St. Seaport ((C) **212/791-7999**). There also a **Lemongrass Grill** downtown, 84 William St. at Maiden Lane ((C) **212/809-8038**).

FOOD COURTS

On the top floor of the **Pier 17** pavilion at South Street Seaport, a sparkling big food court enjoys the kind of picture-window river views normally reserved for the toniest restaurants. The various food vendors whose booths surround the public seating include several ethnic varieties; there's often live music as well. The food court in the **World Financial Center** in Battery Park City features a cluster of sit-down, table-service restaurants, but the ambience is casual enough for kids, and there are takeout options, including a Cosi sandwich shop.

6

Exploring New York City with Your Kids

Yes, everybody knows that New York City is a world-class sightseeing destination. Yet visiting parents may be baffled by it at first—many of its top museums are not inherently suited for youngsters (the Frick Museum won't even admit anyone under 10), real estate is too tight for anything like a theme park, and though there are four children's museums—one in Manhattan, one in Brooklyn, one on Staten Island, and one out on Long Island (see chapter 11)—none of them is as central to local kids' lives as their counterparts in Boston, Chicago, San Francisco, or even Indianapolis. Many of its famous family attractions get so crowded, especially on weekends and school holidays, that tourists face waiting seemingly forever in line. (*Insider tip:* If you're visiting during the school year, try hitting the popular museums in the mornings, when the local kids are in school.)

But New York City's charms are inexhaustible, and as soon as you start thinking out of the tourist box, the city will open its best-kept secrets for you. My advice? For one thing, don't sell your children short: They may appreciate those smaller specialty museums, historic houses, and botanic gardens more than you'd expect. For another thing, don't be afraid to get on a subway and zip to the outer boroughs. Remember, kids love subway rides, and on weekends especially it's the way to go. Spend a day in **Brooklyn** in Prospect Park, dividing your time between the Wildlife Center and the Carousel, or pop over to the Brooklyn Botanic Garden and the Brooklyn Museum—incredibly, these are all within a few minutes' walk of one another. Flushing Meadows is my destination of choice in **Queens,** where you can see both the New York Hall of Science and Queens Wildlife Center in one easy go. In the **Bronx,** the huge Bronx Zoo and the equally huge New York Botanical Garden are right across the road from each other. Getting to **Staten Island** is even more fun because you get to take a ferry ride, and the children's museum there is only a short bus ride from the ferry docks.

Many museums court families by designing weekend and holiday workshops for kids—these are detailed in chapter 8, where you'll also find everything you'll need to know about having fun outdoors in New York's great parks, playgrounds, and neighborhoods.

SIGHTSEEING SUGGESTIONS

If you're trying to cram a lot of sightseeing into a short time, you may want to consider buying a **City Pass,** which gives you entry to five popular attractions: the **American Museum of Natural History,** the **Museum of Modern Art,** the **Guggenheim Museum,** the **Empire State Building** observation deck, and

What's in a Name?

Here's a trivia quiz to test your kids' knowledge of New York City history:
1. Who was the Hudson River named after?
2. Who was the Verrazano Bridge named after?
3. Where does the downtown street name Wall Street come from?
4. Where does the name Harlem, for the uptown neighborhood, come from?
5. Why is the street leading down to South Street Seaport named Fulton Street?
6. What does the name of the New York Mets refer to? (*Hint:* Think of the opera and the big art museum.)
7. What other two area sports teams have names that rhyme with the Mets?
8. Why is Times Square called Times Square?
9. Carnegie Hall, the famous concert hall at 57th Street and Seventh Avenue, is named after whom? And how do you get there?
10. Who is buried in Grant's Tomb?

ANSWERS: 1. English explorer Henry Hudson, who sailed up the river in 1609. 2. Italian explorer Giovanni da Verrazano, the first European to enter the Narrows, in 1524. 3. In the original Dutch settlement, a wall was built at that point to keep out invaders. 4. Nieuw Haarlem was a separate Dutch settlement in the mid-1600s, named after the Dutch city of Haarlem. 5. Ferry service, operated by steamship inventor Robert Fulton, crossed the river at that point, linking Manhattan to Brooklyn (until the completion of the Brooklyn Bridge in 1883). 6. It's short for Metropolitans. 7. The New York Jets football team and the New Jersey Nets basketball team. 8. Because the headquarters of the *New York Times* newspaper is there (an earlier paper, the *New York Herald,* lent its name to Herald Square, a few blocks south at 34th St.). 9. It's named for the man who built it, industrialist/philanthropist Andrew Carnegie (his former mansion is now the Cooper-Hewitt Museum). How do you get there? Practice, practice, practice. 10. Duh—it's Grant, of course (that's Ulysses S. Grant, Civil War commander and U.S. president), alongside his wife, Julia.

the **Circle Line** cruise around Manhattan. Good for a 9-day period, passes cost $53 for adults and $44 for children ages 6 to 17. Buy them at the admission desk of any of these attractions or online at www.citypass.com. The Guggenheim might not otherwise be on a family's agenda, but the other four sights all have tremendous kid appeal, and you'd still save money on the adult pass if you only did those five (it comes out about even on the kid pass, because the art museums don't charge admission for children).

If You Have Only 1 Day

Talk to the animals at the **Central Park Zoo,** followed by a spin on the nearby **Carousel.** Grab a hot dog for lunch in the park; then head up Central Park West to the **American Museum of**

Natural History, with its magnificent dinosaur bones and wildlife dioramas. If you've got enough stamina, wind up with an hour or so at the **Children's Museum of Manhattan,** a couple of blocks away on West 83rd Street.

If You Have 2 Days

Spend day 1 as above. On day 2, start out at **Rockefeller Center** (if you're early enough you can join the crowds watching the *Today* show broadcast live), where you can hang over the railing at Rockefeller Plaza and delve into the concourse to see the underground city in action. Go up to the **Top of the Rock** for a view of Manhattan's glittering cityscape, then cross Fifth Avenue to slip into **St. Patrick's Cathedral.** Swing over to Madison Avenue, where you can grab a sandwich to eat while you wait for your reserved time slot at the **Sony Wonder Technology Lab.** (Optional Midtown alternatives, depending on your kids' tastes, are the **Museum of Television and Radio** and the **American Folk Art Museum.**)

After a spell at the museum, head west to the neon razzmatazz of **Times Square,** where, depending on your age, you can either take a spin on the Ferris wheel at **Toys "R" Us** or watch *TRL Live* being broadcast through the windows at the **MTV Studio.** (Interested in the theater? Check out what's being offered at the **TKTS** half-price ticket booth for tonight's shows.) If you've still got the energy, end your day with a visit to the pricey-but-memorable **Madame Tussaud's New York** on 42nd Street, capped by dinner at one of Times Square's many theme restaurants (see chapter 5).

If You Have 3 Days

Spend days 1 and 2 as above. On day 3, get up early to be first in line for the Circle Line ferry to the **Statue of Liberty** and **Ellis Island.** If you get out on Liberty Island, know that her inside staircase has been closed indefinitely (although you can visit exhibits inside the base), but viewing her close up is still awesome. Proceed via the ferry to Ellis Island, where you can pick up lunch at the more-than-decent snack bar (Liberty Island has no food services) and browse around the fascinating immigration displays (my kids like Ellis Island better than the statue). Catch the ferry back to Manhattan, where you've got three options: Zip over to the **National Museum of the American Indian,** do a lobby-hopping tour around the Wall Street area (see chapter 7), or take a cab over to **South Street Seaport** for a peek into Manhattan's 19th-century maritime past.

If You Have 4 Days

Spend days 1 to 3 as above. With older kids, start out day 4 by taking the hour-long tour of the **United Nations,** have an early lunch in the Delegates' Dining Room, and then cab it uptown for an afternoon at the **Metropolitan Museum of Art.** If you have younger kids, start out at the Metropolitan first thing in the morning (when the crowds are lighter and the guards a trifle more patient), have lunch at an East Side coffee shop, then go to **Central Park playgrounds** so your youngsters can let off some steam. Work your way up Fifth Avenue to 103rd Street, where you can pop in to check out the toy gallery at the **Museum of the City of New York,** and end your day with a stroll through the **Conservatory Garden.**

If the Weather's Cold

To cram the most into 1 day with a minimum of exposure to the elements, start out at the **American Museum of Natural History;** then scoot across Central Park on the 79th Street crosstown bus (just as quick as a taxi) and dive into the **Metropolitan Museum of Art.** Or do it the other way around, depending on which you think your child will want more time for. Both have good on-site cafes, so you won't have to venture outside to eat.

If the Weather's Hot

East River breezes make **South Street Seaport** a refreshing spot in summer, and you can always duck inside the air-conditioned shops and museums when the sun beats down too strongly. As the sun moves westward, so should you: Cab it across town to **Battery Park City,** where you can take in an afternoon movie at the AMC multiplex, emerging in time to stroll down the breezy Esplanade along the Hudson and watch the sun set behind Lady Liberty—or even walk down to South Ferry and take a spin on the **Staten Island Ferry.** Another good warm-weather refuge is the **Cloisters,** the Metropolitan's medieval art annex located up in Fort Tryon Park, where you can chill out amid the dim light and cool stone of transplanted European chapels.

Tip: Don't be tempted to do the Statue of Liberty and Ellis Island on a really hot day—though the ferry ride may be refreshing, the wait in line for the boat will be unbearable.

If You've Got a Sitter

Take advantage of the opportunity to dawdle in one of the art museums kids aren't as happy in—like the **Frick,** the **Whitney Museum of American Art,** or the **Asia Society Galleries,** all on the Upper East Side. Then window-shop along tony **Madison Avenue,** where designer boutiques cluster from the 80s on down to 57th Street. Another child-free option may be to prowl around the Wall Street area: Visit the **New York Stock Exchange,** venerable **Trinity Church,** and the surprisingly small but ornate **City Hall.** Go out to dinner at an elegant restaurant; then catch either a **Broadway show** or a concert at **Carnegie Hall** or **Lincoln Center.** For complete details on all such grown-up activities, pick up a copy of *Frommer's New York City.*

1 Kids' Top 10 Attractions

American Girl Place 𝕬𝕬   **Ages 4 to 14.** Just a store? Try telling that to the legions of 'tween-age girls, dolls lovingly clasped in their arms, who converge on this Midtown site as if they were pilgrims heading to Mecca. If you've been on Mars for the past few years—or if you only have sons (which is the same thing)—you may not know about these expensive, beautifully made 18-inch dolls, each with her own carefully researched back story presented in a series of middle-grade-level books. Originally developed by Wisconsin-based Pleasant Company, the line has been acquired by Mattel, but the quality level remains high, and there are several good spin-off products like modern-era American Girls of Today, Bitty Babies, and human-child-size clothing to match the doll's outfits. At American Girl Place New York, as at the original American Girl Place in Chicago and the new Los Angeles branch, this concern shines through.

Technically, it is possible to visit without spending a penny, although if you can swing that, you are a better parent than I am (or a worse parent, in your daughter's opinion). Besides the three floors of American Girl merchandise, there is an excellent **cafe** upstairs (p. 112), a **theater** presenting a quite respectable show (see chapter 10), and a small **art gallery** displaying original illustration art for the books. On the second floor, detailed and delightful **historical dioramas** present each of the American Girl dolls in her time period. Often, craft activities and special celebrations are on tap, and if your daughter has brought her own Felicity or Kayla or Samantha or whomever, she can have the doll's hair restyled in the **doll salon.**

Warning: Boys may be allergic to this place. If possible, pack them off to the nearby Sony Wonder (later in this chapter), the Top of the Rock observation deck (later in this chapter), or the Build-A-Bear Workshop down the street (see chapter 9), and let your daughter have her day in the sun.

Where to Eat: The **American Girl Cafe** (p. 112), serving lunch, weekend brunch, afternoon tea, and dinner, is an important part of the total experience. Reserve well in advance (for school vacation times, up to 6 months ahead!).

609 Fifth Ave. (at 49th St.). ⒸＣ 877/AG-PLACE. www.americangirl.com. Free admission. Sun–Tues 10am–7pm, Wed–Sat 10am–9pm; in summer months opens daily 9am. Closes 5:30pm Labor Day, Dec 24, and Dec 31; closed Thanksgiving and Dec 25. Subway: E, V to Fifth Ave./53rd St.; B, D, F, V to 47th–50th sts./Rockefeller Center.

American Museum of Natural History 🦕🦕🦕 All ages.

This is the city's one real don't-miss if you're with kids. The excitement begins even in the subway station below (B and C trains to W. 81st St.), where the walls feature wonderful ceramic bas-reliefs of dinosaurs, insects, birds, and mammals. When you enter the rotunda at the top of the Central Park West steps, a rearing skeleton of a mommy dinosaur protecting her baby from a small, fierce predator clues you in that the dazzling fourth-floor **dinosaur halls** are the perennial star attraction; they feature interactive consoles, glass-floored walkways that bring you up to the dino's eye level, and please-touch displays illustrating key points of evolution. But our favorite sights are the superb dioramas in the **North American Mammals** section (first floor)—the grizzly bear raking open a freshly caught salmon, majestic elks lifting their massive antlers, wolves loping through eerie nighttime snow—or, on the floor above, the bi-level **African Mammals Hall,** where you can circle around a lumbering herd of perfectly preserved elephants or check out the giraffes browsing by their water hole.

A circuit of the first floor alone could take a whole day. The PC-but-never-preachy **Hall of Biodiversity** features an immense multimedia re-creation of an African rainforest and a display of Earth's entire family tree, with more than 1,500 specimens and models spread out along a 100-foot wall. We love the dimly lit **Ocean Life room,** where a gargantuan model of a blue whale swims overhead; it has informally become known as the place where toddlers can stretch their legs, racing and twirling around the vast open space. Around the corner, the less-well-visited **North American Forest dioramas** are our family secret—a peaceful part of the museum where you can hunt for blue jays in oak trees and rattlesnakes behind the cactus. Most people hurry through here to get to the interactive **Human Biology and Evolution** exhibits, which seem always full of busy grade-schoolers. Past that lies the **Mineral and Gem room,** where little kids can thrust their hands into a huge geode while older kids gape in awe at the jewels on display.

The museum is not all animals, by any means (remember that Margaret Mead was only one of many brilliant anthropologists whose research was supported by this museum over the years). Studying Native Americans? On the first floor, by the 77th Street entrance, is the astounding collection of **Northwest Coast Indian** totem poles immortalized by J. D. Salinger in *Catcher in the Rye.* The haunting soundtracks in the **African and Asian peoples** sections (on the second floor) lull you into studying the precisely detailed displays there, too. The stunning **Rose Center for Earth and Space,** a 95-foot-high glass cube, includes an interactive exhibit on the nature of the universe, where you can step on a scale that shows your weight on Saturn, see an eerie phosphorescent model of the expanding universe, and touch cosmic debris.

Uptown Attractions

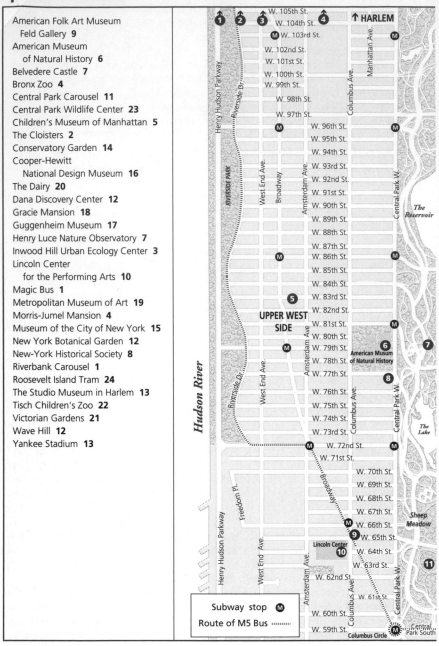

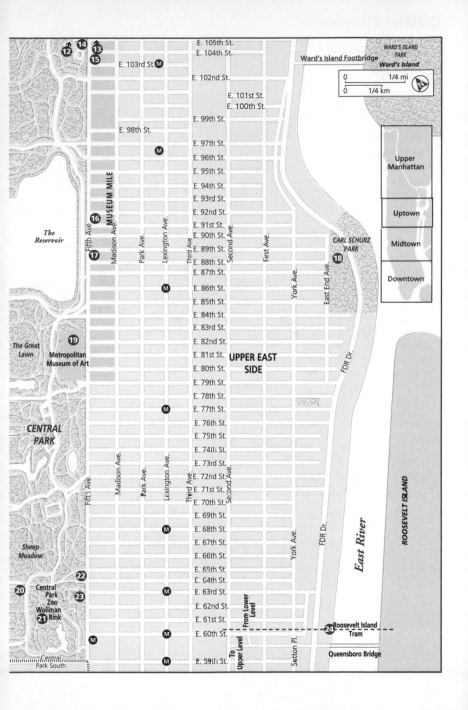

Midtown Attractions

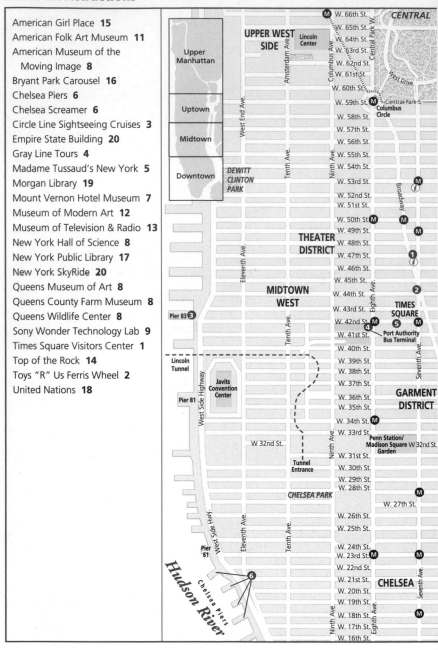

Downtown Attractions

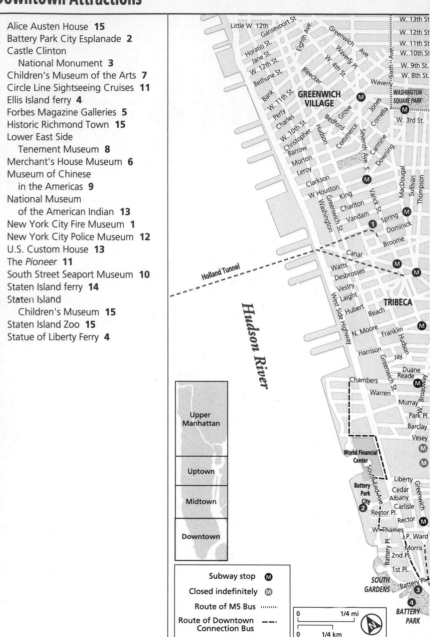

Little W. 12th Gansevoort St W. 13th St
W. 12th St
Greenwich W. 11th St
Horatio St. Eighth Ave. Waverly Pl. Ave. W. 10th St
Jane St. W. 4th St. W. 9th St.
W. 12th St. Sixth Ave. W. 8th St.
Bethune St. Bleecker Waverly
Bank **GREENWICH** WASHINGTON
W. 11th St. **VILLAGE** SQUARE PARK
Perry Bedford Grove Jones Cornelia W. 3rd St.
Charles Hudson
W. 10th St. Commerce Seventh Ave. S. Carmine
Christopher Barrow Downing
Morton
Leroy MacDougal
Clarkson Sullivan
W Houston King Thompson
Greenwich St. Charlton
Washington Vandam Spring
Varick St. Dominick
Broome

Canal

Holland Tunnel

Watts
Desbrosses
Vestry
Laight **TRIBECA**
West Side Highway Hubert Beach
N. Moore Franklin
Harrison Jay Hudson
Duane Greenwich
Reade
Chambers Broadway
Warren
Murray
Park Pl.
Barclay
Vesey
World Financial
Center Liberty
Battery Cedar
Park Albany
City Carlisle
Rector Pl. Rector
W. Thames J.P. Ward
Battery Pl. Morris
2nd Pl.
1st Pl. **SOUTH**
GARDENS Battery Pl.
BATTERY
PARK

Hudson River

Upper
Manhattan

Uptown

Midtown

Downtown

Subway stop Ⓜ
Closed indefinitely Ⓜ
Route of M5 Bus ········
Route of Downtown — · · —
    Connection Bus

0   1/4 mi
0   1/4 km

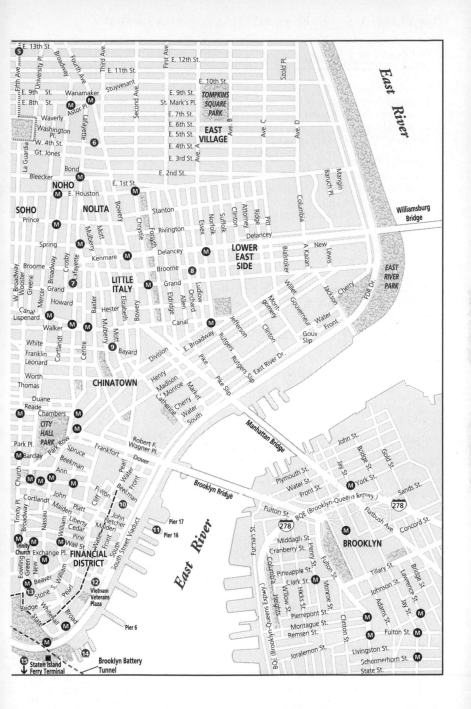

Natural History Museum Treasure Hunt

The American Museum of Natural History is so vast, kids can easily tire if you trudge from hall to hall with no organizing purpose. Here, then, is a treasure hunt designed by my sons, Hugh and Tom, to keep your kids busy exploring. Younger kids may get through only one floor in an afternoon, but persist—I swear, it's all here.

First Floor

1. **North American Mammals**—Where is the rabbit hiding from the lynx?
2. **Ocean Life**—Who's talking back to the orca? (*Hint: Orca* is another name for a killer whale.)
3. **New York State Environment**—How many baby chipmunks are sleeping in the spring burrow?
4. **Human Biology and Evolution**—Find the cave of mammoth bones.
5. **Minerals and Gems**—Where are the rocks that glow in the dark?

Second Floor

6. **African Peoples**—Find the xylophone.
7. **Birds of the World**—How many stuffed penguins are there?
8. **Asian Peoples**—Who's getting married?
9. **Rose Center**—How soon after the Big Bang did our solar system start to form?

Third Floor

10. **African Mammals**—Who's watching the ostriches fight the wart hogs?
11. **Reptiles and Amphibians**—Which is the crocodile, and which is the alligator?

Fourth Floor

12. **Saurischian Dinosaurs**—Find the fossil dinosaur teeth.
13. **Ornithischian Dinosaurs**—Touch the triceratops horn.

ANSWERS: 1. Behind the bush. 2. The leopard seal. 3. Four. 4. Toward the end of the exhibit, in the Earliest Architecture display. 5. In the first gem room, the southeast corner. 6. Midway through the hall, on the west wall, across from the guys in straw skirts who look like Cousin Itt from The Addams Family. 7. Twenty in all—16 adults, 4 babies. 8. In the Chinese section, a bride in her ornate ceremonial sedan chair. 9. Eight billion years. 10. The mouselike elephant shrew, behind a dead log. 11. Facing each other by the entrance at the north end of the hall—the gator (on your right) has the snub snout; the croc (on your left) has the pointy snout. 12. On the south wall. 13. On the east wall.

The **Discovery Room,** on the first floor by the 77th Street entrance (near the immense outrigger canoe), is a special spot where kids 5 and older can touch and feel and fiddle with items related to the displays; it's open weekday afternoons from 1:30 to 5:10, Saturday and Sunday 10:30am to 1:30pm and 2:15 to 5:15pm. "Meet the Scientist" events are held on occasional Saturdays throughout the school year. Squirreled away in a back corner of the second floor is the **Natural Science Center,** a

Brooklyn Attractions

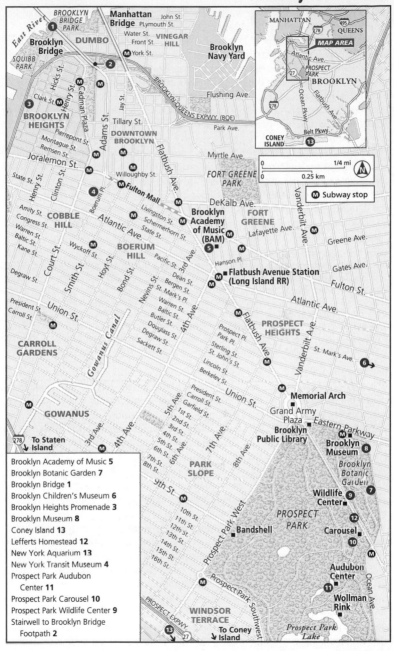

Brooklyn Academy of Music **5**
Brooklyn Botanic Garden **7**
Brooklyn Bridge **1**
Brooklyn Children's Museum **6**
Brooklyn Heights Promenade **3**
Brooklyn Museum **8**
Coney Island **13**
Lefferts Homestead **12**
New York Aquarium **13**
New York Transit Museum **4**
Prospect Park Audubon
Center **11**
Prospect Park Carousel **10**
Prospect Park Wildlife Center **9**
Stairwell to Brooklyn Bridge
Footpath **2**

delightful hands-on workshop where kids 4 and older can explore the natural life of New York City (Tues–Fri 2–4:30pm, Sat–Sun 1–4:30pm).

Here comes my only quibble with the museum: On top of the already significant admission price, there are substantial extra fees, even for members, for special exhibits, and even for regular features such as the space show at the **Hayden Planetarium** and the various films shown in the **IMAX theater** (see below for prices). These can add up awfully fast to make a visit here quite expensive. Believe me, there's enough to do here that you don't need to go for the extras (I personally find the space shows a letdown). Shops at every turn lure you to spend more money, though there are always at least a few inexpensive items.

Where to Eat: The excellent **Museum Food Court** (open 11am–4:45pm) offers a wide range of sophisticated sandwiches, salads, fruit, and snacks as well as hot food, including hamburgers and french fries. On weekends, you can also grab a light meal at the **Dinersaurus Cafe** (on the 4th floor by the 77th St. elevators) and **Cafe 77** (by the 77th St. entrance on the first floor). Since you can reenter the museum with your admission tag, consider popping out into the neighborhood to **Rain, Pizzeria Uno, Monsoon,** or **T & R Pizzeria** (see chapter 5), only a block or two away.

Central Park W. (at 79th St.). (*C*) 212/769-5100; for reserved tickets to Space Show and other special exhibits, (*C*) 212/769-5200. www.amnh.org. Suggested admission for **nonmembers:** $14 adults, $11 students and seniors, $8 children 2–12.; nonmember admission plus IMAX ticket $21 adults, $16 students and seniors, $12 children 2–12; nonmember admission plus Space Show $22 adults, $17 students and seniors, $13 children; nonmember admission plus Space Show plus IMAX $30 adults, $23 students and seniors, $19 children. Admission for **members** free; added fee for Space Show $11 adults, $7 children; added fee for IMAX $10 adults, $6 children; added fee for both IMAX and Space Show $15 adults, $10 children. Children under 2 admitted free. Daily 10am–5:45pm (Rose Center open till 8:45pm first Fri each month). Closed Thanksgiving and Dec 25. Limited parking available on-site (enter on W. 81st St. btwn Central Park W. and Columbus Ave.). Subway: B, C to 81st St./Museum of Natural History; 1 to 79th St.

Bronx Zoo 😺😺 **All ages.** The big kahuna of New York City's wildlife parks, the Bronx Zoo is a world-class facility in every way. It covers 265 acres and boasts more than 4,000 animals, from Siberian tigers and snow leopards to condors and vultures to naked mole-rats and meerkats. Though there's a scattered number of indoor exhibits— the deliciously creepy **World of Darkness** (nocturnal animals); the **World of Reptiles; the **Monkey House; the **Giraffe House; the **Mouse House;** and my family's favorite, **Jungle World**—most of the animals live outdoors in large enclosures re-creating as closely as possible the species' native environment. Kids under 5 may get frustrated by the long walks between animals and the fact that certain creatures may be viewable only at a distance. This doesn't mean they won't love the zoo—it just means you've got to organize your visit sensibly.

You can run into several added charges once you get inside the gates, so I recommend opting for the Pay One Price ticket plan—it not only saves you money, it also saves time, because you can bypass individual ticket booths inside. From April to October several rides help you navigate the park—an **open-sided tram** ($3) that rattles in a big loop around the main part of the zoo, the **Skyfari** cable car ($3) that soars high over the treetops (handy for cutting across, but hardly any animals are visible), and the narrated **Bengali Express monorail ride** ($5, May–Oct) in the Wild Asia section. The monorail is worth the extra money, since it's the only way you can see Wild Asia at all, and the guide en route helps you spot all the lions and antelopes patrolling their roomy open-air habitats. There's also a $3-per-person charge for the **Children's Zoo,** open April to October, which is surprisingly fun even for 8- or 9-year-olds, with lots of learn-by-doing exhibits (like a spider-web rope climb and a prairie-dog burrow that kids can climb through), and a petting zoo. If you want to take a camel ride in the Wild Asia section, that's another $5; my son Tom says it's the biggest rip-off at the park. The zoo also tacks on $3 for each of its two star exhibits, the **Congo Gorilla Forest** and the **Butterfly Zone** (open June–Sept only). Both of them are fascinating— on a good day you can practically go snout-to-snout with our huge simian cousins through a wide glass window or have immense tropical butterflies land on your outstretched hand. (Note that the new **Tiger Mountain** gives you the same close-up access to its big striped cats for no extra charge.) With all these extras, you could easily spend over $100 on a full day for a family of five. Since a 1-year family membership costs $120 anyway, consider joining, especially if you're likely to visit another of the city's four Wildlife Conservation parks any time during the next year; you'll be supporting valuable conservation efforts as well.

During winter, when many of the outdoor animals aren't on view, the park lures visitors with fanciful animal sculptures spangled with lights, as well as the indoor exhibits (still enough species on view to fill a smaller zoo); there's a certain pleasure in visiting during this uncrowded season.

The zoo has several entrances: I recommend the Southern Boulevard/Crotona entrance, which brings you in near the Children's Zoo and the elephants, or the Asia entrance (pedestrians only, closest to the subway station), which brings you in near Wild Asia and Jungle World. In any case, study the zoo map as soon as you enter, and plot which animals you want to visit and the simplest route to pass them. Operate on the assumption that you can't see everything in 1 day, even if your kids are good walkers. Relax, take your time, and enjoy yourselves.

Getting There: By **bus,** BxM11 express buses (call © **718/330-1234**) run about every 15 to 30 minutes from stops along Madison Avenue in Manhattan. At 24th, 54th. And 99th streets; the fare is $5 per person one-way (free for a child under 45 in. riding on an adult's lap). By **train,** take Metro-North from Grand Central Terminal to Fordham Road, change to the Bx9 bus, and ride to the zoo's Southern Boulevard entrance. By **subway,** take the no. 2 to the Pelham Parkway station; walk west 1 block to Boston Road, turn left and go to first traffic light, turn right, and go straight to the zoo entrance. A **taxi** might cost $20 to $35 one-way, depending on your Manhattan starting point or destination. By **car,** take exit 6 off the Bronx River Parkway.

Where to Eat: The zoo's **Dancing Crane Cafe** is open year-round, and three open-air cafes operate seasonally. Expect fast-food-ish menus, with slightly high (but not outrageous) prices. Pack a picnic lunch if you can—there are plenty of places to sit and eat outdoors.

In Bronx Park, Bronx River Pkwy. and Fordham Rd. © **718/367-1010.** www.wcs.org or www.bronxzoo.com. Admission $12 adults, $9 seniors, $9 children 2–12, free for children under 2; pay-1-price tickets (include 6 exhibits and/or rides) $25 adults, $19 students, children, and seniors; admission fees optional Wed, but charges still apply to ticketed exhibits and rides. Stroller rental $6, with $5 deposit (inquire at park entrances). Parking $8. Apr–Oct Mon–Fri 10am–5pm, Sat–Sun and holidays 10am–5:30pm; Nov–Mar daily 10am–4:30pm.

Central Park Wildlife Center and Tisch Children's Zoo ★★ All ages. Beautifully landscaped, this pair of tiny zoos is perfect for young animal lovers—there's nothing bigger than a polar bear here, you can get pretty close to every species on display, and you don't have to walk very far to see everything. The centerpiece of the main zoo is the oval **Sea Lion Pool,** which has glass sides so everyone can watch the sea lions swimming underwater. A few steps to the west is **Monkey Island,** where a troop of snow monkeys scramble over the rocks and a few swans glide on the water.

To the north lies the **Polar Circle,** with a big flock of penguins indoors and polar bears outside, cavorting in and out of their rock-edged pool. Up on the hill behind Monkey Island is the **Temperate Territory,** which stars an otter, some ducks, and a pair of shy red pandas; at the south end you can stand on the bridge over a mucky turtle pond and look for frogs sunning themselves. The greatest number of species in the zoo are inside the **Tropical Zone,** a two-story enclosed aviary with plenty of glass tanks arranged along the wall, featuring exciting creatures like piranhas and bats and snakes—not to mention our favorites, the golden lion tamarins, whose wizened faces remind us of the flying monkeys from *The Wizard of Oz.* Be sure to climb to the upper levels and stand out on the stairways, looking for the bright plumage of tropical birds flitting from tree to tree. Always warm and humid, the Tropical Zone is a great refuge on a chilly day. As soon as you go through the main zoo's gates, check signs near the entrance to see when the sea lion and penguin feedings are scheduled; there's often a crowd for these, but it's fun to see the animals scamper over to their keepers for their fish. (No, they don't do tricks.)

The **Tisch Children's Zoo** is a short stroll north, on the other side of the Delacorte Arch. Much of this friendly hilltop spot is a walk-through aviary, which my older son, the budding ornithologist, finds incredibly cool. My kids also love the waterfall they can stick their hands through, with a dusky little grotto full of fish tanks behind it. Wooden bridges cross over a tidy central pond, cedar-chip paths circle around (strollers are useless here—park yours by the gate), and at the back is a giant spider web kids can clamber over. Children can get right up close to most of the animals here, so who cares if none of them is an exotic species?

Where to Eat: If you can, pack a picnic lunch and eat it at outdoor tables in the cafeteria courtyard. Otherwise, you'll have to go with the **zoo cafeteria** (there aren't many choices in the park), which has a limited menu, with a few sandwiches, salads, and fast-food items. At least there's a special kids' meal that may include animal crackers. There's usually also a cart selling drinks and ice cream in the central courtyard. Note that drinks are served without straws, since a straw tossed into an animal's enclosure could be harmful.

In Central Park, near the park entrance at Fifth Ave. and 64th St. ⓒ 212/439-6500. Admission (includes both zoos) $8 adults, $4 seniors, $3 children 3–12, free for children 2 and under. Mon–Fri 10am–5pm; Sat–Sun 10am–5:30pm (closes 4:30pm Nov–Mar). Subway: N, R, W to Fifth Ave./59th St.; 6 to 68th St.

Ellis Island Immigration Museum 𝕶𝕶𝕶   Ages 4 & up. Our first time here, my

son was 5, and we only got off the ferry on a whim after visiting the Statue of Liberty—and we discovered that Ellis Island was even *more* fun. Every time we return, we notice more things that we hadn't seen before. From the mountain of ragtag luggage stacked right inside the front doors, to the cramped dormitories and medical examination rooms upstairs (cough the wrong way, and you could be sent right back to Europe), to the family heirlooms immigrants brought with them in the **Treasures from Home** collection—this place really brings history to life. We can't help but linger over the first-floor **Peopling of America** exhibit, with a life-size "family tree" and huge three-dimensional bar graph tracking immigration patterns over the years. The second-floor **Registry Hall** is awesome, with its soaring vaulted ceiling faced with white tile; this is where new arrivals waited in endless lines to be interviewed by immigration officials. And the **Wall of Honor** outside, where some 420,000 immigrants' names are inscribed in steel, is fun even though no one in our family ever ponied up the dough to have a relative's name enshrined—we look up two or three family names anyway. There's a self-guided audio tour, or you can pick up handsets at various displays to hear narration; the stirring documentary *Island of Hope, Island of Tears* runs frequently throughout the day, but we chose instead to watch a delightful little play with young actors reenacting the immigration experience. We normally spend nearly 2 hours here and always leave looking forward to our next visit.

Getting There: The **ferryboats** make frequent trips, running a loop from Battery Park to Liberty Island to Ellis Island and back to Battery Park (from New Jersey, you can board ferries in Liberty State Park). In Battery Park, you can buy tickets at Castle Clinton, where there are some interesting exhibits to help pass the time before your ferry. The wait in line can take a while, and security procedures include metal detectors, bag searches (bags larger than a milk crate aren't allowed on the ferry), and waiting in several different holding pens—perhaps an appropriate introduction to the immigrant experience. Once on the ferry (best views are from the top deck on the right-hand side), you can disembark at either island and board a later boat to continue your trip. Schedules vary, but the service generally runs daily starting at 9am (the last trip starts around 3:50pm); allow at least half an hour beforehand to clear security. Boats depart every 30 minutes (every 20 min. on busy weekends); sailing time is about 15 minutes to Liberty Island, another 10 minutes to Ellis Island, and 10 minutes back to Manhattan. The fare is $10 for adults, $8 for seniors, and $4 for children 4 to 12. For information and current schedules, call ✆ **212/269-5755** or go to **www.circle lineferry.com.** For advance tickets, call ✆ **800/600-1600.**

Where to Eat: There's a big, clean **cafeteria** on the site, as well as a snack bar on the ferry. Bring a picnic lunch if you can—there are plenty of places to sit out and eat.

On Ellis Island in New York Harbor. ✆ 212/363-3200. www.ellisisland.com. Free admission. Mon–Fri 9:30am–5pm; Sat–Sun 9am–5:30pm (extended hours in summer). Closed Dec 25. Subway: 4, 5 to Bowling Green; 1, 9 to South Ferry.

Madame Tussauds New York ⚡ **Ages 7 & up.** Transplanted from London, this wax museum to the stars has adapted its slightly creepy signature attraction to the Big Apple by featuring wax replicas of quintessential New Yorkers such as former mayor Rudolph Giuliani, Woody Allen, Joe DiMaggio, Yoko Ono, Jacqueline Kennedy Onassis, Donald Trump, and Andy Warhol. (Never fear, they'll still have Tussauds favorites like Princess Di and the Beatles.) The admission fees are outrageous, granted, but I have to admit we had a whopping good time here, prowling through room after room of these meticulously crafted effigies. Evening hours mean that you can fit this into your schedule after most of the regular museums have closed for the day. Young children may get freaked out by the all-too-lifelike statues; it's better for kids old enough to recognize the celebrities and the great figures from the past. Be sure to bring a camera—we went through a whole roll as my sons posed themselves next to statue after statue (the obligatory rabbit-ear fingers held behind Gandhi's head . . .). I have to confess, we skipped the ghoulish section re-creating the French Revolution, which is rife with blood and dismemberment (another Tussauds trademark).

234 W. 42nd St. (btwn Seventh and Eighth aves.). ✆ 800/246-8872. www.nycwax.com. Admission $29 adults, $26 seniors, $23 children 4–12. Mon–Thurs 10am–10pm; Fri–Sun 10am–11:30pm. Subway: A, C, E to 42nd St./Port Authority; N, Q, R, S, W, 1, 2, 3, 7, 9 to 42nd St./Times Sq.

Metropolitan Museum of Art ⚡⚡ **All ages.** Even though this is the city's number-one tourist attraction, many families we know never take their young kids here. Big mistake. You can have a great time at the Metropolitan, even with toddlers, so long as you remember two rules: Go at their pace, not yours (forget about standing transfixed for 10 min. in front of that wonderfully serene Vermeer), and don't let the gruff museum guards intimidate you. They're the city's most fervent believers that children should be seen and not heard—they'll level stern, disapproving glares if your child so much as skips for joy or exclaims above a whisper. Naturally, don't let youngsters touch the precious works of art or press their fingers against glass cases, but otherwise, let your own common sense prevail.

Granted, the $20 admission price can be off-putting, but remember that children under 12 get in free. And it's only a suggested donation—if you think your kids' attention spans are too short for a lengthy visit, don't be shy about paying less. A better strategy to get your money's worth, however, is to inquire at the information desk about what children's programs may be available that day—these are free with admission, and they're a brilliant way to get the kids immersed in the collection.

The echoing marble-clad Great Hall tells you as you enter that this is a Serious Art Museum. If there's a long ticket line at the booths in front of the entrance, go to the right, past the cloakroom—the booth at the north end is generally quicker. My kids love to climb the awesome central stairway up to the European painting galleries, the museum's prize jewel, but we generally veer off and skip those galleries—they go on forever, boring the pants off most kids.

Here are the galleries kids are more likely to enjoy: the **arms and armor** (first floor), the extensive **Egyptian rooms** (also on the first floor—make a beeline for the glorious mummies), **musical instruments** (second floor, off the American Wing's courtyard), the **Costume Institute** (ground floor—rotating installations will be of varying interest to kids), and the **European** and **American period rooms** (all over the place). On the first floor of the **American Wing,** a side gallery displays vintage baseball cards, and a whole gallery of grandfather clocks ticks away on the second floor. Older kids who are beginning to appreciate art may go for the **Impressionist gallery** (second floor) or the **Lehman Pavilion,** set up like the townhouse of a wealthy collector—it's art in small enough doses that it doesn't overwhelm.

Our favorite corner, hands down, is the **courtyard of the American Wing,** a light-filled open space with plantings, benches, and statues kids can actually relate to (a mountain lion and her cubs, a pensive Indian brave). Bring lots of small change for them to throw into the pool here and in the pool in front of the Egyptian Wing's momentous **Temple of Dendur** (but *not* in the Chinese scholars' court goldfish pool in the second-floor Asian art galleries!). In the Japanese galleries, find the room overlooking the Temple of Dendur; off the musical instruments gallery, find the balcony overlooking the mounted knights in armor. Get the idea? Wander around this immense museum, keep your eyes open, and be willing to walk away from anything that doesn't interest your children.

The huge **museum gift shop** has a lot of good stuff for kids (see "The Best Shops That Just Happen to Be in Museums," on p. 242).

Where to Eat: The **museum cafe** beneath the Lehman Pavilion is set up with an array of food stations (hot food, deli, salad bar, and the like), which makes it easy to beeline for what your kids will like; we've never run into a seriously long line. Child meals come packaged in cute yellow cardboard taxis. Or, since your museum badge allows re-entry, go outside and sit on the splendid Fifth Avenue steps (one of the city's best impromptu grandstands) to eat a hot dog bought at a nearby pushcart.

1000 Fifth Ave. (at 82nd St.). ℂ 212/535-7710. For daily tours and programs call ℂ 212/570-3930. www.met museum.org. Suggested donation (includes same-day admission to the Cloisters) $20 adults, $10 students and seniors, free for children 12 and under. Tues–Thurs and Sun 9:30am–5:30pm; Fri–Sat 9:30am–9pm. Closed Jan 1, Thanksgiving, and Dec 25; open some school holiday Mondays (check website). Strollers not permitted Sun (back carriers available at 81st St. entrance). Subway: 4, 5, 6 to 86th St.

South Street Seaport and the Seaport Museum ℞ **All ages.** One of the reasons why New York became the biggest city in the United States was its prominence as a port, something that's easy to forget in these days of jet travel and internet communications. But down here, in this charming jumble of restored warehouses and maritime shops on the cobblestone East River waterfront, you'll go straight back to New York Harbor's clipper-ship heyday. Like its counterparts in Boston and Baltimore, some of South Street Seaport has been converted into a 21st-century "festival marketplace," and you can spend a fun day here just with the shops and restaurants, pier-side entertainers, and wide-open East River views. If you fork over admission to the Seaport Museum, however, you'll discover a whole new dimension. There's a small but interesting hands-on **children's museum** at 165 John St.; a **gallery** presenting rotating historic exhibits; a 19th-century **printing shop** at 211 Water St.; a **boatbuilding shop** at the corner of John and South streets; and best of all, several **historic ships** to climb onto, including the gallant four-masted barque *Peking* and the imposing wrought-iron sailing ship *Wavertree*. **Harbor cruises** on the *Zephyr* or the historic *Pioneer*, an 1885 schooner, also leave from here (see "Boat Tours," later in this chapter). Special children's workshops and storytelling hours are organized all over the place—pick up a schedule at the visitor center or call ⓒ **212/748-8758.** What with the ocean air whipping in off the estuary, you'll feel like old salts before the day is through.

12 Fulton St. (btwn Water and South sts.). ⓒ **212/748-8600.** www.southstseaport.org. Admission $8 adults, $6 students and seniors, $4 children 5–12. Apr–Oct Tues–Sun 10am–6pm; Nov–Mar Fri–Mon 10am–5pm. Subway: 2, 3, 4, 5 to Fulton St.; A, C to Broadway/Nassau St.

Statue of Liberty ℞℞ **Ages 3 & up.** The symbol of New York is impressive enough from across the harbor, but close up—man, this chick is *big*. It gives me vertigo just to look up at her. (In fact, younger kids may be frightened by the sheer scale of Lady Liberty.) At present, visitors cannot climb up inside the statue, but ranger-led tours explore the promenade (right inside the entrance is displayed her original torch, replaced at the statue's centennial in 1986), or go to the 10th-floor observatory to look at fascinating exhibits and peer up through a glass ceiling into her copper-clad steel skeleton. Timed-pass tickets for these tours must be reserved in advance, although a certain number are available on a walk-in basis at the ferry ticket office at Castle Clinton. Even if you don't have a tour reservation, it's fun to stroll around Liberty Island to gaze out over the harbor. For some kids, the ferry ride over may be more fun than the statue itself.

Getting There: The **ferryboats** make frequent trips, running a loop from Battery Park to Liberty Island to Ellis Island and back to Battery Park (from New Jersey, you can board ferries in Liberty State Park). In Battery Park, you can buy tickets at Castle Clinton, where there are some interesting exhibits to help pass the time before your ferry. The wait in line can take a while, and security procedures include metal detectors, bag searches, and waiting in several different holding pens—you'll come to appreciate the statue's poem about huddled masses yearning to be free. (Keep in mind that if you're carrying belongings that can't fit into a milk crate, you won't be allowed onto the ferry to Liberty or Ellis islands.) Once on the ferry (best views are from the top deck on the right-hand side), you can disembark at either island and board a later boat to continue your trip. Schedules vary, but the service generally runs daily starting at

The While-Waiting-in-Line-at-Lady-Liberty Quiz

1. The Statue of Liberty weighs
   a. 225 tons.
   b. 25 tons.
   c. 225 pounds (when she's been to her step-aerobics class).

2. The statue's full official name is
   a. The Gatekeeper of Liberty.
   b. Liberty Enlightening the World.
   c. Liberty Looking for a Lost Contact Lens.

3. Sculptor Frédéric-Auguste Bartholdi is said to have modeled the statue after
   a. the Mona Lisa.
   b. Napoleon Bonaparte's girlfriend.
   c. his mommy.

4. Emma Lazarus's poem *The New Colossus* ("Give me your tired, your poor . . .") is engraved
   a. on the tablet Liberty cradles in her arm.
   b. on a plaque inside the base of the statue.
   c. on a tattoo on every park ranger's left bicep.

5. The engineer who designed the statue's tricky steel skeleton is also known for
   a. the Eiffel Tower in Paris.
   b. the Brooklyn Bridge.
   c. the Spaceship Earth sphere at Epcot.

9am (the last trip starts around 3:50pm); allow at least half an hour beforehand to clear security. Boats depart every 30 minutes, every 20 minutes on busy weekends; sailing time is about 15 minutes to Liberty Island, another 10 minutes to Ellis Island, and 10 minutes back to Manhattan. The fare is $10 for adults, $8 for seniors, and $4 for children 4 to 12. For information and current schedules, call ✆ **212/269-5755** or go to **www.circlelineferry.com**. For advance tickets, call ✆ **800/600-1600**.

Where to Eat: There's a **snack bar** on the ferry but no food services on Liberty Island itself. (There are some at Ellis Island.) If you bring a picnic lunch, watch out for marauding seagulls.

On Liberty Island in New York Harbor. ✆ **212/269-5755** for ferry schedules; ✆ **212/363-3200** for information. For tour reservations, call ✆ **866/782-8834** (✆ 212/269-5755 from outside U.S.) or order online at www.statue reservations.com. Free admission; service charge for tour reservations $1.75 per person. Aug–June daily 9am–6:15pm; July daily 8:30am–4:30pm. Closed Dec 25. Subway: 4, 5 to Bowling Green; 1, 9 to South Ferry.

United Nations 🍀🍀 **Ages 8 & up.** Technically it's not even part of New York City, but an international zone all its own—step onto U.N. property and you can say you visited each of its 192 member nations in one day. This stunning East River site, its serene lawns and gardens cantilevered cleverly over the FDR Drive, makes a grand setting for that memorable architectural design: the low dome of the General Assembly

6. The French intellectual who first proposed the idea for the statue was
   a. the Marquis de Lafayette.
   b. Edouard René Lefebvre de Laboulaye.
   c. Pepe Le Pew.

7. Once completed and shipped in sections to the United States, the statue almost wasn't erected because
   a. Americans lost the instructions on how to put it together.
   b. Americans hadn't raised enough money to build a pedestal for it.
   c. everybody thought it was so ugly.

8. Lady Liberty looks green because
   a. the statue's hammered-copper sheathing has oxidized as expected.
   b. pollution from New York Harbor has corroded it.
   c. she gets seasick from watching the ferries chug past all day.

9. The statue's nose is
   a. 4½ feet long.
   b. 10 feet long.
   c. 100 feet long (she could use some plastic surgery).

10. The Statue of Liberty was given to the people of the United States by the people of France
    a. because there was no room for it in Paris.
    b. in repayment of old war debts.
    c. to symbolize a special friendship between the two countries.

ANSWERS: 1. a 2. b 3. c 4. b 5. a 6. b 7. b 8. a 9. a 10. c.

building tucked in at the base of the sheer glass plinth of the Secretariat Building. You'll mingle with an international cast of characters, African and Asian and Scandinavian and Middle Eastern and Latin American bureaucrats chattering in a Babel of different tongues: It really brings home to me how big the world is and what an amazing feat it is to get all these people to agree on *anything*.

Walk past the long line of flagpoles (one for every member nation) to reach the visitors entrance at 46th Street and First Avenue; go through security and proceed through the lobby to get on a **guided tour** in English. These run every 10-30 minutes and last nearly an hour (call ✆ 212/963-7539 to find out about tours in other languages). These information-loaded talks fill you in on the organization's history while you cruise around to the complex's major highlights—the General Assembly Hall, the Security Council chamber, and other major meeting halls. The modernist interiors, mostly furnished in sleek Scandinavian style, look a little worn and frayed since their 1950s inception, but there are many details that will impress the kids—the earpieces for simultaneous translations, the glassed-in booths for TV cameras, the horseshoe-shaped Security Council table, and massive pieces of internationally commissioned art and sculpture. A sobering exhibit of relics from the 1945 bombing of Nagasaki and Hiroshima reminds us of why the U.N. was formed in the first place; an exhibit on the horrors of landmines reminds us why it still is necessary.

The various U.N. agencies operate year-round, so there's always plenty of activity on the grounds. But things heat up when the General Assembly is in session, from the third Tuesday in September until sometime near the end of December. The **Gift Center** downstairs is great for finding unusual international handcrafts, including a delightful collection of dolls of all nations.

Where to Eat: There is a quick coffee shop near the gift shops, but for a more special experience, try the **Delegates Dining Room** (reservations required—call ℂ **212/ 963-7625,** and be sure to bring a photo I.D.; jackets are required for men, and no sneakers or shorts are allowed), open to the public Monday through Friday from 11:30am to 2:30pm. Even if it's not exactly packed with high-level diplomats, the river views are great.

On the East River from 42nd to 48th sts. (entrance at First Ave. and 46th St.). ℂ **212/963-TOUR.** www.un.org. Admission $12 adults, $8 students, $8.50 seniors, $7 ages 5–14; children under 5 not admitted on tours. Mon-Fri 9:30am–4:45pm; Sat–Sun10am–4:30pm Mar-Dec. No tours Jan 1, Thanksgiving, Dec 25; limited schedule Sept–Oct. Subway: S, 4, 5, 6, 7 to 42nd St./Grand Central. Bus: M15, M27, M42, M104.

2 Best Views

Battery Park City Esplanade   **All ages.** The Statue of Liberty, Ellis Island, the Verrazano Bridge, and the Jersey City skyline punctuate the harbor views from this landscaped riverside walkway in a stunning residential/office development at the lower edge of Manhattan. People loll on the benches reading the *Times,* coffee mugs in hand; dog owners walk frisky pets on leashes; in-line skaters and cyclists weave patiently around pedestrians; and children hang on the inward-curved railings watching yachts cruise past on their way to the boat basin at the north end. No panhandlers, no T-shirt vendors, no ice cream carts—it's a wonderfully civil scene.

On the Hudson River, between Chambers St. and Battery Place. Subway: A, C to Chambers St.

Brooklyn Heights Promenade ⚘ **All ages.** The calm here is so palpable, you'd never know that the Brooklyn-Queens Expressway is rumbling underneath this cantilevered promenade. On one side are the back gardens of lovely Brooklyn Heights town houses; on the other, the East River and a drop-dead view of Lower Manhattan and the harbor. It faces west, which means that the view is especially terrific near sunset. Best of all, if you're with little kids, there's a superb neighborhood playground at the south end, near Pierrepont Street. Combine this with a walk across the Brooklyn Bridge or a visit to the New York Transit Museum (p. 170), and you've got a great day trip.

West of Columbia Heights (btwn Montague and Cranberry sts.), Brooklyn Heights, Brooklyn. Subway: 2, 3 to Clark St.; then follow Clark St. west to reach the Promenade.

Empire State Building ⚘ **Ages 6 & up.** The Empire State Building is the classic skyscraper observation deck—after all, this is where Cary Grant and Deborah Kerr missed their rendezvous in *An Affair to Remember* and Tom Hanks and Meg Ryan made theirs in *Sleepless in Seattle.* And, of course, this is where Fay Wray and King Kong had their own kind of rendezvous. Shabby as much of the building has become, its Art Deco lobby is still impressive, and the location puts you squarely in the middle of Manhattan, with close-up views to all sides. Tickets for the observation deck are sold up on the second floor concourse, where you can also waste some money on the **New York SkyRide** attraction (see later in this chapter). Elevators whiz you up to the small enclosed observation deck on the 86th floor (change elevators at the 80th floor), which also has narrow outdoor promenades on all sides, though the parapets are too high in many places for youngsters to see over. If you invested the extra $14 downstairs, you can go even further up to get porthole-type window viewing from the 102nd floor (1,250 ft. up). An excellent tape, available for $6, tells you exactly what you're looking out at—not a bad investment if you're an out-of-towner. Gift shops in the main lobby and on the 86th floor sell all kinds of New York City, Empire State Building, and (of course) King Kong knickknacks.

350 Fifth Ave. (at 34th St.). ℂ 212/736-3100. www.esbnyc.com. Admission $16 adults, $14 seniors and students 12–17, $10 children 6–11, free for children under 5. Daily 8am–midnight (July–Aug also open Thurs–Sat until 2am). Subway: B, D, F, N, Q, R, V, W to 34th St./Herald Sq.

Top of the Rock 🌟 **Ages 6 & up.** Though the Empire State Building deck is higher, I'd recommend the Deco-detailed observation terraces atop Rockefeller Center's GE Building, especially for folks who get uneasy with heights—they're cleaner, roomier, and more securely enclosed with big glass panes that don't hinder the view. The 67th floor deck is mostly indoors, a boon if the weather's rainy or cold; an escalator takes you on up to floor 69, where wide terraces ring the building (this is the only level where you can take in views to the west), and stairs lead up to the narrower 70th floor outdoor deck. The elevator ride up is fun—the elevator car has a glass ceiling that allows you to look right up the shaft as you zoom upward; another fun feature is the Target Breezeway on floor 69 where colored lights behind opaque white panels switch on and off in response to people's movements around the room.

30 Rockefeller Center (entrance 50th St. between 5th and 6th aves.). ℂ 212/698-2000. www.topoftherocknyc.com. Admission $18 adults, $11 children 6–12, $16 seniors. Daily 8am–midnight. Subway: B, D, F, V to 47th–50th sts./Rockefeller Center.

3 More Manhattan Museums

American Folk Art Museum **All ages.** For whatever reason, even young kids get the point of folk art—in fact, young kids sometimes enjoy this stuff more than older kids who think they know what "good" art is. The shows here change continually, but every time we've visited, my children have been charmed by the paintings and sculptures and collages, all by untutored artists, past and present—quilts, weather vanes, bottle-cap sculptures, an immense canvas covered with obsessively tiny handwriting, whatever. If your kids are only good for about 20 minutes of museum-going, pop into the small **Feld Gallery** annex on the Upper West Side (2 Lincoln Sq., on Columbus Ave. between 65th and 66th sts.; 1 train to 66th St./Lincoln Center; open Tues–Sun noon–7:30pm), where admission is free. The gift shop features a selection of toys you won't see everywhere else (see "The Best Shops That Just Happen to Be in Museums," on p. 242).

45 W. 53rd St. (btwn Fifth and Sixth aves.). ℂ 212/265-1040. www.folkartmuseum.org. Admission $9 adults, $7 students and seniors, free for children under 12; free to all Fri 5:30–7:30pm. Tues–Sun 10:30am–5:30pm (Fri until 7:30pm). Closed Mon and legal holidays. Subway: E, V to Fifth Ave./53rd St.

Children's Museum of Manhattan 🌟 **Ages 10 & under.** My children have begun to outgrow this place, but at one time in our lives it was a lifesaver. Best for the under-8 crew, it's full of things they can touch, and boasts space for them to run and jump, make-believe environments, and opportunities to experiment. The museum's four floors also include a playroom especially for 4-and-unders; a carpeted reading room with a puppet theater where kids can do their own impromptu shows; a few computers for older kids to mess around on; an interactive "TV station" where they can project themselves into a broadcast; and an activity-packed basement area that's periodically remodeled with a new literary theme. The outdoor Summer Splash is fun, too, I'm told, though it seems to be closed whenever we're visiting. Young readers may appreciate the fun upstairs corridor that pays homage to various children's-book authors. There are always daily activities (check schedules when you enter) like face painting, storytelling, and shows in the auditorium. On rainy days and during school vacations, the joint gets pretty crowded, and the high-ceilinged spaces reverberate with noise, but it's still worth checking out.

212 W. 83rd St. (btwn Broadway and Amsterdam Ave.). ℂ 212/721-1223. www.cmom.org. Admission $8 adults and children, $4 seniors, free for children under 1. Wed–Sun 10am–5pm; also open Tues 10am–5pm in summer; open school holidays. Subway: 1 to 79th or 86th St.; B, C to 81st St./Museum of Natural History.

Children's Museum of the Arts   Ages 10 & under.
Smaller than the Children's Museum of Manhattan (see above), this is a good alternative if you're downtown, with lots of hands-on stuff for kids. Various art projects are set up; youngsters are encouraged to explore rhythm instruments; a couple of computers loaded with graphics programs are available; children's art from around the world is on display; and there's a small Monet-themed play area where infants and toddlers can work off their extra energy. There are loads of creative workshops scheduled, usually for toddlers in the morning and school-age kids in the later afternoons and on weekends. On rainy or cold weekends, it's crowded to the rafters, so be warned.

182 Lafayette St. (btwn Broome and Grand sts.). ℂ 212/274-0986. www.cmany.org. Admission $8, free for children under 1; pay as you wish Thurs 4–6pm. Wed–Sun noon–5pm (Thurs till 6pm); open school holidays. Subway: 6 to Spring St.; N, R, W to Prince St.

The Cloisters 𝕲𝕲   All ages.
Of course your kids aren't into medieval art—that's not the point. For families, the point of the Cloisters, the Metropolitan's beautiful medieval art annex, is the sheer weirdness of it—a conglomeration of chapels and courtyards and refectories lifted from European convents and monasteries, brought in packing crates to America, and reconstructed here on a bluff-top site in Fort Tryon Park. Wander from room to room, soaking up the time-stands-still atmosphere; go out on the terrace for splendid views of the Hudson River and the New Jersey Palisades, and poke around the monks' herb garden. Talk with your kids about unicorns before you go—there's one fascinating gallery devoted to a series of tapestries depicting a unicorn hunt (a medieval version of an adventure comic strip?).

It's a long trek up here, but your children might actually enjoy the bus ride, which won't take forever if you're coming from the Upper West Side (combine the Cloisters with visits to St. John the Divine and Riverside Church for a full day of Gothic-ness). If you're doing this in the same day as the Metropolitan (which makes sense, since your pricey admission covers both sites), compare what you see up here to the Met's first-floor medieval galleries.

In Fort Tryon Park, at 193rd St. and Fort Washington Ave. ℂ 212/923-3700. www.metmuseum.org. Suggested donation (includes same-day admission to Metropolitan Museum of Art) $20 adults, $10 students and seniors, free for children 12 and under. Tues–Sun 9:30am–5:15pm (closes at 4:45pm Nov–Feb). Closed Jan 1, Thanksgiving, and Dec 25. Free parking. Subway: A to 190th St. Bus: M4 to the end of line.

Cooper-Hewitt National Design Museum   Ages 5 & up.
Check to see what exhibit is currently running at this Smithsonian branch devoted to design and decorative arts: A surprising number of them appeal to kids (clothing, furniture, advertising

Rainy Days & Mondays

Given that Monday is New York City's standard museum closing day, many a visitor on a tight schedule has been disappointed to find sights shuttered up on Monday. A number of family-friendly attractions are open on Monday, however, including the following:

- American Museum of Natural History
- Cooper-Hewitt National Design Museum
- Ellis Island and the Statue of Liberty
- Empire State Building/New York Skyride
- Guggenheim Museum of Art
- Madame Tussauds New York
- Merchant's House Museum
- Museum of Modern Art in Queens
- National Museum of the American Indian
- New York Public Library
- New York Unearthed
- New York Transit Museum's satellite gallery in Grand Central Station
- Queens County Farm Museum
- South Street Seaport Museum
- Top of the Rock
- The Toys "R" Us Ferris wheel
- United Nations
- Yankee Stadium

All five of the city's zoos are open 7 days a week as well. The New York Botanical Garden and Brooklyn Botanic Garden, while usually closed on Monday, are open on Monday during 3-day holiday weekends. And to accommodate the schoolchildren who are their core audience, three outer-borough attractions—the Brooklyn Children's Museum, the New York Hall of Science, and Historic Richmond Town—stay open on Mondays during the summer school vacation period.

posters), and the accompanying material is usually so lucid that even a young kid can grasp what's interesting about the displays. What's more, it gives you a chance to get inside industrial tycoon Andrew Carnegie's surprisingly homey neo-Georgian mansion—don't forget to check out the beautiful plaster ceilings, and point out to kids how low some of the doorways are (Carnegie, a short man, wanted the house built to *his* scale). My older son fell in love with the elegant leaded-glass conservatory. There's a nice garden out back and a super gift shop with a number of clever toys and kids' books; it's set in Carnegie's library—look at the inlaid designs in the wood paneling (see "The Best Shops That Just Happen to Be in Museums," on p. 242).

2 E. 91st St. (at Fifth Ave.). © 212/049-8400. www.cooperhewitt.org. Admission $12 adults, $7 students and seniors, free for children 12 and under; free to all Tues 5–9pm. Mon–Thurs 10am–5pm; Fri 10am–9pm; Sat 10am–6pm; Sun noon–6pm. Closed major holidays. Subway: 4, 5, 6 to 86th St.

What Goes Around Comes Around: New York's Carousels

My kids are suckers for old-fashioned merry-go-rounds, no matter how corny the music, and luckily for us, New York is well supplied with them. The best-known is probably the vintage 1908 **Central Park Carousel** (midpark near 64th St.; open daily year-round) with its elaborately carved wooden horses spinning around for 4 minutes to creaky tunes like "Rainy Days and Mondays"; it's not far from either the zoo or the Wollman Rink, another plus. Our other antique choice is also near a good zoo: the **Prospect Park Carousel** (Flatbush Ave. entrance, Prospect Park, open Thurs–Sun and holidays), which has giraffes and zebras and other exotics in addition to horses, all painted in fanciful pastels.

These being postmodern times, however, a new generation of retro carousels has sprung up recently, just as meticulously handcrafted but often with a clever twist. The **Bryant Park Carousel** (in Bryant Park, between 40th and 42nd sts. along Sixth Ave., open daily) may be small but it's enchanting, with a riot of pastel floral decorations and a deer, a frog, and a bunny alongside the traditional horses. Though its ornate style is French-inspired, it was manufactured in good old Brooklyn, by the same firm that also made the distinctive **Riverbank Carousel** (Riverbank State Park, 145th St. and Riverside Dr.; open Fri–Sun in summer); this one is most memorable, with its wonderfully whacked-out steeds designed by New York City kids themselves. The lucky schoolchildren whose drawings were chosen to be reproduced— fanciful creatures like winged frogs replacing the traditional horses—were awarded free rides for life. Now there's a lottery worth winning.

Forbes Magazine Galleries *Value*   **All ages.** An obsessive collector, publishing magnate Malcolm Forbes had enough money to turn his obsessions into a strange and wonderful little museum. Basically, he collected five things: toy boats, toy soldiers, Monopoly games, medals and trophies, and lavishly bejeweled Fabergé eggs. The eggs were recently sold, for a princely sum, but that leaves plenty that kids do love. This labyrinth of small galleries won't tax youngsters' attention spans, though they should be warned ahead that this is a sedate don't-touch kind of place. (No strollers permitted inside, either.) The display windows aren't always low enough for small children, so expect to do a lot of lifting. Your kids may not want to linger as long as you do over the minutiae of the collection—remember, Forbes was a grown-up when he collected this stuff, with an adult's idea of what made something valuable. But there's still enough here to make kids press their noses against the glass for a good half-hour or so, more if they're older.

60 Fifth Ave. (at 12th St.). © 212/206-5548. www.forbesgalleries.com. Free admission. Tues–Wed and Fri–Sat 10am–4pm. Closed major holidays. Subway: N, Q, R, W, 4, 5, 6 to 14th St.; L to Union Sq.

Guggenheim Museum   **Ages 6 & up.** The Guggenheim's rotating exhibits of 20th-century art may or may not appeal to your kids—Norman Rockwell maybe yes, Mark Rothko maybe no. No matter. The main reason for including this museum in your NYC itinerary is the museum building itself: Frank Lloyd Wright's glorious, streamlined, totally wacky inverted spiral, which displays the art along one long ramp coiling down around a huge central atrium. I mean, can you imagine doing the Guggenheim on a *skateboard?* Since kids 11 and younger get in for free, it may be worthwhile to pay the adult admission just so you can enjoy this visionary interior for half an hour. In any case, the side galleries display some artworks kids might enjoy, by such masters as Degas, Cézanne, and Picasso.

1071 Fifth Ave. (at 89th St.). ℂ 212/423-3500. www.guggenheim.org. Admission $18 adults, $15 students and seniors, free for children 11 and under. Fri–Wed 10am–5:45pm (until 7:45pm Fri) Subway: 4, 5, 6 to 86th St.

Lower East Side Tenement Museum 🎨🎨 **Ages 5 & up.** A collection of 19th-century tenement buildings has been converted into this brilliant small museum that picks up the immigrant story where Ellis Island leaves off—in the poor neighborhoods where the new arrivals landed. Once you've seen these bare, cramped living quarters, all too authentically furnished, your kids may never fight again over sharing a bedroom. (It's the perfect antidote to all those ornate period rooms at the Metropolitan Museum.) The restored tenement apartments can only be seen via hour-long guided tours; book ahead to make sure you get onto the right tour. Furnishings and other artifacts tell the stories of immigrants from different homelands and eras of immigration; the best one for kids would be the living-history tour of the Confino apartment, Sephardic Jews who emigrated from Turkey around 1916, which features costumed interpreters. It's held only on weekend afternoons, and tours are limited to 15 people, so reserve in advance, especially for Sunday. Weekend walking tours widen the scope to include the whole neighborhood—they're wonderful if your kids are old enough to keep up with the pace.

108 Orchard St. (below Delancey St.). ℂ 212/431-0233. www.tenement.org. Tours $15 adults, $11 students and seniors (except Confino Program $14 adults, $10 students and seniors). Gallery/ticket office open daily 11am–5:30pm. Advance tickets available through TicketWeb (ℂ 866/811-4111; www.ticketweb.com). Subway: J, M, Z to Essex St.; F to Delancey St.

The Morgan Library **Ages 8 & up.** The Morgan Library's refined gallery space exhibits prints and drawings, which may or may not be of interest to your kids—past shows about A.A. Milne or St. Exupery's *The Little Prince* were totally delightful for youngsters, but that isn't always the case. What kids will appreciate is the wing J. P. Morgan actually used as a library, especially his elegant wood-paneled study with its ceiling-high shelves of rare books, gorgeously bound in leather.

225 Madison Ave. (at E. 36th St.). ℂ 212/685-0008. www.morganlibrary.org. Admission $12 adults, $8 students and seniors, free for children 12 and under. Tues–Thurs 10:30am–5pm, Fri 10:30am–9pm, Sat 10am–6pm, Sun 11am–6pm. Closed holidays. Subway: 6 to 33rd St.

Museum of Chinese in the Americas **Ages 5 & up.** Nestled in the atmospheric heart of Chinatown, this museum mounts fascinating rotating exhibits, mostly drawn from its huge collection of photographs and artifacts—tiny shoes for a Chinese woman's bound feet, tin tea canisters, brocaded Chinese opera costumes, the heavy irons used in a laundry. Located on the second floor of a shabby old school building, the gallery is a stunning surprise, with 15 angled translucent walls creating the illusion of being inside a giant Chinese lantern. Saturday afternoons are a great time to visit, to take advantage of free hands-on workshops for kids (teaching about paper folding, shadow puppets, etc.) or in-depth themed walking tours of Chinatown (tours $12 adults, $6 students and seniors, children 5 and under free).

70 Mulberry St. (at Bayard St.). *C* **212/619-4785.** www.moca-nyc.org. Suggested admission $3 adults, $1 students and seniors, free for children 11 and under. Tues–Sun noon–6pm (also closed Mon in summer). Subway: N, Q, R, W, 6 to Canal St.

Museum of Modern Art (MoMA) 𝄞𝄞 **All ages.** The "modern" in the museum's name no longer means cutting edge, but its galleries do provide a retrospective of the best in 20th-century art, from Picasso to Pollock, from Rodin to Rothko, and its newly expanded Midtown space should finally give MoMA room to display more daring stuff. The very young may be blissfully happy here because they don't care whether a painting looks like anything; preschoolers who've just learned how to make a tree look like a tree may be baffled by a canvas covered with mere spatters of paint, but they'll get the bright images of Andy Warhol's pop art or the moody intensity of van Gogh. My older son fell permanently in love with Picasso after a Sunday afternoon here, while my younger son prefers the meticulous architectural models. My daughter's favorite spot is the splendid central sculpture garden.

Though the adult entrance fee is high, kids under 16 get in free, so your visit here may end up costing no more than an afternoon at the American Museum of Natural History (once you've paid AMNH's extra fees for IMAX and the sky show and special exhibits). Saturday activities for kids include special tours for 4-year-olds, gallery talks for ages 5 to 10, interactive activity workshops for the entire family, and programs of classic short films chosen for a family audience.

11 West 53rd St. (btwn Fifth and Sixth aves.). *C* **212/708-9480.** www.moma.org. Admission: $20 adults, $16 seniors, $12 students, children under 16 free when accompanied by an adult; Fri 4–8pm, pay what you wish. Wed–Mon 10:30am–5:30pm (until 8pm Fri). Subway: E, V to Fifth Ave.

Museum of Television & Radio **Ages 5 & up.** In this sleek Midtown museum (with a sister branch in L.A.), junior couch potatoes can gorge on all kinds of broadcast media, from vintage commercials to 1960s sitcoms to TV coverage of the first moonwalk. Get here early in the day and make a reservation to use the library, where you can search the database on a Mac and then call up a program on an individual console with headphones. If you can't get a reservation, at least stop by the fifth-floor radio-listening room to sample sound bites from timely preselected programs or attend any of the screenings running frequently in a number of cushy small theaters. Weekends are the best time for kids, when there are hands-on workshops in the morning and uncrowded screenings of top international children's TV shows in the afternoon; the staff is genuinely friendly to youngsters. If your child's hooked on TV Land, plan for hours of browsing.

25 W. 52nd St. (btwn Fifth & Sixth aves.). *C* **212/621-6600** or 212/621-6800. www.mtr.org. Admission $10 adults, $8 students, $5 children 13 and under. Tues–Sun noon–6pm (until 8pm Thurs). Closed major holidays. Subway: E, V to Fifth Ave./53rd St.

Museum of the City of New York 𝄞 *Finds* **Ages 3 & up.** If you're on Museum Mile already, your kids may enjoy this more than the art museums further south (be sure to skip across the street afterward to Central Park's lovely Conservatory Garden— see p. 177). The biggest draw for kids is the spectacular exhibit of dolls and dollhouses in the Toys Gallery, though some kids I know like to come here just to parade up and down the gorgeous staircase in the entrance hall. Prowling through recreated bedchambers and parlors and gazing at displays of famous New Yorker's fashionable outfits is a great way for kids to peek back in history. Theater lovers won't want to miss the Broadway exhibit, displaying posters and mementos from the Great White Way (including a costume Barbra Streisand wore in *Funny Girl*). My daughter, Grace, was blown away upon seeing the black net "shadow" that Wendy sewed back onto Peter Pan's toes in the old Mary Martin musical—that's the kind of cool stuff this museum has hidden away.

1220 Fifth Ave. (at 103rd St.). ℭ 212/534-1672. www.mcny.org. Suggested admission $9 adults; $5 students and seniors, children 12 and under free; $20 families. Tues–Sun 10am–5pm. Subway: 6 to 103rd St. Bus: M1/M2/M3/M4.

National Museum of the American Indian *(Value)* **Ages 5 & up.** A branch of the Smithsonian, this museum enjoys a fabulous setting in the ornate 1907 U.S. Customs House, a Beaux Arts gem that was a principal site in the movie *Ghostbusters II*. To enter the exhibition galleries, you pass through the awesome Great Rotunda—don't miss looking up at the painted dome. The museum has vast holdings, only a small portion of which are on display here (especially now that the Smithsonian has opened its main NMAI museum on the Mall down in Washington DC). It isn't big on inter-activity, but wend your way through the series of rooms and you should be able to find something of interest, particularly if your kids have studied Native American culture in school—a hanging bison hide they can stroke, a glass case filled with hundreds of moccasins, mysterious Mesoamerican clay figures, or some eye-opening art by con-temporary Native American artists.

1 Bowling Green, beside Battery Park. ℭ 212/514-3700. www.nmai.si.edu. Free admission. Daily 10am–5pm (Thurs till 8pm). Closed Dec 25. Subway: 4, 5 to Bowling Green; R, W to Whitehall St./South Ferry.

New York City Fire Museum **Ages 3 & up.** Though small, this two-story museum in a converted firehouse is worth the money if your kids are as much into fire trucks as my son was at a certain age. There's an awesome collection of antique fire engines, including several horse-drawn ones (the horses aren't on display, unfortunately, but there's a stuffed fire dog that used to be the mascot of one Brooklyn firehouse). A lot of the museum is most interesting to adults patient enough to pore over the memen-tos of 19th-century firefighting, but there are enough bells, alarms, pickaxes, and noz-zles to hold the youngsters' interest for 45 minutes or so. Best of all, there are usually retired firefighters on hand eager to explain each apparatus to admiring youngsters.

278 Spring St. (btwn Varick & Hudson sts.). ℭ 212/691-1303. www.nycfiremuseum.org. Suggested admission $5 adults, $2 students and seniors, $1 children 11 and under. Tues–Sat 10am–5pm; Sun 10am–4pm. Subway: 1 to Hous-ton St.; C, E to Spring St

New York City Police Museum *(Value)* **Ages 6 & up.** With everything from vin-tage uniforms to a mock-up of a crime scene and a computer simulation of what it would be like to be confronted with a gun-wielding criminal, this collection of police memorabilia should mesmerize any child who's into cops and robbers. Confiscated weapons (including Al Capone's machine gun), counterfeit money, old patrol cars and motorcycles, badges and radios and alarms and nightsticks . . . the mind boggles. It's staffed by NYPD officers and has a clear bias toward supporting law enforcement.

100 Old Slip. (at South St.). ℭ 212/480-3100. www.nycpolicemuseum.org. Suggested admission: $5 adults, $3 stu-dents and seniors, $2 children 11 and under. Tues–Sun 10am–5pm. Subway: 1, R, W to Rector St.; J, M, Z to Broad St.; 4, 5 to Bowling Green.

New-York Historical Society **Ages 4 & up.** Rotating exhibits here will be of varying interest to children, but we've enjoyed several of them in recent years—the blockbuster Alexander Hamilton exhibit, for example, exhibits of Presidential cam-paign memorabilia, or the occasional opportunity to gaze upon John James Audubon's stunning original art for his classic *Birds of America.* Older children may be ready to browse through the fourth-floor exhibit space, crammed with treasures from the society's vast holdings—George Washington's camp bed from Valley Forge, the desk where Clement Clarke Moore wrote *A Visit from St. Nicholas,* a glorious collection of Tiffany lamps, and a portrait of an early governor of New York dressed as a woman.

2 W. 77th St. (at Central Park W.) ℂ 212/873-3400. www.nyhistory.org. Admission $10 adults, $5 students and seniors, free for children 11 and under. Tues–Sun 10am–6pm. Subway: B, C to 81st St./Museum of Natural History.

New York Public Library **Ages 10 & up.** Though most little kids fall in love with the noble pair of lions—Patience and Fortitude—poised beside the front steps, the exhibits mounted inside the New York Public Library are usually of interest to older kids only. (But you never know—there was an exhibit on garbage in 1995 that my boys thought was totally cool.) The library does have an extraordinary collection of first editions, manuscripts, letters, prints, maps, and other treasures on paper and often puts together fascinating shows, but whether or not your youngster will be intrigued all depends on the theme. Otherwise, pop in for a few minutes just to gape at the Beaux Arts architecture, from the dignified marble lobby to the extraordinary third-floor Main Reading Room, where anyone can join the scholars and writers at endless ranks of tables poring over research materials from the NYPL's famous stacks. Note that behind the library is **Bryant Park,** which has cafes and its own spiffy little carousel.

The NYPL's **Donnell Branch,** 20 W. 53rd St., between Fifth and Sixth avenues (ℂ **212/621-0636**), may be worth a stop, too, to see the original Winnie-the-Pooh animals displayed in the Central Children's room (generally open noon–6pm, with some minor variations, and closed Sun).

Fifth Ave. at 41st St. ℂ 212/930-0830. www.nypl.org. Free admission. Tues–Wed 11am–7:30pm, Thurs–Sat 10am–6pm. Subway: B, D, F, V to 42nd St.; 7 to Fifth Ave.

Sony Wonder Technology Lab 🌟 ⱱₐₗᵤₑ **Ages 6 & up.** Though no doubt it helps sell Sony products, this wonderful interactive exploratorium isn't annoyingly self-serving. Sony Wonder actually lets people experiment with all types of high-tech equipment, from TV cameras to industrial robots to ultrasound scanners; you can play at being a game designer, movie director, or electronic musician or just mess around in a multisensory interactive environment. When you first enter the lab, you get your own **personal card,** which becomes magnetically encoded with your name and photo; as you continue through four floors of activities, every time you slide the card through the scanner on a new terminal, your name and photo are inserted into whatever program is up. On your way out, you can print out a personalized certificate recording all the activities you tried. To prevent overcrowding, the Sony Wonder folks have set up a timed-ticket system; call 1 week to 3 months ahead to reserve your time slot, especially if you're planning to come before 2pm on a weekday September through June (this place is *very* popular with school groups). If you haven't reserved a slot, you'll be admitted on a first-come, first-served basis, which may mean you'll have to wait in line in the lobby (a comic robot, b.b.wonderbot, helps you pass the time with goofy interactive chat).

550 Madison Ave. (entrance on 56th St.). ℂ 212/833-8100; for reservations call 212/833-5414 Mon–Fri 8am–2pm. www.sonywondertechlab.com. Free admission. Tues–Sat 10am–6pm (until 8pm Thurs); Sun noon–6pm. Subway: E, N, R, V, W to Fifth Ave.

The Studio Museum in Harlem   **Ages 6 & up.** It all depends on what the current exhibition is, but this savvy uptown museum mounts some very interesting art in its cool, high-ceilinged white galleries and often has good Saturday morning family workshops. It's a reasonably sized place for a dose of art viewing, and a good start to a Harlem neighborhood exploration.

144 W. 125th St. (btwn Lenox Ave. and Adam Clayton Powell Blvd.). 🕐 **212/864-4500.** www.studiomuseumin harlem.org. Suggested donation $7 adults, $3 students and seniors, free for children 12 and under. Wed–Sun noon–6pm (Sat opens at 10am). Subway: 2, 3 to 125th St.

4 Museums in the Outer Boroughs

IN BROOKLYN

Brooklyn Children's Museum 👧👧   **All ages.** Technically the oldest children's museum in the country, founded in 1899, the Brooklyn Children's Museum is also one of the best in the country, with an array of hands-on exhibits that will interest kids up to age 14. The emphasis on technology, TV, and video will appeal to older children (witness the pair of hip New York boys, ages 10 and 12, who wandered into a *Sesame Street* exhibit, saw themselves on a monitor, and wound up happily clowning around alongside various *Sesame Street* characters they thought they'd outgrown). There's also an emphasis on nature, with exhibits exploring animals' eating habits and plants' growing habits in a hands-on greenhouse. In the Animal Outpost, staff members bring out the museum's permanent animal inhabitants, including a beautiful and enormous amber-colored python named Fantasia, to demonstrate their traits. In the MusicMix studio, kids can experiment with how various instruments produce sounds; young divas can bust a move in the Mainstage performance area; and children 5 and under can explore the bright tactile learning environment of Totally Tots. Free Friday Family Jam nights in July and August add music, theater, or dance performances at 5pm.

The museum will double in size when its new daffodil-yellow expansion opens in late 2007, adding a new lobby, theater, café, and much more gallery space. But don't worry—while construction proceeds, the exhibits in the existing museum won't be affected.

Getting There: By **subway,** take the no. 3 to the Kingston Avenue station, walk 6 blocks (with traffic flow) on Kingston Avenue to St. Mark's Avenue, and turn left for 1 block. Or take the no. 2 to the President Street station, walk 8 blocks on Nostrand Avenue (against traffic) to St. Mark's Avenue, turn right, and go 2 blocks. By **car,** take Atlantic Avenue east to Brooklyn Avenue, turn right, and drive 4 blocks south; or follow Eastern Parkway east from Grand Army Plaza to New York Avenue, turn left, and go 6 blocks north to St. Mark's Avenue, where you turn right and go 1 block east. Unmetered on-street parking is nearby. An alternative that's fun for kids is the museum's free **Trolley Express,** which runs Saturday and Sunday between 10am and 5pm, making three stops every hour—at Grand Army Plaza (at quarter past the hour), the Brooklyn Museum of Art (at 25 past the hour), and the Brooklyn Children's Museum (at a quarter to the hour). Call the museum for details.

145 Brooklyn Ave. (at St. Mark's Ave.) in Brower Park, Crown Heights. 🕐 **718/735-4400.** www.brooklynkids.org. Suggested admission $5 per person. Weds–Thurs 2–6pm, Fri noon–6:30pm, Sat–Sun 11am–6pm; July–Aug also open Tue 2–6pm.

Brooklyn Museum 👧   **Ages 6 & up.** The superb Egyptian collection, full of over-the-top mummy cases, is the best reason to visit this big underappreciated museum in

Brooklyn, near neighbor to the Brooklyn Botanic Garden and Prospect Park; even if you're going to spend only an hour or so in the museum, there are enough other things to do nearby to justify the excursion. If your kids like history, they can wander past 27 detailed American period rooms from 1675 to 1928, including an eye-popping Moorish-style smoking room from John D. Rockefeller's town house. If they're old enough to appreciate great art, the American and European galleries are strong, with lots of Impressionism and a load of Rodin bronzes. There's also a special gift shop just for kids, as well as lots of weekend drop-in programs for children.

200 Eastern Pkwy., at Prospect Park, Brooklyn. Ⓒ 718/638-5000. www.brooklynart.org. Admission $8 adults, $4 students and seniors, free for children 11 and under. Wed–Fri 10am–5pm; Sat–Sun 11am–6pm (1st Sat of the month 11am–11pm). Parking $3 for 1st hr., $2 per hr. after that. Subway: 2, 3 to Eastern Pkwy.

Jewish Children's Museum   All ages. Multimedia and hands-on are the watchwords for this new museum out in Crown Heights, dedicated to explicating Judaism to youngsters of all faiths. Push buttons to trigger a multimedia "recreation" of Creation; clamber around a large-than-life replica of a Shabbat table setting and shop in a Kosher supermarket; be a newscaster reporting on the miracle of the oil from the war with the Maccabees; feel the rush of the Red Sea parting on either side of you and stand atop Mount Sinai to receive the Ten Commandments alongside Moses—yep, it's all simulated here. There's even a six-hole mini-golf up on the roof, with a Judaic theme, of course. Developed under the guidance of Rabbi Menachem M. Schneerson, otherwise known as the Lubavitcher Rebbe, this handsome facility offers a pretty persuasive reason to head out to Brooklyn.

792 Eastern Parkway (at Kingston Ave.), Brooklyn. Ⓒ 718/467-0600. www.jcmonline.org. Admission $10, children under 2 free. Mon–Thurs 10am–4pm, Sun 10am–6pm. Closed Jan 1 and all Jewish holidays. Subway: 3 to Kingston Ave.

Lefferts Homestead Children's Historic House Museum   All ages. This Dutch colonial farmhouse has been filled with exhibits for kids—old-fashioned toys, puppets, storybook corners, art activities—and absolutely everything in it is touchable. It's a little shabby, but who cares when your kids are allowed to run up and down the stairs and jump off the porch and just enjoy themselves. On summer Sundays, come for the afternoon story hours under the big tree outside, and go on to visit the nearby Prospect Park Wildlife Center (p. 176) and take a spin on the stunning carved animals of the vintage Prospect Park Carousel.

Flatbush Ave., Brooklyn. Ⓒ 718/789-2822. Free admission. Fri–Sun noon–5pm. Subway: B, Q, S to Prospect Park.

New York Transit Museum 🦋 **Ages 3 & up.** The cool thing about this museum is that it's built in a disused subway station, with exhibits sprawling down the tunnels. My boys love the pair of bus cabs they can climb into and pretend to drive and the set of vintage subway cars they can lope through, hanging on straps and swinging around poles. Beyond that, the collection dwells on antique turnstiles and fare boxes, switching apparatuses, and subway station mosaics, all of which are of consuming interest to the adult subway fanatics who flock here (a breed unto themselves, as we met on one of the periodic Nostalgia Train expeditions where vintage cars are taken out for a spin on today's tracks). The sheer amount of stuff makes this place good for an hour, more if your kid is transportation-obsessed.

At the corner of Boerum Place and Schermerhorn St., Brooklyn. Ⓒ 718/243-8601. www.mta.nyc.ny.us/mta/museum. Admission $5 adults, $3 seniors and children 17 and under. Tues–Fri 10am–4pm; Sat–Sun noon–5pm. Subway: 2, 3, 4, 5 to Borough Hall; A, C, G to Hoyt/Schermerhorn sts.; A, C, F to Jay St./Borough Hall.

IN THE BRONX

Yankee Stadium Tour   *Ages 5 & up.* The home of the Bronx Bombers, aka the House That Ruth Built, isn't exactly a museum—a shrine is more like it, at least to confirmed Yankees fans like my sons—and considering that the club is in the process of replacing it with a shiny new stadium nearby, you'd be well-advised to check it out before it truly does become history. One-hour tours give you a great behind-the-scenes glimpse, seeing the view from the press box, learning how the scoreboard operates, gazing upon the plaques to Ruth, Mantle, DiMaggio, and other great Yankees in Monument Park—and best of all, walking through the clubhouse where the players themselves actually suit up. My older son stared at Bernie Williams's guitar, propped up next to his locker, as though it were the Shroud of Turin. Individual tours do not need reservations; just show up several minutes before noon at the event ticket window near Gate 4. You can tour the stadium year-round, which is good to know if your Little Leaguer suffers from baseball deprivation during the off season.

River Ave. and E. 161st St., the Bronx. (Ⓒ 718/579-4531. www.yankees.com. 1-hr. Babe Ruth tour $12 adults, $6 seniors and children 14 and under (in summer $14 adults, $7 seniors and children). Champions tour $17 adults, $12 children and seniors. Reservations accepted for groups of 12 or more. Group tours Mon–Fri 10am–4pm, Sat 10–11am; individual tours Mon–Sun at noon except for home-game days. Subway: B, D, 4 to 161st St.

IN QUEENS

American Museum of the Moving Image ✶✶ *Ages 8 & up.* This superb resource for cinephiles is housed in the Kaufman Astoria Studio, where talkies were made long ago and *Sesame Street* is filmed today (unfortunately, you cannot tour the set). At interactive workstations, you can fiddle with sound effects, dub in new dialogue, call up different soundtracks, create your own digital animation, and even add your face (a la Woody Allen's *Zelig*) to classic movie scenes. Many of the historic artifacts on display—a 1910 wooden Pathé camera, a 1959 Philco TV set, Charlton Heston's chariot from *Ben-Hur*—may mean nothing to youngsters, but the extensive costume gallery should grab them (items like Robin Williams's padded housedress from *Mrs. Doubtfire*), as will the ghoulish masks in the makeup exhibition and the special effects artifacts—you'll see a character model of Yoda from 1980's *The Empire Strikes Back*, before computer animation rendered such puppetry obsolete. There's a fun display of tie-in toys and lunchboxes promoting TV shows from *Howdy Doody* to *The Simpsons*. Classic movie serials are screened every afternoon in Tut's Fever Movie Palace, an over-the-top ancient-Egypt-themed "cinema" designed by Red Grooms and Lysiane Luong. The on-site café is a welcome convenience, too.

35th Ave. and 36th St., Astoria, Queens. (Ⓒ 718/784-0077. www.ammi.org. Admission (includes film and video programs) $10 adults, $7.50 students and seniors, $5 children 5–18, free for children 4 and under. Wed–Thurs 11am–5pm; Fri 11am–8pm (free admission after 4pm); Sat–Sun 11am–6:30pm. Subway: N, W to Broadway; G, R, V to Steinway St.

New York Hall of Science ✶✶ *Ages 3 & up.* Like the wonderful Imaginarium in San Francisco, this is a completely hands-on museum that makes learning really fun— you can pedal furiously on a bicycle to turn a huge propeller; you can watch a bank of rotating electric fans create wind; you can hunt for microbes and fungi with microscopes; you can use colored Plexiglas tiles to make your own rainbow; you can watch your brother get really huge and then really tiny as he walks across an optically distorted room. Put your ear to glass pipes, and you can hear different pitches; stand in front of a special light scope, and you can cast three different-colored shadows at once.

When we first started coming here, the exhibits weren't over our 4-year-old's head, yet they were plenty fascinating enough for my husband, who's no slouch when it comes to physics. Best of all, no activity takes more than a minute to execute, which means that kids sprint from one to another instead of hogging a demo station—we never had to wait our turn to try anything. Museum staffers were performing all kinds of cool demonstrations down on the main floor, but my boys were too busy to watch them. And the Science Playground (additional $4; appropriate for kids 6 and older; closed Jan–Feb) is an awesome huge space with loads of interactive activities indoors and out, including a gigantic teeter-totter, a light-activated kinetic sculpture, windmills, and a water-play area.

There's a limited cafe here, but you'd be better off packing a lunch—there aren't many options in the neighborhood. Definitely combine the science museum with a stop at the nearby Queens Wildlife Center and/or Queens Museum of Art (later in this chapter).

47–01 111th St., Flushing Meadows-Corona Park, Corona, Queens. ℭ 718/699-0005. www.nyscience.org. Admission $11 adults, $8 children 5–17 and seniors, $2.50 children 2–4, free for children under 2; free to all Fri after 2pm during school year. Sept–June Tues–Thurs 9:30am–2pm, Fri 9:30am–5pm, Sat–Sun noon–5pm; July–Aug Mon–Fri 9:30am–5pm, Sat–Sun 10am–6pm. Closed major holidays. Parking $7. Subway: 7 to 111th St.

Queens County Farm Museum   All ages. Still a working farm, this 18th-century homestead is a bucolic spot of fields and orchards and barns full of animals, with ongoing demonstrations of agricultural arts—plowing, planting, apple picking, reaping, milking cows, birthing foals, incubating chicks, and so on. Plan your trip to come on a weekend, when you can go inside the simple three-room frame farmhouse, built in 1772, and go on a hayride ($4). From mid-September through October, weekend visitors can try to find their way through a giant corn maze ($7 adults, $4 children 4–11).

73–50 Little Neck Pkwy., Floral Park, Queens. ℭ 718/347-3276. www.queensfarm.org. Free admission. Mon–Fri 9am–5pm (grounds only); Sat–Sun 10am–5pm (house and grounds). Subway: E, F to Kew Gardens/Union Tpk.; then Q46 bus to Little Neck Pkwy.

Queens Museum of Art   Ages 8 & up. Besides the fact that it's parked next to the Unisphere, that famous stainless-steel globe from the 1964 World's Fair, the chief reason for children to visit this museum of 20th-century art is the Panorama, an awesomely huge three-dimensional re-creation of the New York skyline. Originally built in 1964, it's been faithfully updated; laser-light shafts stand in place of the World Trade Center, replicating the Tribute in Light that marked the towers' place for a few months after the 9/11 tragedy. The lights are timed to show the progress of a day every nine minutes. Kids will love picking out familiar landmarks; anyone who enjoys dollhouses, Polly Pockets, and MicroMachines can marvel over the incredibly detailed small-scale rendering of a city that's often all too large-scale.

NYC Building (next to the Unisphere), Flushing Meadows-Corona Park, Queens. ℭ 718/592-9700. www.queensmuseum.org. Admission $5 adults, $2.50 students and seniors, free for children under 5. Wed–Fri 10am–5pm; Sat–Sun noon–5pm; July–Aug open until 6pm (and until 8pm Fri). Subway: 7 to Willett's Point/Shea Stadium—walk south over ramp into park and head for the Unisphere.

ON STATEN ISLAND

Historic Richmond Town ℱ Ages 5 & up. Somewhat off the beaten track, this 100-acre re-creation includes 27 buildings spanning the 17th to the early 20th centuries—which may create a disjointed effect for historical purists, but kids generally don't care. Three little streets are set up like a small village, and kids can run in and out of the house, shops, inns, and schoolhouses (there's even a couple of outhouses!) and basically just have a ball. Many buildings were moved here from other sites on Staten Island; they range from a neoclassical courthouse to a little schoolhouse dating from 1695, the oldest elementary school building in the country. Costumed interpreters are in action July and August, demonstrating crafts like basket weaving, spinning, weaving, tinsmithing, and printing. A good full day's expedition.

441 Clarke Ave., Staten Island. ⓒ 718/351-1611. www.historicrichmondtown.org. Admission $5 adults, $4 seniors, $3.50 children 5–17, free for children 4 and under. Wed–Sun 1–5pm; July–Aug open early (10am) Wed–Fri. From the Staten Island Ferry, take bus no. S74 to Richmond Rd./Court Place.

Staten Island Children's Museum ⟨ℛ⟩ **Ages 10 & under.** Of all the area's children's museums, this one has the loveliest setting—on the lawns and gardens of the Snug Harbor Cultural Center, formerly a home for retired seamen. There's already plenty to do on-site, with weekend workshops and a host of interactive exhibits that help children explore the wonders of water, insects, computers, and animals (there's more of an emphasis on natural sciences here than at its more urban counterparts). *A bonus:* You get here via the Staten Island ferry, with only a short added bus ride from the terminus.

1000 Richmond Terrace, Staten Island. ⓒ 718/273-2060. www.statenislandkids.org. Admission $5, free for children under 1. Tues–Fri noon–5pm, Sat–Sun 10am–5pm; July–Aug Tues–Sun 10am–5pm (until 8pm Wed). From the Staten Island Ferry, take the S40 bus (Richmond Terrace) to the Snug Harbor center, with its black wrought-iron gate. The museum is in Building M.

5 Best Rides

Coney Island   All ages. Open in summer months, this cluster of small private amusement parks is on the rebound, with the spruced-up boardwalk, the new Brooklyn Cyclones ballpark, and the New York Aquarium within easy walking distance. At 10th Street, **Astroland** (www.astroland.com) stars the vintage **Cyclone** roller coaster ($6), built in 1927, which offers riders over 54 inches tall the thrill of an eight-story drop at one point. **Demo's Wonder Wheel** park (www.wonderwheel.com) next door at 12th Street features the landmark **Wonder Wheel** ($5), an ingenious double Ferris wheel built in 1920 that circles high over the boardwalk. For those who like to stay closer to earth, there are bumper cars; tilt-a-whirls; carousels; and kiddie rides, including the teacups seen in *Uptown Girls.* The area also has minigolf, go-carts, and even a freak show, not to mention the original Nathan's hot dog stand.

Coney Island Boardwalk, Surf Ave., Brooklyn. ⓒ 718/372-5159. www.coneyisland.com. Admission to parks free; rides $2.50–$6. Parks open weekends only Apr–May and Sept–Oct; daily noon to midnight June to Labor Day. Subway: D, F, N, Q to Coney Island/Stillwell Ave.

New York SkyRide ⟨*Overrated*⟩ **Ages 5 & up.** "Passengers" are seated on a large platform that begins to tilt and jolt and careen wildly while a big screen shows you "crashing" your way around New York landmarks, with lots of ear-splitting recorded sound effects. There's zero sightseeing information—it's just a crazed 8-minute simulation of speeding through the cityscape. Count on a long line, up to 30 minutes at times. Not worth the tourist-soaking price.

In the Empire State Building (2nd floor), Fifth Ave. at 34th St. ⓒ 888/SKYRIDE or 212/279-9777. www.skyride.com. Admission $18 adults, $14 children 12–17, $13 seniors and children 5–11; combination tickets with Empire State Building, $28 adults, $18 seniors and children 12-17, $20 children 5–11. Daily 10am–10pm. Subway: B, D, F, N, Q, R, V, W to 34th St.

Roosevelt Island Tram *Value* **All ages.** A pair of big red cable cars swing over the East River alongside the 59th Street/Queensboro Bridge to Roosevelt Island. Though most of the trip is actually over an unglamorous wedge of East Side real estate, it does go over the river, and you're high up enough to get good views of Manhattan up and down. There are few seats—only a narrow hard bench at either end of a car that holds 30 or so—so get onboard quick to grab a seat by the front windows. Once you're on Roosevelt Island, site of a former smallpox hospital, you can turn right around and ride back—or you can take a ride on the red shuttle bus to loop around this island housing development, a sprawl of modern apartment blocks with lots of riverside green space and little playgrounds tucked away everywhere. The village's main street looks like something out of the 1960s British TV series *The Prisoner*—a curved main street cutting between bland shop fronts (one of everything: post office, library, church, deli, Chinese restaurant, bank, school). Getting there on the cable car is more than half the fun.

Manhattan terminus: Second Ave. and 60th St. © 212-832-4540. www.rioc.com. Fare $2. Subway: 4, 5, 6 to 59th St.

Staten Island Ferry *Value* **All ages.** Walk right on at the South Ferry Terminal, and you can chug across New York Harbor, past the Statue of Liberty, to Staten Island, where you walk around the barriers and get on again for the return ride. The whole round-trip should take about an hour. Most of the ferry decks are now glassed in, alas, but the views are still great. A friend of mine tells me that his mother used to herd her kids onto the ferry on hot summer nights to sleep when their un-air-conditioned apartment got too hot; that's the kind of wonderful institution the Staten Island Ferry is in the hearts of New Yorkers.

Departing from S. Ferry in Battery Park. © 718/727-2508. Free tickets. Subway: R, W to Whitehall St.; 1, 9 to South Ferry.

Toys "R" Us Ferris Wheel **All ages.** Inside the three-story atrium of this immense Times Square toy-o-rama, there's an honest-to-goodness big Ferris wheel with fun, funky cars resembling licensed characters and toy icons like Uncle Moneybags from Monopoly. For the money, it seems a fairly short ride; my kids had just as much fun riding for free up and down in the store's glass-walled elevators.

1514 Broadway (at 44th St.). © 800/869-7787. Tickets $3, children under 2 free. Children under 40 in. must be accompanied by an adult.. Mon–Thurs 10am–10pm, Fri–Sat 10am–11pm, Sun 11am–9pm. Subway: N, Q, R, S, W, 1, 2, 3, 7 to 42nd St./Times Sq.

Victorian Gardens **Ages 2 to 12.** In summer months Central Park's skating rink is overtaken by this squeaky-clean kiddie amusement park, featuring maybe a dozen rides. Don't expect any terrifying roller coasters or vintage charm, but it's a great Manhattan option for a summer afternoon, and there are rarely any lines. My daughter and her pals especially love the old-fashioned Family Swinger, the Kite Flyer, and the mist tunnel.

Wollman Rink, Central Park (enter E. 62nd St.). © 212/982-2229. www.victoriangardensnyc.com. Admission Mon–Fri $6.50, Sat–Sun $7.50; children under 36 in. free with paid adult. Rides $2 each (climbing wall $10). Unlimited-ride wristband $12 Mon–Fri, $14 Sat–Sun. Open mid-May to mid-Sept Mon–Fri 11am–7pm; Sat–Sun 10am–8pm. Subway: F to 57th St.; N, R, W to Fifth Ave./59th St.

6 Historic Houses

Alice Austen House *Ages 6 & up.* Many things about pioneer photographer Austen's house make it a great bet for kids. First, it's really just a cozy cottage, a low-slung gingerbread-trimmed bungalow with rolling lawns that offer dynamite views of

New York Harbor. Second, Austen herself is such an appealing character, a spunky turn-of-the-20th-century woman who started taking pictures when she was 10 and just never stopped. Lots of her work is on display, and the garden has been replanted according to her photos of the original grounds. Third, you get to ride the Staten Island Ferry over. What more could you ask for?

2 Hylan Blvd., Staten Island. (C) 718/816-4506. www.aliceausten.org. Admission $3 adults, free for children 12 and under. Thurs–Sun noon–5pm. From the Staten Island Ferry terminal, take the S51 bus 2 miles to Bay St./Hylan Blvd. Walk 1 block toward water; museum is on right.

Gracie Mansion **Ages 8 and up.** Dating back to the early 19th century, this yellow frame house—formerly a wealthy family's country house—has since 1942 been the official residence of the mayor of New York. The current mayor, Michael Bloomberg, chooses to live in his much nicer Upper East Side townhouse, so visitors can tour the residential areas for the first time in years, as well as the public rooms on the main floor. The tours last 45 minutes, and it's not much of a window into the past—many restorations have wiped original features and furnishings away—but it's a lovely home, nonetheless.

Carl Schurz Park, East End Ave. at 90th St. (C) 212/570-4751 for tour reservations. Admission $7 adults, $4 seniors, free for children. Wed 10am, 11am, 1pm, and 2pm. Subway: 4, 5, 6 to 86th St.

Merchant's House Museum ❀ **Ages 8 & up.** The most interesting thing about the Tredwell family—who lived in this house continuously from 1835 to 1933—is that they weren't famous or unusual at all, just a stable, prosperous, upper-middle-class family whose house and furniture happened to survive intact, wallpaper and all, until it became a house museum in the mid-20th century. The house itself is a fairly notable example of Greek Revival, but your kids will probably be more struck by the old-fashioned furnishings and clothing (poignant details like a piece of needlework tossed onto a table, never to be finished). A nice trip back in time on a quiet side street not far from NYU and the East Village's funky St. Mark's Place.

29 E. 4th St. (btwn Bowery and Lafayette St.). (C) 212/777-1089. www.merchantshouse.com. Admission $8 adults, $5 students and seniors, free for children 11 and under. Thurs–Mon noon–5pm. Subway: 6 to Astor Place or Bleecker St.

Morris-Jumel Mansion **Ages 10 & up.** Dating back to 1765, this imposing mansion with its Georgian front columns had a major brush with history when Gen. George Washington used it as his headquarters in 1776. As they tour the house, however, your kids may become more interested in Eliza Jumel, the wealthy, brazen 19th-century woman who lived here for many years, during her marriage to, and after her divorce from, Aaron Burr. It's too bad this big, elegant mansion is off the beaten path for tourists.

65 Jumel Terrace (at 160th St.). (C) 212/923-8008. Admission $4 adults, $3 students and seniors, free for children 12 and under. Wed–Sun 10am–4pm. Subway: C to 163rd St.

Mount Vernon Hotel Museum and Garden ❀ **Ages 6 & up.** Back in the 1820s and 1830s, when this part of the Upper East Side was considered a country retreat, the Mount Vernon Hotel was a fashionable day resort for genteel travelers. What's surprising is how much this site still feels like a retreat, surrounded by city as it is: The surrounding gardens, planted in 18th-century style, offer a welcome whiff of horticulture, and eight period rooms inside this former carriage house—restored by the Colonial Dames of America—re-create what life in the old inn might've been like. Considering its convenient location, it's curious that this museum isn't better known. Guided tours, which leave on the hour from the gift shop, may be a bit slow for young children, but are worth it.

421 E. 61st St. (btwn First and York aves.). ☎ 212/838-6878. www.mvhm.org. Admission $8 adults, $7 students and seniors, free for children 12 and under. Tues–Sun 11am–4pm (June–July Tues till 9pm). Closed major holidays and Aug. Subway: N, R, W to Lexington Ave./59th St.; 4, 5, 6 to 59th St.

7 Zoos & Aquariums

Aside from the following, check out the **Bronx Zoo/Wildlife Conservation Park** (p. 152) and the **Central Park Wildlife Conservation Center** (p. 153).

New York Aquarium   All ages. After an hour-long subway ride from Manhattan—an adventure in itself—you hit the ocean at Coney Island beach, skirting the amusement parks, and walk to the left down the boardwalk to the aquarium. In summer, you may need to plan a full day so you can also enjoy the beach or the rides, or even get a ticket for a Brooklyn Cyclones game (see chapter 10). We've gone in spring, which is not optimal—many of the exhibits are outdoors, and it was still too chilly to linger while watching the otters, penguins, and walruses on their rocky sea-cliff habitats—but out of season has its own charm, with the beach deserted and the ocean misty, cold, and gray. The kids still had a ball in the interactive **Explore the Shore** exhibit and the recreated salt marsh; and the sharks, of course, are creepily fascinating any time of year. Time your schedule so you can catch the sea lion demonstrations, too. Pack a lunch if you're going in the cooler months, when the outdoor snack bar may be closed and nearby boardwalk joints are boarded up.

Surf Ave. and W. 8th St., Coney Island, Brooklyn. ☎ 718/265-3400 or 718/265-FISH. www.nyaquarium.com or www.wcs.org. Admission $12 adults, $9 seniors and children 2–12. Mon–Fri 10am–5pm; Sat–Sun and holidays 10am–5:30pm. Parking $10. Subway: F, N, Q to W. 8th St./NY Aquarium.

Prospect Park Wildlife Center ⚐   All ages. Of all New York City's zoos, this one is right at the level of preschoolers and young grade-schoolers. The fanciful abstract sculptures arching over the walkway from the side entrance tell you right away you're in kid territory, and on it goes, to the Animals in Our Lives petting zoo and the outdoor Discovery Trail, where kids can hop like a wallaby, squat on their own lily pads, or huddle inside a giant turtle shell. There's a mini-amphitheater built in front of the glass-enclosed environment where a troop of hamadryas baboons scamper around—somebody here knows which animals kids most like to watch. It's small, clean, safe, and tons of fun. Once you're out here, make it a full day by visiting nearby Lefferts Homestead (p. 170), New York's only historic house set up just for kids, and taking a ride on the gorgeous antique Prospect Park Carousel (p. 164), only steps from the zoo entrance. The subway ride from Manhattan isn't all that long, leaving you off only a block or so from the zoo.

450 Flatbush Ave., Prospect Park, Brooklyn. ☎ 718/399-7339. www.wcs.org. Admission $6 adults, $2.25 seniors, $2 children 3–12, free for children 2 and under. Mon–Fri 10am–5pm; Sat–Sun 10am–5:30pm. Subway: B, Q, S to Prospect Park.

Queens Wildlife Center   All ages. Though it may not rate a trip out to Queens from Manhattan on its own account, this smart little zoo is a natural add-on to a New York Hall of Science excursion (p. 171) and a good excuse for a tramp through the old World's Fair grounds. The zoo's focus is on North American species (don't expect exotics here, though my sons considered the American bison plenty exciting) arranged along a handsomely landscaped walking trail. You feel surrounded by wilderness, yet the pathway is actually pretty short—it won't tax young legs—and the loop shouldn't take more than 15 or 20 minutes. Across the park road is a mini farm with domestic animals that'll satisfy the yen for feeding and stroking warm furry creatures.

53–51 111th St. (at 54th Ave.), in Flushing Meadows Park, Queens. (C) **718/271-1500.** www.wcs.org. Admission $6 adults, $2.25 seniors, $2 children 3–12, free for children 2 and under. Mon–Fri 10am–5pm; Sat–Sun 10am–5:30pm. Subway: 7 to 111th St. (Queens).

Staten Island Zoo   All ages. The little Staten Island Zoo isn't under the umbrella of the Wildlife Conservation Society, as are the other zoos around here, and it's definitely a poor cousin. But you may want to combine this with a visit to the Staten Island Children's Museum (p. 173), especially if you're into snakes—the reptile collection is a standout. The 8 acres are also home to a small aquarium and a fair number of birds. You won't see a lot of large animals, but several small mammal species that kids love to gaze at—the red panda, bushbabies, otters, meerkats, and the colorful snout of a mandrill. Feeding times are frequent attractions, and there's a small children's zoo, for younger kids who like their nature hands-on.

614 Broadway, Barrett Park, Staten Island. (C) **718/442-3101.** www.statenislandzoo.org. Admission $7 adults, $5 seniors, $4 children 3–14, free for children 2 and under; admission by donation Wed after 2pm. Daily 10am–4:45pm. Closed Thanksgiving, Dec 25, and Jan 1. Free parking. From the Staten Island Ferry, catch the S48 bus, get off at Broadway and Forest Ave., turn left, and go 2½ blocks up Broadway.

8 Gardens

Brooklyn Botanic Garden 🎔🎔   **All ages.** Every month, something new is blooming at this 52-acre garden beside the Brooklyn Museum and across from Prospect Park. Starting in spring, Daffodil Hill dazzles the eye with a field of stunning yellow; then delicate pink cherry blossoms fringe the Japanese Pond (local Japanese families flock in for blossom viewing). A riot of roses fills the Cranford Rose Garden as summer sets in, and thickets of rhododendron bloom near the Eastern Parkway entrance. There's also a fragrance garden for the blind, coupled with a sweet little Shakespeare Garden featuring all sorts of plants mentioned in Shakespeare's plays. Year-round, you can stroll through the **Steinhardt Conservatory,** with its outstanding bonsai collection, orchids, water lilies, and the Trail of Evolution, a pathway lined with increasingly sophisticated plant forms. You'll also find a cafe, a lovely gardening gift shop, and frequent weekend programs for children and families. Kids may get a kick out of the Celebrity Path, inlaid with the names of famous Brooklynites from Mae West to Woody Allen.

900 Washington Ave. (at Eastern Pkwy.), Brooklyn. (C) **718/623-7200.** www.bbg.org. Admission $5 adults, $3 students and seniors, free for children 15 and under; free Tues and Sat until noon. Tues–Fri 8am–6pm; Sat–Sun and holidays 10am–6pm (Oct–Mar closes 4:30pm). Open holiday Mon; closed Thanksgiving, Dec 25, and Jan 1. Subway: 2, 3 to Eastern Pkwy.; B, Q, S to Prospect Park; 2, 3, 4, 5 to Franklin Ave.

Conservatory Garden *Finds*   **All ages.** Central Park's only patch of formal garden is a delightful surprise in Manhattan and rarely crowded because it's so far uptown. Walk through glorious wrought-iron gates (which once fronted the Fifth Ave. mansion of Cornelius Vanderbilt II), and turn left to find the Children's Garden, with beds of flowers blooming around a wishing well with a statue of the children from Frances Hodgson Burnett's *The Secret Garden.* The central section of the garden is a long lush lawn flanked by a pair of walkways lined with flowering trees; the northern end has a circular design, with a fountain of the Three Graces surrounded by flower beds—a spectacular blaze of tulips in spring and chrysanthemums in fall. On spring and summer weekends, there's nearly always a wedding party here getting photographed. With restrooms and a fair-weather outdoor cafe, it's a welcome refuge, a perfect place to let your kids stretch their legs after a Museum Mile trek.

Central Park at 105th St. ⓒ **212/360-2766**. www.centralparknyc.org. Free admission. Daily 8am–dusk. Free tours Apr–Oct Sat 11am. Subway: 6 to 96th St., then walk up Fifth Ave.

New York Botanical Garden 𝆑𝆑 **All ages.** This lushly planted 250-acre park—five times bigger than the Brooklyn Botanic Garden (see above)—is a real magnet for families. The stunning 8-acre **Everett Children's Adventure Garden** (separate admission $3 adults, $2 seniors and students, $1 children 2–12) tempts youngsters with cunning mini trails and mazes and topiaries and fanciful sculptures, not to mention hands-on stations where they can learn about pollination, chlorophyll, root systems, and all that good stuff. Other highlights are the Wild Wetland Trail, which leads through a natural ecosystem; the Ruth Rea Howell Family Garden, where young city-dwellers can plant, weed, water, and compost tidy little garden plots; the 19th-century Snuff Mill, perched on its riverside terrace; a **rock garden** (admission $1 adults; 50¢ students, seniors, and children 2–12); a huge formal rose garden; a steep rhododendron valley; and the immense Victorian-era greenhouse complex of the **Enid Haupt Conservatory** (admission $5 adults; $4 students, seniors, and $3 for children 2–12), which alone makes the garden a delightful destination year-round.

A narrated **tram** ($2 adults, $1 children 2–12) swings around the grounds to help you cover the territory. Spring is intoxicating here, what with the huge stands of azaleas, magnolias, dogwood, and lilacs, but it's a blast even in winter, when the Holiday Garden Railway exhibit is set up in the Conservatory—a large-scale model train wending its way through fanciful landscapes and cityscapes. Although the botanical garden is right next to the Bronx Zoo (p. 152), you'd have to be very ambitious (and very good walkers) to do both justice in 1 day, since their sites are so spread out—but if you're game, it can be done.

Getting There: Metro-North trains from Grand Central Terminal make the 20-minute trip to the Botanical Garden Station; cross Southern Boulevard, and you're at the entrance. One-way fare is $4.50 off-peak or $6 peak. By **car,** take the Henry Hudson Parkway to the Mosholu Parkway; at the end of the Mosholu, turn right onto Kazimiroff Boulevard, and follow the garden perimeter to the entrance. By **subway,** take the 4 or D to Bedford Park Boulevard. Walk east 8 blocks or take the Bx26 bus to Garden.

200th St. and Kazimiroff (Southern) Blvd., the Bronx. ⓒ **718/817-8700**. www.nybg.org. Admission to grounds only, $6 adults ($5 Bronx residents), $3 seniors, $2 students, $1 children 2–12, free for children under 2. Combination ticket (covers all extra charges) $20 adults, $18 students and seniors, $5 children 2–12; free to all Wed. Tues–Sun and Mon holidays 10am–6pm (Nov–Mar till 5pm). Parking $20.

Wave Hill 𝆑 **All ages.** A very suburban enclave in the Bronx, Riverdale has some fine houses on its Hudson River shore, notably this 28-acre estate with two mansions and extensive gardens. Over the years many famous people lived here, as tenants or as guests (writers Mark Twain and William Makepeace Thackeray, conductor Arturo Toscanini, Theodore Roosevelt); at one time the Tudor-style house was also the official residence of Great Britain's ambassador to the U.N. But there's not much to see inside the houses—just let your kids play on the grounds, which offer one of the few unobstructed views across the Hudson to the magnificent New Jersey Palisades.

Nobody minds if youngsters run on the grass, and the formal gardens are world-famous. My kids' favorites are the Aquatic Garden, with a pair of pergolas enclosing a formal pool; the nook-filled Wild Garden; and a terraced series of small walled gardens showing off cactuses and alpine flowers. Below the mansions' smooth lawns sprawls a 10-acre woodland with walking trails that give kids a nice bit of a hike. Excellent children's workshops are held on weekends in the learning center; call or check the website for a current schedule.

Getting There: The **MTA** (℃ **718/330-1234**) bus no. BxM1 (from the East Side) or BxM2 (from the West Side) goes to 252nd Street; then walk west across the parkway bridge and follow the signs to the main gate. The fare is $5 one-way; a child under 45 inches may sit on a parent's lap for free. Or take the **Metro-North train** (℃ **212/ 532-4900**) to the Riverdale stop, walk up 254th Street, turn right on Independence Avenue, and go to the main gate at 249th Street. The one-way fare is $4.75 peak and $3.50 off-peak. By **car,** take the Henry Hudson Parkway to the 246th Street exit and drive straight north to 252nd Street; turn left to cross the parkway overpass, turn left at the light, and drive south to 249th Street, where you turn right and follow it to the Wave Hill gate.

675 W. 252nd St., Riverdale, the Bronx (entrance at 249th St. and Independence Ave.). ℃ **718/549-3200.** www. wavehill.org. Admission $4 adults, $2 students and seniors, free for children 5 and under; free to all Tues, Sat before noon, and daily Dec–Feb. Tues–Sun 9am–5:30pm (mid-Oct to mid-May closes 4:30pm, June–Aug Wed till 9pm).

9 Nature Centers

Note that Central Park is covered in depth on p. 194 in chapter 8.

The Dairy   All ages. This charming 19th-century structure, with patterned roof tiles and gaily painted gingerbread trim, actually started life as a dairy, back in the days when people grazed cows on Central Park's meadows (children could stop here to buy a cool cup of milk fresh from the udder). There aren't too many Guernseys left in Manhattan, so nowadays the Dairy is the park's chief visitor information center, with a roomful of displays about the park's landscape. There are always a few hands-on activities for youngsters, and it's a pleasant short stroll from either the carousel, the zoo, or Wollman Rink.

In Central Park, midpark at 65th St. ℃ **212/794-6564.** Free admission. Tues–Sun 10am–5pm. Subway: 6 to 68th St.; A, B, C, D, 1, 9 to 59th St./Columbus Circle.

Dana Discovery Center ⍟ **All ages.** After Harlem Meer was dredged out in the early 1990s and its banks beautifully relandscaped, this pretty structure on its north shore opened as a nature-study center, bringing visitors uptown for the first time in years. Weekend family workshops run year-round (usually at 1pm, but call for schedules), and a room overlooking the Meer's serene waters is set up with hands-on nature exhibits. Stroll around the Meer to the neighboring Conservatory Garden (p. 177).

In Central Park at 110th St., near Fifth Ave. ℃ **212/860-1370.** www.centralpark.org. Free admission. Tues-Sun 10am–5pm (closes 4pm in winter). Subway: 2, 3 to 110th St. Bus: M2, M3, or M4 to 110th St./Fifth Ave.

Henry Luce Nature Observatory at Belvedere Castle ⍟ **All ages.** Inside this tiny folly of a castle, built in 1872 as an optical illusion to make the lake to the south look bigger (the woods of the Ramble have since grown so high they now obscure the lake view), children enjoy interactive exhibits on Central Park's natural habitats. But the real thrill is outside, where visitors can stand on the rocky terrace hanging high over Turtle Pond and the outdoor **Delacorte Theater,** or walk onto the castle's upper-level terraces for some super views of the Upper West Side, including the American Museum of Natural History. This castle even has a U.S. Weather Service station on top—note the twirling weather vanes on the tower. Stroll down the hillside west of the castle, a neatly planted **Shakespeare Garden** (appropriate, since the neighboring Delacorte is home to the Public Theater's free Shakespeare in the Park series), or scamper down the long slope to the east, where turtles and ducks populate the adjacent pond.

In Central Park, midpark at 79th St. ℭ **212/772-0210.** Free admission. Daily 10am–5pm. Subway: B, C to 79th St.

Inwood Hill Urban Ecology Center   All ages. This Art Deco canoe house, tiled in aqua and white, holds weekend walking tours of the surrounding park, with its marsh, meadow, and steep rock cliffs. A telescope inside the center lets kids zoom in on details of the neighboring marsh and meadow; other exhibits include hands-on geology displays, an aquarium, and a flip-book of pictures of the native plants and animals. Few Manhattanites venture up to this northern tip of the island, but it's a stunning site.

Inwood Hill Park, 218th St. and Indian Rd. ℭ **212/304-2365.** Free admission. Wed–Sun 10am–4pm. Subway: 1 to 215th St., then walk several blocks to Indian Rd.

Prospect Park Audubon Center ℱ **All ages.** In a magnificently restored century-old terra-cotta boathouse on the shore of a 60-acre man-made lake, the Audubon Society's Brooklyn outpost offers two stories of child-friendly exhibits on the local bird population—songbirds, waders, raptors, woodpeckers, and the rest of the avian crew. Kids can pore over books, videos, feathered models, and computer simulations, all against a background of piped-in birdcalls. Nature walks and boat tours of the lake start from the boathouse as well.

The Lake, Prospect Park, Brooklyn. ℭ **718/287-3400.** Free admission. Thurs–Sun and holidays noon–5pm (Jan–Mar weekends only). Subway: B, Q, S to Prospect Park; Q to Parkside Ave.

---

10 Kid-Friendly Tours

BUS TOURS

Gray Line Tours Double-Decker Bus Tours   All ages. Though lengthy narrated bus tours can make some younger children squirm like crazy, they're convenient for seeing a lot of sights without running your kids ragged. Hop-on/hop-off tours provide a happy medium—you get driven around and spoon-fed information, and when your kids get restless, you just jump off at the next stop, expecting to get back on again later.

Operating both red double-decker buses and bright red trolley buses, Gray Line offers so many options, it could make your head spin. Besides the 2-day **Grand Tour,** which would take 5 hours if you didn't hop on and off, there's a **Lower Manhattan loop,** an **Upper Manhattan loop,** the **Grand Tour plus Statue of Liberty 2-day option,** and the **Lower Manhattan plus Statue of Liberty 1-day option.** More traditional escorted sightseeing tours—the kind where you have to stick with the same groups of bus pals throughout—include both half-day and full-day Manhattan routes that involve a buffet lunch, as well as escorted Harlem tours (the Sun version includes a gospel church service).

Main stop at Port Authority Bus Terminal (42nd St. and Eighth Ave.). ℭ **800/669-0051** or 212/397-2600. www.gray linenewyork.com. Full city tour $50 adults, $40 children under 12; Upper or Lower Manhattan loop $40 adults, $30 children under 12; Statue of Liberty/Ellis Island grand tour $65 adults, $45 children under 12; free for children under 5 if sitting in adult lap. Daily 8am–6pm.

Magic Bus (M5 city bus) _Value_ **All ages.** It's an ordinary city bus route, but it happens to rumble past a host of sights you'd like to see in its 90-minute loop, and you may even get some narration over the PA. You can board anywhere along the route, which is marked with a dotted line on the three city maps in this chapter. I recommend catching the bus at 125th Street and Riverside Drive, where you'll first wheel past **Grant's Tomb** (122nd St.) and gleaming neo-Gothic **Riverside Church** with its carillon bell tower (120th St.). You'll proceed down handsome residential **Riverside Drive** (Riverside Park and the Hudson lie out the right-side window) to 72nd Street, where the route jogs east to Broadway and then south past **Lincoln Center.** At Columbus Circle it turns east and goes across 59th Street—also called Central Park South because it borders the south side of the park (look to your left)—where it turns right at the ornate **Plaza Hotel** at 58th Street. Down Fifth Avenue you'll go, past **Tiffany & Company** (on your left on the south side of 57th St.); **St. Patrick's Cathedral** (on your left at 51st St.); **Rockefeller Center** (on your right from 51st to 48th sts.); the main research library of the **New York Public Library** with its famous stone lions (on the right from 42nd to 40th sts.); the **Empire State Building** (on the right at 34th St.); the narrow wedge-shaped **Flatiron Building** (on the left at 23rd St.); to the white arch of **Washington Square** (facing the foot of Fifth Ave.). After circling the square, you'll go back north up Sixth Avenue, which from 16th to 23rd streets takes you past **Ladies' Mile,** the late-19th-century department store district (many of the old stores have been recently restored for new megastore tenants like Barnes & Noble and Bed, Bath & Beyond); the Herald Square shopping intersection where **Macy's** department store presides at 34th Street; **Bryant Park** (on your right from 40th to 42nd sts.), which was the site of a World's Fair in 1853; more of Rockefeller Center, including **Radio City Music Hall** (on your right at 50th St.); and back to 59th Street to retrace the route back north, as far as 178th Street.

Recommended starting point: 125th St. and Riverside Dr. Fare $2, exact change or MetroCard.

BOAT TOURS

Chelsea Screamer **Ages 7 & up.** Twice as long and a trifle more sedate than _The Beast_ (see Circle Line, below), the _Chelsea Screamer_ narrated speedboat cruise lasts a full hour, tooling past the Statue of Liberty around the tip of Manhattan to the Brooklyn Bridge and back. You'll be out on an open deck and churning up a fair bit of wake. Buy tickets on the dock 30 minutes before departure; groups of eight or more can make reservations.

Board at Pier 62, Chelsea Piers, W. 23rd St. at the Hudson River. ℂ 212/924-6262. www.chelseascreamer.com. Fare $20 adults, $15 children 3–12, free for children under 2. Mid-May to Oct Sat–Sun 1:30pm, 2:45pm, 4pm, 5:15pm. Subway: 1, C, E to 23rd St. Bus: M23 west on 23rd St.

Circle Line Sightseeing Cruises _(×_ **Ages 3 & up.** Circle Line dominates the market on from-the-water sightseeing cruises, operating out of three locations: Midtown at the Hudson River end of 42nd Street, downtown at South Street Seaport's Pier 16, and even farther downtown at Battery Park. The experience of being out on the water with the wind in your hair is marvelous by itself, but getting a mini course in New York history and architecture is a definite bonus. Go early in your trip to get a firm sense of Manhattan as a whole.

Starting from 42nd Street, the classic New York City experience is the **3-hour tour** ($29 adults, $23 seniors, $16 children 12 and under) that chugs around the entire Manhattan island in a low-slung steamer. Sit on the left-hand side of the boat for the best views. On the first leg, you deconstruct the Midtown skyline, get a good look at the Chelsea Piers, pass Battery Park City, and swoop past Ellis Island and the Statue of Liberty. Then the boats cut across New York Harbor and go up the east side of the island, past Wall Street and South Street Seaport, and under the East River bridges, getting a view of the other end of Midtown, with the United Nations looming over the river at 42nd Street. You'll continue north past the Upper East Side, seeing the mayor's official Gracie Mansion. You get to go through Hell Gate (where the East River merges with the Harlem River), glimpse Yankee Stadium on the Bronx bluffs to your right, and slide through Spuyten Duyvil (Spite the Devil), where the Harlem River empties into the Hudson. There's not so much to see on the northern end of the island, but the guides gamely fill in with lots of trivia. (It really is the guide that makes the trip—the first time I went, the narrator was full of wonderful obscure trivia, but a more recent cruise with a lazier guide dragged a bit.) When you pass under the George Washington Bridge, look out for the little red lighthouse featured in Hildegarde H. Swift's classic children's book *The Little Red Lighthouse and the Great Grey Bridge*.

Also **departing from 42nd Street** are 2-hour **semicircle cruises** ($24 adults, $20 seniors, $13 children 12 and under), which go as far as the U.N. and then loop back; and 75-minute **Liberty Cruises** ($19 adults, $16 seniors, $11 children 12 and under), which steam past Liberty and Ellis islands. But if your kids are like my 9-year-old and his friend, they'll want to do the 3-hour circuit instead because it's cool to go *all the way around*. That's the *point*, Mom. Of course, you can always save time *and* score coolness points by taking the high-speed boat *The Beast* (daily May–Sept, weekends only Oct; $17 adults, $11 children 12 and under, must be over 40 in.), its hull painted with huge chomping shark teeth to look like it's eating the waves before it. Cruising at speeds up to 45 mph, the Beast buzzes past the New York skyline, pausing briefly at the Statue of Liberty, and then zips back to port, all within an adrenaline-pumping 30 minutes.

From the Seaport, there's a similar high-speed boat called *The Shark* (daily June to mid-Sept; $17 adults, $15 seniors, $11 children 4–12), as well as the hour-long narrated *Zephyr* harbor cruise (daily May to mid-Sept; $20 adults, $16 seniors, $13 children 4–12), which crosses the harbor to swing past Ellis Island and the Statue of Liberty and then back to the Seaport. **From Battery Park,** a 1-hour narrated **harbor cruise** ($10 adults, $8 seniors, $4 children 4–12, free for children 3 and under) is available from the same slips used by the ferries to Liberty and Ellis islands.

There are restrooms and a snack bar onboard.

© **212/563-3200.** (1) Pier 83, at the foot of W. 42nd St. at the Hudson River. www.circleline42.com. Parking $20. Bus: Westbound M42 to the Hudson River. (2) Pier 16 at South St. Seaport. www.circlelinedowntown.com. Subway: 2, 3, 4, 5 to Fulton St.; A, C to Broadway/Nassau St. (3) Battery Park, slips 2 and 3; buy tickets at Castle Clinton. *©* 212/269-5755 www.circlelinedowntown.com. Subway: 4, 5 to Bowling Green; 1 to South Ferry.

The Pioneer **All ages.** Two-hour harbor cruises aboard a historic schooner depart a couple of times a day (schedules vary) from South Street Seaport. The time-warp experience of setting sail from this old seaport is somewhat diluted by the views of very modern downtown skyscrapers and the chug of barges, tugboats, and tour boats on the water around you, but it could still be a memorable throwback to an earlier era. New York viewed from the water is quite a sight.

Departing from Pier 16 at South St. Seaport. *©* **212/748-8590.** www.southstseaport.org. Admission $25 adults, $20 students and seniors, $15 children 12 and under.

PRIVATE GROUP TOURS

Small Journeys, Inc   All ages. These custom-designed group tours are too expensive for individual families, but if you can hook up with another two or three broods, go for it, because Steven Kavee and his guides really gear their tours to kids' interests. The company also designs behind-the-scenes field trips for school groups, going on-site to meet professionals in fashion, art, theater, music, interior design, whatever. Transportation costs—whether by van, by limo, by bus, or on foot—are additional, depending on the sights involved. Arrange well in advance.

114 W. 86th St., New York, NY 10024. *© 212/874-7300* or *© 914/762-4700. $250 per group for 4-hr. tour.

WALKING TOURS

For detailed strolls around the city and even Brooklyn, you may want to check out *Frommer's Memorable Walks in New York.* Take into account, however, that some of the walks (such as the Greenwich Village literary tours) may not be of much interest to kids.

Several organizations run a number of tours; check the schedules in the *Big Apple Parent,* the *New York Family,* or the *New York ParentGuide,* available free at children's bookstores and clothing stores all over town.

ARTime (*© 718/797-1573*), as its name implies, runs walking tours oriented toward the fine arts, usually focusing on museums and galleries. Because they don't cover as much physical ground as some of the neighborhood and architectural tours (no more than 2 or 3 blocks between art galleries), they're quite suitable for younger kids—so long as the kids are into art. Tour guides gear their talks to children aged 5 to 10. Tours last about 1½ hours and cost $25 for one adult plus a child and $5 for each additional child (an extra adult tagging along is free). You can usually book a tour in advance—they run from October to June, the first Saturday of every month at 11am.

Big Onion Walking Tours (*© 212/439-1090;* www.bigonion.com) are designed primarily for adults, but kids 8 and up will respond to many of their lively topics, which often touch on the multiethnic dimensions of New York's mosaic. Tours can last as long as 2½ hours; they cost $15 for adults, $12 for students and seniors.

The **Grand Central Partnership** (*© 212/883-2420*) sponsors a free 1½-hour walking tour along East 42nd Street—an area that includes such Midtown classics as the Chrysler Building, the Daily News Building, and the old Bowery Savings Bank. With its historical/architectural emphasis, this may be a bit scholarly for kids under 10, but the length (and the price) make it worth trying out. Tours depart Friday at 12:30pm from the Whitney Museum at Phillip Morris, 120 Park Ave., at 42nd Street. Kids might also enjoy the 1-hour lunchtime tour of Grand Central Station run by the **Municipal Arts Society** (*© 212/935-3960* for reservations and details, 212/439-1049 to get a schedule by mail; www.mas.org), which meets every Wednesday at 12:30pm (suggested donation $10; call the society to find out where to meet). Other Municipal Arts Society tours explore the city's architecture and neighborhoods from an urban-design perspective; they may run as long as 7 hours and cost between $12 and $15, but the knowledgeable, enthusiastic guides make it worthwhile. For some of the popular weekend tours, you may need to reserve a couple of weeks in advance; call for times.

Street Smarts NY (*© 212/629-1886;* www.streetsmartsny.com) runs weekend walking tours that might be of interest to older children, depending on the theme, such as "Greenwich Village Past and Present" or "Manhattan Murder Mysteries." They cost $10.

7

Neighborhood Strolls

Manhattan is one of the greatest walking cities in the world. On this densely packed island, it seems there's something new to see every half a block—an intriguing shop, a museum, a beautiful piece of architecture, or an eccentric fellow pedestrian. Even children who normally drag their feet when forced to walk from the far end of a parking lot may cover several blocks without noticing, absorbed by the continual stream of sights. Almost every place you want to go can be reached on foot, often more quickly, and for sure more cheaply, than via taxi, subway, or bus. And along the way you'll get a great window on the way New Yorkers live.

If you're already planning to go to one of the neighborhoods described in this chapter to visit an attraction, restaurant, or store, allow a little more time to explore the immediate area. Most of them are worth a visit simply so you can drink in the kaleidoscope of street life that is New York.

1 Midtown

LOBBY HOPPING

Start at the biggie: the **Empire State Building** (p. 160), 34th Street and Fifth Avenue, whose streamlined 1931 interior includes murals of the Seven Wonders of the World. Then head up Fifth Avenue to the **New York Public Library** at 41st Street, where you can walk up the steps between the famous lions (Patience and Fortitude) and peek into the ornate lobby, eternally cool in white marble. Turn east onto 42nd Street to pop into **Grand Central Terminal** on the north side of 42nd Street at Park Avenue, which, though technically not a lobby, has a gloriously restored main room that'll knock your socks off. Gaze up at the constellations painted or electrically twinkling on the soaring azure ceiling; check out the elegant waiting room; and then descend into the marbled catacombs to find a shopping concourse and a food court, populated with commuters scurrying for their trains. Try out the whispering gallery in the large tiled vault outside the Oyster Bar—if two people face the walls in diagonal corners, they can hear each other's softest speaking voices. One block further east on 42nd Street, on the northeast corner of 42nd and Lex, you can duck into the **Chrysler Building,** whose steel-tipped Deco spire is so notable on the skyline. The small lobby is surprisingly warm and rich looking (think luxury-car glove compartment), with black marble and inlaid wood. Continue east to the end of 42nd Street to visit the **United Nations** (p. 158); even if you don't plan to do a U.N. tour, walk around the U.N. complex's beautiful Rose Garden, with broad paved walkways overlooking the East River.

ROCKEFELLER CENTER AREA

The heart of Midtown is Rockefeller Center, a huge streamlined office/retail complex of pale limestone built in the 1930s by the famously wealthy Rockefeller family. Start on

Fifth Avenue between 49th and 50th streets at the **Channel Gardens,** which lie between the British building on the north and the French building on the south (like the English Channel lies between Britain and France—get it?). The Channel Gardens slope down to **Rockefeller Plaza,** the center's heart. Beneath the colossal gilded statue of the Greek god Prometheus, in winter there's a jewel of an ice-skating rink, in summer an open-air restaurant (the Rock Center Café). Behind Prometheus, where the giant Christmas tree stands every December, rises **30 Rockefeller Plaza,** home of the NBC TV network; if you're here between 7 and 10am, stop outside the glass pagoda on the north side of 49th Street to watch the *Today* show being broadcast live. Hosts Meredith Viera and Matt Lauer often take to the streets outside to film various segments.

Head across 50th Street toward Sixth Avenue (excuse me, Avenue of the Americas) to find the entrance for the **Top of the Rock** observation deck (p. 161) atop 30 Rockefeller Center; from here you'll get a dynamite view of the entire city. Once you've come back down to earth, roam inside 30 Rock's lobby, studying the monumental lobby murals. Take the escalators down from the lobby and you can prowl around the maze of concourses and tunnels connecting all the Rockefeller Center buildings in an underground world of shops and restaurants (good to know about on rainy days). Leaving 30 Rock through the Sixth Avenue entrance, turn around to see the glittering mosaics decorating the portico. My own kids' favorite 30 Rock doorway, however, is on 50th Street; they never fail to get a kick out of the massive stone bas-relief figures framing the doors, jauntily dressed in nothing but attitude and a little city soot. My sons are convinced the one on the left is intentionally mooning **Radio City Music Hall** across 50th Street. Go west to Sixth Avenue for the best views of Radio City's neon-jazzed streamlined facade. This landmark Art Deco theater still has some live stage shows as well as a continual lineup of pop concerts; see chapter 10 for details.

Return to Fifth Avenue along 50th Street and turn left to pass the **International Building,** with its famous bronze statue of Atlas carrying the world. Across the street is Rockefeller Center's famous neighbor, **St. Patrick's Cathedral,** seat of the Archdiocese of New York. You may want to step inside for a look at this graceful late-19th-century Gothic-style church—if you're lucky, there'll be a wedding to watch.

TIMES SQUARE

There was a time, not so long ago, when New York families strenuously avoided the Times Square area when out on the town with their kids. Those days are gone: the old sleazy Forty Deuce has given way to the New 42nd Street, a family-friendly theme park of cinemas and restaurants and shops, with just enough neon razzle-dazzle left to deliver that trademark Big Apple thrill.

If you start at the intersection of 42nd Street and Seventh Avenue and head west on 42nd Street, you'll pass two gloriously restored theaters—Disney's ornate **New Amsterdam Theater** on the south side of the street and the **New Victory Theater** on the north—both of which specialize in family entertainment; farther west on the south side, you'll find a bustling theater-themed 24-hour McDonald's and the New York branch of **Madame Tussauds** (p. 155). Toward the end of the block, two megamultiplex cinemas face off across 42nd Street closer to Eighth Avenue—the 13-screen **Loews** (with an homage-to-Broadway lobby and a great retro neon sign flashing on the facade) and the 25-screen **AMC Empire,** which boasts the gilded moldings and frescoed dome of an old Broadway theater as its lobby. Flanking them are two new chain hotels: a Hilton on the south side and a Westin across the street. Take a moment at the Hilton's street entrance to admire the adorable little bronze figures by Tom Otterness scampering about the doorway.

If you head north up Broadway from 42nd Street, your kids may not allow you to cruise past the **Toys "R" Us** flagship store at the northeast corner of Broadway and 47th Street without stopping in. Older kids may ask to stop between 44th and 45th streets to peer up into the floor-to-ceiling windows of the **MTV studio** on the mezzanine level of 1515 Broadway; a line forms on the sidewalk every afternoon to join the studio audience for *TRL*. (Early mornings, ABC's *Good Morning America* gang holds court on the southeast corner of 44th and Broadway, and later in the afternoon *Late Night with David Letterman* may be filming segments on the street outside the **Ed Sullivan Theater,** up at 53rd and Broadway.) Tourists flock into the bright and busy restored theater lobby that now features the **Times Square Visitors Center** on Seventh Avenue between 46th and 47th streets, and hopeful theatergoers line up for half-price tickets at the **TKTS** booth on the mid-Broadway island.

You don't need to pay any entrance fee just to marvel at the intersection's immense high-definition advertising signs, designed to be as bright and as gimmicky as possible. Despite the changes in display technology, one advertiser has remained constant: For decades there's been a **Coca-Cola** sign facing south at 47th Street. Just plant yourselves on one of the mid-Broadway islands and crane your neck. Don't be ashamed to gawk; we all do.

2 Downtown

WALL STREET LOBBY HOPPING

The narrow urban canyons of this skyscraper-crammed neighborhood are another iconic Manhattan sight, familiar even to youngsters—they're the prototype of many a futuristic movie and video-game landscape.

Begin at the corner of Broad and Pearl streets, where the modern **85 Broad St.** building pays tribute to the archaeological past: The curved lobby shows where old Stone Street used to run, and the Pearl Street sidewalks outside contain glassed-over pits revealing foundations of the old **Stadt Huys,** the town hall of 17th-century Nieuw Amsterdam. Follow Pearl Street down to State Street, and turn left. Even if you're not visiting the **National Museum of the American Indian** (p. 167), go inside the **Alexander Hamilton Customs House** on Bowling Green, Broadway, and State Street, across from Battery Park. Just past the museum's front desk (admission is free) is the glorious Grand Rotunda, with a huge circular ceiling mural celebrating New York history. Outside, Bowling Green may be a simple patch of concrete today, but in the Revolutionary era there was a famous riot here, in which outraged colonists toppled a statue of the English king; you can still see the broken spikes on the iron fence, which originally were topped by little crowns.

Heading up Broadway, you'll pass the venerable Gothic-style **Trinity Church,** tucked among the skyscrapers at the head of Wall Street (Alexander Hamilton and Robert Fulton are among the famous New Yorkers buried in its graveyard). Wall Street marks the limits of the original Dutch settlement, where a wooden wall was built in 1653 to protect the settlers. Turn right down Wall Street to see, on the north side, the Greek Revival **Federal Hall,** with its statue of George Washington marking the spot where our first President took his oath of office in 1789; turn right down Broad Street to see the **New York Stock Exchange** (8 Broad St.), with mythological figures crowding its triangular pediment.

Fun Fact

From 1913 until 1974, New York City could boast of the tallest building in the world. The **Woolworth Building** was the tallest from 1913 to 1930, when it was supplanted by the **Chrysler Building** on 42nd Street. The Chrysler Building didn't hold its title very long—it was taken over a few months later, in 1931, by the **Empire State Building,** which ruled until the **World Trade Towers** arrived in 1972. New York lost the crown soon, however, when the Twin Towers were edged out by Chicago's Sears Tower in 1974.

Return to Broadway and turn right (north); between Dey and Fulton streets, **195 Broadway**—built from 1915 to 1922 as AT&T headquarters—looks like a wedding cake stacked with several levels of classical columns (in fact it has more exterior columns than any other building in the world). Go in the lobby to see even more columns. Then proceed up to the **Woolworth Building** at Park Place and Broadway, which was the world's tallest building from 1913 to 1930. The Woolworth Building was a prime example of Gothic skyscraper design, and the lobby's sculptured ceiling is worth several minutes' study. Ask your kids to look for the self-portrait of the architect hugging his building in his arms and a Scrooge-like caricature of Mr. Woolworth hoarding his wealth.

GREENWICH VILLAGE

Start in the heart of the Village, **Washington Square,** with its white triumphal arch at the foot of Fifth Avenue. The red-brick houses facing the north side of the square look totally 19th-century, dating from a time when Greenwich Village really was a separate country village. Much of the rest of Washington Square is now surrounded by the modern buildings of **New York University,** but the park's crowd is an eclectic swirl of all sorts of New Yorkers, not just college students. Weekends usually attract street performers, and on many afternoons there are informal speed-chess competitions going on beneath the shade trees at the southwest corner of the park.

For a taste of the bohemian Village, go south from the park (down Thompson, Sullivan, or MacDougal) to **Bleecker Street,** lined with cheap ethnic restaurants and long-established music clubs. Turn right to go west on Bleecker Street. Three vintage coffeehouses cluster around the intersection of Bleecker and MacDougal: **Caffe Dante** (83 MacDougal St.). **Café Figaro** (southeast corner of Bleecker and MacDougal sts.), and **Caffe Reggio** (119 MacDougal St.), holdouts from the Village's beatnik days. At Sixth Avenue, Bleecker takes an unpredictable angle north, like many West Village streets, and changes into an Italian neighborhood, with some great food shops selling coffee, bread, pastries, cheese, and sausage.

Return to Sixth Avenue, and go north to West 9th Street; the castlelike red-brick building on your left is **Jefferson Market,** originally a courthouse and now a branch of the public library. Its lovely outdoor garden is usually open to the public in the afternoon. Turn right (east) onto West 11th Street. The brick wall on your right surrounds a tiny cemetery, one of several belonging to **Shearith Israel,** the oldest Jewish congregation in the country. Continue down the block, lined with classic brick townhouses, until you see one that's startlingly modern: **18 W. 11th St.** Inside the large picture window, the owner's stuffed Paddington bear is usually dressed in a timely fashion, with a yellow slicker on if it's raining or a Yankees or Mets cap in baseball season, depending on which team is winning. Soon after, you'll be back at Fifth Avenue—turn right to get back to Washington Square or left to make a stop at the Forbes Magazine Galleries (p. 164), with its collections of toy soldiers and toy boats.

THE EAST VILLAGE

The funky East Village is a magnet for preteens and teenagers determined to score high on the hipness scale. Start on **Astor Place,** the busy intersection of Fourth Avenue, Lafayette Street, and East 8th Street, where sidewalk peddlers usually hawk everything from hammered silver jewelry to vinyl LPs to well-thumbed paperbacks to secondhand lamps and furniture. The hulking brownstone building to the south is **Cooper Union,** a progressive school of architecture, art, and engineering founded in 1859. Head east on what should be 8th Street, here called **St. Mark's Place;** busy day and night, the block of St. Mark's between Third and Second avenues is lined with vintage-clothing stores, bookstores, coffeehouses, and cafes. Beatniks hung out here in the 1950s, hippies in the 1960s, punks in the 1970s. (Incongruously, this neighborhood also has long-established enclaves of Ukrainian immigrants, centered on 7th St., and Russian immigrants, on 9th and 10th sts., as you can see if you stroll around farther.)

At Second Avenue, you may want to turn left and go 2 blocks north to the field-stone **St. Mark's-in-the-Bowery Church,** the city's oldest continually used church building—Peter Stuyvesant, the famous governor of the Dutch colony of Nieuw Amsterdam, used to worship here. In fact, this area used to be his farm, and **Stuyvesant Street,** which angles south back to Astor Place, is named for him. Stroll past the early-19th-century town houses on Stuyvesant Street and try to imagine what the Village looked like back then—before the beatniks, hippies, and punks took over.

If you're looking for club-kid coolness, follow St. Mark's Place until it ends at Avenue A. (Manhattan widens here, requiring a set of lettered avenues to be added east of the numbered ones—hence the neighborhood's nickname, Alphabet City.) You'll be at **Tompkins Square** (bounded by Ave. A, E. 7th St., Ave. B, and E. 10th St.), much spruced up since the late 1980s, when it held a resident camp of homeless people. Nowadays this neighborhood, long the low-rent-or-no-rent domain of squatters, struggling artists, and drug dealers, is significantly gentrified, and Avenue A is lined with edgy shops and cafes, well worth scoping out.

CHINATOWN

Begin on **Canal Street,** the major thoroughfare cutting across Manhattan at this point; Canal Street used to be the northern boundary of Chinatown before its population spilled over into Little Italy and the Lower East Side. Walk east from Centre Street to the Bowery on the south side of Canal Street, where a string of produce and fish stores pile their wares on the sidewalks. Point out to your kids the Chinese lettering on every sign and the pagoda-shaped pay-phone stations. Turn right (south) at the Bowery. On the Bowery's east side, a gargantuan statue of the Chinese philosopher Confucius dominates the little plaza in front of **Confucius Plaza,** a modern red-brick residential development.

Continue south on the Bowery 2 blocks to the frantic intersection called **Chatham Square,** with its big Chinese arch in the middle. Then backtrack on the Bowery a few steps to narrow sloping Pell Street, where you turn left. A Hong Kong–like jumble of restaurants and neon signs, Pell leads you west 1 block to busy Mott Street, a crowded and decidedly unglitzy shopping street. Barbecued ducks hang in glass shop fronts, candy shops sell pastel-colored imported sweets, and twanging recorded music leaks out into the street. Turn right on Mott and go 1 block to Bayard Street, where you should turn left and go 1 block to Mulberry. The **Museum of Chinese in the Americas** (p. 165) is on your right and **Columbus Park** is on your left, where Chinatown residents old and young congregate.

LITTLE ITALY

There's not much left to this classic tenement neighborhood, what with Chinatown encroaching on the south and SoHo on the west; you and your kids can easily do the whole bit in half an hour, even if you stop along the way to check out the authentic little shops. On weekends Mulberry Street becomes a pedestrian mall, which makes it even easier to traverse with young ones. From Canal Street, walk up **Mulberry Street** to Houston Street, past several Italian restaurants that thrive on the tourist trade; don't miss **Umberto's Clam House** at 129 Mulberry St., site of a famous 1973 Mafia hit when a wiseguy named Joey Gallo was rubbed out.

On Mulberry and the streets branching off it, look for stores selling religious medals and figures and others selling glorious foodstuffs—fresh pastas, imported olive oil and vinegars, Baci chocolates, and tangy gelati (Italian ices). At the intersection of Mulberry and Broome streets, **Caffé Roma,** 385 Broome St., is a great old-fashioned tile-floored pastry shop where you can stop for cannoli and espresso. Look above the shop signs to see the tracery of iron fire escapes hanging out over the street, a distinguishing feature of these turn-of-the-20th-century tenement buildings, which slumlords designed to cram in as many small rooms as possible onto the narrow lots.

LOWER EAST SIDE

Once a teeming slum for waves of new immigrants, the Lower East Side has been "discovered" by artistic types, ever on the lookout for cheap apartments. The main shopping drag, **Orchard Street,** though still full of discount-clothing and dry-goods stores (mostly Jewish-owned and shut up tight on Sat), now also has renovated storefronts and trendy boutiques. While you'll admire the changing retail mix and classic tenement architecture, lure your kids to walk with the promise of a good nosh. Start out at **Kossar's** (367 Grand St., between Essex and Norfolk sts.), a glorious time warp of a bagel factory where customers can watch the bakers slide trays full of ring-shaped dough into a vintage oven. The bialys are incredibly dense and flavorful, especially when you get them warm. Return to Orchard Street, turn right, and head north to Broome Street for the fascinating **Lower East Side Tenement Museum** (p. 165), which explores the district's immigrant past. Pickle lovers (you know who you are), don't miss **Guss's Pickles** (85 Orchard St., between Grand and Broome sts.), where Peter Reigert worked in the film *Crossing Delancey.* Window-shop your way north 4 more blocks to East Houston Street, where you can take care of whatever appetite you may have: **Katz's Delicatessen** (E. Houston St. at Ludlow St., 1 block east of Orchard) has sit-down service for Jewish favorites such as blintzes, corned beef, and luscious salami sandwiches; the long-established family deli **Russ and Daughters** (179 E. Houston St., between Orchard and Allen sts.) specializes in cheese, whitefish, and herring; and **Yonah Schimmel's Knishes** (137 E. Houston St., at Forsyth St.) offers an amazing selection of those Yiddish delicacies—pockets of thin dough stuffed with everything from kasha to blueberries to sweet potatoes.

New York Top 10 Movie & TV Sites

If New York didn't exist, Hollywood would've had to invent it to get the perfect movie set. Film companies shoot on location here so often, my kids learned from an early age what it means when we run into a phalanx of trailers, lighting equipment, and headset-wearing production assistants: *They're making a movie!* Here are 10 of the most famous sites around town.

1. **Columbia University Low Library steps** (Upper West Side, 117th St. between Broadway and Amsterdam Ave.)—where *Spider-Man* recovers after his fateful spider bite, where Mary-Kate Olsen tries to save Ashley's scholarship in *New York Minute,* and where three fired Columbia professors decide to go into business as *Ghostbusters.*

2. **Tom's Diner** (Upper West Side, 112th St. and Broadway)—where Jerry and his pals from *Seinfeld* hold their endless discussions, while Jerry eats cornflakes, Elaine devours big salads, and George tries to avoid the bill.

3. **Grove and Bedford streets** (Greenwich Village)—where TV's *Friends* live, in the apartment building on the southeast corner. Go a little farther west to where Grove crooks north and peer through a gate to see the fountain where they splash around in the credits.

4. **14 Moore St.** (TriBeCa)—where the *Ghostbusters* set up office in an old firehouse (it's still a working firehouse).

5. **The Plaza Hotel** (Midtown, 59th St. and Fifth Ave.)—where Eloise scampers in the many Eloise TV movies, and Macaulay Culkin rings up a whale of a room service bill in *Home Alone 2.*

3 Uptown

MORNINGSIDE HEIGHTS

The upper end of the Upper West Side, this neighborhood is Manhattan's college town. The place to start, however, is at 112th Street and Amsterdam Avenue, on the front steps of the Episcopal **Cathedral Church of St. John the Divine.** This will be the largest cathedral in the world if they ever finish building it; they've been at it for over a century, since 1892, but if your kids have studied medieval history at all, they'll know that most of the great European cathedrals took a couple of centuries to complete, too. St. John the Divine is so huge that the Statue of Liberty could fit under the central dome, and the tiny-looking figure of Christ you see in the rose window over the front doors is actually life-size. Notice how only two of the arches over the front doors have statues in them; empty niches in the other arches await future stone-carvers' work. Go inside and stroll around, stopping on the north aisle at Poet's Corner, where paving stones honor selected American poets. Go out to the garden just south of the cathedral to see the Children's Fountain, a fanciful huge sculpture surrounded by peewee sculptures created by local schoolchildren. On the lawns of the surrounding cathedral close, you can sometimes spot a pair of peacocks strutting and preening.

6. **The Empire State Building** (Midtown, 34th St. and Fifth Ave.)—where Tom Hanks and Meg Ryan meet in *Sleepless in Seattle,* just like the reuniting lovers did in the many versions of *An Affair to Remember.* And who could forget what *King Kong* did to this place?

7. **55 Central Park West** (Upper West Side)—where the ancient spirit Gozar must be driven out of Sigourney Weaver in *Ghostbusters* (the top of this varicolored Art Deco building looks significantly different in the movie, though—an elaborate rooftop was matted in). Later in the movie, the nerdy accountant played by Rick Moranis roams glassy-eyed outside Tavern on the Green, the festively lit restaurant across the street in Central Park.

8. **The American Museum of Natural History** (Upper West Side, Central Park West at 79th St.)—where the mermaid in *Splash* escapes, where Cary Grant works on his dinosaur in *Bringing Up Baby,* and where the Macy's parade begins in *Miracle on 34th Street.* And don't forget that *Friends'* Ross Geller works here as a paleontologist.

9. **The front steps of the New York Public Library** (Midtown, Fifth Ave. at 41st St.)—where Holly Golightly researches eligible millionaires in *Breakfast at Tiffany's,* an apparition flips open card catalogues in the opening of *Ghostbusters,* and Peter Parker sees his beloved uncle slain in *Spider-Man.*

10. **The central fountain in Lincoln Center Plaza** (Upper West Side, 64th St. and Broadway)—where Bialystock and Bloom dance in *The Producers.*

Go north on Amsterdam Avenue to 117th Street, where you can pass through wrought-iron gates into **Columbia University,** New York's Ivy League college. As you cross the campus, notice the broad steps of Low Memorial Library on your right; kids will recognize it as the place Peter Parker visited for a fateful high-school field trip in *Spider-Man.* Exit the campus through the matching set of gates onto Broadway and cross the street to enter the gates of **Barnard College,** Columbia's all-women sister college. Or head north on Broadway to 120th Street: Columbia's **Teachers College** is the big, dark, red-brick building on the northeast corner (read the roll call of history's greatest teachers inscribed around the roofline). The **Union Theological Seminary** is the medieval-looking gray stone complex on the northwest corner of 120th Street, complemented by the red-brick **Jewish Theological Seminary** on the northeast corner of Broadway and 122nd Street. Turn left on 120th Street and go west to Riverside Drive, where **Riverside Church** stands on the right. If its pale limestone reminds you of a Gothic version of Rockefeller Center, it's no coincidence, since John J. Rockefeller was one of its founders in 1930. Across Riverside Drive and several yards north sits the columned neoclassical **Grant National Memorial Monument,** where President Ulysses S. Grant and his wife, Julia, are buried. (Ask your kids the corny old joke: "Who's buried in Grant's Tomb?") Admission is free—step inside and peer down into the sunken chamber where their dark marble tombs are laid (kinda creepy, if you think

Fun Fact

The Brooklyn Bridge took 16 years to build, from 1867 to 1883, and it seemed to have a bit of a curse on it—the original designer, John A. Roebling, died from tetanus contracted when his foot was crushed while surveying the site, and his son, Washington, who took over the job, fell ill with the bends after diving into the river to supervise the workmen laying the pilings. A virtual invalid afterward, Washington Roebling watched the bridge going up through a telescope from his house in nearby Brooklyn Heights, while his wife actually supervised much of the completion of the project.

about it). The high-ceilinged memorial offers excellent exhibits about Grant's life and the Civil War he won for the Union, but my kids' favorite part is outside, in the plaza around the tomb, with its nutty mosaic benches designed by New York public school students.

4 Brooklyn

CROSSING THE BROOKLYN BRIDGE

As thrilling a sight as this beautiful brown-hued East River bridge is from afar, with its Gothic-style towers and lacy mesh of cables, the view from the bridge is even more thrilling. A **boardwalk-like pedestrian walkway** goes all the way across, raised slightly above the car traffic. One mile long, it should take about half an hour to traverse—except you'll be tempted to stop more than once to ooh and ahh at the vision of Manhattan's skyscrapers thrusting upward, with the great harbor and Verrazano Bridge beyond.

Why has the Brooklyn Bridge captured the popular imagination so much more than its neighbors to the north, the Manhattan and Williamsburg bridges? Well, for one thing, it was the very first steel-wire suspension bridge in the world when it opened in 1883. Until then, the only way to get from Manhattan to Brooklyn, at that time separate cities, had been via ferry (crossing from Manhattan's Fulton St. to Brooklyn's Fulton St., both named after steamship inventor Robert Fulton, who operated the ferry company).

Since then, however, the Brooklyn Bridge has become a byword in New York lore. The standard old joke defines a con artist as a guy trying to sell rubes the deed to the Brooklyn Bridge ("Brother, have I got a bridge to sell you. . . ."). Cocky teenage hoodlums have proved their bravado by shinnying up its cables, and suicides with a flair for the dramatic have plummeted to their deaths from those same cables into the tidal currents below. The bridge has appeared in countless movies and TV shows, its outline practically synonymous with New York City.

The Manhattan entrance ramps to the bridge begin by the plaza in front of the city's **Municipal Building,** along Centre Street just south of Chambers Street; pedestrian ramps on the other side empty out into Brooklyn's downtown, which is a bit of a wasteland on weekends, but it isn't a far walk from here to **Brooklyn Heights,** one of the loveliest brownstone neighborhoods you'll ever see. Go armed with a map. If your kids aren't hardy urban trekkers, walk halfway to get the view and then double back to Manhattan. Be aware that things get awfully windy once you're over the water!

8

For the Active Family

Don't make the mistake of assuming that New Yorkers are soft, flabby city people—on the contrary, we end up walking much more than car-dependent suburbanites do, and the city's complement of huge parks makes it super easy to ride bikes, play tennis, jog or stroll, toss a Frisbee, fly a kite, skate, or skateboard (not to mention feed ducks or squirrels and watch boats lazily drift past).

But New York parents as a breed tend to be too compulsive to just laze around in the parks—at the drop of a hat, they'll enlist their children in classes for anything from chess and computers to horseback riding and fencing. Staying active in New York is a year-round proposition, and neither the dog days of summer nor the ice days of winter slow down kids' activities. Though many classes and workshops require full-series enrollment, I've listed below a number of drop-in classes that are available for visiting families, or for local kids who want to do something on the spur of the moment.

1 Green New York: The Top Parks

Though New York is studded with squares where you can find a patch of grass and some benches, it has only a handful of parks large enough for a real exploration. Some of these are somewhat off the beaten track: **Flushing Meadows–Corona Park** in Queens (take the no. 7 train to 111th St. or Willets Point/Shea Stadium) and **Van Cortlandt Park** in the Bronx (take the no. 1 train to 242nd St.) are both loaded with recreational facilities, but they're so big and spread out, you can't just ramble around aimlessly. **Fort Tryon Park,** at the northern end of Manhattan (take the A train to 190th St.), a wooded strip of park on high ground overlooking the Hudson River, is lovely but off the beaten path—it's not worth a special trip unless you're already coming to visit The Cloisters (which you definitely should do—p. 162). Then there's compact **Riverbank State Park,** perched over the Hudson River at the western end of 145th Street, which offers a slew of top-notch recreational facilities (see "Sports & Games," later in this chapter) but hardly any untrammeled grass. For other green pleasures in the city, see "Gardens" and "Nature Centers" in chapter 6.

New Yorkers, however, more than make do with the five great parks listed below. The larger three—Central Park, Riverside Park, and Prospect Park—were laid out in the 19th century by the team of Frederick Law Olmsted and Calvert Vaux, a pair of inspired amateurs who virtually invented the art of urban landscape design. These guys really knew how to maximize space, with twisting paths and artful hills and dales that make you feel as though you've left the city as soon as you're 10 paces inside the park. Later, park commissioners slapped on recreational amenities like tennis courts and playgrounds that may not strictly have been what Olmsted and Vaux envisioned, but nothing has seriously marred the beauty of these detailed landscapes.

Central Park 🎠🎠🎠 At 840 acres, this park—one of the world's greatest—is a vital resource for the city. Set right in the middle of things, with frequent entrances cut into its low brownstone wall, it separates the Upper West Side from the Upper East Side, lying between Midtown at the south end and Harlem at the north end. It's big enough to give you a real sense of escape, and when you're walking around the park, the only roads you have to deal with are the circular park drive and one cross-cut at 72nd Street; both are closed to car traffic weekdays 10am to 3pm and 7 to 10pm, as well as 7pm Friday to 6am Monday (holidays are traffic-free, too). Four other east-west streets cross the park—66th, 79th, 86th, and 96th—but they're cunningly hidden beneath overpasses, so you'll never notice them.

The section of the park below 72nd Street is somewhat formal. Starting at 59th Street and Fifth Avenue—where **horse-drawn carriages** line up to give tourists a ridiculously overpriced (about $34 for 20 min.) ride through the park—you'll find the **Pond,** a picturesque small body of water reflecting Midtown skyscrapers. Just northwest of this lie the **Wollman Rink** (p. 215), where you can ice-skate in winter and enjoy a variety of amusement park rides at the **Victorian Gardens,** and **the Dairy** visitor center (p. 179); from the Dairy, follow a path west under an arch to the **Central Park Carousel** (p. 164). The **ball fields** west and south of here are fun even for spectators on summer weekday evenings, when some very competitive after-work leagues slug it out. As you walk up the West Drive past the **Tavern on the Green** restaurant (p. 99), your kids may be interested to know that it was originally built as a sheepfold in 1870 when the **Sheep Meadow,** the broad fenced-in green lawn on your right, still was used for grazing sheep. The **Mineral Springs Pavilion,** just north of the Sheep Meadow, has a snack bar and restrooms.

Go north across 72nd Street to **Strawberry Fields,** a gem of a bit of landscape laid out in memory of Beatle John Lennon, who lived across Central Park West from here in the Dakota apartment building. My kids, all of them next-generation Beatlemaniacs, love to hang out here. It seems there are always flowers laid in tribute to Lennon on the black-and-white mosaic medallion that reads IMAGINE. Across the drive to the northeast lies the **Lake,** a body of water larger than the Pond—large enough, in fact, for boating. To rent rowboats, cross the park along the 72nd Street Transverse. Along the way, though, stop off at two postcard views that your kids may recognize from scores of movies and TV shows: Turn left at **Cherry Hill Fountain** and walk over lovely **Bow Bridge,** or take either the lakeside path or 72nd Street to **Bethesda Terrace,** a grand lakeshore plaza featuring the **Bethesda Fountain.** The lakeside path continues, winding north to the **Loeb Boathouse** (✆ **212/517-2233**), where you can rent boats and also get something to eat at the Boathouse snack bar (the Park View restaurant here is an upscale affair and not particularly child-friendly, alas). The boathouse is open March through October daily from 9am to 4pm, depending on the weather; rowboat rental is $10 per hour (cash only, $30 deposit required; maximum five people per boat).

Across East Drive and just above 72nd Street, the **Conservatory Water** is a fun area even for the littlest ones, with its large serene formal pool—the *Alice in Wonderland* statue at the north end features a giant mushroom that just begs to be clambered on. From April to October you can rent one-quarter-scale radio-controlled model sailboats ($10 per hr.) from a stand beside the boathouse (shades of *Stuart Little*). There's a cafe on the pond's east side, which also has restrooms. Stroll back south through a shady green strip with winding paths, passing a couple of good playgrounds (see "The Playground Lowdown," below). As you head downhill toward a rugged stone arch,

Central Park Attractions

Information ⓘ
Subway stop Ⓜ
Path of Animal
  Statue Walk - - - - -

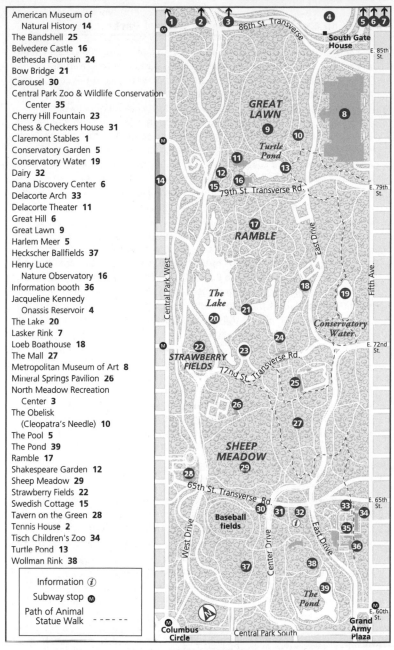

Stalking the Animal Statues in Central Park

In the course of half an hour's walk, you and your kids can bag a couple dozen animals in the wilds of Central Park—statue animals, that is.

Start on the northwest corner of East 79th Street and Fifth Avenue. A few steps into the park, on your right are **(1–3) three bronze bears,** a copy of a Paul Manship statue that's in the Metropolitan Museum directly north. Continue on the path into the park, going through a vaulted tunnel under the East Drive and veering to your left (south) to reach the east end of Turtle Pond. There you'll find King Jagiello of Poland astride a **(4) magnificent horse.** Stroll uphill to your left to the drive and walk downtown (south) on the road, keeping to the right-hand jogging path if there's car traffic in the park. About halfway down the hill, atop a massive rock outcropping on your right, crouches a **(5) bronze panther,** peering out of the foliage ready to pounce on unsuspecting joggers.

Cross the East Drive at the pedestrian crossing near the Loeb Boathouse and walk down a short, steep grassy slope to a path leading south to the Conservatory Water. The Alice in Wonderland statue at the pond's north end has not only the **(6) White Rabbit** but also the **(7) Cheshire Cat,** Alice's **(8) kitten Dinah,** and **(9) assorted mice,** along with the usual number of children climbing all over the giant mushrooms. Swing around to the west side of the pond to find the **(10) Ugly Duckling** waddling past the statue of Danish storyteller Hans Christian Andersen.

Take either path leading south from the Conservatory Water up the hill to the 72nd Street Transverse; cross 72nd Street, turn right to cross the circular drive, then veer left to follow the drive southward. On your right, the ground rises to the Rumsey Playground (less a playground these days than a plaza for special events). Set amid the steps rising to Rumsey's entrance gate is a big **(11) stone goose,** with who else but Mother Goose riding on its back. (Walk around to identify carved scenes from various nursery rhymes.) Go west, away from the drive, past Rumsey downhill to the plaza in front of

expect to see a gaggle of sidewalk performers on weekends, some of whom are delightful to watch—allow for a little dawdling time. Passing through the arch brings you to the **Tisch Children's Zoo,** then south to the **Delacorte Arch,** with its delightful glockenspiel chiming every hour, and finally to the **Central Park Wildlife Center** (p. 153).

North of the Lake, the **Ramble** is a compact wilderness that's easier than you'd think to get lost in; navigate with care, and stick to daylight hours when there are plenty of other folks around (it's known as the best place in the park for a mugging, rare as they may be). Situated on a major North American flyway, this is, against all odds, a bird-watcher's paradise right in the middle of the big city; the **Henry Luce Nature Observatory** (p. 171) at the nearby Belvedere Castle can provide you with equipment to find and identify several species. Look overhead for nests and along the lake's marshy northern shore for frogs.

the Bandshell (watch for roller-skaters on weekends!). At the western edge of the plaza, you'll find a **(12–13) pair of eagles** devouring a hapless **(14) mountain goat.** Bear right to return to the 72nd Street transverse, where a left turn will take you west. On your left, just before 72nd Street meets the West Drive, look up on another big outcropping to find the **(15) falcon** lighting on the glove of the Falconer.

Retrace your steps a short distance east on 72nd Street to the Dead Road, a broad asphalt lane bordering the Sheep Meadow, where skaters and volleyball games proliferate on warm-weather weekends. Turn right and follow the Dead Road south to find the Indian hunter with his faithful **(16) dog.** Turn left, following the circular drive past the foot of the Mall; cross under the drive via a brick-vaulted tunnel (try out the echoes). The path swings uphill on the east side of the drive to reach one of the most famous animal statues in the park, **(17) Balto the sled dog,** hero of a 1995 animated film.

From here the path leads south through another underpass past the gates of the Children's Zoo; look for a **(18–19) pair of goats** prancing atop the zoo's wrought-iron entrance arch. On through a second underpass, you'll come up to the redbrick Delacorte Arch. In a niche to the right of the arch is a bronze **(20) dancing bear,** and the glockenspiel on top of the arch features **(21–26) a hippo, a goat, a penguin, a kangaroo, an elephant, and a bear**—plus a **(27–28) pair of monkeys** squatting on top, hammering the bells. The musical clock performs on the hour and half-hour; stick around to watch if possible. Then proceed south on the walkway past the Central Park Zoo; at the southern end of the zoo's redbrick structures, turn to your right to see another niche with a **(29) dancing goat** inside.

After stalking all this sculpted prey, your kids may well feel as mine did: "Mom, can we see some live animals now?" And here you are, right near the gates of the zoo, ready to grant their wish.

Above 79th Street, two museums dominate the park: the **Metropolitan Museum of Art** (p. 155), inside the park at East 82nd Street, and the **American Museum of Natural History** (p. 143), facing the park at West 79th Street and Central Park West. Midpark, between them, lies the **Great Lawn,** a huge stretch of grass and ball fields where crowds happily congregate in summer for gatherings ranging from Metropolitan Opera concerts to special events like Disney premieres and major rock concerts. At the south end of the Great Lawn, **Turtle Pond** protects a habitat for turtles, ducks, and dragonflies. To the west of it lie the **Delacorte Theater,** home of summer's free Shakespeare in the Park (and another essential set of restrooms); the picturesque wooden **Swedish Cottage** (p. 263), where daily marionette shows are held; and up on the hill, the **Shakespeare Garden** and **Belvedere Castle** with its nature center.

Between 86th and 96th streets, the major feature of the park is the **Jacqueline Kennedy Onassis Reservoir,** named in 1995 in honor of the former First Lady who lived for years nearby at 1040 Fifth Ave. (at 85th St.). A cinder track makes a 1½-mile loop around the reservoir, much of it lined with cherry trees that are breathtaking in spring; we prefer, however, to walk along the bridle path circling the reservoir, where experienced riders can bring their mounts from the **Claremont Stables** (p. 213). Walking here, you've got a very good chance of sighting horses. North of the reservoir is the tan stucco **Tennis House** (see "Tennis" under "Sports & Games," later in this chapter), which also has restrooms.

Above 96th Street the east side of the park has two big attractions: the **Conservatory Garden** (p. 177), at 105th Street and Fifth Avenue, which has restrooms, and **Harlem Meer,** the graceful pond at the northeast corner of the park, where the **Dana Discovery Center** (p. 179) runs nature workshops and hands out fishing poles so even youngsters can try their hand at angling in the meer. Midpark, right off of the 97th Street Transverse, the **North Meadow Recreation Center,** undiscovered by many Manhattanites, has lots of sports facilities, including well-groomed ball fields, handball courts, basketball courts, and climbing walls. See "Sports & Games," later in this chapter, for more details; the staff here will even lend you equipment for free (call ℭ **212/348-4867** to reserve equipment, and be sure to bring a valid photo ID).

On the west side of the park, a stroll above 96th Street will take you to a picturesque and little-known area at West 100th Street: the **Pool,** a willow-fringed pond with a lively waterfall at the east end; my kids love to hang over the railing on the bridge and watch the cascading waters beneath. North of here, the **Great Hill** has a high, broad lawn perfectly suited to picnics. At the top of the park, at 110th Street, is the **Lasker Rink,** which converts in summer into the **Lasker Pool.**

Be wary about going too deep into the park this far north, however, because it's less populated and the surrounding neighborhoods include some risky elements. I readily take my kids to the Pool and Harlem Meer on weekend days, and lots of families we know skate at Lasker Rink, but the social scene is rougher in summer, when the rink turns into a pool.

From 59th to 110th sts., between Central Park W. (Eighth Ave.) and Fifth Ave. ℭ **212/310-6600;** visitor's center 212/794-6564; event hot line 888/NY-PARKS or 212/360-3456. www.centralparknyc.org. Subway: 1 to 59th St./Columbus Circle; N, Q, R, W to 57th St./Seventh Ave.; N, R, W to Fifth Ave./59th St.; B, C to any stop from 59th St./Columbus Circle to 110th St.; 4, 5, 6 to any stop from 59th St. to 103rd St.

Riverside Park 𝒜𝒜 Long, narrow Riverside Park really shows off designer Frederick Law Olmsted's ingenuity: Beneath it lie miles of underground railroad tracks, while the Henry Hudson Parkway, a major thoroughfare out of the city, bisects it lengthwise (you can't always get to the river shore as a result). But between West 83rd and West 96th streets, Riverside Park features a broad paved **promenade** with stone railings where you can lean over and gaze west over the Hudson; the pavement here makes it super for leisurely biking and skating, though you'll have to weave through strolling crowds on summer Sundays. The **dog run** near 86th Street always manages to entertain children even if they don't have a pooch to exercise, and the **community garden** along the median strip at 91st Street is simply glorious.

The southern end of Riverside Park, from 72nd to 83rd streets, is flatter and more open than the rest of the park, and it is unbelievably beautiful in spring, when all the flowering trees unfurl. If you want to fly a kite, this can be a good place for it, with breezes blowing in from the river. Above 96th Street, the park gets more rustic and less crowded, with some very steep paths plummeting down the slope from Riverside Drive

At 72nd Street, 79th Street, and 86th Street, paths dip under the West Side Highway to the park's lower section, which hugs the banks of the Hudson River. At the southern end, the **72nd Street recreational pier** offers a wonderful view up and down the Hudson; a wide riverside path leads north from there to the **79th Street Boat Basin**—a marina full of bobbing houseboats, not all necessarily seaworthy. The grassy shade behind the esplanade makes a good place for a picnic, or you can stop for a casual meal at the **Boat Basin Café** (p. 104). Follow the bike path on north, past a platoon of ball fields and tennis courts and a sister cafe at 105th Street; the bike path meanders along the river more or less all the way to the George Washington Bridge.

Between the Hudson River and Riverside Dr., from 72nd to 153rd sts. $\mathcal{C}$ **212/496-2103.** Subway: 2, 3 to 72nd St. or 96th St.; 1 to any stop from 72nd St. to 125th St.

Prospect Park $\mathcal{R}\mathcal{R}$ Designers Frederick Law Olmsted and Calvert Vaux considered this park their crowning achievement. The main draws for kids are the super trio of attractions on the park's east side, along Flatbush Avenue: the **Prospect Park Audubon Center** (p. 180), the **Lefferts Homestead Children's Historic House Museum** (p. 170), and the **Prospect Park Carousel** (p. 164). Across Flatbush Avenue, you'll find the **Brooklyn Museum** (p. 169) and the **Brooklyn Botanic Garden** (p. 177), which aren't part of the park proper but were always considered part of the overall scheme. On weekends and holidays from noon to 5pm, a free hourly trolley runs continually among all these attractions (call $\mathcal{C}$ **718/965-8999** for schedule).

The focus for nature lovers in Prospect Park is in the park's southern end at the **Boathouse,** a glorious Italianate tiled structure dating from 1905, where the **Audubon Center** ($\mathcal{C}$ **718/287-3400,** admission free, Thurs–Sun and holidays 10am–5pm) offers two floors of exhibits, nature workshops for kids, and nature walks, both ranger-led and self-guided, along the Lullwater and through the wooded Ravine. **Electric-boat tours** leave from the landing in front of the boathouse for $5 per ride for ages 13 and up, $3 for children under 13 (April–Oct Thurs–Sun and holidays noon–4:30pm). If you prefer to power yourself, you can rent four-person pedal boats ($15 per hr. with a $10 deposit). Prospect Park's own **Wollman Rink** sits on the northern shore of the 60-acre lake.

If outdoor play is on your agenda, head for the **Long Meadow,** 90 acres of rolling greensward just inside the park's ornate entrance on Grand Army Plaza. Warm-weather weekends always see plenty of picnic action on the meadow, with lots of families tossing Frisbees and working on little sluggers' pitching arms; it's not so great for kite-flying, since the meadow is set down in one huge gentle hollow. Brooklyn's sizable Middle Eastern and Caribbean populations give cookout hours here a special spicy aroma. In winter the slopes along the edges of the meadow are just the ticket for trying out that new sled or pair of cross-country skis. The park's circular drive follows a 3.5-mile loop that's great for biking or in-line skating.

Bounded by Prospect Park W. (Ninth Ave.), Eastern Pkwy., Flatbush Ave., Parkside Ave., and Prospect Park S., Brooklyn. $\mathcal{C}$ **718/965-8951,** events hot line 718/965-8999. www.prospectpark.org. Subway: 2, 3 to Grand Army Plaza or Eastern Pkwy.; Q to Prospect Park or Parkside Ave.; F to 15th St./Prospect Park.

Carl Schurz Park $\mathcal{R}$ Though not as extensive as its West Side counterpart, Riverside Park, Carl Schurz Park—named after a prominent 19th-century German immigrant who was a newspaper editor, senator, and cabinet member—offers some very good East River views, and behind them, a few delicious green landscaped dells to wander through. Along the river, **John Finley Walk** (which actually continues south for several blocks past the park) is a paved promenade with wide-open views of the Triborough Bridge to the northeast, the railroad bridge spanning the rough waters of Hell Gate (a name that never fails to titillate my children), and across the river, the small lighthouse on the northern tip of Roosevelt Island; otherwise, it's just warehouses and boxy modern apartment complexes across the water.

No bikes or skating are allowed, but there's an enclosed **dog run** just inside the park about halfway up; come right before dinnertime, and watch the dogs romp. Walk to the north end of the promenade, where it loops around **Gracie Mansion,** the mayor's yellow clapboard residence (built as a country house in 1799, when this still was country); stand by the railing and face south to see how this tranquil park is built over four lanes of car traffic, on the busy FDR Drive—another good example of New York City maximizing its real estate.

Along the East River from E. 84th to E. 90th sts. Subway: 4, 5, 6 to 86th St.

Hudson River Park 🐾🐾   The long-term plan is to create a nearly continuous strip of park along Manhattan's Hudson shore from Battery Park to West 59th Street. Don't expect to find big lawns and woods; this is a narrow strip of landfill, much of it devoted to a paved riverside esplanade. But it's Manhattan's best-developed strip of riverside, and its determined reopening after the 9/11 tragedy sent a strong signal to New York (and the world) that downtown Manhattan would prevail.

The oldest section, city-run **Battery Park,** is southernmost, occupying the tip of Manhattan Island. An expanse of grass with some fine old trees, it's crisscrossed by paved paths and dotted with statues; round brownstone **Castle Clinton National Monument** stands here, where you can purchase ferry tickets to the Statue of Liberty and Ellis Island—the ferries embark from Battery Park's waterfront pilings. Hot-dog carts, T-shirt vendors, and street musicians are allowed in Battery Park.

Battery Park City comes next, a large office/retail/residential development built in the early 1980s, with a beautiful **Esplanade** serving as its spine. The heart of the complex— the World Financial Center's tony retail mall, the **Winter Garden Atrium**—features a cascade of marble steps leading to a huge glass window, outdoor plaza, and yacht basin. At the southern end, the **Museum of Jewish Heritage** presides over a terrace with great harbor views; the garden area around **South Cove** is fun for kids, where they can scamper over a small bridge and up into a postmodern gazebo echoing the Statue of Liberty's crown.

North of Battery Park City, the park traces the Hudson shore north to 59th Street, with a bike path, recreational piers, and loads of athletic facilities tucked between busy West Street and the river, with strips of fiercely green lawn and flower-filled planters wherever possible. It's hardly a place to get away from it all—but on a sunny afternoon, when the wide sky arches overhead and the broad Hudson sparkles a stone's throw away, it's an exhilarating place to be.

West of West St., from W. 59th St. to the bottom tip of Manhattan. ℂ **212/627-2020.** www.hudsonriverpark.org. Subway: 1, 2, 3 to Chambers St. and stations north; E to World Trade Center; 4, 5 to Bowling Green.

2 The Playground Lowdown

CENTRAL PARK

Central Park's "adventure playgrounds," most built in the 1980s, feature imaginative designs incorporating lots of places to climb, jump, slide, and hide out, as well as lots of sand to dig in or safely land on. In the 1990s, a new generation of playground arrived, with rubber-mat ground surfaces (as opposed to asphalt) and large, complex structures of metal bars coated with tough plastic, usually in primary colors. The playgrounds are surrounded by iron palings so kids don't wander away unsupervised; they all have drinking fountains, operational from Memorial Day to Labor Day, though only the Heckscher Playground has restrooms, and many have sprinklers to make summertime play a whole lot cooler (which makes up somewhat for the city's appalling lack of decent public pools).

The playgrounds listed below have bucket swings for toddlers and babies and either tire swings or flat swings for older kids. The Parks Department keeps playground equipment decently well maintained, often with the help of neighborhood parents who join in for monthly cleanup days.

THE WEST SIDE   The large **Heckscher Playground,** midpark at 62nd Street, has a large sandbox, two areas with swings and slides (one for smaller children, one with tire swings for older kids), a large central area covered in springy astroturf that's great for picnicking or kicking a ball around, sprinklers in the summer (a blessing because there isn't much shade), and a great boulder outcropping abutted by raised walkways.

Just north of Tavern on the Green, the **West 67th Street Playground** has two sections: a 1970s-era playground atop a small hill and a smaller fenced area across the path with some newer primary-colored climbing structures and a set of bucket swings. The hilltop area is deliciously shady and better than most of this vintage, with undulating concrete forms, a nice bi-level brown timber treehouse, and sprinklers set in a little concrete amphitheater that spills running water into a long raised basin. The sightlines aren't too bad, but the sand could be cleaner.

The well-shaded **Diana Ross Playground** at West 81st Street—so named because the singer donated money to the park after violent incidents marred her Central Park concert in the early 1980s—was one of the first adventure playgrounds, and now it could use some refurbishment. The weathered wood structures, set in sandpits, are complex enough to inspire some really fun games, with webs of chains to climb on, suspension bridges to bounce on, and fireman's poles to slide down. But the design isn't geared to younger kids, who may have some trouble climbing where they want to go (which means you'll have to climb up after them to give them a boost). There are two hulking climbing structures set right in the middle; the sightlines can be a problem. Two giant pluses: There are public restrooms nearby (next to the Delacorte Theater— usually dirty but infinitely preferable to soiled undies), and you're only a block north of the American Museum of Natural History.

A nautical theme prevails at the **West 84th Street Playground,** which has boat-shaped climbing structures, rowboats to rock in, fish designs around the sprinklers, and lots of shade. A stone's throw away, the **Spector Playground** at West 85th Street sits on a rise of land with lots of picnickable grass around it. Its two best features are the nice fenced-off toddler area (baby swings, sandbox, sprinklers) and an irresistible rambling wooden treehouse with a giant rope to swing on, Tarzan-style. Many of the playground's structures are set in sand, however, and a long wooden bridge arches over the middle of the immense sandpit, which makes sightlines problematic if you're in the toddler area and trying to keep an eye on older kids down by the treehouse. The paved sprinkler area gets very active in summer. Across the drive are some bucket swings midpark in the shady cool of the **Pinetum.**

Manhattan Playgrounds

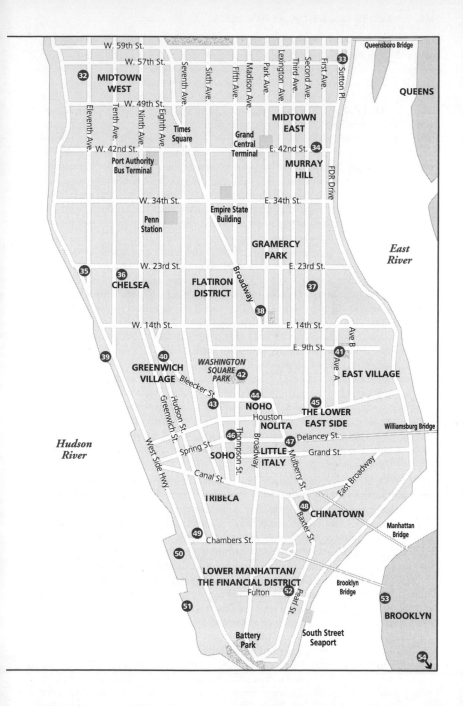

The delightful **Safari Playground** at West 91st Street is an imaginative playscape where children scramble over a herd of hippo sculptures and hop in and out of a green rowboat embedded in the pavement. It has no swings or slides and only two rudimentary climbing structures, but kids hardly notice—they're so busy with jump ropes and hopscotch and sidewalk chalk and running in and out of the sprinklers. With picnic tables and lots of shade, it attracts swarms of preschoolers. At West 93rd Street, the **Wild West Playground** is extremely popular with uptown families, especially in summer, when sprinklers send water rushing down the long central gully into a circular wading pool at the far end. Four square fort-like wood towers at the center make this a great spot for playing all sorts of war games; three of the towers anchor big sandpits surrounded by low wooden palisades, with tire swings, slides, a bouncy suspension bridge, and weathered wood climbing structures (the fourth has a rubber-mat surface that's good for playing ball). The towers in the center make the sightlines a bit of a problem, and the combination of water gully and sandpit means lots of wet gravelly muck in your kids' shoes when you get home.

At West 96th Street, the newer **Rudin Playground** is set on an island between two busy transverse roads, meaning a bit more noise and exhaust than at other playgrounds; the gate leads straight out to Central Park West, which can also be a problem. But in other respects it's a pleasant place, with a central paved sprinkler area, a vine-hung pergola shading a set of benches, and a trio of brightly colored climbing gyms that modulate from low toddler-friendly structures to a fairly demanding set of parallel bars and swinging rings. There's only one small concrete-edged sandbox, but there are lots of well-shaded bucket swings for babies.

The **West 99th Street Playground** is past its prime and looks it, but athletic kids can have a blast on its weathered wood structures, especially the concrete mountain with interior tunnels for reaching the top of a big metal slide. Essentially one large sandpit surrounded by asphalt, it's rarely crowded, but sightlines can be a problem since the benches are on the perimeter. The gang here is fairly mixed, mostly neighborhood folks, but for whatever reasons, it seems to be kept less tidy than playgrounds farther south. There are good lawns nearby for picnicking, and right across the drive are the North Meadow playing fields.

THE EAST SIDE   At East 67th Street, the **Rustic Playground** is one of the park's most imaginative play spaces. You enter through a leafy wooden arbor; straight ahead is an arched stone bridge that looks very much like the famous Bow Bridge over the Lake to the north, connecting a pair of lushly planted islands. On your left is a midsize sandpit with a slide; on your right, a terrace with picnic tables. Best of all, behind the stone bridge, steps lead up a steep rock outcropping to the top of a long curved metal slide actually set into the face of the rock; daredevil kids in the know bring a square of corrugated cardboard to sit on to make the slide superfast, sort of like a waterless log-flume ride. The big problem with the Rustic Playground is you can't see past the bridges and islands in the center; if one of your children is doing repeat trips down that slide—it can be addictive—you can't monitor the rest of the playground if your other children are elsewhere. Still, it's a wonderful place for a pre- or post-zoo frolic.

The **East 72nd Street Playground** is another dinosaur from the era of brown timber, brick pyramids, metal slides, and concrete. These hulking shapes make the sightlines pretty bad, and the ground surface, mostly sand, looks a bit dirty. It's quite shady, though, and the entrance is set safely inside the park. Kids in this neighborhood prefer to go to the **James Michael Levin Playground,** set well inside the park near East

76th Street, with a small iron entrance gate everyone conscientiously keeps latched. The centerpiece of this graceful wide-open playground is a fountain featuring scenes from classic fairy tales; kids swarm between the climbing structure near the gate and a decent-size concrete sandbox at the other end, with plenty of open pavement in between for skating, hopscotch, and the like. Sightlines are super, and the people here are pretty well behaved, but the place gets crowded after school. On the north side of East 79th Street, the **Pat Hoffman Friedman Playground** is a well-sheltered small area behind a replica of the Metropolitan Museum's American Wing's statue *Three Bears* by Paul Manship; there's not much here except bucket swings, a tiny concrete sandbox, a metal slide, and a few climbing bars. It's a handy place for a quick stop right after a visit to the Metropolitan, though only the 4-and-under set will be satisfied.

With its series of glazed-brick pyramids, the **Ancient Playground** at East 84th Street pays homage to the neighboring Metropolitan Museum's Egyptian Temple of Dendur, visible through the glass wall right across the road. Hulking concrete banks around the edges give this playground a bunker-like quality, and, wedged between two busy transverse roads, it's about as bucolic as an interstate gas station. Most of the benches are set up at one end, grouped around concrete chessboard tables, which means babysitters congregating there can't always adequately supervise their charges. But it's an extremely popular after-school spot for elementary school kids, who have great fun leaping all over the pyramids, thundering up and down the metal slides, and taking furious spins on the rope swings. An enclosed area at the far end makes a safe toddler haven with a sandbox and bucket swings.

The popular **East 96th Street Playground** sits at the top of a short, steep rise from Fifth Avenue. A good-size toddler area is set off by iron palings in the center; other separately defined areas include a rubber-matted zone with tire swings and wooden pilings to climb on; a large modern metal-bar structure with all sorts of bridges, ladders, towers, and plastic slides; a cool little treehouse platform in a shady back corner; and a paved expanse surrounding a big water sprinkler. Sightlines are very good.

The well-shaded **East 100th Street Playground** has a coil of red steel that becomes a run-through tunnel of spraying water in summer; the climbing structure is particularly imaginative, with lots of inspiring nooks for all sorts of make-believe. Best of all, this playground is wheelchair-accessible. It's adjacent to an extensive lawn that sees lots of ball playing and picnic action on weekends. On the east shore of Harlem Meer, at 108th Street, the **Bernard Family Playground** features a large steel-bar climbing apparatus, painted maroon and forest green, mounted on black rubber matting. It also has a small, clean sandbox; a paved sprinkler section; and a few bucket swings. Only a few yards away, there's a marvelous tiny sand beach where small children can happily dig, sift, and mold sand beside the lapping meer water.

RIVERSIDE PARK

The **Henry Neufield Playground** at West 76th Street is commonly known as the **Elephant Park,** after a set of five plump little stone pachyderms set around an open expanse of asphalt. This pleasant playground also has two modern climbing structures, a fenced swing area, a small fenced sandbox with very clean sand, and restrooms (hallelujah!) actually kept decently clean. There's an active set of basketball courts next to it. The only drawback is that traffic roars on the West Side Highway right past the bushes on the other side of the back fence. At the **River Run Playground** at West 83rd Street, a sprinkler feeds into a sculpted replica of the Hudson River; this, in turn, flows along the playground, toward a whimsical 35-foot sandbox, with sculptural forms of castles, classical gods, and woodland animals frolicking around it. Parents appreciate another form of running water here—the working restrooms.

The **Hippo Park** (down a steep hill from Riverside Dr., at W. 91st St.) derives its nickname from the wonderful hippopotamus sculptures in the middle, which children can climb on. It has swings for both tots and big kids, smallish sandboxes, and sprinklers in summer. An energetic group of neighborhood parents has organized drop-in arts and crafts classes in summer, as well as regular attendants to keep the restrooms clean and safe.

A few blocks north at 97th Street and Riverside Drive, the **Dinosaur Park** also has sculptures (dinosaurs, naturally) and a huge sprinkler area, great for cooling off in summer, though it gets crowded after school. There are restrooms here as well. Set alongside the Riverside Drive promenade on the park's upper level, the **West 110th Street Playground** has small climbing structures, bucket swings, and little sandboxes that make it best for toddlers. The farthest north, the shady **Claremont Playground,** at West 124th Street (right behind Grant's Tomb), has spouting porpoise sprinklers, a sandbox shaped like a huge rowboat, and—ta-da!—more restrooms.

THE UPPER WEST SIDE

Sandwiched between Riverside and Central parks, the West Side has plenty of access to playgrounds, though few between the parks. If you're at the American Museum of Natural History, it may be handy to stop on Amsterdam Avenue at 77th Street (northeast corner) at the **Tecumseh Playground,** which features a rootin' tootin' Western theme, with climbing structures shaped like Conestoga wagons and longhorn cattle. On West 92nd Street between Central Park West and Columbus Avenue, the **Sol Bloom Playground** not only has two great climbing structures (one toddler-scaled) on a soft red-and-black checkerboard surface, but also is the focus of lots of neighborhood athletics, with basketball hoops, a paved softball diamond, and a handball court.

THE UPPER EAST SIDE

The **Carl Schurz Park Playground** ⟨⋆⟩, at 84th Street and East End Avenue, is my top choice on the East Side. This large, well-shaded playground has several multilevel climbing structures of red-and-green plastic-coated steel and weathered wood—ladders, slides, bridges, steering wheels, climbing chains, and sliding poles provide plenty of playtime interest. It also has a separate sprinkler area and lots of open pavement in the middle that just cries out for a rousing game of Red Rover or Prisoners All. You'll see lots of little girls in uniforms in the afternoons, after nearby Chapin and Brearley schools let out. Adjacent Carl Schurz Park (p. 199) has a superb riverside promenade.

St. Catherine's Playground, on the west side of First Avenue between 67th and 68th streets, is undeniably urban—iron palings, asphalt paving, traffic churning past on three sides—but it's definitely a welcome spot in this near-Midtown neighborhood, roomy and fairly shady with a couple of terraced levels. There's a set of happening basketball and handball courts on the other side of a chain-link fence. **John Jay Park,** on 76th Street east of York Avenue, has some nice up-to-date climbing structures for toddlers in the shady outer area and some for older kids inside the chain-link fence. There are also wide-open asphalt surfaces to run (and fall) on, a small East River lookout, and an outdoor pool open in summer (see "Swimming" under "Sports & Games," later in this chapter).

Ruppert Park (89th to 90th sts., along Second Ave.) has limited playground equipment, but smaller children have fun frolicking on the landscaped series of terraces, with lots of curved paths, flowerbeds, and benches for play-date tête-à-têtes. The

Hunter School Playground, on Madison Avenue between 94th and 95th streets, is notable for its Madison Avenue entrance, which incorporates a redbrick castle-like facade, the remnant of a demolished turn-of-the-20th-century National Guard armory. (A similar armory, still intact, is down Park Ave. between 66th and 67th sts.) Though this playground is open to the public only after school hours, it may be worth a special detour to let your kids scamper up and down the steps between the stout brick towers, through a wide arch that just cries out for a moat and drawbridge.

MIDTOWN

At the east end of 42nd Street, the **Tudor City** residential complex is set on a terrace above First Avenue; halfway up the stairs that rise on the south side of 42nd Street just past Second Avenue is a small fenced playground with a rubberized surface and primary-colored climbing structures. Overlooking the river, **Sutton Place Park** is set in a quiet cul-de-sac where East 57th Street dead-ends just past Sutton Place. This tiny brick-paved play area—a few steps down from street level, on a terrace above the FDR Drive, with lots of shade and some great views of the 59th Street Bridge arching over the East River—is best for infants and toddlers, since there's no playground equipment to speak of, just wooden benches, one absurdly small iron-fenced sandbox, and a large bronze wart hog (Pumbaa!) on a pedestal.

Over on the far West Side, in a grimy neighborhood once called Hell's Kitchen (nowadays more gentrified and relabeled Clinton), the **DeWitt Clinton Park** playground (between 52nd and 53rd sts. on Eleventh Ave.) is set behind a balding set of ball fields, with the West Side Highway rumbling beyond a fence. Still, the playground equipment is excellent, set in pleasant shade, with a nicely executed Erie Canal theme (DeWitt Clinton was the politician who got the Erie Canal built a couple centuries ago—but you already knew that, right?).

CHELSEA, THE FLATIRON DISTRICT & GRAMERCY PARK

Chelsea Waterside Park, right across 11th Avenue from the Chelsea Piers recreational complex at 23rd Street, has a cheery little playground nestled beside the turf athletic fields. It's got some nice water jets and a sand play area, and best of all, it's designed to be wheelchair-accessible. Named for the clergyman who wrote *A Visit from St. Nicholas* (better known as *The Night Before Christmas*), **Clement Clarke Moore Park** (southeast corner of Tenth Ave. and 22nd St.), is a shady, paved corner lot with a few benches, concrete sculptures, and one rubberized-steel climbing structure.

In the Flatiron District, the most centrally located are the two small but heavily populated playgrounds in **Union Square,** side by side near Broadway and 16th Street. The fenced-in one has a smart rubber-coated steel climbing gym in happy primary colors, with hordes of toddlers swarming all over it; outside the fence, many kids still insist on clambering over an older playground's outmoded metal structures, which look like geodesic dome skeletons. The Union Square Greenmarket, operating Monday, Wednesday, Friday, and Saturday, is only a few steps away, which makes playground picnics very handy. Somewhat off the beaten track in the Gramercy Park area is **Augustus Saint-Gaudens Park** (19th St. and Second Ave.), which has shade; good climbing structures; and lots of open pavement, some with basketball hoops.

GREENWICH VILLAGE & THE EAST VILLAGE

The focal point of the Village, **Washington Square Park,** at the foot of Fifth Avenue (between 4th and 6th sts., though the names are changed here for a couple of blocks), has on the north side a bustling playground with lots of up-to-date climbing struc-tures, set off by a fence from the rest of the park. A pair of greenish tortoises spout water from their beaks in summer. Older kids may be attracted more to the **Mercer Playground,** a long narrow strip on the west side of Mercer Street between Bleecker and West 3rd streets; instead of climbing equipment, it features a long skating path, a spray shower, plantings, and benches for socializing. Farther west, at Sixth Avenue and Bleecker Street, the **32 Carmine Street Playground** is buffered by a redbrick wall from the surrounding traffic; go through the iron gate, and you'll find swings and wooden climbing structures in an asphalt-paved yard. Or follow Bleecker Street west to the point where it dead-ends at Hudson Street to find the always-hopping **Bleecker Street Playground,** fenced off with iron palings. It's got swings, a sandbox, picnic tables, and a stretch of asphalt just big enough for hopscotch or a round of double-dutch jump-roping. Way over west on the banks of the Hudson, the new **Pier 51** play-ground in Hudson River Park (west of West Street, at Jane Street) has not only has the usual slides, poles, and ladders, it also takes advantage of its riverside location with viewing scopes and a boat hull that children can clamber over.

Once-derelict **Tompkins Square Park** has become a leafy haven in the increasingly gentrified East Village, and it has no fewer than three good-size fenced-off play-grounds with black rubberized ground surfaces and rubber-coated metal play struc-tures in bold primary colors (my kids are downright envious of such an abundance). The biggest and busiest is along Avenue A at East 9th Street; the other two are along East 7th Street. After a vigorous play session, head down the avenue for pizza at Two Boots (p. 132).

SOHO, LOWER EAST SIDE & CHINATOWN

The **Thompson Street Playground,** on the east side of Thompson Street between Prince and Spring streets, is a welcome romping spot in oh-so-urban SoHo; it has large red timber climbing structures on an asphalt surface. Good for stretching limbs in fair weather, it's about halfway between the New York Fire Museum and the Chil-dren's Museum for the Arts, both on Spring Street. At the corner of Mulberry and Spring streets in Little Italy, the **De Salvio Playground** has a couple of bright mod-ern climbers set in a pleasant fenced-in corner lot, neatly paved with a few benches under the trees.

Tucked between First Street and Houston Street just west of First Avenue, the neatly enclosed **First Street Playground** is the pleasantest Lower East Side playground for younger kids, with lots of shade trees and colorful coated steel climbing structures. In tree-shaded **Columbus Park,** at Worth Street between Baxter and Mulberry streets in Chinatown, hordes of Asian and Asian-American children scramble over the climb-ing structures and dangle on the swings, while elderly men play chess nearby.

TRIBECA & LOWER MANHATTAN

Washington Market Park, on Greenwich Street between Chambers and Duane streets, is an inviting open space, a 2½-acre lawn sprouting up where the city's rough-and-tumble wholesale food markets used to be. The gentle rises of the grassy area, punctuated with a delightful gazebo, are perfect for picnics and Frisbee games, and there's a fanciful maritime-themed wrought-iron fence at the south end, where P.S. 234 sits. The tidy playground is enclosed along the park's eastern wall.

The **Wagner Park Playground** ⍟, at the west end of Chambers Street, is a thriv-ing enclosed area across the esplanade from the river. The super climbing structures, made of weathered wood and royal-blue steel, provide bridges and platforms where kids can scamper above ground; on ground level are three good-size sand areas, one wheelchair-accessible. The northern section is set aside for toddlers, with a delicious bronze dodo set in a tiny splashing area; there's another sprinkler area for older kids, with a stone elephant and hippo. At the southern end is one of the coolest pieces of playground equipment in the city: a red steel whirligig seating eight, powered by pedals mounted beneath every other seat. Though most of the playground is unshaded, several wooden arbors along the sides allow parents and sleeping babies to duck out of the sun. Go up the esplanade to the fanciful sculpture park with its wade-in fountain, too.

Across the street from South Street Seaport, iron fences surround a triangular lot at Fulton and Pearl streets, where the **Pearl Street Playground** has a delightfully complicated climbing structure where kids can let off steam.

BROOKLYN

At the south end of the Promenade in Brooklyn Heights, the excellent **Pierrepont Street Playground** has restrooms (not always clean, however), a separate yard for the very young, lots of shade trees, and loads of slides. Add to that plenty of neighborhood buzz and a peerless view across the East River to Manhattan. The **Imagination Playground** in Prospect Park (east side of the park, near the Lincoln Rd. entrance) is as fanciful as its name promises: a bronze dragon spouts water, a black-and-white-striped bridge twists like a helix, child-size masks are mounted for children to peek through, and a central sculpture features the little boy Peter and his dog Willie from Ezra Jack Keats's beloved children's books.

3 Sports & Games

BASEBALL

Organized Little League games around the city in spring snap up most of the groomed baseball fields on spring weekends; after work, grown-up leagues fill the parks on weekday evenings. Central Park has some very nice fields: at the **Great Lawn** (midpark between 81st and 86th sts.), **Heckscher Ballfields** (midpark between 63rd and 66th sts.), and the **North Meadow** (midpark between 97th and 100th sts.). Anyone can reserve a ball field for use; call the Parks & Recreation department at © 212/ 408-0226) and find out what's available for the time you want. The cost is $10 per 2-hour session (after 5:30pm, $8 gets you a 1½-hr. session). If you don't want to get that formal, try the North Meadow facilities, which are sometimes free on a walk-in basis, provided no one has reserved them; a handful of other Manhattan parks, including **DeWitt Clinton Park** (between 52nd and 53rd sts. on Eleventh Ave.) and **Riverside Park** (west of Riverside Dr., in the section north of 103rd St.—take stairs down from the promenade level), have baseball diamonds with chain-link backstops that are usually free for pickup games.

If your slugger just wants to work on batting form, check out **batting cages** at **The Baseball Center NYC,** 202 W. 74th St., between Broadway and Amsterdam Avenue (© 212/362-0344; $50 per half-hr., $80 per hr., for one to five players); the **Chelsea Piers Field House,** 23rd Street and the West Side Highway, Pier 62 (© 212/336-6500 or www.chelseapiers.com; $2 per 10 balls); in **Hudson River Park** on West St., just north of Chambers St. (© 212/627-2020, www.hudsonriverpark.org, $2 per 15 balls); or at **Randall's Island Family Golf Center,** across the Triborough Bridge on Randall's Island (© 212/427-5689, $2 for 15 balls).

BASKETBALL

Several city-run playgrounds have asphalt half courts where some pretty aggressive games of one-on-one take place. The famous courts at **Sixth Avenue and West 4th Street**—known as "The Cage"—are a breeding ground for serious hoop-dreamers; the action (not to mention the trash talk) is so fast and furious, kids are better off watching than playing. *Insider tip:* The McDonald's across 4th Street has an upstairs seating area with picture windows overlooking the courts, practically as good as a skybox. Intrepid kids may be able to get a pickup game at **St. Catherine's Playground** (First Ave. between 67th and 68th sts.), in **Central Park**'s courts just northeast of the Great Lawn (midpark at 85th St.), **Riverside Park** courts at West 76th Street, the **Sol Bloom Playground** (W. 92nd St. between Central Park W. and Columbus Ave.), or **Goat Park** (Amsterdam Ave. and 99th St.)—named after Earl "the Goat" Manigault, a high-jumping, high-scoring street player who watched his peers win NBA offers while his own life unraveled in disappointment and drug addiction. Manigault redeemed himself by running athletic programs for kids in this very park, for which he will be forever remembered.

If you didn't bring your own ball, head to the paved outdoor courts at Central Park's **North Meadow Recreation Center** (midpark, just north of the 97th St. transverse road); at the recreation center's offices right next to the courts, you can borrow a basketball, along with a whole bag full of other sports equipment. If pickup games aren't your style, organize a group of kids and book a basketball court at the **Chelsea Piers Field House,** Pier 62 at Chelsea Piers, 23rd Street and the West Side Highway (© **212/ 336-6500** or www.chelseapiers.com; $155 per hour to reserve a court, $8 to walk in and play; call for availability).

BICYCLING

The circular drive in **Central Park** is probably the city's most popular biking road, a 6-mile-long circuit that includes a couple of fairly grueling hills; younger kids may want to stick to the relatively flat lower loop, which shortcuts across at 72nd Street, or even the footpath looping around the Great Lawn, midpark from 81st to 86th streets; it's off-limits to bikes, but trikes are usually tolerated. The wide sidewalk bordering the park walls is also good for young riders, with few cross streets to negotiate; follow it up either Fifth Avenue or Central Park West. Park drives are closed to traffic weekdays 10am to 3pm and all weekend long, from 7pm Friday to 7am Monday. Bike traffic circles the park clockwise.

For more ambitious cyclists, the marked **Hudson River bike path** runs all the way from the Battery Park at the southern tip of the island to the George Washington Bridge, which crosses the Hudson at 181st Street. One section, around 125th Street, is still hard to navigate; you may have to turn to city streets for a few blocks at this point. But otherwise, it's smooth, level, and clear sailing all the way, with some amazing river views. The trail begins with the **Battery Park Promenade,** then runs north along West Street, past Greenwich Village and then Chelsea Piers. Things get pretty urban as you follow the bike lane beside the West Side Highway through Midtown, but at 72nd Street, you'll enter **Riverside Park.** The path cruises along through Riverside's lower section and continues north of 125th Street as a strip of green tucked between the river and the West Side Highway, neatly paved and landscaped.

Riverside Park also offers a flat, wide promenade from 83rd to 96th streets, perhaps better for younger bikers. And like Central Park, Riverside is bordered by wide sidewalks, either of asphalt or of distinctive hexagonal paving stones, so you can cruise along the west side of Riverside Drive from 79th Street up to 125th Street with very few cross streets to worry about.

On weekends, there's little traffic in **Lower Manhattan,** so you may have fun circling around the deserted skyscrapers. Just south of City Hall, broad entrance ramps lead onto the Brooklyn Bridge, with broad bike/pedestrian lanes leading you over the river (see "Crossing the Brooklyn Bridge," on p. 146).

The circular road in Brooklyn's **Prospect Park** is another great traffic-free place to ride on weekends; it's only 3½ miles long and has just one really tough hill.

Now here's the catch: Very few of Manhattan's many bicycle rental shops stock bikes for kids; apparently, the insurance costs are too prohibitive. The ones that do are **Larry & Jeff's Bicycles Plus,** 1690 Second Ave., between 87th and 88th streets (© 212/722-2201), charging $8 per hour, $30 for a full day (daily 10am–8pm); and **Pedal Pusher,** 1306 Second Ave., at 69th Street (© **212/288-5592;** Wed–Mon 10am–6pm, charging $6 per hour, $25 per day).

BOWLING
Bowlmor Lanes   Down in the Village, 42-lane Bowlmor survives as a sort of hip throwback, with a long sleek bar, a restaurant, a VIP lounge, and lots of postmodern date bowling (deejays, glow-in-the-dark pins, nude bowling parties, and so on), alongside some ferocious league action at night. Daytimes, though, are relatively uncrowded, which is good for families, because no one under 21 is allowed after 5pm. There's automatic scoring, and gutter bumpers are available to keep kids' balls in the alley. *Trivia fans take note:* The first *Bowling for Dollars* TV game show was shot here, and Nixon bowled here regularly in the 1950s.

110 University Place (btwn 12th and 13th sts.). © 212/255-8188. www.bowlmor.com. Bowling for children 11am–5pm daily. Mon–Thurs $7.95 per person per game, Fri $8.95, Sat $9.25, Sun $8.95. Shoe rental $5. Subway: N, Q, R, W, 4, 5, 6 to 14th St.; L to Union Sq.

Chelsea Piers AMF Bowling 🅖   This sparkling 40-lane facility at Chelsea Piers (it's in the next building south from the Field House) sees lots of family action on weekends. There's also a games arcade, and waiters from the on-site restaurant will bring food right to your lane. Gutter bumpers are much in demand here.

Pier 60 at Chelsea Piers, 23rd St. and the West Side Hwy at the Hudson River. © 212/835-2695. www.chelseapiers.com. Daily 9am–11pm (open until 3am Fri–Sat). Mon–Fri 9am-5pm $6 per person per game, Sat–Sun 9am–5pm $8; Mon–Tues after 5pm $8, Wed–Sun after 5pm $8.75. Shoe rental $5. Subway: C, E, F, N, R, V, W, 1 to 23rd St. station. Bus: M23 across 23rd St.

Leisure Time Bowling   Budding bowlers brave the unattractive bus terminal to find this surprisingly clean and modern 30-lane complex, which offers kids bumper bowling and a relatively low-key scene.

625 Eighth Ave., in the Port Authority Bus Terminal, 2nd level (enter at 40th St. and Eighth Ave.). $6 per person per game; $9 after 5pm Fri–Sat. Shoe rental $5. Subway: A, C, E to 42nd St./Port Authority.

Harlem Lanes   Gospel Bowling on Monday nights? Let me guess: This must be Harlem. Just off the 125th Street strip, this sleek new 24-lane facility occupies two floors of the same building as the Alhambra Ballroom; the third floor is best for families, while more of a lounge atmosphere prevails on the 4th floor. Tuesday nights are officially family night, but kids are welcome here anytime. The café has some tempting food, from Jamaican meat patties and jerk chicken to Cajun BBQ shrimp.

2110-2118 Adam Clayton Powell Blvd. at 126th St., 3th and 4th floors. ℃ 212/678-2695. www.harlemlanes.com. Mon–Thurs 11am–11pm, Fri–Sat 11am–2am, Sun 11am–9pm. $5.50 per person per game Mon–Thurs before 6pm, $7.50 Mon–Thurs after 6pm, $7.50 all day Fri–Sun. Shoe rental $4.50. Subway: 2, 3, A, B, C, D to 125th St.

CHESS

It's possible to play at the outdoor chessboards beside the **Central Park Chess and Checkers House,** midpark at 67th Street, just west of the Dairy; the boards are built into the stone tables and you can pick up chess pieces at the Dairy. The real scene for kids, however, is in Greenwich Village, where two chess stores sit a few doors away from each other on Thompson Street between 3rd and Bleecker streets: **Chess Forum,** 219 Thompson St. (℃ **212/475-2369**), and the **Chess Shop,** 230 Thompson St. (℃ **212/475-9580**). Loads of kids stream in to play, especially on Saturday, and the charges are minimal—children play for free at the Chess Forum. Either store can also arrange lessons at $30 per hour.

CLIMBING

Three venues in Manhattan cater to young climbers with walls scaled to their size: the **Chelsea Piers Field House,** Pier 62, 23rd Street and the West Side Highway, (℃ **212/336-6500,** $25 per half hour, for children 5–16: call for schedule); the **Extra Vertical Climbing Center,** 61 W. 62nd St. between Broadway and Columbus Ave. (℃ **212/586-5718,** www.extravertical.com, $9 first climb, $5 additional climbs; child lesson $65, parent plus child $130; ages 5 and up, open weekdays 3–10pm, weekends noon–8pm, summers daily noon–10pm); and the **North Meadow Recreation Center,** Central Park, midpark at 97th Street (℃ **212/348-4867,** ext. 14), which offers open climb sessions at no charge for kids ages 8 to 17, Sunday from 11am to 1pm and Tuesday from 5:30 to 7:30pm.

FISHING

Believe it or not, you actually can fish in Manhattan. At the north end of Central Park, the **Harlem Meer** has been stocked with fish; April to October, take your kids before 3pm to the Dana Discovery Center on the north shore (near E. 110th St.; ℃ **212/ 860-1370**) and the staff will give them simple fishing poles and some bait. The Urban Park Rangers also run occasional Hudson River fishing sessions in the summer off the **70th Street Pier** at the south end of Riverside Park; call the rangers at ℃ **212/ 427-4040** or check out **www.nycgovparks.org** for upcoming schedules.

GOLF

Golf Club at Chelsea Piers   This is truly an amazing facility: a four-level driving range, where 52 golfers at a time can slam balls out into a huge open space bounded by high-tech mesh, all the while enjoying incredible Hudson River views. Stalls are heated for year-round play, and you don't have to lug around buckets of balls—a computerized system in the floor slides a new ball up on your tee as soon as you've hit the previous one. You pay for as many balls as you wish and get a magnetized card to swipe in a slot at the tee; the computer subtracts how many you hit and you can come back whenever you want to hit the rest. There's also a 1,000-square-foot practice putting green, and pros are available for lessons at the attached Jim McLean Golf Academy.

Pier 59 at Chelsea Piers, 23rd St. and the West Side Hwy., at the Hudson River. ℃ 212/336-6400. www.chelseapiers. com. Minimum charge $20, which gets you 80 balls at peak times, 118 other times. Apr–Sept daily 6am–midnight; Oct–Mar daily 6:30am–11pm. Subway: C, E, F, N, R, V, W, 1, 9 to 23rd St. station. Bus: M23 across 23rd St.

Randall's Island Family Golf Center   Randall's Island is one of the city's best-kept sports secrets; with lots of ball fields, it's a haven for amateur athletes and a quick drive across the Triborough Bridge from Manhattan. Along with a driving range, batting cages, a golf shop, and a snack bar, there's a nifty minigolf course at this golf complex on the island. If you don't have a car, you can take a shuttle bus ($10), leaving from Modell's sporting goods store at 86th Street and Third Avenue every hour on the hour (3–8pm weekdays, 10am–5pm weekends).

On Randall's Island. ✆ 212/427-5689. Driving range $12 for bucket of 153 balls, $8 for 68 balls. Minigolf $6 adults, $4 children under 16. Batting cages $2 for 15 pitches. Mon 11am–11pm; Tues–Sun 6am–11pm. Free parking; shuttle available (see above).

GYMNASTICS

Chelsea Piers Field House   The city has many gymnastics facilities, but most are available only for those taking scheduled classes. The Field House is your best option for drop-in sessions, but what a fabulous resource this is. It boasts an indoor climbing wall scaled perfectly for young climbers and a gymnastics area you have to see to believe—spring floors, in-ground trampolines, deep foam pits for practicing dismounts, and loads of bars, beams, rings, horses, and vaults. Kids 4 and older can check out the Field House at an Open Gym session, while children 6 months to 3 years old can occupy themselves happily in the Toddler Gym, a separate playroom with soft climbing structures.

Pier 62 at Chelsea Piers, 23rd St. and the West Side Hwy., at the Hudson River. ✆ 212/336-6500. Admission $10 to Toddler Gym, $25 to Open Gym & Climb. Call for schedule. Subway: C, E, F, N, R, V, W, 1, 9 to 23rd St. station. Bus: M23 across 23rd St.

HORSEBACK RIDING

Bronx Equestrian Center   Right off the Hutchinson Parkway on City Island, this small stable offers not only lessons and ring riding, but also trail rides in quiet woodlands. Pony rides are available for younger riders.

Shore Rd. S., City Island, the Bronx. ✆ 718/885-0551. Trail rides $30 per hr.; private lesson $40 per half-hr., $45 per 40 min., $50 per hr. Pony rides $5. Daily 9am–7pm.

Claremont Stables ⟲   The only riding stables close to Central Park, Claremont occupies a charming 1892 building. There are lots of classes for kids 6 and up, riding in an indoor ring—English saddle only. Call a day or two in advance to schedule. Experienced riders can take their mounts into nearby Central Park for $50 per hour; the bridle trail runs nearly the length of the park, looping around the reservoir. Thundering along the shady trails, clattering under landmark arched bridges, is a wonderful experience. You must wear shoes with enough of a heel to catch hold in a stirrup; helmets are required, but the stable provides them free of charge.

175 W. 89th St. (btwn Columbus and Amsterdam aves.). ✆ 212/724-5100. $55 per hr. group lesson, $65 per half-hr. private lesson. Mon–Fri 6:30am–7:30pm; Sat–Sun 8am–5pm. Subway: B, C, 1 to 86th St.

Kensington Stables (Value   To me, this is one of the best horseback deals in New York City, provided the schlep to Brooklyn doesn't daunt you. For $25 per hour, you can join a guided trail ride through leafy Prospect Park, riding either English or Western saddle; because there's a guide along, even inexperienced riders can join in. Lessons at the stable can be English or Western saddle. Call ahead if you want to book a lesson; drop-ins are welcome for the trail rides.

51 Caton Place, Brooklyn. ✆ 718/972-4588. $45 per hr. private lesson, $25 per half-hr. private lesson; $35 per hr. group lesson for 3 or more. Daily 10am–sundown. Subway: F to Fort Hamilton Pkwy.

New York City Riding Academy   Yet another of the many sports options on Randall's Island is this up-and-coming riding stable in a quiet area on the East River shore, a good bet for beginners. Riding is all Western saddles and in a ring; there are ponies for smaller riders.

Wards Island Park (take E. 102nd St. footbridge from Manhattan; by car, go over Triborough Bridge, follow road past golf center and psychiatric hospital, continue past baseball fields and turn right). ℂ **212/860-2986**. Lesson $30 per half-hr. Daily 9am–6pm.

Riverdale Equestrian Centre   Founded by former Olympians Rusty Holzer and Ashley Nicoll Holzer, this 21-acre stable in spacious Van Cortlandt Park offers quality instruction and well-cared-for mounts, with some spacious outdoor rings and jumping instruction. All saddles are English; riders must be over 6. Call a few days in advance to book lesson time.

In Van Cortlandt Park at W. 254th St. and Broadway, Riverdale, the Bronx. ℂ **718/548-4848**. www.riverdaleriding.com. $85 per hr. private lesson, $45 per half-hr. private lesson; $65 per hr. semiprivate lesson (for advanced riders only), $40 per half-hr. semiprivate lesson. Mon–Fri 11am–7pm; Sat–Sun 11am–5pm. Subway: 1 to 242nd St. Bus: Liberty Lines BxM3.

ICE-SKATING

Lasker Rink   Cheaper and less crowded than its Central Park cousin the Wollman Rink, uptown's Lasker is well populated by families on weekends. The ice here doesn't get as chewed up as Wollman's, but the rental skates are not of great quality.

In Central Park at 110th St. and Lenox Ave. ℂ **212/534-7639**. Admission $4 adults, $2 children. Skate rental $3.75. Nov–Mar daily 11am–3pm and 4–7pm. Subway: 2, 3 to 110th St.

Riverbank State Park   This roomy, open-air rink on Riverbank's topmost level is very much in demand with school hockey teams, but public skating sessions are leisurely and pleasant—a boon for tentative young skaters. It's rarely crowded, though some fast and furious teenage skaters here don't always watch out for little ones. In summer it converts to a roller rink.

145th St. and Riverside Dr. ℂ **212/694-3642**. Admission $4.50 adults, $2.50 children 12 and under. Skate rental $3.50. Late Oct to Mar Fri 6–9pm; Sat–Sun noon–3pm and 4–7pm. Subway: 1 to 145th St. Bus: M11, Bx19.

Rockefeller Plaza Rink   No doubt the most famous rink in town—and the easiest to find if you're a first-time visitor staying in a Midtown hotel—the Rockefeller Plaza Rink does have undeniable charm, especially in December, when you get to skate under the gargantuan Christmas tree. The golden statue of Prometheus reclines at rink-side, and tourists crowd around the railings above, staring down as you pirouette around (though the ice is sunken far enough below street level that you're hardly aware of your audience). It's expensive (particularly around the holidays), you have to pay again if you want to skate for more than 45 minutes, and the rink is so small you can't get up much speed; there's usually a crowd, which means a wait in line to get in as well as a bit of jostling once you're on the ice. But do it once for the glamour of it.

Lower Plaza, Rockefeller Plaza (off Fifth Ave. between 49th and 50th sts.). ℂ **212/332-7654**. Admission in shoulder season (Oct and early Jan through Apr) weekdays $9 adults, $7 children 11 and under; weekends and holidays $13 adults, $8 children 11 and under; skate rental $7. Admission in high season (Nov–New Year's) weekdays $13–$14 adults, $9–$10 children 11 and under; weekends and holidays $15–$17 adults, $12 children 11 and under; skate rental $8. Skating sessions daily Oct–Apr; call for exact schedule. Subway: B, D, F, V to 47th–50th sts./Rockefeller Center.

Sky Rink ⟨ℛ⟩   Open 7 days a week year-round, this facility offers not one but two permanent ice rinks—the benefit of permanent ice being that the skating surface has more give than ice rinks laid down on top of other surfaces. (This is how Sky Rink justifies its relatively high prices.) The East Rink is booked up pretty solid with figure-skating classes and hockey programs, but the West Rink is open for general skating sessions every afternoon, somewhere between noon and 6:30pm, and some evenings to 9pm (call for the current schedule). If you're a good enough skater to look around, you can gaze out the windows to a wide-open Hudson view. It's a special treat to skate here in summer, wearing a T-shirt and shorts.

Pier 61 at Chelsea Piers, 23rd St. at the Hudson River. ℂ 212/336-6100. www.chelseapiers.com. Admission $11 adults, $8.50 children 12 and under. Skate rental $6; helmet rental $3; coin-operated lockers 75¢ (bring 3 quarters). Call for schedule of public skating sessions. Subway: C, E, F, N, R, V, W, 1 to 23rd St. Bus: M23 across 23rd St.

Wollman Rink   Central Park's chief skating rink, at the southern end of the park nearest to Midtown, makes a super place to spin around the ice outdoors, with a rock-music soundtrack piped in and a skyscraper skyline rising right beyond the trees. After school and on weekends, the ice can be thronged, but since skaters aren't limited to set session times, you can still get your money's worth if you hang out at the rink for a while, maybe refortifying yourself with food and hot chocolate from the snack bar while the Zamboni re-slicks the ice surface.

In Central Park—enter at E. 62nd St. ℂ 212/439-6900. www.wollmanrink.com. Admission Mon–Thurs $9.50 adults, $4.75 seniors and children 12 and under; Fri–Sun $12 adults, $5 children 12 and under, $7.50 seniors. Skate rental $5. Oct–Mar Mon–Tues 10am–2:30pm, Wed–Thurs and Sun 10am–9pm, Fri–Sat 10am–11pm.

IN-LINE SKATING & ROLLER-SKATING

In **Central Park,** the top place for skating on weekends is the plaza by the Bandshell (just south of 72nd St., at the end of the Mall). The entire 6-mile loop of the circular drive is generally popular with skaters on weekends, though it includes some challenging hills that may be too much for young skaters; they should stick to the so-called Inner Loop, from 72nd Street down to 60th Street, which is mostly level. **New York Skate Out** (ℂ 212/486-1919 or 917/257-7648; www.nyskate.com) organizes skating lessons and tours for kids ($25 per session) weekend mornings and Tuesday through Thursday after school, meeting at the Fifth Avenue entrance at 72nd Street; it runs a free kids' skate Saturday from 3 to 4pm.

Other favorite skating pavements around the city are the promenade in Riverside Park, West 83rd to 96th streets; the Upper East Side's walkway on the bank of the East River from 60th Street on north; the riverside Promenade in Battery Park City; and the skate path of Hudson River Park from Chambers Street up to 59th Street.

Skate-rental outlets have proliferated in Manhattan, but not all rent skates in children's sizes. Try **Blades Board & Skate** at one of its Manhattan locations (see p. 244); the branch at 120 W. 72nd St., between Columbus Avenue and Broadway (ℂ 212/787-3911), is closest to Central Park. If you don't have your own wheels, you'll have to go to the following rinks, where skates are available for use at the rink only.

Riverbank State Park   Perched above the banks of the Hudson, this sizable roofed rink catches lots of cooling breezes in summer, though it's an uptown trek.

145th St. and Riverside Dr. ℂ 212/694-3642. Admission $1. Skate rental $4. May–Sept Mon–Thurs 3–6pm; Fri–Sun 2–5pm and 6–9pm. Subway: 1 to 145th St. Bus: M11.

Roller Rink   A pair of open-air roller-skating rinks is set out on the northernmost of Chelsea's recreational piers. Though roller-hockey leagues keep the rinks busy, at least one or the other is open for general skating Saturday 1 to 5pm. In-line-skating instruction is offered as well. Between the rinks, the Skate Pit has been set up for those who want to do stunt skating or skateboarding (see "Skateboarding," below).

Pier 62 at Chelsea Piers, 23rd St. and the West Side Hwy., at the Hudson River. (C) 212/336-6200. www.chelsea piers.com. Admission $8 adults, $7 children 12 and under. Skate rental (including protective gear) $19 adults, $14 children. Credit card deposit required. Subway: C, E, F, N, R, V, W, 1, 9 to 23rd St. Bus: M23 across 23rd St.

KAYAKING

During the summer months, the **Downtown Boathouse** ((C) 646/613-0740; check www.nycgovparks.org for updated schedules) organizes free kayaking Saturday and Sunday on the Hudson River at **Pier 40** (West St. near Houston St.) and at 72nd St. and the river. Life jackets, kayaks, and paddles are provided; you can take a kayak out onto the water for 20 minutes. Come wearing a bathing suit, or a T-shirt and shorts that you don't mind getting wet.

SKATEBOARDING

Primo sites in Manhattan for trick skateboarders include Midtown's **Penn Plaza** (next to Penn Station), the **Seagram Building** on Park Avenue and 52nd Street, and the **Grace Building** plaza at 43rd Street and Sixth Avenue; in and around **Union Square** (14th to 17th sts., Broadway to Park Ave. S.) and the island around the cube sculpture at **Astor Place** (E. 8th and Lafayette sts., in the East Village); and, downtown, spots near City Hall, including the **Police Plaza** and the **Brooklyn Banks,** those swerving concrete ramps around the entrance to the Brooklyn Bridge. But the party's always moving: visit www.5050skateboarding.com for more suggestions.

Ramps have been set up for aggressive skateboarding in **Riverside Park,** at about 108th Street, west of the promenade ((C) 212/408-0239; May–Oct; admission $3), at the **Hudson River Skate Park** (West St. just north of 30th St., free), and at **Chelsea Piers,** Pier 62, 23rd Street and the West Side Highway ((C) 212/336-6200; admission $14; open Mon–Thurs 4–7pm, Sat–Sun 11am–5pm.). The primo sources for boards, either sale or rental, is **Blades Board & Skate;** of its several locations all over town, the handiest for these skateboarding sites are at 120 W. 72nd St., between Broadway and Columbus Avenue ((C) 212/787-3911).

SWIMMING

This is one severe shortage in New York's recreation facilities: There are very few clean, well-run pools open to the public. If you're visiting, and a place to swim is important to you, zone in one of the hotels that has its own pool (see chapter 4). If you live here, and you're dying to take a swim, enroll your child in swim classes, or join a health club.

An option worth knowing about is the drop-in swim pass at the Upper East Side's **Asphalt Green,** York Avenue between 90th and 91st streets ((C) 212/369-8890, www.asphaltgreen.org). A family of four can buy a day pass for $44 ($5 each additional child); call for family swim hours. Asphalt Green has two marvelous, clean pools: one 25-yard long outdoor pool, and an Olympic-size 50m (164-ft.) indoor pool, with a raised lower section ideal for young swimmers. The city's only other Olympic-size pool is at **Riverbank State Park,** 145th Street and Riverside Drive ((C) 212/694-3665), which also offers a smaller outdoor pool in summer; use of the Riverbank pools is far cheaper than Asphalt Green, at $2 for adults and $1 for kids 15 and under, free for children under 5, and it's available daily from 9am to 6pm.

To be frank, I wouldn't advise taking your kids to swim in the city parks' pools, which often are overrun, less than sanitary, and vulnerable to delinquent behavior. For the record, there are city-run indoor pools at **Carmine Street,** Clarkson Street and

Seventh Avenue South (© 212/242-5228); and **West 59th Street,** 533 W. 59th St., between Tenth and Eleventh avenues (© 212/397-3159). The city's outdoor pools, open July and August only, include **John Jay Park,** East 77th Street and Cherokee Place, just east of York Avenue (© 212/794-6566), and Central Park's **Lasker Pool,** midpark at East 106th Street (© 212/534-7639).

TENNIS

Very few public tennis courts are available in Manhattan, where most serious tennis players belong to private clubs. **Riverside Park** offers two sets, one at 116th Street and Riverside Drive, the other a well-maintained set of 10 clay courts at 96th Street in the lower section of the park. Play is first-come, first-served, but there's not usually much of a wait. At the city's premier public facility, the **Central Park Tennis Center,** midpark at West 93rd Street, matters are somewhat more complicated. Players who have bought an annual tennis permit ($100 adults, $20 seniors, $10 juniors) can make advance reservations by phone for $7 by calling weekdays from 10am to 2pm or 4 to 7pm (© 212/316-0800 for information and reservations). Anyone else can get a single-play ticket for $7 at the Tennis Center on the day of play, entitling you to an hour of court time (2 hr. for doubles players). You can sign up for a specific court time—in person only—or put your name on the no-show list to take the next available court; players who don't show up 15 minutes before their booked court time get bumped, so plenty of folks from that stand-by list do get to play. When the hourly bell rings, there's a mass exodus from the courts—26 Har-Tru and 4 hard courts. If you don't have your own racquet, you can rent one at the pro shop ($5 for 1 hr.), and they do have kid-size racquets. The Tennis Center is open daily from 6:30am to 8pm, April to November. Staff pros also offer lessons; call for prices and availability.

It may be worth an excursion into Queens just to play on the site of the U.S. Open, the **U.S.T.A. National Tennis Center** in Flushing Meadows–Corona Park (take the no. 7 subway to the Shea Stadium stop). Call the center at © 718/760-6200 to reserve a court, no more than 2 days in advance. Per-hour fees for outdoor courts are $16 before 4pm and $24 after 4pm; for indoor courts, which are open year-round, per-hour rates are $32 before 4pm and $45 after 4pm. The center is open daily from 8am to midnight.

TRAPEZE

Yes, that's right—in New York City your child can take a trapeze lesson, in a special trapeze arena right beside the West Side Highway in Hudson River Park, run by **Trapeze School New York** (West Street between Vestry and Debrosses sts., © 917/797-1872; www.trapezeschool.com). Classes are offered even for total novices, so long as they are 6 years or older; don't worry, Mom, all sorts of reassuring nets and harnesses are provided. As you might expect, it'll cost you plenty—classes last 2 hours and cost $47–$75, depending on the skill level and time of day, and that's on top of an initial $22 registration fee. Still, it's an exhilarating experience, and those I know who've done it thought it was worth every penny. Take lots of videos.

4 Classes & Workshops

ART & SCIENCE WORKSHOPS

Dana Discovery Center   Summer weekends usually see free entertainment out on the plaza here, and arts-and-crafts workshops, science displays, puppet shows, and the like are regularly held inside this beautiful pondside facility, a short walk north of the Conservatory Garden.

In Central Park at the Harlem Meer, 110th St. at Lenox Ave. ℂ 212/860-1370. Tues–Sun 10am–5pm. Subway: 2, 3 to 110th St. Bus: M2, M3, M4 to 110th St./Fifth Ave.

Metropolitan Museum of Art Indisputably one of the world's great museums, the Met scores big points with families for its frequent programs—they require no reservations and are free with museum admission, which means you can drop in on the spur of the moment and have a transforming experience. Hello Met!, an introduction to the museum, is held daily at 2pm for kids 5 to 12 and their parents; kids zero into on a few specific artworks via sketching and conversation in daily workshops (called Start With Art for ages 3–7, Art Mornings for ages 5–12, Look Again on weekends), and there are occasional 6pm Art Evenings as well for ages 6 to 12 and their families. My children and I did workshops at least once a week one summer, and they never failed to be fascinating. Check in at the information desk in the entrance hall to find out what's happening when.

Uris Auditorium, Metropolitan Museum of Art, 1000 Fifth Ave. (at 82nd St.). ℂ 212/535-7710; for program schedules, call ℂ 212/570-3930. www.metmuseum.org. Suggested museum admission $20 adults, $10 students and seniors, free for children 12 and under. Tues–Thurs and Sun 9:30am–5:30pm; Fri–Sat 9:30am–9pm. Subway: 4, 5, 6 to 86th St.

92nd Street Y Affiliated with the YMHA (Young Men's Hebrew Association), this is one of the city's greatest cultural resources, with loads of evening programs in music and the arts, and a vast roster of sign-up classes for adults and children. Call to ask what is currently available on a drop-in basis.

1395 Lexington Ave. (at 92nd St.). ℂ 212/996-1100. www.92y.org. Subway: 4, 5, 6 to 86th St.

DROP-IN CRAFTS

Craft Studio Plasterwork painting is a big draw here—superheroes, harlequin masks, rainbows, cars, picture frames, puppies, kittens, dinosaurs, you name it, you can paint it (with a little help from the friendly staff). You pay according to the price of the piece you choose. Terra-cotta pots are available for painting (think Mother's Day presents), as are assorted other ceramic items. The space is roomy and well lit, with a rainforest decor, and the shop carries a good number of excellent crafts and toys.

1657 Third Ave. (btwn 92nd and 93rd sts.). ℂ 212/831-6626. Mon–Sat 10am–6pm; Sun 11am–6pm. Subway: 4, 5, 6 to 86th St.; 6 to 96th St.

Little Shop of Crafts Pick a piece of precast plaster from wall racks—there are over 1,000 pieces to choose from—and you can paint it whatever colors you choose, daub on designs in finger wax, sprinkle glitter all over, and just generally make it your own masterpiece. There's no charge except the price of the plaster pieces, which are $13 and up. The staff helps out as much as you need; teenagers labor intently for hours over incredibly detailed curlicues, while little kids are allowed to happily slap on paint as they please. They also carry a full line of functional pottery pieces to decorate; you can't take them home for about a week, but shipping is available for out-of-towners. Bead crafts and T-shirt painting are also on the menu, or you can stuff your own cuddly cloth animal to take home.

431 E. 73rd St. (btwn First and York aves.). ℂ 212/717-6636. www.littleshopny.com. Mon–Tues 11am–6:30pm; Wed–Fri 11am–10pm (after 6pm adults only); Sat–Sun 10am–6:30pm. Subway: 6 to 77th St.

New York Kids' Top Five Cheap Thrills

1. Ride in the front car of the subway train, standing at the front window to watch the train hurtle down the tunnel.
2. Stand on the street gratings above a subway line when the train comes thundering along underneath.
3. Run into the middle of a flock of pigeons, and make them all fly up at once.
4. In a skyscraper elevator, stand on tiptoe when the elevator starts to go up, and lower to a squat as you speed upward.
5. On the double-long accordion-style city buses, sit in the seats right in the hinge so you can swivel when the bus turns a corner.

Make   The ceramic items that customers paint here must be glazed and fired in a kiln, which means you pick them up a week after you've painted them—not as good on the instant-gratification score as the plaster-painting shops described above. On the other hand, you'll end up with a real piece of pottery, from a mug to a piggybank to a pitcher to a platter, a keepsake that's also functional. My kids are always delighted to see me using the mugs they made for me for Mother's Day.

(1) 1566 Second Ave. (btwn 81st and 82nd sts.). 🕻 212/570-6868. www.makemeaning.com. Subway: 4, 5, 6 to 86th St. (2) 506 Amsterdam Ave. (btwn 84th and 85th sts.). 🕻 212/579-5575. Subway: 1 to 86th St. (3) 59 Greenwich Ave. (at Seventh Ave.). 🕻 212/647-7899. Subway: 1, 2, 3 to 14th St.; L to Union Sq. Open daily 10am–7pm (until 10pm Thurs–Fri); after 5pm, adults only. Cost is base charge for item ($5–$60), plus $6 per half hour work time.

MUSEUM WEEKEND WORKSHOPS

On weekends, a number of major Manhattan museums seek to attract families by offering children's workshops, usually free with museum admission. Times vary, so be sure to call ahead.

The **Children's Museum of Manhattan,** 212 W. 83rd St., between Amsterdam Avenue and Broadway (🕻 212/721-1223; www.cmom.org; admission $8, free for children under 1), always has a lineup of fun workshops, often themed to holidays. The **Children's Museum of the Arts,** 182 Lafayette St., between Broome and Grand streets (🕻 212/274-0986; www.cmany.org, admission $8, free for children under 1), sets up hands-on art projects every day, providing materials for kids to create anything from papier-mâché masks to found-art collages to giant mobiles; weekend projects are even more ambitious. Midtown's **Museum of Television and Radio,** 25 W. 52nd St, between Fifth and Sixth avenues. (🕻 212/621-6600; www.mtr.org; admission $10 adults, $8 students, $5 kids 13 and under), has fun Saturday workshops, including a series in which kids can re-create old radio scripts. The magnificent **Cathedral of St. John the Divine,** 1047 Amsterdam Ave., at 114th Street (🕻 212/662-2133; www.stjohndivine.org), offers family medieval art workshops Saturday mornings at 10am for a $5 fee (cathedral admission is free). Up in Riverdale, **Wave Hill,** 675 W. 252nd St., the Bronx (🕻 718/549-3200; www.wavehill.org; admission $4 adults, $2 students, free for kids under 6), organizes superb hands-on children's workshops combining arts and crafts with nature study, helping children appreciate the estate's magnificent gardens and Hudson River landscape.

Sunday is workshop day at these two excellent Judaic museums, which are closed for the Sabbath on Friday and Saturday: The **Jewish Museum,** 1109 Fifth Ave., at 92nd Street (© **212/423-3200;** www.thejewishmuseum.org; admission $10 adults, $5 students, free for kids under 12); and down in Battery Park City, the **Museum of Jewish Heritage—A Living Memorial to the Holocaust,** 18 First Place, at Battery Place (© **646/437-4200;** www.mjhnyc.org; admission $10 adults, $7.50 students, free for kids under 5).

At least once a month, the **Asia Society,** 725 Park Ave., at 70th Street (© **212/288-6400;** www.asiasociety.org, admission $10 adults, $5 students, free for kids under 16), comes up with really super workshops exploring various facets of different Asian cultures—Chinese storytellers, Indonesian puppets. And less frequently, the **China Institute,** 125 E. 65th St., between Park and Lexington avenues (© **212/744-8181;** www.chinainstitute.org; admission $3 for adults, $3 for children), offers similar workshops usually around the Chinese New Year or connected with current rotating shows in its galleries.

If art is your child's special interest, don't miss the workshops offered by the **Museum of Modern Art,** 11 W. 53rd St., between Fifth and Sixth avenues (© **212/708-9400;** www.moma.org; admission $20 adults, $16 seniors, $12 students, free for children 15 and under), which organizes Saturday tours for 4-year-olds, gallery talks for children ages 5 to 10, hands-on classes for the entire family, and family-oriented programs of classic short films. The **Whitney Museum of American Art,** 945 Madison Ave., at 75th Street (© **212/570-3600;** www.whitney.org; admission $15 adults, $10 students, free for kids under 12); the **American Folk Art Museum,** 45 W. 53rd St., between Fifth and Sixth avenues (© **212/265-1040;** www.folkartmuseum.org; admission $9 adults, $7 students, free for kids under 12; $1 materials fee for workshops); and the **Studio Museum in Harlem,** 144 W. 125th St., between Lenox Avenue and Adam Clayton Powell Boulevard (© **212/864-4500;** www.studiomuseum inharlem.org; admission free for workshop participants), present frequent art workshops highlighting aspects of their collections or current exhibitions.

9

Shopping with Your Kids

New York City kids are trained to be conspicuous consumers, with a wide range of options for spending money—deluxe children's clothing boutiques, toy stores crammed with imported marvels, wondrous hobby shops, and comic-book and trading-card dealers stocked with rarities. Some of these can be downright overwhelming, not to mention astronomically priced (come on, what kid really needs that $450 party frock from Bonpoint, that $500 set of antique toy soldiers from Classic Toys, or that $800 dollhouse from Tiny Doll House?). And while adults can safely indulge in mere window-shopping, it's a rare kid who's content to look without trying to coerce you to buy.

One happy thing about Manhattan toy stores is that most of them have a wall of under-$5 toys to pacify your child if you decide against that $150 Playmobil castle. Otherwise, it's best to know what you're shopping for and head straight for the store most likely to have it.

1 The Shopping Scene

SHOPPING HOURS & SALES TAX

Neighborhood stores are generally open daily 10am to 6pm, though some of the upscale East Side boutiques are closed on Sunday. Stores that are open on Sunday may not open until noon, however. Some small Midtown boutiques are closed on weekends, but not the tourist-dependent Fifth Avenue showcases. Street fairs and flea markets are generally weekends-only operations.

New York City has an **8.25% sales tax,** although on clothing and shoe purchases, you don't have to pay sales tax until you spend over $110. Takeout food, groceries, and services are exempt from sales tax.

SHOPPING DISTRICTS

THE UPPER WEST SIDE   Lots of families live in this neighborhood, and its toy and clothing shops tend to be down-to-earth. You'll probably be here at some point anyway, visiting the American Museum of Natural History or the Children's Museum of Manhattan, so check out the outstanding toy stores between 79th and 86th streets, **Penny Whistle Toys** and **West Side Kids,** or the cute, trendy girls' clothing at **Berkeley Girl.** The **Time Warner Center** at Columbus Circle features mostly upscale adult boutiques, but it might be a fun stop just for the chic ambience (and for the air-conditioned cool in the summer).

THE UPPER EAST SIDE   This is the best area of town, hands-down, for pricey, gorgeous kids' clothes and precious toy boutiques. If you're shopping without kids in tow, a serious Madison Avenue expedition could take all day—all the designer kids' boutiques are here, between 62nd and 96th streets (**Jacadi** and **Bonpoint** even have two Madison Ave. locations). Shops along Lexington and Third avenues are a little more reasonable, and there are some darling finds there, especially in the toy realm: **Mary Arnold Toys**, the **New York Doll Hospital**, **A Bear's Place**, and **Big City Kites** (and **Hombons** is definitely worth the extra walk over to First Ave.). On East 86th Street, **Barnes & Noble** has one of the city's biggest and best children's book departments. Older boys can augment their card collections at **Alex's MVP Cards** or get into model-making and RPG games at **Games Workshop**.

MIDTOWN   Primarily a business area, Midtown doesn't have many children's stores, but what it does have is choice (and designed as much for tourist gawping as for actual shopping). **American Girl Place** is without question an essential stop for girls between the ages of 6 and 12, with the flagship store of **Build-A-Bear Workshop** just down Fifth Avenue a huge draw for younger boys and girls as well. The truly impressive **Toys "R" Us** flagship store in the Times Square area is worlds away from the chain's usual strip-mall outlets. The cleverly designed **Niketown** and **NBA Store** are magnets for sports-loving older kids. A number of big department stores reign over Midtown, including **Saks Fifth Avenue** and **Macy's,** as well as several chain stores in **Manhattan Mall,** Sixth Avenue at 32nd Street (② **212/465-0500**), a surprisingly bright and busy vertical mall with glass elevators shooting up and down the central atrium—a very un-Manhattan refuge.

CHELSEA   There's one reason for shopping in Chelsea if you have kids: **Books of Wonder,** the dean of children's bookstores in Manhattan.

GREENWICH VILLAGE   Between **Forbidden Planet** and **Village Comics,** Greenwich Village is the place to interest older kids who are into comics, trading cards, vintage records, and sci-fi/fantasy stuff. It's also chess central on Thompson Street just south of Washington Square, where the **Chess Shop** and the **Chess Forum** sell some beautiful chess sets and let kids play for hours. Funky-but-chic clothes rule down here, in stores like **Ibiza Kidz, Bombalulu's,** and **Peanut Butter & Jane,** and then there's the costume-jewelry clutter at **GirlProps.** Older kids whose idea of fashion lies more at the grunge end of the spectrum may want to troll Broadway below Astor Place, where warehouse-like stores sell vintage clothes, army surplus, and Doc Martens.

THE EAST VILLAGE   The shops here are just plain way out, especially when it comes to toys and accessories. Work your way across East 9th Street, and you'll see what I mean—starting with the relatively staid **Dinosaur Hill** and funky-but-chic clothing boutiques **Lilliput** and **Tigers, Tutus, and Toes,** then getting stranger as you go Avenue A to **Alphabets.**

SOHO & TRIBECA   Parents down here tend to be loft-living urban pioneers with a highly developed visual sense, and the kids' stores reflect this with a very cool, sophisticated, miniature-adult sensibility (**Just for Tykes, Julian and Sara, Babylicious,** and **Les Petits Chapelais**). One cool TriBeCa option is the haircut salon/toyshop **Whipper Snippers.** The line between kids and club kids gets blurry down here, with aggressively ironic boutiques like **KidRobot.**

WALL STREET   This area is hardly a target zone for shopping with kids. **South Street Seaport** features a characterless mix of midrange chain stores and odd theme boutiques; a number of discount children's clothing stores like **Conway's** are scattered around the Fulton Street and Broadway area. The **World Financial Center** has few shops kids will be interested in, but the Winter Garden Atrium is a stunning space with a long cascade of marble steps that toddlers seem to find irresistible.

STREET MARKETS

The long-running Sunday flea market on the Upper West Side at **P.S. 44,** Columbus Avenue at 76th Street, has loads of junk to sort through in the schoolyard, with loads of friendly West Siders jostling one another. On Saturday and Sunday the **Annex Flea Market,** Sixth Avenue at 26th Street ($1 parking/admission), has some finds if you're into nostalgia and kitsch.

The **Union Square Greenmarket,** 16th Street between Broadway and Park Avenue South, runs Monday, Wednesday, Friday, and Saturday and has some truly glorious produce from rural New York State, New Jersey, and Pennsylvania. There's a bustling playground directly south of the greenmarket, so pick up lunch (crisp Macoun apples, fresh cheddar cheese, hearty seven-grain bread), and eat on a bench while the kids clamber away.

From May to October various stretches of Manhattan streets are closed to traffic for **street fairs,** featuring booths selling everything from T-shirts to audiotapes to potted palms and hand-knit Peruvian sweaters. The food booths are even more fun—sizzling-hot stir-fries, heaping tacos, or foot-long hot dogs. Sometimes, there'll be a petting zoo or one of those inflated bouncing castles. You tend to see the same vendors weekend after weekend, and little that's for sale is really special. But the main things are the crowd, the sunshine, and the car-free strolling. Look for posters in neighborhood store windows.

2 Shopping A to Z

My listings are mainly for kid-specific stores and merchandise. If you want to check out what New York offers adult shoppers, see *Frommer's New York City.*

BOOKS

Note that many of these bookstores offer story hours and appearances by children's book authors—for details see "Story Hours" in Chapter 10.

Bank Street College Book Store   This narrow, bright uptown store has a wonderful selection of over 40,000 titles and an extremely knowledgeable staff. It's connected to an outstanding education college, so there's also a great section for parents and teachers. 610 W. 112th St. (at Broadway). ② **212/678-1654.** www.bankstreetbooks.com. Subway: 1 to 110th St.

Barnes & Noble   Far from being bland mall outlets, the Manhattan branches of this megastore have great children's sections (especially the 86th St. and 21st Street locations), with informed salespeople, frequent story hours, and plenty of room for kids to frolic, where the salespeople never complain if your toddler pulls every board book off the shelf and leaves it on the floor. The store's cafes are a good option for a midday snack, too, and there are big clean restrooms available. (1) 240 E. 86th St. (btwn Second and Third aves.). ② **212/794-1962.** Subway: 4, 5, 6 to 86th St. (2) 2289 Broadway (at 82nd St.). ② **212/362-8835.** Subway: 1 to 79th St. (3) 1972 Broadway (at 66th St.). ② **212/595-6859.** Subway: 1 to 66th St./Lincoln Center. (4) Citicorp Building (at Third Ave. and 54th St.). ② **212/750-8033.** Subway: E, V to Lexington Ave./53rd St. (5) Rockefeller Center, 600 Fifth Ave. (at 48th St.). ② **212/765-0590.** Subway: B, D, F, V to 47th–57th sts./Rockefeller Center. (6) 675 Sixth Ave. (at 21st St.). ② **212/727-1227.** Subway: F, V to 23rd St. (7) Union Sq., 33 E. 17th St. (btwn Broadway and Park Ave.). ② **212/253-0810.**

Subway: N, Q, R, W, 4, 5, 6 to 14th St.; L to Union Sq. (8) 396 Sixth Ave (at 8th St.). ℭ 212/674-8780. Subway: A, B, C, D, E, F, V to W. 4th St. (9) 4 Astor Place (btwn Broadway and Lafayette St.). ℭ 212/420-1322. Subway: 6 to Astor Place.

Bookberries   A cozy little carpeted nook has been partitioned off for kids in this small East Side store. The selection is fairly good, though the picture books may be haphazardly alphabetized—probably because so many little hands have pulled them out—a good sign. 983 Lexington Ave. (at 71st St.). ℭ 212/794-9400. Subway: 6 to 68th St.

Books of Wonder   One of the few specialty children's bookstores left in town, this great Chelsea shop has a lot of hard-to-find titles, as well as collectors' items (the Oz books, original Nancy Drews, illustrators' original art). The staff is friendly, helpful, and knowledgeable. 18 W. 18th St. (btwn Fifth and Sixth aves.). ℭ 212/989-3270. www.booksofwonder.net. Subway: 1 to 18th St.

Borders   This chain megastore has a large and welcoming children's section, with plenty for older kids as well as picture books for the younger set. The atmosphere is very conducive to browsing. www.borders.com. (1) 10 Columbus Circle (at Eighth Ave.). ℭ 212/823-9775. Subway A, B, C, D, 1 to 59th St./Columbus Circle. (2) 461 Park Ave. (at 57th St.). ℭ 212/980-6785. Subway: 4, 5, 6 to 59th St. (3) 550 Second Ave. (at 31st St.) in Kips Bay Plaza. ℭ 212/685-3938. Subway: 6 to 33rd St. (4) 2 Penn Plaza (7th Ave. and 31st St.). ℭ 212/244-1814. Subway: 1, 2, 3 to 34th St. (5) 100 Broadway (at Pine St). ℭ 212/964-1988. Subway: 2, 3, 4, 5 to Wall St.

Coliseum Books   This rambling Midtown bookstore has a huge stock, with a surprisingly large amount of titles for kids. 11 W. 42nd St. (btwn Fifth and Sixth aves.). ℭ 212/803-5890. Subway: B, D, F, V to 42nd St./Fifth Ave.

Ivy's Books *(Finds)*   Used and new children's books, smartly selected, can be found in a small section at the back of this bright and charming book-lover's shop (next-door Murder Ink can steer you to the best in mystery novels written for kids). 2486 Broadway (btwn 92nd and 93rd sts.). ℭ 212/362-8905. Subway: 1, 2, 3 to 96th St.

Logos Bookstore *(Finds)*   Near Carl Schurz Park, this pleasant shop has a good children's corner at the back, near the small but leafy outdoor garden, a delightful place for reading in fair weather. While the store's specialty is religious books, this isn't heavily emphasized in the kids' selection, which does include some interesting titles from smaller publishers. 1575 York Ave. (btwn 83rd and 84th sts.). ℭ 212/517-7292. Subway: 4, 5, 6 to 86th St.

Scholastic Store   Big, bright, and glossy, this outlet of the big children's publisher has an obvious motive for selling Scholastic books, activities, and tie-in toys, but considering how many titles your kids love are published by Scholastic—from Clifford the Big Red Dog to Harry Potter—it's a worthwhile SoHo stop. 557 Broadway (btwn Prince and Spring) ℭ 212/343-6166. www.scholasticstore.com. Subway: N, R, W to Prince St.

Seventh Ave Books   In the spirit of Park Slope, this book-lovers' co-op has a wealth of new and used titles for youngsters. 202 7th Ave., Brooklyn. ℭ 718/840-0020. Subway: F to 7th Ave.

Shakespeare & Co.   The East Side branch of this local chain offers a decent children's section, with pint-size chairs and a carpet for in-store reading. The selection is intelligent, if skewed toward "worthy" picture books and classics. 939 Lexington Ave. (btwn 68th and 69th sts.). ℭ 212/570-0201. www.shakeandco.com. Subway: 6 to 68th St.

Westsider Books   This excellent little used-book store—narrow and dusky, with books to the ceiling—has a small children's section with some real finds. 2246 Broadway (btwn 80th and 81st sts.). ℭ 212/362-0706. Subway: 1 to 79th St.

CANDY, CHOCOLATE & SWEETS

Chocolate Bar   Cashing in on the designer chocolate vogue, this boutique in the chic Meatpacking District will intrigue older kids who've outgrown stuffing their faces with Hershey's Kisses. You can sit down and sip a cocoa or latte while you're browsing. 48 Eighth Ave. (btwn Jane and Horatio sts.). © 212/366-1541. www.chocolatebarnyc.com. Subway: A, C, E to 14th St.

Dylan's Candy Bar   The creation of Ralph Lauren's daughter, Dylan's is a sweet-shoppe-themed bi-level boutique full of specialty candy, from imported sweets to store-brand designer chocolates. There's some hard-to-find stuff here, though prices can be, as I overheard one dad growl, "obscene." A nice special-occasion treat; its glossy shopping bags are a status symbol among the younger set. 1011 Third Ave. (at 60th St.). © 646/735-0078. Subway: 4, 5, 6 to 59th St.

Hershey's Time Square Store   Gigantic Hershey bars, buckets of Kisses, and other lavish souvenir packages of Hershey brand confectionery are piled ceiling-high in this bright and busy Times Square boutique, along with T-shirts, stuffed animals, and all manner of candy tie-ins. 1593 Broadway (at 48th St.). © 212/581-9100. www.hershey gifts.com. Subway: 1 to 50th St.; N, R, W to 49th St.

Li-Lac Chocolates   A Greenwich village institution founded in 1923, this charming shop sells handmade chocolates molded into a delightful variety of shapes. (1) 40 Eighth Ave. (at Jane St.). © 212/924-2280. www.lilacchocolates.com. Subway: A, C, E to 14th St. (2) Park Ave. and 42nd St., The Food Market at Grand Central Terminal. © 212/370-4866. Subway: S, 4, 5, 6, 7 to 42nd St./Grand Central.

Mondel Chocolates *Finds*   This old-fashioned little shop in the Columbia University area has beautiful handmade chocolates and other gift items for the sweet tooth in your family. Closed Sunday July through August. 2913 Broadway (near 114th St.). © 212/864-2111. www.mondelchocolates.com. Subway: 1 to 116th St.

CLOTHING

BABY & PRESCHOOLER CLOTHES

babyGap   Although there are babyGap departments inside several of the GapKids stores (see "Everyday Clothing," below), these branches have extra space devoted to baby sizes up to 4XL. Sturdy, simple knits with a casual sense of style, like all Gap clothes. (1) 1535 Third Ave (at 87th St.). © 212/423-0033. Subway: 4, 5, 6 to 86th St. (2) 734 Lexington Ave. (at 59th St.). © 212/751-1543. Subway: 4,5,6 to 59th St. (3) 680 Fifth Ave. (at 54th St.). © 212/977-7023. Subway: E, V to 5th Ave. (4) 1466 Broadway (at 42nd St.). © 212/382-4500. Subway: N, Q, R, S, W, 1, 2, 3, 7, 9 to 42nd St./Times Sq. (5) 60 W. 34th St. (at Broadway). © 212/760-1268. Subway: B, D, F, N, Q, R, V, W to 34th St. (6) 122 Fifth Ave. (at 17th St.). © 917/408-5580. Subway: N, Q, R, W, 4, 5, 6 to 14th St.; L to Union Sq. (7) 11 Fulton St. (at Front St.). © 212/374-1051. Subway: J, M, Z, 2, 3, 4, 5, 6 to Fulton St.

Babylicious   Although this Tribeca boutique also stocks fun toys, accessories, and gifts, it's the groovy playclothes, in sizes up to 4T, that really stand out—downtown styles that'll make your pre-schooler look like the budding rock star or supermodel that he/she probably is. Closed Sunday. 51 Hudson St. (btwn Duane and Jay sts.) © 212/406-7440. www.babyliciousnyc.com. Subway: 1, 2, 3 to Chambers St.

Bombalulu's *Finds*   Funky, casual, colorful clothing in sizes up to age 12—wearable but with a sense of fun. Lots of toys, too. 101 W. 10th St. (btwn Sixth and Greenwich aves.). © 212/463-0897. www.bombalulus.com. Subway: A, B, C, D, E, F, V to W. 4th St.

Manhattan Clothes Shopping

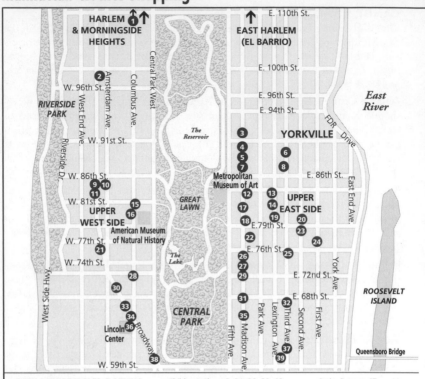

BABY & PRESCHOOLER CLOTHING
BabyGap **8, 41, 42, 49, 60, 74**
Babylicious **71**
Bombalulu's **63**
Bonne Nuit **36**
Calypso Enfants **70**
Catamimi **12**
Didi's Children's Boutique **5**
Farmer's Daughter and Son **44**
Flora and Henri **27**
Greenstones & Cie **7, 15**
Jacadi **35, 38**
Julian & Sara **66**
Just for Tykes **66**
Karin Alexis **2**
Koh's Kids **72**
La Layette **39**
Les Petits Chapelais **65**
Lester's **20**
Magic Windows **7**
Plain Jane **10**
Prince and Princess **22**
Z'Baby Company **28**

EVERYDAY CLOTHING
Baby Depot at Burlington
   Coat Factory **57**

Children's Place **8, 21, 30, 32, 48,**
   55, 56, 61, 68
Conway's **51, 52, 53, 55, 56, 73, 75**
Daffy's **41, 46, 55, 60**
Gap Kids **8, 12, 34, 39, 40, 43, 45,**
   47, 49, 55, 60, 74
Gymboree Store **11, 17, 25, 33, 37**
H&M **54, 55**
New York City Kids **50**
Old Navy **1, 54, 59, 69**

FASHIONS--GIRLS
All Dressed Up **14**
Bambini **17**
Berkeley Girl **16**
Bonpoint **4, 31**
Ibiza Kidz **64**
Infinity **12**
Jacadi **3, 35, 38**
Julian & Sara **66**
Koh's Kids **72**
Lester's **20**
Lilliput **67**
Marsha D.D. **6**
M.W. Teen **7**
Morris Brothers **9**
Peanut Butter & Jane **62**

Petite Bateau **17**
Small Change **19**
Space Kiddets **58**
Spring Flowers Children's
   Boutique **29, 37, 43**
Talbots Kids **23, 43**
Tutti Bambini **24**
Zitomer Department Store **26**

FASHIONS--BOYS
Greenstones & Cie **7, 15**
Lester's **20**
Morris Brothers **9**
Peter Elliot Jr. **18**
Small Change **14**
Talbots Kids **23, 43**

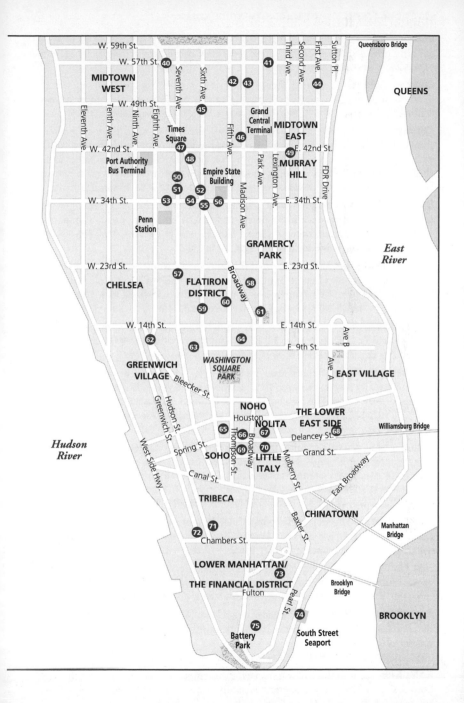

Bonne Nuit This lingerie shop also carries some beautiful layette items and simply cut girls' dresses in lovely fabrics, up to age 10. 30 Lincoln Plaza (at 63rd St.). ℂ **212/489-9730.** Subway: 1 to 66th St./Lincoln Center.

Calypso Enfants Imported French designer ensembles for newborns to size 10 draw fashion-conscious downtown parents to this SoHo shop. 426 Broome St. (btwn Crosby and Lafayette sts.). ℂ **212/966-3234.** Subway: B, D, F, V to Broadway/Lafayette St.

Catamimi These French kids' clothes (mostly size 8 and under) show an ineffable sense of style, with sassy prints and deep-colored solids cut into simple, roomy clothes with real flair. The store has a bold, clean look and friendly staff. The clothes aren't cheap, but they're casual and sturdy enough that you'll get wear out of them. Closed Sunday July–August. 1125 Madison Ave. (at 84th St.). ℂ **212/987-0688.** Subway: 6 to 96th St.

Didi's Children's Boutique Toys and simple, handmade children's clothing with a minimalist sense of style are like a breath of fresh air on upper Madison. Imported stuff doesn't come cheap, though. Closed Sunday. 1196 Madison Ave. (btwn 88th and 89th sts.). ℂ **212/860-4001.** www.didis.com. Subway: 4, 5, 6 to 86th St.

Farmer's Daughter and Son Amid the fluid, casual women's clothes at this Midtown shop, you'll find a limited but tasteful selection of little-children's clothes, plus a few wholesome toys. Well worth a stop if you're nearby. Closed Sunday. 1001 First Ave. (at 55th St.). ℂ **212/421-0484.** Subway: E, V to Lexington Ave./53rd St.

Flora and Henri This shop showcases a delightful designer line of drapey, vintage-inspired knits in sizes newborn to 12. Closed Sunday July–August. 943 Madison Ave. (btwn 74th and 75th sts.). ℂ **212/249-1694.** www.florahenri.com. Subway: 6 to 77th St.

Greenstones & Cie Upper-scale imported kids' clothes, in cuts and fabrics that kids can actually play in. Sizes run from newborn to 12 years (the East Side shop carries up to size 8 only). The East Side location is closed Sunday. (1) 442 Columbus Ave. (at 81st St.). ℂ **212/580-4322.** Subway: B, C to 79th St. (2) 1184 Madison Ave. (btwn 86th and 87th sts.). ℂ **212/427-1665.** Subway: 4, 5, 6 to 86th St.

Jacadi Imported from France, this quality line of baby clothes (and stuff for older kids) features stylish simplicity in rich colors and pastels, with cottons and knits that last. (1) 1281 Madison Ave. (btwn 91st and 92nd sts.). ℂ **212/369-1616.** www.jacadiusa.com. Subway: 4, 5, 6 to 86th St. (2) 787 Madison Ave. (btwn 66th and 67th sts.). ℂ **212/535-3200.** Subway: 6 to 68th St. (3) 1841 Broadway (at 60th St.). Subway: 1 to 59th St./Columbus Circle.

Julian & Sara This tiny SoHo shop sells lovely, upscale things in sizes for newborns to 16 years, for girls and boys. 103 Mercer St. (btwn Prince and Spring sts.). ℂ **212/226-1989.** www.julianandsara.com. Subway: N, R, W to Prince St.

Just For Tykes In a glossy loftlike gallery, this SoHo shop has a well-chosen line of nursery furnishings, baby toys, and clothing up to size 4. 83 Mercer St. (btwn Broome and Spring sts.). ℂ **212/274-9121.** www.justfortykes.com. Subway: N, R, W to Prince St.

Karin Alexis Every item in this charming Upper West side boutique is designed by the shop's owner and made right in New York. Sturdily constructed and cut roomy for toddler play, they have a funky charm that makes mothers happy. 2587 Broadway (btwn 97thd and 98th sts.). ℂ **212/769-9550.** www.karinalexis.com. Subway: 1, 2, 3 to 96th St.

Koh's Kids This is the TriBeCa source for contemporary, casual clothes for the newborn to size 8 set, including American labels like Cozy Toes. 311 Greenwich St. (btwn Chambers and Reade sts.). ℂ **212/791-6915.** Subway: 1, 2, 3 to Chambers St.

La Layette   Lace, smocking, and embroidery turn these infant clothes (to size 2) into frilly fashion statements; if you don't mind seeing a newborn spit up Similac over that $150 moiré silk dress, indulge yourself. Other new-baby gifts are engraved silver picture frames, hand-painted nursery furniture, personalized pillows, and lovely ruffley crib bedding. Closed Sunday and Saturday July-August. 170 E. 61st St. (btwn Lexington and Third aves.). ✆ 212/688-7072. www.lalayette.com. Subway: 4, 5, 6 to 59th St.

Les Petits Chapelais   The French-made designer fashions in this darling SoHo boutique are refreshingly child-appropriate, sturdy looking, and colorful. Sizes 0 to 8. 142 Sullivan St. (btwn Spring and Prince sts.). ✆ 212/625-1023. www.lespetitschapelais.com. Subway: C, E to Spring St.

Lester's   The layette department at this roomy East Side clothing shop features imported and designer styles at fairly reasonable prices. 1534 Second Ave. (at 80th St.). ✆ 212/734-9292. www.lestersnyc.com. Subway: 6 to 77th St.

Magic Windows   Here you'll find East Side–conservative, traditional baby clothes (sizes up to 6X), all in pastel blues and pinks, as well as a collection of preteen clothing. The tiny white cotton sweaters are adorable. 1186 Madison Ave. (at 87th St.). ✆ 212/289-0028. Subway: 4, 5, 6 to 86th St.

Plain Jane   There are only a few baby clothes here, and they're all darling, particularly items like a nutty one-piece knit that'll make your infant look like a Campbell's Soup can. Somebody here is having fun. Closed Sunday. 525 Amsterdam Ave. (btwn 85th and 86th sts.). ✆ 212/679-5424. www.plainjanekids.com. Subway: 1 to 86th St.

Prince and Princess   The name tells you all you need to know about the fabulous imported clothes for boys and girls at this haughty, tiny shop. You don't have to have aristocratic connections to shop here, but chances are you do. Closed Sunday. 41 E. 78th (btwn Park and Madison aves.). ✆ 212/879-8989. www.princeandprincess.com. Subway: 6 to 77th St.

Z'Baby Company   Handily located on both the West and East sides, Z'Baby has a park-straddling hipness in its casual clothes (boys' sizes newborn to 10, girls up to 14) with upscale labels like Petit Bateau, Alphabet, and Lilly Pulitzer. My toddler son fell in love with a $200 black leather baby biker jacket here; alas, I told him he'll have to wait until he's old enough to drive his own Harley. (1) 100 W. 72nd St. (at Columbus Ave.). ✆ 212/579-BABY. Subway: B, C, 1, 2, 3 to 72nd St. (2) 996 Lexington Ave. (at 72nd St.). ✆ 212/472-2229. Subway: 6 to 68th St.

EVERYDAY CLOTHING

Baby Depot at Burlington Coat Factory   Clothing up to size 16, boys' and girls', can be found on the third floor of this big discount store in the megastore shopping district wedged between Chelsea and the Flatiron District. The brands are quite respectable—Carter's, Buster Brown, Guess—but not very appealingly displayed, jammed onto racks under fluorescent lighting. 707 Seventh Ave. (btwn 22nd and 23rd sts.). ✆ 212/229-1300. www.coat.com. Subway: F, V to 23rd St.

Children's Place   This chain store sells its own label of bright, simply cut casual wear in sizes newborn to 12 (up to size 8 in some stores). It's like a slightly cheaper version of the Gap, in all respects, but to fill out a wardrobe, a $10 polo shirt or plain $14 sundress isn't a bad idea. www.childrensplace.com. (1) In the Manhattan Mall, 901 Sixth Ave. (at 33rd St.), 2nd level. ✆ 212/268-7696. Subway: B, D, F, N, Q, R, V, W to 34th St./Herald Sq. (2) 173 E. 86th St. (btwn Third and Lexington aves.). ✆ 212/831-5100. Subway: 4, 5, 6 to 86th St. (3) 2187 Broadway at 77th St. ℭ **917/441-9807.** Subway: 1 to 79th St. (4) 1164 Third Ave. (at 68th St.). ℭ **212/717-7187.** Subway: 6 to 68th St.(5) 1450 Broadway (at 41st St.), ℭ **212/398-4416.** Subway: N, Q, R, S, W, 1, 2, 3, 7 to Times Sq. (6) 22 W. 34th St. (btwn Fifth and Sixth aves.). ℭ **212/904-1190.** Subway: B, D, F, N, Q, R, V, W to 34th St./Herald Sq. (7) 36 E.16th St. (at Union Sq.). ℭ **212/529-2201.** Subway: N, Q, R, W, 4, 5, 6 to 14th St.; L to Union Sq. (8) 142 Delancey St. (at Essex St.). ℭ **212/979-5071.** Subway: F, J to Essex/Delancey St.

Conway's   Budget-conscious parents can be spotted all over town carrying Conway's pink plastic bags, bulging with basic clothing bought at low prices. Conway's has heavily colonized the 34th Street shopping district, and it has locations downtown among the discount stores as well. (1) 11 W. 34th St. (btwn Fifth and Sixth aves.). ℭ **212/967-1370.** Subway: B, D, F, N, Q, R, V, W to 34th St./Herald Sq. (2) 49 W. 34th St. (btwn Fifth and Sixth aves.). ℭ **212/967-6454.** Subway: B, D, F, N, Q, R, V, W to 34th St./Herald Sq. (3) 1333 Broadway (at 35th St.). ℭ **212/967-3460.** Subway: B, D, F, N, Q, R, V, W to 34th St. (4) 450 Seventh Ave. (btwn 34th and 35th sts.). ℭ **212/967-1371.** Subway: 1, 2, 3 to 34th St. (5) 225 W. 34th St. (btwn Seventh and Eighth aves.). ℭ **212/967-7390.** Subway: 1, 2, 3 to 34th St. (6) 45 Broad St. (btwn Broadway and Beaver sts.). ℭ **212/943-8900.** Subway: 4, 5 to Bowling Green. (7) 151 William St. (btwn Fulton and Nassau sts.). ℭ **212/374-1072.** Subway: A, C to Broadway/Nassau St.

Daffy's   The price is definitely right at this smart discount clothing chain that has a sizable children's department, thanks to popular demand. For straightforward play and school clothes, most items are under $20, and I'm talking perfectly acceptable quality and styles. www.daffys.com. (1) 111 Fifth Ave. (at 18th St.). ℭ **212/529-4477.** Subway: N, Q, R, W, 4, 5, 6 to 14th St.; L to Union Sq. (2) 335 Madison Ave. (at 44th St.). ℭ **212/557-4422.** Subway: B, D, F, V to 42nd St./Fifth Ave. (3) 1311 Broadway (at 34th St.). ℭ **212/736-4477.** Subway: B, D, F, N, Q, R, V, W to 34th St./Herald Sq. (4) 125 E. 57th St. (btwn Park and Lexington aves.). ℭ **212/376-4477.** Subway: 4, 5, 6 to 59th St.

Gap Kids   You know the look—jeans, khakis, sweatshirts, T-shirts, denim jackets. You've gotta hand it to them: Gap Kids provides a mix-and-match backbone for kids' wardrobes, giving the casual look a spin of adultlike cool. Wait for sales, and you can clean up. (1) 1535 Third Ave (at 87th St.). ℭ **212/423-0033.** Subway: 4, 5, 6 to 86th St. (2) 2300 Broadway (at 83rd St.). ℭ **212/873-2044.** Subway: 1 to 86th St. 1988 Broadway (at 67th St.). ℭ **212/721-5304.** Subway: 1 to 66th St./Lincoln Center. (3) 734 Lexington Ave. (at 59th St.). ℭ **212/751-1543.** Subway: 4,5,6 to 59th St. (4) 250 W. 57th St. (at Broadway). ℭ **212/315-2250.** www.gap.com. Subway: A, B, C, D, 1 to 59th St./Columbus Circle. (5) 545 Madison Ave. (at 55th St.). ℭ **212/980-2570.** Subway: 4, 5, 6 to 59th St. (6) 680 Fifth Ave. (at 54th St.). ℭ **212/977-7023.** Subway: E, V to 5th Ave. (7) 1212 Sixth Ave. (at 48th St.). ℭ **212/730-1087.** Subway: B, D, F, V to 47th–50th sts./Rockefeller Center. (8) 657 Third Ave. (at 42nd St.). ℭ **212/697-3590.** Subway: S, 4, 5, 6, 7 to 42nd St./Grand Central. (9) 1466 Broadway (at 42nd St.). ℭ **212/382-4500.** Subway: N, Q, R, S, W, 1, 2, 3, 7 to 42nd St./Times Sq. (10) 60 W. 34th St. (at Broadway). ℭ **212/760-1268.** Subway: B, D, F, N, Q, R, V, W to 34th St. (11) 122 Fifth Ave. (at 18th St.). ℭ **917/408-5580.** Subway: N, Q, R, W, 4, 5, 6 to 14th St.; L to Union Sq. (12) 11 Fulton St. (at Front St.). ℭ **212/374-1051.** Subway: J, M, Z, 2, 3, 4, 5, 6 to Fulton St.

Gymboree Store   This clothing chain has some fun looks for younger kids: durable knits in bold colors and kindergartenish prints. Cut roomy for easy moving, they're a sensible, reasonably stylish bet for everyday wear. www.gymboree.com. (1) 1332 Third Ave. (at 76th St.). ℭ **212/517-5548.** Subway: 6 to 77th St. (2) 1120 Madison Ave. (btwn 83rd and 84th sts.). ℭ **212/717-6702.** Subway: 4, 5, 6 to 86th St. (3) 1049 Third Ave. (at 62nd St.). ℭ **212/688-4044.** Subway: 4, 5, 6 to 59th St. (4) 2015 Broadway (at 69th St.). ℭ **212/595-7662.** Subway: 1 to 66th St./Lincoln Center. (5) 2271 Broadway (btwn 81st and 82nd sts.). ℭ **212/595-9071.** Subway: 1 to 79th St.

H & M Not every NYC branch of this value-conscious clothing company carries their children's lines, but you can find them at both 34th Street locations and the Harlem branch. Sizes up to 13 years, for both boys and girls, are designed to be durable, easy to move in, and also fashion-conscious, with an eye to classic looks (and therefore good for hand-me-downs two seasons from now). H & M's Dubbster label puts a big emphasis on denim every which way, while the L.O.G.G. designs are suitable even for prepsters. www.hm.com. (1)1328 Broadway (at 34th St.). © 646/473-1165. Subway: B, D, F, N, Q, R, V, W to 34th St./Herald Sq. (2) 435 Seventh Ave. (at 34th St.). © 212/643-6955. Subway: 1, 2, 3 to 34th St. (3) 125 W. 125th St. (btwn Fifth and Lenox aves.). © 212/665-8300. Subway: 2, 3 to 125th St.

New York City Kids Almost everything is under $100 at this discount store in the Garment District, and with labels like Timberland, that's netting you some substantial savings. There is a tendency toward children's clothes that look like Mini-Me versions of what parents wear—lots of little boys' three-piece suits and girls' glam-o-rama party dresses. 495 Seventh Ave. (btwn 36th and 37th sts.). © 212/868-6925. Subway: 1, 2, 3 to 34th St.

Old Navy Featuring sturdy, classic casual wear in the Gap mold, this clothing chain has plenty of presence in NYC these days—good news for parents who don't want to spend a bundle. Prices are as down-to-earth as the superwearable styles. www.oldnavy. com. (1) 610 Sixth Ave. (at 18th St.). © 212/645-0663. Subway: F, V to 14th St.; L to Sixth Ave.; 1 to 18th St. (2) 503-511 Spring St. (entrance on Broadway btwn Spring and Broome sts.). © 212/226-0838. Subway: B, D, F, V to Broadway/Lafayette St.; 6 to Spring St. (3) 150 W. 34th St. (at Broadway). © 212/594-0049. Subway: B, D, F, N, Q, R, V, W to 34th St./Herald Sq. (4) 125th St. and Frederick Douglas Blvd. (in Harlem USA Mall). © 212/531-1544. Subway: A, B, C, D, 2, 3 to 125th St.

FASHIONS—GIRLS

All Dressed Up Filling a strategic important market niche in Manhattan, this Upper East Side boutique provides drop-dead party gowns for pre-teens—just the thing for getting through the stream of bar/bat mitzvahs that inevitably occupy one's seventh-grade social calendar. Lovely, appropriate dresses, with just the right hint of sophistication. 1201 Lexington Ave. (btwn 82nd and 83rd sts.). © 212/452-3181. Subway: 4, 5, 6 to 86th St.

Bambini This beautiful, humorless, blond-wood store stocks European children's clothes (brand names like Simonetta and Cacharel) and shoes. The clothes are indeed handsome, but at princess prices—$49 for a dead-plain polo shirt or $375 for a stunning smocked party frock. 1088 Madison Ave. (btwn 81st and 82nd sts.). © 212/717-6742. Subway: 6 to 77th St.; 4, 5, 6 to 86th St.

Berkeley Girl Fashion-conscious West Side girls sizes 7 to 16 can outfit themselves in the latest styles in this busy boutique across from the Natural History Museum. They'll know the labels, from Diesel to Lucky to Lilly Pulitzer. 410 Columbus (btwn 79th and 80th sts.). © 212/877-4770. www.berkeleygirl.com. Subway: B, C to 81st St.

Bonpoint This stunning boutique takes the cake—it has the most expensive and probably the most beautiful children's clothes in town (up to size 16 girls and 12 boys). Everything sold is the store's private label, and the fabrics are gorgeous, no question about it; the styles are classic, chic, and perfectly cut. Closed Sunday. (1) 1269 Madison Ave. (at 91st St.). © 212/722-7720. www.bonpoint.com. Subway: 4, 5, 6 to 86th St. (2) 811 Madison Ave. (at 68th St.). © 212/879-0900. Subway: 6 to 68th St.

Ibiza Kidz This Village shop sells some dreamy children's clothes with a bohemian sensibility, as well as shoes, books, and toys. The look is stylish, not grungy, with a sense of whimsy. 61 Fourth Ave. (btwn 9th and 10th sts.). ℭ **212/228-7990** or 212/375-9984. www. ibizakidz.com. Subway: N, R, W to 8th St.

Infinity   As a friend of mine says, "At a certain age, all girls want to look like either a construction worker or a tramp." This is the store for both looks. T-shirts and jeans and skimpy knit dresses rule, along with lots of the huge dumpy backpacks every school kid has to have. Infinity doesn't necessarily try to be hip; it just stocks what kids like to wear, damn the parents. Bring your preteen here to prove you do indeed get it. Closed Sunday in summer. 1116 Madison Ave. (at 83rd St.). ℭ **212/517-4232**. www.infinity nyc.com. Subway: 4, 5, 6 to 86th St.

Jacadi   A French chain, Jacadi sells expensive, stylish, sturdy clothes, cut for comfort, for boys and girls up to age 12. Each season's line is color-coordinated, handy for mixing and matching, and the store looks tidy and very put-together as a result. www. jacadiusa.com. (1) 1296 Madison Ave. (at 92nd St.). ℭ **212/369-1616**. Subway: 4, 5, 6 to 86th St. (2) 787 Madison Ave. (btwn 66th and 67th sts.). ℭ **212/535-3200**. Subway: 6 to 68th St. (3) 1841 Broadway (at 60th St.). Subway: 1 to 59th St./Columbus Circle. (4) 1260 Third Ave.(at 72nd St.), ℭ **212/ 717/9292**. Subway: 6 to 68th

Julian & Sara   The upscale, style-conscious clothes at this SoHo store attract downtown girls up to size 14. 103 Mercer St. (btwn Prince and Spring sts.). ℭ **212/226-1989**. www. julianandsara.com. Subway: N, R, W to Prince St.

Koh's Kids   Located in TriBeCa, this shop provides fun clothes for newborns to 10-year-olds. 311 Greenwich St. (btwn Chambers and Reade sts.). ℭ **212/791-6915**. Subway: 1, 2, 3 to Chambers St.

Lester's   This is an East Side staple for clothing and shoes, ages newborn to 12—most of the stock is imported, and designer styles abound, but the prices aren't too wild. The girls' clothes trend toward more daring looks. 1534 Second Ave. (at 80th St.). ℭ **212/734-9292**. Subway: 6 to 77th St.

Lilliput   An East Village sensibility rules in this crammed-full shop carrying play clothes and spunky fashions in sizes up to 18; expect labels like Diesel, CP and Company, and Petit Bateau. A battery of wind-up toys and a good-size selection of tulle skirts for dress-up fun gives you a clue to the spirit of the place. 265 Lafayette St. (btwn Prince and Spring sts.). ℭ **212/965-9567**. www.lilliputsoho.com. Subway: B, D, F, V to Broadway/Lafayette St.

Marsha D. D.   The lineup of casual clothes here is strong on urban hipness and streetwise sophistication. The buyers are right on top of every street trend, every season. Closed Sunday. 1574 Third Ave. (btwn 88th and 89th sts.). ℭ **212/534-8700**. Subway: 4, 5, 6 to 86th St.

Morris Brothers   Older girls, and those who want to look older than their age, stop in here for the season's slacker must-haves, whether it be a Paul Frank T-shirt or Juicy shorts. 2322 Broadway (at 84th St.). ℭ **212/724-9000**. Subway: 1 to 86th St.

M. W. Teen   When you graduate from Magic Windows (see "Baby & Preschooler Clothes," earlier in this chapter), you get to buy precociously chic party dresses from M. W. Teen next door. The clothes really are pretty, if a trifle too adult for my taste—but then, my daughter's not a teenager yet. 1188 Madison Ave. (at 87th St.). ℭ **212/289-0181**. Subway: 4, 5, 6 to 86th St.

Peanut Butter & Jane   Packed to the rafters, this utterly wonderful small store carries real-life clothes at hipster prices—leopard print leggings, tie-dyed T-shirts, camouflage jackets, and cotton dresses in dusky floral prints. Both the sporty and the dressy items have a funky sense of style; sizes go up to 12 for girls. There are lots of dress-up costumes as well, to feed the imagination, and the clutter of toys in the back is irresistible. My friends in the West Village view this shop as a life-support system. 617 Hudson St. (at Jane St.). ℭ 212/620-7952. Subway: A, C, E, 1, 2, 3 to 14th St.; L to Eighth Ave.

Petite Bateau   As the flagship store for this upscale clothing label, this is a good source for French style (meaning country-club-ish clothes of which *Maman* would approve). Carries clothing for boys and girls up to size 18. 1094 Madison Ave. (at 82nd St.). ℭ 212/988-8884. www.petitebateau.com. Subway: 4, 5, 6 to 86th St.; 6 to 77th St.

San Francisco Clothing   This East Side women's clothing store has a surprisingly darling line of little girls' clothing, in well-cut mini-preppie styles and top-quality fabrics. Don't let the wood-paneled decor and snooty staff put you off—with play clothes under $50 and dresses under $75, this is an upscale shop worth checking out. Closed Sunday. 975 Lexington Ave. (btwn 70th and 71st sts.). ℭ 212/472-8740. www.sanfranciscoclothing. com Subway: 6 to 68th St.

Small Change   As expensive children's clothing shops go, this isn't a bad choice for that special party dress. The store buyers clearly have a sense of style. Closed Sunday. 1196 Lexington Ave. (at 83rd St.). ℭ 212/772-6455. Subway: 6 to 79th St.

Space Kiddets   Come here for some very cute downtown-trendy stuff for wee ones—it can be pricey, but the sales are good. Closed Sunday. 46 E. 21st St. (btwn Broadway and Park Ave. S.). ℭ 212/420-9878. www.spacekiddets.com. Subway: N, R, W, 6 to 23rd St.

Spring Flowers Children's Boutique   In the realm of upscale children's clothing, Spring Flowers strikes a healthy balance: The big-skirt party gowns run only $75 to $175. You can find some casual wear and shoes, but it's the dress-up stuff that catches the eye, round racks bulging with petticoats and pinafores. Imported brand names include Cacharel, Le Petit Bateau, Sophie Dess—all the usual suspects. Closed Sunday. www.springflowerschildren.com. (1) 1050 Third Ave. (at 62nd St.). ℭ 212/758-2669. Subway: 4, 5, 6 to 59th St. (2) 905 Madison Ave. (at 72nd St.). ℭ 212/717-8182. Subway: 6 to 68th St. (3) 538 Madison (at 55th St.). ℭ 212/207-4606. Subway: 6 to 51st St.

Talbots Kids   For all the country-club matron image of the adult Talbots store, this junior version (for newborns to teens) is surprisingly bright and casual and cool, like a Gap without the grunge. Clothes are tailored but stylish, with a coherent mix-and-match look. For classic-cut winter coats, sweaters, and other wardrobe staples, it can't be beat. (1) 1523 Second Ave. (at 79th St.). ℭ 212/570-1630. www.talbots.com. Subway: 6 to 77th St. (2) 527 Madison Ave. (at 54th St.). ℭ 212/758-4152. Subway: 6 to 51st St.

Tutti Bambini   Carrying a wide range of labels—imported, made in the U.S.A., whatever—this busy little East Side shop knows its look: funky and fun. It carries sizes up to 10, with brand names like Lili Gaufrette, Victoria Kids, JKKS, and Charlie Rockets, and tends toward designs adults wouldn't mind wearing. Most of the other shoppers I saw had kids in tow, which means they were picking out clothes the kids themselves like to wear—always a good sign. 1480 First Ave. (btwn 77th and 78th sts.). ℭ 212/472-4238. Subway: 6 to 77th St.

Zitomer Department Store   Bursting at the seams, this drugstore's upstairs children's clothing department has some very upscale imported clothes (dresses in the $50–$500 range) that manage to look cheesy in the fluorescent light, jammed together on chrome racks as they are. But don't be put off by that; it's worth a stop if you're on a quest for something special. 969 Madison Ave. (btwn 75th and 76th sts.). ☎ 212/ 737-5560. www.zitomer.com. Subway: 6 to 77th St.

FASHIONS—BOYS

Greenstones & Cie   Big on sweaters and corduroys, this shop embraces a kind of yacht-club look (every sweater has a design, it seems). Good for boys who wouldn't be caught dead in the Poindexter outfits sold elsewhere on Madison Avenue. Lots of items that are well-nigh irresistible. (1) 442 Columbus Ave. (at 81st St.). ☎ 212/580-4322. Subway: B, C to 79th St. (2) 1184 Madison Ave. (btwn 86th and 87th sts.). ☎ 212/427-1665. Subway: 4, 5, 6 to 86th St.

Jay Kos   Come here for fine menswear scaled down to boys' sizes. Hey, they've gotta change out of their T-shirts and sweats sometime. Closed Sunday. 988 Lexington Ave. (btwn 71st and 72nd sts.). ☎ 212/327-2382. Subway: 6 to 68th St.

Lester's   This is the place for boys to buy a real suit, with knowledgeable fitters and tailors available and a wide range of styles to choose from. More casual clothes are stocked, too. 1534 Second Ave. (at 80th St.). ☎ 212/734-9292. Subway: 6 to 77th St.

Morris Brothers   Best for older kids' clothing, Morris Brothers has two specialties: outfitting your child for camp and outfitting your adolescent to look reasonably cool, with labels like Billabong and Quicksilver that have plenty of street cred. It's also a decent source for winter hats, socks, underwear, pajamas, sweats, and jeans. Very solid, if not a bargain. 2322 Broadway (at 84th St.). ☎ 212/724-9000. Subway: 1 to 86th St.

Peter Elliot Jr.   Prep-school boys who want to dress like their investment-banker dads do very well at this Madison Avenue men's shop. There's nothing like learning the value of good tailoring and top-quality fabrics from an early age. Closed Sunday July-August. 1067 Madison Ave. (at 80th St.). ☎ 212/570-5747. Subway: 6 to 77th St.

Small Change   The prices can be high ($280 for a boy's navy blazer!), but this East Side store understands its upscale customers and their private-school needs. Closed Sunday. 1196 Lexington Ave. (at 83rd St.). ☎ 212/772-6455. Subway: 4, 5, 6 to 86th St.

Talbots Kids   For khaki pants and polos and sweaters in solid colors and traditional stripes, this place has the advantage of one-stop shopping. When my sons finally agree to wear a navy blazer and rep tie, this is where we buy them—they fit, they look great, and I don't have to pay through the nose for something they'll wear only a dozen times. Button-down Oxford-cloth shirts, too—go all the way. www.talbots.com. (1) 1523 Second Ave. (at 79th St.). ☎ 212/570-1630. Subway: 6 to 77th St. (2) 527 Madison Ave. (at 54th St.). ☎ 212/758-4152. Subway: 6 to 51st St.

COMIC BOOKS, CARDS & COLLECTIBLE FIGURES

All these stores have a wide stock of cards and/or comics, but whether they've got that rare item you're looking for is always a question. If you're really on a quest for something special, call the whole lot until you strike gold. Otherwise, drop in for a browse at whichever shop you're nearest.

Alex's MVP Cards   This friendly neighborhood store specializes in comics and sports cards and wax packs, as well as a decent supply of nonsports toys and supplies. 256 E. 89th St. (at Second Ave.). ☎ 212/831-2273. Subway: 4, 5, 6 to 86th St.

Chameleon Comics   Here you'll find Marvel comics and sports cards. Closed Sunday. 3 Maiden Lane (btwn Nassau St. and Broadway). ☎ 212/732-8525. www.chameleoncomics.com. Subway: A, C to Broadway/Nassau St.; 2, 3, 4, 5 to Fulton St.

Collector's Universe   A store for true aficionados, this large Midtown place stocks comic books—millions of comic books—as well as covering all ends on sports and superheroes. Closed Sunday. 124 E. 40th St. (btwn Park and Lexington aves.), 1st floor. © 212/ 922-1110. Subway: S, 4, 5, 6, 7 to 42nd St./Grand Central.

Cosmic Comics   This is a good source for comics, in addition to action figures, nonsports trading cards, T-shirts, models, trade paperbacks, and videos. 10 E. 23rd St. © 212/460-5322. www.cosmiccomics.com. Subway: 6 to 23rd St.

Forbidden Planet   This overwhelming store is a valuable source for comics and assorted sci-fi and fantasy paraphernalia. 840 Broadway (at 13th St.). © 212/473-1576. www.fpnyc.com. Subway: N, Q, R, W, 4, 5, 6 to 14th St.; L to Union Sq.

Gotham City Comics   A wide-ranging stock of comics, sports cards, action figures, and T-shirts, with some rarities—it's one of those places where collectors could browse happily for a long time. 796 Lexington Ave. (at 62nd St.), 2nd floor. © 212/980-0009. Subway: 4, 5, 6 to 59th St.

Gotta Have It   The trove of sports collectibles here includes a good stock of sports cards, including plenty of rarities. Closed Sunday. 153 E. 57th St. (btwn Lexington and Third aves.). © 212/750-7900. www.gottahaveit.com. Subway: 6 to 59th St.

Jim Hanley's Universe   Comic books old and new, plus fantasy role-playing games, can be found here. 4 W. 33rd St. (btwn Fifth Ave. and Broadway). © 212/268-7088. www.jhuniverse.com. Subway: B, D, F, N, Q, R, V, W to 34th St./Herald Sq.

Kidrobot   Purveying what the store itself describes as "urban vinyl action figures," this tiny SoHo shop is often packed with club kids and slacker hipsters. You'll know your kid would dig this place if he/she recognizes these product lines: Homies, Kubriks, Dunnys, and Stifkas. 126 Prince St. (btwn Greene and Wooster sts.). © 212/966-6688. www.kidrobot.com. Subway: N, R, W to Prince St.

St. Mark's Comics   Anything comic-related can be bought here, including books, magazines, action figures, and toys; the shop has its own subculture buzz. (1) 11 St. Mark's Place (btwn Second and Third aves.). © 212/598-9439. Subway: 6 to Astor Place (2) 148 Montague St., Brooklyn. © 718/935-0911. Subway: M, R, 2, 3, 4, 5 to Court St./Borough Hall.

Toy Tokyo   Near the grungy hipness of St. Mark's Place, this fascinating little store specializes in Japanese imports of vinyl figures, sought by connoisseurs (of which your son may be one). 121 Second Ave. (at 9th St.). © 212/673-5424. www.toytokyo.com. Subway: 6 to Astor Place.

Village Comics   This store is renowned in the comic collector community as a superb source for Marvel cards, action figures, toys, and other collectors' supplies, as well as comics. 214 Sullivan St. (btwn W. 3rd and Bleecker sts.). © 212/777-2770. www.village comics.com. Subway: A, B, C, D, E, F, V to W. 4th St.

CRAFTS, MODELS & TRAINS

Bruce Frank   For the child who wants to go beyond stringing plastic beads to attempt some more advanced jewelry making, this snug little shop selling Indonesian art and antiques carries an absolutely amazing selection of handmade and ethnographic beads. 215 W. 83rd St. (btwn Broadway and Amsterdam Ave.). © 212/595-3746. www. brucefrankbeads.com. Subway: 1 to 86th St.

Craft Studio   The rainforest-themed site for plaster-painting parties has an excellent front section with lots of crafts kits, art materials, puzzles, and other toys. Walk in and paint on plaster, wood, or terra-cotta pots. Their private parties have 10 different craft themes, from doll-making to chocolate to PJs and puppets.

Closed Sunday July-August. 1657 Third Ave. (btwn 92nd and 93rd sts.). © 212/831-6626. www. craftstudionyc.com. Subway: 6 to 96th St.

Games Workshop   Manhattan now has three branches of this U.K.-based chain of stores, selling its own line of character models and hosting elaborate fantasy-game tournaments. For certain boys, it's a sort of clubhouse. www.gamesworkshop.com. (1) 1457 Third Ave. (at 83rd St.). © 212/744-1390. Subway: 4, 5, 6 to 86th St.. (2) 269 72nd St. (at Amsterdam Ave.). © 212/362-0726. Subway: 1, 2, 3 to 72nd St. (3) 54 E. 8th St.(at University Place). © 212/982-6314. Subway: A, B, C, D, E, F, V to W. 4th St.

Jan's Hobby Shop   This stocked-to-the-rafters shop is a wondrous source for all kinds of wooden models—in everything from balsa wood to mahogany—as well as plastic model kits (loads of Revell planes and race cars) and die-cast metal items for collectors. The display cases of military models are awesome. 1435 Lexington Ave. (btwn 93rd and 94th sts.). © 212/861-5075. Subway: 4, 5, 6 to 96th St.

Red Caboose   New York's most intense model-railroad shop, the Red Caboose has been selling all gauges and scales of trains since 1942, as well as equipment and supplies desired by modelers. The stock of train and automobile kits is growing all the time, too. Closed Sunday (except during the holiday season). 23 W. 45th St. (btwn Fifth and Sixth aves.); enter the lobby and go downstairs at the back. © 212/575-0155. www.theredcaboose.com. Subway: B, D, F, V to 47th–50th sts./Rockefeller Center.

Train World   True electric-train fanatics may want to venture out to this huge store for train sets. Closed Sunday. 751 McDonald Ave., Brooklyn. © 718/436-7072. www.trainworld. com. Subway: F to Ditmas Ave.

DEPARTMENT STORES

Bloomingdale's   Bloomie's prides itself on glitz, which doesn't translate well into family-oriented merchandise. The layette department is extravagant, geared toward pregnant shopaholics going on a final binge before the demands of motherhood put their shopping days to an end. The kids' clothing departments are claustrophobic and overpriced, and there's no toy department to speak of. 1000 Third Ave. (at 59th St.). © 212/705-2000. www.bloomingdales.com. Subway: 4, 5, 6 to 59th St.

Lord & Taylor   This slightly dowdy Midtown matron stocks traditional layette stuff and children's clothes. Its meticulous window displays at Christmas are the best in town—collectors of American Girl dolls will want to linger over the detailed historic scenes with their tiny costumed moving figures. 424 Fifth Ave. (at 39th St.). © 212/391-3344. www.lordandtaylor.com. Subway: B, D, F, V to 42nd St.

Macy's   Macy's flagship in Midtown is one of the world's biggest department stores, with a solidly middle-class orientation. The children's departments are huge and carry a broad range of merchandise, including lots of sturdy playwear for boys and girls. This is the only Manhattan department store with a significant toy department, though the selection is fairly run-of-the-mill; my kids actually get more of a kick out of the electronic-games department or the sample room setups on the vast furniture floor. At Christmastime, Macy's still mounts a Santaland, a state-of-the-art extravaganza with long lines and Santa himself taking requests. 151 W. 34th St. (from Broadway to Seventh Ave.). © 212/695-4400. www.macys.com. Subway: B, D, F, N, Q, R, V, W to 34th St.

Prowling the Pet Stores

When your child decides he or she can no longer tolerate another museum or toy store, try this boredom-buster: Visit one of Manhattan's many pet stores. Whether or not you're actually in the market to buy a pet, it never hurts to drop by and take a look. If your child is fascinated by exotic fish, try **New World Aquarium,** 204 E. 38th St., between Second and Third avenues (© 646/865-9604), or **Aqua Star Pet Shop,** in Little Italy at 172 Mulberry St., between Grand and Broome sts., © 212/431-4311. If your kids demand to see puppies and kittens, stop at **American Kennels,** 798 Lexington Ave., between 61st and 62nd streets (© 212/838-8460), or **Pets-on-Lex,** 1271 Lexington Ave., between 77th and 78th streets (© 212/426-0766).

Saks Fifth Avenue   Sleek and chic, Saks does best for the very young, with a fairly good infant-wear department, but it has recently upgraded its departments for older kids with special themed characters and fun events. Worth including in your Rockefeller Center expeditions, especially since the store's restaurant, **Café SFA** (p. 115), is such a winner. 611 Fifth Ave. (at 50th St.). © 212/753-4000. www.saksfifthavenue.com. Subway: B, D, F, V to 47th–50th sts./Rockefeller Center.

DOLLS & DOLLHOUSES

American Girl Place   Buying an American Girl doll may be the first serious investment of a girl's life, and it's a sizable expenditure, not to be taken lightly. Whom to choose? Molly, the spunky World War II–era girl with the glasses and pigtails? Victorian Samantha, the lonely rich orphan in her fur-trimmed cloak? Addy, the runaway black slave? Each of these beautifully made 18-inch dolls has her own story; a series of books written about her; and a dozen or so detailed, historically accurate outfits. American Girl Place—one of only three stores (the others are in Chicago and Los Angeles) where you can buy these dolls in person, rather than by catalog or online—is like a shrine for young doll owners, and many bring their dolls with them to worship here. Besides the historical dolls, other doll lines such as Bitty Babies, Hopscotch School, Angelina Ballerina, and American Girls of Today are displayed, along with books, accessories, and a fair number of clothes for the doll owners themselves. The store also boasts a doll hair salon, a theater (see chapter 10), and a usually booked-up café (p. 112). Closed Monday. 609 Fifth Ave. (at 49th St.). © 877/AG-PLACE. www.american girl.com. Subway: E, V to Fifth Ave./53rd St.; B, D, F, V to 47th–50th sts./Rockefeller Center.

Manhattan Doll House Shop   Besides a truly awesome selection of kits and finished dollhouses, this Gramercy store has all the furnishings, right down to electrical fixtures. Full-size dolls are also repaired and sold, with a specialty in Madame Alexander. Closed Sunday. 236 Third Ave. (btwn E. 19th and 20th sts.). © 877-DOLLHSE. www.manhattan dollhouse.com. Subway: 6 to 23rd St.

Mary Arnold Toys   This top-notch East Side toy shop includes an outstanding doll section—Madame Alexander, Corolle, Götz, and the like. Closed Sunday. 1010 Lexington Ave. (btwn 72nd and 73rd sts.). © 212/744-8510. Subway: 6 to 77th St.

New York Doll Hospital   Since 1900, young New Yorkers have climbed the stairs to this musty space bearing their precious dolls and stuffed animals in need of repairs. You can also buy antique and discontinued dolls and kitschy collectibles like a Charlie McCarthy doll, a Howdy Doody, a Daddy Warbucks tie-in from the movie *Annie*, or a Pee Wee Herman doll. A wonderful jumble of dolls' heads, arms, and legs on the floor gives the place a slightly Twilight Zone–ish atmosphere. No credit cards are accepted. Closed Sunday. 787 Lexington Ave. (btwn 61st and 62nd sts.), 2nd floor. ℭ 212/838-7527. Subway: 4, 5, 6 to 59th St.

Rexall Gifts   The pharmacy aspect of this Upper East Side shop has been more or less squeezed out by the collectible dolls and paraphernalia for American Girl dolls, among others. (Not, unfortunately, American Girl dolls themselves—for those, you'll have to go down to Midtown.) There's not much, but what's available is choice. Closed Sunday. 1335 Madison Ave. (btwn 93rd and 94th sts.). ℭ 212/831-2354. Subway: 6 to 96th St.

Tiny Doll House   In this small, well-organized shop, rows of perfectly put-together miniature rooms flank the side walls, while a few empty doll mansions preside regally over the center of the room. Wallpaper, carpeting, lamps, cutlery—a tasteful selection of all the tiny furnishings you'll ever need. Before you go inside, warn little would-be customers not to touch, as the staff is somewhat gun-shy about kids breaking the delicate miniatures. Closed Sunday. 314 E. 78th St. (btwn First and Second aves). ℭ 212/744-3719. www.tinydollhouse.com. Subway: 6 to 77th St.

GAMES

Chess Forum   Competing head-to-head with the Chess Shop right up the street, the Chess Forum is big on chess lessons for kids, along with selling a large variety of exquisite sets for chess, backgammon, cribbage, and dominoes. Celebrity customers include David Lee Roth, Sean Lennon, Yoko Ono, and Harvey Keitel. 219 Thompson St. (btwn 3rd and Bleecker sts.). ℭ 212/475-2369. www.chessforum.com. Subway: A, B, C, D, E, F, V to W. 4th St.

Chess Shop   Come here for exotic chess sets, esoteric chess manuals, and a slew of related computer software, as well as clocks for speed chess. 230 Thompson St. (btwn 3rd and Bleecker sts.). ℭ 212/475-9580. www.chess-shop.com. Subway: A, B, C, D, E, F, V to W. 4th St.

Compleat Strategist   This specialist shop stocks a fairly mind-boggling array of games, from chess and backgammon to military simulations and role-playing games, but doesn't neglect board games for the younger set, including some noncompetitive games for nonreaders. Fun for browsing. Closed Sunday. 11 E. 33rd St. (btwn Fifth and Madison aves.). ℭ 212/685-3880. www.compleatstrategist.com. Subway: 6 to 33rd St.

Neutral Ground   Along with selling an eclectic array of games, especially role-playing games, this store sponsors Magic the Gathering tournaments, role-playing campaigns, and miniature battles. Check their website to get a monthly calendar of events. 122 W. 26th St., 4th floor (btwn Sixth and Seventh aves.). ℭ 212/633-1288. www.neutralground.com. Subway: N, R, W, 1 to 28th St.

GIFTS & GADGETS

Alphabets   The East Village sensibility of this wacky gift-a-torium translates well to more mainstream neighborhoods; central to the concept is lots of campy kids' stuff—Etch-a-Sketch and Mr. Potato Head, yes, but also some truly goofball stuff like a chess set with the Simpson family (Homer and Bart, that is)—which is probably bought by as many adults as children. Loads of one-of-a-kind T-shirts abound. www.alphabetsnyc.com.

(1) 115 Ave. A (at 7th St.). ℂ **212/475-7250**. Subway: 6 to Astor Place. (2) 47 Greenwich Ave. (btwn Sixth and Seventh aves.). ℂ **212/229-2966**. Subway: 1, 2, 3 to 14th St. (3) 2284 Broadway (btwn 82nd and 83rd sts.). ℂ **212/579-5702**. Subway: 1 to 79th St.

E.A.T. Gifts   Next door to the absurdly overpriced E.A.T. cafe, this gift store isn't really designed for kids—it's crowded and there's an annoying "don't touch" factor—but somehow, every time we wander in, there's something one of my children can't live without. Little gift books, bath toys, tiny shaped soaps and crayons, chocolate novelties—it's like quicksand for the reluctant shopper. 1062 Madison Ave. (btwn 80th and 81st sts.). ℂ **212/861-2544**. Subway: 6 to 77th St.

Hammacher Schlemmer   You want gadgets? They've got gadgets—high-quality gadgets to do everything under the sun, including some things you've never thought of doing before. Older kids and adults get a kick out of the unique and ingenious products, and don't worry if most items are way out of your price range—the ratio of browsers to buyers is usually pretty high. Closed Sunday.. 147 E. 57th St. (btwn Lexington and Third aves.). ℂ **212/421-9000**. www.hammacher.com. Subway: 4, 5, 6 to 59th St.

HAIRCUTS

Cozy's Cuts for Kids   Spanking clean and bright, Cozy's plays videos to keep kids happy in the chair—which may be a regular barber chair or a yellow Jeep. Après-cut, the little shavers get lollipops, balloons, and favors—all the usual bribes. Cozy's has enough quality toys to double as a toy store, which unfortunately means you've got to ward off toy requests when you come in only for a haircut, but what the hey, at least you have no trouble getting the kids in the door. Closed Sunday. www.cozyscutsforkids.com (1) 1125 Madison Ave. (at 84th St.). ℂ **212/744-1716**. Subway: 4, 5, 6 to 86th St. (2) 1416 Second Ave. (at 74th St.). ℂ **212/585-2699**. Subway: 6 to 77th St. (3) 448 Amsterdam Ave. (btwn 81st and 82nd sts.). ℂ **212/579-2600**. Subway: 1 to 79th St.

Kids Cuts   If you're in Midtown, this small salon may be more convenient; its slightly lower prices also reflect the fact that it's not part of the Upper East Side yupscale hub. They cut adult hair as well, which is a real bargain. Closed Sunday July through August. 201 E. 31st St. (at Third Ave.). ℂ **212/684-5252**. www.kidscutsny.com. Subway: 6 to 33rd St.

Kidville   There's a multitude of classes and activities for little kids at this bright and busy Upper West Side hangout, but even if you haven't registered in a class, you can still drop by for a haircut. 466 Columbus Ave. (btwn 82nd and 83rd sts.). ℂ **212/362-7792**. Subway: 1 to 79th St.

Paul Mole   Well known for stylish men's cuts, the Paul Mole salon also has a thriving business in cutting the hair of those stylish men's children (mostly sons). Closed Sunday July through August. 1031 Lexington Ave. (at 74th St.). ℂ **212/535-8461**. Subway: 6 to 77th St.

Whipper Snippers   Patient, cheery haircutters ply their scissors downtown at this bright and busy salon/toyshop, run by savvy neighborhood parents. 106 Reade St. (btwn W. Broadway and Church St.). ℂ **212/227-2600**. www.whippersnippers.com. Subway: A, C, 1, 2, 3 to Chambers St.

JEWELRY & ACCESSORIES

Claire's   Costume jewelry, hair doodads, and a grab-bag of slumber-party-worthy gift items make these bouncy chain shops a hit with 'tweens. www.claires.com . (1) 2267 Broadway (btwn 81st and 82nd sts.). ℂ **212/877-2655**.. Subway: 1 to 79th St. (2) 720 Lexington Ave.

(at 58th St.). ℭ 212/644-8665. Subway: 4, 5, 6 to 59th St. (3) 1385 Broadway (btwn 37th and 38th sts.). ℭ 212/302-6616. Subway: B, D, F, N, Q, R, V, W to 34th St. (4) 89 South St. Seaport (2nd floor). ℭ 212/566-0193. Subway: 2, 3, 4, 5 to Fulton St.; A, C to Broadway/Nassau St.

GirlProps Inexpensive does not mean cheap—that's the watchword of this groovy costume-jewelry shop in SoHo, where you can pick up tons of plastic adornments for a buck or two. Some of the stuff here drifts into Goth and punk paraphernalia for club kids, so be prepared to divert. www.girlprops.com. (1) 153 Prince St. (btwn W. Broadway and Thompson St.). ℭ 212/505-7615.. Subway: N, R, W to Prince St. (2) 33 E. 8th St. (btwn Fifth Ave. and University Pl.). ℭ 212/505-7615. Subway: N, R, W to 8th St.

Ricky's For hair ornaments, youthful makeup, and dress-up stuff (you should see this store around Halloween), Ricky's has a definite cool quotient, especially with teens and 'tweens. www.rickysnyc.com. (1) 144 E. 8th St. (btwn Mercer and Greene sts.). ℭ 212/254-5247. Subway: N, R, W to 8th St. (2) 590 Broadway (btwn Houston and Prince sts.). ℭ 212/226-5552. Subway: N, R, W, 6 to Spring St. (3) 383 Fifth Ave. (btwn 35th and 36th sts.). ℭ 212/481-6701. Subway: B, D, F< N< Q, R, V, W to 34th St. (4) 1189 First Ave. (at 64th St.). ℭ 212/879-8361. Subway: 6 to 68th St. (5) 112 W. 72nd St. (btwn Broadway and Columbus Ave.). ℭ 212/769-3678. Subway: 1, 2, 3 to 72nd St. (6) 1380 Third Ave. (btwn 78th and 79th sts.) ℭ 212/737-7724. Subway: 6 to 77th St. (7) 472 Columbus Ave. (at 83rd St.). ℭ 212/724-4590. Subway: 1 to 86th St.

MAGIC & GAGS

Abracadabra Harry Potter fans can indulge some serious fantasies at this ever-growing magic superstore, so large it even has a stage and a cafe on-site. Its several thousand feet of space are stocked with every magic trick, costume, and gag under the sun. Warning to parents of skittish youngsters: Some of the masks on display are extremely lifelike and gruesome as all get out. Closed Monday. 19 W. 21st St. (btwn Fifth and Sixth aves.). ℭ 212/627-5194. www.abracadabrasuperstore.com. Subway: F, V to 23rd St.

Martinka Magic Co. Houdini himself once owned this outfit, which claims to be the oldest magic shop in the country. There's something subtle in the air here, like a Twilight Zone set just waiting for creepy things to start happening. Closed Sunday. 45 W. 34th St. (btwn Fifth and Sixth aves.), 6th floor. ℭ 212/279-6079. www.martinka.com. Subway: B, D, F, N, Q, R, V, W to 34th St.

Tannen's Magic Amateur or professional, magicians shop here, and the array of equipment is impressive. In the interests of developing future magicians, Tannen's also runs magic camps (for ages 12–20) and hosts a fall magic conference in the Catskills; magic is serious business here. Closed Sunday.. 45 W. 34th St., Suite 608 (btwn Fifth and Sixth aves.). ℭ 212/929-4500. www.tannens.com. Subway: B, D, F, N, Q, R, V, W to 34th St.

MUSIC

Bleecker Bob's Golden Oldies Like a scene out of the movie *High Fidelity*, this famous Village hangout still has bins full of vinyl, with some very obscure albums, and staff who really know their arcane music trivia. Older kids who are into esoterica and nostalgia might dig it. 118 W. 3rd St. (btwn Sixth Ave. and MacDougal St.). ℭ 212/475-9677. www.bleeckerbobs.com. Subway: A, B, C, D, E, F, V to 4th St.

Colony Music Center Nobody ever sells sheet music anymore—well, except for Colony, which has a mind-blowing assortment of song sheets and scores for your budding musician, including jazz, rock, and every Broadway show tune ever written. Even better, you'll be rubbing shoulders with real professional musicians as you browse the narrow aisles. The huge selection of easy piano books is great for beginners, and—who knew?—it's also the world's largest karaoke dealer. 1619 Broadway (at 49th St.). ✆ 212/265-2050. www.colonykaraoke.com. Subway: 1 to 50th St.

House of Oldies   Like Bleecker Bob's (see above), the House of Oldies prides itself on hard-to-find vintage recordings, especially 45s and LPs. If your kids don't know what a "record" is, bring them here for a history lesson. Closed Sunday and Monday. 35 Carmine St. (btwn Bleecker and Bedford sts.). ✆ 212/243-0500. www.houseofoldies.com. Subway: A, B, C, D, E, F, V to W. 4th St.

Manny's Music   On Midtown's Music Row, Manny's is one store that welcomes kids to fiddle around on the instruments for sale. 156 W. 48th St. (btwn Sixth and Seventh aves.). ✆ 212/819-0576. Subway: B, D, F, V to 47th–50th sts./Rockefeller Center.

Tower Records   The name's a bit of a misnomer, since there's precious little vinyl for sale anymore. But Tower remains a massive source for recorded music. www.tower records.com. (1) 725 Fifth Ave. (at 57th St.). ✆ 212/838-8110. Subway: N, R, W to Fifth Ave./59th St. (2) 692 Broadway (at 4th St.). ✆ 212/505-1500. Subway: 6 to Bleecker St.

Virgin Megastore   Everybody's favorite hip Brit tycoon Richard Branson moved into Times Square in a big way with this three-story megamart for recorded music—along with a bookstore, cafe, and movieplex. The music selection is good and deep, and there are lots of listening posts around so you can sample the sounds before you buy. Dig the smoke-blowing weird bronze facade of the Union Square branch. www.virginmegastore.com. (1) 1540 Broadway (at 45th St.). ✆ 212/921-1020. Subway: N, Q, R, S, W, 1, 2, 3, 7 to 42nd St./Times Sq. (2) 52 E. 14th St. (at Park Ave.). ✆ 212/598-4666. Subway: N, Q, R, W, 4, 5, 6 to 14th St.; L to Union Sq.

SHOES

East Side Kids   Free popcorn is dispensed to shoe-shopping kids, which means the place looks like a pigsty by the end of the day. But the range of shoes is wide, some chic and some totally playground-friendly. Closed Sunday. 1298 Madison Ave. (btwn 92nd and 93rd sts.). ✆ 212/360-5000. www.eastsidekids.com. Subway: 6 to 96th St.

Harry's Shoes for Kids   This frantically bustling West Side shoe store finally spun off its children's shoe operation into a separate store up the street. Fashion is less the point here than solid quality. Broadway (btwn 83rd & 84th sts.). ✆ 212/874-2034. www.harrys-shoes. com . Subway: 1 to 86th St.

Ibiza Kidz   This Village kids boutique sells shoes from newborn through women's sizes, as well as books and stuffed animals. The stock shows some real flair. 61 Fourth Ave. (btwn 9th and 10th sts.). ✆ 212/228-7990 or 212/375-9984. www.ibizakidz.com. Subway: N, R, W to 8th St.

Lester's   This all-purpose children's clothing store provides one-stop shopping with a full-service shoe department in the back. 1534 Second Ave. (at 80th St.). ✆ 212/734-9292. Subway: 6 to 77th St.

Little Eric   Style is the watchword—get your 4-year-old shod here if you want to wow the admissions officer at your Brearley or Buckley interview. Yes, they've got plain patent-leather Mary Janes and classic penny loafers in peewee sizes, but also cowboy boots and other trendy styles. 1118 Madison Ave. (at 83rd St.). ✆ 212/717-1513. Subway: 4, 5, 6 to 86th St.

The Best Shops That Just Happen to Be in Museums

My husband and I sometimes regret the habit we started with our kids: persuading them to go to museums by promising a stop in the gift shop afterward. Believe me, we've been burned more than once when the final gallery of a museum dumps you out into a schlocky souvenir-a-torium. On the other hand, we got into this routine in the first place because so many New York City museums have really excellent gift shops, often selling items for children than you can't find anywhere else. Some are so good, we shop there without visiting the museum at all. So when you're out and about in New York City, don't forget the following wonderful museum boutiques (see Chapter 6 for more details about these and other NYC museums).

The renowned gift shop at the **Metropolitan Museum of Art** (1000 Fifth Ave. at 82nd St., ☎ 212/535-7710, closed Mon) takes top honors in my mind. Sensibly, you don't have to pay museum admission to enter this huge two-story shop. The large children's department on the upper level includes plenty of beautiful books, craft kits, coloring books, art materials, dolls, puzzles, and games. Echoing the Met's great arms and armor galleries, there are loads of toy knights here, as well as toy Roman legionnaires and charioteers (in tribute to the vast classical art galleries) and Egyptian trinkets (tying into the mummies on display).

Further north along the Upper East Side's Museum Mile, three other excellent choices are the **Cooper-Hewitt National Design Museum** (2 E. 91st St. at Fifth Ave., ☎ 212/849-8300, closed Mon), which offers some very clever toys and books in a gorgeous stately home setting; the **Jewish Museum** (1109 Fifth Ave. at 92nd St., ☎ 212/423-3200, closed Sat), a super source for children's books about Judaism as well as toys, games, and puzzles (plus the best dreidel selection in town); and **The Museum of the City of New York** (1220 Fifth Ave. at 103rd St., ☎ 212/534-1672, closed Mon), which has a pleasant selection of toys and books, in line with its excellent toy galleries inside.

Naturino   This spare, chic boutique is the prime source for imported children's shoes by Naturino, Moschino, and Oilily. Closed Sunday July-August. 1184 Madison Ave. (btwn 86th and 87th sts.). ☎ 212/427-0679. www.naturinonewyork.com. Subway: 4, 5, 6 to 86th St.

Shoofly   A whimsical collection of designer hats for kids hangs from tree branches poking out of one wall; low shelves, bins, and steamer trunks overflow with a wild assortment of shoes, sandals, socks, mittens, hair bows, belts, and ties, running the gamut from goofy to glam, all the way up to a women's size 9. It's always fun shopping here, even if you don't buy. The prices aren't outlandish, but the sense of style is—just what little New Yorkers need to look really cool. 42 Hudson St. (btwn Duane and Thomas sts.). ☎ 212/406-3270. www.shooflynyc.com.. Subway: 1, 2, 3 to Chambers St.

Stride Rite   Carrying the Stride Rite standard on the Upper East Side, Stride Rite looks like a super-treehouse, with separate areas (each decked out with boredom-fighting

On the Upper West Side, the intelligent toys and books sold at the **Children's Museum of Manhattan** (212 W. 83rd St. between Broadway and Amsterdam Ave., ✆ 212/721-1234, closed Mon in summer, Mon–Tues during the school year) never fail to delight. Some of the stock features tie-ins to special exhibits, but there's always a wide range of wholesome, educational-yet-fun items for kids 10 and under. At the nearby **American Museum of Natural History** (Central Park West at 79th St., ✆ 212/769-5100, open daily), you'll have to pay admission to visit most of the gift shops, with the exception of the Planetarium Shop near the West 81st Street entrance. If you're inside the museum anyway, though, you'll find an impressive array of educational toys, games, stuffed animals, and nature books in the main shop near the Central Park West entrance; smaller boutiques tucked around the museum may be geared to special exhibitions or particular interests. The AMNH also makes sure to stock lots of inexpensive impulse-buy items, knowing full well how the gift-shop bribe works for families.

If you're in Midtown, a trio of museums along West 53rd Street between Fifth and Sixth Avenues offer a fun shopping diversion for kids: the **Museum of Modern Art** (11 W. 53rd St., ✆ 212/708-9400, closed Tues); the **American Folk Art Museum** (45 W. 53rd St., ✆ 212/265-1040, open daily), and the **Museum of Arts and Design** (40 W. 53rd St., ✆ 212/956-3535, open daily; moving to 2 Columbus Circle in spring 2008). The MoMa shop is famous for its art books and visually appealing *objets*, but the narrow little gallery at the folk art museum gets a higher rating for its small-but-brilliant selection of things that will strike kids' fancy.

Finally, some of the city's best places for stuffed animals are the gift shops at the various zoos. While you might not go to the Bronx or Prospect Park just to visit the zoos' boutiques, the one at the **Central Park Zoo** (in Central Park, near the park entrance at Fifth Ave. and 64th St., ✆ 212/439-6500, open daily) is incredibly handy, displaying even more plush species than the zoo's live ones. Again, it's outside the admission barriers, so anyone can walk in.

activities) for different age groups. An essential stop for durable midpriced shoes and for wider feet. 1241 Lexington Ave. (at 84th St.). ✆ 212/249-0551. www.striderite.com. Subway: 4, 5, 6 to 86th St.

Tip Top Kids   Bright, cheerful, and relaxed, this children's annex to Tip Top Shoes is the antidote to crazed Harry's Shoes (see above): You can almost always get waited on immediately, the staff handles children with good humor, and the selection offers quality shoes at fair prices. Brands like Elefanten, Aster, Timberland, Sperry, and Bass, as well as Stride Rite and Adidas are popular here. 149 W. 72nd St. (btwn Broadway and Columbus Ave.). ✆ 212/874-1004. www.tiptopshoes.com. Subway: 1, 2, 3 to 72nd St

SHOWER & BABY GIFTS
Little Extras   Though there are a few toys here for older kids (pacifying gifts for displaced older siblings, perhaps), baby gifts reign: music boxes, picture frames, picture

albums, nursery lamps, soft wall hangings, baby towel sets, silver cups and spoons and rattles, personalized footstools, and toy chests. This place never lets me down when I'm en route to a shower, christening, or bris and need a present in a hurry. Closed summer Sundays. 676 Amsterdam Ave. (at 93rd St.). ℂ 212/721-6161. Subway: 1, 2, 3 to 96th St.

Tiffany & Co.   Wanna score points? A silver spoon, rattle, teething ring, or baby cup from Tiffany's is still the classy way to celebrate a new arrival, and no new parent minds duplicates of these classics. Get the spoon or cup engraved for an extra touch; you can do it all by phone or online, though visiting this fabled store is usually a pleasure. All except the cup are under $100, so why not go for it? A child is born only once. 727 Fifth Ave. (at 56th St.). ℂ 212/755-8000. www.tiffany.com. Subway: N, R, W to Fifth Ave./59th St.

SOFTWARE & ELECTRONIC GAMES

Electronics Boutique/Game Stop   Racks full of computer software and accessories, as well as those GameBoy, PlayStation2, and X-Box games kids think they can't live without. The staff make it their business to know about the latest hot games, even if it means steering you away from a rip-off. Our family makes a supply stop here at least once a month. www.ebgames.com. (1) 30 Rockefeller Center, concourse level. ℂ 212/765-3857. Subway: B, D, F, V to 47th–50th sts./Rockefeller Center. (2) 901 Sixth Ave. (at 33rd St.). ℂ 212/564-4156. Subway: B, D, F, N, R, V to 33rd St. (3) 1282 Broadway (at 33rd St.). ℂ 212/967-9070. Subway: B, D, F, N, Q, R, V, W to 34th St. (4) 1470 Third Ave. (at 83rd St.). ℂ 212/288-5370. Subway: 4, 5, 6 to 86th St. (5) 128 E. 86th St. (btwn Park and Lexington aves.). ℂ 212/423-1844. Subway: 4, 5, 6 to 86th St. (6) 2330 Broadway (btwn 84th and 85th sts.). ℂ 917/441-4160. Subway: 1, 2, 3 to 86th St. (7) 2764 Broadway (at 106th St.). ℂ 212/864-4292. Subway: 1 to 103rd St. (8) 251 W. 125th St. (btwn Seventh and Eighth aves.). ℂ 212/749-7434. Subway: 1 to 125th St. (9) 324 First Ave. (at 19thSt.) ℂ 212/995-0085. Subway: L, N, Q, R, W, 4, 5, 6 to 14th St./Union Sq. (10) 107 E. 14th St. ℂ646/602-1483. Subway: N, Q, R, W, 4, 5 to 14th St.; L to Union Sq. (11) 743 Broadway (btwn 7th and 8th sts.). ℂ 212/979-7678. Subway: 6 to Astor Place; N, R, W to 8th St (12) 687 Broadway (btwn W. 3rd and W. 4th sts.). ℂ 212/473-6571. Subway: N, R, W to 8th St. (13) Pier 17 at South St. Seaport, 2nd floor. ℂ212/227-1945. Subway: 2, 3, 4, 5 to Fulton St.; A, C to Broadway/Nassau St.

SPORTS STUFF

Blades Board & Skate   In-line skaters and skateboarders gear up at this chain of specialty stores, where you can have your own board custom-built for $500 or so. Get your helmets and kneepads here as well. Rentals are available. See chapter 8 for skateboarding info. www.blades.com. (1) 120 W. 72nd St. (btwn Broadway and Columbus Ave.). ℂ 212/787-3911. Subway: B, C, 1, 2, 3 to 72nd St. (2) 659 Broadway (at Bleecker St.). ℂ 212/477-7350. Subway: B, D, F, V to Broadway/Lafayette St. (3) 901 Sixth Ave. (btwn 32nd and 33rd sts., in the Manhattan Mall). ℂ 212/563-2448. Subway: B, D, F, N, Q, R, V, W to 34th St./Herald Sq.

Eastern Mountain Sports   This place is big on camping gear and outdoor wear, along with equipment for climbing walls—the ideal place to buy a sleeping bag that doesn't have Mickey Mouse or Batman all over the lining. 591 Broadway (at Houston St.). ℂ 212/966-8730. www.ems.com. Subway: B, D, F, V to Broadway/Lafayette St.

Mets Clubhouse Shop   Mets fans stock up on blue-and-orange team paraphernalia and memorabilia here. You can buy game tickets, too. Let's go, Mets! 143 E. 54th St. (at Lexington Ave.). ℂ 212/888-7508. Subway: E, V to Lexington Ave./53rd St.; 6 to 51st St.

Modell's   When you gotta go to Mo's, you gotta go. Though not totally kid-oriented, Mo's is an important destination for any family harboring a young athlete because of its sheer size and its attention to some of the less mainstream sports. Equipment, clothing, and some sports fan gear as well—it's hard to get out of here without buying more than you expected. www.modells.com (1) 1535 Third Ave. (btwn 86th and 87th sts.). ⊙ **212/996-3800.** Subway: 4, 5, 6 to 86th St. (2) 200 Broadway (btwn Fulton and John sts.). ⊙ **212/964-4007.** Subway: 2, 3, 4, 5 to Fulton St. (3) 51 E. 42nd St. (btwn Vanderbilt and Madison aves.). ⊙ **212/661-4242.** Subway: S, 4, 5, 6, 7 to 42nd St./Grand Central. (4) 234 W. 42nd St. (btwn Seventh and Eighth aves.). ⊙ **212/764-7030.** Subway: A, C, E to 42nd St./Port Authority. (5) 1293 Broadway (btwn 33rd and 34th sts.). ⊙ **212/244-4544.** Subway: B, D, F, N, Q, R, V, W to 34th St./Herald Sq. (6) 55 Chambers St. (btwn Broadway and Elk St.). ⊙ **212/732-8484.** Subway: 1, 2, 3, A,C to Chambers St. (7) Harlem USA Mall, 300 W. 125th St. (btwn St. Nicholas Place and Eighth Ave.). ⊙ **212/280-9100.** Subway: A, B, C, D, 1, 2, 3 to 125th St. (8) 606 W. 181st St. (at St. Nicholas Place). ⊙ **212/568-3000.** Subway: 1 to 181st St.

NBA Store   This three-story player in the Fifth Avenue Parade of Theme Stores celebrates hoop dreams in a big way, with lots of gleaming blond hardwood floors, high ceilings, and fun b-ball-themed merchandise. The jerseys in stock show a decided preference for New York–area teams (Knicks, Nets, Liberty) but there's plenty for fans of all stripes. The on-site cafe is reasonably priced and offers burgers, chicken fingers, and shakes—your usual arena food. 666 Fifth Ave. (btwn 52nd and 53rd sts.). ⊙ **212/515-6221.** Subway: E, V to Fifth Ave./53rd St.

Niketown   This glitzy temple to sports and sneakers is more of a museum/attraction than a place to buy shoes, with several interactive stations where kids can measure their feet, test their reach and reflexes, and generally try to be like Mike (or Tiger, perhaps, these days). 6 E. 57th St. (btwn Fifth and Madison aves.). ⊙ **212/891-6453.** Subway: N, R, W to Fifth Ave./59th St.

Paragon Sports   Paragon is good for rugged sports clothing and total gear, including lots of camping equipment, ski stuff, and a golf department with a tiny putting green. 867 Broadway (at 18th St.). ⊙ **212/255-8036.** www.paragonsports.com. Subway: N, Q, R, W, 4, 5, 6 to 14th St.; L to Union Sq.

Princeton Ski Shop   Large, bright, and modern, this ski-equipment shop has a great selection of gear for all members of the family. Some price tags run high, but this is skiing, after all—you'll pay a lot more if you wait until you get to the resort to buy those goggles, gloves, and parkas. 21 E. 22nd St. (btwn Broadway and Park Ave. S). ⊙ **212/228-4400.** Subway: N, R, W, 6 to 23rd St.

Scandinavian Ski and Sports Shop   The array of quality ski equipment and clothing here is huge, and the ladies really know the meaning of service. There's a decent stock of cycling, camping, and tennis gear, too. Look for end-of-season sales. Closed Sunday. 16 E. 55th St. (btwn Fifth and Madison aves.). ⊙ **212/757-8524.** Subway: F to 57th St.

Sports Authority   Though not quite as comprehensive as Mo's, this is another good clean Midtown source for sports equipment and apparel, as well as tickets and fan gear to support a pro-sports spectating habit. www.sportsauthority.com (1) 845 Third Ave (at 51st St.). ⊙ **212/355-9725.** Subway: E, V to Lexington Ave.; 6 to 51st St. (2) 636 Sixth Ave. (at 19th St.). ⊙ **212/929-8971.** Subway: F, N, R, V, W to 23rd St.

Yankees Clubhouse Shop   Bronx Bomber fans can indulge their merchandise-buying addictions here. Also a good source for tickets. (1) 393 Fifth Ave. (btwn 36th and 37th sts.). ⊙ **212/685-4693.** Subway: 6 to 33rd St. (2) 110 E. 59th St. (btwn Park and Lexington aves.). ⊙ **212/758-7844.** Subway: 4, 5, 6 to 59th St. (3) 745 Seventh Ave. (at 49th St.). ⊙ **212/391-0360.** Subway: t to 50th St. (4) 245 W. 42nd St. (btwn Broadway and Eighth Ave.). ⊙ **212/768-9555.** Subway: N,

Q, R, S, W, 1, 2, 3, 7, 9 to 42nd St./Times Sq.; A, C, E to 42nd St./Port Authority. (5) Pier 17 at South St. Seaport (outside on cobblestones). ℂ212/514-7182. Subway: 2, 3, 4, 5 to Fulton St.

STROLLERS, CRIBS & FURNITURE

Albee Baby Carriage Co.   This store may be crowded and a little grimy and disorganized, but what these folks don't know about nursery equipment ain't worth knowing. There's always an unwieldy mother-to-be collapsed in a glider rocker, looking glassy-eyed as she (and her mother and/or husband) order a couple thousand dollars' worth of baby stuff—I wonder how many labors have started here over the years. Closed Sunday. 715 Amsterdam Ave. (at 95th St.). ℂ 212/662-5740. Subway: 1, 2, 3 to 96th St.

Baby Depot at Burlington Coat Factory   Toil up to the third floor of this discount emporium to find a Toys "R" Us–ish collection of layettes, cribs, strollers, car seats, and clothing. The prices are fairly low—just don't expect top-of-the-line furnishings for your nursery. 707 Seventh Ave. (btwn 22nd and 23rd sts.). ℂ 212/229-1300. www.coat.com. Subway: F, V to 23rd St.

Bellini   At this expensive baby-furniture boutique, the service can be offhand (unless, of course, you're spending a bundle). The look is pretty with an edge of fun, nothing too unusual. If you want to start your infant off with upscale tastes, this is where to do it. 1305 Second Ave. (btwn 68th and 69th sts.). ℂ 212/517-9233. www.bellini.com. Subway: 6 to 68th St.

Just For Tykes   Here's one-stop shopping for baby furniture and other tot essentials, upscale and handsome, in a sliver of a SoHo boutique. 83 Mercer St. (btwn Broome and Spring sts.). ℂ 212/274-9121. www.justfortykes.com. Subway: N, R, W to Prince St.

Kids Supply Co.   This boutique sells some intriguing children's furniture, featuring warm woods and bold colors and a sophisticated sense of style. Quality stuff, built to withstand children. Closed Sunday July through August. 1343 Madison Ave. (at 94th St.). ℂ 212/426-1200. www.kidssupply.com. Subway: 6 to 96th St.

Little Folks Shop   Little Folks sells a solid range of nursery outfittings and strollers, plus layettes and clothes up to size 7. Closed Saturday. 123 E. 23rd St. (btwn Park and Lexington aves.). ℂ 212/982-9669. www.littlefolksnyc.com. Subway: 6 to 23rd St.

Plain Jane   This kicky little West Side boutique specializes in antique nursery furniture, country-look bedding, quilts, and some newer stuff with a retro sensibility— truly one-of-a-kind items like a $500 decoupaged toy chest accented with kids' faces straight from some *Dick and Jane* primer. Closed Sunday. 525 Amsterdam Ave. (btwn 85th and 86th sts.). ℂ 212/595-6916. www.plainjanekids.com. Subway: 1 to 86th St.

Planet Kids   Big, bright, and bustling, this store has a wide range of furnishing and paraphernalia for babies and toddlers. www.planetkidsny.com. (1) 247 E. 86th St. (btwn Third and Second aves.). ℂ 212/426-2040. Subway: 4, 5, 6 to 86th St. (2) 2688 Broadway (at 104th St.). ℂ 212/864-8705. Subway: 1 to 103rd St.

Schneider's   This downtown source offers not only nursery essentials but furniture for kids' and even teenagers' bedrooms, as well as strollers, car seats, and layette must-haves. Closed Sunday. 41 W. 25th St. (btwn Sixth Ave. and Broadway). ℂ 212/228-3540. www.schneiders baby.com. Subway: F, V, N, R, W to 23rd St.

THEME STORES

NBA Store   This three-story player in the Fifth Avenue parade of theme stores celebrates hoop dreams in a big way. 666 Fifth Ave. (btwn 52nd and 53rd sts.). ℂ 212/515-6221. Subway: E, V to Fifth Ave./53rd St.

Niketown   Eye-popping design and lots of sports videos build the buzz at this sneaker palace. 6 E. 57th St. (btwn Fifth and Madison aves.). ⓒ 212/891-6453. Subway: N, R, W to Fifth Ave./59th St.

The World of Disney   The Disney Corporation's 3-story Fifth Avenue flagship store borrows liberally from Disney theme parks to present a big glossy stage set of an emporium. You'll find not only tons of Disney-themed merchandise, but also lots of interactive areas: Shoppers can visit the Princess Castle Court for glittery costume jewelry and crafts, Goofy's Candy Company sweets boutique (similar to Candy Land at the Times Square Toys "R" Us), a make-your-own Mr. Potato Head room, a Friendship Room where Disney characters provide several daily photo ops, and a MultiMedia Zone with listening stations and gaming stations for trying out the latest Disney products. 711 Fifth Ave. (at 55th St.). ⓒ 212/702-0702. www.worldofdisney.com. Subway: E, V to Fifth Ave

TOYS

A Bear's Place   This store has an immense stock of equipment for mothering baby dolls, along with wooden toys, games, puppets, big teddy bears, dolls, and the entire line of imported Battat toys for babies and toddlers. You can order some hand-painted nursery furnishings here, too. Closed Sunday July-August. 789 Lexington Ave. (btwn 61st and 62nd sts.). ⓒ 212/826-6465. Subway: 4, 5, 6 to 59th St.

Big City Kites   Beyond all the great wind-worthy kites promised in the name, this handy little shop stocks loads of other flying toys, from Frisbees to balsa-wood gliders; a serious collection of yo-yos and juggling equipment rounds out the inventory. A good stop if you're on the way to Central Park on a windy spring afternoon. Closed Sunday. 1210 Lexington Ave. (at 81st St.). ⓒ 212/472-2623. www.bigcitykites.com. Subway: 4, 5, 6 to 86th St.

Build-A-Bear Workshop   The two-story flagship location of this mall-based chain is quite impressive, with a number of only-in-New-York items as well as a full line of international bear outfits and accessories. Both boys and girls have a blast choosing a limp bear form and seeing it stuffed right before their eyes (not to mention getting to put a red satin heart inside, or even a voice box with their own recorded message on it). Downstairs offers a party room and the cheery Eat With Your Bear Hands Café— not a bad bet if you've been shopping for hours and couldn't get a reservation at American Girl Place just up the street. Attached is a boutique where Friends 2B Made cloth dolls can be custom-made as well. 565 Fifth Ave. (at 46th St.). ⓒ 212/871-7080. www.buildabearworkshop.com. Subway: S, 4, 5, 6, 7 to 42nd St./Grand Central.

Children's General Store   This charming toy boutique is a welcome addition to the shopping at Grand Central Terminal, offering some unusual handmade and imported toys you won't see in most other stores. The emphasis is on well-made toys with a certain imagination-sparking value. (1) Grand Central Terminal, Lexington Passage. ⓒ 212/682-0004. Subway: S, 4, 5, 6, 7 to 42nd St./Grand Central. (2) 168 E. 91st St. (btwn Lexington and Third aves.). ⓒ 212/426-4479. Subway: 4, 5, 6 to 86th St.

Cozy's Cuts for Kids   Besides haircuts (see listing earlier in this chapter), Cozy's deals in a small stock of well-chosen toys, including lots of arts and crafts. www.cozyscutsforkids.com (1) 1125 Madison Ave. (at 84th St.). ⓒ 212/744-1716.. Subway: 4, 5, 6 to 86th St. (2) 1416 Second Ave. (at 74th St.). ⓒ 212/585-2699. Subway: 6 to 77th St. (3) 448 Amsterdam Ave. (btwn 81st and 82nd sts.). ⓒ 212/579-2600. Subway: 1 to 79th St.

Didi's Children's Boutique   On cool, spare, back-lit white shelves, you'll find beautiful, almost museum-quality imported toys. Closed Sunday. 1196 Madison Ave. (btwn 88th and 89th sts.). ℂ 212/860-4001. www.didis.com. Subway: 4, 5, 6 to 86th St.

Dinosaur Hill   Selling imported toys, mobiles, wooden blocks, art supplies, and puppets—notably an extensive line of handmade marionettes—this airy East Village shop also has a battery of under-$2 stuff so no child will have to leave empty-handed. 306 E. 9th St. (near Second Ave.). ℂ 212/473-5850. www.dinosaurhill.com. Subway: 6 to Astor Place.

FAO Schwarz   Risen like a phoenix from the ashes of corporate bankruptcy, this Manhattan toy mecca has re-emerged as a sleek, streamlined multi-story temple of conspicuous consumption. The focus is on larger-than-life stuffed animals, collectible Barbies and other dolls, antique toys, elegant dress-up clothes, top-of-the-line art kits, high-end electronic cars and robots (what kid doesn't want his or her own mini-Mercedes?), and a panoply of other toys you won't find at any mall. Costumed characters, story hours, craft activities, and a soda shoppe add to the deluxe ambiance. Even if you don't intend to buy, stroll around and gawk to your heart's content; it's one of those only-in-Manhattan experiences your kids will remember. 767 Fifth Ave. (at 58th St.). ℂ 212/644-9400. www.faoschwarz.com. Subway: N,R,W to Fifth Ave.

Geppetto's Toybox   Kids and collectors alike shop at this light-filled Greenwich Village boutique, its varnished blond-wood surfaces echoed by the number of quality wooden toys. The selection tends toward high-end dolls, collectible bears, and artist-designed toys, as well as some very sturdy playthings for infants and toddlers. 10 Christopher St. (btwn Greenwich Ave. and Gay St.). ℂ 212/620-7511. www.nyctoys.com. Subway: 1 to Christopher St.

Hombons   Crowded into this storefront is a deep selection of stuff to play with, best for its arts-and-crafts materials, puzzles, board games, Playmobils, and other small-motor activities. It's definitely a place that rewards a long, slow browse. 1500 First Ave. (btwn 78th and 79th sts.). ℂ 212/717-5300. Subway: 6 to 77th St.

Kay-Bee Toys   Sometimes you need a chain toy store to get that Malibu Barbie or G.I. Joe your kid is pining for. Utterly mass-market, but very dependable. Manhattan Mall, 901 Sixth Ave. (at 33rd St.). ℂ 212/629-5386. www.kbtoys.com. Subway: B, D, F, N, Q, R, V, W to 34th St.

Kidding Around   This shop brings the uptown toy-buying aesthetic to downtown—imports and educational toys in a clean well-lighted space. There's lots of rugged plastic wildlife in baskets on the floor. 60 W. 15th St. (btwn Fifth and Sixth aves.). ℂ 212/645-6337. www.kiddingaround.us. Subway: N, Q, R, W, 4, 5, 6 to 14th St.; L to Union Sq.

Mary Arnold Toys   One of the best toy stores in town, Mary Arnold's is intelligently laid out with nooks where children can fiddle and browse without clogging the aisles. Quality toys—Legos, Brios, Playmobils—many shelves of board games, lots of dress-up costumes, and a very impressive doll department make this a never-fail destination to satisfy kids of any age or interest. Closed Sunday. 1010 Lexington Ave. (btwn 72nd and 73rd sts.). ℂ 212/744-8510. Subway: 6 to 77th St.

The Nest   Educational toys—puzzles, blocks, board books, manipulatives—fill a corner of this Tribeca gathering place for downtown moms and tots. 36 N. Moore St. (btwn Hudson and Varick sts.) ℂ 212/219-3130. www.thenestny.com. Subway: 1 to Franklin St.

Penny Whistle Toys   This outstanding shop has more or less defined what upscale New York parents want in a toy store: imported, quality, educational toys, well made but with a sense of fun. Nothing too precious; nothing too commercial. Mechanical bears outside both stores blow soap bubbles in fair weather, which makes it very hard to get your kids past without stopping. (1) 448 Columbus Ave. (at 81st St.). © **212/873-9090.** Subway: B, C to 79th St. (2) 1283 Madison Ave. (at 91st St.). © **212/369-3868.** Subway: 4, 5, 6 to 86th St.

Robot Village   This interactive little store tucked away on an Upper West Side side street makes a great play date or party destination; kids can gather around worktables and create their own robots, from a number of age-appropriate materials, or stage battles with the robots they have already created. Everything from books to wind-up toys to robot kits to collectible robots to batteries—it's pretty much the robot capital of Manhattan. Closed Monday. 252 W. 81st St. (btwn Broadway and West End Ave.). © **212/799-7626.** www.robotvillage.com. Subway: 1 to 79th St.

The Scholastic Store   Lots of quality educational toys as well as book tie-ins are to be found in this airy, bright store downstairs from the publisher's SoHo offices. There's even room to play with them, and lots of in-store events to keep things hopping. Intelligently stocked and refreshingly free of blatant self-promotion. 557 Broadway (btwn Prince and Spring sts.). © **212/343-6166.** www.scholasticstore.com. Subway: N, R, W to Prince St.

Stationery & Toy World   There's a delightfully unpretentious clutter of mass-market toys amid the spiral notebooks and ballpoint pens at this friendly West Side storefront. A good place for reward and bribe toys and fun little surprises. Closed Sunday July-August. 125 W. 72nd St. (btwn Columbus Ave. and Broadway). © **212/580-3922.** Subway: 1, 2, 3 to 72nd St.

Toys "R" Us   I give in—this is a fabulous toy store, and my kids never let us have an excursion to Times Square without pleading to visit it. The space is huge, bright, sparkling clean, and full of fun, from the amazing scale models of New York landmarks in the Lego section to the pink Barbie clubhouse to the adorable Candyland-themed sweet shop upstairs. Though the stock is fairly mass market, they have everything on hand, and the prices are (surprise!) not jacked up to pay Manhattan rents. *One warning:* There's a menacing animatronic dinosaur out of Jurassic Park in the back corner of the second floor, in case you've got a skittish younger child. 1514 Broadway at 44th St. © **800/869-7787.** www.toysrus.com. Subway: N, Q, R, S, W, 1, 2, 3, 7, 9 to 42nd St./Times Sq.

West Side Kids   This superb West Side store has lotsa Legos, T.C. Timber, Playmobils, some truly elegant dolls and stuffed animals, every crafts kit known to youth, an impressive board-game selection, and a whole wall of superb imported infant and toddler items. The staff is knowledgeable, the selection intelligent and responsible. When I've got a birthday or Christmas coming up and have no time to troll the stores, I can count on one-stop shopping here. 498 Amsterdam Ave. (at 84th St.). © **212/496-7282.** Subway: 1 to 86th St.

Whipper Snippers   Considering the shortage of great stores for kids way downtown, it's good news that this upbeat haircut salon is also a super toy store, with all the quality toys like Lego, Playmobil, and Groovy Girls that you won't mind buying. 106 Reade St. (btwn W. Broadway and Church St.). © **212/227-2600.** www.whippersnippers.com. Subway: A, C, 1, 2, 3 to Chambers St.

Zittles   This East Side drugstore's toy department just kept expanding and crowded out the second floor; now it's got its own name and a floor to itself. Finally, this overflowing selection of toys has room to be properly displayed, even with a little flair. For a good mix of quality items and unsnobby mainstream toys, it's a source worth knowing about. 969 Madison Ave. (btwn 75th and 76th sts.). © **212/737-2040.** www.zitomer.com. Subway: 6 to 68th St.

10

Entertainment for the Whole Family

Being the theater capital of the United States doesn't necessarily make New York City the children's theater capital—most of those struggling actors and playwrights and directors are too intent on breaking into the Big Time to pay much mind to kid stuff. On the other hand, the major classical-music venues—Lincoln Center and Carnegie Hall—have in the past few years seen the wisdom of introducing children to music *early*, perhaps because impresarios realize (with panic) that their core audience is rapidly aging and needs to be replaced. In any case, there's a lot of talent hanging around this city, and when enterprising organizers decide to put on a show for young audiences, the production values are generally high.

New York parents tend to be culture hounds, so plays and concerts for children are usually well attended—which means that, as for adult productions, you've got to reserve in advance. Compared to the $100 you can pay for orchestra seats in the big Broadway theaters, ticket prices for kids' events aren't usually outrageous, though a few major annual events—like the Big Apple Circus and *The Nutcracker*—get away with higher prices.

FINDING OUT WHAT'S ON Both the weekly Time Out New York (www. timeoutny.com) and its offspring Time Out Kids (www.tonykids.com) have up-to-date, detailed listings of cultural events

kids would enjoy, as does the website gocitykids.com. The local parents' monthly Big Apple Parent (www.parentsknow. com), which carries a calendar of upcoming kids events, can usually be picked up free at public libraries, toy stores, and kids' clothing stores.

The Theatre Development Fund lists current theater offerings online at www. tdf.org/search. You can get event listings for **Lincoln Center** by calling © 212/ 546-2656 or visiting www.lincolncenter. org. For events in **city parks,** which are plentiful in summer (and often free!), call © 888/NY-PARKS or go online to www. nycgovparks.org.

Every Friday the *New York Times* (www.nytimes.com) runs a "Family Fare" column in its Weekend arts section, and you may also find useful listings in *New York* magazine (www.newyorkmetro. com) and the *Village Voice* (www.village voice.com).

For a complete listing of current Broadway and off-Broadway shows, visit **www.playbill.com**. Not only do they give you all the basic information, you can also sign up to receive a regular update via e-mail, informing you which shows offer discounted tickets of anywhere from 10% to 50%.

GETTING TICKETS The Radio City Christmas show and seasonal runs like *The Nutcracker,* the Big Apple Circus, and the Ringling Bros. and Barnum & Bailey

Circus should be reserved weeks or even months in advance, as should Broadway plays and popular long-running shows. For pro-sports events, ticket availability is a matter of how well the team's been doing lately, though even rotten season records haven't freed up Knicks or Jets tickets, whose venues are long sold out to season ticket holders. You can usually find scalpers hovering around Madison Square Garden, but you'll pay through the nose and might be sold bogus tickets; using a ticket agent would be a safer bet if your youngster desperately wants to see a game.

Madison Square Garden events and major theater productions offer their tickets through **Ticketmaster** (© 800/755-4000, 212/307-4100, or 212/307-7171; www.ticketmaster.com) or through **Tele-Charge** (© 800/432-7250 or 212/239-6200; www.telecharge.com). **Madison Square Garden** events also have their own box office (© 212/465-MSG1; www.thegarden.com). For smaller children's theater companies and puppet shows, contact the box office numbers in separate listings below (some are simply answering machines where you leave your number so the organizer can call you back).

Same-day tickets for many Broadway, off-Broadway, and Lincoln Center events can be bought in person at the **TKTS booths** (© 212/768-1818; www.tdf.org) in Midtown on the pedestrian island called Duffy Square at 47th Street and Broadway (open daily 3–8pm for evening performances, Wed and Sat 10am–2pm for matinees, Sun 11am–3pm for matinees and 3pm–closing for evening shows). The earlier you line up, the more options you will have. Most tickets are sold at half price, though some are discounted only 25%, but you'll have to have cash or traveler's checks—no plastic. A $3 TKTS service charge is added. TKTS often has long lines, which move fairly fast but not fast enough for restless small kids. (*Tip:* Window 6, the "Play Only" window, often has a shorter wait.) The surrounding assemblage of wild lit-up signs can provide some distraction while you're waiting, and sometimes mimes and jugglers and street musicians work the crowd. But if you can swing it, one parent should take the youngsters for a walk while the other hangs out in line.

1 The Big Venues

Brooklyn Academy of Music (BAM) Theater, dance, music, puppetry—an impressively international selection of productions rolls through BAM in the course of a year, with a tendency toward the avant-garde. A handful of reasonably priced performances are suited to youngsters, especially the 2-day BAM Kids Film Festival in the spring. Age levels are specified for each performance. 30 Lafayette Ave., Brooklyn. © 718/636-4100. www.bam.org. Subway: B, Q, 2, 3, 4, 5 to Atlantic Ave.; C to Lafayette Ave.; G to Fulton St.; D, M, N, R to Pacific St.

Lincoln Center With resident companies including the Metropolitan Opera, New York City Ballet, New York City Opera, New York Philharmonic, Film Society, Jazz at Lincoln Center, and the Lincoln Center Theater (all covered in various sections below), something exciting is always brewing at this world-class arts center—with an increasing amount geared for families. 65th and Broadway. © 212/875-5456. www.lincolncenter. org. Subway: 1 to 66th St./Lincoln Center.

Madison Square Garden B-ball, hockey, WWE wrestling, the circus, ice shows, and rock concerts occupy this large arena in a grubby part of Midtown. It can be an intimidating space for a small child, but older kids will recognize it for what it is: a big-league venue with lots of urban electricity. Tickets for most events here are also handled through Ticketmaster. The **Theater at Madison Square Garden,** part of the Garden complex, hosts concerts and live touring stage shows like *Sesame Street Live.* Seventh Ave. between 31st and 33rd sts. ℭ **212/465-MSG1.** www.thegarden.com. Subway: A, C, E to 34th St./Penn Station; 1, 2, 3 to 34th St.

New Victory Theater   This lovely renovated century-old theater on 42nd Street has an impressive lineup of entertainment totally for kids. You'll find high-profile talent such as London's Young Vic Theatre Company, Theater for a New Audience, Circus Oz, Mabou Mines, and the Peking Acrobats, as well as idiosyncratic acts like the Flying Karamazov Brothers, the Flaming Idiots, and Thwack. Target age groups vary, but there are significant offerings for that tricky age group of 8- to 12-year-olds—too old for puppet shows but still too young for many Broadway shows. There are many special workshops and meet-the-cast events as well, especially through the Victeens program. New York parents have learned to book tickets far in advance, even if they've never heard of the artists; the runs are generally only 3 weeks long and often sell out. The season is September through June, with extra showtimes during holidays and spring vacation. 209 W. 42nd St. (btwn Seventh and Eighth aves.). ℭ **646/223-3020** or 212/239-6200 (Telecharge). www.newvictory.org. Tickets $10–$35. Subway: N, Q, R, S, W, 1, 2, 3, 7 to 42nd St./Times Sq.; A, C, E to 42nd St./Port Authority.

Radio City Music Hall   The Art Deco interior of this Rockefeller Center showcase is a marvel in itself, but kids probably won't notice—they'll be too busy gaping at the vast proscenium of the stage. Besides mounting its own live stage shows twice a year (see "Seasonal Events," below), Radio City hosts concerts, including the occasional family show. 1260 Sixth Ave. (at 50th St.). ℭ **212/307-7171** (Ticketmaster). www.radiocity.com. Subway: B, D, F, V to 47th–50th sts./Rockefeller Center.

Symphony Space   Besides the Just Kidding (see the listing for Symphony Space under "Weekend Shows," below) and Film Factory series (see "Films," later in this chapter), this recently renovated Upper West Side theater hosts an eclectic variety of events: international dance troupes, Gilbert & Sullivan operettas, and, in spring, a really great series of short-story readings by famous actors and writers. 2537 Broadway (at 95th St.). ℭ **212/864-5400.** www.symphonyspace.org. Subway: 1, 2, 3 to 96th St.

2 Seasonal Events

Big Apple Circus   **All ages.** This beloved one-ring circus performs in a tent (heated, of course) at Lincoln Center from October to January. In 2¼ hours, the Big Apple Circus manages to pack in clowns, elephants, trapeze artists, bareback riders, and something for everyone. Skilled circus artists and a sophisticated sense of humor make this a good show for adults who'd rather be charmed than stunned. A splendid time is guaranteed for all. In Damrosch Park at Lincoln Center, Broadway and 64th St. ℭ **212/307-4100.** (Mailing address: 505 Eighth Ave., 19th Floor, New York, NY, 10018.) www.bigapplecircus.org. Tickets $38–$125, free for children under 2. Subway: 1 to 66th St./Lincoln Center.

Cirque du Soleil   **Ages 10 & up.** Not your ordinary bigtop show by any means, Cirque du Soleil sets up its colorful tents on Randall's Island from April to July. Productions change from year to year, but they're always sophisticated visual spectacles, a creative blend of acrobatics, dance, music, and traditional clowning with an edgy twist. Shows tend to run 2 ½ hours long. On Randall's Island. ℭ **800/678-5440** or 514/790-1245. www.cirquedusoleil.com. Tickets $42–$95. Buses: X80 event buses leave from Lexington Ave. and

Street Performers

When former Mayor Giuliani cleared away the vagrants and the squeegee men from New York City streets, the crime rate plummeted, but the number of street performers also dwindled. They're still around, however—keep on the lookout. Top spots for catching jugglers, acrobats, break dancers, and magicians are at South Street Seaport, by the Statue of Liberty ferry line in Battery Park, by the TKTS line in Duffy Square, on the Central Park pathways just north of the children's zoo around 65th Street, at Bethesda Terrace just north of 72nd Street in Central Park, on the steps leading up to the Metropolitan Museum of Art, and by the fountain in Washington Square Park.

The subways see their fair share of freelancers—there's actually a great space set up for them in the Times Square and Grand Central stations, near the Times Square shuttle platform. The 34th Street station for the B, D, F, N, Q, R, V and W trains often attracts good musicians as well, including an Andean pipe band that's really primo.

There's no guarantee these people will be any good, of course. Standouts in my mind include the guy who plays electric harmonica on the Times Square platforms in Midtown; the Crowtations Motown-singing hand puppets near 72nd Street in Central Park; the magician with the 1960s political agenda who works under the trees near the children's zoo; and a man who tangos very romantically with a dummy of a woman. Remember, you're under no obligation to give these people money, but if you think they're good, you should. Unlike panhandlers, these people are at least doing something for their money.

East 125th St. Ferry: NY Waterway ferries run to Randall's Island from East 34th St (© 800/53-FERRY, www.nywaterway.com). Parking $10.

Nutcracker ⟡⟡⟡ **Ages 10 & up.** The city's best *Nutcracker* is staged every December by the New York City Ballet, with several stunning effects (like a Christmas tree that grows up out of the stage to gi-normous proportions). At the New York State Theater in Lincoln Center, Broadway and 63rd St. © 212/870-5570. www.nycballet.com. Tickets $20–$98. Subway: 1 to 66th St./Lincoln Center.

Nutcracker *(Finds* **Ages 5 & up.** The New York Theater Ballet's abbreviated version of Tchaikovsky's holiday classic ballet lasts about 1 hour, cutting out a lot of the first act to focus on the magical elements of the story. Alongside the classical ballet elements, bits of juggling have been thrown in, and Herr Drosselmeyer has some speaking parts to set up the story. Children are allowed—even expected—to make noises and jump out of their seats. A nice introduction to the ballet for younger audiences. Florence Gould Hall, 55 E. 59th St. (btwn Park and Madison aves.). © 212/355-6160 or © 212/307-4100 (Ticketmaster). Tickets $30 adults, $25 children 12 and under. Subway: 4, 5, 6 to 59th St.; N, R, W to Lexington Ave./59th St.

Radio City Music Hall Christmas Show **Ages 3 & up.** The Rockettes gotta perform somewhere, and this is it. Radio City's elegant Art Deco interior, with its immense stage, cries out for a stage extravaganza like this—lots of music, lavish stage effects, corny holiday motifs, and that classic precision kick line. The Christmas Spectacular runs early November to the first week in January, usually one show a day until the holidays loom close, when up to five shows a day are performed. It's an annual tradition, and the magic still works, dazzling the Nickelodeon generation. 1260 Sixth Ave. (at 50th St.). ℰ 212/307-1000 (Ticketmaster). Tickets $39–$129. Subway: B, D, F, V to 47th–50th sts./ Rockefeller Center.

Ringling Bros. and Barnum & Bailey Circus   Ages 6 & up. This glitzy, humongous circus takes up residence at the Garden for 6 weeks every spring, beginning in late March, starring death-defying aerialists, wild animal acts, lumbering elephants, snarling bears, hordes of clowns, the whole shebang. Smaller kids may be overwhelmed by the sheer size of the Garden, not to mention the flashing lights and eardrum-blasting music. Adults may be overwhelmed by the barrage of vendors selling junk food and junky souvenirs at wildly inflated prices. Still, it's the Greatest Show on Earth and pretty darn impressive. At Madison Square Garden, Seventh Ave. between 31st and 33rd sts. ℰ 800/755-4000, 212/465-MSG1, or 212/307-7171 (Ticketmaster). www.ringling.com. Tickets $10–$50. Subway: A, C, E, 1, 2, 3 to 34th St.

Shakespeare in the Park   Ages 10 & up. From June to August of each summer, The New York Public Theater produces two free shows at the outdoor Delacorte Theater in Central Park, at least one of them by Shakespeare. Recent years have included the much-loved *A Midsummer Night's Dream*, a musical of *Two Gentlemen of Verona*, and *Macbeth*. The line to get tickets forms early each day (9 or 10am), snaking around the Great Lawn, but once the box office opens it moves quickly, and all tickets are soon distributed. The wait can be tedious, but it's a small price for free theater in a beautiful setting. At the Delacorte Theater, Central Park. ℰ 212/260/2400. www.publictheater.org. Tickets free (limit 2 per person in line). Subway: B, C to 81st St.

3 Weekend Shows

Henry Street Settlement Abrons Arts Center   Ages 4 to 12. On weekends this Lower East Side cultural center—a longtime mainstay of the neighborhood—runs a series for kids and their parents at 2pm, with performances twice a month. The company does a wide variety of shows, including dance performances, plays based on updated fairy tales, improv sessions, and puppet shows, all nicely multicultural and very professional. I recommend you call for reservations a week in advance. Check the website—the schedule is continually subject to change. 466 Grand St. (at Pitt St.). ℰ 212/ 598-0400. www.henrystreet.org. Tickets $10 adults, $5 children 4–12. Subway: F to Delancey St.; S to Grand St.; J, M, Z to Essex St.

Symphony Space   Ages 5 & up. October through April, the Just Kidding series presents weekend performances for kids—often concerts with stars like Tom Chapin or the a cappella group the Persuasions, or film and story telling. Eclectic, multicultural, and fun. 2537 Broadway (at 95th St.). ℰ 212/864-5400. www.symphonyspace.org. Tickets generally $20 adults, $12 children under 12. Subway: 1, 2, 3 to 96th St.

4 Theater
LONG-RUNNING SHOWS

It's always hard to predict which Broadway and off-Broadway shows will still be running by the time you read this (much less by the time you get to New York), but these seven are a pretty safe bet—they've been running for a long time with no sign of letting up. Most of them (except *The Lion King*) are usually available for half price at the TKTS booth at 47th Street and Broadway.

Aida **Ages 9 & up.** The most mature of the long running Disney musicals, *Aida* updates the classic Verdi opera with a soaring score by Elton John and Tim Rice that focuses on the timeless love story of an interracial couple. A large cast creates a dazzling stage spectacle. At the Palace Theater, 1564 Broadway (between 46th and 47th sts). © 212/307-4747 or 800/755-4000. www.disneyonbroadway.com. Tickets: $25–111. Subway: N, Q, R, S, W, 1, 2, 3 to 42nd St./Times Square.

Beauty and the Beast 🅰 **Ages 5 & up.** The beloved Disney film has been turned into a surprisingly affecting Broadway musical (2½ hr. long) that keeps regular Broadway hours—8pm shows Wednesday through Saturday, 2pm matinees Wednesday and Saturday, a 1pm Sunday matinee, and an early-bird 6:30pm Sunday night show. At the Lunt-Fontanne Theatre, 205 W. 46th St. (at Broadway). © 212/575-9200. www.disneyonbroadway.com. Tickets $30–$95. Subway: 1 to 50th St.

Blue Man Group **Ages 8 & up.** Faces painted blue, this trio has been committing weird mayhem onstage since 1992, with lots of flashing strobes and percussion effects. The hip performance-art elements are directed to adults, but preteens dig the show, too. It runs slightly under 2 hours. At the Astor Place Theater, 434 Lafayette St. (btwn E. 4th St. and Astor Place). © 212/254-4370 or 212/307-4100 (Ticketmaster). www.blueman.com. Tickets $69 and $79. Subway: 6 to Astor Place.

The Circle of Friends **Ages 6 & up.** You don't have to own an American Girl doll to enjoy this sprightly musical, starring a rotating cast of talented youngsters who are refreshingly not stagey. The story weaves together memorable incidents from the books about American Girl characters, each a little window into that character's unique historical era. Original songs are memorable, and the dialogue is snappy yet natural. There are usually two afternoon shows a day Wednesday through Sunday during the school year, expanding to four shows Tuesday through Sunday in summer. Running time is about 75 minutes. Call at least a month ahead to be sure of obtaining tickets, but don't hesitate to try at the last minute. For the younger set, ages 3 to 6, check out ***Bitty Bear's Matinee***, a family participation production that runs 40 minutes long with varying performance times. At American Girl Place, 609 Fifth Ave. (at 49th St.). © 877/AG-PLACE. www.americangirl.com. Tickets $32 for Circle of Friends, $20 for Bitty Bear. Subway: E, V to Fifth Ave./53rd St.; B, D, F, V to 47th–50th sts./Rockefeller Center.

The Lion King 🅰🅰🅰 **All ages.** Still a hot ticket, this adaptation of a Disney animated movie is worth planning your trip around. Tony-winning director Julie Taymor discarded glitzy special effects and made stage magic instead with puppets, dancers, masks, billowing cloths, and imagination, drawing strongly on African folk traditions. This show is genuinely moving, even—dare I say it?—better than the movie. Call for tickets many months in advance, line up outside for same-day returns, or splurge on a ticket agent, but somehow get your children to see this play. At the New Amsterdam Theater, 214 W. 42nd St. (btwn Seventh and Eighth aves.). © 212/282-2900 or 212/307-4747 (Ticketmaster). www.disneyonbroadway.com. Tickets $25–$100. Subway: N, Q, R, S, W, 1, 2, 3 to 42nd St./Times Sq.

Stomp **Ages 8 & up.** What kid hasn't made music by tapping a broom handle on the floor or crashing two pot lids together? This troupe of eight athletic-looking dancers does the same sort of rhythmic stuff with everyday objects for an hour and a half, and it's undeniably captivating. Early evening performances Saturday and Sunday make it possible to see this without being out too late. At the Orpheum Theater, 126 Second Ave. (btwn 7th and 8th sts.). ℂ 212/477-2477 or 212/307-4100 (Ticketmaster). Tickets $37–$65. Subway: 6 to Astor Place.

Tarzan   Ages 4 & up. Another adaptation of a Disney movie, this musical is much along the lines of *The Lion King*—with big spectacles, a large cast, and a crowd-pleasing plot peppered with family comedy. Tickets should most definitely be purchased in advance if possible, as it is the most recent of Disney musicals to open. At the Richard Rodgers Theater, 226 W. 46th St. and Broadway. ℂ 212/307/4747 or 800/755-4000. Tickets $51.25-111.25. Subway: N, Q, R, S, W, 1, 2, 3 to 42nd St. Times Square.

CHILDREN'S THEATER COMPANIES

ManhattanTheater Source   Ages 5 & up. This bustling Greenwich Village theater organization works two or three hour-long productions for kids—both musicals and straight plays—into their yearly schedule. A recent example: *The Waking Prince*, a spin-off of the Cinderella story from the prince's point of view. 177 MacDougal St. (btwn 8th St. and Waverly Place). ℂ 212/260-4698. www.theatersource.org. Tickets $12. Subway: A, B, C, D, E, F, V to W. 4th St.

New Perspectives Theatre   Ages 4 & up. New Perspectives' World Voices series comprises eight different productions a year, Saturdays and Sundays at 11am and 1pm, many of them adaptations of various ethnic fables. Shows run about an hour, including a preshow activity. Middle school and high school students can also enjoy two Shakespearean performances performed throughout the year. 456 W. 37th St. ℂ 212/730-2030. www.newperspectivestheatre.org. Tickets $8 ($6 per person for families of 4 or more). Shakespeare shows $15 adults, $12 students. Subway: A, C, E to 34th St.

Paper Bag Players   Ages 4 to 9. January to March, this veteran troupe presents original 1-hour plays with a pleasant edge of nuttiness, on Saturday at 2pm and Sunday at 1 and 3pm. The company's trademark is using everyday materials like paper bags and corrugated cardboard for all the costumes, sets, and props, giving the productions a homegrown look that somehow makes them very appealing to kids. Each year they perform in various locations throughout the city. ℂ 212/663-0390. www.the paperbagplayers.org. Tickets $10–$25.

Shadow Box Theatre   Ages 4 & up. The children's theater-in-residence at the Brooklyn YWCA specializes in original musicals with multicultural themes, featuring singing, dancing, and puppetry. November to May they present four or five productions, each running about a month, with weekday and weekend performances. They also do various performances in Manhattan as well as Brooklyn. Call ahead for a schedule. At the YWCA, 30 Third Ave. (at Atlantic Ave.), Brooklyn. ℂ 212/724-0677. (Mailing address 325 West End Ave., New York, NY 10023.) www.shadowboxtheatre.org. Tickets $5.55–$10. Subway: 2 to Nevins St. Some shows also in Manhattan at F.I.T., 7th Ave. and 27th St. Subway: 1, N, R to 28th St.

Theater for a New Audience   Ages 8 & up. This top-notch off-Broadway company devotes itself to the classics, mostly Shakespeare. By no means for children only, its vigorous productions do attract lots of school groups because they're a great way to introduce youngsters to the Bard. From January to April there are two or three productions, playing Tuesday to Saturday nights, with a Saturday matinee. At The American Palace Theatre, 111 W. 46th St. (btwn Broadway and Sixth Ave.). ℂ 212/229-2819. www.tfana.org. Tickets

$10–$60, $10 for those under 25. Subway: B, D, F, V to 47th–50th sts./Rockefeller Center; N, Q, R, S, W, 1, 2, 3, 7 to 42nd St./Times Sq.; N, R, W to 49th St.

Theatreworks USA **Ages 5 & up.** One of the city's top choices for kids, this long-running troupe presents witty, vivid musical versions of classic books like *The Lion, the Witch, and the Wardrobe, Charlotte's Web,* or *The Boxcar Children,* as well as some original story scripts. They put on a dozen or so plays each year, with several performances of each, so you can count on something every weekend at 2pm from September to March. Children under age 4 are not admitted. At the Auditorium at Equitable Tower, 787 Seventh Ave. (at 51st St.). (*C*) 800/497-5007 or 212/647-1100. www.theatreworksusa.org. Tickets $25 (some performances free). Subway: 1 to 50th St.; N, R, W to 49th St.; B, D, E to Seventh Ave.

Thirteenth Street Repertory Theater **Ages 4 & up.** Alongside its grown-up productions, this Greenwich Village company puts on two original children's shows on Saturday and Sunday at 1 and 3pm year-round. With recorded music and special effects, shows like *Danger Dinosaurs* and *Rumple Who?* are perfectly calibrated for a young audience, with healthy doses of humor. Reservations are recommended a couple of days in advance of the performance. 50 W. 13th St. (btwn Fifth and Sixth Aves.). (*C*) 212/675-6677 or 212/352 3101. www.13thstreetrep.org. Tickets to children's shows $7. Subway: 1, 2, 3, N, Q, R, W, 4, 5, 6 to 14th St.; L to Union Sq.

Tribeca Performing Arts **Ages 3 & up.** Offering a mixed bag of events—some starring kids, others with adult performers, others with puppets or dancers or actors performing in sign language—this downtown arts center brings to town a full season of children's entertainment with its Family, Folk, and Fairy Tale series (Oct–June Sat or Sun at 1:30pm). Past productions have included musical versions of classics like *Hans Brinker* and *The Reluctant Dragon,* as well as retellings of children's books such as *The House at Pooh Corner.* 199 Chambers St. (btwn Greenwich St. and the West Side Hwy.). (*C*) 212/220 1460. www.tribecapac.org. Tickets $15 adults, $10 children 12 and under. Subway: A, C, 1, 2, 3 to Chambers St.

Victory Theatrical **Ages 3 to 10.** Strongly promoting hands-on learning, this company provides preshow arts-and-crafts workshops on Saturday and Sunday beginning at 1pm before a 2pm show. The company usually performs two shows a year with original music. Past shows include *The Velveteen Rabbit.* Check the website for weekday performances during school vacations as well. At the YWCA, 610 Lexington Ave. (at 53rd St.) or 5 W. 63rd (btw Broadway and Central Park West). (*C*) 212/866-5170. www.literallyalive.com. Tickets $15 for show, $20 for show plus workshop. Subway: for Lexington Ave. site, E, V to Lexington Ave./53rd St. or 6 to 51st St.; for 63rd St. site, 1 to 66th St.

KIDS ONSTAGE

City Lights **Ages 4 & up.** Several times a year, students 7 to 18 who've taken classes at the City Lights school perform—an original play in the winter and a musical (like *West Side Story*) in the spring. A junior musical for younger children is performed in May as well. Other events include stage readings for family audiences. Presently between home bases, City Lights performs at various theaters around town; check the website for directions to current venues. Mailing address: 300 W. 43rd St, Ste. 402, NY, NY 10036. (*C*) 212/262-0200. www.clyouththeatre.org. Tickets $12 adults, $8 children.

New Media Repertory Company **Ages 3 to 7.** These performances are by and for kids, with lots of participation from the youthful audience. A new original non-musical adventure story, written by New Media's director, Miranda McDermott, is presented in February and March on Saturday at 3pm. The young performers are students at the program's acting workshops. Reservations are essential. 512 E. 80th St. (btwn York and East End aves.). ℂ 212/734-5195. Tickets $10. Subway: 6 to 77th St.

TADA!   Ages 3 & up. The most energetic and successful of NYC's theater schools for kids, TADA! has even performed at the White House. A diverse group of professional kid performers, ages 8 to 17, stars in TADA!'s sprightly original musicals. They play weekends in January, March, and December (including one Fri night show, unusual for children's companies; two Sat matinees; and two Sun matinees). In July— when most other children's entertainment dries up—TADA! comes to the rescue with weekday shows as well. Even adults without children have been known to see TADA!'s shows, which tells you something about how lively they are. 15 W. 28th St. (btwn Broadway and Fifth aves.) ℂ 212/252-1619. www.tadatheater.com. Tickets $18 adults, $8 children. Subway: 1, N, R, W to 28th St.

5 Concerts

The Amato Opera Theatre *(Finds)*   **Ages 5 & up.** One of the oldest arts organizations in the United States, the delightfully intimate Opera Amato in Greenwich Village offers from October through May a special children's series, Opera in Brief— 90-minute shows on Saturday mornings at 11:30am, usually condensed versions of kid-pleasers like *Hansel and Gretel* and *Amahl and the Night Visitors*. This is a wonderful opportunity to introduce your children to the beauty of opera. 319 Bowery (near 2nd St.). ℂ 212/228-8200. www.amato.org. Tickets $30 adults, $25 children, seniors and students. Subway: 6 to Bleecker St.; F, V to Second Ave.

Brooklyn Center for the Performing Arts   Ages 3 & up. The center's Family-Fun Series presents six productions a year, plus an annual December *Nutcracker* ballet ($35 adults, $18 children 12 and under). It's a multicultural grab bag of cultural events appealing to kids—circuses, puppet shows, jugglers, classical-music concerts, plays, and ballet. Performances in 2006 included productions of *Seussical* and *A Kid's Life: The Musical.* The Brooklyn Center Performing Arts Complex, 2009 Campus and Hillel Place (Flatbush and Nostrand aves.), Brooklyn. ℂ 718/951-4500. www.brooklyncenter.com. Tickets $15–$20. Subway: 2 to Flatbush Ave.

Carnegie Hall Family Concerts *(Value)*   **Ages 6 & up.** Six or seven Saturdays a year, October through May, Carnegie Hall presents hour-long concerts at 2pm, preceded by 1pm activities like demonstrations, craft workshops, and storytelling. Performers might include anyone from the Chicago Youth Symphony Orchestra to classical-music stars such as cellist Yo-Yo Ma and clarinetist Richard Stoltzman. Advance reservations recommended. At Carnegie Hall, 881 Seventh Ave (at 57th St.). ℂ 212/247-7800. www.carnegiehall.org. Tickets $8. Subway: N, Q, R, W to 57th St./Seventh Ave.

CarnegieKids *(Value)*   **Ages 3 to 6.** These 45-minute weekday morning concerts are designed especially for preschoolers and kindergarteners, using storytellers and musicians who interact with the children in the audience, letting them sing and move around to the music. The program occurs in November and again in March, Monday through Friday, with shows at 10 and 11:30am. Kaplan Space at Carnegie Hall, corner of 57th St. and Seventh Ave. ℂ 212/247 7800 www.carnegiehall.org. Tickets $3, by mail order or reservation only. Subway: N, Q, R, W to 57th St./Seventh Ave.

Jazz for Young People   Ages 5 & up. Under the aegis of superstar trumpeter Wynton Marsalis, this series consists of 1-hour shows (at 11am and 1pm) on 2 Saturdays a year, one in October and one in May, in Jazz at Lincoln Center's sparkling new Rose Theater in the Time-Warner Center on Columbus Circle. 33 W. 60th St. (at Broadway). ℂ 212/721-6500 for tickets, 212/258-9800 for information. www.jazzatlincolncenter.org. Tickets $30–$60 for 2-performance series. Subway: A, B, C, D, 1 to 59th St./Columbus Circle.

Jazz Standard   Ages 5 & up. The Jazz Standard Youth Orchestra, an ensemble of about 20 gifted high school musicians, entertains during a jazz brunch for children, Sunday from 1 to 3pm (shows start at 2pm) from September through June Delicious food is catered from the acclaimed barbecue restaurant Blue Smoke downstairs. Reservations recommended. 116 E. 27th St. (btwn Park and Lexington aves.). ℂ 212/576-2232. www.jazz standard.com. $5 donation. Subway: 6 to 28th St.

Little Orchestra Society   Ages 3 to 12. Two series—Happy Concerts for Young People (ages 6–12) and Lolli-Pop Concerts (ages 3–5)—are designed to introduce kids to classical music, using first-class professional artists (moonlighting Philharmonic members, New York City Ballet stars, and the like). This organization has been around since the 1950s, and the quality is top-notch. The Lolli-Pop series, held at the **Kaye Playhouse** at Hunter College (68th St. between Park and Lexington aves.), uses cutesy costumed figures to help teach wee ones about music; it is a three-concert series with four performance times for each, two on Saturday and two on Sunday, and it's so popular that you pretty much have to buy a whole series (at $99 a head; $40 for single tickets, if there are any seats left) to get in. It's easier to score tickets for Happy Concerts; there are two Saturday performances for each of the three concerts per year, but they are held in a much larger space, Lincoln Center's **Avery Fisher Hall** (Broadway at 65th St.). Happy Concert subscription prices range from $24 to $126, with individual tickets ranging from $10 to $50. There are also some nonsubscription events every year, like *Peter and the Wolf* and the annual Menotti's *Amahl and the Night Visitors,* a fully staged opera with live animals—the works. Mailing address: 330 W. 42nd, 12th Floor, New York, NY 10036-6902. ℂ 212/971-9500. www.littleorchestra.org.

Meet the Music   Ages 6 to 12. The Chamber Music Society of Lincoln Center puts in its bid for young audiences with this upbeat Sunday afternoon series. Even modern pieces by Aaron Copland or Andrew Lloyd Webber might be performed, so long as they're played by a small group of musicians, one player to a part. With narrators, props, and audience participation, the concerts engage fidgety youngsters admirably. Merkin Concert Hall, 129 W. 67th St. (btwn Broadway and Amsterdam Ave.). ℂ 212/875-5788. www.chambermusicsociety.org. Tickets $28 $50. Subway: 1 to 66th St./Lincoln Center.

Young People's Concerts   Ages 6 to 12. Want to turn your kid into a hard-core classical-music fan? Four Saturdays a year the New York Philharmonic trots out musicians like violin prodigy Sarah Chang and conductors Kurt Mazur and Leonard Slatkin to introduce kids to major selections from the classical repertory—not just the chestnuts like *Eine kleine Nachtmusik,* but also pieces by moderns like George Gershwin and Charles Ives. Topping it off, free 12:45pm interactive Kid Zone Live sessions precede the 2pm concerts. Older kids (12–17) can graduate to Philharmonic Teens, which gives them discount seats to the orchestra's weekday Rush Hour Concerts (at 6:45pm). Often rush tickets can be purchased for select concerts up to ten days before. There are often free pre- and post-concert meet-the-artist events. Avery Fisher Hall, Lincoln

Center, Broadway and 64th St. ℂ **212/721-6500** or 212/875-5656. www.newyorkphilharmonic.org. Tickets $5–$25. Subway: 1 to 66th St./Lincoln Center.

6 Films

If it's standard feature-film fare you want, Manhattan is packed with cinema screens, including the busy 12-screen **Sony Lincoln Square complex** at 68th and Broadway, where each theater entrance evokes a different classic New York movie palace; and the multiplex **Loews** and **AMC Empire** cinemas, both located on West 42nd Street between Broadway and Eighth Avenue. For more unusual films geared for a young audience, here are your choices:

AMNH IMAX Theater   Ages 3 & up. The screen at the Natural History Museum isn't quite as huge as the one at the Sony IMAX (see below), but unless you get out your measuring tape, you'd never know. The main thing is that your whole field of vision is occupied, which somehow doubles the sensory impact of a movie—something to consider before you take young, skittish children inside. You have a choice of IMAX movies every day, some more intense than others, though all have an educational bent. Whether you're in outer space, underwater, or deep in the rainforest, the sights and sounds tend to include a speeding camera taking you on a visual thrill ride that swoops over rising and falling terrain, the hallmark of the IMAX experience.

Buy the combination ticket when you enter, or stop by the ticket counter near the museum's 77th Street entrance. There's a movie every 45 minutes or so, though school groups get first dibs on seats weekday mornings (the public is then admitted on a first-come, first-served basis). The museum is open daily year-round, except on Thanksgiving and Christmas. At the American Museum of Natural History, Central Park W. at 79th St. ℂ 212/769-5200. www.amnh.org. Tickets (includes museum admission) $21 adults, $16 seniors and students over 12, $12 for ages 2–12. Subway: B, C to 81st St./Museum of Natural History.

BAMKids Film Festival   Ages 2 to 13. For 2 days each spring (generally a weekend in Feb or Mar), BAMKids treats its young audience to an array of international feature-length films and shorts. Selections have ranged from animated favorites like *Babar: King of Elephants* to quality classics like *The Red Balloon.* Guest appearances by featured animators and directors make the experience for youngsters even more meaningful. Call for a schedule. At the Brooklyn Academy of Music (BAM) Rose Cinemas, 30 Lafayette Ave., Brooklyn. ℂ **718/636-4130.** www.bam.org. Tickets $10 adults, $6 kids. Subway: B, Q, 2, 3, 4, 5 to Atlantic Ave.; C to Lafayette Ave.; G to Fulton St.; D, M, N, R to Pacific St.

Children's International Film Festival *(Finds*   **Ages 3 & up.** Held in March, this excellent festival brings a wide range of films and videos, from commercial features to animation to shorts and documentaries from around the world, screened at venues around town. And how's this for interactive: Young viewers get to vote to award festival prizes for certain portions of the program. Way cool. 295 Greenwich St. (at Chambers). ℂ 212/349-0330. www.gkids.com. Ticket prices for individual films vary.

Film Factory   Ages 5 & up. Symphony Space's film series for kids groups feature-length films around a common theme, to be shown at 11am on Saturday mornings over the space of a few weeks, with fun follow-up activities. Leonard Nimoy Thalia Movie Theater, Symphony Space, 2537 Broadway (at 95th St.). ℂ **212/864-5400.** www.symphonyspace.org or www.tickets.com. Tickets $10. Box office Tues–Sun noon–7pm. Subway: 1, 2, 3 to 96th St.

Fresh Air Flicks   Ages 5 & up. This is the pedestrian New Yorker's version of a drive-in movie: outdoor movies, screened in New York City parks on summer evenings. The movies may not be first-run (try classics like *Annie Hall, Ghostbusters,* or *West Side Story*), but admission's free, and you can spread out a blanket and have a picnic while you're claiming your spot. Locations include Bryant Park, Washington Square Park, and Riverside Park (at both 70th and 103rd sts.). ℭ **212/NEW-YORK**. www.nycgovparks.org.

Movies for Kids   Ages 4 & up. This special Lincoln Center series shows movies at 2pm sporadically from October through June. The selection each month is organized along a specific theme—one on cars, for instance, included *Chitty Chitty Bang Bang* and *The Phantom Tollbooth.* Most are full-length features, with some shorts or cartoons thrown in; generally these are American films, but occasional series focus on international movies from anywhere from Africa or Iran to Scandinavia. At the Walter Reade Theatre in Lincoln Center, 165 W. 65th St. and Broadway, plaza level. ℭ **212/621-0621**. www.filmlinc.com. Tickets $10 adults, $7 students, $5 children 6–12. Subway: 1 to 66th St./Lincoln Center.

Museum of Television and Radio   Ages 3 & up. What's called the International Children's Television Festival runs in November, offering screenings on Saturday and Sunday afternoons of outstanding live and animated kids' TV shows from around the world. Curated screenings the rest of the year may attract kids, too, like summer 2004's look at TV superhero series. 25 W. 52nd St. (btwn Fifth and Sixth aves.). ℭ **212/621-6800** or 212/621-6600. www.mtr.org. Tickets $10 adults, $8 students, $5 children 12 and under. Subway: E, V to Fifth Ave./53rd St.

New York Public Library   Ages 3 to 8. Along with story hours, children's rooms at several Manhattan branch libraries may run an hour-long program of short films once a month, many of them made from children's books—*Madeline, Curious George, Doctor deSoto,* and so on. Various branches around Manhattan. For a monthly schedule, contact the NYPL at 8 W. 40th St., New York, NY 10018 (ℭ **212/221-7676** or 212/869-8089; www.nypl.org), or stop by any branch to pick up schedule brochure.

Sony IMAX Theater   Ages 3 & up. Not just IMAX but 3-D IMAX—awesome. The screen is eight stories high, and you get this cool headset that puts you in the extraspatial dimension. Needless to say, there isn't a lot of film material for this format and some of the offerings aren't 3-D. But Sony has managed to get movies that go beyond documentaries into actual storytelling features—like *Across the Sea of Time,* which tells of a young Russian immigrant boy searching for relatives in Manhattan (think of it as a live-action *An American Tale*). Features like *Michael Jordan: To the Max* will definitely excite sports fans young and old. Most shows run about 45 minutes to an hour. Target ages for the scheduled films vary, so check ahead—and as always with IMAX, consider whether your youngster is suited to the medium's heightened sensory impact. At Sony Lincoln Square, Broadway and 68th St. ℭ **212/336-5000**. Tickets $15 adults, $12 children 12 and under. Subway: 1 to 66th St./Lincoln Center.

7 Dance

American Ballet Theatre   Ages 8 & up. On this enormous stage, the spring season (May–June) features both modern works and some classic story ballets like *Swan Lake* and *Coppelia* just the thing for budding ballerinas. Check the website for hands-on workshops for youngsters, occasionally held in conjunction with performances. Metropolitan Opera House, Lincoln Center, Broadway and 64th St. ℭ **212/362-6000**. www.abt.org. Tickets $20–$145. Subway: 1 to 66th St./Lincoln Center.

Dance Theater Workshop **Ages 4 & up.** One of the city's leading promoters of modern dance, the workshop presents among other things a Family Matters series, Sunday matinee events appropriate for parents and kids of all ages (not necessarily purely dance). The season usually runs September to June. 219 W. 19th St. (btwn Seventh and Eighth aves.). ℂ 212/924-0077. www.dtw.org. Tickets $10–$20. Subway: C, E to 23rd St.; 1 to 18th St.

Ice Theatre of New York (Value) **Ages 5 & up.** Unlike typical ice-show companies, Ice Theatre leads figure skating strongly in the direction of dance, even commissioning noted nonskating choreographers to create new pieces for their lyrical, intriguing performances. With guest artists like Nancy Kerrigan and Paul Wylie, the skaters take to the ice in free lunchtime shows January through March at **Rockefeller Center** (last Wed of the month) and **Riverbank State Park** (145th St. and Riverside Dr.; last Thurs of the month); other performances (not free) are at the **Sky Rink** at Chelsea Piers (23rd St. at the Hudson River) in October. ℂ 212/929-5811 or 212/307-7171 (Ticketmaster). www.icetheatre.org. Tickets $25 adults, $20 children 12 and under.

Joyce Theater **Ages 6 & up.** This Chelsea theater devoted to modern dance does an admirable job of bringing in young audiences. Touring dance companies booked into the Joyce are asked to design special Saturday family matinees, with dancers showing up in the lower lobby afterwards, still in costume, to meet audience members and give autographs. 175 Eighth Ave. (at 19th St.). ℂ 212/242-0800. www.joyce.org. Tickets $32–$42 adults, $10–$20 kids. Subway: C, E to 23rd St.; 1 to 18th St.

New York City Ballet **Ages 10 & up.** For technique, many critics feel this troupe surpasses its Lincoln Center cousin, the ABT (see above), but young balletomanes may not get the point of NYCB's more abstract pieces, following the tastes of founder George Balanchine. However, this is where the city's best *Nutcracker* is staged every December (see "Seasonal Events," earlier in this chapter). The ballet offers two seasons—April through June and Thanksgiving through February—with nightly performances (except Mon) and weekend matinees. New York State Theater, Lincoln Center, Broadway and 64th St. ℂ 212/870-5570. www.nycballet.com. Tickets $32–$70. Subway: 1 to 66th St./Lincoln Center.

New York Theater Ballet **Ages 5 & up.** Besides its splendid condensed *Nutcracker* (see "Seasonal Events," earlier in this chapter), this classical dance troupe presents three other ballets each season, often based on fairy tales. The quality of the dancing is excellent, and costumes are lovely, though sets are minimal on this relatively small stage. Geared for young audiences, these productions stress the storytelling elements of dance and don't run too long—which makes them great introduction to traditional ballet. At Florence Gould Hall, 55 E. 59th St. (btwn Park and Madison aves.). ℂ 212/355-6160 (theater box office), or 212/307-4100 (Ticketmaster). www.nytb.org. Tickets $15-30. Subway: 4, 5, 6 to 59th St.; N, R, W to Lexington Ave./59th St.

8 Magic Shows

Monday Night Magic **Ages 10 & up.** A fabulous showcase for serious magicians, Monday Night Magic varies from week to week; some performances are less appropriate for children than others (they won't admit anyone under 8 years old), so go on the website to see what this week's program offers. Acts range from hilarious to eerie to borderline raunchy, with card tricks, knife-throwing, balloon tricks, and all the sleight-of-hand you could want. Performances run year-round, every Monday night at

8pm. St. Clements Theater, 423 W. 46th St. (between 9th and 10th aves.). ℂ 212/615-6432 or www. telecharge.com for tickets. www.mondaynightmagic.com. Tickets $30–$33. Subway: A, C, E to 42nd St.

9 Puppet Shows

Leni Suib Puppet Playhouse Ages 2 to 5. The Leni Suib Puppet Playhouse has been running for years and years; Leni Suib is a major player in the puppet world, up there with Bill Baird and Burr Tillstrom. Every weekend from September to May, kids can take in a different show, with different puppets and a different theme (nonpuppet antics, like juggling and mime, are often thrown in, just to keep things hopping). Showtimes are Saturday, usually at 10:30am, noon, and 1:30pm (call for exact times). Reservations aren't accepted (except for groups of 10 or more), so get there 20 minutes before showtime to be sure of a seat. At Asphalt Green, 555 E. 90th St. (btwn York and East End aves.). ℂ 212/369-8890. Tickets $8 (subject to change). Subway 4, 5, 6 to 86th St.

Papageno Puppet Theater (Finds Ages 3 to 9. Named after the famous character from Mozart's *Magic Flute,* this low-key children's puppet company led by former opera singer Susan Delery Whedon presents musical shows using hand and rod puppets, based on familiar stories like *Thumbelina, Peter and the Wolf,* and *Hansel and Gretel,* as well as more modern tales like *Puff the Magic Dragon.* Performances are Saturday and Sundays at 11:30am and 1:30pm every other weekend throughout the school year. Reservations required. 462 Columbus Ave. (in party room of Ray's Pizza), between 82nd and 83rd sts. ℂ 212/874-3297. Tickets $7. Subway: B, C to 81st St./Museum of Natural History.

Puppetworks—Park Slope Ages 3 to 7. Using both hand puppets and marionettes, these puppeteers retell classic children's stories. The season runs year-round, with performances on weekends at 12:30 and 2:30pm. Reservations are required. 338 6th Ave., Brooklyn. ℂ 718/965-3391. www.puppetworks.org. Tickets $8 adults, $7 children. Subway: F to 7th Ave.

Swedish Cottage Marionette Theatre (Value Ages 3 to 10. This alpine-looking cottage holds a small stage where near-life-size marionettes prance and caper in hour-long productions of classic fairy tales—recorded soundtrack, spot lighting, full scenery, the works. Because these are such elaborate shows, one production (usually a classic fairy tale) is designed per year and performed year-round. A puppeteer prefaces performances with a helpful mini seminar on puppetry. The pace is leisurely, and the sense of humor is gentle. Call 3 or 4 weeks in advance for a reservation—there are usually one or two shows a day, but they fill up fast with school groups and birthday parties. Closed Mondays in the school year, closed Sundays in summer. In Central Park (West Dr. at 81st St.). ℂ 212/988-9093. www.centralparknyc.org. Tickets $6 adults, $5 children; reservations required. Closed mid-Aug through Sept. Subway: B, C to 79th St.

10 Spectator Sports

Brooklyn Cyclones (Value Ages 6 & up. The hardest-to-get sports ticket in town just may be for this Mets-affiliated Class A minor-league franchise out in Brooklyn, which debuted in Coney Island in 2001. Folks line up before dawn the day season tickets go on sale, and individual tickets often sell out within an hour after online ticketing opens. However, in keeping with the Cyclones' populist profile, there are always a limited number of general admission tickets offered at the box office at 10am on home game days. KeySpan Park strives for the way-back-when feel of the Brooklyn

Milestones in New York Sports History

In all the major pro sports, the lucrative New York area market sustains at least two teams, and at some period (baseball in the 1950s, hockey today), three teams. New Yorkers, spoiled by years of sport success, aren't big on rooting for underdogs (with the exception of the 1969 Mets). Then again, we aren't used to having underdogs, maybe because New York money enables team owners to buy the best talent available, from Babe Ruth to Wayne Gretzky to Alex Rodriguez. New York fans, hooked on those championship titles, still can't get enough. Here's the sort of thing we're talking about:

- **1921–23:** Two New York baseball teams—the Giants and the Yankees— meet in the World Series for 3 consecutive years. The Giants win the first 2 years; the Yankees finally take the title in 1923, establishing a taste for victory they'll never shake.
- **1927–28:** Two consecutive World Series victories for the Yankees, both of them four-game sweeps. Babe Ruth sets his home-run record at Yankee Stadium in 1927.
- **1928:** New York Rangers win hockey's Stanley Cup for the first (but not the last) time.
- **1936–37:** Two more Yankees–Giants World Series match-ups—the Yankees win both times.
- **1938–39:** The Yankees continue their streak, sweeping the Cubs and then the Reds to make four World Series titles in a row.
- **1941:** The Yankees beat the Brooklyn Dodgers in the World Series.
- **1947:** Another Dodgers vs. Yankees Series; the Yankees win.

Dodgers' old Ebbets Field, with only 7,500 seats, alcohol-free sections, billboards advertising local small companies, and a view of Coney Island's parachute jump and boardwalk. A great place to spot good young players on their way up, and to recapture the charm that made baseball America's Game. KeySpan Park, 1904 Surf Avenue between W. 17th and 19th sts., Coney Island. ✆ 718/449-8497. www.brooklyncyclones.com. Tickets $7. Subway: D, F, Q to Coney Island/Stillwell Ave.

New Jersey Devils **Ages 8 & up.** Winners of the 1995 and 2000 Stanley Cups, the Devils have stolen the thunder from the New York area's older hockey teams, the Rangers and the Islanders. The season runs from October to mid-April, and though much of the arena gets sold out with season tickets, individual tickets for cheaper seats may be available. It's always worth checking the day of a game to see if some seats have been released. Continental Airlines Arena, East Rutherford, NJ. ✆ 201/507-8900, 212/307-7171 (for single-game tickets), or 212/307-7171 (Ticketmaster). www.newjerseydevils.com. Tickets $20–$90. Parking $8. For game-time bus service from Manhattan's Port Authority Bus Terminal, call New Jersey Transit at ✆ 800/772-2222.

New Jersey Nets **Ages 8 & up.** The 2001–02 season was a magical one for the Nets, who won the Eastern Conference championship and battled the LA Lakers for the national title. Who could have known that trading Stephon Marbury for Jason

- **1949–56:** New York dominates baseball, with one of its teams winning the World Series every year—the Yankees for 5 years straight, and then the Giants in 1954, the Dodgers in 1955 (finally beating the Yankees!), only to have the Yankees vanquish the Dodgers again in 1956. Six World Series in this 8-year period are "Subway Series"—the Yankees face the Dodgers five times and the Giants once.
- **1961:** Yankee Roger Maris breaks Babe Ruth's home-run record.
- **1969:** The New York Jets win the Super Bowl; the "Miracle" Mets win the World Series.
- **1970:** The New York Knicks take the NBA championship (and again in 1973).
- **1980–83:** The New York Islanders dominate hockey, winning the Stanley Cup 4 years in a row.
- **1986:** The Mets win another World Series.
- **1987:** The Giants win the Super Bowl (and again in 1991).
- **1994:** The Rangers win another Stanley Cup.
- **1995:** This year, it's the New Jersey Devils' turn to win the Stanley Cup.
- **1998–2000:** The Yankees make regular World Series visits, winning three in a row, including the first-ever Subway Series against the Mets in 2000.
- **2000:** The New Jersey Devils win another Stanley Cup.
- **2001:** In a highly emotional post–September 11 end of season, the Yankees win their fourth consecutive World Series berth—only to lose in the seventh game to the Arizona Diamondbacks.
- **2003:** The New Jersey Devils win the Stanley Cup once more.

Kidd would pay off so well? With the Knicks sliding so badly, the Nets are the metropolitan area's current b-ball darlings. The regular season runs from November to mid-April. Continental Airlines Arena, East Rutherford, NJ. © **800/7NJ-NETS**, 201/935-3900 (for single-game tickets), or 201/507-8900 (Ticketmaster). www.nba.com/nets. Tickets $15–$500. Parking $8.

New York Giants   Ages 8 & up. With a seeming revolving door of coaches, the Giants dance in and out of contention. Because football teams play only once a week, there are few home games in the course of their September-to-December season, and just about the whole stadium goes with season ticket holders—to get tickets you have to know somebody or *be* somebody or spring for a scalper. On game days, there's a New Jersey Transit bus from Port Authority Terminal, Eighth Avenue between 40th and 42nd streets—call © **212/564-1114** for information. **Warning:** It's an open-air stadium, so it gets bitterly cold by the end of the season. At Giants Stadium in the Meadowlands, East Rutherford, NJ. © **201/935-8222** or 201/935-3900 for single-game tickets. www.giants.com. Tickets $40 and $50. Parking $10.

New York Islanders   Ages 8 & up. A lively force in recent NHL seasons, the Islanders skate on their home ice out on Long Island (hence the name) from October to mid-April. Take the Long Island Rail Road from Penn Station, Seventh Avenue between 31st and 33rd streets, to Hempstead (bus service nearby) or Westbury (take a taxi to the Nassau Coliseum). To reach the coliseum by car, take the M4 exit off the Meadowbrook Parkway. At Nassau Coliseum, Hempstead Tpk., Uniondale, NY. ℂ **800/882-ISLES,** or 631/888-9000 (Ticketmaster). www.newyorkislanders.com. Tickets $25–$140.

New York Jets   Ages 8 & up. Playing in the same stadium as the Giants, the Jets have had some loser seasons in the recent past, but Jets fans are die-hards, and both individual and season tickets are totally sold out—you'll need connections, ticket agents, or a scalper to attend a game, and be sure they will take their profits off the top. On game days there's a New Jersey Transit bus from Port Authority Terminal, Eighth Avenue between 40th and 42nd streets—call ℂ **212/564-1114** for information. The regular season runs September through December. At Giants Stadium in the Meadowlands, East Rutherford, NJ. ℂ **516/560-8200.** www.newyorkjets.com. Tickets $55 and $70. Parking $10.

New York Knicks   Ages 8 & up. The Knicks play 41 regular-season home games a year from November to mid-April. Though the team has suffered from injuries and managerial changes the past few volatile seasons, getting tickets is still tough, unless you're Spike Lee. There's still hope: On the day of the game, the box office sometimes releases a small number of tickets (call ℂ **212/465-6040**), and there are always scalpers who'll be happy to let you pay top dollar for tickets. At Madison Square Garden, Seventh Ave. between 31st and 33rd Sts. ℂ **212/465-MSG1,** 212/465-JUMP, 800/4NBA-TIX, or 212/307-7171 (Ticketmaster). www.nyknicks.com. Tickets $40–$285. Subway: A, C, E to 34th St./Penn Station; 1, 2, 3 to 34th St.

New York Liberty   Ages 5 & up. The success of professional women's basketball surprised all the pundits, who never expected the public to respond so immediately to its brand of clean, fast, non-trash-talking basketball. Kids, especially girls, have been an important part of the Liberty's audience all along (it helps that its June–Aug season coincides with school vacation); plenty of on-court activities during the breaks, along with a lively dog mascot who patrols the stands looking for kids to shake paws with, boosts the entertainment quotient for younger ones. At Madison Square Garden, Seventh Ave. between 31st and 33rd sts. ℂ **212/465-MSG1** or 877/WNBA-TIX (Ticketmaster), 212/564-WNBA for info. www.nyliberty.com. Tickets $10–$230. Subway: A, C, E to 34th St./Penn Station; 1, 2, 3 to 34th St.

New York MetroStars   Ages 6 & up. Playing from March to October, the MetroStars have built an audience from all those kids and parents who've been bitten by the soccer bug through youth leagues, and they are usually contenders for the U.S. Cup. Games are generally Wednesday nights or weekend days or evenings. Sitting outdoors in the Meadowlands is a lot nicer in summer than in November. For game-time bus service from Manhattan's Port Authority Bus Terminal, call New Jersey Transit (ℂ **800/772-2222**); **NY Waterway** (ℂ **800/533-3779**) also offers a service for $35. At Giants Stadium in the Meadowlands, East Rutherford, NJ. ℂ **201/935-3900;** for tickets, 888/4-**METROTIX,** or 212/307-7171 and 201/507-8900 (Ticketmaster). www.metrostars.com. Tickets $18–$60. Parking $10.

New York Mets   All ages. With the 2005 hiring of Omar Minaya as general manager and William Randolph as head coach, the Mets have become National League contenders in a big way, dominating their division throughout the 2006 season (take that, Atlanta Braves). Open-air Shea Stadium makes a fine place to spend a summer afternoon; seats cost considerably less than they do for the other sports, and unlike the theater, you don't have to worry about keeping your child quiet. Even night games are a distinct possibility—if your kids get bored or sleepy, you can always leave early. The regular season runs mid-April through early October; throughout this stretch, 81 home games are played at Shea. Tickets are best purchased in advance, but you may still be able to get tickets at the stadium on game day if you don't care about sitting close. The food is typical arena fare: nachos, hot dogs, and soda. **NY Waterway** runs a Mets Express ferry to the ballpark ($14 adults, $10 children 11 and under, or $50 for game ticket plus transportation); call ℂ **800/533-3779** or order from www.ny waterway.com. Ferries depart from Weehawken, New Jersey, South Street Seaport, 34th Street at the East River, and 90th Street at the East River. At Shea Stadium in Flushing, Queens. ℂ **718/507-METS** or 718/507-TIXX. www.mets.com. Tickets $9–$43, free for children under 32 in. Subway: 7 to Shea Stadium.

New York Rangers   Ages 8 & up. The Rangers play 41 hockey games, mostly at night, at Madison Square Garden during their season, from October to mid-April. Celebrities and CEOs pay as much as $500 for prized behind-the-bench seats, but in "Blue Heaven"—the cheap seats high above the ice—true hockey fans make Rangers games an audience participation sport. Rangers tickets usually sell out a couple of months before the season starts, so buy in advance. At Madison Square Garden, Seventh Ave. between 31st and 33rd sts. ℂ **212/465-MSG1** or 212/307-7171 (Ticketmaster), 212/308-NYRS for info. www.newyorkrangers.com. Tickets $25–$150. Subway: A, C, E to 34th St./Penn Station; 1, 2, 3 to 34th St.

New York Yankees   All ages. Yankees fans have never minded watching their team roll effortlessly over all the competition. The beloved but aging team that won consistently from 1996 on was inevitably dismantled at the end of the 2001 season, leaving only Derek Jeter and Bernie Williams, but owner George Steinbrenner spent megabucks to acquire a whole new team of stars such as Alex Rodriguez, Gary Sheffield, Hideki Matsui, and Johnny Damon (late of the rival Boston Red Sox). And guess what? They're all Yankees now and we love them! New York's American League team plays 81 home games at grand old Yankee Stadium from mid-April to early October; order tickets in advance or buy them at the stadium ticket office on game day (when they're playing well, ticket availability gets tight toward fall). The refreshments here run in the traditional peanuts and popcorn and Cracker Jack vein, along with hot dogs and jumbo sodas. Show up a couple of hours early and you may be able to watch batting practice. To make it a really special outing, take the **NY Waterway** Yankee Clipper ferry to the stadium ($14 adults, $10 children 11 and under, or $56 for game ticket plus transportation); call ℂ **800/533-3779** or order from www.nywaterway.com. Ferries depart from Weehawken, New Jersey, South Street Seaport, 34th Street at the East River, and 90th Street at the East River. At Yankee Stadium in the Bronx. ℂ **718/293-6000** or 212/307-1212 (Ticketmaster). www.yankees.com. Tickets $8–$65. Subway: B, D, 4 to 161st St.

Staten Island Yankees *Value* **Ages 6 & up.** The Yankees' Class A minor-league team hasn't quite achieved the retro glamour of their local rivals the Brooklyn Cyclones, but the quality of play is high, and their ballpark is a pleasantly low-key place to watch the major-league stars of tomorrow show off their goods. Best of all, it's easy to get to, being within walking distance from the Staten Island Ferry terminal (all this and a cool boat ride, too!). Richmond County Bank Ballpark at St. George, 75 Richmond Terrace, Staten Island. ℂ **718/720-9200.** www.siyanks.com. Tickets $8–$18. Parking $4.

11 Story Hours

Babylicious   The weekly Thursday morning story hour at this cozy Tribeca children's boutique is geared for youngsters aged 3 months to 4 years, so expect the picture books to be short and sweet—and expect everyone to be tolerant of wee ones' natural behavior. 51 Hudson St. ℂ **212/406-7440.** Subway: 1 to Franklin St.

Barnes & Noble **Ages 2 to 7.** Many of these bookstores hold lively, well-attended weekend story hours. Call ahead, or check www.barnesandnoble.com to make sure of dates and times, but in general the East 86th Street branch holds Saturday story hours at 11am, Citicorp branch Saturdays at 2pm, Union Square Sundays at 2:30, Astor Place Mondays at 4:30pm, and Sixth Avenue at Eighth Street Wednesdays at 3:30pm. (1) 240 E. 86th St. (btwn Second and Third aves.). © **212/794-1962.** Subway: 4, 5, 6 to 86th St. (2) 2289 Broadway (at 82nd St.). © **212/362-8835.** Subway: 1 to 79th St. (3) 1972 Broadway (at 66th St.). © 212/ **595-6859.** Subway: 1 to 66th St./Lincoln Center. (4) Citicorp Building (at Third Ave. and 54th St.). © **212/750-8033.** Subway: E, V to Lexington Ave./53rd St. (5) 675 Sixth Ave. (at 21st St.) . © **212/727-1227.** Subway: F, V to 23rd St. (6) Union Sq., 33 E. 17th St. (btwn Broadway and Park Ave.). © **212/253-0810.** Subway: N, Q, R, W, 4, 5, 6 to 14th St.; L to Union Sq. (7) 396 Sixth Ave. at 8th St. © **212/674-8780.** Subway: B, C. D. E. F. V to W. 4th St. (8) 4 Astor Place (btwn Broadway and Lafayette St.). © 212/ **420-1322.** Subway: 6 to Astor Place.

Books of Wonder **Ages 3 to 7.** This great Chelsea shop runs friendly story hours on Sunday at noon. 18 W. 18th St. (btwn Fifth and Sixth aves.). © **212/989-3270.** www.booksof wonder.net. Subway: 1 to 18th St.

Borders Books At these large, welcoming chain stores, well-stocked children's departments usually hold weekly story hours for pre-schoolers: the Park Avenue branch has a Saturday 1:30pm story time, Columbus Circle holds them Wednesdays at 2:15pm, and the Second Avenue store has them at 3pm on Thursdays. Check www. borders.com for updates. (1) 10 Columbus Circle (at Eighth Ave.). © **212/823-9775.** Subway A, B, C, D, 1 to 59th St./Columbus Circle. (2) 461 Park Ave. (at 57th St.). © **212/980-6785.** Subway: 4, 5, 6 to 59th St. (3) 550 Second Ave. (at 31st St.) in Kips Bay Plaza. © **212/685-3938.** Subway: 6 to 33rd St. (4) 2 Penn Plaza (7th Ave. and 31st St.). © **212/244-1814.** Subway: 1, 2, 3 to 34th St. (5) 100 Broadway (at Pine St). © **212/964-1988.** Subway: 2, 3, 4, 5 to Wall St.

Bryant Park In this handsome Midtown park behind the central branch of New York Public Library, story hours are conducted on alternate summer Saturdays at noon, in cooperation with the excellent Bank Street College Book Store. Bryant Park, 42nd Street between Fifth and Sixth aves. For details contact Bank Street College Book Store, © 212/ **678-1654** or www.bankstreetbooks.com. Subway: B, D, F, V, 7 to 42nd St.

Central Park **Ages 2 to 8.** June through September, there are story hours here every Saturday at 11am, rain or shine. At the Hans Christian Andersen Statue, on the west side of Conservatory Water (at 74th St.). www.centralparknyc.org. Subway: 6 to 77th St.

Logos Bookstore This pleasant Upper East Side shop holds story hours every Monday at 3pm. 1575 York Ave. (btwn 83rd and 84th sts.). © **212/517-7292.** Subway: 4, 5, 6 to 86th St.

New York Public Library (Value) **Ages 2 to 8.** Nearly every weekday, some Manhattan branch library holds a story hour or shows short films about children's books or holds some kind of cool workshop—and it's all free. You can contact the NYPL at 8 W. 40th St., New York, NY 10018 (© **212/221-7676**), for a monthly brochure of events for children, or visit its website at www.nypl.org/events. Better yet, stop by the **Donnell Library,** 20 W. 53rd St. (© **212/621-0618**), the main children's branch for the system, to pick up a brochure—while you're there, don't miss the original Pooh animals and Mary Poppins's umbrella on display. Various branches around Manhattan.

Scholastic Store   Weekly story hours are held Tuesdays and Thursdays at 11am at the big, bright SoHo flagship of the Scholastic publishing house. Saturdays often feature interactive events planned around Scholastic titles—which luckily include such winners as the Harry Potter books, Klutz activity kits, and the adventures of Captain Underpants. Check events at www.scholasticstore.com. 557 Broadway (btwn Prince and Spring) ℂ 212/343-6166. Subway: N, R, W to Prince St.

12 Arcades

Chelsea Piers AMF Bowling   **Ages 8 & up.** A well-lighted, clean space at the back of this bowling alley has a dozen or so relatively wholesome games involving car-driving or shooting or ball-throwing skills. Makes for a good amusement stop if you're at the Piers anyway. Between Piers 59 and 60 at Chelsea Piers, 23rd St. and the West Side Hwy. at the Hudson River. ℂ 212/835-2695. www.chelseapiers.com. Subway: C, E, F, N, R, V, W, 1 to 23rd St. Bus: M23 across 23rd St.

ESPN Zone   **Ages 8 & up.** Games here, on an upper floor of this clean and glossy theme restaurant (thus less walk-in street trade, which is a plus), tend to be sports-oriented—baseball, hockey, soccer, driving simulators, that sort of thing, rather than sci-fi–based shoot-'em-ups. Children under 18 are not admitted without an accompanying adult, which lessens the teen hangout factor. 1472 Broadway (at 42nd St.). ℂ 212/921-3776. www.espnzone.com. Subway: N, Q, R, S, W, 1, 2, 3, 7 to 42nd St./Times Sq.

Game Time Nation   **Ages 8 & up.** This pseudo-living-room setting offers a public place to play video games on platforms like Xbox and PlayStation 2. Fees vary according to whether or not you're playing with a friend or whether you're joining an online game. You get your own couch and coffee table, just like home; games are projected onto a 32-inch flat screen TV, which is sure better than home for most kids I know. The slacker clientele is cool with kids, and you can buy refreshments on-site (a necessity for those marathon sessions . . .). 111 E. 12th St. (btwn Fourth and Third aves.). ℂ212/228-4260. www.gametimenation.com. From $4 per half-hr., single player, up to $26 per 4-hr. double-player session. Subway: L, N, Q, R, W, 4, 5, 6 to Union Square.

11

Side Trips from New York City

Though New York City has enough attractions to keep even the most active child busy and interested, sometimes it's a relief to get away from the jangle of honking horns and crowded streets for a little while. When the weather's nice, a day trip from Manhattan can be just the ticket.

The following places are all within an hour of the city. A car would be the most convenient way to travel, but all are also reachable by train (or even, in the case of Philipsburg Manor, boat).

If you're interested in exploring farther afield, you might want to check out *Frommer's Wonderful Weekends from New York City.*

1 Edison National Historic Site

45 min. W. of Manhattan

"I always invented to obtain money to go on inventing," Thomas Edison once said. Yes, he was a gifted chemist and visionary, but he was also a shrewd businessman who amassed a fortune. While the Edison Laboratories in West Orange, New Jersey, were still under renovation at press time, that site is expected to reopen in 2007; meanwhile, Edison's imposing mansion a mile from the labs gives you a personal glimpse into the life of this man whose very name became synonymous with "genius."

ESSENTIALS

If you're driving, take either the Lincoln or Holland tunnels (the George hat traffic slows down the tunnels) and take either the Garden State Parkway or the New Jersey Turnpike to I-280 westbound (exit 145 from the Garden State, exit 15-W from the NJ Turnpike). Follow I-280 west to exit 10; turn right at the end of the exit ramp, go to the end of the street, and make a left onto Main Street. At the second light, Park Way, you can turn left to reach the Edison home, Glenmont (pass through a gatehouse, follow Park Way to Glen Ave., turn right, then left onto Honeysuckle Ave.). If you continue on Main Street two more blocks you will reach Lakeside Avenue and the Edison Laboratories.

New Jersey Transit (℗ **800/772-2222;** www.njtransit.com) bus #21 takes you to the Mississippi Loop in West Orange; a cab from there to Glenmont costs around $TK.

WHAT TO SEE & DO

Glenmont   Already a successful inventor and businessman, Edison bought this grand 29-room red Queen-Anne-style mansion in Llewellyn Park for his second wife, Mina. All the original furnishings are here. Downstairs rooms reflect the formal Victorian style of the era, with lots of ornate carved wood, damask wall-coverings, and stained-glass windows; things get comfier upstairs in the family living room, where

Edison's children sometimes helped him look up scientific references in shelves full of books. In the master bedroom, you can see the imposing bed where all three Edison children were born, and where Edison himself died. An heiress in her own right, Mina presided over the elegant mansion, raising their children and throwing lavish dinner parties, which workaholic Thomas did his best to avoid. As a businessman, Edison saw the benefits of putting on a high-class social front, but he didn't enjoy socializing. One thing's for sure: this was probably the first house in the neighborhood with a phonograph, let alone the Home Projecting Kinetoscope—the Edison children must have been very popular for play dates.

Honeysuckle Ave., Llewellyn Park, West Orange NJ. € 973/324-9973. www.nps.gov/edis. Admission free. Wed–Sun 9am–5pm; tours on the hour 10am-4pm. Closed Dec 25 and Jan 1.

The Edison Laboratories   Though Edison's first lab was in Menlo Park, New Jersey, this larger West Orange complex was in operation for over 40 years and accounted for over half of his patents. Notice how closely the ivy-covered red-brick buildings are set together—Edison designed it this way so he wouldn't waste too much time scurrying from chemistry lab to machine shop to drafting room. The kids may be surprised to learn that, of the 1,093 patents credited to Edison—the most any American has ever obtained—many were actually invented by other scientists who worked for him. Walking around the restored lab complex, you can visualize his team of some 200 researchers, hired to refine and improve existing inventions. There were light bulbs before Edison's, but his was more reliable, long-lasting, and easy to manufacture; the telegraph, the phonograph, the stock ticker, the movie camera and projector were all devices that other scientists pursued at the same time, but Edison's versions *worked better*. Another 10,000 workers in the attached factory (not part of the historic site) then mass-produced these inventions for commercial sale—he controlled the entire cycle. Accessories, too—there's a music recording studio you can peek into, where Edison engineers made sure phonograph customers would have something to play on their new machines.

11 Main St. and Lakeside Ave., West Orange NJ. € 973/736-0550. www.nps.gov/edis. Admission free. Hours to be announced upon reopening.

2 Garden City, Long Island

50 min. E of Manhattan

Across the road from the Nassau Coliseum, one of the New York area's best-kept secrets is quietly growing into a museum powerhouse. Eventually, this Mitchel Field complex is planned also to include a science-and-technology museum, a firefighting museum, and even a vintage carousel. But the two museums that have already opened definitely make this worth the hour's drive from Manhattan. We spent a day here—the morning at the children's museum, the afternoon at the aviation museum—and there wasn't time enough to see and do everything.

ESSENTIALS

If you're driving, take the Long Island Expressway to exit 38 for the Northern Parkway. You'll quickly see signs for the Meadowbrook Parkway South (exit 31A). From the Meadowbrook, take exit M4 West, which will take you onto Charles Lindbergh Boulevard. The museums are on the right side after the traffic light.

Long Island Rail Road (🕿 **718/217-5477;** www.mta.nyc.ny.us/lirr) trains from Penn Station will take you to the Garden City station or the Mineola station. One-way adult fares are $5.25 to $8.25, depending on time of travel. A cab ride from either station to the museum costs about $6.

WHAT TO SEE & DO

The Long Island Children's Museum The two-story LICM echoes with children's excitement. The ground floor is geared for the younger set, with a special **Totspot** play area for under-5s, the ever-popular **bubble room,** and a mazelike climbing structure called **Climb-It** (which cleverly has a ramp, so it's wheelchair-accessible). The **Toolbox** area attracts young tinkerers to its carpentry worktables, where kids can discover the principles of simple machines, and my kids enjoyed **Sandy Island,** which was much more of a science lab than we expected—various stations demonstrated wave motions, sediment patterns, and erosion, with plenty of sand samples to peer at under microscopes.

Older kids will gravitate upstairs. In the **Communication Station,** kids explore various modes of communication, from speaking tubes to Morse Code telegraphs to telephones. The **mock TV station** is a big hit—your kids may want to see themselves projected on a giant TV screen as big-time news broadcasters—and the adjacent radio station lets them practice being DJs and putter around with sound effects. We had a ball in the **Music Gallery,** testing different drums and xylophones; the sequestered **Lullaby Nook** here is the perfect place to calm down wee ones, with its headphones tuned to restful songs from around the world. **It's Alive** focuses on animal habitats (including human ones), and **Bricks and Sticks** is full of young block-builders. Children 6 and up enjoy an exhibit called **What If You Couldn't . . .,** which aims to sensitize kids to disabilities: There are wheelchairs and crutches to experiment with, Braille to touch, lenses showing what the world looks like to people with diminished sight, a phone that plays only muted conversation, and writing as it might appear to a dyslexic child. But my personal favorite area was **Patterns,** which sounds simple—computer monitors and wooden blocks where you can fiddle around with recurrent visual images—but made us delay lunch for at least 40 minutes, even though we were starving. I'm making a beeline for it on our next visit.

Like all children's museums, this one can get noisy and chaotic at times, depending on the ages of the school groups milling around. The ticket policy is set up to prevent overcrowding, though, so call in advance to get a time slot.

11 Davis Ave., Garden City, NY (museum entrance on Charles Lindbergh Blvd.). 🕿 516/224-5800. www.licm.org. Admission $9, free for children under 1 and members. Tickets are sold for specific time slots when crowded; in inclement weather, call ahead for schedule. Wed–Sun 10am–5pm Sept–June; Tues–Sun 10am–5pm July–Aug.

Cradle of Aviation Museum ☆ *Finds* Right next door to the Long Island Children's Museum, this is like a miniversion of Washington's Air and Space Museum, fascinating but not overwhelmingly big. It's focused on Long Island's aviation history—this site is, after all, where Lindbergh took off on his historic flight to Paris. Famed aviatrix Harriet Quimby trained here, and major companies like Curtiss and Grumman were located a stone's throw away. The local-history hook really means something.

Walk into the glass atrium and there's a supersonic F-11 Tiger suspended overhead; from the gallery's catwalk entrance, you can gaze straight ahead at an authentic 1909 Bleriot monoplane, a *Spirit of St. Louis* sister plane, and Grumman Wildcats, Hellcats, and Tomcats; around the corner, in the space exploration section, there's an original

1972 lunar landing module displayed in a rugged mock moonscape. A new hangar, opened in August 2004, displays even more of the collection's really big aircrafts, including an F-14 and the nose of a speed-record-setting El Al 707. There are plenty of hands-on activities—a hot-air balloon you can inflate, cockpits you can climb into, and a mesmerizing monitor displaying current air traffic across the U.S. For an additional $2 you can spend 20 minutes executing a simulated mission to Mars, an activity that includes 4 minutes on a better-than-average motion simulator. There's also an IMAX show every hour. Loads of volunteers, many of them retired engineers and pilots, mill about, eager to share their knowledge; a number of them personally helped to restore the planes on display.

1 Davis Ave., Garden City, NY (museum entrance on Charles Lindbergh Blvd.). © 516/572-4111. www.cradleof aviation.org. Admission $9 adults, $8 kids 2–14; IMAX tickets $8.50 adults, $6.50 kids 2–14; museum plus IMAX $15 adults, $11 kids 2–14. Sept–May Tues–Sun 10am–5pm; holiday Mon 9:30am–5pm; daily 9:30am–5pm June–Aug. Closed Dec 25 and Jan 1.

WHERE TO EAT

The Long Island Children's Museum has a cafeteria space, but you'll have to bring your own food or buy snacks at the vending machines. The Cradle of Aviation is better equipped foodwise, with the **Red Planet Cafe** selling sandwiches, packaged salads, and drinks. Otherwise, you can drive to the end of Charles Lindbergh Boulevard, keeping right at the fork, and turn left onto Stewart Avenue for the usual mix of chain restaurants in strip malls.

3 Playland

50 min. N of Manhattan

Remember the movie *Big*, when Tom Hanks's younger self made his fateful wish to be big after missing the height requirement for a roller coaster? That was shot at Playland. A pleasant antidote to the big, overhyped mega-theme parks that proliferate in the rest of the country, this old-timey collection of rides and games in a conveniently close seaside suburb is like a window into a kinder, gentler past.

ESSENTIALS

By **car**, take I-95 north to exit 19 in Rye (Playland Pkwy.) and then follow the signs to Playland. Parking costs $5 Tuesday to Friday, $7 Saturday and Sunday, and $10 holidays. Senior citizens with a valid ID only pay $1 except for holidays.

Metro-North Railroad trains take about 45 minutes from Grand Central Terminal to the Rye station. Adult one-way fares are $8.50 peak and $6.25 off-peak; children travel for 75¢. From the Rye station, take bus no. 75 to Playland. Metro-North also organizes Playland packages, which include train and bus fare and a book of Playland tickets. These packages are likely to be cheaper than buying train tickets and Playland tickets separately; call Metro-North (© **800/METRO-INFO** or 212/532-4900; www.mta.nyc.ny.us/mnr, or www.mtainfo.com) for details.

ENJOYING THE PARK

No mere rinky-dink midway, Playland is actually listed on the National Register of Historic Places. In 1923, the Westchester County Park Commission decided to create an "unequaled seaside public park to provide clean, wholesome recreation for the people of Westchester County"; Playland opened in 1928, right on Long Island Sound, and has lived up to its promise ever since. It's been kept up beautifully, with neat landscaping, landmark Art Deco buildings, and old-fashioned charm: striped awnings, painted wooden fences enclosing the rides, and festive-looking ticket booths.

Playland features so many rides, food stalls, games, and other amusements, I can't list them all. Kids 5 and under should be steered straight to **Kiddyland,** which has rides tailored to their size like The Kiddy Whip, Kiddyland Bumper Cars, and the Demolition Derby. For older kids, the most thrilling rides are probably the vintage wooden **Dragon Coaster** (tame by Busch Gardens standards, but enough to make me lose my lunch), the **Hurricane Coaster,** the **Crazy Mouse,** and **Power Surge.** My daughter and I, however, had more fun on retro rides like the **Ferris wheel;** the **Whip;** and best of all, the one-of-a-kind **Derby Riders,** a circular track where you plunge forward on steel horses that race twice as fast as carousel nags. I'm embarrassed to tell you how many times we rode that one. Plan on several hours here; your kids will insist on it.

In addition to the rides, Playland has a beach, a pool, an ice rink, minigolf, and a lake for boating, which are open seasonally.

Playland Pkwy., Rye, NY. ℂ 914/813-7010. www.westchestergov.com. Free admission, but rides each require 2-4 points from a point card: $20 for a 24-point card, $28 for a 36-point card, $35 for a 6-hr unlimited ride card. May–Sept noon–midnight; days of operation vary (check website for details).

WHERE TO EAT

Playland offers many types of food in **concession stands**—and just the kind of junky food kids go crazy for. There are also attractive picnic areas.

4 Philipsburg Manor

45–50 min. N of Manhattan

Leafy, suburban Tarrytown is one of those Hudson Valley towns that has been there since colonial days and still maintains pockets of quiet charm. It's a great place to visit the past, since there are four historic homes in relative proximity: Philipsburg Manor, Sunnyside (Washington Irving's home), Van Cortlandt Manor in Croton-on-Hudson, and the Rockefeller estate, Kykuit. Of the four, Philipsburg offers the most for children, but you could easily visit two homes in 1 day if your crew has the stamina.

ESSENTIALS

By **car,** take I-95 or the Henry Hudson Parkway/Saw Mill River Parkway north to the New York State Thruway (I-87), and go west toward the Tappan Zee Bridge. Get off I-87 at exit 9, Tarrytown, the last exit before the Tappan Zee Bridge. Go left on NY 119 and then take a quick right onto U.S. 9 north. Philipsburg Manor is 2 miles north on the left.

Metro-North (ℂ 800/METRO-INFO or 212/532-4900; www.mta.nyc.ny.us/mnr) offers local train service from Grand Central Terminal directly to Philipsburg Manor (a 50-min. ride) or express train service to Tarrytown (a 40-min. ride). One-way adult fares are $7 to $9.25, depending on when you travel; children's fares are 75¢ (ages 5–11 with an adult). If you get off at the Philipse Manor station, you can walk to your destination (⅓ mile). From the Tarrytown station, you'll need to take a cab, which costs about $6. Call for details.

NY Waterway (ℂ 800/53-FERRY for reservations) runs a Sleepy Hollow Cruise once a day, on weekends and holidays, from Pier 78 at West 38th Street and Twelfth Avenue. A shuttle bus meets the ferry in Sleepy Hollow. The fare (including boat, bus, and Philipsburg Manor admission) is $46 for adults, $25 for children 12 and under. The ferry departs at 10:30am and returns at 6pm. The estimated time on the ferry is 1½ hours, but the full-day round-trip takes 7½ hours and also includes sightseeing at Sunnyside.

For information on children's workshops and special events at any of the four historic homes in the area, check out **Historic Hudson Valley's** website at **www.hudson valley.org**.

VISITING THE MANOR

An 18th-century colonial farm with a working gristmill, a yard full of animals, a farmhouse, and a tenant house, Philipsburg Manor fascinates school-age children. A long wooden bridge crosses the millpond near the entrance, leading on to the main house; long and close to the water, the bridge is fun to run across, sweeping you straight into the 18th century once you reach the other side.

Guides decked out in 18th-century dress demonstrate various farm activities of that era: milling, sheep shearing, plowing, and dairying. Every half-hour a guide gives a **tour of the farmhouse,** where the wealthy Philipse family once lived. The **stone manor house,** built between 1682 and 1720, includes interesting details of colonial life, including a night box to guard candles from rat attacks and a big white mound in the kitchen you later learn is sugar (the guide allows kids several guesses on that one). However, it was African slaves who actually worked the property for the Philipse family, laboriously threshing their wheat and grinding it into flour (there was indeed slavery outside of the South, folks), and their lives centered more on the **barnyard.** Children under 8, who may have started to weary during the house tour, will perk up when they see the sheep, chickens, cows, and cats wandering about the barnyard, though they won't be allowed to pat the animals. Just be aware that with the pond and the stream so close, parental supervision is necessary at all times.

U.S. 9, Sleepy Hollow, NY. (© 914/631-8200. www.hudsonvalley.org. Admission $10 adults, $9 seniors, $6 children 6–17, free for children 5 and under. Wed–Mon 10am–5pm. Closed Thanksgiving, Dec 25, and Jan–Feb.

WHERE TO EAT

To the left of the gift shop is a small **cafe** where you can buy decent gourmet-type sandwiches or salads (under $6). There's not much here to entice children, though, so it might be easier to bring a picnic lunch and eat at the tables by the millstream.

5 Maritime Aquarium at Norwalk

1 hr. NE of Manhattan

Focusing on the marine ecology of Long Island Sound, the Norwalk aquarium is just as pleasant a place to view marine life as the New York Aquarium in Coney Island (p. 176), and if you've got a car, it's perhaps easier to get here; it's certainly easier to get here from Manhattan than it is to visit the superb Mystic Aquarium at the other end of Connecticut.

ESSENTIALS

By car, take I-95 heading east/north to the South Norwalk exit (exit 14) off I-95 and follow the signs to the Maritime Center; it's about a 6-minute drive from the highway. Or take the Hutchinson River Parkway north, which becomes the Merritt Parkway in Connecticut; take exit 39A, and follow the signs on U.S. 7 to the Maritime Center. Parking at the center costs up to $5.

Metro-North trains (☏ **800/METRO-INFO** or 212/532-4900; www.mta.nyc.ny.
us/mnr) to South Norwalk cost $9.25 to $12 for adults, 75¢ for children 5 to 11, and
are free for children under 5. Travel time is about 60 minutes. From the South Norwalk station, take a short taxi ride or walk—it's only about 3 blocks. When you get
off the train, turn left, and go down the stairs at the end of the platform; turn right at
the bottom of the stairs, walk under the bridge, and go 1½ blocks to the first traffic
light, at the intersection of Main and Monroe streets. Turn left onto Main Street, and
go to the next traffic light; then turn right onto Washington Street. Go under another
bridge, and continue past shops and restaurants to the next traffic light, at the corner
of Washington and Water streets. You'll see the large red-brick Maritime Aquarium on
your left.

EXPLORING THE AQUARIUM

Go up freestanding stairs in the lobby and across a midair bridge to the second-floor
entrance, where carpeted walkways lead through a softly lit series of **20 marine habitats,** progressing from salt marsh to the ocean depths. You'll see a thousand or so
marine creatures of more than 125 species, all native to Long Island Sound; my kids'
favorites were the sleek speckled harbor seals that flop around an indoor/outdoor pool
in the lobby (watch them being fed at 11:45am, 1:45pm, and 3:45pm), but the
bright-eyed otters in the woodland shoreline habitat run a close second. Sand tiger
sharks circle and glare at you through the glass in enormous ocean tanks; immense,
primeval-looking loggerhead turtles paddle like wise old grandpas in another tank;
while jellyfish shimmer deductively in the Jellyfish Encounter. Kids who want to get
really close to sea creatures—sea stars, horseshoe crabs, whelks—can linger at the
Touch Tank or, if they're bold enough, pet a live ray at the **Ray Touch Pool.**

Two-story **Maritime Hall** has loads of interactive educational displays on fish, but
my son and brother-in-law were absorbed by the displays on navigation and the
wooden-boat workshop. The second-floor **Ocean Playscape** is a colorful marine-
themed play area for children under 5. Aside from regular exhibits, the aquarium
always has on tap some intriguing traveling exhibit or other, as well as an **IMAX theater** with a rotation of megascreen natural-history films. An excellent gift shop lies in
wait at the end of your day.

N. Water St., Norwalk, CT. ☏ **203/852-0700.** www.maritimeaquarium.org. Admission $11 adults, $9.50 seniors,
$8.50 children 2–12; IMAX tickets $8.50 adults, $7.50 seniors, $6.50 children 2–12; museum plus IMAX $16 adults,
$15 seniors, $12 children 2–12. Daily 10am–5pm (till 6pm July to Labor Day); evening IMAX shows Fri–Sun. Closed
Thanksgiving and Dec 25.

WHERE TO EAT

The **Cascade Café** on the second floor offers some good seafood, not all of it fried, at
reasonable prices. It's open daily from 10am to 4pm.

Appendix A:
For International Visitors

New York's global media profile might make it appear familiar, but movies and TV, music videos, and news images distort as much as they reflect. The gap between image and reality can make certain situations puzzling for the foreign—or even the domestic—visitor. This chapter will help prepare you for the more common issues or problems that you may encounter.

1 Preparing for Your Trip

ENTRY REQUIREMENTS

Check at any U.S. embassy or consulate for current information and requirements. You can also obtain a visa application and other information online at the **U.S. State Department's** website, at **www.travel. state.gov**.

VISAS The U.S. State Department has a **Visa Waiver Program (VWP)** allowing citizens of certain countries to enter the United States without a visa for stays of up to 90 days. At press time, these included Andorra, Australia, Austria, Belgium, Brunei, Denmark, Finland, France, Germany, Iceland, Ireland, Italy, Japan, Liechtenstein, Luxembourg, Monaco, the Netherlands, New Zealand, Norway, Portugal, San Marino, Singapore, Slovenia, Spain, Sweden, Switzerland, and the United Kingdom. Citizens of these countries need only a valid passport and a round-trip air or cruise ticket in their possession upon arrival. If they first enter the United States, they may also visit Mexico, Canada, Bermuda, and/or the Caribbean islands and return to the United States without a visa. Further information is available from any U.S. embassy or consulate. Canadian citizens may enter the United States without visas; they need only proof of residence.

Citizens of all other countries must have (1) a valid passport that expires at least 6 months later than the scheduled end of their visit to the United States, and (2) a tourist visa, which may be obtained without charge from any U.S. consulate.

To obtain a visa, the traveler must submit a completed application form (either in person or by mail) with a 1½-inch-square photo and must demonstrate binding ties to a residence abroad. Usually, you can obtain a visa at once or within 24 hours, but it may take longer during the summer rush from June through August. If you cannot go in person, contact the nearest U.S. embassy or consulate for directions on applying by mail. Your travel agent or airline office may also be able to provide you with visa applications and instructions. The U.S. consulate or embassy that issues your visa will determine whether you will be issued a multiple- or single-entry visa and any restrictions regarding the length of your stay.

British subjects can obtain up-to-date visa information by calling the **U.S. Embassy Visa Information Line** (© **0891/200-290**) or by visiting the American Embassy London's website at www.usembassy.org.uk.

Irish citizens can obtain up-to-date visa information through the **Embassy of the USA Dublin,** 42 Elgin Rd., Dublin 4, Ireland (© **353/1-668-8777;** or by checking out http://dublin.usembassy.gov.

Australian citizens can obtain up-to-date visa information by contacting the **U.S. Embassy Canberra,** Moonah Place, Yarralumla, ACT 2600 (© **02/6214-5600**) or by checking the U.S. Diplomatic Mission's website at http://us embassy-australia.state.gov/consular.

Citizens of **New Zealand** can obtain up-to-date visa information by contacting the **U.S. Embassy New Zealand,** 29 Fitzherbert Terr., Thorndon, Wellington (© **644/472-2068**), or get the information directly from the "For New Zealanders" section of the website at http://us embassy.org.nz.

MEDICAL REQUIREMENTS Unless you're arriving from an area known to be suffering from an epidemic (particularly cholera or yellow fever), inoculations or vaccinations are not required for entry into the United States. If you have a medical condition that requires **syringe-administered medications,** carry a valid signed prescription from your physician— the Federal Aviation Administration (FAA) no longer allows airline passengers to pack syringes in their carry-on baggage without documented proof of medical need. If you have a disease that requires treatment with **narcotics,** you should also carry documented proof with you— smuggling narcotics aboard a plane is a serious offense that carries severe penalties in the U.S.

For **HIV-positive visitors,** requirements for entering the United States are somewhat vague and change frequently. According to the latest publication of *HIV and Immigrants: A Manual for AIDS Service Providers,* the Immigration and Naturalization Service (INS) doesn't require a medical exam for entry into the United States, but INS officials may stop individuals because they look sick or because they are carrying AIDS/HIV medicine.

If an HIV-positive noncitizen applies for a nonimmigrant visa, the question on the application regarding communicable diseases is tricky no matter which way it's answered. If the applicant checks "no," INS may deny the visa on the grounds that the applicant committed fraud. If the applicant checks "yes," or if INS suspects the person is HIV-positive, it will deny the visa unless the applicant asks for a special waiver for visitors. This waiver is for people visiting the United States for a short time, to attend a conference, for instance, to visit close relatives, or to receive medical treatment. It can be a confusing situation. For up-to-the-minute information, contact **AIDSinfo** (© **800/448-0440** or 301/519-6616 outside the U.S.; www.aidsinfo.nih.gov) or the **Gay Men's Health Crisis** (© **212/367-1000;** www.gmhc.org).

DRIVER'S LICENSES Foreign driver's licenses are mostly recognized in the U.S., although you may want to get an international driver's license if your home license is not written in English.

PASSPORT INFORMATION

Safeguard your passport in an inconspicuous, inaccessible place like a money belt. Make a copy of the critical pages, including the passport number, and store it in a safe place, separate from the passport itself. If you lose your passport, visit the nearest consulate of your native country as soon as possible for a replacement. Passport applications are downloadable from the websites listed below.

Note: The International Civil Aviation Organization has recommended a policy requiring that *every* individual who travels by air have a passport. In response, many countries are now requiring that children must be issued their own passport to travel internationally, where before those under 16 or so may have been allowed to travel on a parent or guardian's passport.

FOR RESIDENTS OF CANADA

You can pick up a passport application at one of 28 regional passport offices or most travel agencies. Canadian children who travel must have their own passport. However, if you hold a valid Canadian passport issued before December 11, 2001, that bears the name of your child, the passport remains valid for you and your child until it expires. Passports cost C$85 for those 16 years and older (valid 5 years), C$35 children 3 to 15 (valid 5 years), and C$20, children under 3 (valid 3 years). Applications, which must be accompanied by two identical passport-size photographs and proof of Canadian citizenship, are available at travel agencies throughout Canada or from the central **Passport Office,** Department of Foreign Affairs and International Trade, Ottawa, ON K1A 0G3 (℃ **800/567-6868;** www.dfait-maeci.gc.ca). Processing takes 5 to 10 days if you apply in person, or about 3 weeks by mail.

FOR RESIDENTS OF THE UNITED KINGDOM

As a member of the European Union, you need only an identity card, not a passport, to travel to other EU countries. However, if you already possess a passport, it's always useful to carry it. To pick up an application for a standard 10-year passport (5-year passport for children under 16), visit the nearest Passport Office, major post office, or travel agency. You can also contact the **United Kingdom Passport Service** at ℃ **0870/571-0410** or visit its website at www.passport.gov.uk. Passports are £33 for adults and £19 for children under 16, with another £30 fee if you apply in person at a Passport Office. Processing takes about 2 weeks (1 week if you apply at the Passport Office).

FOR RESIDENTS OF IRELAND

You can apply for a 10-year passport, costing €57, at the **Passport Office,** Setanta Centre, Molesworth Street, Dublin 2 (℃ **01/671-1633;** www.irlgov.ie/iveagh). Those under age 18 and over 65 must apply for a €12 3-year passport. You can also apply at 1A South Mall, Cork (℃ **021/272-525**), or over the counter at most main post offices.

FOR RESIDENTS OF AUSTRALIA

You can get an application from your local post office or any branch of Passports Australia, but you must schedule an interview at the passport office to present your application materials. Call the **Australian Passport Information Service** at ℃ **131-232,** or visit the government website at www.passports.gov.au. Passports for adults are A$144 and for those under 18 are A$72.

FOR RESIDENTS OF NEW ZEALAND

You can pick up a passport application at any New Zealand Passports Office or download it from their website. Contact the **Passports Office** at ℃ **0800/225-050** in New Zealand or 04/474-8100, or log on to www.passports.govt.nz. Passports for adults are NZ$80 and for children under 16 NZ$40.

CUSTOMS
WHAT YOU CAN BRING IN

Every visitor more than 21 years of age may bring in, free of duty, the following: (1) 1 liter of wine or hard liquor; (2) 200 cigarettes, 100 cigars (but not from Cuba), or 3 pounds of smoking tobacco; and (3) $100 worth of gifts. These exemptions are offered to travelers who spend at least 72 hours in the United States and who have not claimed them within the preceding 6 months. It is altogether forbidden to bring into the country foodstuffs (particularly fruit, cooked meats, and canned goods) and plants (vegetables, seeds, tropical plants, and the like). Foreign tourists may bring in or take out up to $10,000 in U.S. or foreign currency with no formalities; larger sums must be declared to U.S. Customs on entering or leaving, which includes filing form CM 4790. For more specific information regarding U.S. Customs and Border Protection, contact your nearest U.S. embassy or consulate, or the **U.S. Customs and Border Protection** office (© **202/927-1770** or www.customs.us treas.gov).

WHAT YOU CAN TAKE HOME

U.K. citizens returning from a non-E.U. country have a customs allowance of: 200 cigarettes; 50 cigars; 250 grams of smoking tobacco; 2 liters of still table wine; 1 liter of spirits or strong liqueurs (over 22% volume); 2 liters of fortified wine, sparkling wine, or other liqueurs; 60 cubic centimeters (ml) perfume; 250 cubic centimeters (ml) of toilet water; and £145 worth of all other goods, including gifts and souvenirs. People under 17 cannot have the tobacco or alcohol allowance. For more information, contact HM Customs & Excise at © **0845/010-9000** (from outside the U.K., 020/8929-0152), or consult their website at www.hmce.gov.uk.

For a clear summary of **Canadian** rules, request the booklet *I Declare,* issued by the **Canada Customs and Revenue Agency** (© **800/461-9999** in Canada, or 204/983-3500; www.ccra-adrc.gc.ca). Canada allows its citizens a C$750 exemption, and you're allowed to bring back duty-free one carton of cigarettes, one can of tobacco, 40 imperial ounces of liquor, and 50 cigars. In addition, you're allowed to mail gifts to Canada valued at less than C$60 a day, provided they're unsolicited and don't contain alcohol or tobacco (write on the package "Unsolicited gift, under $60 value"). All valuables should be declared on the Y-38 form before departure from Canada, including serial numbers of valuables you already own, such as expensive foreign cameras. *Note:* The C$750 exemption can only be used once a year and only after an absence of 7 days.

The duty-free allowance in **Australia** is A$400 or, for those under 18, A$200. Citizens age 18 and over can bring in 250 cigarettes or 250 grams of loose tobacco, and 1,125 milliliters of alcohol. If you're returning with valuables you already own, such as foreign-made cameras, you should file form B263. A helpful brochure available from Australian consulates or Customs offices is *Know Before You Go.* For more information, call the **Australian Customs Service** at © **1300/363-263,** or log on to www.customs.gov.au.

The duty-free allowance for **New Zealand** is NZ$700. Citizens over 17 can bring in 200 cigarettes, 50 cigars, or 250 grams of tobacco (or a mixture of all three if their combined weight doesn't exceed 250g); plus 4.5 liters of wine and beer, or 1.125 liters of liquor. New Zealand currency does not carry import or export restrictions. Fill out a certificate of export, listing the valuables you are taking out of the country; that way, you can bring them back without paying duty. Most questions are answered in a free pamphlet available at New Zealand consulates and Customs offices: *New Zealand Customs Guide for Travellers, Notice no. 4.* For more information, contact **New Zealand Customs,** The Customhouse, 17–21 Whitmore St., Box 2218, Wellington (© **0800/428-786** or 04/473-6099; www.customs.govt.nz).

HEALTH INSURANCE

Although it's not required of travelers, health insurance is highly recommended. Unlike many European countries, the United States does not usually offer free or low-cost medical care to its citizens or visitors. Doctors and hospitals are expensive, and in most cases will require advance payment or proof of coverage before they render their services. Policies can cover everything from the loss or theft of your baggage and trip cancellation to the guarantee of bail in case you're arrested. Good policies will also cover the costs of an accident, repatriation, or death. See "Health, Insurance & Safety," in chapter 2, for more information. Packages such as **Europ Assistance's "Worldwide Health-care Plan"** are sold by European automobile clubs and travel agencies at attractive rates. **Worldwide Assistance Services, Inc.** (© **800/821-2828;** www.worldwide assistance.com) is the agent for Europ Assistance in the United States.

Though lack of health insurance may prevent you from being admitted to a hospital in nonemergencies, don't worry about being left on a street corner to die: The American way is to fix you now and bill the living daylights out of you later.

INSURANCE FOR BRITISH TRAV-ELERS Most big travel agents offer their own insurance and will probably try to sell you their package when you book a holiday. Think before you sign. **Britain's Consumers' Association** recommends that you insist on seeing the policy and reading the fine print before buying travel insurance. **The Association of British Insurers** (© **020/7600-3333;** www.abi. org.uk) gives advice by phone and publishes *Holiday Insurance,* a free guide to policy provisions and prices. You might also shop around for better deals: Try **Columbus Direct** (© **020/7375-0011;** www.columbusdirect.net).

INSURANCE FOR CANADIAN TRAVELERS Canadians should check with their provincial health plan offices or call **Health Canada** (© **613/957-2991;** www.hc-sc.gc.ca) to find out the extent of their coverage and what documentation and receipts they must take home in case they are treated in the United States.

MONEY
CURRENCY The U.S. monetary system is very simple: The most common

bills are the $1 (colloquially, a "buck"), $5, $10, and $20 denominations. There are also $2 bills (seldom encountered), $50 bills, and $100 bills (the last two are usually not welcome as payment for small purchases). All the paper money was recently redesigned, making the famous faces adorning them disproportionately large. The old-style bills are still legal tender.

There are seven denominations of coins: 1¢ (1 cent, or a penny); 5¢ (5 cents, or a nickel); 10¢ (10 cents, or a dime); 25¢ (25 cents, or a quarter); 50¢ (50 cents, or a half dollar); the new gold-colored "Sacagawea" coin worth $1; and, prized by collectors, the rare, older silver dollar.

Note: The "foreign-exchange bureaus" so common in Europe are rare even at airports in the United States, and nonexistent outside major cities. It's best not to change foreign money (or traveler's checks denominated in a currency other than U.S. dollars) at a small-town bank, or even a branch in a big city; in fact, leave any currency other than U.S. dollars at home—it may prove a greater nuisance to you than it's worth.

TRAVELER'S CHECKS Though traveler's checks are widely accepted, make sure that they're denominated in U.S. dollars, as foreign-currency checks are often difficult to exchange. The three traveler's checks that are most widely recognized—and least likely to be denied—are **Visa, American Express,** and **Thomas Cook.** Be sure to record the numbers of the checks, and keep that information in a separate place in case they get lost or stolen. Most businesses are pretty good about taking traveler's checks, but you're better off cashing them in at a bank (in small amounts, of course) and paying in cash. *Remember:* You'll need identification, such as a driver's license or passport, to change a traveler's check.

CREDIT CARDS & ATMs Credit cards are the most widely used form of

Travel Tip

Be sure to keep a copy of all your travel papers separate from your wallet or purse, and leave a copy with someone at home should you need it.

payment in the United States: **Visa** (Barclaycard in Britain), **MasterCard** (EuroCard in Europe, Access in Britain, Chargex in Canada), **American Express, Diners Club, Discover,** and **Carte Blanche;** you'll also find that New York vendors may accept international cards like **enRoute, Eurocard,** and **JCB,** but not as universally as Amex, MasterCard, or Visa. There are, however, a handful of stores and restaurants that do not take credit cards, so be sure to ask in advance. Most businesses display a sticker near their entrance to let you know which cards they accept. (*Note:* Businesses may require a minimum purchase, usually around $10, to use a credit card.)

It is strongly recommended that you bring at least one major credit card. You must have a credit or charge card to rent a car. Hotels and airlines usually require a credit card imprint as a deposit against expenses, and in an emergency a credit card can be priceless.

You'll find **automated teller machines (ATMs)** on just about every block—at least in almost every town—across the country. Some ATMs will allow you to draw U.S. currency against your bank and credit cards. Check with your bank before leaving home, and remember that you will need your personal identification number (PIN) to do so. Most accept Visa, MasterCard, and American Express, as well as ATM cards from other U.S. banks. Expect to be charged up to $3 per transaction, however, if you're not using your own bank's ATM.

One way around these fees is to ask for cash back at grocery stores that accept ATM cards and don't charge usage fees. Of course, you'll have to purchase something first.

ATM cards with major credit card backing, known as "debit cards," are now a commonly acceptable form of payment in most stores and restaurants. Debit cards draw money directly from your checking account. Some stores enable you to receive "cash back" on your debit card purchases as well.

SAFETY

GENERAL SUGGESTIONS Tourist areas in Manhattan are generally safe, and the city has experienced a dramatic drop in its crime rate in recent years. Still, crime is a national problem, and U.S. urban areas tend to be less safe than those in Europe or Japan. You should always stay alert, use common sense, and trust your instincts. If you're in doubt about which neighborhoods are safe, don't hesitate to make inquiries with the hotel front staff or the local tourist office.

Avoid deserted areas, especially at night, and don't go into public parks after dark unless there's a concert or similar occasion that will attract a crowd.

Avoid carrying valuables with you on the street, and keep expensive cameras or electronic equipment bagged up or covered when not in use. If you're using a map, try to consult it inconspicuously—or better yet, study it before you leave your room. Hold on to your pocketbook, and place your billfold in an inside pocket. In theaters, restaurants, and other public places, keep your possessions in sight.

Always lock your room door—don't assume that once you're inside the hotel you are automatically safe and no longer need to be aware of your surroundings. Hotels are open to the public, and in a large hotel, security may not be able to screen everyone who enters.

DRIVING SAFETY An inviolable rule of thumb for New York: Don't even think of driving within the city. Like many cities, New York has its own arcane rules of the road, confusing one-way streets, incomprehensible street-parking signs, and outrageously expensive parking garages. Public transportation—whether buses, subways, or taxis—will get you anywhere you want to go quickly and easily, and that's where you'll be most comfortable.

If you do drive to New York in a rental car, return it as soon as you arrive, and rent another when you're ready to leave the city. Always keep your car doors locked. Never leave any packages or valuables in sight, because thieves will break car windows. If someone attempts to rob you or steal your car, don't resist. Report the incident to the police department immediately.

SIZE CONVERSION CHART

Women's Clothing

American	4	6	8	10	12	14	16	
French	34	36	38	40	42	44	46	
British	6	8	10	12	14	16	18	

Women's Shoes

American	5	6	7	8	9	10
French	36	37	38	39	40	41
British	4	5	6	7	8	9

Men's Suits

American	34	36	38	40	42	44	46	48
French	44	46	48	50	52	54	56	58
British	34	36	38	40	42	44	46	48

Men's Shirts

American	14½	15	15½	16	16½	17	17½
French	37	38	39	41	42	43	44
British	14½	15	15½	16	16½	17	17½

Men's Shoes

American	7	8	9	10	11	12	13
French	39½	41	42	43	44½	46	47
British	6	7	8	9	10	11	12

2 Getting to the U.S.

In addition to the domestic airlines listed in chapter 2, "Planning a Family Trip to New York City," many international carriers serve John F. Kennedy International and Newark airports. **British Airways** (© **0845/77-333-77,** 0870/55-111-55 in the U.K., or 800/AIRWAYS in the U.S.; www.britishairways.com) has daily service from London as well as direct flights from Manchester and Glasgow. **Virgin Atlantic** (© **01293/747-747,** 01293/511-581 in the U.K., or 800/862-8621 in the U.S.; www.virgin-atlantic. com) flies from London's Heathrow to New York.

> **_Tips_ Prepare to Be Fingerprinted**
>
> Starting in January 2004, many international visitors traveling on visas to the United States will be photographed and fingerprinted at Customs in a new program created by the Department of Homeland Security called **US-VISIT.** Non–U.S. citizens arriving at airports and on cruise ships must undergo an instant background check as part of the government's ongoing efforts to deter terrorism by verifying the identity of incoming and outgoing visitors. Exempt from the extra scrutiny are visitors entering by land or those from 28 countries (mostly in Europe) that don't require a visa for short-term visits. For more information, go to the Homeland Security website at **www.dhs.gov/dhspublic.**

Canadian readers might book flights on **Air Canada** (© **888/247-2262;** www.aircanada.ca), which offers direct service from Toronto, Montreal, Ottawa, and other cities.

Aer Lingus flies from Ireland to New York (© **0818/365000** in Ireland, or 800/IRISH-AIR in the U.S.; www.aerlingus.ie). The following U.S. airlines fly to New York from most major European cities: **Continental** (© **0800/776-464** in the U.K., or 800/525-0280 in the U.S.; www.continental.com); **United** (© **0845/844-4777** in the U.K., or 800/864-8331 in the U.S.; www.ual.com); **American** (© **0208/572-5555,** 0845/778-9789 in the U.K., or 800/433-7300 in the U.S.; www.aa.com); and Delta (© **0800/414-767** in the U.K., or 800/221-4141 in the U.S.; www.delta.com).

Qantas (© **13-13-13** in Australia, or 800/227-4500 in the U.S.; www.qantas.com.au) and **Air New Zealand** (© **0800/737-000** or 800/262-1234 in the U.S.; www.airnewzealand.co.nz) fly to the West Coast and will book you straight through to New York City on a partner airline.

AIRLINE DISCOUNTS The smart traveler can find numerable ways to reduce the price of a plane ticket simply by taking time to shop around. For example, overseas visitors can take advantage of the APEX (Advance Purchase Excursion) reductions offered by all major U.S. and European carriers. For more money-saving airline advice, see "Getting There," in chapter 2. For the best rates, compare fares and be flexible with the dates and times of travel.

IMMIGRATION & CUSTOMS CLEARANCE Visitors arriving by air, no matter what the port of entry, should cultivate patience and resignation before setting foot on U.S. soil. Getting through immigration control can take as long as 2 hours on some days, especially on summer weekends, so be sure to carry this guidebook or something else to read. This is especially true in the aftermath of the World Trade Center attacks, when security clearances have been considerably beefed up at U.S. airports.

People traveling by air from Canada, Bermuda, and certain countries in the Caribbean can sometimes clear Customs and Immigration at the point of departure, which is much quicker.

3 Getting Around the U.S.

BY PLANE Some large airlines (for example, Northwest and Delta) offer travelers on their transatlantic or transpacific flights special discount tickets under the name **Visit USA,** allowing mostly one-way travel from one U.S. destination to another at very low prices. These discount tickets are not on sale in the United States and must be purchased abroad in conjunction with your international ticket. This system is the best, easiest, and fastest way to see the United States at low cost. You should obtain information well in advance from your travel agent or the office of the airline concerned, since the conditions attached to these discount tickets can be changed without advance notice.

BY TRAIN International visitors (excluding Canada) can also buy a **USA Rail Pass,** good for 15 or 30 days of unlimited travel on Amtrak (© **800/USA-RAIL;** www.amtrak.com). The pass is available through many overseas travel agents. Prices in 2004 for a 15-day pass were $295 off-peak, $440 peak; a 30-day pass costs $385 off-peak, $550 peak. With a foreign passport, you can also buy passes at some Amtrak offices in the United States, including locations in San Francisco, Los Angeles, Chicago, New York, Miami, Boston, and Washington, D.C. Reservations are generally required and should be made for each part of your trip as early as possible. Regional rail passes are also available.

BY BUS Although bus travel is often the most economical form of public transit for short hops between U.S. cities, it can also be slow and uncomfortable—certainly not an option for everyone (particularly when Amtrak, which is far more luxurious, offers similar rates). **Greyhound/Trailways** (© **800/231-2222;** www.greyhound.com), the sole nationwide bus line, offers an **International Ameripass** that must be purchased before coming to the United States, or by phone through the Greyhound International Office at the Port Authority Bus Terminal in New York City (© **212/971-0492**). The pass can be obtained from foreign travel agents or through Greyhound's website

(order at least 21 days before your departure to the U.S.) and costs less than the domestic version. In 2004, passes cost as follows: 4 days ($160), 7 days ($219), 10 days ($269), 15 days ($329), 21 days ($379), 30 days ($439), 45 days ($489), or 60 days ($599). You can get more info on the pass at the website, or by calling © **402/330-8552.** In addition, special rates are available for seniors and students.

BY CAR Unless you plan to spend the bulk of your vacation time in New York City, where walking is the best and easiest way to get around, the most cost-effective, convenient, and comfortable way to travel around the United States is by car. The interstate highway system connects cities and towns all over the country; in addition to these high-speed, limited-access roadways, there's an extensive network of federal, state, and local highways and roads. Some of the national car rental companies include **Alamo** (© 800/462-5266; www.alamo.com), **Avis** (© 800/230-4898; www.avis.com), **Budget** (© 800/527-0700; www.budget.com), **Dollar** (© 800/800-3665; www.dollar.com), **Hertz** (© 800/654-3131; www.hertz.com), **National** (© 800/227-7368; www.nationalcar.com), and **Thrifty** (© 800/847-4389; www.thrifty.com).

If you plan to rent a car in the United States, you probably won't need the services of an additional automobile organization. If you're planning to buy or borrow a car, automobile-association membership is recommended. **AAA (American Automobile Association;** © **800/222-4357)** is the country's largest auto club and supplies its members with maps, insurance, and, most important, emergency road service. The cost of joining runs from $63 for singles to $87 for two members, but if you're a member of a foreign auto club with reciprocal arrangements, you can enjoy free AAA service in America. See "Getting There," in chapter 2, for more information.

FAST FACTS: For the International Traveler

Also see "Fast Facts: New York City," in chapter 3 for more New York City–specific information.

Automobile Organizations Auto clubs will supply maps, suggested routes, guidebooks, accident and bail-bond insurance, and emergency road service. The **American Automobile Association (AAA)** is the major auto club in the United States. If you belong to an auto club in your home country, inquire about AAA reciprocity before you leave. You may be able to join AAA even if you're not a member of a reciprocal club; to inquire, call AAA (© **800/222-4357**). AAA is actually an organization of regional auto clubs; so look under "AAA Automobile Club" in the White Pages of the telephone directory. AAA has a nationwide emergency road service telephone number (© 800/AAA-HELP).

Business Hours Offices are usually open weekdays from 9am to 5pm. Banks are open weekdays from 9am to 3pm or later and sometimes Saturday mornings. Stores typically open between 9 and 10am and close between 5 and 6pm from Monday through Saturday. Stores in shopping complexes or malls tend to stay open late: until about 9pm on weekdays and weekends, and many malls and larger department stores are open on Sunday.

Currency & Currency Exchange See "Entry Requirements" and "Money" under "Preparing for Your Trip," above.

Drinking Laws The legal age for purchase and consumption of alcoholic beverages is 21; proof of age is required and often requested at bars, nightclubs, and restaurants, so it's always a good idea to bring ID when you go out. Beer and wine often can be purchased in supermarkets, but liquor laws vary from state to state.

Do not carry open containers of alcohol in your car or any public area that isn't zoned for alcohol consumption. The police can fine you on the spot. And nothing will ruin your trip faster than getting a citation for DUI ("driving under the influence"), so don't even think about driving while intoxicated.

Electricity Like Canada, the United States uses 110–120 volts AC (60 cycles), compared to 220–240 volts AC (50 cycles) in most of Europe, Australia, and New Zealand. If your small appliances use 220–240 volts, you'll need a 110-volt transformer and a plug adapter with two flat parallel pins to operate them here. Downward converters that change 220–240 volts to 110–120 volts are difficult to find in the United States, so bring one with you.

Embassies & Consulates All embassies are located in the nation's capital, Washington, D.C. Some consulates are located in New York, and most nations have a mission to the United Nations here. If your country isn't listed below, call for directory information in Washington, D.C. (© **202/555-1212**) or log on to **www.embassy.org/embassies**.

Australia: Embassy in Washington D.C. (© 202/797-3000; www.austemb.org); Consulate General in New York City, 150 E. 42nd St. (© 212/351-6500). **Canada:** Embassy (© 202/682-1740; www.canadianembassy.org); Consulate General, 1251 Ave. of the Americas (© 212/596-1628; www.canada-ny.org). **Ireland:** Embassy (© 202-462-3939; www.irelandemb.org); Consulate General, 345 Park

Ave. (℃ 212/319-2555). **New Zealand:** Embassy (℃ 202/328-4800; www.nzemb. org); Consulate General, 780 Third Ave. (℃ 212/832-4038). **United Kingdom:** Embassy (℃ 202/462-1340; www.britainusa.com); Consulate General, 845 Third Ave. (℃ 212/745-0200; www.britainusa.com).

Emergencies Call ℃ **911** to report a fire, call the police, or get an ambulance anywhere in the United States. This is a toll-free call. (No coins are required at public telephones.)

If you encounter serious problems, contact the **Traveler's Aid International** (℃ **202/546-1127**; www.travelersaid.org) to help direct you to a local branch. This nationwide, nonprofit, social-service organization geared to helping travelers in difficult straits offers services that might include reuniting families separated while traveling, providing food and/or shelter to people stranded without cash, or even emotional counseling. If you're in trouble, seek them out.

Gasoline (Petrol) Petrol is known as gasoline (or simply "gas") in the United States, and petrol stations are known as both gas stations and service stations. Gasoline costs about half as much here as it does in Europe (about $3 per gallon at press time), and taxes are already included in the printed price. One U.S. gallon equals 3.8 liters or .85 Imperial gallons.

Holidays Banks, government offices, post offices, and many stores, restaurants, and museums are closed on the following legal national holidays: January 1 (New Year's Day), the third Monday in January (Martin Luther King, Jr. Day), the third Monday in February (Presidents' Day, Washington's Birthday), the last Monday in May (Memorial Day), July 4th (Independence Day), the first Monday in September (Labor Day), the second Monday in October (Columbus Day), November 11 (Veterans Day/Armistice Day), the fourth Thursday in November (Thanksgiving Day), and December 25 (Christmas). Also, the Tuesday following the first Monday in November is Election Day and is a federal-government holiday in presidential-election years (held every 4 years; 2004, 2008, and so on).

Legal Aid If you are "pulled over" for a minor infraction (such as speeding), never attempt to pay the fine directly to a police officer; this could be construed as attempted bribery, a much more serious crime. Pay fines by mail or directly into the hands of the clerk of the court. If accused of a more serious offense, say and do nothing before consulting a lawyer. Here, the burden is on the state to prove a person's guilt beyond a reasonable doubt, and everyone has the right to remain silent, whether he or she is suspected of a crime or actually arrested. Once arrested, a person can make one telephone call to a party of his or her choice. Call your embassy or consulate.

Mail If you aren't sure what your address will be in the United States, mail can be sent to you, in your name, c/o General Delivery at the main post office of the city or region where you expect to be. (Call ℃ **800/275-8777** for information on the nearest post office.) The addressee must pick up mail in person and must produce proof of identity (such as a driver's license or passport). Most post offices will hold your mail for up to 1 month and are open Monday to Friday from 8am to 6pm, Saturday from 9am to 3pm.

Generally found at intersections, mailboxes are blue with a red-and-white stripe and carry the inscription U.S. MAIL. If your mail is addressed to a U.S. destination, don't forget to add the five-digit postal code (or zip code) after the two-letter abbreviation of the state to which the mail is addressed. This is essential to prompt delivery.

At press time, domestic postage rates were 23¢ for a postcard and 37¢ for a letter. For international mail, a first-class letter of up to one-half ounce costs 80¢ (60¢ to Canada and Mexico); a first-class postcard costs 70¢ (50¢ to Canada and Mexico); and a preprinted postal aerogramme costs 70¢.

Measurements See the chart on the inside front cover of this book for details on converting metric measurements to U.S. equivalents.

Taxes The United States has no value-added tax (VAT) or other indirect tax at the national level. Every state, county, and city has the right to levy its own local tax on all purchases, including hotel and restaurant checks, airline tickets, and so on.

Telephone, Telegraph, Telex & Fax The telephone system in the United States is run by private corporations, so rates, especially for long-distance service and operator-assisted calls, can vary widely. Generally, hotel surcharges on long-distance and local calls are astronomical, so you're usually better off using a **public pay telephone,** which you'll find clearly marked in most public buildings and private establishments as well as on the street. Convenience grocery stores and gas stations always have them. Many convenience groceries and packaging services sell **prepaid calling cards** in denominations up to $50; these can be the least expensive way to call home. Many public phones at airports now accept American Express, MasterCard, and Visa credit cards. **Local calls** made from public pay phones in most locales cost either 35¢ or 50¢. Pay phones do not accept pennies, and few will take anything larger than a quarter.

You may want to look into leasing a cellphone for the duration of your trip.

Most long-distance and international calls can be dialed directly from any phone. **For calls within the United States and to Canada,** dial 1 followed by the area code and the seven-digit number. **For other international calls,** dial 011 followed by the country code, city code, and the telephone number of the person you are calling.

Calls to area codes **800, 888, 877,** and **866** are toll-free. However, calls to numbers in area codes **700** and **900** (chat lines, bulletin boards, "dating" services, and so on) can be very expensive—usually a charge of 95¢ to $3 or more per minute, and they sometimes have minimum charges that can run as high as $15 or more.

For **reversed-charge or collect calls,** and for person-to-person calls, dial 0 (zero, not the letter O) followed by the area code and number you want; an operator will then come on the line, and you should specify that you are calling collect, or person-to-person, or both. If your operator-assisted call is international, ask for the overseas operator.

For **local directory assistance** ("information"), dial ☎ **411;** for long-distance information, dial 1, then the appropriate area code and 555-1212.

Telegraph and telex services are provided primarily by Western Union. You can bring your telegram into the nearest Western Union office (there are hundreds across the country) or dictate it over the phone (☎ **800/325-6000**). You can also telegraph money, or have it telegraphed to you, very quickly over the Western Union system, but this service can cost as much as 15% to 20% of the amount sent.

Most hotels have **fax machines** available for guest use (be sure to ask about the charge to use it). Many hotel rooms are even wired for guests' fax machines. A less expensive way to send and receive faxes may be at stores such as **The UPS Store** (formerly Mail Boxes Etc.), a national chain of retail packing service shops. (Look in the Yellow Pages directory under "Packing Services.")

There are two kinds of telephone directories in the United States. The so-called **White Pages** list private households and business subscribers in alphabetical order. The inside front cover lists emergency numbers for police, fire, ambulance, the Coast Guard, poison-control center, crime-victims hot line, and so on. The first few pages will tell you how to make long-distance and international calls, complete with country codes and area codes. Government numbers are usually printed on blue paper within the White Pages. Printed on yellow paper, the so-called **Yellow Pages** list all local services, businesses, industries, and houses of worship according to activity with an index at the front or back. (Drugstores/pharmacies and restaurants are also listed by geographic location.) The Yellow Pages also include city plans or detailed area maps, postal zip codes, and public transportation routes.

Time The continental United States is divided into **four time zones:** Eastern Standard Time (EST), Central Standard Time (CST), Mountain Standard Time (MST), and Pacific Standard Time (PST). Alaska and Hawaii have their own zones. For example, noon in New York City (EST) is 11am in Chicago (CST), 10am in Denver (MST), 9am in Los Angeles (PST), 8am in Anchorage (AST), and 7am in Honolulu (HST).

Daylight saving time is in effect from 1am on the first Sunday in April through 1am on the last Sunday in October, except in Arizona, Hawaii, and Puerto Rico. Daylight saving time moves the clock 1 hour ahead of standard time.

Tipping Tips are a very important part of certain workers' income, and gratuities are the standard way of showing appreciation for services provided. (Tipping is certainly not compulsory if the service is poor!) In hotels, tip **bellhops** at least $1 per bag ($2–$3 if you have a lot of luggage) and tip the **chamber staff** $1 to $2 per day (more if you've left a disaster area for him or her to clean up). Tip the **doorman** or **concierge** only if he or she has provided you with some specific service (for example, calling a cab for you or obtaining difficult-to-get theater tickets). Tip the **valet-parking attendant** $1 every time you get your car.

In restaurants, bars, and nightclubs, tip **service staff** 15% to 20% of the check, tip **bartenders** 10% to 15%, tip **checkroom attendants** $1 per garment, and tip **valet-parking attendants** $1 per vehicle.

As for other service personnel, tip **cab drivers** 15% of the fare; tip **skycaps** at airports at least $1 per bag ($2–$3 if you have a lot of luggage); and tip **hairdressers** and **barbers** 15% to 20%.

Toilets You won't find public toilets or "restrooms" on the streets in most U.S. cities, but they can be found in hotel lobbies, bars, restaurants, museums, department stores, railway and bus stations, and service stations. Large hotels and fast-food restaurants are probably the best bet for good, clean facilities. If possible, avoid the toilets at parks and beaches, which tend to be dirty; some may be unsafe. Restaurants and bars in resorts or heavily visited areas may reserve their restrooms for patrons. Some establishments display a notice indicating this. You can ignore this sign or, better yet, avoid arguments by paying for a cup of coffee or a soft drink, which will qualify you as a patron.

Appendix B:
Useful Toll-Free Numbers & Websites

AIRLINES

Air Canada
℃ 888/247-2262
www.aircanada.ca

Air Jamaica
℃ 800/523-5585 in U.S.
℃ 888/359-2475 in Jamaica
www.airjamaica.com

Air New Zealand
℃ 800/262-1234
or -2468 in the U.S.
℃ 800/663-5494 in Canada
℃ 0800/737-767 in New Zealand
www.airnewzealand.com

Airtran Airlines
℃ 800/247-8726
www.airtran.com

Alaska Airlines
℃ 800/252-7522
www.alaskaair.com

American Airlines
℃ 800/433-7300
www.aa.com

American Trans Air
℃ 800/225-2995
www.ata.com

America West Airlines
℃ 800/235-9292
www.americawest.com

British Airways
℃ 800/247-9297
℃ 0345/222-111 or
0845/77-333-77 in Britain
www.british-airways.com

BWIA
℃ 800/538-2492
www.bwee.com

Continental Airlines
℃ 800/525-0280
www.continental.com

Delta Air Lines
℃ 800/221-1212
www.delta.com

Frontier Airlines
℃ 800/432-1359
www.frontierairlines.com

Jet Blue Airlines
℃ 800/538-2583
www.jetblue.com

Mexicana
℃ 800/531-7921 in the U.S.
℃ 01800/502-2000 in Mexico
www.mexicana.com

Midwest Express
℃ 800/452-2022
www.midwestexpress.com

North American Airlines
℃ 718/656-2650
www.northamair.com

Northwest Airlines
℃ 800/225-2525
www.nwa.com

Olympic Airways
℃ 800/223-1226 in U.S.
℃ 80/111-44444 in Greece
www.olympic-airways.gr

Southwest Airlines
℃ 800/435-9792
www.southwest.com

Spirit Airlines
℃ 800/772-7117
www.spiritair.com

TACA
℃ 800/535-8780 in U.S.
℃ 503/267-8222 in El Salvador
www.taca.com

United Airlines
℃ 800/241-6522
www.united.com

US Airways
℃ 800/428-4322
www.usairways.com

Virgin Atlantic Airways
℃ 800/862-8621 in Continental U.S.
℃ 0293/747-747 in Britain
www.virgin-atlantic.com

MAJOR HOTEL & MOTEL CHAINS

Best Western International
℃ 800/528-1234
www.bestwestern.com

Clarion Hotels
℃ 800/CLARION
www.clarionhotel.com
or
www.hotelchoice.com

Comfort Inns
℃ 800/228-5150
www.hotelchoice.com

Courtyard by Marriott
℃ 800/321-2211
www.courtyard.com or
www.marriott.com

Days Inn
℃ 800/325-2525
www.daysinn.com

Doubletree Hotels
℃ 800/222-TREE
www.doubletree.com

Econo Lodges
℃ 800/55-ECONO
www.hotelchoice.com

Fairfield Inn by Marriott
℃ 800/228-2800
www.marriott.com

Four Seasons
℃ 800/819-5053
www.fourseasons.com

Hampton Inn
℃ 800/HAMPTON
www.hampton-inn.com

Hilton Hotels
℃ 800/HILTONS
www.hilton.com

Holiday Inn
℃ 800/HOLIDAY
www.holiday-inn.com

Howard Johnson
℃ 800/654-2000
www.hojo.com

Hyatt Hotels & Resorts
℃ 800/228-9000
www.hyatt.com

Inter-Continental
Hotels & Resorts
℃ 888/567-8725
www.interconti.com

ITT Sheraton
℃ 800/325-3535
www.starwood.com

La Quinta Motor Inns
℃ 800/531-5900
www.laquinta.com

Marriott Hotels
℃ 800/228-9290
www.marriott.com

Motel 6
℡ 800/4-MOTEL6
(800/466-8356)
www.motel6.com

Omni
℡ 800/THEOMNI
www.omnihotels.com

Quality Inns
℡ 800/228-5151
www.hotelchoice.com

Radisson Hotels International
℡ 800/333-3333
www.radisson.com

Ramada Inns
℡ 800/2-RAMADA
www.ramada.com

Red Lion Hotels & Inns
℡ 800/RED-LION
www.redlion.com

Red Roof Inns
℡ 800/843-7663
www.redroof.com

Renaissance
℡ 800/228-9290
www.renaissancehotels.com

Residence Inn by Marriott
℡ 800/331-3131
www.marriott.com

Ritz-Carlton
℡ 800/241-3333
www.ritzcarlton.com

Sheraton Hotels & Resorts
℡ 800/325-3535
www.sheraton.com

Super 8 Motels
℡ 800/800-8000
www.super8.com

Travelodge
℡ 800/255-3050
www.travelodge.com

Westin Hotels & Resorts
℡ 800/937-8461
www.westin.com

Wyndham Hotels and Resorts
℡ 800/822-4200 in Continental U.S.
and Canada
www.wyndham.com

Index

See also Accommodations and Restaurant indexes, below.

RESTAURANTS

FROMMER'S® COMPLETE TRAVEL GUIDES

Alaska
Amalfi Coast
American Southwest
Amsterdam
Argentina & Chile
Arizona
Atlanta
Australia
Austria
Bahamas
Barcelona
Beijing
Belgium, Holland & Luxembourg
Belize
Bermuda
Boston
Brazil
British Columbia & the Canadian
  Rockies
Brussels & Bruges
Budapest & the Best of Hungary
Buenos Aires
Calgary
California
Canada
Cancún, Cozumel & the Yucatán
Cape Cod, Nantucket & Martha's
  Vineyard
Caribbean
Caribbean Ports of Call
Carolinas & Georgia
Chicago
China
Colorado
Costa Rica
Croatia
Cuba
Denmark
Denver, Boulder & Colorado Springs
Edinburgh & Glasgow
England
Europe
Europe by Rail
Florence, Tuscany & Umbria

Florida
France
Germany
Greece
Greek Islands
Hawaii
Hong Kong
Honolulu, Waikiki & Oahu
India
Ireland
Israel
Italy
Jamaica
Japan
Kauai
Las Vegas
London
Los Angeles
Los Cabos & Baja
Madrid
Maine Coast
Maryland & Delaware
Maui
Mexico
Montana & Wyoming
Montréal & Québec City
Moscow & St. Petersburg
Munich & the Bavarian Alps
Nashville & Memphis
New England
Newfoundland & Labrador
New Mexico
New Orleans
New York City
New York State
New Zealand
Northern Italy
Norway
Nova Scotia, New Brunswick &
  Prince Edward Island
Oregon
Paris
Peru
Philadelphia & the Amish Country

Portugal
Prague & the Best of the Czech
  Republic
Provence & the Riviera
Puerto Rico
Rome
San Antonio & Austin
San Diego
San Francisco
Santa Fe, Taos & Albuquerque
Scandinavia
Scotland
Seattle
Seville, Granada & the Best of
  Andalusia
Shanghai
Sicily
Singapore & Malaysia
South Africa
South America
South Florida
South Pacific
Southeast Asia
Spain
Sweden
Switzerland
Tahiti & French Polynesia
Texas
Thailand
Tokyo
Toronto
Turkey
USA
Utah
Vancouver & Victoria
Vermont, New Hampshire & Maine
Vienna & the Danube Valley
Vietnam
Virgin Islands
Virginia
Walt Disney World® & Orlando
Washington, D.C.
Washington State

FROMMER'S® DAY BY DAY GUIDES

Amsterdam
Chicago
Florence & Tuscany

London
New York City
Paris

Rome
San Francisco
Venice

PAULINE FROMMER'S GUIDES! SEE MORE. SPEND LESS.

Hawaii

Italy

New York City

FROMMER'S® PORTABLE GUIDES

Acapulco, Ixtapa & Zihuatanejo
Amsterdam
Aruba
Australia's Great Barrier Reef
Bahamas
Big Island of Hawaii
Boston
California Wine Country
Cancún
Cayman Islands
Charleston
Chicago
Dominican Republic

Dublin
Florence
Las Vegas
Las Vegas for Non-Gamblers
London
Maui
Nantucket & Martha's Vineyard
New Orleans
New York City
Paris
Portland
Puerto Rico
Puerto Vallarta, Manzanillo &
  Guadalajara

Rio de Janeiro
San Diego
San Francisco
Savannah
St. Martin, Sint Maarten, Anguila &
  St. Bart's
Turks & Caicos
Vancouver
Venice
Virgin Islands
Washington, D.C.
Whistler

FROMMER'S® CRUISE GUIDES

Alaska Cruises & Ports of Call | Cruises & Ports of Call | European Cruises & Ports of Call

FROMMER'S® NATIONAL PARK GUIDES

Algonquin Provincial Park
Banff & Jasper
Grand Canyon

National Parks of the American West
Rocky Mountain
Yellowstone & Grand Teton

Yosemite and Sequoia & Kings
Canyon
Zion & Bryce Canyon

FROMMER'S® MEMORABLE WALKS

London
New York

Paris
Rome

San Francisco

FROMMER'S® WITH KIDS GUIDES

Chicago
Hawaii
Las Vegas
London

National Parks
New York City
San Francisco

Toronto
Walt Disney World® & Orlando
Washington, D.C.

SUZY GERSHMAN'S BORN TO SHOP GUIDES

France
Hong Kong, Shanghai & Beijing
Italy

London
New York

Paris
San Francisco

FROMMER'S® IRREVERENT GUIDES

Amsterdam
Boston
Chicago
Las Vegas

London
Los Angeles
Manhattan
Paris

Rome
San Francisco
Walt Disney World®
Washington, D.C.

FROMMER'S® BEST-LOVED DRIVING TOURS

Austria
Britain
California
France

Germany
Ireland
Italy
New England

Northern Italy
Scotland
Spain
Tuscany & Umbria

THE UNOFFICIAL GUIDES®

Adventure Travel in Alaska
Beyond Disney
California with Kids
Central Italy
Chicago
Cruises
Disneyland®
England
Florida
Florida with Kids

Hawaii
Ireland
Las Vegas
London
Maui
Mexico's Best Beach Resorts
Mini Mickey
New Orleans
New York City

Paris
San Francisco
South Florida including Miami &
the Keys
Walt Disney World®
Walt Disney World® for
Grown-ups
Walt Disney World® with Kids
Washington, D.C.

SPECIAL-INTEREST TITLES

Athens Past & Present
Best Places to Raise Your Family
Cities Ranked & Rated
500 Places to Take Your Kids Before They Grow Up
Frommer's Best Day Trips from London
Frommer's Best RV & Tent Campgrounds
in the U.S.A.

Frommer's Exploring America by RV
Frommer's NYC Free & Dirt Cheap
Frommer's Road Atlas Europe
Frommer's Road Atlas Ireland
Great Escapes From NYC Without Wheels
Retirement Places Rated

FROMMER'S® PHRASEFINDER DICTIONARY GUIDES

French | Italian | Spanish